Interrogating Gazes

European University Studies
Europäische Hochschulschriften
Publications Universitaires Européennes

Series XVIII
Comparative Literature

Reihe XVIII   Série XVIII
Vergleichende Literaturwissenschaft
Littérature comparée

Vol./Band 137

PETER LANG

Bern · Berlin · Bruxelles · Frankfurt am Main · New York · Oxford · Wien

Montserrat Cots, Pere Gifra-Adroher
& Glyn Hambrook (eds.)

Interrogating Gazes

Comparative Critical Views
on the Representation of Foreignness
and Otherness

PETER LANG

Bern · Berlin · Bruxelles · Frankfurt am Main · New York · Oxford · Wien

Bibliographic information published by die Deutsche Nationalbibliothek
Die Deutsche Nationalbibliothek lists this publication in the Deutsche
Nationalbibliografie; detailed bibliographic data is available on the Internet
at ‹http://dnb.d-nb.de›.

British Library Cataloguing-in-Publication Data: A catalogue record for this book
is available from The British Library, Great Britain

Library of Congress Cataloging-in-Publication Data

Interrogating Gazes/Miradas Interrogantes : Comparative Critical Views
on the Representation of Foreignness and Otherness /
Montserrat Cots, Pere Gifra-Adroher & Glyn Hambrook (eds.).
pages cm. – (Europäische Hochschulschriften. Reihe 18, Vergleichende
Literaturwissenschaft ; Band 137 = Publications Universitaire Européennes. Série 18,
Littérature comparée ; Band 137 = European University Studies. Series 18,
Comparative Literature, ISSN 0721-3425 ; vol. 137)
ISBN 978-3-0343-1312-4
1. Other (Philosophy) in literature. 2. Comparative literature. 3. Travel writing.
4. Cosmopolitanism in literature. 5. Identity (Psychology)–Cross-cultural studies.
6. Globalization in literature. I. Cots, Montserrat, editor of compilation.
II. Gifra-Adroher, Pere, 1966- editor of compilation.
III. Hambrook, Glyn, editor of compilation.
PN56.O69I59 2014
809'.93353–dc23

2013029490

ISSN 0721-3352
ISBN 978-3-0343-1312-4 pb.   ISBN 978-3-0351-0603-9 eBook

© Peter Lang AG, International Academic Publishers, Bern 2013
Hochfeldstrasse 32, CH-3012 Bern, Switzerland
info@peterlang.com, www.peterlang.com

Printed in Switzerland

Contents

6

8

11

Acknowledgments

Neither the Xenographies II Congress in September 2011 nor the publication of this book would have been possible without the involvement and generous support of various organisations and institutions. The editors' thanks go in the first place to the Spanish Ministry of Education whose funding has been essential in bringing this book to fruition (FFI2011-13732-E). Next, they would like to acknowledge the institutional and scientific support that two academic societies have lent to this project: the Sociedad Española de Literatura General y Comparada (SELGYC) and the British Comparative Literature Association (BCLA). Their involvement provided the Xenographies II Congress with an international reach that made it possible to explore the most recent avenues of comparative literature. The editors also wish to express their gratitude to all the units of Pompeu Fabra University and the University of Wolverhampton that have backed this project both financially and administratively, in particular the Centre for Transnational and Transcultural Research (Wolverhampton) and the Departament d'Humanitats and Institut de Cultura (Pompeu Fabra).

The editors are grateful to all the delegates who attended the conference and especially to the invited speakers, professors Leonardo Romero Tobar, Richard Hitchcock, Eloy Martín Corrales and the late Noel Polk. It is with great sadness that they lament the loss of the latter, who passed away during the preparation of this volume. The editors are indebted to them for their work and the academic rigour that they bring to this book. Thanks are also due to the scientific committee with members from various European universities who have assured the quality of the papers through a process of blind reviewing. The same gratitude goes to the expert who anonymously reviewed the final manuscript and also to the editorial team at Peter Lang for guiding the book to publication.

Finally, the editors would like to acknowledge the collaboration they have received from various members of the research project "Relevancia de la Literatura Comparada", coordinated by Dr Antonio Monegal and funded by the Spanish Ministry of Education (FFI2011-28728). At various points they were also fortunate to count on the flawless editing skills of Marta Manso, Eric Ramos, Noelia Rivas and Raquel Maspoch. To them and all the others who have helped in the completion of this volume they give their heartfelt thanks.

Preface

The essays gathered in this volume are the outcome of an inspiring and timely collaboration between two major European comparative literature associations, the Sociedad Española de Literatura General y Comparada (SELGYC) and the British Comparative Literature Association (BCLA). The volume comprises a selection of the papers delivered at "Xenographies II", an international, trilingual conference (English, Castilian, Catalan) hosted by Pompeu Fabra University, Barcelona (8-11 September 2011), the second of two scholarly encounters —the first took place at the University of Wolverhampton, United Kingdom, in September 2009— exploring the representation of the foreign(er) in literature and other discourses. The conference received the support of a scientific committee with members from several European universities and attracted over one hundred delegates delivering over ninety papers, including four plenary lectures. These two conferences, together with other research activities have acquired the collective designation of Xenographies project. The origins of this initiative go back to a BCLA Executive Committee meeting in 2008 at which Glyn Hambrook received the committee's blessing to formally propose the collaborative endeavour that, following preliminary discussions in Madrid with Professor Montserrat Cots (who had just assumed the presidency of SELGYC) and Dr Javier Pardo (also of the SELGYC's Executive Committee), acquired the guise of the aforementioned first joint conference. This event was attended by forty delegates from Spain, the United Kingdom and other countries.

This volume is the third and most recent refereed publication deriving from the project. The first and second published outputs were special issues of, respectively, SELGYC's journal *1616. Anuario de Literatura Comparada* and the BCLA's *Comparative Critical Studies*.[1] The present

---

1   The special issue ("Xenografías") of *1616*, vol. 1, was published in 2011. The special issue of *Comparative Critical Studies* vol. 9, issue 2 ("Xenographies") was published in 2012 and edited by Glyn Hambrook, Benjamin Colbert and Pedro Javier Pardo.

book, *Interrogating Gazes/Miradas interrogantes*, explores different ways of approaching the topics of foreignness and otherness, as well as of constructing the figures of the foreigner and the Other. It does so through multiple academic gazes which interrogate these issues from various standpoints, questioning at the same time the theoretical foundations on which the essays in the book are based. The book is divided into two main sections. The first one, titled Sights and Insights into Foreignness, examines the representation of specific images of foreigners, whereas the second one, titled Exploring Otherness, deals with the notion of the Other in a more abstract sense.

Many of the papers included here focus on travel writing and the impact that the traveller's gaze has had on the construction of otherness and the foreign(er). National stereotypes are discussed in a significant group of essays. There are also a substantial number of papers devoted to examining how otherness is both experienced and envisaged by minority groups whose identity is continuously affected by gender, politics and religion. Another relevant contribution of this volume has to do with its multidisciplinary approach to the image of the foreign(er) and the Other, as many of the contributors come from such different academic fields as history, music, art and, needless to say, literature. In this respect, the chronological boundaries of the research presented here oscillate between the late eighteenth and the early twenty-first centuries. A number of the essays significantly broaden the concept of culture also by studying new cultural forms often connected to the information technologies. The reader will discover, in short, that the construction of the Other does not only manifest itself in the Gothic novel of the past but also in the digital literature of the present. Finally, this volume also reflects the international scope of the Xenographies project, as it includes contributions not only from European researchers but also from scholars from South America, Taiwan and Australia.

The Xenographies Project has already served positively the cause of comparative literature in a variety of ways. Firstly, in bringing together two major comparative literature associations, it has created a formal international network of academic collaboration and interchange that has prompted, among other things, a timely comparison of and mutual reflection on respective methodologies and approaches. Secondly, and in so doing (and as the range of approaches deployed in the present volume demonstrates), it has carried the Xenographies project into the realm of the current debate on comparative literature's future and function that came into being with the formulation of the "New Paradigm" in the late twentieth century. This debate was given further impetus, in the English-speaking academic world at least, by the publication of Gayatri Chakravorty Spivak's controversial and catalytic *Death of a Discipline* (2004). The interdisciplinarity represented across and within the essays gathered in this volume provides further evidence of this. Thirdly, it has placed comparative literary research at the heart of European and international *cuestiones palpitantes* both within and, more significantly, beyond the academic world. The foreigner and foreignness, as specific manifestations of the Other and otherness, have become conceptual touchstones in contemporary debates on global and transnational —and national— identity, particularly in relation to migration and multiculturalism in all their guises and the complex, multifaceted phenomenon known as "Globalization".

Finally, on an institutional level, the Xenographies Project offers further evidence of Pompeu Fabra University's commitment to comparative literary study and the place of honour that the former academic home of Claudio Guillén occupies in Iberian, European and international comparatism; and at the same time, albeit on a more modest scale, the project has helped to establish a research base for the discipline in one of the institutions closely associated with the venture, the University of Wolverhampton. The success of the first Xenographies conference, as well as that of a previous BCLA workshop conference, "Literature Travels" (Wolverhampton, 2005) formed part of the evidence that secured approval for the inauguration of a new research unit at this university, the Centre for Transnational and Transcultural Research (CTTR). Founded in February 2010 under the joint direction of Dr Glyn Hambrook and Dr Benjamin Colbert, the CTTR is in effect the home for comparative literary research in the institution.

In the British context, this is more than merely local news: it is part of an encouraging national trend. With the decline of student interest in foreign language study in the United Kingdom since the beginning of the new millennium, it is comparative literature that on many instances has not only rushed in to fill the void in intercultural competence created by the consequent crisis in university modern languages departments but also gamely presumed to bring to the attention of the academic community the current indispensability of an authentically international aca-

demic outlook and provision. In the case of Spain, the field of comparative literature has enjoyed a long tradition of philological erudition that
made itself manifest in many departments of languages and literatures.
Today, however, it has strengthened its position in the academic community not as a purveyor of knowledge in foreign languages but as critical literary model with a broader scope. It is not a coincidence that comparative literature in Spain is often connected to literary theory departments of recent creation.

The editors of and contributors to this volume are aware that it appears at a time when the vogue for explorations of otherness in its multiple forms has passed from being the fashion to the very substance of
much contemporary enquiry. Consequently, the volume aspires to stand
out against a backcloth woven from numerous cognate enterprises. *Foreignness* appears here, therefore, as a specific and distinct form of otherness and, indeed, of identity in general; yet specificity and distinctive-
ness do not imply reductive exclusivism. In other words, they are like
two sides of the same coin. Foreignness, as these essays most ably demonstrate, is itself a plural, multifaceted concept, a signifier amenable to a
range of credible and compelling interpretations, ready and able to acquire a variety of inflections without succumbing to gratuitousness. It
offers a most apposite conceptual hub for this endeavour, one that without being dissolved in the waters of an expansive otherness, can nevertheless be duly radicalised as a particular, flexible form thereof.

By way of conclusion, a brief exploration of the term "Xenography"
is appropriate here. "Xenography" is in the context of our initiative a
neologism less by coinage than by appropriation. The adjectival form
"xenographic" exists already as a scientific and specifically medical term
used, possibly with a certain disregard for etymology, to mean "across
species". The term has been used in the Humanities since the 1830s to
refer simply to use of another language, including speaking in tongues.[2]
Elsewhere, it has been defined as "the art of representing otherwise",
that is, the use of modes of representation different from the culturally

2   See William Cobbett's definition of "xénographie" as "xenography, knowledge of
     foreign languages" in *A New French and English Dictionary* (London, 1833), 408;
     for xenography as a form of psychic "glossalalia", see Alan Gault, *Mediumship and
     Survival: A Century of Investigations* (London: Heinemann, 1982), 101.

enshrined or orthodox.[3] The range of meanings assigned to the term mitigates without flippancy the assignation of yet another meaning to the term on this occasion. This is justified because it is timely and relevant: today, when, certainly no less than in previous times, a sense of foreignness not only around "us" (whoever "we" happen to be) but also within,[4] can emerge, with sudden poignancy or in a gradually pervasive manner, constantly or intermittently, in guises that range from the confusing and threatening to the consolatory and emancipatory. The former range from the long-established setting apart of outsider from insider —for Sophocles, Aeschylus, and Euripides, writes Kristeva, "barbarian meant 'incomprehensible', 'non-Greek' and finally 'eccentric' or 'inferior'" (51)— to more recent radical "otherings" in the name of progress. "The politics of civilisational identity [separates] a 'civilised culture' from 'violent cultures'" (2000: 18), claims Talal Asad,[5] for whom the designation of foreigner comes to be applied to entities that are *intended* to be excluded:

> The idea of European identity […] is not merely a matter of how a more inclusive name can be made to claim loyalties that are attached to local or national ones. It concerns exclusions and the desire that those excluded recognise what is included in the name. It is a symptom of anxieties (2000: 12).

These anxieties, as Michael Cronin explains, are propagated in and through a purportedly civilising process itself. "States which are invited to open themselves to the flows of Western capital and the ministrations of transnational corporations compensate by acting out dramas of national sovereignty in the cultural arena", affirms Cronin, who continues

---

3   See Michele Grossman, "Xen(ography) and the Art of Representing Otherwise: Australian Indigenous Life-Writing and the Vernacular Text", *Postcolonial Studies*, 8: 3 (2005): 277-301.
4   "The foreigner is within us. And when we flee from or struggle against the foreigner, we are fighting our unconscious —that 'improper' facet of our impossible 'own and proper'. Delicately, analytically, Freud does not speak of foreigners: he teaches us how to detect foreignness in ourselves. That is perhaps the only way not to hound it outside of us", Julia Kristeva, *Strangers to Ourselves*, translated by Leon S. Roudiez (Columbia: U of Columbia P, 1991), 191.
5   Talal Asad, "Muslims and European Identity: Can Europe Represent Islam?", in Elizabeth Hallam & Brian V. Street (eds.), *Cultural Encounters. Representing "Otherness"* (London & New York: Routledge, 2000), 11-27.

with the following observation: "Hence the prevalence of moral panics around foreign migrants, foreign customs, foreign beliefs, and foreign languages" (311).[6]

As one who seeks to break such pernicious spells by drawing attention to and celebrating the unsuspected proximity or even familiarity of the foreign, Cronin reminds us that "whereas formerly, the foreign, the exotic, the Other, was held to be over the border or beyond the mountains or over the sea, now the Other is next door, or across the street or in the same office" (307, after Hall). It is in the spirit of these assumptions that the contributions gathered in this volume might help to redefine the "foreigners" and "others" in us and around us.

---

6   Michael Cronin, "The Expanding World. Translation, Mobility and Global Futures",
    in Mona Baker, Maeve Oldham & María Calzada Pérez (eds.), *Text and Context*,
    (Manchester: St Jerome, 2010), 303-317.

I

Sights and Insights into Foreignness:
Travel Writing and Other Discourses

RICHARD HITCHCOCK

Reflections on the Vogue for Spain in England, 1800-1850

Clearly Spain was not unknown to the English prior to the nineteenth century, but it did not become what one might call fashionable until certain factors coalesced. Some of these may have overlapped but, when taken *en conjunto* they may be said to have accounted for the burgeoning popularity of the Iberian Peninsula in Britain. The most prominent and perhaps obvious factor was the English intervention in the Peninsular War. It has been calculated that there were perhaps upwards of 200,000 men who served with Wellington's armies; not all survived (indeed, there were around 50,000 fatalities), but some 150,000 would have returned with their impressions of five years campaigning, many with a knowledge of Spanish, some with Spanish wives, the officers with mementoes, including books —the Marquis of Worcester (1792-1853), an aide-de camp to Wellington (1812-1814), even brought a dog (Sancho) back with him, later cherished by the family.

Quite a number, of high and low rank, wrote their accounts, published in England, and conveying sundry opinions on Spain and its inhabitants. One may particularly draw attention to the fact that a number of the British aristocracy served as officers in the Peninsula, aristocrats who in peace-time would have made the Grand Tour of Europe (Paris, Geneva, Vienna, Venice, Rome), but who were now *force majeure* made aware of cities such as Salamanca, Madrid and Zaragoza. The attractions of the Grand Tour of the eighteenth century had not been exhausted, but the more adventurous spirits were eager for different experiences, and so looked to Spain and Portugal. It is quite remarkable, in retrospect, that a number of young noblemen should go to the Peninsula as civilians, in effect, tourists whilst the Peninsular War was still in progress. Some had an introduction to Wellington himself and would visit him whilst he was campaigning. For example, a threesome, all grandees, The Hon. George Bridgman, later Lord Bradford, Lord John Russell, later Prime Minister, and the Hon. Robert H. Clive toured Portugal, Spain, Sicily and Malta between 1812 and 1814, when the war was at its height. They visited General Trant, the governor at Oporto; they viewed the site of the battle of Salamanca en route for Madrid. In a letter to his mother dated October 9, 1812, Bridgman wrote:

> We went to-day to the immortal field of Arapiles, it is a sad sight, however, for the ground is still covered with unburied carcasses of men and horses, on which flocks of vultures were feeding; the stench even at this distant period of above eleven weeks is very great (1875: 32).

At one point, they "rode to see our position in front, and saw the French descend in large columns, apparently to attack us. We gave way a little, when Lord Wellington brought down the First Division, upon which the French immediately retired without engaging" (1875: 39-40). They later joined in the retreat from Burgos, once Wellington raised the siege, and at the end of the year, were enjoying society in Madrid. One might further add that, at several points, Bridgman expresses his determination to learn Spanish. He wrote: "I have picked up a good deal of the language from my grammar, and talking with the peasants, and I can read it tolerably with occasional assistance from the dictionary". He also "laid out" [spent] £60 on books, including "a large folio of the maps of Spain by Lopez" for dispatch back to England (1875: 53-4).

From this and from other evidence in the letters, one can make the following deductions. Firstly, that there existed what might be called a kind of war tourism for the elite; this was not for the sake of voyeurism, but rather an extension of, or even substitute for the Grand Tour, and not for the faint-hearted, and only available to those with both wealth and connections in high places, as well as an adventurous spirit. Secondly, such tourists, and there were others apart from those mentioned, made an effort to learn the language. This would suggest that they did not regard themselves as superior, but recognized that a knowledge of Spanish would assist them in their pursuit of understanding and appreciating the country and its past, just as French was a *sine qua non*, and Italian was learnt by travellers to Italy for a better appreciation of that country's past. Bradford, by his own admission, sought to acquire Spanish so that he could read the books that he bought. These three noblemen mixed in the most exalted circles, and back in England after their long absence, would not only freely communicate their impressions, but also had a library to continue their interest. Indeed, Russell wrote two works with a Spanish theme, which he published in 1822. The first, a novella about a young English soldier called *The Nun of Arrouca*, perhaps because the trio visited this place at the start of their tour in Portugal [Russell was soon to regret this youthful exuberance, and tried to withdraw all copies from sale]; the second was *Don Carlos, Or A Persecution, A Tragedy in Five Acts* (1822), which ran into five editions. Thirdly, the rank and file of the soldiery represented an influence of a quite different nature, certainly unquantifiable but by no means negligible.

Amongst the prominent visitors to the Peninsula in wartime one may count Lord Holland, accompanied by his wife. They had been to Spain on several previous occasions, the first in 1793 when Lord Holland met Argüelles in Oviedo, and in October 1808 they "roamed in and out of the theatre of war in ambassadorial style" (1850: 148; 1989: 52). They spent four months in Sevilla in 1809, holding court in the grand manner. One of their guests was José María Blanco, later known as Blanco White. Holland House in London was to have immense significance, not only for the exiled Blanco White, but as a central focus for Spanish culture and politics. Less well known is William Jacob MP (1761-1851), who spent two years (1809-1810) in the south of Spain, principally Seville, and whose letters, published in 1811, comprise a full and accurate account of the *status quo* in the Peninsula. In 1809, he met "Padre Blanco, so well known throughout Spain as the author of the patriotic semanario", "a priest without bigotry, a philosopher without vanity" (1811: 145). There are a number of lesser known figures who, on returning to England, published the account of their journeyings.[1] Before the advent of the War, Reverend George Whittington had sought to provide some information about Spain that was neither historical nor driven by tourism. Darwin's uncle, whose letters were not published until the twentieth century, revealed that travel in Spain and Portugal during the early part of the War was a hazardous undertaking. How many others who went to

---

1   For example, [Rev. George Downing Whittington], *Travels through Spain and Part of Portugal, with commercial, statistical, and geographical details*, 2 vols (London: Richard Phillips, 1808); Sir Francis Sacheverell Darwin, *Travels in Spain and the East 1808-1810* (Cambridge: The University Press, 1927). The author was an uncle of Charles Darwin.

the Peninsula, but did not record their experiences, may never be determined...

There was another way through which the Peninsular War had an
impact on the English; I refer to the supply routes. John Bowring (1792-
1872) was sent to Spain as a clerk for an English merchant in 1812 and
again in 1813 when he witnessed the siege of San Sebastián, July 28 to
August 31. "His principal dealings were with local suppliers and Wellington's officers, when the headquarters of the British army were at
Lesaca south of the river Bidassoa. He was in charge of the cargo of
wheat and stores for the British army" (Hitchcock 1993: 44). Subsequently, he remained trading in the South of France and in Spain until
the end of 1814. Although Bowring had acquired a grounding in foreign
languages, including Spanish, during his schooling, it may be reasonably
assumed that his interest grew through the contacts he made then and in
later visits.

A second substantial source for the increase in awareness of Spain
was the embroilment of many Spaniards in the political turmoil following the restoration to the throne of Fernando VII in 1814. This resulted in
the exile of Spanish liberals in London, an event that was to be repeated
in 1823 with the collapse of the *trienio*. White had come to England earlier, and had founded a journal, the *Español* in 1810. In this, writing
both under his name and under a pseudonym, White criticised the Cortes
at Cadiz for not taking a robust attitude towards the French, incurring
their wrath for his support of the coup against Spain in Caracas, perhaps
through the influence of his friend, Andrés Bello. White had settled in
Oxford at the time of the influx of the political refugees to London in
1814, and stood apart from them. For the first period of exile, one might
name Bartolomé José Gallardo, scholar and librarian of the Cortes, a
major polemical figure in Spanish politics in the first half of the century,
and Antonio Puigblanch (1775-1842) whose notorious *The Inquisition
Unmasked* was published in London in 1816.[2] This topic had already
been made familiar to the English reading public in 1810, with the publi-

---

2   A. Puigblanch, *The Inquisition Unmasked: Being An Historical And Philosophical
     Account of the Tremendous tribunal, Founded on Authentic Documents; and Exhib-
     iting the necessity of its Suppression, as a Means of Reform and Regeneration.*
     Translated from the author's enlarged copy by William Walton, Esq., 2 vols (Lon-
     don: Baldwin, Cradock, and Joy, 1816).

cation of Stockdale's *History of the Inquisition*.[3] It was Puigblanch, who also came to England after 1823, who was responsible for this self-advertisement:

> La Cataluña en todos los tiempos reputada no muy literata es la más interesada en promover las miras del Dr. P., no solo por el mérito tal cual fuere de sus anunciadas obras, sino también por lo que pueda el ejemplo de un patricio estimular a la Juventud Catalana (quoted in Allison Peers 1924: 319).

Ángel Anaya published an *Essay on Spanish Literature* in London in 1818 directed toward "the English student", which he described as "a mere sketch of the progress of Literature in Spain". He conducts "An Inquiry into the causes of the prejudice existing against Spanish literature", and appends "Some specimens of language and style in prose and verse, taken from various Castilian authors", which include extracts from Luzán, Campomanes and Cadalso, all of the eighteenth century. The author was, in effect, making a plea for the reinstatement of Spanish into the European canon, vigorously rejecting Montesquieu's opinion that Spain had produced no more than one good work, which is *Don Quixote* (1818: vi, 31-5, 125-76). Anaya's book contains the Publisher's catalogue of "Books for the Use of Schools", including sections for French, Italian and Spanish. This list comprises twenty-six works, all published by Boosey and Sons which, taken as a whole, demonstrate an unmistakable intention to stimulate an interest in Spanish amongst their clientele.

During this second decade of the nineteenth century, personal accounts of the Peninsular War came out: Steele's *Notes of the War in Spain*, not published until 1824, is noteworthy for the map of Cadiz, signalling its political significance and its prevalence over the three tourist icons of Sevilla, Córdoba and Granada. Poems with a Peninsular War theme, such as Crocker's *The Battle of Talavera* with his own notes on the battle, which ran into ten editions between 1809 and 1816, were also

---

3   John Joseph Stockdale, *The History of the Inquisitions; including the Secret Transactions of those Horrific Tribunals*, illustrated with Twelve Plates (London: Printed for J. J. Stockdale, 1810). The Inquisition was a topic that appealed to British readers. A decade after Puigblanch's book, an abridged translation of Juan Antonio Llorente's *Histoire critique de l'Inquisition espagnole* (Paris, 1817-1818) was made available to them under the title *History of the Inquisition of Spain* (London: Whittaker, 1826).

extremely popular. Poetic evocations of this kind clearly struck chords. These circumstances go some way toward explaining the heightened awareness of Spain in England during the first two decades of the nineteenth century, but it is evident that there have to have been other factors.

Lord Holland (1773-1840), a prominent Whig politician was a dominant member of society in London; he entertained Spanish diplomats and grandees, and had a fine library of Spanish books which, it seems, he was content to lend out. The records of these loans survive, and provide a fascinating insight into contemporary interests and requirements: Jeremy Bentham borrowed three legal works in Spanish; Southey, three Spanish sources as background for his narrative poem, *Roderick, the Last of the Goths*; Blanco White, the *Anales* of Sevilla, and "Eleven Spanish pamphlets of 1821"; and Dr McCrie, Pellicer's *Ensayo de una Biblioteca* (1874: 180-83). It was McCrie who later published an authoritative account of the Reformation in Spain, based on Spanish sources (1829). Lord Holland found time himself to write *Some Account of the Life and Writings of Lope Felix de Vega Carpio*, and see it through to a second, enlarged edition.[4]

Robert Southey, later to be poet laureate, in contrast, lived in Keswick, and not in the grand manner. He had travelled extensively in Spain and Portugal, and through his familiarity with Spanish literature has sound claims for being considered the first English Hispanist. His *Letters written during a short residence in Spain and Portugal* went into two editions before 1800, and in the Preface to his translation of *Amadis de Gaul*, he wrote: "Perhaps others may not see the beauty which I perceive; the necessity of dwelling on every sentence has produced in me a love for the whole", words indicative of his engagement with his subject, and of his literary perspicacity (Lobeira 1872: xxvi).[5] In a letter in 1818, he described his own achievements: "I have read widely in Spanish poetry; and might in historical and literary recollections call myself half a Spaniard, if, being half a Portuguese also, this would leave any room for the English part of my intellectual being". He did not mix in the same

---

4   Henry Richard Lord Holland, *Some Account of the life and Writings of Lope Felix de Vega Carpio* (London: Longman, Hurst, Rees, and Orme, 1806); *Some Account of the Life and Writings of Lope Felix de Vega Carpio and Guillen de Castro*, 2 vols. (London: Longman, 1817).

5   The translation was first published in 4 vols. in 1803.

circles as Lord Holland, but does record a dinner in Holland House in 1813, possibly his first visit there, where he met Byron (1912: 286, 217).

The romantic ardour for Spain may be observed in works by Walter Scott, Lord Byron, and Mrs Felicia Hemans among others. These were fuelled in part by the histories of Spain, and of Spanish literature in existence, such as Friedrich Bouterwek's *History of Spanish literature*, translated into English, but there may have been another significant factor, the Gothic novel. The fashion for Gothic fiction of which Walpole's 1764 *Castle of Otranto* was a prototype led to authors reaching further and further afield in their quest for suitably remote settings for their stories of mystery and the supernatural. In the early days of the genre, the tales were frequently set in medieval Germany or Italy. When this potential had been exhausted, authors turned to Spain; a number of the titles suggest a Spanish setting for the horrors to be unfolded within.

In the 1820s, the short-lived resurrection of liberalism in Spain (1820-1823) attracted the attention of radicals such as Jeremy Bentham who, with the aid of his newly acquired confidant, John Bowring, concocted a draft constitution for the Cortes, and maintained correspondence with the Conde de Toreno, the President. Bowring was Bentham's controversial choice as the first editor of the influential *Westminster Review* in 1824. A key behind-the-scenes and little-known figure in these years was the naval officer Edward Blaquiere (1779-1832) who introduced Bowring to Bentham, and who, in a series of letters from Spain, provided an unrivalled first-hand account of the political upheavals: "The revolution of 1820 is, in fact, one of the sublimest instances of forbearance, magnanimity and self-denial that history will have to record" (1822: 349). A similar but slighter publication which owed much to Blaquiere, who wrote the Introduction, was *The Anecdotes of the Spanish and Portuguese Revolutions* (1823), by Count Giuseppe Pecchio (1785-1835), a Milanese nobleman with liberal leanings who later married an Englishwoman and settled in England. In a letter from Madrid dated July 25, 1821, he identifies the "Forces operating against the Constitution", incorporating "all those who are accustomed to live by favours and gifts; the clergy including archbishops, bishops, chapters, canons &, who lose their enormous revenues"; and "nearly all the old generals" (68). The frontispiece to his book is a portrait of Rafael de Riego y Núñez (1785-1823), the charismatic general who was hanged when the French took Madrid in 1823, and whose name is synonymous with liberty in Spain.

If the Romantic image of Spain had received a boost in the aftermath of the Peninsular War, it went into abeyance in the 1820s. Serious students of Spain interpreted the political situation, and many distinguished refugees stamped the imprint on London, but the impetus for visiting the country waned, with noblemen preferring the traditional haunts of Paris and the Grand Tour. England still maintained a healthy trade with Spain, and retained consuls in cities such as Málaga. However, with the accession of William IV to the throne of England in 1830, a new adventurous spirit seemed to have been released (although I am not necessarily implying any connexion). Richard Ford (1796-1858) spent three years in Spain (November, 1830-October, 1833), establishing a home for himself and his family in Sevilla, from where he embarked on a number of journeys through Spain. Whilst there, one might say that he "Hispanified", that is to say, he learnt the language, dressed in Spanish apparel, and became absorbed in Spanish mores, culture and history. It was an archetypical Romantic gesture to opt to rent apartments in the Alhambra in the summer, where he could indulge in his hobby of watercolouring, welcome guests, and enjoy the cool of the ruins. The reason why he chose to move his wife and family to Andalucía traditionally given is his wife's delicate state of health, but this has always struck me as ludicrous. It was surely imprudent to expose his wife, in particular, let alone his three young children to a climate where cholera was known to be rife. A more credible explanation suggests itself, namely Ford's own nature, his spirit of enterprise, his immense even arrogant self-belief in his own capabilities, and his devil-may-care attitude to life. He thought nothing of running risks, which in some measure accounts for the extraordinary commercial success of his *Hand-Book*. One must not underestimate the scholarship that underpins this work, which almost singlehandedly set down the markers for travel to Spain in the Victorian era, and unleashed a torrent of tourists, many clutching a copy of Ford's indispensable guide-book.

However, travel in the Peninsula was not all like this; Inglis's *Rambles in the Footsteps of Don Quixote* of 1837, with characteristic illustrations by George Cruickshank, was so shallow as to be a caricature, whereas George Borrow's *Bible in Spain* was a work on an altogether more exalted plane (1843). This achieved what may justly be described as an astounding if unanticipated success, being reprinted six times in the year of publication, 1843. In the Preface, Borrow wrote: "I am no tourist, no writer of books of travels"; "the present work is devoted to an account of what befell me in Spain whilst engaged in distributing the Scriptures" (xx); "I was, as I may say, from first to last adrift in Spain" (x); "though various books have been published about Spain, I believe that the present [book] is the only one in existence which treats of missionary labour in that country" (x). Borrow did not come from a privileged background, but perhaps in common with Bowring, he went through life with an enormous chip on his shoulder. He was a writer with an exceptional talent for bringing his characters to life by description and through dialogue, as in his masterpiece *Lavengro* (1851). When in England, he was a refugee in his own country; when in Spain a wanderer with no fixed objective, buoyed up by his facility for languages; he spoke Spanish with the Spaniards, Romani when with gypsies, even snatches of Hebrew and Arabic where and when required. He was not driven by any so-called missionary ardour; selling Bibles on behalf of the British and Foreign Bible Society was the ostensible motive for his journeys in Spain, but this was a pretext for his numerous objectives: to wit, to urge himself towards the limits of endurance, to suffer or relish day-to-day experiences, to sail without exception close to the wind, to prove himself, and perhaps, above all, to be noticed. He was a showman *par excellence*. It is ironical that someone whose principal goal was arguably to exalt and promote his own image should, almost as an accidental by-product have removed the veil from Spain, laid it bare for countless English-speaking readers, avid for vicarious experiences.

So two books published in the 1840s, one wittingly and one unwittingly, brought into being a vogue for Spain, which was to wax and wane over the decades but which was never to be extinguished. Travelling in Europe from thenceforward comprised Spain as well as the "Grand Tour" countries, as a passport, issued on June 1, 1850, in Italy, by the British Minister Plenipotentiary in Italy, written in French, entitling Lady Walrond, her daughter, a servant and a chambermaid to pass freely through France, Spain and Portugal.

There is much that I have had to omit in this overview, but my reflections to date lead me to conclude that it was a set of sundry, often divergent circumstances that attracted people's attention to Spain. To apply some perspective to all this, it could be argued that in the first half of the nineteenth century the British people knew more about India than the Iberian Peninsula.

Bibliography

Allison Peers, E. 1924. "The Literary Activities of the Spanish 'emigra-
    dos' in England (1814-1834)", *Modern Language Review* 19, 315-
    24; 445-58.

Anaya, A. 1818. *An Essay on Spanish Literature, Containing its History,
    from the Commencement of the Twelfth Century, to the Present
    Time,* London, Boosey and Sons.

Blaquiere, E. 1822. *An Historical Review of the Spanish Revolution,
    Including some Account of Religion, Manners, and Literature, in
    Spain,* London, G. & W. B. Whittaker.

Borrow, G. 1843. *The Bible in Spain; or, The Journeys, Adventures, and
    Imprisonments of an Englishman in an Attempt to Circulate the
    Scriptures in the Peninsula,* 3 vols., London, Murray.

Darwin, F. S. 1927. *Travels in Spain and the East 1808-1810,* Cam-
    bridge, The University Press.

G. A. H. F. B. 1875. *Letters from Portugal, Spain, Sicily, and Malta,*
    London, Chiswick Press.

Hitchcock, R. 1993. "John Bowring, Hispanist and Translator of Spanish
    Poetry", in J. Youings (ed.), *Sir John Bowring 1792-1872. Aspects
    of His Life and Career,* Exeter, The Devonshire Association, 43-53.

Jacob, W. 1811. *Travels in the South of Spain, in Letters written A. D. 1809
    and 1810,* London, J. Johnson & W. Miller.

Llorente, J. A. 1826 [1817-18]. *History of the Inquisition of Spain, from the
    Time of its Establishment to the Reign of Ferdinand VII,* London,
    Whittaker.

Lobeira, V. 1872 [1803]. *Amadis of Gaul,* translated from the Spanish
    Version of Garciordonez de Montalvo by Robert Southey, A New
    Edition, 3 vols., London, John Russell Smith.

Lord Holland, H. R. 1806. *Some Account of the life and Writings of Lope
    Felix de Vega Carpio,* London, Longman, Hurst, Rees & Orme.

—. 1817. *Some Account of the Life and Writings of Lope Felix de Vega
    Carpio and Guillen de Castro,* 2 vols., London, Longman.

—. 1850. *Foreign Reminiscences,* edited by his son, Henry Edward Lord
    Holland, London, Longman, Brown, Green & Longmans.

M'Crie, T. 1829. *History of the Progress and Suppression of the Reformation in Spain in the Sixteenth Century*, Edinburgh, Blackwood; London, Cadell.

Murphy, M. 1989. *Blanco White. Self-Banished Spaniard*, New Haven & London, Yale UP.

Pecchio, G. 1823. *The Anecdotes of the Spanish and Portuguese Revolutions*, London, G. & W. B. Whittaker.

Princess Marie Liechtenstein. 1874. *Holland House*, 2 vols., vol. II, London, Macmillan.

Puigblanch, A. 1816. *The Inquisition Unmasked: Being An Historical And Philosophical Account of the Tremendous tribunal, Founded on Authentic Documents; and Exhibiting the necessity of its Suppression, as a Means of Reform and Regeneration.* Translated from the author's enlarged copy by William Walton, Esq., London, Baldwin, Cradock, & Joy, 2 vols.

Southey, R. 1912. *Letters of Robert Southey, a Selection*, M. H. Fitzgerald (ed.). London, Henry Frowde, Oxford UP.

Stockdale, J. J. 1810. *The History of the Inquisitions; Including the Secret Transactions of those Horrific Tribunals*, London, J. J. Stockdale.

[Whittington, G. D.]. 1808. *Travels through Spain and Part of Portugal, with Commercial, Statistical, and Geographical Details*, 2 vols., London, Richard Phillips, 1808.

MIQUEL BERGA BAGUÉ

Catalans at War: Representations of Catalonia during the Spanish Civil War

Langdon-Davies, the English journalist and author who —like Graves in Majorca or Brenan in Andalusia— came to Spain in the aftermath of the First World War in search of a rural arcadia, away from the horrors of mechanical civilisation, settled first in the Catalan Pyrenees and later on in the unspoilt Costa Brava of the 1920s. He was the author of the first full book devoted to Catalan culture and society in the twentieth century. His *Dancing Catalans* (1929), took the sardana, the typical dance of Catalonia, as a metaphor of the ideals of Catalan *Noucentisme*, a program of national reconstruction based on order, culture and an idealized version of the Greek classical past. The publication came out in time for the International Exhibition of Barcelona in 1929 and the book was a considerable success, both in Britain and the United States. Langdon-Davies's next book about Catalonia was a vivid account of the first months of the war with the knowledge of an eye-witness and a foreigner totally familiar with the language and the people of Catalonia. *Behind the Spanish Barricades* was published in November 1936 and became a best-seller with subsequent editions in the United States. When the book came out George Orwell was in the process of preparing to set out for Barcelona the following month, December 1936.

The militant enthusiasm and political fascination that pervades Langdon-Davies's account of the first months of the war was to be deeply modulated by the harsh realities of the development of the war and the growing political conflicts in the Republican side in Orwell's now famous account *Homage to Catalonia*, published in 1938. During the war, Langdon-Davies stood as the *typical* good-hearted fellow traveller of the Communist strategy (he was the author of the dismissive review of *Homage to Catalonia* in the communist *Daily Worker*) and Orwell the symbol of the dissident leftist who through his involvement with the POUM militias was to learn, precociously, the evils of Stalinism. By the end of the war, both writers were on the same side: fervent anti-Stalinists who stood for democratic socialism and full of regret and compassion for the Spanish people suffering the exhaustion of defeat and war, and now facing the harsh dictatorship of General Franco.

It is against the background of those important books on the war in Catalonia by English writers that I want to focus on the works of a woman writer, Nancy Johnstone, who wrote two extraordinary, yet practically forgotten, books about her experiences in trying to run, with the help of her husband, a small hotel in Tossa de Mar, at the heart of the Catalan Costa Brava. In *Hotel in Spain* (1937) and *Hotel in Flight* (1939), both published by Faber & Faber, the author documents her experiences in Catalonia from 1934 to 1939.

Spain began to be seen, in the 1930s, as an attractive destination by some adventurous Britons. The country was gloriously cheap and still contained the promise of a rural Arcadia. The fact that, for the majority, Spain "was distant and unimportant, a country which at best was non-threatening by virtue of its reduced circumstances" (Shelmerdine 2002: 367) did not stop a number of English writers from settling in that remote Peninsula. To them, wounded and jaded by a cynicism brought on by life in the metropolis of the empire, this new journey was extremely appealing. In Spain, an inexpensive, quiet life amid exotic surroundings was virtually guaranteed; a peaceful place of plenty that was ideal for dedicating oneself to writing. It was in this spirit that Nancy and Archie Johnstone took the same step when they discovered the remote Tossa de Mar. Their perceptions of Spain were somehow typical of the British left: the Spanish Republic was carrying out a sort of peaceful revolution that would allow the new Spain to take her place among the democratic nations of Europe and get rid of the country's reactionary evils, that is, the military, the landlords and the clergy (Buchanan 2007: 1-22).[1]

Archie was a veteran Scottish journalist who had spent years working in London's Fleet Street, mostly for *The News Chronicle*. He was a man approaching forty whose life took a radical change of direction thanks to his younger partner's enthusiasm for the adventure of living

---

1   For a study of the ideological profile of British travellers during the same period see Schweizer (2001). For a general survey of travellers to Spain during the Civil War see Chapter 5 —"La Guerra Civil Española (1936-1939)"— in J. Ruíz Mas (2003: 92-108).

and working abroad. Nancy, born and raised in Bath in the genteel atmosphere of well-off country folk, had the restless temperament of her Irish ancestors. She would soon be thirty. She was a confident and determined young woman and she was convinced that one of her responsibilities was to infect her husband with the bug for an alternative life. She was certain that in Tossa they would find a way of making a living and live like kings, with the added advantage of being able to give full vent to their literary aspirations. In fact, they were by no means the first foreigners in Tossa. The place already had its regular visitors and every year more "newcomers" swelled their numbers.

In October 1934 —while the Johnstones were purchasing the plot of land in Tossa on which they would build their curious hotel— *ART* magazine published a special issue dedicated to the colony of foreign artists, mostly German fugitives of the Nazi regime, that had grown up there. In "Tossa, Babel de les arts",[2] Rafael Benet appraised the number of visitors and residents in that corner of the coastal world that is, at the same time, "a market garden —where strawberries can be picked all year round— watered by a stream in which wild turtles live" (Benet 1934-35: 3). Some of the residents mentioned in Benet's article, such as the painter Oskar Zügel or the architect Fritz Marcus, both German, appear extensively in Johnstone's books on Catalonia. Among the newcomers, the angelic Marc Chagall stands out, the great painter-poet who, according to Benet, "with his blue eyes has come to drink in the blueness of Tossa" (Benet 1934-35: 20). Chagall in his turn was to contribute his own special dedication to that issue of *ART* magazine: *Tossa, paradis bleu.* Nancy Johnstone, despite the rumblings of political instability heard on radios in Tossa (in that very October of 1934 President Companys declared Catalonia an independent state[3]), also felt that she had come to live and work in a blue paradise. A year later, *Casa Johnstone* was already part of the town's seafront and the Johnstones were an integral part of the expat community. The hotel's first season was a success.

---

2   *ART*, vol. 2 (October 1934-July 1935), publication of the Junta Municipal d'Exposicions d'Art, Barcelona. For a full study of the period, see the catalogue of the exhibition curated by G. Bosch and S. Portell, *Berlín>Londres>París>Tossa... La tranquil·litat perduda* (2007).

3   The announcement, though, did never materialize and a few days later Companys and his government were all imprisoned by the Spanish authorities.

The political situation in Spain was going from bad to worse and generated great interest among the British public. With the outbreak of the War the need to supply the public with eye-witness accounts of the situation increased. The Johnstones "were amazed to hear that we were trapped among wild Bolsheviks, who were howling outside our houses for our blood, while the rebels, tactfully called 'insurgents' in *The Times*, were doing their utmost to arrive in time to save us from Something Worse than Death" (Johnstone 1937: 283). Similarly disheartening was the realization of the extent to which the Catalans had a blind faith in the democratic principles of the English nation. They were deeply convinced Britain would never let them down.

Johnstone's narrative is always amusing and rich in characters: their Catalan neighbours, the German refugees, the guests (with their absurd questions and worries!), the perfect assistant (Walter Leonard), the English journalists... And then, of course, as the war went on and on, the chronicle of how expectations were to be reconsidered and how the hotel was used for all sorts of purposes: a home for British journalists covering the war or for poets recovering from the shock, like Auden himself; a temporary headquarters for dubious commissars; a rest house for relief workers; and a refuge for children (under the auspices of the International Solidarity Fund) through the days of the greatest food scarcity and to the bitter end when they took the children to safety just before Tossa fell to General Franco's troops.

The process of publication of Johnstone's books on Catalonia is marked by the events of the war. It is significant that it is Frank Jellinek, the author of a remarkable book on the civil war[4] and a regular guest at Casa Johnstone, who recommended publication to Faber & Faber, the prestigious publishing house headed by T.S. Eliot.[5]

After the success of the first season for Casa Johnstone, the magnificent outlook for the summer of 1936 was set back, as would be so many

4   *The Civil War in Spain* (London: Gollancz, 1938). Orwell published a positive review of the book in spite of the author's communist sympathies and discrepancies over the May Events of 1937 and the suppression of the POUM. They maintained a correspondence on the matter that suggests mutual respect and admiration.

5   The presence of a number of distinguished visitors in Casa Johnstone, usually invited by the Catalan government as the war dragged on, has been seen as part of a movement of "Spanish war tourism" intended to produce favourable publicity abroad (Garcia 2010: 221).

things, by the military coup and its consequences. Up until then, the account of the Johnstones had resembled that sub-genre of travel literature —the "Home Abroad" register— that has proved to be such a rich vein in English literature. However, the book's indisputable added value is directly linked to the Johnstones' decision to reject the offer of repatriation made by the British government to the residents and to stay in Tossa in spite of the war. They refused to "let down" the people of their adopted home and so decided to see out the war in Tossa de Mar. And this is how a hypothetical "A Year in the Costa Brava" becomes the most complete and continuous chronicle about the life of some English people in Catalonia during the Civil War.

The narrative sequence that begins with the discovery of the "blue paradise" ends with the tragic flight from a lost paradise. It is the painful transition from managing a charming hotel to its conversion into a home for refugee children. And, in narrative style, it is the same sequence that goes from a prose that is open and fresh, to an eyewitness account full of adverse circumstances; from joy to sorrow and from irony, eventually, to sarcasm. Private life and personal voice are continuously modulated by the current of the story that, even in a foreign country, ends up frustrating the expectations of an untroubled and happy life with which the author began her journey. Perhaps it is for this reason that the most noteworthy reviews of Johnstone's *Hotel in Flight*, which were published once the Civil War was over, are by two English writers who had experienced it intensely.[6] The first is George Orwell, the author of *Homage to Catalonia* (1938), and the second is Ralph Bates, author of *The Olive Field* (1936), someone who knew Republican Spain well and who was a summer visitor to Tossa. Bates played a leading role in the organisation of the International Brigades and became editor of the British contingent's magazine *Volunteer for Liberty*.

Both reviewers look upon Johnstone's account with a measure of condescension. However, they value her extraordinary courage in saving the refugee children that stayed in the hotel, as well as her account of daily life until the end of the war, far from the political dispute and the

---

6   See Orwell's "The Spanish War" and Bates's "Postscripts on Spain". In general, we may say that Johnstone's books were widely and positively reviewed at the time of publication in leading publications like *The Times Literary Supplement*, *The New York Times*, *The Scotsman* or *The Saturday Review*, among others.

fighting on the front. Both critics coincide in highlighting the final chapters of *Hotel in Flight*, with the Johnstones protecting their children in the Edison Theatre in Figueres during the horrible days of 1939 when defeat and flight turned the town into a hell. And, above all, the critics emphasize the bitter but vigorous account of Johnstone's arrival in France and the life in the improvised concentration camps that the exiled Spanish were forced to suffer.

The ordeal of the road to the French border in an overloaded lorry with sixty children, with Franco's troops chasing them, is described in sober tones. Nancy Johnstone ends her narrative with a vivid account of life in the French camps when "refugees poured into France with no thought of the future" and she was fully devoted to keeping "her" thirty children together in Les Haras barracks which had been converted into a refugee camp. The children were finally sent off to a permanent home somewhere and Nancy had to see them depart from Perpignan railway station without knowing the train's final destination: "I gave them and Leonor all the money I had, several hundred francs, and promised to send more. I swore I would never abandon them. At last it was so painful that I tore myself away and rushed out of the station" (Johnstone 1939: 363). She went back to Perpignan and spent weeks there helping Spanish refugees and meeting up with friends from Tossa and Barcelona. She and Archie worked mostly with Quaker relief organizations for as long as they could. It was depressing work due to the scarcity of money and supplies. Not surprisingly, the amusing tone of her narrative through all kinds of circumstances is put to the test at the very end of the book and the last lines cannot help the bitter, sarcastic tone of despair:

> The relief work depended on what help the British Government cared to give. Voluntary organizations were drained. But one organization was still going strong. A contingent of plus-four clad gentlemen arrived from England to shoot painlessly the wandering, starving Spanish mules. It seemed a pity that they did not first shoot painlessly the cooped-up, starving Spanish refugees (Johnstone 1939: 378).

Johnstone's autobiographical account provides an exceptional testimony of a social, cultural and political micro-climate —that of Tossa de Mar— during the most distressing period for Catalonia in modern times, that which goes from the events of October 1934 to the exodus of 1939. In as far as they represent a woman's view and the most comprehensive account of the Civil War in Catalonia, Johnstone's narratives can now be seen as a complementary counterpart to the other two English writers who left substantial eye-witness accounts of the period.

If John Langdon-Davies wrote a vivid journalistic account of the war and the revolutionary atmosphere during the first months of the conflict in *Behind the Spanish Barricades* (1936), and George Orwell covered the key events of May 1937 in the streets of Barcelona in *Homage to Catalonia* (1938), Johnstone's books offer a full background of the war in Catalonia written away from the trenches but lived through a similarly engaged political stance. Langdon-Davies's and Orwell's accounts are taken, as it were, to the very end of the war by Nancy Johnstone, to include the personal testimony of a British citizen who experienced, alongside the defeated Republicans, the exodus towards France and life in the concentration camps. The recent publication of a Catalan translation of *Hotel in Spain* and *Hotel in Flight*, presented in a single volume,[7] seems to offer —seventy-two years later— a sort of poetic justice to Nancy Johnstone's extraordinary record of life among the Catalans in dire circumstances.

Bibliography

Bates, R. 1940. "Postscripts on Spain", *The Saturday Review* (11 May 1940), 6-15.
Benet, R. 1934-35. "Tossa, Babel de les Arts", *ART* 2: 1 (October 1934-July 1935), 3-30.
Bosch, G. & S. Portell. 2007. *Berlín>Londres>París>Tossa... La tranquil·litat perduda,* Girona, Fundació Caixa Girona.
Buchanan, T. 2007. *The Impact of the Spanish Civil War on Britain.* Eastbourne, Sussex Academic Press.
Garcia, H. 2010. "Potemkin in Spain? British Unofficial Missions of Investigation to Spain during the Civil War", *European History Quarterly* 40, 217-39.

---

7   Nancy Johnstone, *Un hotel a la costa* (2011). This is an edited translation of the two books in a single volume.

Jellinek, F. 1938. *The Civil War in Spain*, London, Gollancz.

Johnstone, A. 2001 [1952]. *In the Name of Peace*, Honolulu, UP of the Pacific.

Johnstone, N. 1937. *Hotel in Spain*, London, Faber & Faber.

—. 1939. *Hotel in Flight,* London, Faber & Faber.

—. 2011. *Un hotel a la costa*, M. Berga (trans.), Barcelona, Tusquets.

Langdon-Davies, J. 1936. *Behind the Spanish Barricades*, London, Secker & Warburg.

Orwell, G. 1938. *Homage to Catalonia*, London, Secker & Warburg.

—. 1939. "The Spanish War", *The Adelphi* (December 1939), 125-26.

Ruíz Mas, J. 2003. *Libros de viajes en lengua inglesa por la España del siglo XX*, Madrid, Grupo Editorial Universitario.

Shelmerdine, B. 2002. "The Experiences of British Holidaymakers and Expatriate Residents in Pre-Civil War Spain", *European History Quarterly* 32: 3, 367-90.

Schweizer, B. 2001. *Radicals on the Road: The Politics of English Travel Writing in the 1930s*, Charlottesville, UP of Virginia.

ISABELLE BES HOGHTON

El mallorquín en la literatura de viajes francesa del siglo XIX

A lo largo del siglo XIX, algo más de una veintena de viajeros franceses, entre los cuales, André Grasset de Saint-Sauveur, Isidore Taylor, George Sand, Charles Dembowski, Jean-Joseph Bonaventure Laurens, Joséphine de Brinckmann, Léopold Alfred Gabriel Germond de Lavigne, Charles Davillier, Paul Henry, Abdon Mathieu, Gaston Vuillier, André Hallays, Edouard Conte y Marius Bernard, visitaron Mallorca. Estos literatos y artistas románticos y posrománticos dejaron una visión muy peculiar de la isla y de sus habitantes. Marcada por la representación romántica del insular, la figura del mallorquín acabó por fundirse con la del "afortunado" y del "buen salvaje". Tras una rápida presentación del concepto de "afortunado" y "buen salvaje" en la literatura francesa de la Ilustración y principios del XIX, estudiaremos cómo esta concepción peculiar del insular marcó la visión de los viajeros a Mallorca.

En Francia, desde la época colonial, existía una dicotomía entre el hombre civilizado y el salvaje. Si en los siglos XVI-XVII se hablaba del buen civilizado y del bárbaro salvaje, en el XVIII, la situación se invirtió con el barón de Lahontan (*Diálogos con un salvaje*, 1704), que popularizó el personaje del "buen salvaje", vigoroso, sencillo, generoso, que desconoce la corrupción de las ciencias y de las artes, y que es feliz porque obedece a la naturaleza. Marmontel (*Los Incas*, 1777), Rousseau (*Discurso sobre el origen y los fundamentos de la desigualdad entre los hombres*, 1755) y Bernardin de Saint-Pierre (*La choza india*, 1790) consolidaron esta figura del buen salvaje "libre, sano, bueno y feliz". Con este último, al que hay que añadir *Pablo y Virginia* (1787), que retrataba la felicidad de la sociedad primitiva de la isla de Francia (actual isla Mauricio), el habitante de las islas acabó por fundirse por completo con la figura del popular "Viernes" de Defoe, bueno y feliz.

Si desde la Antigüedad, el imaginario de la isla estaba relacionado con el paraíso terrenal a través del mito de las islas afortunadas (Hesíodo, *Los Trabajos y los Días*, 170-173; Píndaro, *Olímpicas, II*; Homero, *Odisea, IV*: 563-568), fueron Jean-Jacques Rousseau y Jacques Henri Bernardin de Saint-Pierre quienes iban a afianzar este mito del paraíso insular en Francia a finales del siglo XVIII. Rousseau comparaba lo que había vivido en la isla de San Pedro a la felicidad de los Afortunados: "Es la vida de los afortunados en el otro mundo, y yo hacía de ello en adelante mi felicidad suprema en éste" *(368)*. Bernardin de Saint-Pierre, por su parte, convertía la isla Mauricio en un lugar de amor y belleza, de felicidad primitiva con una humanidad sin pecado, virgen de toda corrupción social.

Al principio del siglo XIX, el mito de la isla paraíso con sus "afortunados" seguía muy vigente. A lo largo del siglo, la imagen de Mallorca se vio afectada por este mito, como atestigua la obra de referencia del siglo XIX, el *Grand dictionnaire universel du XIXe siècle* de Pierre Larousse (1867-1890), que describe su "clima suave y templado", su "fertilidad prodigiosa", y sus mallorquines "alegres", "humanos, francos, hospitalarios" (Larousse 1873: X, 984). George Sand confirmaba en su *Invierno en Mallorca* esta imagen del insular que propagaba cualquier obra sobre las Baleares de la época:

> En todas las geografías descriptivas que he consultado, he encontrado en el artículo *Baleares* esta breve indicación que confirmo aquí, sin perjuicio de señalar más tarde las consideraciones que atenúan su verdad: "Estos insulares son *muy afables* (sabido es que en todas las islas, la raza humana se clasifica en dos categorías: los que son antropófagos y los que son muy afables). Son amables, hospitalarios, es muy raro que cometan un crimen, y el robo casi es desconocido entre ellos" (38).

El viajero que visitaba Mallorca, una isla "perdida" en el Mediterráneo y casi desconocida en Francia, solo podía esperar encontrar en ella a un hombre lejos de la civilización, un hombre en estado natural.[1] Y fue, en efecto, lo que quiso retratar a sus coetáneos. Olvidó por completo al habitante de la ciudad, para interesarse solo por el habitante del campo que le daba la imagen buscada del insular. Si mencionaba, a veces, al

---

1   Joséphine de Brinckmann escribe en una carta del 26 de junio de 1850 que en el continente se considera generalmente a las Baleares "como países perdidos por la civilización" (317). Marius Bernard sigue afirmando al final del mismo siglo: "Mallorca, Menorca, Ibiza son, para nosotros, como islas muy lejanas, casi desconocidas, pobladas de insulares apenas civilizados" (202).

habitante de la capital, Palma, únicamente era para lamentar su europeización tanto en su forma de vestir como en sus costumbres (Taylor 1860: 251). Hacia finales del siglo, este mismo viajero rehuía Sóller, "la ciudad del trabajo y de la industria"[2] (Conte 1895: 148). Allí volvía a encontrar a los obreros de la Francia industrial con "el pañuelo escarlata atado debajo de la barbilla" (Conte 1895: 148) que mostraban su "dependencia del juego, la bebida y la costumbre de ir al bar para matar la tarde, que los Mallorquines de los demás cantones pasan en familia" (Conte 1895: 151).[3]

El único elemento de la sociedad mallorquina todavía no alcanzado por el progreso y parado en un tiempo primitivo era el *pagès*. Los campesinos ofrecían al viajero "la naturaleza cogida *in fraganti*" (Laurens 2006: 87) y componían "un cuadro viviente que recuerda a los segadores de Léopold Robert" (Laurens 2006: 88). Los pastores mallorquines, con su piel de cabra parda en la espalda, le llevaban a "la más alta antigüedad" y agudizaban su imaginación romántica. Su descripción roza frecuentemente el arquetipo, como nos muestran varios ejemplos. Por un lado, Charles Dembowski afirma que el pastor "[d]esconoce la *cuchilla-da*, acaba sus disputas con puñetazos, hace medias de punto o canta durante su tiempo libre, y venera a San Antonio igual que a Dios y a la Virgen" (I, 299). Por otro, Marius Bernard observa: "Y, por la tarde, mientras que, en la puerta, esperamos la hora del sueño, unos campesinos, —*pageses*—, regresan del campo con los sonidos idílicos de la flauta y de la guitarra que preceden a su pequeña tropa" (228). Y también André Hallays, al final del siglo, "con su atavío bíblico y sus caras labradas de arrugas", los compara con los "pastores de una Natividad pintada por Ribera" (1899: 336).

Se insistió hasta la exageración en la bondad, la dulzura y la felicidad de este pueblo campesino. Según la tradición que Estrabón inició

---

2   Los textos en francés en la versión original han sido traducidos por la autora.
3   Antònia Morey observa que, a partir de 1880, Sóller desarrolla y mecaniza la manufactura de algodón (150) y concluye que a partir de la segunda mitad del siglo los fundamentos de un nuevo modelo social y económico caracterizado por la industrialización se ponen en marcha en las Baleares (157). Manuel Santana, en el capítulo "Les transformacions socials" de esta misma obra, afirma que en el último tercio del siglo, una serie de transformaciones sociales y económicas, entre las cuales, la aparición de una nueva burguesía capitalista y de una clase obrera, cambia progresivamente las bases estructurales tradicionales de la sociedad (213).

con su retrato de los insulares felices, todos los viajeros, incluso Grasset de Saint-Sauveur —que había sido mucho más crítico de la isla que halagador—, volvieron a repetir lo que poco a poco se transformó en un cliché. Ilustrado, sea por anécdotas (Taylor 1860: 252-53), sea por datos judiciales (Dembowski 1841: 300) o simples exclamaciones (Grasset de Saint-Sauveur 1807: 299), la pureza de este pueblo pacífico, bueno y feliz inundó las páginas de los relatos de viaje. Según éstos, las casas tenían las puertas abiertas en los pueblos (Conte 1895: 161; Henry 1884: 78), las cárceles estaban abandonadas por falta de malhechores (Conte 1895: 162) y no había lugar designado para las ejecuciones (Taylor 1860: 252). Asimismo, los campesinos y los niños eran muy amables y corteses hacia el extranjero, saludándole, siempre quitándose el sombrero, acompañándole a veces un poco a lo largo del camino (Vuillier 1982: 50; Davillier 1874: 785), o acogiéndole con mucha cordialidad en su casa, que ponían a su disposición gratuitamente (Dembowski 1841: 303; Grasset de Saint-Sauveur 1807: 297). Ya sean del principio o del final de siglo, casi todos los viajeros afirmaban que el mallorquín desconocía el robo y el asesinato; el abate Abdon Mathieu alegó incluso que "los movimientos revolucionarios apenas hacen sentir ahí sus nefastas repercusiones" (209).

El poco grado de civilización del insular fue descrito de manera muy positiva por la mayoría de los viajeros porque presentaba esta imagen del otro tan esperada en las islas. George Sand, sin embargo, lo percibió de manera más negativa. Lejos de estar encantada por esta sociedad, fue feliz tras su regreso a Francia de haber "abandonado los salvajes de la Polinesia por el mundo civilizado" (205). Su retrato de esta sociedad primitiva está en total oposición con la descripción bucólica de los amores de los campesinos mallorquines que hace Charles Dembowski. George Sand no buscaba en absoluto en hacer soñar a su lector, llevándole a los tiempos más remotos de la pastoral antigua, sino que le presentaba, al contrario, la dura realidad a la cual se enfrentó: un campesino ignorante, en un estado primigenio de la evolución humana, "apenas […] más hombre que los seres adormilados en la conciencia del bruto", un "mono", como se atrevió a llamarle (182).[4]

Desgraciadamente fue esta caracterización negativa y muy subjetiva de este pueblo que marcó a los historiadores y geógrafos de la época. En la obra *L'Univers ou Histoire et description de tous les peuples, de leurs religions, mœurs et coutumes*, en el apéndice del tomo sobre España, el capítulo "Îles Baléares et Pityuses" (1847) de Frédéric Lacroix adoptaba enteramente la opinión de la escritora, afirmando que el testimonio de los viajeros, que citaban hechos, era más de fiar que la aserción de los geógrafos. Definía al pueblo balear por su ausencia de civilización, que no debía a sí mismo sino a las instituciones sociales, a las autoridades locales y al gobierno central "que no hacen nada para instruir y civilizar este pueblo, más digno de compasión que de reprobación" (9). Algunos años más tarde, la primera guía publicada en Francia sobre las Baleares, hablaba de nuevo de mallorquines "fanáticos, supersticiosos, indolentes y de una extrema ignorancia" (Germond de Lavigne 1866: 742) y hacía recaer la culpa de ello sobre el gobierno, los monjes y la Inquisición. Esta guía iría hasta animalizarlos nuevamente, ya no como "monos", según la célebre escritora romántica, sino como "cabras":

En invierno, se cubren de una capa gris que se parece al hábito de los monjes, o de una gran piel de cabra de África con el pelaje a la vista. Cuando andan en grupos con sus pieles leonadas atravesadas de una raya negra en la espalda y cayendo de la cabeza a los pies, se les tomaría fácilmente por un rebaño andando con las patas de atrás. Casi siempre al ir al campo o al regresar a casa, uno de ellos anda delante, tocando la guitarra o la flauta, y los demás siguen en silencio, pisándole los talones, y bajando la nariz con un aire lleno de inocencia y estupidez (Germond de Lavigne 1866: 743).

A pesar de dichas críticas, en la descripción de sus fiestas tradicionales, tanto religiosas como paganas, el insular seguía siendo un "afortunado", un hombre sencillo, feliz, que goza del momento. En el relato de viajes, cualquiera que sea la época, el viajero o el destino, la fiesta tradicional

---

4   Ella misma añade: "Y, sin embargo, este campesino mallorquín tiene dulzura, bondad, costumbres apacibles y una naturaleza calma y tranquila. No ama el mal y no conoce el bien. Se confiesa, reza y sueña sin cesar en merecer el paraíso, pero ignora los verdaderos deberes de la humanidad. No es menos odioso que un buey o un carnero, pues apenas es más hombre que los seres adormilados en la conciencia del bruto" (182).

presenta siempre una fuente inagotable de exotismo para el viajero. Las fiestas son pretexto de largas descripciones pintorescas. Además de retratar lo exótico y lo insólito, presentan al lector otros elementos igualmente buscados: estética y pintoresquismo. La fiesta, por un procedimiento de fragmentación pictórica, fue transformada en escena de género y, tal como afirma Daniel-Henri Pageaux, "la realidad española [y mallorquina] está totalmente teatralizada según las leyes de la composición pictórica" (64).

La feria del ganado, por ejemplo, descrita por Grasset de Saint-Sauveur, fue objeto de un encantador cuadro campestre. Es uno de los únicos pasajes del *Voyage* en el que el cónsul se vuelve lírico y se deja llevar por su sensibilidad para dar al lector una descripción extremadamente pintoresca:

> La llanura está cubierta de pequeños tenderetes. Ahí, en medio de los rebaños balantes, unos grupos de jóvenes sentados en la hierba, a la sombra de un olivo, hacen una comida campestre; allí, otros se entregan al baile al sonido de un rústico candil; un extranjero aparece, se apresuran a invitarle a participar al festín o al baile: se alegran cuando acepta (298).

La fiesta de Santa Catalina Tomás en Palma es también otra escena de género, con su primer plano y su segundo plano, que nos pinta al mallorquín de antaño, de unos tiempos muy inocentes en que las santas obraban grandes milagros. Esta escena iba a conmover tanto al abate Mathieu, en lo más profundo de su alma, que sus "ojos se llenaron de dulces lágrimas" (Mathieu 1887: 212). Esta muestra de tal inocente piedad en la isla encantaba a un religioso que se enfrentaba cada día a una Francia cada vez menos piadosa:

> Cada año la ciudad de Palma celebra su fiesta con un entusiasmo indescriptible: una cabalgata en la cual los heraldos, provistos de antorchas y brillantemente vestidos de trajes antiguos de los más extraños, andan en parejas delante del carro triunfal donde se encuentra, en compañía de otras jóvenes, una tierna niña que representa a la pequeña campesina Tomasita; hasta una hora avanzada de la noche, recorren así las calles de la ciudad al sonido de la música y cantando el cántico popular compuesto en su honor. Es a la vez sencillo, recreativo y verdaderamente conmovedor para el que posee el precioso tesoro de la fe cristiana (Mathieu 1887: 211-12).

El cuadro insólito de la fiesta de San Antonio, con su mezcla de profano y de sagrado, característica de los pueblos poco civilizados, también

deleitó al viajero romántico. La imagen primitiva que el viajero romántico prodigaba del habitante se hace patente en el relato de Charles Dembowski, que describe así el exotismo de la fiesta:

> El día de mi llegada, se celebraba en este pueblo la fiesta de San Antonio, patrón de
> Mallorca. Un sacerdote estaba instalado en la escalinata de la Casa Consistorial, y
> rociaba con agua bendita a la larga procesión de cerdos y mulos que desfilaba de-
> lante de una estatua del santo. Campesinos enmascarados en honor al carnaval lle-
> vaban a estos animales, y en el momento de la bendición, depositaban su ofrenda
> ante la imagen del santo, sobre un plato de plata que sujetaba un joven clérigo
> (300).

Un pueblo bien aferrado a sus tradiciones populares de antaño, del tiempo de la inocencia, de la ingenuidad, de la felicidad sencilla, un pueblo
no corrompido por la civilización, la modernidad, la industrialización.
Esa es la imagen de Mallorca y de sus habitantes que los viajeros quisieron dar a los lectores. Si esta representación de la isla afortunada, de la
isla paraíso, ya estaba presente durante el siglo de las luces, el siglo XIX
la consolidó, añadiendo una nueva perspectiva. Los filósofos despecia-
ban el arcaísmo, lo primitivo, todo lo que el viajero decimonónico buscaba, interesándose solamente por aportar el progreso a este lugar tan
atrasado en sus técnicas agrícolas e industriales. Es con esta búsqueda
insaciable del tiempo pasado, de la pre-modernidad, que los viajeros
huyen de una Francia en plena transformación para refugiarse en un espejismo de exotismo y color local.

Bibliografía

Bernard, M. 1895. *Autour de la Méditerranée, Les côtes latines,
L'Espagne (De Tanger à Port-Vendres),* vol. 1, Paris, Henri Laurens.
Brinckmann, J. de. 1852. *Promenades en Espagne pendant les années
1849 et 1850,* Paris, Frank libraire-éditeur.
Conte, E. 1895. *Espagne et Provence-Impressions,* Paris, Calmann Lévy.
Davillier, J. C. 1874. *L'Espagne,* Paris, Hachette.
Dembowski, C. 1841. *Deux ans en Espagne et en Portugal pendant la
guerre civile: 1838-1840,* 2 vols., Paris, Gosselin.

Germond de Lavigne, L. A. G. 1866. *Itinéraire descriptif, historique et artistique de l'Espagne et du Portugal*, Paris, Hachette.

Grasset de Saint-Sauveur, A. 1807. *Voyage dans les Îles Baléares et Pithiuses; fait dans les années 1801, 1802, 1803, 1804 et 1805*, Paris, Léopold Collin.

Hallays, A. 1899. "Majorque", in *En flânant. Les idées, les faits et les œuvres*, Paris, Pavillon de Hanovre, 327-39.

Henry, P. 1884. "Un mois en Espagne", *Revue de l'Anjou*, Angers, Germain et G. Grassin.

Lacroix, F. 1847. "Îles Baléares et Pithyuses", in J. Lavallée & A. Guéroult (eds.), *Espagne depuis l'expulsion des maures jusqu'à l'année 1847. L'Univers Pittoresque. Histoire et description de tous les peuples*, vols. 30-31, Paris, Firmin Didot.

Laurens, J. J. B. 2006. *Recuerdos de un viaje artístico a la isla de Mallorca*, Palma, Olañeta.

Larousse, P. 1866-1876. *Grand dictionnaire universel du XIXe siècle*, 17 vols., Paris, Vve. P. Larousse.

Mathieu, A. 1887. *L'Espagne, Lettres d'un Français à un ami*, Madrid, Imprimerie de Henri Rubiños.

Morey Tous, A. 2008. "Les transformacions econòmiques al segle XIX", in E. Belenguer (dir.), *Història de les Illes Balears. Del segle XVIII Borbònic a la complexa contemporaneïtat*", vol. III, Barcelona, Edicions 62, 139-57.

Pageaux, D.-H.1996. *Le bûcher d'Hercule*, Paris, Honoré Champion.

Rousseau, J.-J. 1967. *Œuvres complètes*, Paris, Editions du Seuil.

Sand, G. 1995. *Un invierno en Mallorca*, Palma, Luís Ripoll.

Santana Morro, M. "Les transformacions socials", in E. Belenguer (dir.), *Història de les Illes Balears. Del segle XVIII Borbònic a la complexa contemporaneïtat*", vol. III, Barcelona, Edicions 62, 213-30.

Taylor, I. S. J. 1860. *Voyage pittoresque en Espagne, en Portugal et sur la côte d'Afrique, de Tanger à Tétouan*, Paris, Lemaître.

Vuillier, G. 1982. *Voyage aux îles Baléares, Les Baléares vues en 1888*, Paris, Les Editions Errances.

Eduard Cairol

Les noces d'Itàlia i Alemanya: un cas entre antropologia, literatura i teoria de l'art

La Itàlia idealitzada

L'any 1829, un jove pintor alemany, Friedrich Overbeck (1789-1869), va donar per acabat el quadre programàticament titulat *Les noces d'Itàlia i Alemanya*, [en alemany *Italia und Germania*] començat el 1811. Es tractava, tal i com no resulta gens difícil endevinar, de tot un manifest estètic, gestat en el context de la petita "revolució" representada per l'abandonament —per part de l'artista i alguns dels seus col·legues en aquesta institució— de l'Acadèmia de Belles Arts de Viena, l'any 1810, per establir-se a la capital italiana i perfeccionar així el seu ofici a través del contacte directe amb les obres dels primitius mestres italians del Quattrocento, Correggio i el primer Rafael.

En el quadre, dividit en dues parts molt clares, gairebé simètriques l'una de l'altra, dues figures femenines abillades amb vestit d'època i retallades cadascuna sobre un paisatge característic, entrellacen delicadament les seves mans en el curs d'una conversa plena de complicitat, dibuixant amb els braços un oval suggerent. La noia de l'esquerra, situada al davant d'una petita església camperola i d'una serralada suau en darrer terme, du els cabells foscos cenyits per una corona de llorer d'inspiració clàssica. A l'igual que la de la dreta, amb el cabell rossenc pentinat en trenes i una actitud que sembla suplicant, es tracta clarament d'un arquetipus, de la representació simbòlica d'una idea o al·legoria, i no pas del retrat individualitzat de cap dona real.

Però, ¿com ha pogut arribar l'artista a una tal concepció, amb caracteritzacions tan contrastades? I sobre quines idees se sosté?

La imatge d'Itàlia i dels italians ha estat, ja des dels temps clàssics, objecte d'una complexa elaboració en el marc de la cultura occidental moderna. En aquesta elaboració, marcada per la idealització, s'hi barregen diversos motius. D'una banda, la nostàlgia —gairebé una invariant antropològica— pel "paradís original", convertit després en "paradís perdut". Per altra part, el desig —molt més relacionat amb l'evolució de la nostra cultura— de restaurar la plenitud i l'esplendor de l'Antiguitat clàssica. Com és obvi, tots dos motius es confonen en una figura característica de la supervivència de les estructures mítiques en un context secularitzat. Així, com ha estudiat molt bé Dieter Richter, la recerca del paradís terrenal s'ha anat desplaçant amb el pas dels segles cap al Sud, convertit des de començaments de l'edat moderna en arquetipus de la felicitat i de la plena realització ontològica de l'home. Al seu torn, Itàlia ha estat, durant molts segles, la reserva gairebé única d'obres artístiques i testimonis arqueològics de l'Antiguitat, el coneixement directe de les quals era considerat des del Renaixement per les elits europees com un element imprescindible en la formació del caràcter. Aquest és precisament l'origen, de la institució del "viatge a Itàlia" a partir del segle XVII.

Des d'aquesta perspectiva, però, la imatge dels italians en el cas de la literatura alemanya pot resultar sorprenent. En efecte, ja el propi Goethe sembla una mica perplex davant dels excessos populars del Carnaval presenciat a Roma l'any 1757, una festa on "un pot comportar-se de manera tan irracional i esbojarrada com vulgui" i en la qual "gairebé tot està permès" (522).[1] Però, igual o més pintoresca és encara la seva caracterització de la població autòctona durant la seva visita a Nàpols. Així, "n'hi ha prou amb passejar-se pels carrers i amb tenir els ulls ben oberts per trobar-se amb els quadres més inimitables" (234). Per una banda, hi ha el fet que la vida del poble napolità transcorre fonamentalment al carrer, provocant multitud d'escenes de picaresca o si més no d'una certa exòtica teatralitat, sobretot per a un observador que ve del Nord d'Europa. És el que succeeix, per exemple, amb motiu de la festivitat de sant Josep, patró dels *frittauroli*, o venedors ambulants de fregits, que ho celebren davant de les portes de les cases, i amb fogons i paelles preparats per a l'ocasió. Però, també en general, "la gent fa vida al carrer, asseguda al sol sempre que lluu" (204). En definitiva, a Nàpols, tothora "innombrables persones corren pels carrers de manera confusa"(204). Per altra part, hi ha la misèria regnant. Tal i com fa notar Goethe, "és cert que a cada pas es veuen persones mal vestides, i fins i tot amb la roba en parracs" (353). Per últim, hi ha la presència ostensible de la reli-

---

1   Totes les traduccions al català dels textos citats en aquest treball són meves.

gió en el curs de la vida de la gent, com ara quan la pietat popular invoca "la sang de sant Genaro, de la mateixa manera que la resta dels pobles recorren a la sang per tal de defensar-se contra la mort i el diable" (232).

Molt curiosament, aquests trets són els mateixos que ens apareixen a la crònica de la seva estada a Nàpols —cent anys més tard— en l'escriptor, també alemany, Walter Benjamin. Per a ell, desconcertat davant del caos de la ciutat, "els desheretats segueixen sent els guies en aquest indret" (25). També, com ja passava en Goethe, la presència de la religió en les seves manifestacions més irracionals resulta xocant als ulls de l'observador procedent de l'Europa més septentrional. Així, "si [el Catolicisme] desaparegués de la superfície de la terra, potser l'últim lloc no seria Roma sinó Nàpols" (23). Per fi, el més inquietant de la ciutat és probablement ara la permeabilitat que manifesten entre si diversos ordres de coses, com la vida privada i l'existència pública. Com constatarà Benjamin amb gran perplexitat, "l'existència, el més privat dels assumptes per als europeus del Nord, és aquí una qüestió col·lectiva" (32).

La proximitat a la naturalesa

Amb tot, la contradicció entre la imatge idealitzada d'Itàlia i la irracionalitat del poble italià és, de fet, més aparent que no real. El propi Goethe, llegit amb atenció, ens pot ajudar a resoldre-la. En efecte, el que es desprèn en últim terme de la seva descripció és que els napolitans es lliuren, per sobre de tot, a "viure la vida". Amb espontaneïtat i ensems amb fruïció. Amb intensitat i en la seva integritat, sense menystenir la sensualitat. Així, "tots, a la seva manera, no treballen simplement per sobreviure, sinó per gaudir, i fins i tot treballant volen fruir de la vida" (354). Això és el que, paradoxalment, ens permet d'explicar la misèria regnant a Nàpols, on, gràcies al bon temps, no hi ha necessitat de preocupar-se pel demà, al contrari del que succeeix als països del Nord d'Europa, sotmesos a un clima inclement que estimula la previsió i la laboriositat dels seus habitants. I això —o sigui, la *joia de viure*, la sensualitat i la *naturalitat*— és també el que havia anat a buscar Goethe a Itàlia.

De fet, el seu és ben clarament un viatge de *retorn als orígens*, on l'episodi napolità juga un paper decisiu. Efectivament, a Nàpols (etapa meridional incorporada al "viatge a Itàlia" només prou tardanament), en presència de l'exuberant vegetació autòctona, Goethe —que veurà confirmada durant el viatge la seva vocació de naturalista i científic— descobreix la "planta originària" (*Ur-Pflanze*), de la qual deriven tota la resta d'espècies vegetals. Itàlia, per tant, ha revelat a l'autor del *Werther* el rostre de la "naturalesa originària", tant respecte a la botànica *com a si mateix*. Tot plegat, si fa o no fa, el mateix es podria dir també del coneixement de l'Antiguitat i de l'art clàssic adquirit per Goethe de resultes del seu viatge. Ara, tal i com declara repetidament l'autor tot al llarg del text (per exemple, en el moment de la seva arribada a Roma) es pot dir que coneix de debò tot allò que a través de descripcions i de reproduccions només coneixia indirectament. "Només ara —li confessa a Herder en carta de 17 de maig de 1787—, dic, la paraula *Odissea* cobra sentit per a mi" (342). I què és allò que, més precisament, constitueix aquest caràcter propi d'Homer i de tota la literatura i la cultura de l'Antiguitat? Doncs la seva proximitat respecte a la Naturalesa, la seva *naturalitat*.

Es tracta, com és sabut, d'un tema central en la teoria artística i literària, sobretot a partir del segle XVIII, íntimament lligat a l'episodi de la *Controvèrsia entre Antics i Moderns*, i a la seva prolongació en la polèmica entre Classicisme i Romanticisme a la major part dels països europeus. Un tema amb el qual cal tenir molta cura. Perquè, de fet, tota la teoria classicista i àdhuc neoclàssica reclama ja un retorn a la naturalesa en tant que aquesta es reflecteix en les obres dels artistes de l'Antiguitat. I, tanmateix, és el propi concepte de Naturalesa allò que *canvia* substancialment amb el Romanticisme, per ser entesa cada cop més com a espontaneïtat que escapa a tota possible formulació racional (a l'igual que el concepte coetani de "geni"), alhora que la imatge de l'Antiguitat va accentuant també els seus aspectes més irracionals, tal i com quedarà molt palès ja amb Nietzsche. En definitiva, la Naturalesa com a ideal transcendental passa a ser ara allò oposat a la pàtina de refinament que comporta la Cultura, i es concep com el seu *origen* o el "passat transcendental" d'aquesta Cultura.

Les pintoresques caracteritzacions que Goethe fa dels italians a Nàpols —així com les molt posteriors de Benjamin— són, doncs, totalment coherents amb aquesta imatge d'Itàlia i l'Antiguitat com el "passat transcendental" de l'art i de la humanitat. Es tracta, per una altra part, de descripcions que tenen el seu "fonament científic" (o pseudo-científic) en una llarga tradició que es remunta a la pròpia Antiguitat d'aplicació a les

diverses races i nacions de la terra de les velles teories dels quatre tempe-
raments. Així, Montesquieu pren en molta consideració, a *L'Esprit des
Lois* (1748), la diferent idiosincràsia dels pobles i nacions a l'hora
d'aplicar la legislació. Kant, per la seva banda, assajarà l'extensió als
mateixos de les categories estètiques del Bell i del Sublim. Un altre dels
llocs comuns de tota aquesta literatura pseudo-científica és, sense dubte,
la influència del medi. Això també ha estat vist per Montesquieu. Però,
de fet, aquesta mínima exigència de cientificitat es troba a la base de la
que es pot considerar com a autèntica refundació moderna de la disciplina de la Història de l'Art per part de Winckelmann. Segons aquest autor,
és la benignitat del clima grec, juntament amb la qualitat del cel i de la
llum, allò que constitueix l'explicació última del "fenomen grec".

La preferència pel primitiu

Les descripcions del caràcter típic italià fornides ja per Goethe i perpetu-
ades un segle després tot al llarg d'un segle, oculten, en realitat, sota una
capa d'anècdota i de pintoresquisme, tota una elaborada reflexió estètica.
Aquesta reflexió apunta cap al concepte de Naturalesa com a ideal transcendental dels artistes i poetes.

Fixem-nos com, en efecte, els tres motius subratllats anteriorment de
la religiositat, la pobresa i la vida al carrer, presentats pels observadors
com a característics del poble italià, no encobreixen res més que la irracionalitat, l'anarquia i el salvatgisme. Tot plegat es tracta de característiques que convergeixen també en la figura arquetípica del *geni*, tal i com
ha estat progressivament elaborat per la teoria artística durant tot el segle
XVIII —recollint elements clàssics reinterpretats per la filosofia neopla-
tònica del Renaixement italià i posteriorment anglès, de Ficino i de Bru-
no fins a Shaftesbury—, en particular per Diderot i Kant ja a les darreries
de la Il·lustració (Marí 1997). Tal i com afirmarà una mica més tard el
filòsof idealista F. W. J. Schelling, la Naturalesa, com el passat transcendental de la humanitat, s'expressa en l'home a través de l'activitat del
geni artístic, on harmonitzen llibertat i necessitat, natura i cultura.

Aquesta articulació entre les descripcions pintoresques i els ideals
estètics resulta particularment visible en l'obra de Germaine de Staël,

notable escriptora francesa del període napoleònic i, tanmateix, profundament germanitzada en virtut de la seva estreta amistat amb August Wilhelm Schlegel, un dels membres del primer cercle romàntic de Jena. De fet, Madame de Staël (com era coneguda en els ambients intel·lectuals de l'època) és autora d'un autèntic *díptic* que reprodueix, en el pla literari, les *noces* entre Itàlia i Alemanya representades al quadre d'Overbeck. Es tracta, per una part, de l'influent assaig *De l'Allemagne* (1800) i, per altra, de la novel·la *Corinne ou l'Italie*, avui tan poc coneguda, publicada l'any 1840. En aquesta darrera, retrobem tots els tòpics sobre el poble italià que ja coneixem, certament acompanyats d'una consciència crítica no gaire usual en la literatura contemporània, així com les apel·lacions pseudocientífiques al determinisme del clima i la naturalesa que ja coneixem també. Així, i segons Madame de Staël, en efecte, "no hi ha cap mena de luxe, ni bon gust, en la festa de Carnaval" (240). Tot plegat, constitueix una peculiar espècie d'estat d'anòmia o "anarquia moral"; estat que denota una absència de refinament en la civilització: "Tanmateix, la civilització [a Itàlia] hi és molt menys refinada que a altres països. Un podria gairebé trobar alguna cosa de salvatge en aquest poble" (161). Ara bé, aquesta mancança redunda en un gran desenvolupament de la imaginació i l'entusiasme, tal i com es fa patent en la pròpia festa dels Carnavals, qualificada per l'autora de "bacanal de la imaginació". I tanmateix, aquests són —una vegada més— els principals atributs del geni artístic, considerat com a un producte no pas de l'art o de la bona educació sinó de la Naturalesa! En efecte, per a De Staël, "aquesta bona fe en les arts de la imaginació i en tota la resta de coses és el caràcter propi del geni, mentre que el càlcul de l'èxit és gairebé sempre el destructor de l'entusiasme" (1985: 222-23). Així, mentre la dansa francesa resulta remarcable "per l'elegància i per la dificultat dels seus passos" (1985: 148), a Itàlia es caracteritza per "un talent que és molt més a prop de la imaginació i del sentiment" (148).

   Tot plegat, com veiem, es tracta de deduccions amb vagues pretensions de cientificitat, però elaborades intel·lectualment i no de forma empírica, condicionades per múltiples prejudicis i que al seu torn es troben a la base d'arquetipus i imatges culturals que es perpetuen a través de la literatura, les arts i àdhuc de la filosofia, com és el cas, al llarg de segles. Tal i com afirma Peter Burke a *Visto y no visto. El uso de la imagen como documento histórico*, quan es produeix l'encontre entre dues cultures diferents, "el més probable és que les imatges que una fa de l'altra siguin estereotipades" (158). I, segons ens recorda aquest mateix autor, "l'estereotip pot no ser completament fals, però tot sovint exagera determinats elements de la realitat i n'omet uns altres" (158). Els italians han aparegut descrits per Goethe en termes una mica brutals, però això no és res més que l'altra cara de la seva proximitat a la Natura i el seu caràcter original en el sentit d'allò primigeni, encara no pervertit pels refinaments i les sofisticacions de la Cultura. Aquesta proximitat a la naturalesa explicaria també la seva inclinació al Paganisme, fins i tot més enllà de la pàtina representada per la Cristianització. De la mateixa manera, aquesta dosi relativa de brutalitat no es contradiu pas amb la imatge aparentment més edulcorada que presenta l'encarnació d'Itàlia en el quadre-manifest del natzarè Friedrich Overbeck. En efecte, no oblidem pas que aquesta escola pictòrica es caracteritza pel seu anti-academicisme (expressat a través de la ja referida deserció dels seus membres fundadors de l'Acadèmia de Belles Arts de Viena, però també en el seu rebuig de l'obra de Rafael posterior a la fundació de l'Acadèmia) i la seva correlativa imitació dels així anomenats ben significativament pintors *primitius* italians.

Comptat i debatut, no és estrany que els pintors natzarens hagin estat un dels objectes d'atenció de l'historiador Ernst Gombrich a la seva monografia *La preferencia por lo primitivo. Episodios de la historia del gusto y del arte de Occidente* (2002). Es tracta en aquest cas, com a la resta dels episodis estudiats, d'un intent dut a terme per tal de revigoritzar l'art occidental modern a través del *retorn periòdic* a les seves *fonts originals*, allà on s'acumularia una reserva d'energia i de creativitat encara intactes; un d'aquells "retorns" que l'eminent historiador de l'art Erwin Panofsky no ha dubtat a qualificar de successius "renaixements" dins l'art occidental. El període que ens ocupa, encarnat en la figura de Friedrich Overbeck i en el seu manifest estètic *Les noces d'Itàlia i Alemanya*, ha aspirat sense dubte a un "renaixement" o "refundació" d'aquest tipus, similar a aquella altra, assajada a començaments del segle XX pel pintor Pablo Picasso amb *Les senyoretes del carrer d'Avinyó* (1907), o pel compositor rus Igor Stravinsky gairebé als mateixos anys amb *La consagració de la primavera* (1909), totes dues obres constitutives d'una autèntica reivindicació de les maneres "primitives". I un "renaixement" que, en el nostre cas, resultaria inseparable de certes imatges estereotipades d'Itàlia i de la seva contra-imatge dialèctica, Alemanya, unides ara en virtut d'un ambiciós projecte estètic que —seguint el patró de la raó dialèctica, integradora de les contradiccions, que s'imposarà en la filosofia del XIX a partir de Hegel— pretén harmonitzar paganisme i Cristianisme, Natura i Cultura, Antiguitat i Modernitat en l'ideal d'un "nou Classicisme".

Bibliografia

Benjamin, W. 2011. *Denkbilder. Epifanías en viajes*, Buenos Aires, El cuenco de plata.

Burke, P. 2001. *Visto y no visto. El uso de la imagen como documento histórico*, Barcelona, Crítica.

Goethe, J. W. von. 2009. *Viaje a Italia*, Barcelona, Ediciones B.

Gombrich, E. 2003. *La preferencia por lo primitivo*, Barcelona, Debate.

Marí, A. 1997. *L'home de geni*, Barcelona, Edicions 62.

Richter, D. 2011. *El Sur. Historia de un punto cardinal*, Madrid, Siruela.

Staël, M. de 1985. *Corinne ou l'Italie*, París, Gallimard.

CATERINA CALAFAT

Insights into Julian Barnes's Frenchness

Barnesian Francophilia and *La perfide Albion*

This paper analyses Julian Barnes's immense love of French culture, present throughout his considerable literary and journalistic oeuvre, as well as his reviews in literary supplements. Indeed, the reader is reminded of Barnes's Gallicised perspective even in that dimension of his work considered more "English" because of its subject matter.

In spite of the fact that his masterpiece *Flaubert's Parrot* (1984) is an extraordinary homage to Flaubert, until now the impact of Barnes's work on Flaubert in France or in England has been practically negligible: he is not even mentioned in the exhaustive *Dictionnaire Flaubert* (2010)! Another remarkable omission is found in the following apology concerning the "[r]éceptions créatrices de l'œuvre de Flaubert" in the Anglophone world: "Cette extraordinaire variation à la fois sur *Madame Bovary* et sur *Un cœur simple* qu'est *Le Perroquet de Flaubert* de Julian Barnes aurait naturellement pu, elle aussi, donner matière à réflexion" (Chardin 2001: 6-7).

My aim consequently is to draw up in a broader context a long-term plausible project yielding a Barnes French cultural guide, dealing with his particular realm of memory of the British imaginary that only a foreign perspective could reveal. Is he really the most Francophile of British writers when in his work an almost utopian representation of France exists alongside a rather blasé attitude towards his own country? To this end, the essay will pursue two courses of action: first of all, it will compile a catalogue of the most frequent textual elements (characters, spaces, habits, etc.) that might serve as a foundation for the production of a handbook of French culture *à la Barnes,* compared to his vision of English culture. Secondly, another vein would be the field of French language and literature, where I would like to consider his command of

French as a translator. This would initially involve evaluating the French figures and literary works that have had a profound impact on Barnes's written works, with the specific purpose of exploring the extent of the influence of his beloved Flaubert's work and French nineteenth-century literature; surveying his partial and selective portrayal of a cultural France is a must: "The cultural period I am constantly drawn back to is roughly 1850-1925, from the culmination of Realism to the fission of Modernism" (2002: xiv). When he is asked about his early readings in French, he asserts: "When I was fourteen or fifteen I was just beginning to read in French, but the first time I read *Madame Bovary* it was certainly in English [...] So it would be Voltaire, Montaigne, Flaubert, Baudelaire, Verlaine, Rimbaud" (Guignery and Roberts 2009: 66).

With regard to methodology, I will be focussing on the *foreign dimension* in Barnes's work (overseas lectures, travels, correspondence, models, etc.) and proposing the creation of a first corpus of Barnes's texts that accords priority to the most "Gallicised" works: a selection of his many contributions to the *New York Review of Books* or *The New Yorker*, called *Something to Declare* (2002); the pictures of fictional British characters living in France at different times in *Cross Channel* (1996); and literary essays published on a regular basis. As his intentionally idyllic representation of France and the French collides with his deliberately irritating stereotypical image of England and the English, I will follow a strictly contextualised comparative approach, contrasting his blasé vision of English culture (significantly, the title of his last essay, "Daddy's girl" in *New York Review of Books*, in February 2012, is devoted to the biopic of life and legacy of Margaret Thatcher!), in accordance with the notion that "[u]ne sémiotique des cultures se doit [...] d'être différentielle et comparée [...]. En effet, une culture n'est pas une totalité: elle se forme, évolue et disparaît dans les échanges et les conflits avec les autres" (Rastier 2001: 281). Consequentially a second corpus of English culture will be compiled comprising his non-fiction work (mainly *Letters from London*, published in 1995, a collection of fifteen essays including pieces from *The New Yorker*) and his literary work (chiefly from *England, England*, 1998).

Barnes is considered to be an English postmodernist writer. He is nevertheless unique in his possession of a deep knowledge of French culture, be it literary, filmic or artistic —an interesting feature shared by most of the narrators and characters he creates: "Most of the authors of the 1980s were concerned with life in Britain. However, Julian Barnes's light, confident, humorous style demonstrated his interest in France and its culture" (Christopher 2006: 78). Furthermore, his work is truly original since his love of France does not stem from exoticism or clichés:

> I talked about *Le Grand Meaulnes, Le Petit Prince,* Greuze, Astérix, the *comédie larmoyante,* Bernadin de Saint-Pierre, pre-Great War railway posters, Rousseau, Offenbach, the early films of Fernandel and the semiotic significance of the yellow triangular —nay, tricornic— Ricard ashtray (1996: 125).

He is a true exponent of English Francophilia, with his profound insight into French mores, customs and heritage. France appears in all his work, fiction and non-fiction: "Barnes depicts travels as something that [...] helps to shape individual identity, which in turn affects other forms of identity such as a sense of Englishness" (Pristash 2011: 49). Actually Barnes's first book identifies France both as a place and a psychological influence for the English (Moseley 1997: 18).

In this sense, he is able to offer an historical and cultural overview of France where heterogeneous elements come together to form a rich kaleidoscope filled with nuance and contrasts, albeit, of course, highly individual: "Doubtless there was an element of cultural snobbery in my initial preference for things Gallic [...] Is my view of France partial? Certainly" (Barnes 2002: xii-xiv).

If France, or rather the relationship of the English to France and its culture, has remained one of the features in Barnes's work, what could be said about his concept of British civilisation?: "Old England had lost its history, and therefore —since memory is identity— had lost all sense of self" (1998: 259). Pristash considers that the writer uses myth to break apart the collective identity. Instead of merely arguing that England needs to reinvest in its own myths, Barnes depicts these myths as empty and uninspiring (2011: 126). The definition of myth expands from a story or concept based on a communal understanding of historical events to a sense of myth as falsity, as in —it is a myth to consider Englishness a fixed notion, a fallacy (2011: 112).

In reality, his portrayal of England is often deliberately clichéd. The reader sometimes seems to find a succession of unoriginal stereotypes mostly designed to offend or, worse still, irritate the English reader. His malicious comments on even renowned cultural figures provide a simple illustration of this: "I'm saving Virginia Woolf for when I'm dead" (1985: 109). In addition in *Nothing to be Frightened of*, one observes the use of the rather infrequent adverbs like "Englishly" (2008: 94) or "Britishly" (151), because he ironically considers that "[m]issing God is for me rather like Being English: a feeling roused mainly by attack" (77).

The Barnesian mastery of French language

Barnes's mastery of the French language allows him to endow some of his Anglophone characters with French words and expressions. He studied French Literature at Oxford and lived in France for a year as a teacher. Furthermore, in his early twenties he worked as an editorial assistant for the *Oxford English Dictionary*. It is logical to suppose that this three-year training in lexicography explains his characters' frequent use of Gallicisms and his philological interpretations. As an example, *Flaubert's Parrot* operates in the typically postmodern technique of intertextuality: quotations in French, quotations translated into English. In fact fifty quotations are taken from French authors and forty-seven from British authors (Guignery 2005: 47). It is precisely this mastery of French which allows him to indulge not only in translation exercises but also in bilingual plays-on-words, with a translingual element (Petit 1994: 11). Indeed, if we take the concept of heterolinguism, we see that the phenomenon here demands of English readers an immense competence in French culture and language since the Barnesian translation into English does not always appear.

In his last collection of stories, *Pulse* (2011), though not particularly too French, he frequently has recourse to Gallicisms when discussing France, Great Britain and even America in the four short stories concerning friends' dinners at "Phil & Joanna". Thus, the characters comment upon "le coup de foudre" et "le moment supreme" (192) or humoristic reflexions such as the etymology of the word "marmalade", coming from the French "Marie malade", that is, "[t]hat Queen of Scotland who had French connections. [...] The marmalade theory of Britishness" (53, 55). They also refer to the French slang for "balls" or "les valseuses" ("the waltzers"): "female bollocks. Trust the French" (27).

Interestingly, this lover of the French language dares to authoritatively theorise about traductological issues, and often mockingly. For instance, he criticises a translation of Mallarmé, one of the most Anglicised French authors: "Mallarmé is one of the least translatable of the French poets: reading him in English is often like listening to a chamber work for brass band" (2002: 137). It is in his essays that he assesses the English translation of classics such as Voltaire, Maupassant, or Jules Renard. For instance, in a remarkable recent essay (2010) on *Madame Bovary*, Barnes compares accurately certain solutions to six of the fifteen English versions of Flaubert's novel.

A special mention of Barnes's only translation called *In the Land of Pain* which appeared in 2002 should be made. Here, this writer-turned-translator goes beyond introducing the English public to additional elements of French culture, transmitting elements of French culture even among the French: the text, in French *La Doulou*, written by Alphonse Daudet, unknown for many years since it was not published until 1930 —he died in 1897— met with little success in France. In fact, among the most recent studies on Daudet, Anne-Simone Dufief's is noteworthy because she only devotes one short chapter to the *Journal de malade*, "ce journal intime, distinct de ses carnets" (Dufief 1997: 193). Barnes's impeccable translation, the result of thorough research, effectively constitutes a critical edition with extensive footnotes, which sometimes exceed the length of the text itself. This is why the most recent French edition of *La Doulou*, in 2007, includes a preface, notes and a postscript from *In the Land of Pain*.

Barnes's reception of French literature

Barnes's so-called autobiography *Nothing to Be Frightened of* is created in the form of an original essay with reflections on the deaths of important figures of Western culture, sometimes tinged with humour: "I think the company of saints might be distinctly interesting. [...] Dom Perignon was a monk, after all" (2008: 64). References to Anglo-Saxon figures are frequent: "Too many French deaths? Very well, there's a good old British death, that of our national connoisseur of mortal terror, Philip

Larkin" (208), Russell, Edith Wharton, Donne, Somerset Maugham, Nabokov, Arthur Koestler, Ford Madox Ford, George Bernard Shaw, Emily Dickinson. Nevertheless the "Gallic" presence is also remarkable, particularly that of nineteenth-century French writers: Flaubert and Montaigne (10 allusions), Daudet and Zola (5 allusions), the Goncourt brothers, Stendhal and Gautier (3 allusions), Camus (twice). Sand, Balzac, Rimbaud, Voltaire, Gide, Prévert, Rabelais only receive one mention each, as do other philosophers and artists: Pascal, Saint-Simon, Rousseau, Sartre, Braque, Jacques Brel.

The Barnesian alter ego is without doubt Jules Renard (1864-1910), the author of a diary compiling thoughts about life and death, and about the literary world. Barnes even describes "certain similarities" (2008: 159-60), considers him as "one of my dead, French, non-blood relatives" (46) and devotes the last six pages of his autobiography to his last visit to the village where the French writer lived and died.

Barnes's readers may also find highly significant that in the recent *Through the Window* (2012), a compilation of one short story and seventeen previously-published essays, he devotes eight of these pieces to French matters and the overlapping of British, French and American cultures.

Conclusion

In an admirably documented study on Mallarmé, Barnes openly recognises that "if he weren't so French he could easily be English" (2002: 132). Mallarmé's language and poetry had also been studied within the perspective of English influence by Derrida, who finally stated:

> We know, and not only through his biography, that Mallarmé's language is always open to the influence of the English language, that there is a regular exchange between the two, and that the problem of this exchange is explicitly treated in *Les mots anglais*. For this reason alone, *Mallarmé doesn't belong completely to "French literature"* (1992: 125; my italics)

If we subscribe to the words of this most international of French philosophers, we could follow up this twin-track exploration of Barnes's
vocation by asking the same question in relation to Barnes himself.

Even if in one of his last works, *The Sense of an Ending*, Francophilia is present in a more attenuated guise, can it be argued that Barnes
now has a more French literary style? As Rafferty puts it when discussing *Arthur and George* (2005), in which Englishness and a questioning
thereof pervade the entire book, "Julian Barnes has written a deeply English novel, in the grand manner, about the sorts of existential questions
the English on the whole prefer to leave to the French" (2006: 3). Furthermore, we should classify *Nothing to be Frightened of* as a book of
memoirs *à la Jules Renard*.

However, as a twenty-first century English novelist, Barnes confesses he does not write "Flaubertian novels" (Guignery and Roberts
2009: 75). Despite his admiration for his ancestors, Barnes is far from
being trapped in the French literary past: "His choice of writers such as
Flaubert, Daudet, Renard with whom one feels his kinship, might actually be a way to express his fascination for them, *to claim a cultural
identity which is linked to the French literary canon*, but also to suggest
his own obsession with originality" (Guignery 2011: 50; my italics).
Even so, if I were asked if Barnes partially belongs to French literature, I
could only reply: definitely! Therefore, a project aimed at exploring this
is more justified than ever.

Bibliography

Barnes, J. 1985. *Flaubert's Parrot,* London, Picador.
—. 1996. *Cross Channel,* London, Picador.
—. 1998. *England, England,* London, Picador.
—. 2002. *Something to Declare,* London, Picador.
—. 2002. *In the Land of Pain*, London, Jonathan Cape.
—. 2008. *Nothing to be Frightened of,* London, Jonathan Cape.
—. 2011. *Pulse,* London, Jonathan Cape.
—. 2011. *The Sense of an Ending*, New York, Alfred A. Knopf.
—. 2012. *Through the Window*, New York, Vintage.

Chardin, P. 2000. "Avant-propos", in *Réceptions créatrices de l'œuvre de Flaubert,* special issue of *Littérature et Nation* 22, 3-7.

Childs, P. 2011. *Julian Barnes,* Manchester & New York, Manchester UP.

Christopher, D. P. 2006. *British Culture: An Introduction*, London & New York, Routledge.

Derrida, J. & D. Attridge. 1992. *Acts of Literature*, New York, Routledge.

Dufief, A.-S. 1997. *Alphonse Daudet, romancier*, Paris, Honoré Champion.

Guignery, V. 2005. *Flaubert's Parrot. Julian Barnes,* Paris, Armand Colin.

_____. 2011. "'A Preference for Things Gallic': Julian Barnes and the French Connection", in S. Groes & S. Matthews (eds.), *Julian Barnes: Contemporary Critical Perspectives,* New York, Continuum, 37-50.

Guignery, V. & R. Roberts. 2009. *Conversations with Julian Barnes*, Jackson, Mississippi, UP of Mississippi.

Guinot, J.-B. 2011. *Dictionnaire Gustave Flaubert,* Paris, CNRS.

Kempton, A. 1996. "A Barnes Eye View of France", *Franco-British Studies* 22, 92-101.

Moseley, M. 1997. *Understanding Julian Barnes*, Columbia, South Carolina, U of South Carolina P.

Petit, M. 1994. "'Gourstave Flaubear': l'intertextualité contrastive comme procédé métafictionnel dans *Flaubert's Parrot* de Julian Barnes", in M. Duperray (ed.), *Historicité et métafiction dans le roman contemporain des Îles Britanniques*, Aix-en-Provence, Publications de l'Université de Provence, 121-37.

Pristash, C. 2011. "Englishnesses: Traditional and Alternative Conceptions of English National Identity in Novels by Julian Barnes, Angela Carter, John Fowles, and Jeanette Winterson", PhD Thesis, Indiana University of Pennsylvania.

Rafferty, T. 2006. "The Game's Afoot", *The New York Times* 15, <http://www.nytimes.com/2006/01/15/books/review/15rafferty.html> [accessed May 2, 2012]

Rastier, F. 2001. *Arts et sciences du texte*, Paris, PUF.

Maria Zulmira Castanheira

"A Dog and Three Englishmen": Representations of the English and of English National Identity in Alexandre Herculano's *De Jersey a Granville* (1843)

Driven into political exile because of his liberal views and involvement in the struggle against King Miguel's absolutism (1828-1834), Alexandre Herculano (1810-1877), one of the founders of Portuguese Romanticism, emigrated to England in 1831, but relocated soon thereafter to France. His contact with foreign lands, which would prove to be so decisive in the young writer's literary evolution, gave rise to compositions in verse and in prose, directly linked to his experience of exile, among which the memoir titled *De Jersey a Granville* (*From Jersey to Granville*). First published in 1843 in the review *O Panorama* (Lisbon, 1837-1868) and later included by Herculano in his volume *Lendas e Narrativas* (1851), this account, of an autobiographical bent, describes the author's voyage from the Island of Jersey to France in 1831. On board the *chasse-marée* there travelled, besides a group of six Portuguese emigrés and two French sailors and a cabin-boy, a dog and three Englishmen (the order is not arbitrary), the latter becoming the object of the narrating subject's observant and caustically critical gaze.

This essay analyses the perception of the English and of England presented in *De Jersey a Granville*, a text which condenses virtually every recurring trait in the representation of the typical Englishman to be found in nineteenth-century Portuguese literature and which, for this reason, is imbued with a paradigmatic quality. The pain of exile —very strongly felt in the case of Herculano— underlies the entire text, to a large extent conditioning the state of mind with which the writer *looks* at the English who are his fellow-travellers and, from them, at England as a whole.

The author records that the journey to Granville began on "an Autumn day, as fair as the fairest day in Portugal" (Herculano 1996: 7),[1] which at once reveals with what nostalgia the émigré recalls the luminous sky of his country of birth. Herculano's destination, after residing for two months in Plymouth, was now France, that centre of political, social and literary ideas with which the author states he identifies, which he considers a second Motherland and which therefore seems to him to be a place of hope for a new life after the privations experienced in England. Leaving behind the "horrible English roofs of dark slate, like signs of spleen" (1996: 8), the author concentrates his attention on the crew and passengers of the coasting vessel. And it is while enumerating "the collection of animals included between the four planks of the fragile vessel" (1996: 9), in an obvious reference to Noah's Ark (all the more so as the arrival at the French coast is preceded by a violent storm which the narrating subject describes as a sublime spectacle in its terrifying beauty), that the reader first encounters the wit with which Herculano imbues his text.

Among the passengers, besides the Portuguese émigrés, there were "a dog and three Englishmen" (1996: 9): it should be noted that the Englishmen are listed last, which immediately reveals a deliberate intention to slight them. Confined in the very limited space of the vessel, the author is given the opportunity to observe minutely those three sons of England. His gaze seeks out all that is ridiculous and risible in them.

That England gave him shelter when he was a political refugee is insufficient to temper the implacable portrayal which the author draws of "the first nation in the world." Instead of writing about the impressive progress and material might of England, he underscores its intellectual inferiority in relation to France, seeing in it a factor of moral and political weakness. England imposed itself not through ideas but by the might of its Navy and by oppressing the weakest, sowing hatred which Herculano foresees as one day possibly being fatal for a country "whose physiognomy is monstruous and antinomic" (1996: 35). I would highlight the use of the adjective "monstrous", also used by many other writers of Portuguese Romanticism (and beyond) in their critical writing on industrial and utilitarian England, guided by the capitalistic logic of profit, of self-interest, and riven with terrible social inequality.

---

1   Subsequent references are to this edition. The translations are mine.

Not for a moment does Herculano forget that Portugal was among the small, poor countries which suffered as a result of English domination. Two episodes featuring the Englishmen on the journey bring to his mind, with patriotic indignation, England's interference in Portugal's affairs over the centuries, and make him react with animosity to his fellow travellers on this journey. Right at the start, one of them, the oldest, seasick from the rocking of the vessel, thrusts his dizzy head onto the narrator's knees and closes his eyes, leaving Herculano divided between the desire to shove away that head which symbolised the affront to Portuguese sovereignty and the consideration due to elderly persons. In the end, the latter sentiment prevails in spite of everything: "A white head of hair is always worthy of respect, even if it is placed on the trunk of a son of Great Britain" (1996: 16). Later, when night falls and the other two Englishmen go down into the narrow cabin below the deck, the same old man follows them, but on placing his foot on the steep stairs, he slips and falls all the way down with a loud bang, landing on top of his two countrymen, producing "the sound of a keg of beer falling from a height of twenty feet" (1996: 30). Once again, it is his sense of duty and not any liking for the Englishmen which leads him to help the victims.

For Herculano and his contemporaries, it was notorious that if Portugal had had recourse to English help at several moments in its history, especially most recently during the French invasions, such help had come at a high price, for England had always benefited greatly in economic terms from its alliance with Portugal. A markedly Anglophobic attitude thus moulds the schematic portrayal by the narrator of the Englishmen, like him on their way to France. This ironical, sarcastic evocation comprises a series of traits which many other Portuguese literary figures also developed in the 1800s in their representations of the English: their physical and psychological features, the peculiarity of their customs, their gluttony and alcoholism, their religion, their Sunday observances, the climate and language.

In the description of the three Englishmen on board, we find some of the physical features and distinctive sartorial traits which became fixed in the collective consciousness as defining the typical Englishman. One of them, the oldest, possessed "a legitimate British head: hard, heavy and massive, like the government of the English company in Asia" (1996: 16) and a ruddy complexion. As for the other two, brothers, one apparently fifty (Mr. Graham Senior) and the other forty (Mr. Graham Junior), information is more detailed. The former is thin, tall ("a pine-tree", 1996: 29), with sunken cheeks, with a long, fleshy nose, sallow of complexion, enveloped in four overcoats jocularly compared to the output of "half a Leeds factory" (1996: 25); the latter, "an Anglo-Saxon type" (1996: 13), has a "broad, flattened face, blue eyes, dishevelled fair locks, a mouth deeply etched at the extremities of the lower lip, with an air of tedium and pride, as if all the British smoke of charcoal enveloped him in its halo of national glory" (1996: 13). Here are some of the peculiarities which became crystallised as a cliché: the large head, the red face as a result of excessive consumption of alcoholic beverages, the height, corpulence, the unmistakable enormous, heavy overcoat, or on the other hand, the slimness, blue eyes, fair hair, disdainful mouth. The idea prevails of the Englishman as a singular category, unmistakable in his inimitable traits and habits which to the eyes of a foreigner appear unalterable.

Holding firmly to his habits and seemingly following a pattern of monotonous uniformity, the Englishman involuntarily offers up to other peoples the material for the stereotypes of caricature: "Two ridiculous Englishmen are indubitably the two most ridiculous things in the world" (1996: 25) remarks the narrator of *De Jersey a Granville*. In addition to the ever-repeated, always expected gestures, there is a deep national pride, a trait seen as the true essence of the psychology of the English and for that same reason the butt of Herculano's mirth. It is a truism that vanity supplies comedy with an abundance of material. Herculano has a single aim: to criticise the exacerbated patriotism of the British, their sense of civilisational superiority and the arrogance of Portugal's old allies, for whom the Portuguese were no more than "humble creatures" (1996: 31), "savages of Europe" (1996: 22).

England's imperialist voracity appears associated to images of literal gluttony. The literary representation of the Englishman as a person who ate and drank to excess was, incidentally, backed by a long tradition, and Herculano continues it when he defines England and its people in two short but pithy phrases: the "Might [sic] Empire of steam and beer" (1996: 14) and "compatriot of beefsteaks" (1996: 34). His satire on John Bull's haughty country is thus also built up from a critique of British eating habits, for he sees in them proof of a materialistic ravening.

The grotesque side of a son of old Albion when in his cups is another seam explored in *De Jersey a Granville*. One of the Englishmen on board is portrayed in two colours, as already stated: his white hair and florid complexion, a sign of a prolonged habit of ingesting alcohol. Maliciously, the narrator remarks that as a sign of his respect for the water of baptism the old man had sworn never again to let it pass his lips, content with drinking rum, wine and beer. The satire on the alcoholism of the English takes on a further dimension when Mr. Graham Senior, the poet, significantly armed with a "small flask of brandy which he wore over his shoulder and across his chest" (1996: 29), was the protagonist of a scene revealing John Bull's arrogance and aggressiveness: the one in which he demands that the French cabin boy bring him a bottle of brandy or rum. When this is refused, he gets angry and threatens the poor boy with a beating, to assert his wishes —behaviour which allows the narrator to call him "the poet of temperance and brandy" (1996: 39), in a clearly sarcastic tone regarding the Englishman's attitude which bears little resemblance to his status as a poet of the school of Pope and, therefore, the singer of moderation. Obviously, the drinker's lack of sobriety is used to attack the hypocrisy of British society, which under Victoria would make of temperance one of the pillars of respectability.

Another strategy for criticising England is found in the bedrock of the Portuguese Motherland's principles which establish, on the moral plane, the superiority of Portugal over its ambitious ally. Herculano finds them in religion. After declaring that each nation "has its creed, its language, its scent" (1996: 14) and that the smell of mutton and black tea unequivocally points to the three passengers being English, the writer's tone hardens when referring to the proliferation of religious sects in England, "which send each other mutually to hell" (1996: 14). His critique is underpinned by the view of Roman Catholicism as a tie that binds the Portuguese, in contradistinction to the disarray which on the other side of the English Channel was promoted by the multiplicity of creeds. The Church of England, in particular, becomes the target of a violent attack because of the way England observed the Sabbath, with all entertainments banned but with tolerance shown for the clandestine opening of pubs.

The grey ambience of fog and rain contributed to the stultifying blandness of the English Sunday. The climate, a recurring theme in literary representations of England by Portuguese authors, which almost always triggered homesick thoughts of a sun-drenched Motherland, thus could not but be present in Herculano's portrayal, although he does not develop the theme to any great extent. Significant is the fact that the mists of the English sky, so often discussed, are taken as essential in defining the Englishman in general when Herculano refers to him as the "compatriot of mists" (1996: 34).

It also became conventional to establish a close relation between the climate and the melancholy of the English, which often generated suicidal tendencies. It was at the end of the eighteenth-century that, according to Paul Langford in *Englishness Identified* (2000), foreigners, and the English themselves, began to identify melancholy as a pathology of the English soul, brought on not just by the climate but also by the process of industrialisation. Economic prosperity meant leisure time for the well-off, very often bringing with it a degree of tedium likely to lead to suicide.

The Englishman who suffers from spleen, with a deeply rooted unhappiness about life despite his material goods, easily became the butt of satire. In *De Jersey a Granville*, the figure of Mr. Graham Senior, who insists on tormenting his brother and other fellow-travellers by declaiming his "most frigid poetry" (1996: 21), allows Herculano to build up a scene in which spleen and the suicidal impulse are highlighted as underlying features of the English way of being. This is the episode in which the character in question searches in one of his pockets for his little book of verse so as to read from it to the other passengers. As yet not knowing the Englishman's intentions, and seeing the look of entreaty on Mr. Graham Junior's face, the narrator believes he is about to witness one of those acts of desperation to which spleen often led the natives of England:

> I observed this scene; I knew what spleen is capable of, and the fear of an Anglicide went through my mind, as I looked upon the glazed appearance of the one and the distressed and timid gesture of the other. The wind whistled violently, the water was beginning to be tinted with black, and the sky was completely overcast; it was half a British poem. A gun-shot and a corpse flipped into the sea would complete an epic tome. [...] The worthy Mr. Graham was not searching in his pocket for the essence and substance of British ideality and poetry, the suicidal pistol. No! It was a more atrociously murderous thing; it was a thick exercise book covered in microscopic writing, probably containing his unpublished inspirations! (1996: 19, 20).

The taciturnity associated with spleen gave rise to a further distinctive trait which also circulated widely in the form of a stereotype: English laconicism. The extreme brevity of the few words exchanged between Mr. Graham Senior and Mr. Graham Junior becomes a singular type of behaviour worthy of ridicule:

> Mr. Graham Junior, no sooner had his worthy brother stopped reading, turned to him his melancholic face and murmured, after a sigh:
> "Aye! Very good!"
> With the three 'yeses' preceding these words, the sum was of six words or croaks, of which Mr. Graham Junior had delivered himself that day (1996: 25).

It should be noted that the English words with which the author exemplifies the laconic way of being of the natives of England also serve to reference a peculiar aspect of the English language: its markedly monosyllabic nature. In Herculano's critical view, this feature, which renders the language monotonous and dry, is presented as one of John Bull's most typical traits.

Often the substance of jokes, laconicism served as a pretext for numerous nineteenth-century Portuguese authors, among whom Herculano, to attack, with particular venom, a basic identitary factor in the *faithful* ally: their mother tongue. There is an abundance of remarks on the *abstruse* nature of the English language, the absurdities of its spelling and pronunciation and, further, its limited adequacy for the lyrical and dramatic modes —clear proof that for many of the Portuguese writers, journalists and literary critics of the time such a language was far from enjoying the prestige of French.

The author's first comment about the passengers on board the vessel is, pertinently enough, a derogatory remark with regard to their language. Referring to the first part of the journey, the author states that neither the dog nor the Englishmen had uttered "the former a single bark, the latter a single squawk" (1996: 12). The choice of a verb that belittles the three men and places them beyond the limits of the human species, *squawk*, is thenceforth reinforced by the recurring use of other terms which are likewise related to animal voices and sounds whenever the Englishmen's utterances are described: "growl", "bleat", "grunt", "chirp" (1996: 19, 32, 20, 22, respectively).

Going far beyond the strictly linguistic sphere, Herculano makes use of the theme of the English language to stress the political and economic scope of his critique of England. To this end, he sets up an analogy between different peoples' languages and their respective morals and true ethics, which allows him to infer that the English language, with its great differences between spelling and pronunciation and its monosyllabism, is an example of England's lack of loyalty, of its deceitful nature and of its avarice.

Concentrating on the laughable, caricatured features of the Englishman's physical and psychological characteristics, as well as on his customs and tastes, Herculano reduces the Other (England and the English) to a set of stereotypes which became fixed in the collective consciousness of the Portuguese as defining the people to whom Portugal was linked by a centuries-old alliance, and he paints a grotesque picture of mighty, haughty England, shot through with strong anti-British feelings. The result is a narrative which highlights the major role played by humour —used as a means of punishing capitalist and materialistic England and freeing tensions and resentment with respect to the interference of the old ally and *protector* in Portugal's affairs— in the literary representation of the English in nineteenth-century Portuguese literature. Through mirth, weak, small Portugal discredits strong, great England, with this subversive act affirming its identity and autonomy.

Bibliography

Herculano, A. 1843. "De Jersey a Granville (Fragmento.)", *O Panorama* 70 (29 April), 130-33; 73 (20 May), 154-58.
—. 1996. *De Jersey a Granville (1831)*. Verificação de texto por A. C. Lucas, Lisboa, Parque Expo 98.
Langford, P. 2000. *Englishness Identified: Manners and Character, 1650-1850*, Oxford, Oxford UP.

Rosa Cerarols & Antonio Luna-García

Gendering Colonial Writing:
The Experience of Spanish Morocco

Introduction

Travel writing inherently intertwines geography and literature and often becomes a practice of representation that generates imaginaries and imaginative geographies. Similarly, geographical imaginations have to be conceived of as subjective discursive formations of gender that comprise multiple constellations of power, knowledge and geography. When analyzing the geographical imaginations of the European imperial period, postcolonial and feminist revisions show that the relationships between West and East remained most of the time marked by an unequal hierarchy of power, focused in a positioning clearly androcentric.

Spanish foreign policy since the mid-nineteenth century redirected its overseas interests towards territories closer to home. A rising colonialist interest in the Alauite Empire, which began with the Spanish-Moroccan War of 1860, culminated with the designation of a French-Spanish Protectorate in Morocco (1912-1956). It has also been demonstrated that parallel to Spain's increasing interest in this territory, the number of people that were displaced to Morocco and that left written accounts of their travel experiences increased concomitantly. So, as regards the Spanish context and with reference to colonial Morocco, it transpires that more than fifty such travelogues were written by men while only four were composed by women. The exceptional voices displayed in these female accounts makes them worthy of critical attention. Bearing such output in mind, this essay will revisit Spanish travellers' accounts referring to their "domestic" Orient from the perspective of gender. To this end, two war narratives will be analyzed with the aim of identifying similarities and differences in the conception of colonial space.

Theoretical approaches and the geo-historical context

Edward Said postulated in 1978 that the Orient never really existed. It was, he argued, a European mental discourse projecting an image of the Other that tried to define alterity as well as the "real" European and western essence. But Said's contributions in relation to *Orientalism* were developed through too homogeneous a conception of the discourse of Orientalism, incorporating one single colonial subject, unmistakably masculine. He did not reflect on the absence of women in the production of orientalist discourses nor on the nonexistence of women as agents in the creation of colonial culture. Consequently Said reproduced a traditional vision that has remained oblivious to the role of women in the context of colonial expansion (Blunt et al. 1994; Chauduri et al. 1992; García Ramón et al. 1998; Kobayashi 2004; Lewis 2004; McClintock 1995; Melman 1992; Mills 2005; Yegenoglu 1998).

Feminist explorations of the imperial period, by contrast, highlight feminine presence and emphasize the concept of ambivalence. They consider women's complicity in relation to colonialism as well as their possible negation of or resistance to it. At the same time, they emphasize the role of European women as relevant cultural agents in the formation of imperial relationships (Bassnett 2002; García Ramón 2002; McEwan 2000; Melman 1992; Monicat 1996).

To talk of Orientalism in Spain we must refer, first of all, to the notion of Africanism, or more precisely of "marroquismo" (Abel and Cerarols 2008; Martín Corrales et al. 2002; Morales Lezcano 2006; Nogué et al. 1999), because the Spanish Orient, since the end of the nineteenth century, was located in the south and not in the east. However, Spanish involvement in North African issues goes back to the Middle Ages. Spanish military interest manifested itself in a presence in strategic points along he Maghreb's coast, of which the fortified cities of Ceuta and Melilla were the most important.

In fact, the territorial defence of these locations was the source of constant frontier conflicts, some of which grew into Spanish-Moroccan military confrontations of significance, as is the case of the "African War" of 1860 or the Wars of Melilla of 1893 or 1909. Thus, "Africanism" became the national political ideology aimed at rectifying the overseas colonial "disaster of 1898" and a burning issue in Parliament as well as in the national press. At the Conference of Algeciras (1906), Spain was and remained designated, together with France, the power that should administer the Protectorate of Morocco between the years 1912 and 1956.

Gender and colonialism

Since colonial journeys have been fundamentally masculine, the few Spanish feminine travel narratives about colonial sites that have remained must be considered exceptional. First, we will analyze how these narratives are linked with the colonial interests of the period. Next, we will explore how and in which ways the gender variable conditioned (or not) the perception and popularization of colonialism.

Wars in the hinterland of Melilla: Boada and Burgos's contributions

Spanish colonialist practice in Morocco was, from beginning to end, belligerent. In fact, the Spanish-Moroccan wars had a cause-effect relationship with Spanish colonial interests in Africa. For this reason, it is of great interest to know how this symbiotic relationship was treated from male and female perspectives. Two existing narratives that deal specifically with the subject of the Melilla military campaigns and lend themselves to an analysis from the perspective of gender are José Boada's *Allende el estrecho* (1895) and Carmen de Burgos's *En la guerra* (1909).[1]

Carmen de Burgos's narrative departs radically from the canonical and typical journalistic war chronicle written by men. In stark contrast to Boada's narration, Burgos's story ultimately turns into an anti-war mani-

---

1   José Boada was a Catalan journalist and businessman who had a strong connection with the Spanish Africanist movement of the late nineteenth century. For more information, see García-Romeral (2004). Carmen de Burgos was a journalist and feminist writer very advanced in relation to her context and period. She was known as Colombine. For more information, see Núñez (2005) and Bravo (2003).

festo. The contribution of the author to the travel genre, which comprises war seen through the female gaze, refers to an "everyday life" never observed before in this typology of narrative, hitherto always written by men. Thus, the account places little emphasis on military action, such as battles or patrols. In Burgos's narrative the context of the confrontations becomes more relevant: the existence of two opposed sides, the complex gestation of news, the feelings of the soldiers, the women's —mothers, wives, and sisters— sufferings. Her narrative describes the geography of the immediate environment: she incorporates the most human side of the camp and refers to events on the edge of the military action. In short, she enriches the chronicle with multiple information concerning to a great plurality of spaces. Boada, on the other hand, confines himself from the outset to the war. For him, the military campaign is limited to battlefield geography and to the soldiers' drills. Burgos's *En la guerra* is exceptional, in contrast to Boada's account, in its approach and positioning of the author.

Beyond the war-related "news", she recreates the atmosphere of the place and the battlefields, her personal ideology and the feelings of those affected by the conflict, paying special attention to the situation of women. As a journalist, she also manifests a great interest in leaving evidence of how she gathers and writes the news; she is also extremely aware of the relevance of news in the military campaign. Leaving the writing process aside, the author also informs us about what is happening in the surroundings of Melilla. Burgos's point of view does not simply conceive of the military campaign as something exclusive to journalists and soldiers (as does the story of Boada) but rather as something open to the average travel writer. She explains, for example, that she wished to see *prima facie* the "wild tradition" of a conflict that opposed two different races (Burgos 1912: 13, our translation). She also recounts the lives of others who observe and experience the war around Melilla, pointing out on "where" and "how" the conflict is happening. "It was surprising how close the city was to the battlefield", she writes. "The line of fortifications, with cannons along their battlements, began right next to the last houses" (Burgos 1912: 21-22, our translation). She adds that "[w]hile the men fought against the Christians, women, children and old men advanced in queasy confusion towards Melilla" (Burgos 1912: 52, our translation). In short, she takes the reader to that very place where the border between the city and the war zone becomes blurred, and examines the consequences of the war for the most vulnerable elements of the Moroccan population.

Boada's account, on the contrary, emphasizes his personal recreation of place within the context of what he considers to be a war. His narrative emphasises to what extent fighting is a masculine affair. He associates virility with warlike confrontation and (re)constructs an epic discourse where only males can be heroes or martyrs. For the author, the war is a stimulant and the necessary instrument of "revenge". The war happens at the front and therefore, so does the news. In this sense, he emphasizes his tricky movements and describes how he reaches the place where the news is being made, pointing out first his own courage as a reporter and then that of the Spanish soldiers. He recounts one of his heroic deeds with explicit details:

> A cloud of blood passed in front of our eyes; we lost all notion of danger, and, clasping nervously the rifles, bayonets fixed, we all went out to the field, soldiers and journalists, ready to defend to the death the entrance to the fort (Boada 1999: 407, our translation).

With this example he also relates us how he "makes war" against the enemy. Through detailed description of action and the detailed positioning, Boada ends up appearing in favour of the war, accepting it as a necessary step to reaching the territorial goals of Spanish colonialism. As a result, another frictional point appears again between masculine and feminine narrative.

In this sense, Burgos's narrative is more wary of emitting valuable judgments regarding the utility of war. According to Núñez (2005), Burgos's narrative refrains from including an open declaration of all her pacifism in order not to offend the patriotic mission of the soldiers and be censored by the army. Despite appearing cautious and diplomatic, she was also capable of using the literary resources of the period to build a textual background that makes her opposition to the war evident. To this end, she makes the protagonist of her narrative a woman, Alina, wife of one of the commanders. Carmen de Burgos uses the protagonist's voice and gaze to explain her ideology in relation to the war and to foreground everyday life near the front lines.

Accordingly, she explains how the soldiers spend their time off duty or the emotions they experience when letters from Spain arrive. As little to do with war as the event of receiving a letter may seem, it acquires great significance in the narrative of the author because it is a high point in the boring lives of the soldiers. At the same time, it also shows the other side of the war, the lives of those who stay suffering back in Spain, waiting for the return of the soldiers.

Conclusion

With travel accounts, multiple and varied geographical imaginations appear, which, if analysed as discursive formations, can explain the colonial experience relationally. At the same time, the inclusion of feminine narratives in the analysis of colonial discourse gives more complexity to Spanish Orientalism at the same time that it enriches the ensemble of the existing "geographical imaginations" on Morocco. From this point of view, one may affirm that Carmen de Burgos was the first Spanish woman war correspondent and that her texts, in spite of the censorship, served to diffuse antimilitarist points of view.

The contributions of Boada as well as those of Burgos deal with colonialism in direct relation to the war. However, the example of Carmen de Burgos is different from many of the other contemporary chronicles of war and it may be argued that it is due to the fact that she is a woman writer. Both her use of an almost cupriferous language (a feminine literary strategy of the period) and her treatment of the subject depart from the typical aggressive and masculine language that until then had characterized the chronicles of war. Perhaps what is more important here is the message that she wishes to convey: an approach to the depiction of war that comprises a geography full of nuances that enriches itself in the colonial context. The story of Carmen de Burgos, in short, has to be considered exceptional when relating it to its context of production. It is a pioneering example within Spanish literature of how women became capable of intervening in a gendered narrative typology that was clearly produced by and for men. The study of more texts like this will surely help to reassess the role that women played in the consolidation of Spanish travel writing at the beginning of the twentieth century.

Bibliography

Albet, A. & R. Cerarols. 2008. "De viatge pel Marroc: entre el debat colonial i la mirada estereotipada", in M. D. Garcia Ramon, J. Nogué & P. Zusman (eds.), *Una mirada catalana a l'Àfrica. Viatgers i viatgeres dels segles XIX i XX (1859-1936),* Lleida, Pagès, 239-75.

Bassnett, S. 2002. "Travel Writing and Gender", in P. Hulme & T. Youngs (eds.) *The Cambridge Companion to Travel Writing,* Cambridge, Cambridge UP, 225-241.

Bhabha, H. 1994. *The Location of Culture,* London, Routledge.

Blake, S. 1992. "A Woman's Trek. What Difference does Gender Make?", in N. Chaudhuri & M. Strobel (eds.), *Western Women and Imperialism,* Bloomington, Indiana UP, 19-34.

Blunt, A. & C. McEwan (eds.). 2002. *Postcolonial Geographies,* London, Continuum.

—, & G. Rose (eds.). 1994. *Writing Women and Space: Colonial and Postcolonial Geographies,* New York, Guildford Press.

Boada y Romeu, J. 1999 [1895]. *Allende el Estrecho: viajes por Marruecos (1889-1894),* Melilla, Consejería de Cultura; Ceuta: Consejería de Cultura.

Bravo Cela, B. 2003. *Carmen de Burgos, Colombine (1867-1932),* Madrid, Espasa Calpe.

Burgos Seguí, C. de [Colombine]. 1912 [1909]. *En la guerra. Episodios de Melilla,* Valencia, Sempere y Cía.

García Ramón, M. D. 2002. "Viajeras europeas en el mundo árabe. Un análisis desde la geografía feminista y postcolonial", in *Documents d'anàlisi geogràfica* 40, 105-130.

—, A. Albet, J. Nogué & Ll. Riudor. 1998. "Voices from the Margins: Gendered Images of 'Otherness' in Colonial Morocco", *Gender, Place and Culture* 5: 3, 229-40.

—. 2003. "Gender and the Colonial Encounter in the Arab World: Examining Women's Experiences and Narratives", *Environment and Planning D: Society and Space* 21, 653-72.

García-Romeral Pérez, C. 2004. *Diccionario de viajeros españoles,* Madrid, Ollero y Ramos.

Gregory, D. 1995. "Imaginative geographies", *Progress in Human Geography* 19: 4. 447-85.

Kobayashi, A. 2004. "Geography, Spatiality and Racialization: The Contribution of Edward Said", *Arab World Geographer* 7: 1-2, 79-81.

Lewis, R. 1996. *Gendering Orientalism. Race, Femininity and Representation,* London, Routledge.

—. 2004. *Rethinking Orientalism. Women, Travel and the Ottoman Harem,* London & New York, Tauris.

Martín Corrales, E. (ed.) (2002). *Marruecos y el colonialismo español (1859-1912). De la guerra de África a la "penetración pacífica",* Barcelona, Ediciones Bellaterra.

McClintock, A. 1995. *Imperial Leather: Race, Gender and Sexuality in the Colonial Contest,* New York, Routledge.

McEwan, C. 2000. *Gender, Geography and Empire: Victorian Women Travellers in West Africa,* Aldershot, Ashgate.

Mills, S. 1991. *Discourses of Difference. An Analysis of Women's Travel Writing and Colonialism,* London, Routlegde.

—. 2005. *Gender and Colonial Space,* Manchester, Manchester UP.

Monicat, B. 1996. *Itinéraires de l'écriture au féminin: Voyageuses du 19e siècle,* Amsterdam, Rodopi.

Morales Lezcano, V. 2006. *Historia de Marruecos,* Madrid, La Esfera de los Libros.

Nash, C. 1996. "Reclaiming Vision: Looking at Landscape and the Body", *Gender, Place and Culture* 3, 149-69.

—. 2002. "Cultural Geography: Postcolonial Cultural Geographies", *Progress in Human Geography* 26: 2, 219-30.

Nogué, J. & J. L. Villanova (eds.). 1999. *España en Marruecos. Discursos geográficos e intervención territorial,* Lleida, Milenio.

Núñez Rey, C. 2005. *Carmen de Burgos, Colombine en la Edad de Plata de la literatura española,* Madrid, Fundación José Manuel Lara.

Pratt, M. L. 1992. *Imperial Eyes. Travel Writing and Transculturation,* London, Routledge.

Said, E. W. 1978. *Orientalism,* New York, Vintage.

—. 1996. *Cultura e imperialismo,* Barcelona, Anagrama.

Yegenoglu, M. 1998. *Colonial Fantasies: Towards a Feminist Reading of Orientalism,* Cambridge, Cambridge UP.

AGUSTÍN COLETES BLANCO

"Valour and Patriotism": La representación de los españoles en la poesía británica de la Guerra de la Independencia (1808-1814)

"Valour and Patriotism" es el subtítulo de un libro de poesías de Felicia Hemans publicado en Londres y 1808, pocas semanas después de que los periódicos de la capital británica dieran una noticia casi increíble: España se había sublevado contra la ocupación napoleónica, y unos enviados de la Junta General del Principado de Asturias, que había declarado la guerra al emperador de los franceses, se habían presentado inopinadamente en Londres solicitando la ayuda del gobierno británico.[1] A partir de ese momento se desencadena una serie de episodios de colaboración angloespañola que incluye, de manera destacada, una toma de postura por parte de los literatos británicos, y en concreto de los poetas, unánimemente favorable a la causa de los que llaman "patriots" o patriotas españoles. El objetivo de este trabajo es dar algún detalle sobre esa toma de postura, teniendo en cuenta el contenido de este volumen en el que la representación de los extranjeros es esencial. La poesía que surge de este conflicto puede incluirse dentro del género *war poetry*, un importante corpus de poesía de guerra, en este caso un siglo anterior a la más famosa correspondiente a la I Guerra Mundial e incluso a la Guerra Civil española. Mostraremos aquí que dicha poesía no es inferior a ninguna de las otras en calidad, cantidad e impacto sociocultural.[2]

Sorprende comprobar que prácticamente todos los grandes poetas del Romanticismo inglés compusieron poesías sobre la Guerra de la Independencia (o Guerra del Francés en Cataluña) que son favorables a los patriotas españoles y están escritas al hilo mismo de los acontecimientos

---

1 Véase Bainbridge (2005), Laspra Rodríguez (2010) y Sweet-Malynyk (2001) para más detalles. El presente trabajo está vinculado al Proyecto de Investigación Nacional I+D+i MCI FFI2011-23532.

2 Véase Bainbridge (2003), Bennett (1976), Fletcher (2001) y Saglia (2000) para más detalles.

y no posteriormente: es decir, se trata de auténtica literatura de combate, parte integrante del esfuerzo bélico.[3] William Wordsworth tiene una importante serie de sonetos que giran en torno a la guerra en el País Vasco, los guerrilleros españoles o los sitios de Zaragoza, ciudad que es "a bulwark in the soul", un baluarte del alma para el poeta. La mencionada Hemans, una poetisa felizmente recuperada por la crítica y que nada tiene que envidiar a sus compañeros de generación, canta en *England and Spain*, poema largo íntegramente dedicado a la causa patriótica, a los castellanos que "rush, intrepid, to the fight". Como explica en el Prefacio a su obra, Walter Scott dedica la tercera parte de *The Vision of Don Roderick* a lo que llama la "traición" de Bonaparte y su "usurpación" del trono español en la persona de su hermano, acto que no provoca sino el despertar del valor hispano, "that Genius of the land", ese genio de la tierra que, añade, es un clamor desde "wild Biscay", la agreste Vizcaya, hasta "stately Seville", la majestuosa Sevilla. Robert Southey, en su *Carmen Triumphale, for the Commencement of the Year 1814*, dedicado a celebrar las victorias de Wellington en la campaña peninsular, habla también del despertar del heroico pueblo español, que rompiendo sus cadenas y sacudiendo su yugo recaba la ayuda de su antiguo enemigo británico ("First from his trance the heroic Spaniard woke; his chains he broke, and casting off his neck the treacherous yoke, he called on England, on his generous foe").[4] Un par de años antes, Byron había dedicado casi todo el Canto I de *Childe Harold's Pilgrimage*, la obra que como él mismo dice le haría famoso de la noche a la mañana, a la que llama "lovely Spain, renown'd, romantic land", con unos versos que se encuentran entre la mejor poesía de guerra de todos los tiempos. Su actitud claramente favorable a la causa patriótica ("awake, ye sons of Spain! awake! advance!") no le impide componer una serie de potentes estrofas dedicadas, a la manera de los goyescos "desastres de la guerra", a mostrar la descarnada crueldad de este y de todos los conflictos bélicos, lo cual ejemplifica con los cadáveres que, sin distinción de nacionalidad, son pasto de los cuervos en el campo de batalla de Talavera.[5]

3   Véase, sobre literatura politizada, Grenby (2000) y Laspra Rodríguez (2009).
4   Véase respectivamente "And is it among the rude untutored dales" 6, *England and Spain* 3.14, *The Vision of Don Roderick* 46.3-6 y *Carmen Triumphale* 5.1-3.
5   *Childe Harold's Pilgrimage* 35.1 y 37.1. Sobre Byron y su visita a una España en plena guerra, véase Coletes Blanco (2008 y 2010).

Solo la edulcorada visión del romanticismo británico que Matthew Arnold transmitió a la sociedad victoriana, como un fenómeno fundamentalmente escapista tanto en el tiempo como en el espacio, con su gusto por lo exótico, lo medieval y lo ruralizante, y que pasaría a los manuales de literatura de varias generaciones, puede explicar que esta importante vena de compromiso con lo inmediato, y más en concreto con la causa patriótica española, haya pasado tan desapercibida, incluso en Gran Bretaña. A poco que profundicemos, sin embargo, nos daremos cuenta de que, incluso con toda la importancia de lo anterior, estamos solo ante la punta del iceberg. Entre la segunda mitad de 1808 y la primera de 1814 se publican en Inglaterra, sobre el conflicto peninsular, no menos de veinte poemas largos en forma de libro exento. Se trata de obras firmadas por autores hoy considerados de segunda o tercera fila, pero que en su momento gozaron de indudable popularidad, como lo prueba el hecho de haber sido, en varios casos, objeto de múltiples reimpresiones, destacando en este sentido *The Battle of Talavera*, de John Crocker, que al final de la guerra iba por la décima edición.[6] En efecto, es frecuente que estos poemas se publiquen a raíz de una gesta épica del pueblo español, como *The Siege of Zaragoza* de Laura Sophia Temple, o de un triunfo de las armas aliadas, como los titulados *The Battles of Talavera, Salamanca, Vittoria and The Pyrenées*, de Pearson; *The Battles of the Danube and Barrosa* de John Guilliam; o *The Fall of Badajoz* de William Hersee. Es probable que la más temprana de estas poesías sea *Ode to Iberia* de Eyles Irwin, pues su autor fecha la composición el 15 de agosto de 1808, es decir, solo dos meses después de que en la prensa londinense aparecieran las primeras noticias sobre la llegada de los comisionados asturianos. Significativamente, Irwin advierte al lector de que su poema, "being a reflection of passing events, will require few or no notes, to be understood" (7). Estamos pues ante un exponente, representativo con respecto al conjunto, del poeta comprometido con su papel de mediador entre los acontecimientos y el público, mediación que, también en la práctica totalidad de estas obras, más olvidadas aún que las de los grandes clásicos mencionados, sigue ofreciendo una representación

---

6   Véase, para más detalles editoriales sobre este y los demás poemas que se mencionan, la relación de "fuentes primarias" al final de este trabajo.

de los españoles como genuinos luchadores por la libertad.[7] "Spain, and Valour" son sinónimos en el *Portugal* de Grenville. Los españoles son los "brave Allies" en *The Fall of Badajoz*, así como "a gallant people" en el anónimo *Catalonia*. Españoles, portugueses y británicos "bring equal valour to the plain; their worth [is] the same" en el también anónimo *Battle of Albuera*; están "proudly resolved to conquer or be slain" en el *Iberia* de Glanville, y así sucesivamente.[8]

Por último, no se puede ni mucho menos olvidar que, al margen de todas estas aportaciones, está la gran masa de poesías sueltas, de circunstancias, que versan sobre la misma temática y que a lo largo del periodo acotado ven la luz en diarios y revistas británicas. No son distintas de las publicadas en volumen por lo que se refiere a la representación, casi unánimemente positiva, que proyectan de los españoles, el tono empleado o los asuntos tratados: algunos títulos, por poner un mínimo ejemplo, son "To the memory of those who fell in the defense of Saragossa", "Ode to the Patriotic Spaniards", "Song for the Spanish Patriots", "A War-Song, for the Spaniards", "The Spanish Patriots, A New Song" o "On the Death of Lieut.-Gen. Sir John Moore". Con frecuencia se publican anónimamente o con un seudónimo que, en ocasiones, actúa como tenue velo de personalidades con cierta relevancia social, política o intelectual, aunque en otras se trata de simples lectores que aportan su grano de arena a la causa patriótica. Presentan, además, una notable variedad formal en cuanto a extensión, tono y métrica y, desde luego, un nivel medio de calidad literaria más que aceptable. Aunque, realmente, lo que destaca de estas poesías es su elevado número, que está en correlación directa con la cantidad e importancia de los acontecimientos bélicos que reflejan. Durante julio y agosto de 1808 encontramos dos de estas poesías en *The Times*, siete en *The Sun* y otras siete en *The Morning Chronicle*, aunque se lleva la palma *The Morning Post*, con 20 poesías publicadas durante ese mismo periodo. Hay que añadir, naturalmente, las otras muchas publicadas con fecha posterior en esos cuatro diarios, y en al menos las siguientes revistas literarias y misceláneas: *Scotts Magazine*, *Monthly Mirror*, *Athenaeum*, *Universal Magazine*, *Gentleman's Magazi-*

---

7   Para más detalles sobre el papel mediador del poeta y la representación de los españoles, véase Bainbridge (2005) y Laspra Rodríguez (2008).

8   Véase respectivamente *Portugal* 5, *Fall of Badajoz* 69.3, *Catalonia* 22.4, *Battle of Albuera* 15.18-19, *Iberia* 7.

ne, European Magazine, Poetical Register, Poetical Magazine, Monthly Magazine, London Chronicle, Edinburgh Review y *Scots Magazine*, así como en el anuario *The Annual Register* correspondiente a esos años. Como mínimo, unas 500 poesías de circunstancias relativas a la Guerra de la Independencia fueron publicadas a lo largo del periodo acotado en estas y otras cabeceras de la prensa periódica inglesa.

Quisiera, para terminar, referirme brevemente a un par de aspectos de interés. La representación poética de los españoles en estas poesías inglesas tiene también una vertiente histórica: estamos, sostienen algunas de ellas, ante una cruzada, una nueva Reconquista. De la misma manera que los cristianos peninsulares de mil años atrás, víctimas de la traición y la inoperancia de sus gobernantes, habían sufrido la invasión de los sarracenos, pero habían acabado expulsándoles tras una larga lucha, a los españoles de 1808, también víctimas de un gobierno entreguista y corrupto, les había tocado en suerte el protagonizar otro alzamiento contra un nuevo invasor de su tierra y usurpador de su cultura, el odiado Napoleón. Una nueva cruzada, que como tal admitía perfectamente un componente internacional: la ayuda británica, a la que también estos poetas cantan como elemento fundamental del conjunto. Así, la muy conocida "The Burial of Sir John Moore after Corunna" de Wolfe es una elegía en honor del héroe británico caído en La Coruña, mientras que *The Fall of Badajoz* constituye una exaltación del "immortal Wellington", personificación misma de una Britannia guerrera que es "pride and honour of my country dear!" y "of Spain, of Portugal-the valiant friend".[9] Tanta es la exaltación que, en ocasiones, la figura de Wellington llega a eclipsar completamente a cualquier otra, incluida la representación individual o colectiva de los españoles. Es muy cierto que la batalla de Talavera fue uno de los grandes triunfos de Wellington, pero ello no justifica, desde el punto de vista histórico, el hecho de que Crocker prácticamente ignore, en *The Battle of Talavera*, a los 35.000 españoles que al mando del general Cuesta pelearon con pundonor en la batalla. La reconquista histórica había dado comienzo en Asturias; la contemporánea, en cierto modo, también; no sorprende por tanto que Byron se pregunte "where is that standard, which Pelagio bore?", que Southey invoque a "Pelayo and the Campeador" o que Hemans hable de "unconquered Asturias" y de la

9 *The Fall of Badajoz* 69.1-2.

"free blood" de los asturianos.[10] Por otro lado, solo en muy contadas ocasiones se insinúa una representación más crítica de los españoles por parte de estos poetas ingleses, representación que, hay que decir, no contradice la realidad de los hechos. En alguno de sus sonetos patrióticos Wordsworth viene a dar la razón a Bonaparte por haber invadido un país que no merecía otra cosa ("Our groans, our blushes, our pale cheeks declare / That he has the power to inflict what we lack strength to bear"). En *The battle of Barrosa*, John Guilliam alude a "that morn that saw the cowards yield", en indudable referencia a la actitud del general español Manuel Lapeña, que no había acudido en ayuda de los angloportugueses de Graham. En *Catalonia* se achaca la pérdida de Tortosa a la "disunion" de sus "perfidious chiefs", reflejando así unas críticas a la falta de unión entre los propios españoles que venían siendo moneda común entre los diplomáticos y militares británicos desde el comienzo mismo del conflicto. También en *Catalonia* se reprocha a los españoles su actitud reservada ("then, Spaniards, why this cold reserve? Why thus from closer ties refrain?") y se habla de una situación de "dark distrust", desconfianza entre los aliados a la que ya se había referido Jovellanos cuando en carta a Lord Holland, escrita en las horas bajas de 1810, afirmaba en referencia a la angloespañola que "jamás alianza tan fría y tan poco sincera se ha visto en la historia".[11] Finalmente, algunas poesías critican el hecho de que Gran Bretaña apoye la causa de la libertad de un país donde no se ha abolido aún el tráfico de esclavos, como hace una composición publicada anónimamente en *Morning Chronicle* de 14 de septiembre de 1812.

Críticas puntuales al margen, es indudable que tal mediación globalmente positiva entre los acontecimientos y el público lector que lleva a cabo esta pequeña legión de poetas ingleses de todo tipo (consagrados, populares, semidesconocidos, anónimos) tiene consecuencias trascendentales: simplemente, provoca un giro de 180 grados en el paradigma representativo de España en Gran Bretaña. Lo que desde la época de la Gran Armada era una imagen de España como la tierra del fanatismo religioso, la monarquía absoluta, la Inquisición y la leyenda negra se convierte, de la noche a la mañana, en una percepción de la nación espa-

---

10   Respectivamente, *Childe Harold's Pilgrimage* 53.2, *Carmen Triumphale* 8.7 y "There are sounds in the dark Doncesvalles" 10.7.

11   Respectivamente, "Indignation of a high-minded Spaniard" 13, *Battle of Barrosa* 79, *Catalonia* 22-24, y Jovellanos a Holland, 30 agosto 1810.

ñola como baluarte de la libertad frente a la tiranía, y cuna del liberalis-
mo frente al despotismo napoleónico (López de Abiada 2007). Ya no se
habla de un populacho embrutecido y atrasado sino de un valiente pueblo
en armas que se enfrenta románticamente a la máquina militar más poderosa de su tiempo. El *conquistador* cruel y sin escrúpulos y el *grande*
vacuamente altanero dejan paso a una legión de *quijotes* generosos que,
desplegados a lo largo y ancho de la geografía peninsular, luchan fiera-
mente por su independencia. El bandido serrano se convierte en belicoso
guerrillero, terror de los franceses, y hasta la mujer española pasa de ser
una beata oscura y sumisa a una resplandeciente Belona con la figura de
Agustina de Aragón. En el ruedo ibérico un espontáneo a quien nadie
había invitado, Napoleón, sufre la estrepitosa cogida del toro bravo español, como magistralmente refleja Gillray en su famoso grabado "The
Spanish Bullfight or, the Corsican Matador in Danger" de 1808, que vale
más que mil palabras.

Quizás lamentablemente, esta percepción tan positiva no sobrevive a
la propia guerra, como se insinúa ya en algunas poesías de última hora.
"The Good Old Times", publicado en *The Morning Chronicle* de 13 de
junio de 1814, es un sarcástico epigrama sobre las consecuencias inmediatas del fin de las hostilidades: de nuevo entronizados los Borbones
tanto en Francia como en España, lo primero que hacen es reinstaurar el
tráfico de esclavos y la inquisición. "On the Present State of Spain",
publicada en *The Monthly Magazine* dos meses más tarde, es toda una
elegía dictada, dice su anónimo autor, por las lamentables circunstancias
de la España actual, que incluyen "the re-establishment of an unlimited
monarchy, of the Inquisition, of the religious (rather irreligious) orders,
of the convents, etc.", con todo lo cual "Virtue, Freedom and Religion...
retire in sadness".[12] Los muchos viajeros británicos que a partir de entonces visitan una España que se había puesto de moda acabarán comple-
tando la nueva imagen. En buena parte olvidada la percepción positiva
del periodo bélico, la subsiguiente representación de España será la con-
vencionalmente romántica, aún vigente en alguna medida y que en cierto
modo supone una vuelta a la imagen anterior a la guerra. Pero esa ya es
otra historia.

12 *The Monthly Magazine* 38 (agosto 1814): 44.

Bibliografía (i)

Anónimo. 1811. *Catalonia, a poem; with notes*, Edinburgh. Ballantyne.
Anónimo. 1811. *The Battle of Albuera: A Poem*, London. Gale.
Anónimo. 1814. "On the Present State of Spain", *The Monthly Magazine* 38 (agosto), 44.
Barbauld, A. 1812. *Eighteen Hundred and Eleven*, London, Johnson.
Byron, G. G. 1812. *Childe Harold's Pilgrimage*, London, Murray.
Crocker, J. 1813. *The Battle of Talavera*, London, Murray.
Fitzgerald, P. 1813. *Spain delivered*, London, Stockdale.
Glanville, J. 1812. *Iberia [...] War; an ode*, London, Ebers.
Grant, A. M. V. 1814. *Eighteen hundred and thirteen*, Edinburgh, Ballantyne.
Grenville, G. N. 1812. *Portugal. A poem*, London, Longman.
Gwilliam, J. 1811. *The Battles of the Danube and Barrosa*, London, Moyes.
—.1813. *The Campaign: a poem. Battles of Vittoria and the Pyrenees*, London, Wilson.
Hayley, W. 1813. *The stanzas of an English friend to the patriots of Spain*, London, Westley.
Hemans, F. 1808. *England and Spain; or, Valour and Patriotism*, London, Cadell.
—. 1841 [c. 1808]. "There are sounds in the dark Roncesvalles", in *The Works of Mrs Hemans*, London, Cadell, 7: 24.
Hersee, W. 1813. *The Battle of Vittoria. A Poem*, London, Cooper.
—. 1812. *The Fall of Badajoz. A Poem*, Chichester, Mason.
Irwin, E. 1808. *Ode to Iberia*, London, Moyes.
Jovellanos, G. M. de. 1956 [1810]. "Carta a Lord Holland" (30 agosto 1810), in *Obras publicadas e inéditas*, Madrid, Biblioteca de Autores Españoles (BAE), 4: 456.
Pearson, R. 1813. *Battles of Talavera, Salamanca, Vittoria and The Pyrenees*, London, Maiden.
Scott, W. 1811. *The Vision of Don Roderick*, Edinburgh, Ballantyne.
Southey, R. 1814. *Carmen Triumphale*, London, Weeks.
Temple, L. S. 1812. *The siege of Zaragoza*, London, Miller.

Wolfe, C. 1847 [c. 1811]. "The Burial of Sir John Moore after Corunna", in *Remains of the Late Rev. Charles Wolfe*, London, Hamilton, 1847, 25-26.

Wordsworth, W. 1974 [1810-11]. "Poems dedicated to national independence and liberty", in *Poetical Works*, London, Oxford UP, 249-55.

Bibliografía (ii)

Bainbridge, S. 2003. *British Poetry and the Revolutionary and Napoleonic Wars*, Oxford, Oxford UP.

—. 2005. "Napoleon and European Romanticism", in M. Ferber (ed.), *A Companion to European Romanticism*, Oxford, Blackwell, 450-66.

Bennett, B. T. 1976. "Introduction", in *British War Poetry in the Age of Romanticism, 1793-1815*, New York, Garland, 1-25.

Coletes Blanco, A. 2010. *Cartas y poesías mediterráneas*. Por George Gordon Byron. Traducción, edición, introducción, notas e índices, Oviedo, KRK.

—. 2008 "Lord Byron y John C. Hobhouse, testigos y propagandistas de la Guerra Peninsular", in *Actas del VII Congreso de Historia Militar*, Zaragoza, Academia General Militar, 2: 219-222.

Fletcher, I. 2001. "Introduction", in H. Turner, *Against All Hazards. Poems of the Peninsular War,* Staplehurst, Spellmount, ix-xiii.

Grenby, M. O. 2000. "Politicised Fiction in Britain, 1790-1810: An Annotated Checklist", *The European English Messenger* 9: 2, 47-53.

Laspra Rodríguez, A. 2009. "El impacto de los sitios de Zaragoza en el Reino Unido: prensa, arte y literatura", in *Los sitios de Zaragoza y su influencia en la resistencia española a la invasión napoleónica*, Zaragoza, Los Sitios, 32-58.

—. 2010. "Fictionalising History: British War Literature and the Asturian Rising, 1808", in J. Almeida (ed.), *Romanticism and the Anglo-Hispanic Imaginary*, Atlanta, Rodopi, 109-32.

—. 2008. "La literatura romántica inglesa y la Guerra Peninsular: resonancias de un conflicto", *Spagna Contemporanea* 34, 1-25.

López de Abiada, J. M. 2007. "Spaniards", in M. Beller & J. Leersen (eds.), *Imagology*, New York, Rodopi, 242-47.

Saglia, D. 2000. *Poetic Castles in Spain: British Romanticism and Figura-
    tions of Iberia*, Amsterdam, Rodopi.
Sweet, N. & J. Melnyk (eds.). 2001. *Felicia Hemans: Reimagining Poetry
    in the Nineteenth Century*. Basingstoke, Palgrave.

MONTSERRAT COTS

Miradas cruzadas bajo el prisma del humor: *La tesis de Nancy* de Ramón J. Sender

Introducción

La obra literaria de Ramón J. Sender, imponente por su extensión y su diversidad, se considera hoy como uno de los mayores exponentes de la producción novelística española del siglo XX y se yergue como testimonio perenne de la denominada "literatura del exilio". En este contexto, *La tesis de Nancy*, publicada en México en 1962, aparece como una obra menor, juzgada además con una cierta severidad por los estudiosos de Sender: de "intrascendente" la califica, por ejemplo, Marcelino C. Peñuelas (1971: 74). Su posterior incorporación al conjunto novelístico de *Los cinco libros de Nancy* (1984) no redundó tampoco en su beneficio, ya que dicho ciclo tuvo en su conjunto una crítica adversa. En esta pentalogía, *La tesis de Nancy*, aunque constituye la primera parte, cambia su título por el de *Andalucía descubre a Nancy*, mientras que la segunda parte adopta el título de *La tesis de Nancy*. A pesar de la crítica desfavorable, el público ha premiado con su fidelidad la obra, una de las más leídas de Sender, a la par que se han matizado los juicios negativos sobre su última etapa creativa (García Fernández 2001: 579). El propio autor se burlaba de la estrechez de miras de los críticos en el *Epílogo a Nancy (Bajo el signo de Tauro)*: "Esos varones grávidos y envarados encuentran mis libros sobre Nancy demasiado ligeros. No sé qué quieren decir" (Sender 1984: 612).

Si bien es cierto que el núcleo temático de *La tesis de Nancy* puede calificarse de "intrascendente" —la llegada de una joven estadounidense a Sevilla para recabar, in situ y de primera mano, información para su tesis sobre los gitanos y su progresiva integración social a la que contribuye el noviazgo con Curro—, la habilidad lingüística de Sender para encontrar un armazón que permite que la lengua se "erija en vehículo de representación de un mundo nuevo para Nancy" (Borrero y Cala 2001: 565) confiere al texto un humor del que intentaré demostrar la complejidad.

Añado además que, desde la perspectiva de la imagología y de los estudios interculturales, *La tesis de Nancy* cobra una inusitada actualidad: si se entiende esta metodología "como una de las formas de indagación más "concretas" de la aproximación a la alteridad" (Moll 2002: 347), la novela de Sender ofrece un juego de miradas cruzadas que permite observar las relaciones entre dos mundos, España y América, y también percibir algunas de las diferencias entre sus sistemas culturales en un momento determinado de la historia del siglo XX.

Estructura narrativa

La tesis de Nancy es una novela epistolar: Nancy envía diez largas cartas a su prima Betsy de Pensilvania narrándole experiencias, impresiones, descubrimientos. Las cartas evitan fechas, encabezamientos o fórmulas de despedida. En la "Nota previa" que precede a la obra, Sender explica que Betsy le ha enseñado una carta de su prima, que él la ha traducido y le ha pedido nuevas cartas. En el *Epílogo a Nancy*, insiste aún sobre ello: "Según he dicho varias veces los libros sobre Nancy los ha escrito ella misma, puesto que mi tarea ha consistido sólo en retocar sus cartas [...] o traducirlas si las había escrito en inglés" (Sender 1984: 611). Sender se adhiere de esta forma a la tradición de la gran novela epistolar de disimular la autoría y la paternidad de la obra. Remito, por ejemplo, a *Les Lettres persanes* de Montesquieu o a *Les Liaisons dangereuses* de Laclos. Sin embargo, en los cuatro libros del ciclo, el yo de Sender se hace más visible, especialmente en el *Epílogo* en el que toma las riendas de un relato dirigido a Nancy para darle –y darnos– una excelente lección de tauromaquia evocando, con todo lujo de detalles verídicos y bien documentados, un momento áureo del toreo español, el de José Gómez, llamado "el Gallito" y también "Joselito" y el de su rival, Juan Belmonte, conocido como "el Pasmo de Triana".

Como han observado algunos críticos, "Sender insiste en situarse fuera de la narración" (Borrero y Cala 2001: 565). En efecto, Sender juega con los efectos de la ausencia-presencia de su yo real advirtiendo en un breve preámbulo a la carta sexta: "En esta carta Nancy me alude a mí" (1998: 165). También Nancy recuerda las lecciones del profesor de español, estrechando así en la obra la relación entre la vida real —Sender efectivamente enseñó en los Estados Unidos— y el mundo ficcional: "Yo me acordaba de lo que nos dijo un *visiting professor* en sus conferencias sobre don Juan. ¿Te acuerdas? Era Sender" (1998: 166). Pero no solo el yo real de Sender vive en los recuerdos de Nancy sino que él mismo se hace garante de la existencia de Nancy, a la que conoce desde hace años: "Yo no he hablado nunca con la prima de Betsy, aunque la he visto muchas veces en los partidos de fútbol, donde suele actuar de *cheer leader*" (1998: 17). Estas estrategias narrativas potencian, sin duda, la verosimilitud del relato y ayudan a convencer al lector de que, en lo contado, yace una verdad.

Miradas cruzadas: "No hay como los extranjeros para ver nuestras cosas" (Ramón J. Sender, *La tesis de Nancy*. Carta III)

La conclusión a la que llega Nancy sobre la certera visión de los extranjeros, a partir de unas observaciones más que discutibles de Curro sobre el cine americano, invita, en su ingenuidad taxativa, a buen número de reflexiones. Ya Robert Escarpit, en un artículo memorable, partiendo de una observación de Tiresias en la *Odisea* (XI, 121-29), deducía:

> L'étranger est celui qui, pour interpreter une même réalité, possède une autre clef qui lui est fournie par l'expérience collective de son groupe social. C'est ainsi que le même objet qui est interprété comme une rame par l'homme de la cité maritime, est interprété comme une pelle à blé par l'homme de la cité agricole (1964: 240).

La mirada del extranjero, por el distanciamiento que entraña, tiene una capacidad de observación de la realidad ajena desde una óptica objetiva, aunque no por ello escapa a sus propios condicionantes. Esta mirada implica una ambivalencia esencial: por una parte el distanciamiento facilita la vía a un juicio objetivo, susceptible de convertirse en juicio crítico; pero, al mismo tiempo, dicha mirada está sujeta a la presencia latente de estereotipos y prejuicios, debido a complejos mecanismos de percepción: "our way of seeing and judging is conditioned by preconceived notions, prejudices and stereotypes" (Beller 2007: 4).

Los imaginarios colectivos crean mitos y opiniones del extranjero en función de un momento histórico y cultural, así como también por la influencia de textos literarios. A guisa de ejemplo, la célebre Carmen de Mérimée se erigió en un arquetipo de mujer española, sensual y apasionada, que no dejó de seducir el imaginario romántico francés. Sin embargo, "whatever their truth value, the images of national characters, countries and peoples, have acquired an effective recognition value: the reader who encounters literary stereotypes is on familiar ground, recognizes motifs, stock characters and plot situations" (Syndram 1991: 178).

Desde la perspectiva de Nancy, los rasgos identitarios españoles, andaluces y gitanos se superponen en una confluencia variopinta, aunque predomina la observación de los consabidos tópicos sobre España: "Aquí la virginidad es muy importante. A la Virgen María no la adoran por ser la madre de Jesús, sino por ser virgen." (1998: 102); "Aquí los cuernos son tabú. En el país de los toros. ¡Quién iba a pensarlo!" (1998: 116).

A lo largo de su estancia en España, se perfila claramente para Nancy un "aquí" y un "allí", una manera española y una manera americana de entender y ver la vida. Tras una actitud inicial de entusiasmo, Nancy se ve a la postre obligada a reconocer la verdad: la dificultad de conciliar los dos mundos. La novela epistolar facilita el tono intimista de la confesión del fracaso de su experiencia amorosa: "Muchas cosas nos separan" (1998: 75). Las ariscas intervenciones de Curro en contra de los americanos, pobladas ya no solamente de estereotipos sino incluso también de ridículas burlas y de cómica distorsión de la realidad —los hombres son unos cocinillas, beben leche a porrillo, comen maíz hincando el diente en la panocha entera, hay indios con flechas envenenadas detrás de los árboles— no contribuyen a mejorar la relación amorosa. La escasa capacidad de adaptación del gitano andaluz, enquistado en su pequeño mundo y en sus atávicas convicciones, es un excelente ejemplo de incapacidad de acercamiento al Otro. Nancy, siempre lúcida aunque triste, concluye: "Yo me hago andaluza, pero Curro no se hace americano, y eso a veces me duele. Oh, sí, Betsy, me duele, y tú lo comprendes" (1998: 227). Nancy se predispone así para el reencuentro con América.

Tampoco hay que olvidar que la España que refleja la novela de Sender es un país muy alejado del de hoy. El momento histórico de la novela, por algunos índices textuales deducibles, nos retrotrae al año 1958 o al 1961. En la obra se advierte "la suposición de una condición de las culturas como islas o bolas [...]; las culturas son diferentes una a otra y, por lo tanto, se entienden difícilmente entre ellas" (Welsch 2008: 114). En aquel contexto, el "aquí" y el "allí" eran dos realidades muy diferenciadas, como también lo eran en el mundo personal de Sender. El novelista vuelve por primera vez a España en 1974, tras su largo exilio después de la guerra civil. De retorno a San Diego, en un comunicado televisivo, Sender resumía sus propios sentimientos respecto a su "aquí" y a su "allí": "la influencia de América ha sido tremenda en mi caso personal, en el sentido de que me ha dado una noción diferente de la vida, incluso de la vida española. Me ha dado una noción que podemos llamar global o mundial y veo lo español en relación con el globo terráqueo con todos sus problemas" (Watts 1976: 186). Como a Nancy, las vivencias americanas le permitían observar mejor la realidad española.

El humor en *La tesis de Nancy*: "That joke was lost on the foreigner" (Mark Twain, *The Innocents Abroad*, XXVII)

Analizar los mecanismos del humor es tarea compleja porque, como ya observó un olvidado Wenceslao Fernández Flórez "el humor puede hacer reír y puede no hacer reír, sin dejar de ser humor, porque no es eso precisamente lo que se propone, a diferencia del chiste, cuyo éxito culmina en la carcajada" (1957: 7). Ya en la "Nota previa" a su novela, Sender insiste en reivindicar la dimensión lúdica del relato y, previamente, abren el libro unos epígrafes de Cervantes, de Beaumarchais y de T. Dekker en alabanza de la risa y del reír, los tres en sus lenguas originales, a buen seguro para significar lo universal del empeño.

En estas borrosas fronteras entre el humor y la risa, se ha afirmado que el "conocimiento imperfecto del idioma produce hilaridad" (Beinhauer 1973: 26). En este sentido, el extranjero, ya sea por el mal uso del idioma o porque desconoce los implícitos del lenguaje, a menudo interpreta mal una expresión o se le escapa su cabal entendimiento. Nancy, obsesionada por incorporar lo que ella llama "el *slang* español" a sus usos idiomáticos, deduce significados erróneos, con frecuencia por no separar el sentido figurado del recto o por simple desconocimiento de la palabra, lo que provoca la risa del lector. Así, el que a algunos toreros "se les arruga el ombligo", cree que es debido a "alguna alergia", se asombra del enigmático "pelar la pava" porque "aquí sólo se come pavo para Navidad"; y de un "lilaila" comenta: "no sé qué profesión será esa". Sender, a lo largo de la novela, encadena los juegos de palabras, generalmente a partir de la anfibología y de la polisemia, recurriendo también a la antanaclasis, las paronomasias, los homónimos, los heterónimos, los equívocos... y todos aquellos recursos que son aptos para crear una connivencia lúdica. El juego polisémico se revela un método fecundo de creación humorística ya que "permet de construire deux ou plusieurs niveaux de lecture tout au long de la construction phrastique (isotopie) autour de mots dont le sens est double ou triple". (Charaudeau 2006: 32). De ahí que ya se ha observado que *La tesis de Nancy* es un caudal de prácticas lingüísticas idóneas para el aprendizaje del castellano, a la vez que un compendio de expresiones, quizás hoy poco frecuentes, pero no por ello menos dignas de ser recordadas.

Sin embargo, la comicidad no se reduce únicamente a los hallazgos léxicos. Hay en *La tesis de Nancy* otro tipo de humor más incisivo y de mayor alcance. Es el humor que pone de manifiesto los desajustes de las normas sociales o el ridículo de algunos hábitos: "It is also widely accepted that humour typically involves some kind of subversion" (Mulkay 1987: 247). Para este tipo de humor, la mirada del extranjero se revela de extrema eficacia porque, como observaba R. Escarpit, el extranjero tiene otra "clave" para interpretar la misma realidad.

Nancy se convierte paulatinamente en sujeto pensante y desarrolla su propio proceso cognitivo, todo ello sin abandonar la perspectiva ingenua, a veces un tanto asombrada, ante la realidad, uno de los recursos literarios más usados, junto con la explotación de lo ridículo, para desencadenar la risa. Son ejemplos de risa punitiva que se identifica con el "castigat ridendo mores" y que entraña la denuncia social. Así, en la cena en casa del marqués de Estoraque, cuando el aristócrata aprovecha para tocar el muslo de Nancy por debajo de la mesa, ella lo interpreta como un masaje a la rodilla y una costumbre española, por lo que, al marcharse, le da las gracias por ello: "Los otros no comprendían. Yo no estoy segura de comprender tampoco" (1998: 29). Tampoco entiende la costumbre del piropo, que la lleva a interpretar un "está buena" como una amable preocupación por su salud. El extranjero no "comprende" pero su incomprensión es una fuente inagotable de comicidad que pone al descubierto las singularidades o los desaciertos de la sociedad que lo acoge.

Conclusión

En *La tesis de Nancy* confluyen la ingenua mirada de la protagonista y la desilusionada mirada del exiliado Sender. Ambas se combinan para satirizar los desajustes de la sociedad española del momento, aunque bajo prismas distintos. En una amable controversia académica, Linda Hutcheon y Mario Valdés discurrieron sobre las relaciones entre la nostalgia y la ironía, la primera entendida como "is not something you 'perceive' *in* an object; it is what you 'feel' when two different temporal moments, past and present, come together for you and, often, carry considerable emotional weight" (1998-2000: 24). Por su parte, la ironía implica una dialéctica en la que juegan lo dicho y lo no dicho para enriquecer el significado. El humor que Sender transmite en su aparente intrascendente novela funde el inocente humor de Nancy y el humor nostálgico, un tanto desengañado, a veces irónico, del exiliado Sender. El cruce de ambas miradas confiere a la novela una dimensión subversiva de crítica social que se logra precisamente desde la otredad y el alejamiento.

Bibliografía

Beinhauer, W. 1973. *El humorismo en el español hablado. (Improvisadas creaciones espontáneas)*, Madrid, Gredos.

Beller, M. 2007. "Perception, Image, Imagology", in M. Beller & J. Leerssen (eds.), *Imagology. The Cultural Construction and Literary Representation of National Characters*, Amsterdam, Rodopi, 3-16.

Charaudeau, P. 2006. "Des catégories pour l'humour?", *Questions de Communication* 10, 19-41.

Borrero Barrera, M. J. & R. Cala Carvajal. 2001. "De lo literario y lingüístico en *La tesis de Nancy* de Ramón J. Sender", in *Sender y su tiempo. Crónica de un siglo*. Actas del II Congreso sobre Ramón J. Sender. Huesca, 27-31 de marzo de 2001, Huesca, Instituto de Estudios Altoaragoneses, 563-75.

Escarpit, R. 1964. "La visión de l'étranger comme procédé d'humour", in *Connaissance de l'étranger. Mélanges offerts à la mémoire de Jean-Marie Carré*, Paris, Didier, 240-46.

Fernández Flórez, W. 1957. *Antología del humorismo en la literatura universal*, Barcelona, Labor.

García Fernández, J. A. 2001. "*La tesis de Nancy*, espacio para el reencuentro", in *Sender y su tiempo. Crónica de un siglo*. Actas del II Congreso sobre Ramón J. Sender. Huesca, 27-31 de marzo de 2001, Huesca, Instituto de Estudios Altoaragoneses, 577-91.

Hutcheon, L. & M. J. Valdés. 1998-2000. "Irony, Nostalgia, and the Postmodern: A Dialogue", in *Poligrafías. Revista de Literatura Comparada* 3,18-41.

Moll, N. 2002. "Imágenes del 'Otro': La literatura y los estudios interculturales", in A. Gnisci (ed.), *Introducción a la literatura comparada*, Barcelona, Crítica, 347-89.

Mulkay, M. 1987. "Humour and Social Structure", in W. Outhwaite & M. Mulkay (eds.), *Social Theory and Social Criticism. Essays for Tom Bottomore*, Oxford & New York, Blackwell, 243-63.

Peñuelas, M. C. 1969. *Conversaciones con Ramón J. Sender*, Madrid, Magisterio Español.

Peñuelas, M. C. 1971. *La obra narrativa de Ramón J. Sender*, Madrid, Gredos.

Sender, R. J. 1984. *Los cinco libros de Nancy*, Barcelona, Destino.

—. 1998 [1962]. *La tesis de Nancy*, Madrid, Magisterio Español.

Syndram, K. U. 1991. "The Aesthetics of Alterity: Literature and the Imagological Approach", *Yearbook of European Studies* 4, 177-91.

Watts, L. C. de. 1976. *Veintiún días con Sender en España*, Barcelona, Destino.

Welsch, W. 2008. "El camino hacia la sociedad transcultural", in A. Sanz Cabrerizo (ed.), *Interculturas/Transliteraturas*, Madrid, Arco Libros, 108-31.

TOM DICKINS

Attitudes to the Notion of "Foreign", as Reflected in the Czech Lexicon since the End of the Nineteenth Century

Introduction

The aim of this essay (which draws on a number of the author's recent publications, as identified in the bibliography) is to evaluate the Czechs' perceptions of foreign influences, with special reference to their implications for lexical variation and change. The paper highlights some of the stereotypical concepts of the "self" and the "other", as well as broader questions of inclusivism and exclusivism, as evidenced by language usage. Particular attention is paid to the Czechs' evolving attitudes to their principal contact communities, and to the major modern European lexical donors —German, French, Russian and English.

Mayer (2009: 30) has stressed the Czechs' tendency to define their national identity in relation to foreigners —from the Germans to the Austrians, to the Russians, to the Slovaks, and back to the Germans and to Europe. Macura (1983, 2010) and Kosatík (2010) have depicted Czech history more figuratively as a series of "dreams" which involve either the elimination of external threats (especially the threat of German speakers, but subsequently that of the Soviet empire) or the desire to embrace and even subsume other peoples (particularly the Slovaks).

The essay focuses principally on the period from 1918, when the Czechoslovak state was founded, although mention is also made of referents which pre-date this era. The first part of the twentieth century, until 1938, can be characterised as a time of nation building; the second part, from 1938 to 1945, as a struggle for national survival; the third part, from 1945 to 1989, as an age of ethnic entrenchment, based firmly on Herder's model of language-culture-state (1784); and the fourth part, from 1990 to the present day, as the establishment of a new cultural diversity.

The First Republic (1918-1938) was broadly receptive to (non-German) foreign influences, providing they did not threaten the underlying tenets of parliamentary democracy. By contrast, post-1948 Czechoslovakia exploited a combination of national mythopoeia and anti-western ideology to promote a monocultural consensus. Since 1989, enlightened public discourses about identity, and participation in a larger community, have led to a more nuanced approach to the notion of "foreign", but by no means all outsiders enjoy an equal status. Havlík (2007: 2-3) argues that near neighbours, west Europeans, Americans and other peoples from developed capitalist economies are currently seen as "unproblematic", whereas the inhabitants of the former USSR, people from the Far East and Roma are regarded as much more "problematic".

Foreign lexifiers

Excluding Greek and Latin, German was by some margin the major foreign source of vocabulary before 1918, with French occupying second place and English increasingly influential after the turn of the twentieth century. The eighteenth- and nineteenth-century Czech National Revival was marked by a wave of linguistic purism, as discussed by Jelínek (2007) amongst others, which led to the replacement of a great many German terms by Slavonic root words. German influence persisted in naturalised lexemes, such as *křída* < *Kreide* (chalk), as well as in other areas of language, including syntax (*co to je za ...? < was für ein(e)... ist das?* [what sort of ... is it?]). Yet it is perhaps in the spoken language that German influence has remained most conspicuous, as demonstrated by lexical items such as *šmakovat* (to taste good) < *schmecken*.

Unlike German, the Romance languages continued to play a major role in the development of Czech throughout the second half of the nineteenth and early twentieth century. French influence is particularly evident in domains such as fashion and cosmetics, diplomacy, cuisine and the arts, while Italian, as elsewhere, has left its mark principally on musical terminology, food and drink and money-related matters. The main contribution of English began later, and particularly affected the fields of culture, sport and technology.

The influence of French grew further after 1918 as a result of increased political and cultural contacts, including translations of French works into Czech (analysed by Dvořáček 1932). Following the Munich Agreement of 1938, however, there was a renewed puristic reaction to terms from western languages, which reflected the Czechs' sense of betrayal by their "bourgeois" allies. The Czechs' post-war re-evaluation of their relationship with the outside world led to a new alliance with the USSR, which appeared not only to offer a bulwark against German revanchism, but also the prospects of greater social cohesion and equality. The enduring appeal of the Czech "egalitarian ethos", as considered by Holy (1996: 72), is borne out by surveys conducted in June and July 1968, in which 86% of respondents expressed the desire to persist with socialism (cited in Pecka 1996: 206, and Bren 2010: 25).

The reorientation of Czechoslovakia towards the Russian-speaking world after 1945 (and especially after the Communist takeover in 1948) had a significant effect on Czech stylistically, semantically and conceptually. It also led to the adoption of some new terminology, most noticeably in the three areas of public life most closely associated with Communist ideology and Soviet speak: politics, economics and national security (particularly the military). Surprisingly, however, it did not result in a dramatic shift in the overall balance of foreign words in the language. A study by Těšitelová (1990: 112), which drew mainly on research from the 1980s, found that of the 10,000 most common Czech words just ten were from Russian. Despite the endorsement of the Soviet model and of things Russian "from above", any initial enthusiasm "from below" for lexical change on the basis of Russian quickly abated.

In the early years of Communist rule, English influence was heavily suppressed, but neologisms such as *kečup* ([tomato] ketchup) still found their way into the Czech lexicon. There was a revival of interest in, and an increase in exposure to, the Anglophone world in the 1960s, but the Czechoslovak authorities took measures to reassert covert control over lexical usage after the 1968 Warsaw Pact intervention. For example, preference was given to the loan translation *párek v rohlíku* (sausage in a roll) over *hot dog*, and the media actively promoted the use of *odbíjená* (volleyball) over *volejbal*.

The people to whom the Czechs have always had the greatest
affinity —the Slovaks— have tended to feel politically, economically
and linguistically oppressed by the presence of their "elder brother".
Czech helped to shape the Slovak language from the fourteenth to the
nineteenth century as a result of religious and educational contact, and
continued to inform the Slovak lexicon throughout much of the twentieth
century. The process was not altogether one way, but the relationship
was always asymmetrical. Prior to 1918, the ethnic descriptor *Čech*
(Czech/Bohemian) often subsumed the notion of "Slovak", and until
1938 many Czechs continued to treat the Slovak language as a dialect of
Czech (as discussed by Dickins 2009b).

As in other European languages, the number of English borrowings
and internationalisms derived from English has increased exponentially
in recent years. Most of the Anglicisms that have been introduced have
served to fill lexical gaps, but some, such as *houmlesák* for *bezdomec*
(homeless person), would appear functionally surplus to requirements.
Crystal (2004) attributes the rise in English as a global language to a
combination of political (military), technological, economic and cultural
power. The unique political and cultural capital of English is enhanced
by its role as the first foreign language in school, and by the absence of
historical enmity between the Czech- and English-speaking lands.

Czechs' perception of themselves and others

The image which the Czech lexicon projects of its matrix population is
varied and occasionally contradictory. Although the Czechs see
themselves as a cultured and educated people, whose contribution to the
world has exceeded that of many other similar-sized nations, they also
tend to be overtly self-critical. Czech ethnohistoriography accentuates
the importance of the demotic myth, but at the same time portrays the
ordinary person in a largely unheroic light. It is not insignificant that the
two fictional "heroes" who perhaps best personify the Czech nation, that
is, the fairy-tale character *Hloupý Honza* (Stupid Honza; "Silly Billy")
and Hašek's Good Soldier Švejk (1921-1923), are ne'er-do-wells, who
rely on native wit and cunning, rather than reason and honest endeavour,
to overcome the obstacles in their way.

Amongst the various self-deprecating endonyms which have come to define the "average" Czech is *malý český člověk* (the little Czech), which is so widely recognised that it has spawned its own initialism, *MČČ*. According to Holy (1996: 72), the *MČČ* is cautious and mistrustful of those outside his immediate circle, but has acquired the status of "the ideal member of the Czech nation", thanks to his resistance to external oppression. Several of the derivatives of *Čech* have similarly pejorative overtones, including *Čecháček*, which may suggest narrow-mindedness and a tendency to put self-interest first, but is open to a wide range of personal interpretation. Ex-president Havel (cited in Šíp 1999) applied the plural form *Čecháčkové* to the types of Czech whose attitude to the rest of Europe is characterised by parochialism, complacency and xenophobia, while Moravian nationalists have sometimes employed it as a more general ethnophaulism for their Bohemian counterparts.

By contrast, most of the Czech terms for the Slovaks and vice versa are either neutral or suggest a degree of affection. Amongst the more derogatory Czech expressions for the Slovaks are the dated noun *dráteník/dráteníček* ([travelling] tinker), while the Slovaks employ the ironic hypocoristic *pepík* to denote a typical Czech. (This term is also used in Moravia to refer to the Bohemians and in Polish [*pepik/pepiczek*] of the Czechs.) The Czechs' relations with their bigger Slav neighbours —the Poles (sometimes humorously called *Pšonci*, on account of the way they speak)— are likewise generally cordial, despite earlier territorial disputes, and a lack of mutual empathy, as suggested by the Polish metaphor *czeski film* (Czech film), which can refer to virtually anything that is impenetrable.

The recent more conciliatory attitudes of the Czechs to the German-speaking world have been striking, in view of the depth of their erstwhile animosity. Both the Germans and the Austrians now belong firmly in the "unproblematic" camp, but the Czech lexicon still testifies to anti-German sentiment, as evidenced by the old-fashioned derivative of *Němec* (German): *Němčour* (obstinate German), and pejorative exonyms relating to German imperial ambition, such as *nácek* (Nazi). Czech also has a few derogatory terms for Austrians, including the dated cognate of *Rakušan* (Austrian): *Rakušák/Rakušačka* ("loyal" Austrian).

Czech perceptions of the Russian-speaking world have historically been largely positive, despite repeated misgivings over Russian absolutism. According to Sak (1996: 9), "Czech Russophilism was in essence non-political, and drew mainly on literary and metaphysical sources". Pro-Russian sentiment reached its peak in 1945, as a result of the Red Army's role in the liberation of Czechoslovakia, but expressions of goodwill quickly gave way to (private) criticism of the Soviet-directed excesses. Amongst the more hostile descriptors that have been applied to the Russians are the well-established slur *Rusák/Rusáček* (Russky), and the Soviet-era neologism *kolchozník* (collective farm worker).

Attitudes to the Ukrainians, who constitute the largest foreign community in the Czech Republic, have become increasingly negative. Ukrainian migrant workers are amongst the most disadvantaged sector of society and are unpopular, at least in part, because they are felt to be taking "Czech" jobs. The jocular old-fashioned nickname for Ukrainians *Chachlák/Chochlák* or *Chachol/Chochol,* which is derived from Russian, has largely been replaced by the more derogatory expression *Úkáčko.*

Of all the ethnic minorities, only the Roma are viewed with greater disdain than the Ukrainians. Suffice it to say, even the most commonly used designation —*cikán* (gypsy)— has pejorative associations. The Roma desire to be simultaneously outside Czech society and an integral part of it runs counter to the Czechs' normative view of their national ethos. The sense that the Roma do not belong is heightened by linguistic differences, which contribute to the educational under-achievement of the Roma, with its concomitant social implications.

Terms reinforcing inclusivism and exclusivism

The question of ethnic affiliation is illustrated in the Czech lexicon by an extensive range of terms distinguishing between "us" and "them", and "here/(at) home" and "there/abroad", including *náš* (our) and *jejich* (their), *své/svůj* (*vlastní*) (one's own) and *nesvůj/cizí* (someone else's, foreign), *doma* (literally "at home [in our country]") and *venku* ("outside [our country]"). Phrases such as *svůj k svému* (each to his own), used by tradesmen in the late 1880s to encourage support for Czech-run businesses, highlight the importance that the Czechs have attached to the notion of self-dependence. The Revivalist phrase *Národ sobě!* (literally "The nation to itself!"; By the people, for the people!), used as a rallying cry for the collection of funds to construct the National Theatre (*Národní divadlo*), further reflects the idea of the self-reliance of Czech speakers.

The pronoun *náš* (our) can be exclusive, as in *naši remizovali ve Slovinsku* ("ours" [we, the Czechs] drew in Slovenia), but it has also been employed by Masaryk, amongst others, to subsume various ethnics, as in *náš národ* (our [Czech and Slovak] nation) and *naši Němci* (our ['Czechoslovak'] Germans). The construction *u nás* (*doma*) (cf. German "bei uns", French "chez nous"), likewise covers a variety of meanings ranging from ethnic affiliation to more localised attachment. As Judt (cited in Roberts 2005: 173) has observed, the expression allows one "to slide effortlessly from cozy domesticity into ethnocentric exclusivism".

The adjective *cizí* has a similar semantic range to that of German *fremd*, but, unlike its German counterpart, it has yielded pejorative derivatives, such as *cizáci* and *cizáctvo* (undesirable foreigners). The relative frequency of the expression *cizí nadvláda* (foreign hegemony), suggests the extent to which the idea of the burden of foreign oppression has become routinised. Heimann (2009: 148-49) has argued that the Czechs have tended to make a scapegoat of external forces, even in respect of events that cannot be blamed on outsiders, such as the expulsion of the German and Hungarian minorities after the war.

Conclusion

The repeated distinction between Czech and non-Czech, based on age-old territorial claims, has historically reinforced the idea of nationality as a birthright and of the foreigner as an unwelcome outsider. However, attitudes to the notion of "foreign" have changed significantly, as a result of greater regional and European integration, the more general impact of globalisation, and increased personal contacts with foreign cultures and languages. Puristic sentiment, in the narrow sense that it existed in the past, has largely vanished, and most Czechs now recognise the need for lexical innovation, and cultural and linguistic diversity, as a prerequisite for full participation in the international community. Although tensions with "problematic" ethnic groups persist, foreign influences are no longer automatically dismissed as inimical to the interests of the state. Glorious isolation has given way to selective inclusivism.

Bibliography

Bren, P. 2010. *The Greengrocer and his TV. The Culture of Communism after the 1968 Prague Spring*, Ithaca & London, Cornell UP.

Crystal, D. 2004. "The Past, Present and Future of World English", in A. Gardt & B. Hüppauf (eds.), *Globalization and the future of German*, Berlin, Mouton de Gruyter, 27-46.

Dickins, T. 2009a. *Attitudes to Lexical Borrowing in the Czech Republic*, Liberec, Nakladatelství Bor.

—. 2009b. "Češi a slovenština", *Naše společnost* 7: 1, 12-26.

—. 2006. "Russian and Soviet Loanwords and Calques in the Czech Lexicon since the Beginning of the Twentieth Century", *The Slavonic and East European Review* 84: 4, 593-638.

—. 2011. "The Czech-speaking Lands, Their Peoples and Contact Communities: Titles, Names and Ethnonyms", *The Slavonic and East European Review* 89: 3, 401-54.

Dvořáček, J. 1932. "Nejčastější galicismy v novočeské skladbě", *Naše řeč* 16: 3, 65-71; 16: 4, 97-103; 16: 5, 129-37; 16: 6, 161-68.

Heimann, M. 2009. *Czechoslovakia: The State that Failed*, New Haven & London, Yale UP.

Havlík, R. 2007. "Postoje k cizincům a menšinám ve světle sociologického výzkumu", *Paideia: Philosophical E-Journal of Charles University* 4: 1-2, 1-8 [accessed Nov. 20, 2010] <http://userweb.pedf.cuni.cz/paideia/download/havlik.pdf>

Holy, L. 1996. *The Little Czech and the Great Czech Nation*, Cambridge, Cambridge UP.

Jelínek, M. 2007. "Purismus", in J. Pleskalová et al. (eds.), *Kapitoly z dějin české jazykovědné bohemistiky*, Praha, Academia, 540-72.

Jungmann, J. 1849. *Historie literatury české aneb Soustavný přehled spisů českých s krátkou historií národu, osvícení a jazyka*, Praha, České museum, Kněhkupectví F. Řivnáče.

Kosatík, P. 2010. *České snění*, Praha, Torst.

Macura, V. *2010. The Mystifications of a Nation. The "Potato Bug" and Other Essays on Czech Culture,* H. Pichová & C. Cravens (trans. & eds.), Madison, Wisconsin, U of Wisconsin P.

—. 1983. *Znamení zrodu. České obrození jako kulturní typ*, Praha, Československý spisovatel.

Mayer, F. 2009. *Češi a jejich komunismus. Paměť a politická identita*, H. Beguivinová (trans.), Praha, Argo.

Pecka, E. 1996. "Political Culture in the Czech Republic", in F. Plasser & A. Pribersky (eds.), *Political Culture in East Central Europe*, Aldershot, Avebury.

Roberts, A. 2005. *A Dictionary of Czech Popular Culture,* Budapest & New York, Central European UP.

Sak, R. 1996. *Anabáze: Drama československých legionářů v Rusku (1914–1920)*, Praha, H&H.

Šíp, E. 5 August 1999. "Čecháčkové", *Národní osvobození* [in *Britské listy*], <http://blisty.cz/art/10864.html> [accessed June 4, 2009]

Těšitelová, M. 1990. "O přejatých slovech v češtině z hlediska kvantitativního", *Slovo a slovesnost* 51: 2, 111-23.

MARGARITA GARBISU

España en los escritos de John B. Trend: desmontando tópicos

El hispanista y musicólogo inglés John Brande Trend (1887-1958) visitó España con frecuencia en la década de los 20 del siglo pasado: conoció cada rincón de la Península, se empapó de sus diversas costumbres, se mezcló con sus gentes y cultivó una fuerte amistad con músicos, literatos e intelectuales de la época. Trend se dejó embaucar por España, por una España diversa, que quiso compartir con sus conciudadanos.

En este sentido, uno de sus empeños fue dar a conocer una imagen de este país distinta a la que la gente inglesa tenía en mente, que no era otra que una España llena de tópicos y prejuicios: una España que identificaban exclusivamente con el Sur, con una tierra de gitanas, matadores, flamenco, superstición y religiosidad popular. Para hacerlo se valió, claro está, de su pluma, pues Trend escribió multitud de artículos en prestigiosas revistas culturales inglesas así como un buen número de volúmenes de ensayos, la mayoría con contenidos idénticos o similares a los incluidos en sus artículos.

El objetivo del presente texto parte de estos escritos ya que pretende describir cómo con ellos Trend intentó desmontar una serie de tópicos preconcebidos en la mente de sus lectores ingleses. Es mucha la bibliografía de John Trend y resulta imposible abarcarla íntegra desde estas páginas; por este motivo, se van a tomar solamente ejemplos aislados, los considerados más adecuados. Pero cabe antes comenzar con una breve revisión de la trayectoria del hispanista y de su estrecho vínculo con las gentes y la cultura españolas.

Trend y España

1919 y 1937 enmarcan la primera y la última visita de Trend a España; pero existe un antes y un después en este periodo con el año 1933 como línea divisoria, cuando es nombrado catedrático de español en la universidad de Cambridge. Desde entonces sus estancias en la Península se reducen por dos motivos: por el exceso de trabajo y, a partir del 36, evidentemente por la guerra, pero también por su desacuerdo con la España resultante de la contienda. Esta idea debe quedar clara: para Trend España es la de los años veinte y los treinta, la de la Edad de Plata y la Residencia de Estudiantes, y no otra. La España de después de la guerra no existe para él: no escribe ni una sola letra sobre la cultura española de los 40 o los 50 y, por supuesto, no pisa la España de Franco.

En su primer viaje de 1919 llegó a la Península como corresponsal de la revista *The Athenaeum*. Recala en Granada, en donde en seguida contacta con Manuel de Falla[1] y Federico García Lorca. Él mismo lo recuerda en sus obras: "The first time I met Don Manuel de Falla was on a blustering September evening at the *Villa Carmona* on the Alhambra Hill" (1921: 237). En cuanto a Lorca, lo conoció una noche estrellada cuando le escuchó recitar en un local del Albaicín; permaneció con él hasta la madrugada, hora de regresar a casa por las estrechas calles granadinas (1971: 1-2).

Se podría decir que estos dos nombres marcan los dos momentos en la creación ensayística de Trend, con ese 1933 como frontera, ya que dos de sus obras más significativas se centran en ellos: la primera es *Manuel de Falla and Spanish Music* (1929), un volumen monográfico sobre el compositor, y la segunda *Lorca and the Spanish Poetic Tradition* (1956), una compilación de ensayos sobre diversos autores que, previamente, se habían publicado como separatas a cargo de la Universidad de Cambridge. Asimismo estas dos obras son orientativas de su trayectoria pues hasta 1933 prevalece el Trend musicólogo, y a partir de ese año prevalece, por su nuevo cargo, el Trend crítico literario.

---

1   El profesor Nigel Dennis ha editado un volumen que recoge la correspondencia
     entre Trend y Manuel de Falla desde 1919 a 1935; el libro viene introducido por un
     prólogo con su firma, que se ha convertido en escrito de obligada referencia para
     conocer el vínculo del inglés con Falla y con España (Dennis 2007: 7-23).

Por consiguiente, fue como musicólogo cuando se introdujo en la idiosincrasia española, en su cultura, sus lugares y gentes. Desde su primera estancia de 1919, empezó a viajar por la Península; de Granada se traslada a Madrid y allí se vincula con el ambiente de la Residencia de Estudiantes. En *Lorca and the Spanish Poetic Tradition* relata que en los primeros años veinte tuvo la ocasión de escuchar a creadores de diversas generaciones, a Antonio Machado, Unamuno, Juan Ramón Jiménez, Ortega y Gasset, Pedro Salinas, Jorge Guillén o Luis Cernuda, entre otros muchos (1971: 172). Llegaron también las diferentes regiones, donde, de archivo en archivo, de biblioteca en biblioteca, indagó sobre la música antigua española. Visitó las bibliotecas de El Escorial y Palma de Mallorca, la Biblioteca de Cataluña de Barcelona, la del Colegio del Patriarca de Valencia o la Provincial de Cádiz (Dennis 2007: 11). Fruto de estas vivencias e indagaciones nacieron *A Picture of Modern Spain: Men and Music* (1921), *Luis Milán and the Vihuelistas* (1925) o *The Music of Spanish History to 1600* (1926). Asimismo en 1928 publica *Spain from the South,* un libro de viajes que recorre parte de la Península. A todos estos volúmenes hay que añadir los artículos que publicó en revistas como *The Criterion, The Athenaeum, Music and Letters, Times Literary Supplement, The Musical Time* o *Monthly Musical Record.*

En todos estos textos quedó reflejado su profundo conocimiento de España, que excedía, como se ha esbozado anteriormente, lo puramente musical y literario. Trend introduce su propia visión de esta tierra, fruto de horas de observación; una visión plenamente alejada del estereotipo, lo que quiere mostrar a sus lectores. Tal como observa el profesor Nigel Dennis,

> se asigna a sí mismo la responsabilidad de hacer de puente o intermediario entre España e Inglaterra, explicando al público británico el sentido de la cultura españo-la, en su dimensión histórica y actual [...]; un público curioso, sin duda, pero mal informado, que no ve más allá de las leyendas románticas y los estereotipos cultura-les (2007: 10).

Dennis apunta que ya desde sus primeras obras españolas, Trend "se queja de la falsedad o superficialidad que tienen los ingleses de España", país al que veían como una ficción (Dennis 2007: 10); la intención del hispanista es transmitir con sus escritos la España esencial y verdadera que se esconde tras esa ficción, la ficción del tópico.

¿Cómo consigue su objetivo? Se podría afirmar que con la alusión constante a dos argumentos diversos, si bien estrechamente relacionados: por un lado, la denuncia directa del estereotipo y la explicación de su origen y su porqué, y, por otro, la defensa del europeísmo de la cultura española, el europeísmo de sus figuras y de sus artes.

La denuncia del estereotipo español

En *A Picture of Modern Spain: Men and Music,* Trend se lamentaba de que las mujeres inglesas seguían pensando en las españolas en términos de "Carmen", de abanicos y mantillas (1921: 40). Y es que aquí se encuentra, según él, el inicio de todo, pues el tópico se aferra al siglo XIX, a la cultura romántica y específicamente a la ópera *Carmen* del compositor francés Georges Bizet, estrenada en 1875. Trend considera que, a partir de esta ópera, se creó un doble estereotipo que consiguió definir equivocadamente nuestra cultura: el de la mujer española y el de la música española.

Del primero habla claramente en *Spain from the South.* En este libro Trend explica al viajero que la "mujer Carmen", esa mujer morena, gitana y embaucadora, no es la que va a hallar en cada esquina del país; que, al contrario de lo que comúnmente se piensa, en España Carmen no es la regla sino más bien la excepción. La idea errónea —continúa el musicólogo— se extendió por Europa desde el estreno de la ópera, que así la fomentó; pero la culpa de ello no fue ni de Bizet ni de Prosper Mérimée (como es sabido, el autor de la novela corta en la que se inspira la obra musical), sino de los libretistas y traductores del texto que, con su interpretación, transmitieron la falsa visión que derivó en el estereotipo:

No one could say anything against Bizet, a great musician whose work has kept its freshness [...]; and no one can abuse Prosper Mérimée, who knew the Spain of his time inside out and was an admirable writer. The fault lies with the opera-librettists and their translators, who have signally failed to catch the stark quality of the story and the precision of its language (Trend 1928: 7).

Para desmontar este primer cliché, Trend respalda la tesis de que la trama de *Carmen* bien podría haber acontecido, en lugar de en Andalucía, en Hungría, en Rumanía o incluso en Hampshire, al sur de Inglaterra; es decir, en cualquier lugar de la tierra en el que habiten gitanos. Lo importante no es que Carmen viva en Sevilla, sino que Carmen sea gitana. Es su origen gitano lo que define su carácter temperamental y apasionado; por consiguiente —concluye diciendo Trend a sus lectores—, es absurdo identificar a Carmen con la mujer andaluza y, por añadidura, con toda mujer española (1928: 7-8).

En cuanto al segundo estereotipo, el de la música española, Trend denuncia que los ingleses tendían a identificarla, como ocurría con la mujer, con la música flamenca del Sur, que había empezado a despertar interés fuera de España precisamente a finales del XIX. Para desmontar este segundo cliché, Trend recurre en sus escritos al mismo procedimiento que en el estereotipo anterior: por un lado, explica el origen del tópico y, por otro, intenta hacer ver a sus lectores que, del mismo modo que no todas las mujeres de España son "Cármenes", no toda la música española es flamenca. Habla sobre este último asunto en *Manuel de Falla and Spanish Music,* en concreto, en un capítulo dedicado íntegramente a Felipe Pedrell, el músico y musicólogo catalán que centró parte de su investigación en la recuperación de la música popular española (1934: 3-14). Aquí Trend no puede ser más claro cuando afirma que al igual que fuera de Inglaterra solo se considera la céltica como la única música popular inglesa, fuera de España solo se conoce como música popular española la flamenca; pobre visión en ambos casos. Sin embargo, añade el musicólogo, en la Península Ibérica existen multitud de músicas y culturas populares: la del País Vasco, la mediterránea, la gallega, la castellana o la catalana, culturas diversas que Pedrell y algunos otros expertos habían dado a conocer con sus indagaciones.

Pero decíamos que Trend pretende también explicar a sus paisanos el origen del estereotipo musical; a este respecto, les anuncia que parten de un error de base pues esa música flamenca que identifican como española les ha llegado totalmente desvirtuada, plenamente alejada de su verdadera esencia.

En "The Moors in Spanish Music", una crónica publicada en *The Criterion* en 1924, afirma que la verdadera música popular del Sur de

España (que nace de la música popular del XVIII), es el cante jondo.[2] El jondo —afirma— es el cante del sentido trágico de la vida y se vincula siempre con el pueblo gitano. Pero ocurrió que a finales del XIX empezó a ser interpretado de un modo más vulgarizado por gitanos y también por payos vestidos con ropajes de colores (de colores que recordaban a los flamencos). Esta particular interpretación del cante jondo pasó a ser conocida como cante flamenco (1924: 205-206).

¿Consecuencia? Que en esos momentos empezó a olvidarse la verdadera esencia del cante original, esto es, del jondo, y fue el flamenco el que comenzó a traspasar fronteras. A ello —añade Trend en *Manuel de Falla and Spanish Music*— contribuyeron las descripciones excesivamente entusiastas, románticas y religiosas que algunos escritores y estudiosos realizaron de Sur, de la Semana Santa sevillana y de sus saetas, erróneamente interpretadas, contagiadas como estaban por la vulgarización general del jondo. Pocos cantaores eran capaces, según él, de interpretar las saetas en su versión pura, en su versión jonda:

> The glowing descriptions of musical performances in southern Spain given in such number by writers who are not musicians, and the romantic religiosity attributed by certain professors to the singing of *saetas* in Seville during the processions of Holy Week, apply not to the true *cante hondo,* but to a vulgarized form of it which has received the name of *cante flamenco.* The truth seems to be that except for some few *cantaores* and one or two who have grown too old to sing, that which remains of the primitive Andaluz folk-song is only the shadow of what it once was (1934: 26).

En este sentido, Trend relata una curiosa anécdota que le aconteció con Manuel de Falla en una procesión de Semana Santa: el compositor se enojó por la nefasta interpretación de un cantaor y, furioso, exclamó: "They call that singing *saetas*? [...] It sounds like drawing corks —like someone going to be sick! Hush, man [...], for God's sake! Rabbits, man!" (1934: 26).

Precisamente, el inicio de la recuperación del jondo se debió al músico de Cádiz, gracias al famoso festival de Granada que organizó en 1922 con el que quiso reivindicar su esencia e interpretación verdadera. Pero Falla no se quedó solo ahí ya que supo combinar en sus creaciones

---

2   El contenido de esta crónica quedará después recogido en *The Music of Spanish History to 1600* (1926).

esas formas populares con la música del siglo XX, es decir, la tradición española de antaño con la vanguardia europea contemporánea.

El europeísmo de la cultura española

Desde sus obras iniciales, Trend quiso hacer ver a sus lectores ingleses que España no era ese país de bárbaros, retrasado e ignorante que imaginaban, sino un país europeo, más similar a Inglaterra de lo que podían pensar. En *A Picture of Modern Spain: Men and Music,* en su capítulo I, titulado "Spain after the War", afirmaba lo siguiente:

> Travel and conversation with men of very different classes in very different provinces shows convincingly that the European view of life and its values —that mixture of idealism, humanity and common sense with other ingredients not easily described— is more alive today in Spain than in most other countries. Listening to Spaniards I have often felt that they are expressing a point of view which is very "English" (1921: 1).

La comparación de España con el Reino Unido y Europa se acentúa en el capítulo segundo del ensayo, momento en el que Trend se esfuerza especialmente en explicar la avanzada situación de la cultura y educación del país en los años 20. Este capítulo, titulado "Education in Spain", centra su atención en la labor desarrollada por la Institución Libre de Enseñanza, la Junta para Ampliación de Estudios, la Residencia de Estudiantes e incluso la Residencia de Señoritas; incluye asimismo semblanzas de sus artífices, de Francisco Giner de los Ríos, de José Castillejo y de Alberto Jiménez Fraud; con este último mantuvo una larga relación por circunstancias que después se mencionarán.

El hispanista defiende, entusiasta, la labor emprendida por estos intelectuales: quisieron reducir el alto analfabetismo de la población, quisieron que los españoles fueran capaces de contar con criterio propio para opinar y, en definitiva, quisieron sacudir a España de la enorme y nefasta influencia que la Iglesia y el estamento militar había ejercido durante siglos en la educación del país. Y por motivos diversos, no era fácil para ellos, explica Trend:

Their position is, however, harder than it is with us, for at present they are rather isolated, and form a definite set. Culture is not so widespread in Spain as in some other countries; but those who are interested in it are tremendously keen, and their education is not in the least superficial. The army and the aristocracy do not worry about them, the bourgeoisie dismisses them as "high-brow", the Church is, as a rule, their deadly enemy. Yet it is not a one-sided view which sees modern Spain and modern Spanish progress entirely in terms of this little group of idealists (1921: 43).

Su encendida defensa llevó al hispanista a comparar la Residencia de Estudiantes con los *colleges* de Cambridge y Oxford: "The *Residencia* is like [...] certain colleges at Oxford and Cambridge, because of the friendship and social intercourse which exists between the junior and more senior members of it, between undergraduates and dons" (1921: 37). Ya se ha esbozado que mantuvo una especial cercanía con esta institución, de cuyo ambiente y hospitalidad disfrutó en temporadas continuas y alternas. Este vínculo se preservó siempre, por admiración, por nostalgia, pero también porque en 1936 Trend ayudó a Jiménez Fraud en su exilio en Inglaterra.

Como a Jiménez Fraud, durante la guerra socorrió a otros intelectuales (lo intentó con Antonio Machado y con Jorge Guillén) así como a un grupo de refugiados vascos, ciudadanos anónimos, la mayoría de ellos niños, a los que acogió en 1937 en su ciudad. En el verano de ese año Trend viajó por última vez a la España republicana, su España;[3] después nunca regresó a un país que le resultaba adverso y desconocido.

Conclusión

Si Trend convenció o no a sus lectores con sus argumentos es un dato difícil de conocer. Lo que sí sabemos es que siguió defendiendo la esencia de España hasta sus últimas obras. Apoyó la República[4] y mantuvo

---

3   Él mismo así lo afirma: "On my last visit to Spain in 1937, in time of war and invasion" (1941: 2). Se desplazó, en concreto, a Valencia.

4   Así se muestra, por ejemplo, en una carta enviada en el otoño de 1936 al *Times Literary Supplement* en la que "expresa toda la indignación y el dolor" por el asesinato de García Lorca (Dennis 2007: 22).

desde su particular exilio el contacto con los amigos españoles. En 1938 viajó a México, destino de intelectuales exiliados, y allí visitó a José Moreno Villa, Jesús Bal y Gay o al mejicano Alfonso Reyes. Consecuencia de esta estancia, nace en 1940 *Mexico: A New Spain with Old Friends,* volumen que muestra los lugares y las costumbres de aquel país, pero que parte de la evocación de España, de esa España —dice Trend— "que no puede ser nunca destruida y empieza de nuevo en Latinoamérica" (1941: 3).

Como tal quiso mostrársela a los ingleses: una España sin tópicos ni estereotipos, una España plural y diversa, una España europea aunque después truncada. Y también —no hay por qué negarlo— una España algo idealizada en la mente y la memoria del hispanista.

Bibliografía

Dennis, N. 2007. "Prólogo", in N. Dennis (ed.), *Manuel de Falla-J.B. Trend. Epistolario (1919-1935),* Granada, Universidad de Granada. Archivo Manuel de Falla, 7-23.

Trend, J. B. 1921. *A Picture of Modern Spain: Men and Music,* London, Constable.

—. 1924. "The Moors in Spanish Music", *The Criterion* II: 6, 204-19.

—. 1928. *Spain from the South,* London, Methuen.

—. 1934. *Manuel de Falla and Spanish Music.* New York, Knopf.

—. 1941. *Mexico. A New Spain with Old Friends,* Cambridge, Cambridge UP.

—. 1971. *Lorca and the Spanish Poetic Tradition,* New York, Russell & Russell.

PERE GIFRA-ADROHER

Images of Foreigners in Mary Eyre's Travel Books

During the Victorian period, the term "abroad" had a "dreamlike, talis-manic quality" for many women secluded in their homes (Hamalian 1981: x). Some of them, however, did not equate going abroad to a pleasant activity but rather to "the need to alleviate financial distress" (Foster 1990: 9). Mary Eyre belonged to this category. In 1862, unable to keep her home in Hamsptead once she had used up the earnings from her previous two novels, this fifty-year-old writer had to leave England in search of a cheaper life on the Continent. She lived frugally, often travel-ling alone, and gathered enough information to write two travel books: *A Lady's Walks in the South of France* (1865) and *Over the Pyrenees into Spain* (1865). The first book relates the excursions she made with her inseparable dog in the Pyrenees during late 1862 and part of 1863. The favourable reviews it received compelled her publisher, Richard Bentley, to dispatch her further south to gather materials for a second travel book. She set out again in the summer of 1865, travelling to southeast France, Andorra, and on to Spain, as far as Granada. This new literary venture, however, proved traumatic: she was harassed and suffered many ail-ments during the journey. Moreover, despite completing this second book within an extremely short period of time, it met with the rebuff of some critics and presumably yielded less profit than expected. Whether disappointed by such setbacks or physically broken by her excursions, the fact is that her career had, to all intents and purposes, reached its end.

Eyre's travel books originally received a significant critical recep-tion not only because the areas they described were unfrequented by women hikers but also because solitary female travellers exerted an enormous appeal on Victorian readers. Moreover, pedestrian touring was by then fully accepted as a valuable social practice among the Victorian elites (Wallace 1993: 168). Recently, however, few scholars of British travel writing have taken an interest in Eyre (Robinson 1994: 26, 451; Theakstone: 32). This essay attempts to revive interest in this neglected author by focusing on the representation of the French, Andorrans and Spaniards in her two travel books. To do so, it is first necessary to contextualise Eyre's construction of these images of foreigners within the larger discursive structures in which her books appeared. Her representation of foreigners arguably falls within the ideological framework of the two chief discourses that, as Sara Mills contends, constrained women's travel writing during the Victorian period, that is, the discourse of colonialism and that of femininity. The one, Mills observes, demanded "action and intrepid, fearless behaviour from the narrator", whereas the other required "passivity from the narrator and a concern with relationships" (21). Eyre invariably adopts both. On certain occasions she styles herself as a bold woman traveller by almost mimicking the privileged voice of the British coloniser and regarding the foreigners as inferior. On others, she focuses on many aspects of domestic life abroad and interacts with the locals to enhance the sentimental side of her travelogues. Her images of foreigners, partially affected as well by the negative circumstances of her forced sojourn abroad, emerge from these conflicting roles.

In the first travel book, which relies more openly on domestic and feminine discourses, Eyre casts an overall positive light on the French, occasionally counterpointed by her perennial belief in the superiority of British civilization. In the second one, however, she provides images of the Andorrans and Spaniards that clearly betray an extensive use of the discourse of colonialism with scenes where stereotyped characters and menacing multitudes typical of colonial writing abound, conveying either a sinister or an infantilised image of the "native" peoples. I believe that these roles serve Eyre to present her southbound itinerary as a progression from the civilised French to the half-civilised Spaniards via a brief encounter with the wild Andorrans. The construction of such images is not gratuitous, and arguably manifests the author's —or perhaps the publisher's— intention to present both texts as a continuum: a symbolic journey in which the unprotected female traveller, mirroring the colonial male hero, uses her encounters with foreigners to assert her Englishness.

Most of the chapters in *A Lady's Walks in the South of France* relate the excursions that Eyre made around the regions of Béarn and Bigorre, where she visited such places as Pau, Eaux-Bonnes, Argelès, Cauterets or Bagnères de Luchon. Despite her strenuous walks, Eyre's note-taking for her travel book made her feel animated and optimistic. Thanks to her fairly good command of French, she managed to hold long conversations with the locals; she represents the people of these regions as cheerful, hospitable and hard-working, living a thrifty life in their own autarchic world. However, she does not idealise them; they are not mountain folk naturally born to please the foreign tourist, but people already affected by capitalism and increasingly aware of the exchange value of tourism as a commodity. Eyre affirms that the peasants "are astute, close, and avaricious" and "grow rich by saving up sous", yet also adds to their credit that "they do not, upon this, alter their habits or mode of life" (1865a: 330). The variety of regional costumes worn across the region is another trait of the French that Eyre comments on. They are not only picturesque tokens of identity that distinguish people from different valleys, but something that endows them with an air of dignity. The French peasant's dress is "much more respectable-looking and whole than that of our working people", Eyre affirms, for it lends an air of exotic nobility to the natives (1865a: 184). Fascinated by the linguistic diversity of the country, she also positively describes the people who speak Provençal and even translates a few folk-tales from this language. Ironically, her class bias makes her observe that the local *patois* becomes a melodious language specially when spoken by the local upper classes.

Eyre, who contemplated the possibility of becoming an expatriate in the French Pyrenees, rejected it because she found this area lacking in the comforts of Victorian domestic life. Her first book criticises several aspects of French mountain life that she finds either primitive or uncivilised, such as the poor service at hotels, the extreme working conditions to which women are submitted or the beatings of wives by their husbands. However, nothing seems to disturb her as much as the lack of cleanliness and lack of comfort of the local homes and hotels. Her complaints at the presence of fleas and dirt in some of the places where she lodges are constant, and likewise she cannot hide her disgust during her visits to the homes of local propertied landlords who literally share their dwellings with their cattle. This disregard for cleanliness and domestic good manners epitomises for Eyre the primitivism of this good-natured, innocent Pyreneans who stubbornly cling to their old-age customs, but it also evidences the lack of a rural gentry like that of England that could set a high moral and educational example to the rustic peasants. Eyre is always ready to celebrate the domestic achievements of Victorian England. She may acknowledge that the French are aesthetically superior "in all things that strike the eye", but firmly believes "that in the country villages [they] are far behind us, in the common decencies and comforts of civilised life" (1865a: 314). Feminine and colonial discourses coalesce in this travelogue to construct an image of the French that, for all its sympathy, never ceases to stress the superiority of British civilisation.

Eyre further developed her representation of the French in the first chapters of *Over the Pyrenees into Spain*, which trace an itinerary that begins in Paris and proceeds southwards to Nimes, Tarascon, Foix and Ax-les-Thermes. Though travelling across new regions, she keeps insisting on some of her previous ideas about the French, affirming at one point: "The more I see of French life the more I value England, with all her comforts and conveniences even for the poor; her coal-fires, her coppers, her public baths and wash-houses" (1865b: 25). Eyre's second book focuses above all on the inhabitants of the Ariège, whom she regards as a race of plain *montagnards*, sturdy yet courteous, resembling the other French rural folk previously described. She strikes conversations with them, but paradoxically this time she does not seem interested in regional clothing any longer, and her images convey an increasingly bitter tone. Eyre found herself in a region not yet accustomed to receiving many British tourists, let alone a solitary female traveller like herself with a Leghorn hat, an umbrella and iron-hoops. Moreover, she felt physically frail and was writing under her publisher's pressure, a situation that inevitably affected her perception of things foreign. The inhabitants of her next stop, Andorra, had to bear the brunt of Eyre's criticism.

The Principality of Andorra, an off-the-beaten-track destination scarcely visited during the mid-nineteenth century, was often idealised as an independent "republic" of rustic mountain men. Eyre's images of the Andorrans before writing *Over the Pyrenees into Spain* oscillated between the utopian descriptions she had culled in James Erskine Murray's *Summer in the Pyrenees* (1837) and the negative ones she had read in Richard Ford's influential *Handbook for Travellers in Spain* (1845). She had also received mixed impressions from the French who secured her the credentials to travel there. However, her views were ultimately shaped by the bad mule trek that took her to Andorra. During the long trek her physical pain was aggravated and her untrustworthy mountain guide nearly abandoned her. To make matters worse, two Andorran lads threw stones at her near the hamlet of Encamp, eventually running off and leaving her with a bad head injury. The pent-up expectations of the border-crossing ritual present in many travel books become in Eyre's narrative a vile episode of xenophobia and gender violence that can only present to the readers a negative image of the foreigner.

The border aggression perpetrated by the two barbaric youngsters is not the only negative image of the citizens of Andorra that Eyre offers. She bitterly comments, for instance, that in the village of Les Escaldes she was followed and "annoyed by a crowd of little children" who were "hooting, while their relatives rather encouraged them than otherwise" (1865b: 113). Likewise, in one of the inns of the capital, Andorra la Vella, she feels threatened by the appearance of some local men. After noting that "some ten or a dozen bronzed-visaged, swarthy, dark-eyed men, in knee breeches, and plush waistcoats, and with sashes round their waists, were lying grouped in a most picturesque manner", she remarks that near them "round a long deal table, as wild, ragged, and barefooted [...], a set were sitting devouring their supper, and all were shouting, gesticulating, and talking" (1865b: 100-101). The diction of this passage, far from constructing an idealised image of the inhabitants of this old microstate, rather stereotypes them as menacing strangers on the margins of civilization. This cultural construction of the foreigner, on the one hand, may have rung a bell to Eyre's audiences, accustomed as they were to processing images of otherness constructed through the all-present discourse of Imperialism. Yet, on the other hand, it may have well served to enhance the adventurousness of the narrative by presenting the solitary traveller as a vulnerable female in a menacing, masculinised foreign scenario.

Despite her inbred cultural superiority, Eyre still spares a handful of Andorrans from the negative image she builds in her book, albeit in an overtly paternalistic manner. For example, when she talks to the man who acts as her cicerone in the tiny nation —a travelled man by Andorran standards— she says that she would be "very glad that he should see England and her comfortable homes, and carry back with him a higher standard of civilisation and progress than he now possesses" (1965b: 134). Her verdict is categorical: the Andorrans, for all their peaceful existence, are a primitive, uncivil and backward people who lack the industriousness of the northern countries. The contemplation of some hot springs makes her wonder why they have not used this natural resource to more profitable ends rather than for merely washing their clothes.

Similarly, she criticises their refusal to exploit some iron mines for fear that it might trigger foreign interference in their affairs, and concludes her stay affirming that "the best thing that could befall the Andorrans would be to lose [their] boasted independence", which to Eyre "consists only in not progressing with the rest of the world; in being able to remain poor, bigoted, ignorant, dirty, lazy, and vicious" (1965b: 116). The discourse of rural domestic bliss employed by other nineteenth-century travellers to build an idyllic image of the independent Andorrans is, in short, quickly dismantled by Eyre, who replies to such dreams with the Victorian gospel of wealth. Once again, the traveller's gaze alternates between feminine and imperial discourses to approach the Other.

Eyre's reliance on the discourse of colonialism to represent the foreigner as a "subaltern", to use Spivak's term, is also noticeable in her account of her arrival into Spain, which she symbolically presents as a further step away from civilization. Using the image of the indolent Spanish beggar so common in nineteenth-century British travel writing, Eyre relates that as soon as she had crossed the border post that separated Spain from Andorra in the town of La Seu d'Urgell, she encountered

> a tribe of half-naked, barefooted, or hempen-sandalled little vagabonds, whose swarthy, bare little breasts and legs reminded one of English gypsies, to the number of at least thirty, collected together, hooting and shouting at my English hat, I suppose [...] were joined by women and girls, and the whole pack followed me, shouting and screaming, till we reached the very portal leading to [the] hotel (1865b: 144).

She likewise explains that the following day was chased through the streets of the same town by "a tribe of howling, shouting girls, women, and children, and one or two of the lowest class of men" (1865b: 151). The diction employed here, which stereotypes the Spaniards with connotations of primitivism and savagery, is used several times in the Spanish chapters of her book. Eyre visited Barcelona, Madrid and Granada and quite often her gaze focused on crowds and mobs, of which she underscores the primitive and violent traits. The frequent allusion to unbridled native and turbulent crowds is precisely one of the indicative symptoms of the colonial context of travel writing (Frawley 2005: 32).

In Barcelona, despite her efforts to pass unnoticed, Eyre was accosted by a group of curious bystanders whose menacing attitude forced her to seek refuge in a store. This incident makes her conclude that "until

Spaniards allow a well-conducted, modest, quietly-dressed woman in black, to walk their streets and parades without being mobbed, they cannot lay claim to being a civilised nation" (1865b: 206). Several days later, in Granada, she relates that even though she was accompanied by a local guide, she had to endure "the hootings and yellings of the stall-keepers, in the streets", and put up with children who shouted at her merely because she was a single, foreign female. In the light of these incidents, she asserts that "the Spaniards are at present a half-civilised, semi-barbarous race" (1865b: 310). Eyre, who could not speak Spanish and interpret local customs, contrasts the foreigners' primitivism to the superior values she embodies, and she does so by means of binaries. She arrogates to herself concepts such as civilization, modesty, cleanliness and discretion —presented as inherent to the Protestant culture from which she comes— in contrast to the brutality, filth and incivility of her foreign hosts. These binary oppositions typical of the discourse of colonial travel literature establish relations of dominance that women travellers like Eyre also incorporated to their ideological repertoire.

Yet Eyre's focus on crowds does not mean that her images of the Spaniards are always unfriendly. Domestic and feminine discourses also make themselves manifest in her travel book to soften the negative representations. Eyre provides, for instance, interesting views of the Barcelonese women. Likewise, in other stages of her journey she reproduces agreeable conversations with several Spaniards travelling by train with her, and confesses that such moments helped her to revise the stereotypical images that she had culled from literary sources. Eyre affirms that the bookish image of the Spaniard as "a stern, grave, courteous, stately, chivalrous gentleman; somewhat too proud, [...] too jealous as a lover, or a husband, and too fond of gallantry to married women" was not what she encountered; the Spaniards she met were rather "merry, rollicking fellows, always seeking occasion for banter, and prone to laugh like children at the veriest trifle" (1865b: 334-35). Eyre's remarks, stressing the foreigners' infantile traits, demonstrate here the very hierarchy upon which the logic of colonialism is sustained. The female British traveller, like a mother eyeing a child, gazes from her position of cultural power on the exotic spectacle furnished by a people who —despite enjoying fewer comforts than herself— are always happy.

Eyre's encounter with the foreign, as we have seen, arose out of necessity rather than out of pleasure or duty. She was simply a writer who tried to earn a living with her solo travels, not a missionary carrying the torch of civilisation to remote milieus overseas. Throughout her southbound itinerary she could not disentangle herself from the discourses of femininity and colonialism. She demonstrated that the Victorian woman traveller could survive abroad unchaperoned, and that at the same time she could show her cultural superiority to the foreigners she met. The further she travelled, the more she complained and criticised them. "The Ariégois [sic] are bad; the Andorrans worse; the Spaniard worst of all!" (1865b: 153), she wrote. Perhaps the ambivalent use of these discourses helped Eyre to assuage her readers' sense of superiority, but the critics never forgave her for trespassing the bounds of propriety.

Bibliography

Eyre, M. 1865a. *A Lady's Walks in the South of France*, London, Bentley.

—. 1865b. *Over the Pyrenees into Spain*, London, Bentley.

Foster, S. 1990. *Across New Worlds: Nineteenth Century Women Travellers and their Writings*, New York, Harvester Wheatsheaf.

Frawley, M. 2005. "Borders and Boundaries, Perspectives and Place: Victorian Women's Travel Writing", in J. Pomeroy (ed.) *Intrepid Women: Victorian Artists Travel*, Aldershot, Ashgate. 27-37

Hamalian, L. (ed.). 1981. *Ladies on the Loose: Women Travellers of the 18th and 19th Centuries*, New York, Dodd Mead.

Mills, S. 1991. *Discourses of Difference: an Analysis of Women's Travel Writing and Colonialism*, London & New York, Routledge.

Robinson, J. 1994. *Unsuitable for Ladies. An Anthology of Women Travellers*, Oxford & New York, Oxford UP.

Spivak, G. C. 1988. "Can the Subaltern Speak?", in G. C. Spivak, *Marxism and the Interpretation of Culture*, London, Macmillan, 271-313.

Theakstone, J. 2006. *Victorian and Edwardian Women Travellers: a Bibliography of Books Published in English*, Mansfield Center, Connecticut, Martino Publishing.

Wallace, A. 1993. *Walking, Literature and English Culture*, Oxford, Clarendon.

HELENA GONZÁLEZ VAQUERIZO

La alteridad en Kazantzakis: los libros de viaje

Introducción

El extranjero es el Otro, el complemento, la mitad que a uno le falta, también su espejo y a veces su enemigo. La literatura siempre ha sido un vehículo idóneo para representar la alteridad y, a través de las obras de autores especialmente sensibles a las cuestiones de identidad es posible indagar en los modos en que el discurso literario conforma la imagen del extranjero, a menudo implicando el acercamiento a distintas disciplinas y ámbitos de interés.

Nikos Kazantzakis (1883-1957) nació en Creta, pero vivió y viajó por multitud de países de Asia, África y Europa, fue autor de novelas, crónicas de viaje, obras de teatro, poesía, fue traductor y periodista, desempeñó cargos políticos... Conciencia inquieta, que se cuestionaba a sí misma de manera constante, ofrece un amplio campo de trabajo en torno a la alteridad.

Este trabajo trata de poner de manifiesto los mecanismos mediante los cuales se representa al extranjero en la obra de este autor polígrafo, contradictorio y polémico. Son mecanismos eminentemente dialógicos, que dan lugar a una imagen doble de la alteridad, tal y como se podrá comprobar en el análisis de algunos de sus extranjeros: los protagonistas de sus relatos de viaje. En primer lugar se examinarán los mecanismos de representación de la alteridad en Kazantzakis: las oposiciones conceptuales. En segundo lugar se verá cómo estas se activan en las crónicas de viaje y configuran arquetipos literarios que se imponen a las realidades de los países visitados.

Para este autor, como para este trabajo, los extranjeros no son única ni necesariamente los no griegos, sino aquellos que, por razones de diversa índole, son diferentes a él: los Otros. Estos son fundamentalmente de tres clases y las tres se definen de idéntica manera, mediante un mecanismo de oposiciones conceptuales a aquellas categorías en las que él mismo encaja de forma más inmediata: individuo, hombre, cretense. Como individuo el autor se distingue de la masa, que casi siempre es servil, manipulable, falta de criterio e incluso despreciable. Como hombre se distingue de las mujeres, que suelen poseer virtudes y defectos típicamente femeninos. Por último, para un cretense, extranjero es, por encima de cualquier otro, el turco, pues no es griego, ni europeo, ni cristiano, ni occidental.

Kazantzakis es deudor del pensamiento hegeliano y el esquema de contraposición de opuestos vertebra su obra y su pensamiento. No es solo que el extranjero se defina en su obra mediante la antítesis, sino que dicho esquema subyace en todos sus personajes e identidades con el resultado de que estas son siempre contradictorias en sí mismas. La búsqueda de síntesis será por tanto esencial en su vida y en su obra.

Oposiciones conceptuales

El cuerpo y el alma, la vida y la muerte, la realidad y el sueño, o el deseo. Luces y sombras en las que, intermitente, se mueve el pensamiento de Kazantzakis. Deudor del tripartito esquema hegeliano, pasó toda su vida en busca de un absoluto que paliara el desasosiego y la crisis existencial en que la convulsa época que le tocó vivir lo había sumido. El medio para alcanzar esta meta existencial sería siempre una tercera vía, la síntesis de opuestos.

El primer par de opuestos lo forman el individuo y la masa. Como buen discípulo de Nietzsche, a quien consideró uno de sus maestros (Kazantzakis 2002b: 7), Kazantzakis hizo a menudo gala de un individualismo aristocrático, de un desprecio por la servidumbre y la ignorancia de los grupos, a los que nunca quiso atarse. Estos están formados por extraños y encarnan todos los defectos del hombre gregario. En contraposición, el héroe es el individuo solitario capaz de superación, que busca la libertad.

La segunda pareja de contrarios es la del hombre y la mujer. Ella representa para Kazantzakis un misterio a menudo indescifrable; de ahí que las féminas sean en la obra de este autor las "Otras" por antonomasia. Encontramos en ellas los clichés típicos de principios de siglo XX: la mujer es incapaz de aspiraciones intelectuales, su naturaleza la ata a la tierra y a la maternidad, por eso es un peligro para el hombre que quiere ser libre. La mujer es fácilmente dominada por su deseo sexual, que tiene su origen en el instinto maternal. Es además sentimental y débil, dependiente, dulce y manejable. El varón prototípico, huelga decirlo, es la antítesis de todo esto. Estos prejuicios fueron matizados y reformulados a través de los años, y de las relaciones con mujeres y hombres que escapaban a la simplificación. Con el tiempo, el ideal humano de Kazantzakis consistiría en la aceptación por parte del individuo de las dos corrientes, la masculina y la femenina, que lo constituyen y en la síntesis de ambas (2007: 24).

La tercera y última oposición conceptual que examinamos es la de Oriente frente a Occidente. Cuando en 1821 Grecia se desvinculó del Imperio Otomano asociándose a Occidente, se defendió que los griegos, cristianos y civilizados, habían sufrido bajo el yugo de un pueblo inferior, nómada y salvaje como el turco (Volkan y Itzkowitz 1994: 68). El griego se convirtió para sí mismo y para el resto del mundo occidental en el "yo", mientras que el turco se asoció al "otro". Ese "otro" era, como siempre son los "otros", un extraño y un misterio incomprensible. Fruto de la incomprensión es el que se lo tachara de sucio, vago y fanático, que se lo asociara a la duplicidad, la sensualidad y la brutalidad, y también el que se lo temiera.

La isla de Creta no obtuvo la independencia hasta 1898. La distinción griego-turco cobró por este motivo especial relevancia en un territorio que ya desde su posición geográfica —equidistante de Asia, África y Europa— estaba destinado a ejercer de puente entre Oriente y Occidente (Clogg 1998).

En la novela *Libertad o muerte (El Capitán Mijalis)*, publicada por primera vez en 1953, Kazantzakis plasmó el ambiente de su infancia en la isla, cuando aún no se había logrado la independencia, haciéndose eco de las sucesivas revueltas de los griegos, las represalias turcas y las venganzas recíprocas de la población cristiana y musulmana. La novela describe, por tanto, el proceso de la liberación. Pero, más allá de la libertad e independencia políticas, Kazantzakis fue consciente de que la verdadera independencia que debían buscar sus compatriotas era la cultural:

> Liberarse a toda costa del turco, ese fue el primer paso, a continuación, más tarde, comenzó una nueva batalla: liberarse del turco interior —de la ignorancia, la mali-

cia, la envidia, del miedo y la pereza, de las embaucadoras falsas ideas, y finalmente de los ídolos, de todos ellos, incluso de los más reverenciados y amados— (2007: 69).[1]

En sus palabras vemos el retrato negativo del turco, representante de lo peor de un griego. No obstante, parece claro que lo que él denomina "turco interior" no es sino un arquetipo, que puede habitar en todo hombre, independientemente de su nacionalidad. Así, esta descalificación del extranjero es desmentida en boca de uno de los personajes más carismáticos de Kazantzakis, el famoso Zorba. A propósito de su participación en las Guerras Balcánicas (1912-1913) y del cuestionamiento de su adhesión al nacionalismo griego, Zorba explica:

> Momento hubo en que solía decir: "Este es turco; este otro, búlgaro, el de aquí, griego." [...] Degollé, robé, incendié pueblos, violé mujeres, exterminé familias. ¿Por qué motivo? Por la sencilla razón de que eran búlgaros o turcos. [...] Ahora, en cambio, sólo digo: "Este es buena persona, el de más allá un sinvergüenza." Así sea búlgaro o griego, tanto me da. ¿Es bueno? ¿Es malo? Esto es lo único que pregunto hoy en día (2002b: 232).

Arquetipos literarios

Kazantzakis trabajó como corresponsal de distintos periódicos griegos y gracias a ello publicó diversos libros de viaje. También residió largos años en diferentes países centroeuropeos. Los más destacados de sus relatos de viaje son las crónicas de sus viajes a Italia, Egipto, el Sinaí, Jerusalén, Chipre y Morea, así como los monográficos *Viajando. Rusia* (1928); *Viajando. España* (1937); *Viajando. Japón-China* (1938) y *Viajando. Inglaterra* (1941).

El autor no intenta en ninguna de estas crónicas llevar a cabo un análisis sistemático de los pueblos que visita: "He venido a llenar mis cinco sentidos", dirá en una ocasión. "No soy sociólogo —¡Gracias a Dios!— ni filósofo ni turista" (1999: 168). Muy al contrario, la representación de los extranjeros que nos ofrece proviene de forma casi invaria-

---

1   Todas las traducciones son nuestras.

ble de sus propias ideas previas sobre los países: ideas que no son tanto estereotipos compartidos por el sentir más o menos superficial de la época, como arquetipos procedentes de su particular forma de entender el mundo, mediante oposiciones conceptuales, configurados a partir de sus lecturas y profundamente asimilados a los moldes de su pensamiento.

"Doble es el rostro de España", arranca la crónica de la Guerra Civil. "De una parte, la alargada imagen del febril caballero de la triste figura; de otra, la práctica cabeza cuadrada de Sancho" (2002a: 11). Ahí están las dos Españas, tópico literario o tópico a secas, que Kazantzakis extrae a partir del clásico por excelencia de las letras hispanas, el *Quijote*. De este modo hace coincidir las expectativas despertadas por la literatura con las realidades halladas sobre el terreno. Los españoles de Kazantzakis son contradictorios, extremos, apasionados: duros, varoniles y belicosos ellos, poseídas de instinto maternal ellas (2002a: 68-69). En la imaginación del poeta encontramos una España masculina, que deslumbra como un macho de pavo real con sus plumas desplegadas entre dos aguas (2002a: 11).

En Egipto, como en Chipre o Morea, esto es, en aquellos lugares cuyo glorioso y evocador pasado se impone sobre el presente, Kazantzakis apenas si se asoma a la realidad del Otro visitado. Huye al pasado y corrobora sobre el terreno lo que de este le sugirieron sus lecturas. La sociedad egipcia era estática, conservadora y estaba obsesionada con vencer la muerte, de modo que en los campesinos que malviven a orillas del Nilo Kazantzakis encuentra a los hijos de los esclavos de los faraones (2004: 35) y la historia entera de Egipto se entiende como una historia de sumisión (2004: 49).

La isla de Chipre es "la auténtica patria de Afrodita" (2004: 183), una isla cargada de feminidad, donde el dulce aire que se respira hace al visitante peligrosas promesas. Es un patrón en las descripciones de Kazantzakis asociar el paisaje a características femeninas, como sucede en el caso de Chipre, o masculinas, como veíamos en el caso de España y como sucederá también en el desierto.

Así como en Chipre habita la bella Afrodita, junto a las orillas del Eurotas, en el Peloponeso, uno puede reencontrarse con la hermosura de Helena de Troya, sentir "algo femenino y fértil, y peligrosamente encantador" (2004: 213). Morea es el "feliz paraje que con sus antítesis armonizadas dio las flores más excelsas" (2004: 285), Helena y el Taigeto. De nuevo hallamos en el paisaje una feminidad que es doble, que seduce y amenaza al tiempo, y el predominio de la lucha entre los opuestos, que da lugar a la más sublime y armónica belleza. Para los antiguos, como es bien sabido, la armonía es una cuestión fundamental. Se ejercitan por igual el cuerpo y la mente, pues el excesivo desarrollo de uno en detrimento del otro es una "barbaridad", es decir, algo propio de extranjeros.

En cuanto al desierto, el interés principal del viaje de Kazantzakis al monte Sinaí vuelve a ser literario: explorar los escenarios de uno de sus libros preferidos, la Biblia. Mientras recorre el desierto hacia los monasterios, el autor cree descubrir el origen del carácter de la raza hebrea, forjada en la dureza del paisaje y en la experiencia del éxodo, que la hicieron voluntariosa, obsesiva y enormemente resistente (2004: 95).

Por su parte Rusia, donde conviven a la sazón más de cien etnias, es una "peligrosa Babilonia" (2000a: 41) y esto porque la diferencia asusta, cuestiona la identidad, haciendo ver que los pueblos tienen más en común de lo que pudiera parecer. Ante la amenaza de la fragmentación el bolchevique ha opuesto la uniformidad de su Idea, de manera que la diferenciación de los pueblos, sus lenguas, costumbres, usos y carácter, pierda relevancia frente a la adhesión a una misma causa. Se potencia la diferencia, según explican los comunistas al visitante, cómo esta puede ser regulada: el objetivo es que cada hombre sea libre y distinto —pues la homogeneidad empobrecería el conjunto— y que, desde su libertad, se someta a la Idea. La única distinción a la que deberán atender los pueblos es la del comunista frente al burgués: el primero es compañero; el segundo, enemigo (2000a: 44).

Finalmente Asia es para Kazantzakis un misterio. Puesto que no logra profundizar en una cultura harto hermética, se dispone a hacer su viaje con los sentidos, en lugar de con la inteligencia. Y así, al acordarse de Japón, revive la sensual experiencia de ver el pecho de una mujer por vez primera —la mujer que, una vez más, es un misterio (1999: 9)— y el rostro de Japón es el de una máscara. China, el gigante asiático, no resulta asimilable a ninguna categoría. Kazantzakis es incapaz de darle una forma, un rostro, siquiera una máscara. Dirá entonces que en China no hay una raza, una lengua, una religión, sino muchas y que el "amarillo" tiene en su pecho muchas almas.

Conclusión

Pares de oposiciones recorren toda la obra de Kazantzakis y la unifican. Frente a las oposiciones conceptuales que conformaron su forma natural y heredada de sentir al extranjero, el autor opuso la visión, adquirida con la madurez y la experiencia, de la universalidad del espíritu humano y de la hermandad de todos los pueblos y razas:

> Sentía que las fronteras se derrumbaban, los nombres, los países, las razas desaparecían, se unía el hombre al hombre, lloraban, reían, se abrazaban, un relámpago había iluminado su entendimiento y habían logrado ver: ¡eran todos hermanos! (2007: 400).

Sin duda la contraposición y la comparación son mecanismos ineludibles para entender el mundo. Comparamos porque es la primera forma de aproximación al conocimiento de lo nuevo y de lo extraño, después, necesariamente distinguimos, parafraseando a Guillén (2005), lo Uno de lo Diverso. Al final, si somos capaces de reconciliar los contrarios hallaremos la ansiada síntesis que Kazantzakis perseguía con sus oposiciones conceptuales.

Si existe una forma de conocer la alteridad a través de la literatura, esta implica la asunción de que el "otro" será, bien esa parte de nosotros mismos que se revela en la confrontación con los puntos de vista del autor, bien esa otra individualidad, al comienzo extraña pero cada vez más familiar, que se dibuja a partir de sus palabras y a modo del negativo de una fotografía, como nuestro interlocutor.

Cuando la literatura nos ofrece el retrato del extranjero hemos de ser precavidos. Antes de dar crédito a las palabras del autor, debemos tener en cuenta las limitaciones que su visión y la nuestra propia van a imponer a la comprensión de ese Otro. Pues el conocimiento se produce mediante un proceso que dista de ser objetivo (Foucault 1980).

Cuanto más familiarizados estemos con el autor, mayor será nuestra capacidad de ser críticos. Asimismo, cuanto más familiarizados estemos con la alteridad que se nos muestra, es decir, con el país o nacionalidad concretos representados, mayor y más completo será el conocimiento que de este extraigamos. Seríamos así viajeros atentos en el espacio y en el tiempo, sociólogos, historiadores e incluso psicólogos, que reconocerían

en la representación del extranjero sus propias percepciones o las des-
mentirían. Sin olvidar que, al fin, el requisito previo de toda búsqueda y
de toda pesquisa es el de conocerse a sí mismo, porque, en definitiva, la
pregunta por la alteridad es la pregunta por la identidad y por el propio
origen. Responderla es sumamente difícil, tal vez incluso imposible, pero
constituye el objetivo último de toda trayectoria vital que no quiera permanecer en la ceguera.

Bibliografía

Clogg, R. 1998. *Historia de Grecia*, Cambridge, Cambridge UP.
Foucault, M. 1980. *Power/Knowledge: Selected Interviews and Other
    Writings 1972-1977*, New York, Macmillan.
Guillén, C. 2005. *Entre lo uno y lo diverso*, Barcelona, Tusquets.
Kazantzakis, N. 1999. *Taxidevontas B: Iaponia—Kina*, Athina, Kazant-
    zaki.
—. 2000a. *Taxidevontas: Rousia*, Athina, Kazantzaki.
—. 2000b. *Taxidevontas G: Anglia*, Athina, Kazantzaki.
—. 2002a. *Taxidevontas A: Ispania*, Athina, Kazantzaki.
—. 2002b.*Vios kai politeia tou Alexi Zorba*, Athina, Kazantzaki.
—. 2004. *Taxidevontas (Italia, Aigyptos, Sina, Ierousalim, Kypros, o
    Morias*, Athina, Kazantzaki.
—. 2005. *O Kapetan Michalis*, Athina, Kazantzaki.
—. 2007. *Anafora ston Greco*, Athina, Kazantzaki.
Volkan, V. & N. Itzkowitz, 1994. *Turks and Greeks: Neighbours in Con-
    flict*, Cambridge, Eothen Press.

GLYN HAMBROOK

The Concept of the Foreign in Pompeyo Gener's *Literaturas malsanas* and Enrique Gómez Carrillo's *Literatura extranjera*

Introduction

This paper will explore the conceptual and ideological frames within which the notions of foreignness and its corollary, the indigenous, were located, and by which their meaning and connotations were determined during the European fin de siècle, with particular reference to Hispanic engagement with a wider world of European fin de siècle identity politics in relation to literary practice.

Pompeyo Gener's *Literaturas malsanas* (1894) and Enrique Gómez Carrillo's *Literaturas extranjeras* (1895) have recourse to a similar delimitation of foreign and native culture, but offer opposing takes on the significance of foreignness. Gener was a champion of Mediterranean Latin culture in an era of its perceived decadence and decline, and belongs to a school that, taking as its point of departure Lombroso's *L'uomo di genio* (1888), interpreted developments in contemporary literature in terms of Degeneration Theory. Morel's *Traité des dégénérescences* (1857) provided a seminally comprehensive account of this theory, and its reception in Spain has been ably documented by Campos Marín and Huertas (2001). Gener claimed to have written *Literaturas malsanas* before Max Nordau's *Entartung* (1893), a point of reference for many a fin de siècle study of "degenerate genius" (Gener 1900: 389n), was published. Gómez Carrillo, a Guatemalan-born, European-based apologist for French literary culture (Kronik 1967; Hambrook 1991) and advocate of foreign influences as a means of overcoming the Hispanic ideological orthodoxy's resistance to literary modernity, propounded an aesthetic route to cultural regeneration in contrast to Gener's scientific model.

The broad conceptual and ideological parameters of these works are, nevertheless, demonstrably common. For one thing, they deem cultural production to be a manifestation of collective identity based on ethnic precepts, with its concomitant distinction between an indigenous community and exogenous ones. Secondly, both reflect contemporary preoccupations with the relative "health" of these identity communities, particularly the perceived decline or stagnation —actual or potential— of the indigenous "Latin" culture and the role of foreign influences in accentuating or arresting this process.[1]

For Gener the solution lay in collective psychological progress through resistance to a literature-borne degenerative contagion from outside until the epidemic runs its natural course (1900: 379-391), while for Gómez Carrillo, regeneration of Hispanic literary culture through receptivity to foreign influences was the answer.

Identitarian worlds

In both works, the world is divided into zones of identity predicated broadly on the aforementioned biological-evolutionary scheme, which divided Europe into Latin, Nordic and Slavic "races" within a European "macro-race", and considered each in terms of its relative fitness. Each work's world has an Iberian homeland *as part of* the centre, and in terms of contemporary identity politics can be represented by sliding scales of "fitness". Gener's demarcates successively a Mediterranean core community and Latin peoples endowed with a healthy constitution that is, respectively, innate and resilient, and innate but susceptible to degenerative contagion; European Nordic peoples in whose literatures the signs of degeneration, albeit of a temporary nature, are marked and significant; and a pessimism-prone Slavic (Russian) periphery and "Orient" (the "Asiatic" and "Semitic") in whose population degeneration is in differing degrees endemic. Gómez Carrillo's scale of aesthetic originality and

---

1   The review *La Renaissance Latine* and E. Desmolins's *À quoi tient la superiorité des Anglo-Saxons* (1897) are just two of many contemporary publications exploring the theme of Latin decline and regeneration and the rise of the "Nordic" (Germanic, "Anglo-Saxon", Flemish, Scandinavian and Slavic [Russian]) cultures. V. Cacho Viu (1997: 77-115) and L. Calvo Revilla (1998: 74-79, 83-85) provide informed accounts of Spain's place in this new Latin decadence.

dynamism inverts completely Gener's flow chart: Spain (sometimes synonymous with the Hispanic world and occasionally with Latin culture in general) is hampered by cultural stagnation and complacency; France (effectively Paris) is a regenerating intermediary of "indigenous" Latin stock but receptive to the foreign; the foreign Nordic, Slavic and "Oriental" (particularly Chinese) literatures are repositories of new artistic energies and perspectives from the influence of which Hispanic literature, Gómez Carrillo argues, could benefit.

Homelands

The particular character and delimitation of indigenous culture configured in each work offers a useful measure of where foreignness begins. Gener circumscribes a macro-indigenous Latin identity encompassing Spain (Andalusia, Castile and Catalonia), France, Italy and Greece (341), but posits a Mediterranean core identity "por temperamento y por convicción", based on a concept of naturalism defined as evolutionary oneness with nature facilitated by a milieu "en que ha nacido y renacido la civilización humana" and whose native population, "aunque alcancemos la categoría de intelectuales puros" never loses contact with "el mundo sensible, la naturaleza viviente" (75-79). An implicit distinction is made between Mediterraneans and "[l]as razas que pueblan la España Central y sobre todo la Meridional", whose innate propensity to "la hipérbole y a la exageración poco exacta" (26) constitutes a symptom of degenerative tendencies, albeit "de esas que no matan, pero molestan. [...] hijas del vivir una porción de años atrasados" (7), that taint the "other". For Gener, then, foreignness of a sort begins within the Iberian Peninsula.

Gómez Carrillo, on the other hand, tends towards ex-centric conflation, using "en España" as a common reference to the Hispanic world in general, and "nosotros" and "nuestro/a" to embrace a pan-Hispanic readership (2-3). But unlike Gener's Mediterranean *patria*, Gómez Carrillo's homeland has already fallen prey to literary stagnation and intercultural myopia, as he notes in sardonic mimicry of his compatriots' complacency: "Nosotros no tenemos necesidad de renegarnos [...]. Los que hoy hablan en España y América de revolución poética, son visionarios optimistas. [...] Yo no veo [...] sino [...] una gran calma, o, mejor dicho, una gran indiferencia" (2-3).

Europe and Beyond

The Latin French in *Literaturas malsanas* recall the villagers of ambivalent allegiance whose settlements lay between Gener's "fortress Mediterranean" and the advancing degenerate Nordic barbarian hordes, while in *Literatura extranjera* they are portrayed as the vanguard of an army of aesthetic regeneration moving in from the North of Europe and beyond to relieve a Spain occupied by the forces of literary complacency and parochialism. Thus contemporary French writers' interest in Nordic literatures that for Gener amounts to "los bárbaros volviendo sobre las Galias reconquistadas por los latinos" (178) is for Gómez Carrillo a sign of resurgent Latin enlightenment (1-2).

Gener, then, inverts the contemporary belief in the Nordic races' evolutionary strength by reformulating their power not as *vigour* but as the *virulence* of a contagious degenerative disease, a depressive pessimism —principally German "Neobudismo" and Russian "Nihilismo" (5)— to the causes of which "agréguese el refinamiento de la civilización moderna" —that has spread to "los latinos" (281). Gómez Carrillo also problematizes the Latin decadence/Nordic progress binary by introducing an ambivalent note into his advocacy of Nordic literature when he explains that some young French and German writers have grasped the new Nordic sensibility, "y por eso logran concebir obras *desequilibradas y bellas... En el fondo, la enfermedad de esos pueblos* [nórdicos] *vale más que nuestra salud* [My emphasis]" (29). Gómez Carrillo thereby questions the idea that Nordic disquiet is necessarily harmful, implying that even disease can be an appropriate motor to timely change. This position is not entirely incompatible with Gener's claim that "[l]os fenómenos patológicos actuales son síntomas, no de decadencia final, no de agotamiento de razas, sino de esfuerzo, de progreso, de enérgica evolución ascendente" (389-91).

Europe, then, is an ambivalent site. Gener's degeneration-based thesis posits a sliding scale of susceptibility to degenerative afflictions that is directly linked to foreignness: the further from the Mediterranean mean of evolutionary health a community is, the more alien (and threatening) it becomes. Gener identifies as triggers to degenerative pessimism physical factors such as climate, historical factors such as Protestantism (278), and recent circumstances such as "la brutalidad que la lucha para la vida material ha revestido en Inglaterra" or the advent of Prussianforged Imperial Germany, "[l]a nación que con su estado particular ha contribuído más al pesimismo moderno" (278-79). Emphasis on these elements —*moment* and *milieu*— is consistent with Gener's view that degeneration is but part of a cycle of change. When *race* enters the equation, however, the situation acquires quite a different complexion. In Russia, "[o]tra nación que sufre de un estado patológico colectivo" (278), contributory factors such as the social instability caused by rapid but societally uneven development are referred to as causes but in fact are treated as catalysts to a purported "racial" predisposition to extreme pessimism in the guise of "elementos asiáticos, algunos de ellos de origen mogólico", in the Slavic make-up, a "pequeñísima mezcla de sangre amarilla [que] ha bastado [...] para perturbar el cerebro eslavo con un delirio de muerte" (278-79). This factor, for Gener, grounds Slavic fatalism in constitutional rather than circumstantial factors (310), and also serves to explain the depressive influence on Germany of the dominant Prussians, "mezclados de eslavo y de hugrofinés" (280) and therefore "orientalised".

From this derives *Literaturas malsanas*'s notion of endemically, transhistorically degenerate "races", prominent among which are those of "sangre amarilla", largely synonymous with peoples of India (282, 301): "la sangre amarilla es pesimista por esencia" (310); the "semitic" races: "razas [...] condenad[a]s a la desgracia", whose literature therefore "consiste en lamentaciones y apocalipsis" (276) and the legacy of which is a symbolism that is "feo y recargado [...] a la manera hebraica" and a type of writer who "se resiente de semitismo, desde subordinar su pluma al beneficio personal, hasta su modo parabólico de concebir las obras" (100); in short, all "las irrupciones morales y materiales del Oriente" (197) that contributed to the decline of civilization from the decadence of classical antiquity. The Americas too are condemned for their "utilitarismo egoísta, astuto, inmediato" and "el estúpido noticierismo a la norteamericana" (158, 378).

Gener's Latins, however, enjoy a natural resistance to this ingrained pessimism: "El Latino, en general, no puede ser pesimista más que individualmente; [... E]sta raza será siempre refractaria al pesimismo oriental. Aunque el budista nos venga disfrazado [... de] filósofo tudesco, [...] nunca hará aquí prosélitos, siempre será esencialmente exótico entre nosotros" (281-83). For Gómez Carrillo, on the contrary, it is not a matter of defending the homeland against dangerous immigrants but of encouraging Latins to becoming aesthetic migrants themselves. Thus he advocates the initiative of certain French writers, presented here as clear-mindedly Mediterranean as any Generian *genio*, who,

> así como los Pescadores de Islandia abandonan todos los años el azul mediterráneo para ir a buscar en las glaucas aguas del Océano Ártico peces cuyas substancias fortifican, así también se alejan a menudo de París, que es la capital del ingenio claro, para buscar entre la bruma del polo la savia poética que reconforta (2).

What is more, Gómez Carrillo leads by example. He adopts a quasi-foreign, not-exclusively-Hispanic, Latin identity, expounding on French fin de siècle culture from the discursive position —a devotion, but of the balanced, well-informed variety— of an insider, while explicitly retaining a native affiliation to the Spain and Hispanic world whose need of a rehabilitative education in literary culture he perceives as urgent. The idiosyncratic "indigenous" space in which Gómez Carrillo sits is not the beleaguered but inviolate Mediterranean spiritual heartland of Gener, nor a hub of unmitigated complacency, but a neo-Latin communal zone with permeable frontiers that needs to build on its capacity to embrace rather than shun otherness —whence his applause that "la juventud francesa se siente hoy más ávida de sensaciones psicológicas que de placeres superficiales" (2), his frustration that "we Spaniards" grasped only superficially Zola's Naturalism, diluting it with a home-made realism to produce "una bebida más agradable que fuerte" (3), or his scorn for "esa encantadora frivolidad que nuestro público admira" (22). What for Gener is robust "naturalism" is for Gómez Carrillo intellectual limitation. He is also irked by the cultural xenophobia of an intellectual Old Guard who "hicieron la Guerra en nombre de cierta tradición castiza, y [...] nos hablaron [...] de herencia grecolatina", and for whom "todo lo que no nacía en las márgenes del Mediterráneo era [...] cosa bárbara" (71-72) — possibly a swipe at Gener himself. Any sign of a more receptive turn in Spanish attitudes to contemporary foreign literature delights him: "[S]ólo la francesa nos interesa más que la rusa" (71). Gómez Carrillo's insistence on the benefits of a cosmopolitan outlook —the blend of "elementos tártaros, rusos y franceses" in Russian artist María Bashkirtseff, for whom "[l]os escritores interesantes no tienen [...] patria" (65) is not presented as a degenerate mix as in Gener but as "un carácter extrañamente cosmopolita" (60)— yields a response to the Oriental that is diametrically opposed to Gener's: "Bueno es, una vez que otra, salir de nuestro mundo europeo. Los viajes intelectuales a través de países lejanos abren nuevos horizontes a la imaginación y proporcionan a la inteligencia puntos de vista originales. [...] El exotismo bien entendido es cosa excelente" (87); whence the revelation that foreigners are not so foreign as Gener would claim: just as "la lectura de esas novelas [rusas] nos hizo comprender que los hombres del Norte [...] eran más compatriotas nuestros, que D. José María de Pereda" (72), the Latin literary traveller to China who anticipates finding "monstruos espantosos" discovers "hombres civilizados" (88), and, moreover, a "cultura del 'yo'" close to that of fin de siècle European artists and a striking similarity between Chinese seventh-century poetry and that of Wyzewa, Rubén Darío or Baudelaire (98). This notion of cultural proximity, of aesthetic fraternity waiting to be discovered, finds its opposite in Gener's depiction of the foreigner as an atavistic enemy:

> [Dice el decadente]: "Sí! Substituyamos a la Razón, al Pensamiento, al Sentimiento natural, la Pasión. La pasión es lo imprevisto, lo inapercible, un vendeval, la barbarie, la animalidad obrando por los sentidos. Venga, pues, la Pasión, y que ella se substituya a la Belleza... pues la Belleza... ¿qué es? [...] una futilidad greco-latina, una ilusión mediterránea. [...] [L] armonía es teutónica, la Belleza es latina. ¡Muera la Belleza! ¡Muera la Mediodía!" (215-16).

In *Literaturas malsanas*, foreigner-stigmatising derision abounds: Belgian Symbolists and English Pre-Raphaelites are "vagos, indeterminados" (257); Wagner is "un desorbitado", "bárbaro" and "decadente" (211–17); French Symbolists, Decadents and Naturalists are "miopes del arte y de la inteligencia" (83); Russian nihilist literature exhibits "la imaginación delirante de los enfermos de las cárceles" (340).

Conclusion

Gómez Carrillo's "de-othering" of the foreigner to counter stifling aesthetic parochialism and Gener's "hyper-othering" combination of scientific objectivity and demagogy demonstrate yet again how foreignness is a culturally and ideologically determined, relative concept, susceptible to suasive or tendentious exploitation. What is more, it is the fundamental importance that fin de siècle ideology placed on the social function of literature in relation to "racial" identity —as Gómez Carrillo's appeal to its writers and arbiters and Gener's appeal to its consumers show— that allows the concept of foreignness to acquire such a crucial position in contemporary cultural debates.

Bibliography

Cacho Viu, V. 1997. *Repensar el 98*, Madrid, Biblioteca Nueva.

Calvo Revilla, L. 1998. *La cara oculta del 98. Místicos e intelectuales en la España del fin de siglo (1895-1902)*, Madrid, Cátedra.

Campos Martín, R. & R. Huertas. 2001. "The Theory of Degeneration in Spain", *Boston Studies in the Philosophy of Science* 221, 171-87.

Demolins, E. 1897. *A quoi tient la supériorité des Anglo-Saxons*, Paris, Didot.

Gener, P. 1894. *Literaturas malsanas. Estudios de patología literaria contemporánea*, Madrid, Fernando Fe.

—. 1900. *Literaturas malsanas. Estudios de patología literaria contemporánea*, fourth edition, Barcelona, Juan Llordachs.

Gómez Carrillo, E. 1895. *Literatura extranjera*, Paris, Garnier.

Hambrook, G. 1991. "Del poeta a la poesía: La imagen de Charles Baudelaire y de su obra en las crónicas literarias de Enrique Gómez Carrillo", *Estudios de investigación franco-española* 5, 97-111

Kronik, J. W. 1967. "Enrique Gómez Carrillo, Francophile Propagandist", *Symposium* 21, 50-60.

Lombroso, C. 1888. *L'uomo di genio in rapporto alla psichiatria, alla storia ed all'estetica*, Turin, Bocca.

Morel, B. A. 1857. *Traité des dégénescences physiques, intellectuelles et morales de l'espèce humaine et des causes qui produisent ces varietés maladives*, Paris, Baillière.

Nordau, M. 1893. *Entartung*, Berlin, Druckner.

BEGOÑA LASA ÁLVAREZ

Viajeros británicos en la prensa española de principios del XIX: La *Biblioteca británica* de Olive

A principios del siglo XIX, favorecida por razones de tipo político y militar, se aprecia una progresiva anglomanía en España que, aunque difícilmente puede rivalizar aún con la hegemonía cultural francesa, sí que se plasma en el mercado editorial español mediante publicaciones como la *Biblioteca británica* que sale a la luz en 1807. Se trata de una compilación de textos misceláneos que Pedro María de Olive tomó y tradujo de otra colección que con el mismo nombre se estaba publicando en lengua francesa, la *Bibliothèque britannique*. En este sentido, es de destacar el hecho de que, por su origen en Ginebra y la tradicional vinculación de esta ciudad con la cultura anglófona, la *Bibliothèque britannique* constituye uno de los primeros focos en el avance de ésta en el continente europeo, aunque paradójicamente la lengua utilizada para ello fuera la francesa.

La *Bibliothèque britannique* se publicó entre 1796 y 1815 en Ginebra por los hermanos Marc-Auguste y Charles Pictet y su amigo Frédéric-Guillaume Maurice. Esta se publicaba en diversos volúmenes siguiendo una división temática, y Pedro María de Olive dejará de lado los volúmenes dedicados a "Sciences et Arts" y "Agriculture", y traducirá únicamente textos de la sección dedicada a "Littérature". En ésta, como indica David Bickerton, el concepto de literatura se concibe de una manera mucho más amplia que en la actualidad (1986: 490). Así, los propios editores de la revista ginebrina mencionan en el prólogo del volumen 13 dedicado a "Littérature" que en esta sección se incluirán textos sobre educación, economía política, viajes, bellas artes, biografías y obras de imaginación (1800: 4-11). Y aunque sean estas últimas las que más espacio ocupen, les siguen muy de cerca los textos sobre viajes (Bickerton 1986: 513), lo que pone de manifiesto la gran popularidad de este género en esta época. Del mismo modo, la presencia de textos de viajes en la colección española es notable, lo que se corresponde con la importancia concedida a los mismos en la introducción con la que Olive presenta su obra, en la que destaca la curiosidad que suscitan y su originalidad (I, 4-5).

Aunque los españoles del siglo XVIII, comparados con otros ciudadanos europeos, no eran tan aficionados a viajar y por tanto a escribir relatos de viajes (Fabbri 1996), sí que gustaban de leerlos (García Garrosa 2007) y se aprecia en estos momentos un interés creciente por lo que Francisco Lafarga denomina "territorios de lo exótico" (1994). Además, como señala Guillermo Carnero en su estudio sobre colecciones y misceláneas similares a esta que aquí analizamos, los textos de viajes constituían un componente habitual de las mismas (38), y por tanto, como se indica en este mismo trabajo, servían como lectura y comentario en las tertulias y reuniones de la época.

El primer texto que bajo el epígrafe de "Viajes" aparece en el primer tomo de la *Biblioteca británica* lleva por título "Descripción de los Harenes, (o sean serrallos de Alepo) y noticia de las costumbres, ocupaciones y diversiones de las mujeres turcas, sacadas de la Historia natural de Alepo, por Russell" (6-32) y procede del capítulo V del primer libro de *The Natural History of Aleppo* (236-75) de Alexander Russell (1756). Russell era un médico escocés que trabajó para la Levant Company británica desde 1749 a 1753 en Alepo, importante enclave comercial entre Asia y Europa. Tanto Alexander Russell como su hermano Patrick, responsable de una segunda edición de la obra y que también trabajó para la misma compañía, estudiaron en Edimburgo durante los primeros años del conocido como *Scottish Enlightenment*, que supuso un considerable desarrollo de actividades científicas, filosóficas y culturales en las ciudades escocesas más importantes, con la creación de destacadas sociedades y clubes (Starkey 2003). La segunda mitad del siglo XVIII constituye asimismo un periodo en el que proliferaron los viajes. Los motivos por los que se emprendían eran muchos, económicos, científicos, de exploración e incluso turísticos, por el afán de saber y reunir conocimientos propios de la Ilustración, así como por los avances tecnológicos que mejoraron drásticamente los medios de comunicación y que dinamizaron el mercado editorial (Bohls 2005; Thompson 2011: 44-52). El texto de Russell formaría parte obviamente de esta relación, pero además, como su título indica, no solo se centra en el viaje, sino que, tras la estela y bajo la influencia de Linneo y su *Systema Naturae*, junto a aspectos etnográficos, geográficos, culturales, y en este caso, médicos, también describe y clasifica la flora y la fauna del lugar. Como resultado de la publicación del texto de Linneo "[t]ravel and travel writing would never be the same again. In the second half of the eighteenth century, whether or not an expedition was primarily scientific, or the traveller a scientist, natural history played a part in it" (Pratt 1992: 27). Por otro lado, la zona geográfica de la que se ocupa Russell se contempla de forma un tanto diferente, pues si hasta este siglo los historiadores y viajeros habían considerado a los pueblos de Oriente como los enemigos, especialmente por motivos religiosos, la secularización que trajo consigo el siglo ilustrado, supuso una mayor imparcialidad en su acercamiento a ellos (Said 1990: 150).

Los editores de la *Bibliothèque britannique* repararon en un fragmento del libro que por su singularidad y exotismo podría atraer a los lectores occidentales, el de las actividades y las costumbres de las mujeres en los harenes turcos. Además de que por su condición de médicos los Russell tenían acceso privilegiado a estos harenes y podían hablar de ellos por su propia experiencia (I: 13), resulta interesante señalar que el autor de la segunda edición, Patrick, manifiesta en el prólogo que ha ampliado esta parte de la obra (Russell 1794: xii), posiblemente por las mismas causas antes mencionadas. En el texto se explica con bastante detalle cómo viven las mujeres en los harenes y también su relación con los hombres, destacándose en varios pasajes su modestia y su posición de respeto e inferioridad con respecto a ellos, e incluso, comparando su actitud con la de las europeas: "Su ignorancia de la libertad y de los privilegios que gozan las europeas, hacen que no estén mortificadas por ello, y cuando se las habla de tales privilegios, no parece que desean gozarlos por oponerse a sus ideas de honor y de modestia" (I: 11). Por otro lado, resulta interesante mencionar que la misma curiosidad que los occidentales manifiestan por los orientales, la revelan las mismas protagonistas del relato pues le hacen al médico "infinitas preguntas sobre su país, y principalmente sobre las mujeres europeas, sus vestidos, ocupaciones, sus diversiones, sus casamientos, y la educación de sus hijos" (I: 14).

El siguiente texto es "Relación del viaje del Gran Lama para visitar al Emperador de la China" del tomo I de la *Biblioteca británica* (33-51), del que se indica que procede de la traducción de "A Narrative of the Journey of the Teshoo Lama to Visit the Emperor of China" que se publicó en *Oriental Repertory*, un periódico editado por el escocés Alexander Dalrymple en ocho números entre 1791 y 1797 con material sobre la India y China, y patrocinado por la East India Company, compañía para la que trabajó como hidrógrafo en la India (Chambers 1835: 44). Se trata, como el editor indica en los diversos prólogos, de una compilación de textos misceláneos de diversos autores que ha reunido con el propósito de mostrar "everything promoting our knowledge of the East" (Dalrymple 1808: ii). El texto narra, como se indica en el título, el viaje que realizó el Gran Lama desde el Tibet a China para visitar al Emperador, un relato en el que predomina el exotismo, la suntuosidad y unas costumbres un tanto extravagantes para el público occidental.

El tercer texto de la sección sobre viajes del primer volumen de la *Biblioteca británica* se titula "Ferocidad de los salvajes" (181-89), y es traducción de un fragmento de la obra *A Journey from Prince of Wales's Fort in Hudson's Bay, to the Northern Ocean* de Samuel Hearne, que fue el primer europeo que llegó por tierra a la costa ártica de Norteamérica. Un hecho que, según Mary Louise Pratt, diferenciaría a los viajeros o expedicionarios del siglo XVIII respecto de los anteriores, puesto que sus periplos se centraban en descubrir y describir las costas de las nuevas tierras con el fin de elaborar mapas, mientras que los viajeros del siglo ilustrado se adentran y exploran la tierra, movidos en estos momentos por intereses económicos, especialmente en busca de materias primas para la industria en plena expansión (1992: 9). Pero si por algo es conocido el texto de Samuel Hearne es por la masacre de esquimales o inuits que describe y que es precisamente uno de los pasajes que se recoge en la biblioteca de Olive. Cuando se publicó el libro fue objeto de numerosas recensiones y también se tradujo a otros idiomas, destacándose siempre la descripción de esta matanza (McGoogan 2007: xviii). No obstante, además de la comprensible curiosidad, despertó una importante controversia, especialmente entre los historiadores canadienses, que se ha extendido hasta la actualidad, sobre si efectivamente fue Hearne testigo de lo ocurrido, e incluso sobre la veracidad del episodio (McGrath 1993). En el relato incluido en la biblioteca se recogen dos fragmentos del libro de Hearne, y en efecto, el primero describe cómo los indios nativos americanos con los que viajaba el autor y que eran sus guías, matan de forma violenta e inmisericorde a un grupo de esquimales en ese momento indefensos, incluyendo mujeres y niños. Según sus propias palabras, el autor no participa, solo es testigo, pero junto a los hechos, también describe sus sensaciones, consiguiendo dar así un mayor dramatismo a su relato:

"No podré pintar aquí bien el horror y espanto que todo esto me causaba: me esforcé cuanto pude para contener las lágrimas; pero cuando ahora me acuerdo de tan espantosa escena lloro sin poderme contener" (I: 185).

Ya en el volumen segundo de la colección de Olive, el único texto bajo el epígrafe de "Viajes" es el titulado "Carácter y costumbres de los turcos, sacado de la obra intitulada Constantinople ancient and modern, por Mr. Delaway" (124-50), que efectivamente consiste en una compilación de pasajes de *Constantinople Ancient and Modern, with Excursions to the Shores and Islands of the Archipelago and to the Troad* (1797) de James Dallaway. Este, como todos los autores anteriores, trabajaba también para el gobierno británico, como médico y capellán de la embajada, y recopiló en este libro datos y experiencias de su estancia en Constantinopla y alrededores. En el texto de la biblioteca se tocan temas como la religión, el gobierno, y costumbres en cuanto a indumentaria, honras a difuntos y ocio, así como una parte algo más amplia dedicada a las costumbres de las mujeres, en particular a los harenes, un tema que parece que interesaba en la época, al repetirse en ambos volúmenes.

Hemos considerado incluir aquí por su temática un texto de la sección "Historia" del volumen II de la *Biblioteca británica* que lleva por título "Noticia sobre los negros. Sacada de la historia de las indias orientales por Brian Edwards" (225-45). Lo comprenden algunos fragmentos de *The History Civil and Commercial of the British Colonies in the West Indies* (1793) de Bryan Edwards, uno de los hombres más ricos de Jamaica con numerosas plantaciones y esclavos; era anti-abolicionista y consideraba el tráfico de esclavos como un mal necesario (Blouet 2000: 218-219), por este motivo se defiende y defiende a los dueños de plantaciones en el prólogo de su obra, en relación a las inmerecidas críticas vertidas contra ellos por su supuesto maltrato a los esclavos africanos (Edwards 1793: xx-xi).

Tras observar y escuchar a sus esclavos, Edwards describe las características tanto físicas como morales de algunas tribus africanas, como mandingos, koromantines, o eboes. Lo que se destaca en ellos es su salvajismo y ferocidad, o su pusilanimidad, falsedad y tendencia al robo. Como ejemplo, se señala la sublevación que se produjo en Jamaica en 1760 en la que "los negros les dieron muerte [a los criados blancos] con la mayor crueldad bebiendo su sangre mezclada con rum" (II: 229). También afirma Edwards que algunas tribus africanas son antropófagas "y no me queda duda en ello, pues me lo ha asegurado positivamente un

esclavo antiguo de esta nación, diciéndome, aunque con mucha ver-
güenza, porque sus costumbres se habían suavizado con el trato de los
blancos, que siendo mozo tomaba parte en estos festines" (II: 233-234).
A continuación, explica el comportamiento de los esclavos en las plantaciones y en este caso los africanos tampoco salen bien parados. Son falsos, tiranos, rencorosos o bárbaros (II: 135). Entre otras cosas afirma que
"El amor entre los negros es solo un puro instinto, semejante al de los
demás animales" (II: 136), o que "la mayor parte de sus canciones y
bailes consisten en el desorden y grosería" (II: 138); pero uno de los
aspectos que más preocupaba a Edwards era la extensión de las supersticiones y hechicería entre los esclavos, puesto que perjudicaba en gran
manera el orden y funcionamiento de la plantación, y la dificultad que
entrañaba su erradicación. A pesar de que Edwards manifiesta mantener
una relación hasta cierto punto cercana con alguno de sus esclavos, sus
apreciaciones negativas no dejan de ser un síntoma de su creencia en que
el contacto de los africanos con una cultura superior como la europea
resulta favorable para ellos, pues como él mismo decía se suavizan sus
costumbres. Lo que evidentemente sustenta la necesidad del tráfico de
esclavos, su trabajo en las plantaciones y, en última instancia, la presencia colonial de los británicos con su tutela (Thompson 2011: 134).

A través de este somero análisis de los diversos textos de viajes presentes en la *Biblioteca británica* se ha podido apreciar que los escritores
de este tipo de relatos, al igual que los traductores, no son los inocentes
creadores de un texto, sino que sus obras son parte de un proceso de
manipulación que modela y condiciona nuestras actitudes hacia otras
culturas (Bassnett 1993: 99). El punto de vista del escritor está siempre
presente, con todo lo que conlleva, y así lo hace constar ya a finales del
siglo XVIII Patrick Russell, el editor de la segunda edición de *The Natural History of Aleppo*, uno de los textos aquí estudiados, al mostrarse
convencido de que "opinions formed of Men and Manners, from private
experience, must inevitably in the representation to others, take some
tincture from the observer's condition of life, as well as from his constitutional temper" (1794: xii).

Finalmente queremos poner de relieve que, gracias a la *Biblioteca
británica* de Olive, los españoles pudieron acceder a un reducido pero
variado y curioso panorama de la literatura de viajes británica de finales
del siglo XVIII, un género en ascenso también en España. Los lectores
de la Península pudieron así acercarse a diversos continentes y conocer a

sus habitantes y sus costumbres, en algunos casos —como en el de los esquimales o los nativos americanos— posiblemente por primera vez.

Bibliografía

Bassnett, S. 1993. *Comparative Literature. A Critical Introduction*, Oxford, Blackwell.

Biblioteca Británica, o colección extractada de las obras inglesas, de los periódicos, de las memorias y transacciones de las sociedades y academias de la Gran Bretaña, de Asia, de África y de América, 1807, Madrid, Imprenta de Vega y Cia.

Bibliothèque britannique ou recueil extrait des ouvrages anglais périodiques et autres; des Mémoires et Transactions des Sociétés et Académies de la Grande Bretagne, d'Asie, d'Afrique et d'Amérique, en deux séries, 1796-1815, Genève, Impr. de la Bibliothèque britannique.

Bickerton, D. M. 1986. *Marc-Auguste and Charles Pictet, the Bibliothèque britannique (1796-1815) and the Dissemination of British Literature and Science on the Continent*, Genève, Slatkine.

Blouet, O. M. 2000. "Bryan Edwards, F.R.S., 1743-1800", *Notes and Records of the Royal Society of London* 54:2, 215-22.

Bohls, E. A. 2005. "Introduction", in *Travel Writing 1700-1830. An Anthology*, E. A. Bohls & I. Duncan (eds.), Oxford, Oxford UP, xiii-xvii.

Carnero, G. 1998. "El *Remedio de la melancolía y entretenimiento de las náyades*: narrativa, miscelánea cultural y juegos de sociedad en las colecciones españolas de fines del XVIII y principios del XIX", in F. García Lara (ed.), *I Congreso Internacional sobre novela del siglo XVIII*, Almería, Universidad de Almería, 25-52.

Chambers, R. 1835. *A Biographical Dictionary of Eminent Scotsmen*, vol. II, Glasgow, Blackie.

Dallaway, J. 1797. *Constantinople Ancient and Modern, with Excursions to the Shores and Islands of the Archipelago and to the Troad.* London, T. Bensley.

Dalrymple, A. (ed.). 1808. *Oriental Repertory*, London, William Ballantine.

Edwards, B. 1793. *The History Civil and Commercial of the British Colonies in the West Indies,* London, John Stockdale.

Fabbri, M. 1996. "Literatura de viajes", in F. Aguilar Piñal (ed.), *Historia literaria de España en el siglo XVIII*, Madrid, Trotta, 407-23.

García Garrosa, M. J. 2007. "El periplo literario español del *Viaje del joven Anacarsis a Grecia* (1790-1830)", in F. Lafarga, P. S. Méndez & A. Saura (eds.), *Literatura de viajes y traducción*, Granada, Comares.

Hearne, S. 1795. *A Journey from Prince of Wales's Fort in Hudson's Bay, to the Northern Ocean*, London, Strahan and Cadell.

Lafarga, F. 1994. "Territorios de lo exótico en las letras españolas del siglo XVIII", *Anales de literatura española A.L.E.U.A* 10, 173-92.

McGoogan, K. 2007. "Foreword", in S. Hearne *A Journey to the Northern Ocean*, Custer, Canada, Touchwood Editions, ix-xxiv.

McGrath, R. 1993. "Samuel Hearne and the Inuit Tradition". *Studies in Canadian Literature* 18: 2, <http://journals.hil.unb.ca/index.php/scl/article/view/8186/9243> [consultado el 02.VIII.2011]

Olive, P. M. de (dir.). 1807. *Biblioteca Británica*, Madrid, Vega y Cia.

Pratt, M. L. 1992. *Imperial Eyes. Travel Writing and Transculturation*, London & New York, Routledge.

Russell, A. 1794. *The Natural History of Aleppo*, vol. I, London, G. G. & J. Robinson.

Said, E. W. 1990. *Orientalismo*, Madrid, Libertarias.

Starkey, J. C. M. 2003. "Mercantile Gentlemen and Inquisitive Travellers: Constructing *The Natural History of Aleppo*", in C. Foster (ed.), *Travellers in the Near East*, London, Stacey International, 1-35.

Thompson, C. 2011. *Travel Writing*, London & New York, Routledge.

VLADIMIR MONTAÑA MESTIZO

La representación de los extranjeros europeos en la literatura de viajes sobre la Colombia del siglo XIX

Este trabajo tiene como objetivo explorar las representaciones hechas a propósito de los europeos emigrados a Colombia durante la transición postcolonial. Dada la muy reducida población de extranjeros en este periodo y en esta zona geográfica, podemos decir que son pocas las fuentes que nos permiten abordar dicha temática desde un punto de vista sistemático, y es en ese sentido que los relatos de viaje se nos presentan como un instrumento particularmente provechoso. Nuestro trabajo se divide en dos referentes temáticos. Inicialmente intentaremos aproximarnos a la sensación que tuvieron los viajeros acerca de cómo se veía su situación en tanto que extranjeros para el imaginario de los colombianos. Seguidamente intentaremos mostrar las representaciones que tenían los viajeros de los emigrados europeos que se encontraban en tierras americanas.

Representación de los extranjeros

Al abordar la herencia colonial en Colombia, creemos que esta tardará muchos años en desaparecer, no solo en términos políticos y económicos, sino también en cuanto a las propias representaciones de la identidad y de la alteridad. Esta situación nos la dejan entrever dos viajeros franceses de la segunda mitad del siglo XIX, quienes en contextos diferentes y en lugares totalmente diferentes, dejaban claro a sus interlocutores indígenas con respecto a que ellos mismos, por ser franceses, no eran españoles, y que en efecto correspondían a "otro tipo" de blancos. Así, alrededor de 1857, por ejemplo, un indio de la Sierra Nevada de Santa Marta le había ofrecido su hospitalidad al geógrafo Elisée Reclus diciéndole: "¡Soy práctico de la Sierra, conozco bien la montaña y lo conduciré a usted por todas partes!... pregunte por Zamba Simonguama, ¡y verá si los indios saben dar hospitalidad como los españoles!" (Reclus 1861: 77). En este mismo sentido, el médico Charles Saffray en 1869 habría tenido que aclarar a un cacique de la cordillera occidental: "Yo no soy español, pero los blancos de mi país aman y respetan a los indios. Vengo a solicitar vuestra amistad y a ver vuestro país" (Saffray 1873: 118). Según se desprende de las anteriores referencias, podríamos suponer que la representación del foráneo en tanto que "español" parecía un hecho corriente en algunas regiones, y particularmente en zonas indígenas de reducido contacto intercultural.

Un cuadro singular de la representación de los extranjeros nos lo proporciona el diplomático sueco Karl Gosselman, para quien los colombianos del siglo XIX únicamente conocían tres tipos de nacionalidades: "colombianos libres", "pendejos españoles" y "amigos ingleses". No tenemos indicios para considerar cuáles pudieron ser las causas de esa particular benevolencia ante a los "ingleses", aunque podría creerse que la justificaría el vínculo de las legiones británicas a la causa de la Independencia. Pero esta simpatía hacia los ingleses quizás podría tener unas implicaciones más amplias, y es por ello que, según relata el mismo Gosselman, los términos "europeo" e "inglés" podían ser empleados como sinónimos e incluso englobar a los norteamericanos, pues —decía el diplomático sueco— éstos y los ingleses son considerados los mismos, "más aún si con ese criterio ven la independencia norteamericana" (Gosselman 1981: 336). Una percepción semejante habría tenido Saffray casi 45 años después, cuando, tras lanzar una pregunta ingenua a un niño que vendía insectos en una calle, solamente obtuvo una explicación indulgente a propósito de la naturaleza de ese producto cuando el pequeño comerciante se percató de que aquel viajero francés era "un inglés" (Saffray 1872: 94). Intentando explicar el éxito de los ingleses ante a los colombianos, el comerciante de perlas Charles Stuart Cochrane opinaba que era debido al reducido número de extranjeros que pasaban por las alejadas comarcas, y ello, en razón de un cierto exotismo, justificaría la hospitalidad hacia los "foreigners" en general, y hacia los "Englishmen" en particular (491).

El alemán Alfred Hettner, fundador de la geografía regional, nos muestra que en la región de Antioquía, en efecto, todos los extranjeros eran considerados ingleses, pero al mismo tiempo en Santander eran percibidos como alemanes y en Boyacá como italianos. Todo ello tenía un directo vínculo a causa del predominio en los referidos estados de los ingleses como mineros y de los alemanes como comerciantes; al estado de Boyacá, que era muy pobre, no llegaban "*sino tenderos italianos*" (Hettner 1976: 158). Vale bien decir, entonces, que el apelativo genérico de "inglés" no se reconocería sino en ciertos contextos, y que en efecto se realizó el reconocimiento de algunas identidades nacionales específicas sobre la base de interacciones culturales bastante puntuales. Es así como se anotó, por ejemplo, que entre los indios —salvajes— de La Guajira, los franceses eran bien recibidos al haber sido los piratas (nanteses y bretones) aliados de dichos indios en sus incursiones contra los "españoles" (Reclus 1861: 126-27). Pero al igual que ocurría con los ingleses, podríamos sugerir que la representación de los franceses también estuvo en varios momentos marcada por cierta ambigüedad. Así, por ejemplo, cabe tener en cuenta que los franceses con los cuales se interactuaba en las costas caribeñas eran en muchas ocasiones haitianos que se reclamaban pertenecientes a su antigua metrópoli cuando las necesidades prácticas así lo exigían (Reclus 1861: 166-67).

Por todo lo anterior debemos suponer que el apelativo de "inglés", "francés", "alemán" e "italiano", tal como era utilizado por los sectores subalternos del siglo XIX, más que una sinonimia o metonimia frente a lo europeo, demarcaría el espacio de una indefinición de cada proyecto nacional en tierras americanas. Así pues diremos que la adscripción a una identidad nacional europea no se aplicaba de una manera tan sencilla en el siglo XIX a como pudiera creerse en principio. La definición de los "ingleses" de hecho marcaba un referente de naturaleza conceptual diferente al marco simbólico que se construía alrededor de los "franceses". Ahora bien, si estamos de acuerdo con Walter Benjamin en cuanto a la posición de la cultura francesa en el siglo XIX, debemos reconocer entonces que la situación de lo "francés" o de lo "inglés" pudiera resultar referencial o no desde un punto de vista simbólico, dependiendo de dónde fuera enunciada la representación de lo nacional. Isaac Holton, profesor de química e historia natural, de una manera muy sucinta, al describir a sus compañeros de viaje en un barco que iba por el río Magdalena rumbo a Bogotá, nos demuestra de hecho la importancia que entre los propios viajeros tenía la lengua francesa, ya que casi era un requisito incluso entre los angloparlantes y entre todos los que se atribuían la profesión de viajeros (Holton 1857: 81-82).

Representaciones entre los mismos extranjeros

Nos preguntaremos ahora cuál pudo haber sido la representación del
hecho nacional europeo cuando sus ciudadanos se hallaban en el exilio.
Debemos decir que el sentido de identidad nacional no debía operar de la
misma manera, y que el nivel de compromiso con un determinado proyecto nacional dependía de variables heterogéneas en el caso de cada
nación. Reclus opinaba que la diferencia entre los alemanes y los ingleses se debía a que mientras los primeros se podían desprender con mucha
facilidad de "sus ropajes" alemanes adaptándose rápidamente a las culturas locales, los segundos llevaban la patria en sí mismos y no requerían
de nada más para vivir su propia experiencia nacional. Los franceses, por
el contrario, se caracterizarían por tener un mayor apego a sus valores y
a sus costumbres, razón por la cual, en el exilio, se aglomeraban en torno
a pequeñas comunidades rechazando siempre naturalizarse; la comunidad era fundamento de la auto-representación nacional, primando entre
las distinciones de clase (Reclus 1861: 156).

Las representaciones de la identidad y de la alteridad eran por supuesto variables entre los propios europeos y conducían a juicios de valor diferentes. Es desde este punto de vista que podremos entender el
contexto de enunciación del estadounidense Isaac Holton, quien opinaba
que la fama de los "ingleses" no era del todo bien ganada, y que, en
cuanto a él mismo, eran más las vergüenzas que le generaban constantemente los comportamientos de esa "raza" anglosajona que andaba dispersa por todo el mundo (97). En opinión de Reclus los americanos del
Norte, a diferencia de los ingleses, tenían la tendencia a reclamar lo más
rápidamente posible su nacionalidad extranjera a fin de ejercer funciones
públicas, y con ello, activar un espíritu de dominación por el cual serían
mal vistos entre los colombianos (1861: 165-66).

Para el ciudadano sueco Karl Gosselman, la diferenciación de las
nacionalidades europeas se podría ejercer a partir de unos marcadores
circunscritos a la esfera de lo público. La cultura, traducida en lo que
Bourdieu ha denominado *habitus*, podría ser un elemento decisivo a
tener en cuenta en los procesos de representación. Para Gosselman de
este modo las nacionalidades se distinguían básicamente por sus gustos:
el inglés podría pedir el brandy con agua, el francés una taza de café, y el
colombiano chocolate, "siempre que antes no haya pedido a gritos: 'Pon-

che de huevos', que los jóvenes especialmente, toman gustosos" (Gosselman 1981: 41).

Ya en este orden de ideas llegamos al punto en donde la representación del extranjero en un contexto internacional se vinculaba al ámbito de lo público, y fundamentalmente a través del mundo del trabajo y de las relaciones de producción. Así pues, con respecto al escenario del comercio, Gosselman llegó a sostener que los ingleses, norteamericanos y franceses desempeñaban el papel de "agentes" comerciales, mientras que los colombianos eran básicamente los dueños de las embarcaciones (117). Pero contrariamente a como pudiera creerse, este vínculo entre profesión y nacionalidad no resulta tan objetivo. De hecho el perfil ilustrado que tenían algunos europeos los "obligaba" a ocupar ciertas profesiones a las cuales eran ciertamente ajenos. Así, los franceses eran tenidos generalmente como buenos peluqueros, o vendedores de cepillos, jabones o perfumes, pero también como ingenieros, dadas las obras de construcción del Canal de Panamá.

Resulta vistoso el deslizamiento laboral que llevó a cabo un herrero francés al presentarse como ingeniero en una empresa minera colombiana. En aquel caso singular, dicho herrero, que no obstante ejercía como un buen obrero en París, al encontrar unos negociantes que tenían por encargo regresar con un técnico para acometer la empresa de perforación de un pozo en una mina de la zona de Antioquía, emprendió aquella insólita tarea. Dudando en principio, el herrero se procuró una enciclopedia y se dirigió a su nuevo trabajo, con tan poco éxito que, tras ser despedido, tuvo que trabajar como arquitecto de la catedral de la ciudad de Riohacha (Reclus 1861: 163-64). Dicho relato, lejos de ser una simple y picaresca exageración, es un correlato de un caso similar que habría documentado ochenta años antes el misionero jesuita italiano Philippo Salvatore Gilij. En aquella ocasión sería un neogranadino quién le ofrecería al francés, en virtud de su nacionalidad, presentarse como un médico y actuar como tal, de manera que era el propio colombiano quien efectuaba la preparación de los remedios, aunque ganando la clientela a través de la fachada que le proporcionaba el europeo (Gilij 1955: 174). Podemos decir, pues, que era la representación de lo nacional lo que en algunos casos motivaba las dinámicas ocupacionales de la población migrante.

En este punto, nos preguntamos: ¿por qué no podía ser la faceta de agricultor la representación más usual para los inmigrantes y colonos europeos? Y es que en disonancia con el proyecto eugenésico de formación nacional —derivado a la postre de las teorías del mestizaje—, la legislación que promovía la inmigración de europeos resultaba inoperante incluso a pesar de haber sido proclive en gran medida hacia los europeos. Charles Cochrane no dudaría en destacar las ventajas que implicaba la introducción de colonos europeos, y frente a ello opinaba que el gobierno parecía estar lo suficientemente persuadido de ello; de hecho, consideraba que Colombia tenía unas ventajas en términos de productividad que le serían muy beneficiosas en el futuro (87). Gaspard Theodor Mollien, el célebre viajero enemigo de Bolívar, destacaba igualmente la puesta en acción de una "generosa medida del gobierno" que se había ampliado aún más, y que en la época habría puesto unos dos millones de fanegadas para que se distribuyeran "gratuitamente entre las familias extranjeras" que quisieron establecerse en el país, con la condición de roturar la parte correspondiente dentro del año en que la concesión les fuera hecha" (1824: 204). Para el propio Cochrane, sin embargo, las medidas de promoción gubernamental tendientes al fomento de la migración no serían nunca suficientes, y aún cuando reconocía que seguramente el índice de europeos en América aumentaría, ello no tendría una "influencia importante sobre la forma del nuevo gobierno" (232).

Pero como es sabido, el devenir de Colombia como un destino migratorio o de colonización agrícola no resultó ser un proyecto exitoso. Las variables en juego y que supusieron el fracaso fueron varias. Se opinaría por ejemplo que la principal dificultad que encontrarían los europeos en su transformación en colonos sería la resistencia de los grupos indígenas —llamados— "salvajes" (Reclus 1861: 227). Pero además del clima y de los "salvajes", los viajeros también mencionaron las condiciones de explotación a las que se veían sometidos los inmigrantes europeos. Gosselman narra el encuentro con un compatriota suyo, quien tenía como trabajo la penosa labor de reclutar mineros alemanes a base de engaños y promesas truculentas (153). Alfred Hettner por su parte menciona el caso de una cuadrilla de zapateros alemanes que habrían sido seducidos bajo el equívoco proyecto de un empresario colombiano que se proponía venderles zapatos a los indígenas (Hettner 1976: 212). El mismo Reclus describe la situación de una colonia agrícola dirigida por un empresario colombiano, el cual, basándose en la importación de mano de obra genovesa, habría fracasado; sus réditos fueron totalmente diferentes de lo que hubiera sido un proceso espontáneo de colonización, en el cual aquellos mismos campesinos italianos habrían tenido más éxito por sí solos (1861: 145).

Para el suizo Ernst Röthlisberguer, profesor de la Universidad Nacional, el tema de la adaptación de los nuevos colonos europeos, teniendo en cuenta las dificultades inherentes a la naciente república, se vincularía así no solo con las condiciones convergentes al propio fenómeno migratorio, sino con las motivaciones mismas que lo ejercitaron. Era plausible, entonces, que gentes totalmente desposeídas en Europa prefiriesen tener algo en propiedad a cambio de un aislamiento del mundo y de otras duras privaciones. En un sentido paralelo, Reclus mostraría esas tierras, no solamente como ejemplo de abundancia, sino como receptáculo para aquellos que huyeran (como era su caso en tanto que exiliado) de las "prisiones culturales del nuevo mundo" (145). El Dorado no solo era el país del oro sino también el de la libertad. Esta visión optimista sería parcialmente compartida por el coronel John Potter Hamilton, inglés, quien no tendría duda del crecimiento de la emigración de europeos, pero condicionaba dicho proceso a que hubiesen gobiernos bien establecidos y, fundamentalmente, a que hubiese una "tolerancia en asuntos religiosos". Una vez logradas esas premisas, sin duda se vería "el gran poderío físico de las fértiles mesetas de Sur América progresar, ya que poseen quizás los climas mejores del mundo, aun cuando se hallan tan cerca del Ecuador" (Hamilton 1827: 155).

Sea como fuere, la vinculación de la nacionalidad al desempeño de una labor u oficio que dotara a la postre de un sentido de identidad, la reiteración de anécdotas acerca de emigrantes motivados por la búsqueda de El Dorado, fueron muy significativas. Recuerda Hamilton la escena en donde un soldado de la legión británica que combatiera junto a Bolívar, habiendo encontrado una moneda de plata en el suelo, decidió súbitamente patearla aduciendo que él había llegado al destino americano en búsqueda de oro, y que no permitiría mancharse las manos con una moneda de plata (Hamilton 1827: 219). Ya se tratara de la libertad pretendida por Reclus, de los secretos del orden universal que buscaba Humboldt, o de las perlas que pretendía Cochrane, podríamos decir, finalmente, que la búsqueda de un tesoro sería un elemento compartido entre los europeos que emigraron a la Colombia del siglo XIX y esto, desde diferentes lecturas, fue el mensaje recogido por los viajeros acerca de la identidad y de las nacionalidades europeas.

Bibliografía

Benjamin, W. 1991 [1939] *Paris, Capital du XIXe siècle,* Paris, Gallimard.

Cochrane, C. 1825. *Journal of a Residence and Travels in Colombia during the Years 1823 and 1824,* vol. 2, London, Henry Colburn.

Gilij, P. 1955 [1782], *Ensayo de Historia Americana–Estado de la tierra firme,* Bogotá, Editorial Sucre.

Gosselman, C. 1981 [1826]. *Viaje por Colombia: 1825 y 1826,* Bogotá, Talleres Gráficos del Banco de la República, <www.banrepcultural.org/blaavirtual/historia/viajes/indice.htm> [consultado el 18.X.2012].

Hamilton, J. P. 1827. *Travels through the Interior Provinces of Colombia,* vol. 1, London, John Murray.

Hettner, A. 1976 [1888]. *Viajes por los Andes colombianos (1882-1884),* Bogotá, Talleres Gráficos del Banco de la República, <www.banrepcultural.org/blaavirtual/historia/viaand/indice.html> [consultado el 18.X.2012].

Holton, I. 1857. *New Granada: Twenty Months in the Andes,* New York, Harper and Brothers.

Mollien, G. T. 1824. *Voyage dans la République de Colombia en 1823,* vol. 2, Paris, Arthus Bertrand.

Reclus, E. 1861. *Voyage à la Sierra Nevada de Sainte-Marthe: paysage de la nature tropicale,* Paris, Hachette.

—. 1893. "Colombie", in E. Reclus (ed.), *Nouvelle Géographie Universelle. La terre et ses hommes,* vol. 18, Paris, Hachette.

Röthlisberguer , E. 1963 [1896]. *El Dorado: estampas de viaje y cultura de la Colombia suramericana,* Bogotá, Talleres Gráficos del Banco de la República. <www.banrepcultural.org/blaavirtual/historia/eldorado/indice.htm> [consultado el 18.X.2012].

Saffray, C. 1872. "Voyage à la Nouvelle Grenade-De Sainte-Marthe à Turbaco", *Le Tour du Monde* 24, 81-96.

—. 1873. "Voyage à la Nouvelle Grenade-Du Rio Verde à Manizales", *Le Tour du Monde* 25, 113-28.

EDUARD MOYÀ

Forty Years Shaping the Balearics: the Playground of British Travellers and their Imagery of Pleasure (1903–1939)

In 1926 travel writer and novelist Rose Macaulay published *Crewe Train*, a social comedy of manners that criticised the highbrow intellectual circle of London. In the first pages of the novel, the reader perceives how the protagonist's father, tired of the "so busy, so sociable" (3) English parish life, decides to change his occupation and country for a quieter life: "He recalled the island of Mallorca, where he and his wife had once spent a very pleasant spring holiday [...] agreeable and cheap" (3-4). He buys a house in Sóller and "[a]t first he was very happy and peaceful" (4), but then "[t]he English came" (4). The narrator explains how "[a]rtists came, spreading themselves over the town and port, painting their foolish pictures of the landscape and the natives" (4). The protagonists leave the island and decide never to come back.

The story of travel literature in the Balearics in the first forty years of the twentieth century follows a very similar reaction to that portrayed by Macaulay in her novel: travellers to the islands journey with the belief that they are the last witnesses of an idyllic life that is disappearing. Yet, in differing degrees, they themselves, ironically, contribute to its disappearance by portraying and re-creating their idea of paradise for more readers, travellers and tourists.

Travellers to the Balearics in the nineteenth century depict a little developed, scarcely visited destination with few facilities compared to other Mediterranean resorts. This factor makes the journey through the islands a hazardous effort and fills the accounts with rich anecdotes and picturesque encounters. As a result of this contact, Victorians present a variety of images and stereotypes that are sometimes redeployed by subsequent travellers. This article explores how, in the twentieth century, travellers such as Margaret D'Este, Mary Stuart Boyd, J. E. Crawford Flitch, Douglas Goldring, Ada Harrison, Gordon West, and Francis

Caron, amongst many, adopt or reject these images in order to recreate them or formulate new ones regarding the place and the people visited. This article will begin with an analysis of contextual factors and sensibilities in Britain and in the Balearics and then proceed to identify and explore three distinctive periods in the development of the Balearic image by British travellers in the first third of the twentieth century. These are from 1903 to 1914, from 1915 to 1929, and from 1929 to 1939.

The Empire of the mind (1903-1914)

Regarding this first period, travellers find the Balearics in somewhat different circumstances from those found by their predecessors in the previous century. The first hotels are being built in Palma and there is a growing awareness among the local community of the need to develop the tourist industry. British travellers of this period, self-appointed inheritors of a distinctive (and authoritative) way of understanding travel, journey through the islands conscious of their nature as travellers, not as modern tourists.

Although the travellers do not attack the figure of the tourist openly, there is in their accounts, especially in D'Este's *With a Camera in Majorca* (1907), Boyd's *The Fortunate Isles* (1911) and Flitch's *Mediterranean Moods* (1911), a sense of belonging to an exclusive tradition of travellers. This is perceived in their aims and discourses. Their aims lie in the artistic, photographic, and textual representation and preservation of what they present as the last days of a world threatened by a new modern practice: tourism, the result of the industrialisation of the North. Their discourse is similar to their predecessors' inasmuch as they present the Other as an object of meticulous observation. This observation, however, is biased by what the travellers (or travellers before them) considered to be authentic images of the South. In order to present their narratives as the authentic product of travel and observation, the authors reuse accepted, traditional and hegemonic images that concentrate on the picturesquely local or, again, on what others have perceived as local before them. By deploying a traditional discourse and re-creating old images, the travellers, particularly women such as D'Este and Boyd, seem to seek recognition and authority in a long-established masculine literary field.

Despite the fact that these travel accounts are presented as scrupulously factual (following the conventions of non-fictional literature such as travel guides or ethnographic reports), there is a strong deployment of picturesque imagery that is arguably influenced by previous historical or narrative sources. Hence, with D'Este, Harrison and Flitch, Majorca and Ibiza appear quaintly Southern if not Oriental, hardly touched by modern life. Towns appear as "Arab fortresses, white, flat-roofed, and dominated by a single palm" whose beauty seems to be "the illusion of a desert oasis" (Flitch 1911: 169). Arabian traits work as a constant textual reference to previous exoticist and Orientalist discourses.

The trope "Sunny South" used by previous travellers is reutilised by D'Este, Boyd and Flitch (although the latter develops it more philosophically, projecting cultural values onto the land), who see in the sun the epitome of the Mediterranean. All travellers from D'Este to Flitch use a wide selection of colours in the descriptions of the Balearic landscape. Descriptions of food and exotic fruit are also found in their narratives. The olive tree becomes a representation of the connection between ancient times (and wise, shrewd agriculture) and the effects of the sun: "[the olive tree] recalls the antiquity of Mediterranean civilisation, and might well stand for the symbol of it" (Flitch 1911: 111).

The spell woven by Southern images in these accounts is so strong that any landscape not following these patterns of representation is rejected. This is the case for Barcelona, too industrialised to correspond to the idea of quaint Spain (Goldring 1925: 6; West 1939: 37); for Sóller, in some descriptions too rainy and not Southern-looking enough (Boyd 1911: 89) and, especially, for Minorca, which "must be put down as painfully and typically English" (D'Este 1907: 145) due to its recent British history.

Locals are only important if they appear picturesque or, idealistically (and rigidly) exotic. Stereotypes of the industrious old peasant and the lazy Spanish city-dweller appear to be more the result of an ideological projection than of the fruit of reliable observation. In addition, despite the travellers' love of what they consider to be truly local, there is a concealed paternalistic wish to preserve the Other as ancient and primitive, depriving the local people of their chance to progress. In a colonialist context, accepting an evolutionary perception of civilisation, this could be the interpretation of a mature society (the British travellers) depicting an immature, underdeveloped and naïve community (the Balearics). From the cultural relativist perspective, this device is merely the result of the infantilisation of the Other. The confinement of the Balearics to their rigid stereotype is reproduced (possibly unintentionally) by subsequent discourses, such as those of Harrison —portraying the ultra-picturesque— or Goldring.

Ultimately, the discourses of these travellers (D'Este, Boyd, partially Flitch and possibly Harrison) utilise the hegemonic tools deployed by former colonialist travel narratives. They unwittingly consolidate the idea of a hegemonic centre (developed, modern, and moral) and a picturesque periphery (colourfully primitive, lagging behind technologically and morally unconstrained).

Southern utopias (1915-1929)

The First World War scarred a generation of British travellers and writers. In the words of Samuel Hynes, "[t]he mood of bitterness that emerged from the First World War has no like in any other war that England has fought" (1968: 14). Despite winning the war, there was a sense of desolation that led many intellectuals and artists to adopt an acute scepticism in the new era of the machine. This made many of those intellectuals, artists and writers look for alternative ways of life. Gathering old tropes from previous travel narratives on the Mediterranean, many travellers set their sights on the Balearic Islands as the epitome of their desire: a sunny land of abundance unpolluted by the modern, philistine, capitalist modernity that had led them to war. The Balearics, therefore, are presented as personal utopias on which to project the travellers' melioristic fantasies.

In this period of travel (1915-1929) there are discourses as rich as those of Douglas Goldring's *Gone Abroad* (1925) or Ada Harrison's *A Majorca Holiday* (1927), all of which stress the idea of the Other as charged with a positive value, working as a counter-example. The Other is the mirror by means of which British society is reflected, criticised and attacked. The tourist, as the incarnation of an industrialised and consumerist life, is the focus of the travellers' criticism.

Despite having published *Mediterranean Moods* before the First World War (1911), Flitch represents the discursive bridge between two periods of understanding travel in the South. The anxiety of Flitch, as in our era, has more to do with time than with space (Foucault and Miskowiec 1986: 22). This is reflected in his account. Flitch reproduces the fantasised old scenes of nineteenth-century travel narratives (like those of Bartholomew, Clayton, Wood, D'Este, and Boyd) where an idyllic pre-industrialised society lived in accordance with the rhythms of nature. What is modern in Flitch's discourse, however, is the realisation of the pointlessness of wanting to preserve these imagined scenes and the recognition of the ever-consuming power of time. After an epistemological epiphany, the traveller learns that in the Mediterranean the only universal elements that will outlast civilisations and empire are the eternal sea (the same sea as that of the ancients, but which is constantly renewing itself) and the immortal flesh and spirit of youth: "For I was looking on two things that were unconquerable, certainly enduring, always beautiful, and always young—the human flesh and the sea" (1911: 288). Further accounts seem to adopt Flitch's conclusion and reify it.

Goldring presents a sensual paradise that lies in a pleasurable fringe far away from the established centre (symbolised by home, the ruling British upper classes and tourism). Places like Ibiza work as a perfect spatial, temporal and social margin in which the traveller can transgress and return to a playful, leisurely and desired space: "too good to be true: the island of our dreams" (Goldring 1925: 74). Harrison's writing, bringing together discourses from both periods, recreates the islands as a resort for a generation's fantasy for escaping and transgressing under the sun. Ultra-exotic traits define the islands, with the exception of Minorca, not as essentially Mediterranean but no less essentially pleasurable: "One sits for an age warmed through by sun and a sweet formless sensation of thought, watching the sea a thousand times lap over and uncover the same point of rock" (Harrison 1927: 20). The sun is the discursive engine of Harrison's journey. She uses the orange as a metaphor, as a reification of the sun, and a new symbol of the South: flavoursome, sunny, and ready to be consumed in an "ecstasy of freshness" (141). Minorca is excluded from the Southern paradise due to its lack of participation (according to the travellers) in the idea of "South". This, arguably, results in the disproportionately slow evolution of Minorcan tourism in comparison to the rest of the islands.

As regards the representation of people, in the eyes of Goldring, only the marginalised are the true carriers of an exotic, pure essence. They live in a spatial margin (living far from the tourist resorts), and a social one: smugglers, dangerous-looking bandits and untamed Ibizans exemplify Goldring's ideal of the Balearic inhabitant. Between the locals and Teresita —Goldring's English travel partner— an erotic dialogue is established. Harrison reprises the representational discourse of D'Este and Boyd and focuses on the ultra-picturesque element to define the locals. Only the exotic appears to be truly local in the eyes of Harrison. In her compulsion to preserve the Other as picturesquely as possible, she constrains the locals to very rigid patterns of representation, to the extent that Majorcans are considered to be more authentic the more they resemble the Andalusian imagotype, a broader and more recognizable figure (Harrison 1927: 204).

Despite a consciously poignant attack on tourists and the connotations they embody (consumerist behaviour, conceited lack of interest towards anything local, anxiety to collect tourist markers, etc.), many of these travellers fail to provide a convincing alternative. A lack of true dialogue (with the exception of Flitch) leads the travellers to present inflexible and stereotyped portraits. Furthermore, by reifying their fantasies and projections of what the South should be, the travellers turn their utopias into exotic non-places where any transgression is possible. This transgressive exoticism is eventually commercialised in the following years and comes to signify the major branding label and source of income of the islands.

The "Med" is the flesh (1929-1939)

Travel literature in the Balearics in the 1930s shows two of the major symptoms of the era before the Spanish Civil War and the Second World War. On the one hand, a profound scepticism of the establishment leads to revisiting traditional discourses of travel; on the other, there is a vertiginous sense of carefree joy before the presage of a deluge to come.

The first of these is exemplified by Gordon West's *Jogging Round Majorca* (1929), which revisits the traditional travel tropes (especially those of adventure and exploration) in a mocking and ironic way similar to other travel writers of the time (such as Byron, Waugh, and Fleming). Instead of falling back on the security of pure cliché, considered commonplace and touristic (Fussell 1980: 39-40), West emphasises his misadventures as a traveller journeying with a tourist, his wife. Traditional tropes like "the true encounter", "authenticity" or "romance" are presented in a farcical manner rather than to illustrate knowledge of the Other (as previous travellers such as D'Este, Boyd and Flitch tried to do), in order to present anecdote and a light-hearted travel narrative.

Francis Caron's *Majorca: the Diary of a Painter* (1939) presents the generational problem (according to Hynes, that of the Auden generation) of young men facing maturity in a world that seems to have lost the support of old values and morals. The fulfilment of this generation's fantasies results for Caron, and, for a wide expatriate community, in a rite of passage (mainly sexual) to be performed in the South. The Balearics, representative of that Southern model, become the locus of this pleasurable marginal space (again with the exception of Minorca). West's representation of the Balearic landscape includes a certain amount of flirtation and carefree joyousness, providing the reassurance of leisure and *joie de vivre*. This feeling is also shared by Caron who states: "how beautiful life can be! And Majorca, and my room I had absolutely for myself. '[A] tramp's life'—how beautiful it was after school" (1939: 8). Caron's account offers the right erotic tone to consecrate certain spaces and certain activities as openly licit, reminding the reader how "refreshing [it is] to be a man alone on this island" (1939: 97).

Despite mocking several traditional travel tropes in an original way, West utilises all the stereotyped traits of the Southern landscape: turquoise seas and a golden sun at the disposal of the travellers' fantasies. Such scenery, however, is dispossessed of any former value (ancient, quaint and perishable —in the eyes of D'Este and Boyd— or as a model to be followed in the case of Flitch). West's landscapes only work as colourful settings for what is important in the narrative, the travellers' action: "One wants to play at Robinson Crusoe here! One wants to play at desert islands! One wants to make love, to be romantic, to dream all the impossibly-coloured dreams of youth!" (1929: 262). In the case of Caron, the presentation of two clearly separate spaces shows the under-

standing of the artist's perceptions. On the one hand, he presents a day-
time environment, local, sunny and lethargic (not necessarily as a negative term); on the other, a night scene populated by an international
community dedicated to leisure and, especially, to the fulfilment of sexual pleasure:

> I know a lot of married women who are always worrying their husbands because
> they want to be petted and fussed over, and distracting their husbands from the se-
> rious business of making money. Of course their husbands jump at the chance if
> their wives say that they want to go for a little trip alone. Women like that often
> decide to go to Majorca. They like the idea of a warm climate combined with the
> famous Spanish temperament (Caron 1939: 84).

As a result of these perceptions, both West's and Caron's narratives are
peopled by caricatures at the service of the narrators' purpose rather than
by plausible characters. The hollow portraits of these accounts lead the
reader to think that they are the consequence of fantasised projections as
much as of the impossibility of attaining real communication with the
locals. Because of this lack of exchange of ideas with the locals, and
especially a lack of observation, the travel narrative undergoes fictionali-
sation, disassociating itself from the previously non-fictional tones found
at the beginning of the century. Furthermore, it is the travellers, their
companions (Teresita in the case Goldring's account; the Spirit of Joy in
West's) and the expatriate community (in the case of Caron) that become
the protagonists and, as such, gain agency. Their action (not that of the
Other, the depiction of landscape, or the Mediterranean spirit) is what
counts.

Ultimately, accounts like West's and Caron's represent the evolution of the stereotype spread by the European Romantic travellers, who
concentrated on the particularly local. Passion (as essentially Spanish)
was valorised to the detriment of Reason (as naturally non-Spanish).
Future visitors assumed it to be true. Victorians recreated the same discourse including the Balearics as part of the joyful and indolent Sunny
South. Late Victorians (D'Este) and Edwardians (Boyd and Flitch) regarded the Balearics as a source of pleasure for the mind, recognising a
picturesque and exotic way of life on the verge of disappearance. Finally,
the interwar travellers (Goldring, Harrison, West and Caron) legitimated
it as a transgressive space for the fulfilment and pleasure of the senses.

Bibliography

Boyd, M. S. 1911. *The Fortunate Isles: Life and Travel in Majorca, Minorca and Iviza*, London, Methuen.

Caron, F. 1939. *Majorca: The Diary of a Painter*, London, Cassell.

D'Este, M. 1907. *With a Camera in Majorca*, New York & London, Putnam's and Sons.

Flitch, J. E. C. 1911. *Mediterranean Moods: Footnotes of Travel in the Islands of Mallorca, Menorca, Ibiza and Sardinia*, London, Grant Richards.

Foucault, M. & J. Miskowiec. 1986. "Of Other Spaces", *Diacritics* 16: 1, 22-27.

Fussell, P. 1980. *Abroad: British Literary Travel Writing between the Wars*, Oxford, Oxford UP.

Goldring, D. 1925. *Gone Abroad: A Story of Travel, Chiefly in Italy and the Balearic Isles*, London: Chapman and Hall.

Harrison, A. 1927. *A Majorca Holiday*, London, Gerald Howe.

Hynes, S. 1968. *The Edwardian Turn of Mind*, Princeton, NJ, Princeton UP.

Macaulay, R. 1926. *Crewe Train*, London, Collins.

West, G. 1929. *Jogging Round Majorca*, London, Alston Rivers.

Paulina Nalewajko

El retrato del extranjero-peregrino a partir de *Doce cuentos peregrinos* de Gabriel García Márquez

Doce cuentos peregrinos es un libro excepcional en la producción literaria de Gabriel García Márquez. No es una simple recopilación de varios cuentos escritos en un período de tiempo determinado sino un conjunto de historias que persiguen un tema con la misma persistencia con la cual el tema persigue al autor durante años: los latinoamericanos en Europa y sus aventuras extrañas. De esta manía nos informa el mismo autor en el prólogo titulado "Porqué doce, porqué cuentos y porqué peregrinos" que narra la anécdota nostálgica del peregrinaje de los textos y del sufrimiento del autor que durante décadas enteras no puede concluir su obra. Asimismo, impone las pautas de interpretación. Nos enteramos de que al principio el autor tuvo varios temas anotados que debían formar "una colección de cuentos cortos, basados en hechos periodísticos pero redimidos de su condición mortal por las astucias de la poesía" (2007: 6). El objetivo era "escribirlos todos con un mismo trazo, y con una unidad interna de tono y de estilo que los hiciera inseparables en la memoria del lector" (7). Al cabo de décadas de intentos frustrados han surgido doce cuentos escritos en años y lugares distintos que dan "una visión panorámica" (10) de la inmigración latinoamericana en Europa.

No todos los protagonistas son peregrinos en el sentido religioso de la palabra. Algunos están en el Viejo Mundo por primera vez con la firme decisión de cumplir con sus objetivos y volver al continente americano, otros son inmigrantes sin esperanza ni derecho a volver. Son personas de diferentes edades y profesiones, tanto los hombres como las mujeres. La descripción de cada personaje sería solo una reescritura inútil de la obra una vez hecha por el maestro colombiano y además privada de su encanto. Por eso, en el presente trabajo nos centraremos en el análisis de la representación de dos procesos que se realizan en las mentes de los protagonistas y que en nuestra opinión aseguran "la unidad interna de tono y de estilo" que ha deseado el autor. Estos procesos son la percepción y el reconocimiento.

Nuestro análisis parte del caso más extremo de la extranjera-peregrina —la señora Prudencia Linero—, la protagonista del cuento "Diecisiete ingleses envenenados". En su ejemplo podemos observar cómo la experiencia personal impone la manera de percibir el mundo y a los demás. Es una mujer mayor que ha pasado toda su vida en Riohacha casi sin salir de casa, cuidando a su marido gravemente enfermo. Su único pasatiempo en aquella época era la práctica de los ritos católicos y el sueño de su vida, ver al Sumo Pontífice. Después de la muerte del marido, la protagonista decide cumplir su sueño y emprende el viaje por mar a Europa. Ofrece a Dios llevar el hábito hasta la muerte, si le permite llegar a Roma y ver al Papa. La protagonista percibe los obstáculos en el camino como parte de la "penitencia" (151). El problema empieza cuando aparecen unas dificultades distintas de las previstas. La mujer, hasta ahora encerrada entre cuatro paredes, tiene que funcionar sola en la Nápoles de la postguerra que iba a ser solamente la parada en su camino a Roma. Su percepción del mundo se realiza por la comparación de todo lo que encuentra con los pocos elementos que conoce de la vida y del mundo. Las únicas cosas que le consuelan son las que reconoce de América:

> Lo primero que notó la señora Prudencia Linero cuando llegó al puerto de Nápoles, fue que tenía el mismo olor del puerto de Riohacha. [...] se sintió menos sola, menos asustada y distante, a los setenta y dos años de su edad y a dieciocho días de mala mar de su gente y de su casa (141).

En la parte última del cuento, la misma sensación olfatoria y la visión del mar le permiten orientarse cuando se pierde en la ciudad. Esta vez, sin embargo, también los elementos recientemente conocidos se convierten en los objetos de reconocimiento: los hoteles en la playa, los taxis, etc. Todo ello formaba una novedad sujeta a la percepción y ahora son puntos de referencia que permiten ubicarse en la ciudad y encontrarse en el mundo nuevo. Porque para la mujer, este mundo de Nápoles, de Europa, el continente tradicionalmente llamado el Viejo Mundo, es absolutamente nuevo.

Entre los otros viajeros la protagonista se siente sola por llevar ropa distinta, hablar otro idioma y tener costumbres diferentes. Su figura contrasta con el trasfondo formado por otros pasajeros que vuelven a casa, reconocen el puerto, los elementos arquitectónicos de la ciudad, a sus familiares y amigos que les están esperando. La señora Linero todo esto lo percibe por primera vez, lo que agranda el sentimiento de soledad causado por el hecho de que nadie la espera en el puerto:

> pensó que el mal no estaba en el corazón de los otros sino en el suyo, por ser ella la única que iba entre la muchedumbre que regresaba. Así deben ser todos los viajes, pensó, padeciendo por primera vez en su vida la punzada de ser forastera, mientras contemplaba desde la borda los vestigios de tantos mundos extinguidos en el fondo del agua (143).

Respecto al tema de la otredad, Gabriel García Márquez parece preferir el uso del vocablo más amplio "forastero" —su empleo es muy frecuente, por ejemplo, en *La hojarasca*, *Cien años de soledad*, *Vivir para contarla*—, es decir, "que es o que viene de otro lugar", que "extranjero", o sea, "de una nación que no es la propia" (Clave). A partir de esto podemos notar la diferencia entre la percepción de otredad en el continente europeo y en el americano. Los europeos tenemos muy arraigado el concepto de la nacionalidad como el factor primordial que distingue unos grupos de otros. El escritor colombiano suele subrayar el "contraste humano" (Mendoza y García Márquez 1994: 52) que existe dentro de la misma nación colombiana entre los costeños y los colombianos de la cordillera, expresando de esta manera una versión especial suya del determinismo geográfico.

Profundicemos ahora en la expresión "la punzada de ser forastera". La protagonista se siente forastera por primera vez en su vida. Lo percibe como una "punzada", es decir: "1) Dolor agudo, repentino y pasajero, que suele repetirse cada cierto tiempo. 2) Herida hecha con la punta de un objeto" (Clave). El uso de este preciso vocablo sugiere que el sentimiento de ser de otro lugar se percibe de manera tan fuerte y penosa como dolor o herida y que la angustia va a repetirse varias veces.

Esta descripción forma parte de una de las dos series paralelas en las que se basa la construcción del cuento: las impresiones de Nápoles que experimenta la protagonista se asocian con las descripciones del estado emocional de la mujer. Este paralelismo se inscribe en el fenómeno analizado entre otros por Mario Vargas Llosa que distingue las "repeticiones en la materia y en la forma" (1971: 598-607). Rómulo Cosse nombra el fenómeno "el paralelismo estructural" (124-25) y observa (refiriéndose a *Cien años de soledad*) que "esta peculiaridad de seriar segmentos que asumen un mismo carácter sintáctico tiende a inmovilizar el discurso y fijarlo, produciendo la impresión de un cuerpo que proyecta sus fantasmas y por lo tanto de un ensimismamiento repetitivo" (25).

El fragmento que en nuestra opinión mejor demuestra el empleo del procedimiento es el siguiente:

> *Fascinada* por el espectáculo que parecía ejecutado en su honor, pues sólo ella lo agradecía, la señora Prudencia Linero no se dio cuenta de en qué momento tendieron la pasarela, y una avalancha humana invadió el barco con los aullidos y el ímpetu de un abordaje de bucaneros. *Aturdida* por el júbilo del tufo de cebollas rancias de tantas familias en verano, *vapuleada* por las cuadrillas de cargadores que se disputaban a golpes los equipajes, se sintió *amenazada* por la misma muerte sin gloria de los políticos en el muelle (144-45; los subrayados son nuestros).

En un fragmento de apenas unas líneas aparecen referencias a distintas emociones y estados, todas expresadas con la misma estructura: los participios pasados. Primero la mujer queda "fascinada" por la situación que nunca antes ha experimentado. La índole del verbo *fascinar* y de la forma adjetivada *el espectáculo de maravilla* sugieren un sentimiento positivo, lo que contrasta fuertemente con la imagen presentada a continuación de "una avalancha humana" que "invade" el sitio. La multitud de sensaciones —imágenes, sonidos, olores— provoca "el aturdimiento" de la mujer hasta convertirla en un objeto golpeado, "vapuleado" por los cargadores interesados solamente en ganar clientes. La mujer empieza a sentirse "amenazada", la impresión que se repite en varias versiones hasta el final del cuento: "asustada" (154), "sobrecogida" (148), "aterrorizada" (146), "despavorida" (155). El uso repetitivo de participios pasados da la impresión de pasividad e inmovilidad. La cantidad de impresiones y acontecimientos es demasiado grande para la pobre mujer que pasó treinta años "cuidando del cuerpo sin alma de su esposo" (149) y solamente quiso ver al Papa antes de morir.

No se nos informa de si la mujer llega por fin a la audiencia con el Papa. Se suspende la historia cuando, al enterarse de la muerte de diecisiete turistas ingleses a los que vio una vez en el hotel, la protagonista busca refugio en su cuarto:

Otra vez con el nudo de lágrimas en la garganta, la señora Prudencia Linero *pasó* los cerrojos de la habitación. Luego *rodó* contra la puerta la mesita de escribir y la poltrona, y *puso* por último el baúl como una barricada infranqueable contra el horror de aquel país donde ocurrían tantas cosas al mismo tiempo. [...] (156; los subrayados son nuestros).

El dramatismo que domina el fragmento se debe al empleo del paralelismo estructural. Esta vez, sin embargo, se utilizan las formas verbales cortas de la voz activa (Pretérito Indefinido): "pasó", "rodó", "puso". Gracias a esto la escena final gana un fuerte dinamismo, especialmente contrastado con el anterior uso de los participios pasados. La mudanza de las formas verbales realza el cambio brusco en el comportamiento de la mujer que no soporta el contraste del mundo que observa con la vida tranquila que conocía.

Podríamos suponer que el dramatismo comentado no resulta de la condición de extranjera sino de la vida anterior de la mujer limitada a cuidar al marido enfermo. Sin embargo, cambiamos de opinión cuando profundizamos en la situación de los protagonistas del cuento "El rastro de tu sangre en la nieve". Nena Daconte y Billy Sánchez de Ávila están enamorados y felices; se han casado recientemente en Cartagena de Indias. Los conocemos desde distintas perspectivas: primero el autor nos presenta las impresiones de los guardias que les dejan pasar la frontera entre España y Francia. Nos enteramos de que los esposos se identifican con los pasaportes diplomáticos; son jóvenes, bellos y ricos. El funcionario reconoce su estatus material a partir de la ropa, las joyas y el coche que están descritos con esmero. En breve, el punto de vista cambia, adoptando la perspectiva de Nena Daconte gracias a la que conocemos su historia amorosa y otros detalles del pasado de ambos esposos. Nos enteramos de que es ella quien ha recibido la formación en las mejores escuelas de Suiza, que domina unos idiomas perfectamente y que conoce Francia desde niña. El hábito de acordarse de los más pequeños detalles para hacer el viaje más agradable demuestra el lado pragmático de su carácter. Su marido, que ha crecido en libertad absoluta en América, parece un salvaje alegre, fuerte e impávido que siente que no hay "vientos contrarios ni bastante nieve en el cielo para impedir" (197) el cumplimiento de sus metas. También, a partir de las impresiones y los recuerdos de Nena, se nos informa de que la mujer se pinchó el dedo con un ramo de rosas. Las menciones de la herida ignorada al principio van repitiéndose con más frecuencia. Nena se está desangrando y pierde la conciencia en un hospital de Paris. En aquel momento, es la perspectiva de Billy que nos empieza a guiar. El chico está totalmente perdido en la capital de Francia. Su esposa era la que le comunicaba con este mundo nuevo y para él totalmente desconocido. Las más prosaicas actividades se presentan como un esfuerzo hercúleo sin el conocimiento de las reglas que reinan en aquel mundo. Sin Nena, Billy pierde toda su anterior confianza. Intenta visitar a su mujer en el hospital pero le informan de que solo la podrá ver dentro de unos días. A causa de la barrera lingüística no puede acceder a los detalles sobre el estado de salud de su esposa. Busca ayuda en la embajada pero solamente le instruyen de que "estaban en un país civilizado cuyas normas estrictas se fundaban en los criterios más antiguos y sabios, al contrario de las Américas bárbaras, donde bastaba con sobornar al portero para entrar en los hospitales" (216) y que debería esperar hasta el día indicado como día de visitas en el hospital. Eso es lo que hace Billy solo para enterarse de que su mujer murió setenta horas después de su ingreso en el hospital. Casi al final del cuento se nos cita también la perspectiva del funcionario de la embajada que atendió al chico. El oficial "nunca se hubiera imaginado que aquel costeño aturdido por la novedad de París, y con un abrigo de cordero tan mal llevado, tuviera a su favor un origen tan ilustre" (220).

Terminaremos con el análisis de la representación del proceso de reconocimiento en el cuento "Buen viaje, señor presidente". No solo es éste su tema principal sino que también domina el texto en el estrato lingüístico, lo que podemos ver en la estadística de las palabras. En el tomo entero los vocablos derivados del verbo reconocer aparecen treinta y dos veces de las cuales catorce se manifiestan en el cuento analizado.

El cuento narra la historia de un viejo ex-presidente de uno de los países caribeños que busca en Ginebra el remedio para su misteriosa enfermedad y allí le ayuda un matrimonio, una pareja de compatriotas pobres. Nunca nos enteramos de qué país del Caribe han venido exactamente. Todo y todos en este cuento se convierten en los objetos de reconocimiento: primero, el hombre que trabaja en el hospital reconoce al presidente que intenta ingresar de incógnito y le sigue por toda la ciudad. Luego, el presidente reconoce la cara del hombre y espanta al perseguidor.

El caso del presidente es especialmente interesante porque se trata del extranjero que al cabo de décadas vuelve a la ciudad que llegó a conocer bastante bien durante los estudios. El protagonista intenta reconocer el paisaje y a sí mismo:

> Estaba sentado en *el escaño de madera* bajo *las hojas amarillas* del parque solitario, contemplando *los cisnes polvorientos* con las dos manos apoyadas en *el pomo de plata* del bastón, y pensando en la muerte. Cuando vino a Ginebra por primera vez el lago era *sereno* y *diáfano*, y había gaviotas *mansas* que se acercaban a comer en las manos, y mujeres de alquiler que parecían fantasmas de las seis de la tarde, con volantes de *organdí* y sombrillas de *seda*. Ahora la única mujer posible, hasta donde alcanzaba la vista, era una vendedora de flores en el muelle *desierto*. Le costaba creer que el tiempo hubiera podido hacer semejantes *estragos* no sólo en su vida sino también en el mundo (15; los subrayados son nuestros)

En el fragmento citado se nos presenta la imagen de un parque solitario construida a base de solamente unos elementos dispersos: "el escaño de madera", "las hojas amarillas", etc. El procedimiento principal es el contraste entre el pasado y el presente. Lo anterior forma una imagen idílica llena de ternura y nostalgia característica de los recuerdos buenos. El autor consigue este efecto por la acumulación de adjetivos: "sereno", "diáfano", "manso", la mención de mujeres fantasmas y las telas poco comunes. Todo esto crea la impresión de lo extraordinario, lo exótico. La descripción del pasado se realiza en cuarenta y seis palabras mientras que la del presente únicamente en diecinueve. En la segunda aparecen solo dos elementos de los que uno está descrito por un adjetivo ("desierto") que da la impresión de solitud, carencia, destrucción. Todo se concluye con la metáfora conceptual (Lakoff y Johnson 2003) del tiempo que hace "estragos", es decir, de acuerdo con la definición del diccionario Clave: "daño, ruina o destrozo, especialmente los causados por una guerra o por una catástrofe". El tiempo es una fuerza destructora comparada a la guerra o a una catástrofe natural que arruina tanto la vida de las personas como el paisaje, el mundo entero.

A partir de las tres situaciones analizadas podemos suponer que la cantidad de las razones para emprender el viaje y las aventuras que pasan a los viajeros son tan grandes como el número de los inmigrantes latinoamericanos en Europa. Sin embargo, en un tomo de apenas doscientas páginas, Gabriel García Márquez logra crear "la visión panorámica" que era su objetivo. Su secreto parece ser la técnica prestada de un autor inglés: "Graham Greene resolvió ese problema literario de un modo muy certero: con unos pocos elementos dispersos, pero unidos por una coherencia subjetiva muy sutil y real. Con ese método se puede reducir todo el enigma del trópico a la fragancia de una guayaba podrida" (Mendoza y García Márquez 1994: 42).

En *Doce cuentos peregrinos* el premio Nobel colombiano reduce las historias concretas de millones de inmigrantes a doce narraciones empapadas en el ambiente raro, logrado gracias al extrañamiento e hiperbolización de hechos periodísticos. El panorama mantiene la coherencia debido al paralelismo estructural y logra diversidad por el uso del perspectivismo y de los incontables contrastes: entre los dos mundos, los tiempos diversos y sobre todo entre la gente. En este fondo vuelven como eco dos procesos: la percepción y el reconocimiento representados con "las astucias de la poesía". Probablemente todos han padecido alguna vez la "punzada de ser forasteros" pero solamente unos pocos saben expresar este sentimiento inmenso de manera tan lograda y contundente como Gabriel García Márquez.

Bibliografía

Clave: Diccionario de uso del español actual [2003], Madrid, Ediciones SM, [CD].

Cosse, R. 1984. *"Cien años de soledad*: ideología y plasmación narrativa", *Plural* 154, 22-26.

García Márquez, G. 1976. *Cien años de soledad*, Barcelona, Plaza & Janés.

—. 2007. *Doce cuentos peregrinos*, Barcelona, Debolsillo.

—. 1976. *La hojarasca*, Barcelona, Plaza & Janés.

—. 2002. *Vivir para contarla*, Barcelona, Mondadori.

Lakoff, G. & M. Johnson. 2003. *Metaphors We Live By*, Chicago & London, U of Chicago P.

Mendoza, P. A. & G. García Márquez. 1994. *El olor de la guayaba*, Barcelona, Mondadori.

Vargas Llosa, M. 1971. *Gabriel García Márquez. Historia de un deicidio*, Barcelona, Barral.

ISABEL OLIVEIRA MARTINS

The Representation of Otherness:
an American Vassar Girl's Perspective on Spain

By the end of the nineteenth century travel writing was already an established and accepted genre of writing among Americans following a trend that had also by then earned a very special status in Europe. Between 1660 and 1800, travel books appeared at a steady rate in Western Europe and by the end of the eighteenth century more than a hundred collections of travelogues had been printed, some in several editions, and others translated into various languages thus showing that it had become a popular genre as well as a profitable business.

The nineteenth century saw a substantial increase in travelling either by Europeans or Americans, and this was also the century that witnessed the rise of the tourism phenomenon, that is to say the regular travel *en masse*. Conditions had changed for Americans: after the end of the Civil War they had reached a political and social situation which allowed them to travel more and not just for utilitarian reasons but in search of a recreational experience just as their European counterparts had been doing for a long time.

Moreover, technological advances in transportation, namely the railroad and the steam-boat, made it possible for a greater variety of Americans to reach Europe in substantial numbers and visit several areas of the European continent quicker and much more comfortably (Schriber 1997; Decker 2009). Indeed this recreational side of American travelling was sought after to such a degree that it became a social phenomenon that would meet with severe criticism, as was observed in a rather caustic article in *Putnam's Magazine* in May 1868:

> It is not going abroad, in itself, that we condemn, but the aimless, gregarious, material, and, as it were, reckless vagabondage of our people, or, rather, a class of them, which, within the last few years, has increased to a multitude. They herd together in Paris, cling to their whiskey and buckwheats, never explore what is historic, or assimilate with the socially gifted. Idlers, they grow selfish through dissipation; bold

and unrefined, they cherish neither reverence nor admiration for the interests of wisdom and faith. Extravagant, indiscriminate, snobbish, they misrepresent abroad all that is nominally characteristic of our institutions or hopeful in our national life (Tuckerman 1868: 533-534).

If more Americans were travelling, then more travel books began to be published by Americans arguably to correspond to the need for an American perspective of abroad. When Elizabeth Champney, also known as Lizzie, went to Europe from 1874 to 1875 with her husband James Wells Champney —a well known New York genre painter and illustrator who illustrated the majority of Champney's works— she did so at a time that could by then be considered the "Tourist Age" when the market for any kind of new travel books seemed to have reached saturation point. Indeed, as early as 1848, the editors of *Blackwood's Edinburgh Magazine* in an article entitled "Modern Tourism" stated that mass travel was creating not only an undesirable new kind of traveller (the tourist) but also particularly a new breed of female:

> No sooner does the year shake off its robe of snow, and the sun begin to glimmer again, than the whole tribe are in motion; no matter where, all places are alike to their pens, the North Pole or the Antarctic. [...] But our horror is the professional tourist; the woman who runs abroad to forage for publication; reimports her baggage, bursting with a periodical gathering of nonsense; and with a freight of folly, at once empty as air and heavy as lead, discharges the whole at the heads of a suffering people ("Modern Tourism" 1848: 185).

Thus, when in 1883 Champney publishes her work *Three Vassar Girls Abroad*, the first of a series of eleven travel stories for girls that were published up until 1892, she was most certainly aware of all the constraints regarding the publishing of one more travel book and particularly one written by a woman. The complete title of the book —*Rambles of Three College Girls on a Vacation Trip Through France and Spain for Amusement and Instruction; With Their Haps and Mishaps*— clearly shows the author had in mind a specific type of reader which would in turn imply a specific way of writing.

Being herself a graduate of the Vassar class of 1869, Champney became a popular writer of articles and books about her travels in England, France, Morocco, Spain, Portugal and other countries. In this particular work she narrates the recreational journey of three Vassar students across Europe, mainly through France and Spain, a brief visit to Portugal and a short trip across to Tangier. Using a third person narrator, Champney also introduces the reader to a variety of character and personality, since she uses three main characters: Maud Van Vechten, a wealthy society girl who comes to Europe with her sister, Mrs. Arnold, who proposes to spend the summer travelling and to meet her husband, a naval officer, in Nice in the winter; Barbara Atchison, an equally wealthy girl from the West coast and somewhat eccentric; and Cecilia Boylston (pet name Saint), a not so wealthy artist from Boston. This strategy allows the construction of a hybrid narrative, a blend between a travel book and a novel.

Champney's narrative strategy is supported by a "conversational" writing style which allows her to bring together the two main dimensions of a travel book: instruction and pleasure. While describing the three girls' rambles, their attendance at recreational events and particularly their encounters with some male suitors —Armand Le Prince and Mr. Featherstonhaugh— Champney inserts the informational/instructive dimension about history, architecture and customs as well as her characters' opinions about pertinent issues like prejudice, religion and, above all, about the people and places they visit.

Considering that out of sixteen chapters, eight are devoted to Spain (chapters V to XII), this country is definitely the main object of the book. Champney avoids following the itinerary strategy and her main interests regarding Spain are clearly stated from the beginning:

> Over dizzy trestle-work, and through cavernous tunnels, out into blinding sunshine, past riotous cascades, sleepy villages, dusty olive-groves, and long stretches of tawny sun-burnt lands, they whirled into a land of romance and mystery, into the heart of Spain (1883: 91).

Expectations of romance and mystery are fulfilled when the girls are confronted by Granada and the Alhambra, "the crowning delight of their Spanish tour" (1883: 137) and become "thoroughly enthusiastic over the Moorish architecture and traditions with which the place is full" (1883: 150). These expectations corresponded, after all, to an already established and more generalized American view of the Old World.

Washington Irving was one of the earliest American authors to express what may be called an American view of Europe. In the introduction to his remarkably successful *The Sketch Book* —"The Author's Account of Himself"— Irving summarized the main and prevailing American idea about Europe using the voice of his fictional narrator, Geoffrey Crayon:

> But Europe held forth all the charms of storied and poetical association. There were […] the quaint peculiarities of ancient and local custom. My native country was full of youthful promise; Europe was rich in the accumulated treasures of age. […]. I longed to wander over the scenes of renowned achievement—to tread, as it were, in the footsteps of antiquity—to loiter about the ruined castle—to meditate on the falling tower—to escape, in short, from the commonplace realities of the present, and lose myself among the shadowy grandeurs of the past (Irving 1848:10-11).

In general terms, Irving's characterization of Europe shaped later generations of American travel writers that propagated the thoroughly self-conscious American view of Europe. Americans were able to contemplate "the ancient", "the treasures of age", "the ruined castle", and "the falling tower" and hence wander among the deeds of their ancestors, even celebrate them, while they reassured themselves that America was the land of the future and Europe that of the past.

It may therefore not come as a surprise that Irving's *Tales of the Alhambra* was "[the girls'] guide-book", and that "they sought out with avidity every place which he had mentioned, and bought photographs with which to 'inter-lay' their copies of his works" (1883: 143), as stated by the third person narrator, nor that the last chapter concerning Spain consists of an attempt to imitate Irving's tales. The whole chapter (which includes three legends, the girls' asides, and the illustrations) depicts the mystery and the romance mixed with some instructive aspects: it invokes historical and architectural aspects of the construction of an imaginary palace in Seville while describing a love affair between the Moorish architect Aben Cencid's daughter, Aicha, and a young artist Diego Rizzi who exhibits his knowledge of Moorish art. It even appropriates Irving's authorial voice about the Alhambra and, as a whole, it shows on the one hand Champney's ability to deal with artistic matters as a result of living a life surrounded by artists, and on the other hand allows for a romanticized vision of the Moorish past of Spain.

Actually, Champney stresses this aspect on several other occasions and her perception of Spain falls in line thereby with that predominant in Irving's work, and also with that of previous Anglophone travellers in

Spain, such as Henry Swinburne and James Cavanagh Murphy. Although she is not particularly critical of the influence of the Catholic Church upon the Spanish monarchy and state, as those authors were to a greater extent, one notices that the reiterated insistence on the positive nature of Moorish influence helps to ascribe to the clergy the more negative elements. For instance, when visiting the great mosque in Cordoba and while admiring its architecture and history, one of the girls, Barbara, remarks:

> It seems almost a pity, does it not, [...] that Ferdinand and Isabella drove the Moors out of Spain? Even the religion of the country seems to have deteriorated. I am sure that Mohammedan ablutions might be introduced with good effect into the present ritual (1883: 125-26).

This is not a surprising statement since most of the Anglophone travellers were Protestants and when they came either to Spain or Portugal one of the main aspects they focused on was indeed the Catholic religion and its negative influence upon both societies. Nevertheless, if this was more or less justified in earlier travel accounts, when the Inquisition was still active in both countries, when the work was written, at the end of the nineteenth century, it functions as one of those subjects of which it was mandatory to write, not for its specific relevance but because it fulfilled a prevalent convention that would comfort Protestant American readers.

Then again, as there are no more *autos de fé* that can be described in all their gore, religion has to be presented in its picturesque aspects. That is perhaps the reason why Champney devotes a whole chapter to the description of several devotional images of the Virgin, all accompanied by their respective illustrations and comparatively ranked among the sisterhood according to their importance. The general tone is a blend of condescending appreciation, particularly about the fables surrounding some of these icons, a few humorous comments and historical details which do not contradict the final remark: "Wandering through the columned forest of the grand mosque of Cordova one wonders whether the religion which has usurped that of Allah in Spain has less of error in its fabric" (1883: 107).

Nevertheless the religious dimension does not constitute a central aspect of the girls' travels in Spain and Champney's narrative is not full of guidebook-style enumerations of dimensional details. She weaves her information without disturbing the flow of her writing and prefers to indulge in descriptions of monuments, landscapes, and the work of some reputed Spanish painters. Such descriptions are mixed with romantic reveries and quite often the three girls' commentaries and dialogues. The formulaic convention of depicting the local color can be exemplified by the first description of Seville:

> Through street doorways, curtained by a beautifully wrought iron gate, —which gave the interior the mysterious charm which a lace veil adds to a beautiful face— the girls caught glimpses of brilliant gardens […] patios filled with blossoming ole-anders, oriental palms and tree ferns, and the whole gamut of roses. […] In the cen-tre, usually, a cistern or fountain, around which, ivy and passion-vine were matted, now and then they caught the white gleam of statues, the glitter of gayly enameled faience; and sometimes a senora, fan in hand, rose tranquilly from a half hidden chair and glided away from their observation (1883: 127).

Spanish traditions such as the bullfight, the use of the mantilla by the ladies, or guitar playing are approached in indirect ways. In the case of the bullfight, the idea of attending one is suggested by Mrs. Arnold while they are in Madrid in an attempt to divert the girls' attention from the possible arrival of the unwanted suitor of Maud, Armand Le Prince. The dialogue that follows reveals the girls' opinion but is also ambiguous.[1] The mantilla is several times referred to and even bought by the girls. When they are in Seville they learn that a milliner's shop has just opened and is selling French hats. Maud's reaction and the subsequent dialogue establish a conventional response to national customs that pretends to recognize the difference, the "otherness" that is losing ground in face of progress:

> "What a pity!" said Maud; "when the national custom of draping the head and shoulders in a black-lace veil is so much more effective and artistic".

1   "A bull-fight? horrible!"[…]
     "Why not? The spectacle is the national amusement of Spain, you lose one of your opportunities."
     "I don't care," exclaimed Maud, "they are low and vulgar, and brutal, I would as soon think of attending a prize-fight in London, or a cock or dog-fight,"—
     "Or a hanging in Kansas," added Barbara, "or even a New York walking-match. Why we are all of us members of the Society for Prevention of Cruelty to Animals. I think I see myself trotting coolly off to a bull-fight —on Sunday morning too!" (1883: 93-94)

"No national custom can long resist Parisian fashion. The peaked hat of Tyrol, the folded kerchief of the Roman girl, the quaint cap of the German peasant, all give way before it."

"That is true enough, but think how stupid it will be to travel a few years hence, and find everywhere the same regulation hat and feathers. I am filled with resentment against this milliner, whoever she may be, who is trying to do away with the beautiful Andalusian mantilla" (1883: 129-30).

At the end of their stay in Spain, and while taking a stroll in the Alameda, in Granada, the overall picture is one that conveys a stereotypical view:

The band played tumultuously, and the gas jets glittered. The water-carriers cried, *"Agua, agua, mas fria que la nieve!"* The children munched succarillos, or seed-cakes cut out in the shape of bulls, their horns ornamented with bits of blue ribbon. [...] Priests in long, shovel hats, with thong and crucifix hanging by the side of their black gowns, [...] jauntily dressed men whose braided queues proclaimed them to be bull-fighters. Girls in white satin slippers, black-lace mantillas, enormous fans, and dresses of bright pink or blue, coquetted with theatrical-looking men in wide sombreros and cloaks. Beggar-children ran in and out, laughing shrilly, and stopping in the midst of a caper to snuffle, —*"Senorita, yo no tengo padre,"*— and beg for the eighth part of a cent for the love of the mother of God (1883: 182).

But this is the present, one that more than often Champney chooses not to emphasize. In fact, Champney's view of Spanish "otherness" is one that highlights the past, particularly the "oriental past" as has already been mentioned, perhaps because to recognize otherness or to identify the foreign or foreignness can be done by establishing differences from home but to define them one needs a preconceived image or picture.

Even so, the preconceived image of the positive influence of the "oriental", only works when it envisions Spain. When Champney does indeed describe the girls' experience in Tangier the picture is quite different. There they have a near view of the "real Oriental" (as Maud names it) being one that "showed more filth than magnificence" (1883: 220).

The last section of the book therefore functions almost as a deconstruction of what had previously been done in regard to Spain. The Vassar girl's view of this country stands out as being that of a tourist in the sense that Champney witnesses people simply going about their lives, yet she defines those moments as a spectacle to be viewed, a production to be savored, and not as something to be part of or even as something from which she and her readers could really learn anything. The final lines regarding Toledo are revealing about the representation of Spanish "otherness":

> They left Toledo by the grand old Gate of the Sun, and looked back upon the castellated walls with regret. It was not a gay city, certainly, nor a particularly neat one, with its stable-yards invariably occupying the interior court, which was often the reception-room and dining-room as well, of the house. But it was a city with a history, and legends of enchanted palaces dating back to Roderic's time of Greek fire, fabricated for Saracen artillerymen, are still connected with its mysterious underground laboratories and windowless towers (1883: 117).

Whenever reality is disappointing and does not match Champney's expectations and after all those of her readers, then imagination is set in motion.

Bibliography

Champney, L.W. 1883. *Three Vassar Girls Abroad. Rambles of Three College Girls on a Vacation Trip Through France and Spain for Amusement and Instruction. With Their Haps and Mishaps*, Boston, Estes and Lauriat.

Decker, W. M. 2009. "Americans in Europe from Henry James to the Present", in A. Bendixen & J. Hamera (eds.), *The Cambridge Companion to American Travel Writing*, Cambridge, Cambridge UP, 127-44.

Irving, W. 1848 [1819-20]. *The Sketch Book of Geoffrey Crayon, Gent.,* The author's revised edition, New York, George P. Putnam.

"Modern Tourism". 1848. *Blackwood's Edinburgh Magazine* 64 (August), 185-89.

Schriber, M. S. 1997. *Writing Home: American Women Abroad, 1830-1920*, Charlottesville, U of Virginia P.

Tuckerman, H. T. 1868. "Going Abroad", *Putnam's Monthly Magazine* 1: 5 (May), 530-38.

MANUELA PALACIOS

Enriched and Challenged:
Women Writers' Encounters with Foreignness

The foreigner's face is, according to Julia Kristeva in *Strangers to Ourselves*, "like a standing invitation to some inaccessible, irritating journey" (1991: 4). Contemporary Irish and Galician women writers and/or their close relatives have either emigrated in search of better work opportunities or travelled to broaden their horizons. Recent social changes have also brought these writers face to face with the experience of immigration and political asylum. One way or another, the encounter with the foreigner becomes both an "irritating" challenge that unsettles our assumptions about ourselves and our place in the world, and an "invitation" to worlds of unlimited possibilities. Judith Butler's reflection on the death of the sovereign subject in *Giving an Account of Oneself* (2005) has also informed my hypothesis that foreignness tests the limits of our autonomy.

In this article, I will analyse two contemporary poets' inscriptions of foreignness in their writings: the Irish writer Celia de Fréine's poetry collection *imram: odyssey* (2010) and the Galician writer Chus Pato's hybrid text *Hordes of Writing* (2008, 2011). My objective is to explore the confluence of travel, gender and foreignness in order to assess the extent to which discourses on mobility and the encounter with foreignness are gendered. This article examines the ways in which the experience of travel is affected by the subject's gender consciousness and elicits feelings of autonomy or dependency.[1] In line with Kristeva's aforementioned observation, I will also explore the tensions between attraction and challenge that take place during the encounter with the foreigner. The analysis of de Fréine's and Pato's literary texts will be sup-

1   This article is part of the research projects "Us and Them" and "Ex-sistere" on women's discourses on foreignness and mobility in Irish and Galician literatures, funded by the Spanish Ministerio de Economía y Competitividad (FFI 2009-08475 and FFI2012-35872).

plemented with a few reflections, by a number of Irish and Galician women writers, on the experience of travel.[2] The authors' testimonies can be read alongside their creative writing in a productive rather than a limiting dialogue, opening signification, rather than reducing it.

When women travel, they confront not only the challenges of foreignness but also the restrictions that their own social background imposes on women's mobility. Women's travel is conditioned to various, though far from foreseeable, degrees by the following factors: social class, economic means, cultural level, the consideration of travel as a more or less necessary asset in life, moral and religious injunctions about the propriety of women's behaviour, women's family commitments and age, official regulations and extra-official discourses on women's mobility at a given time, and by the choice of destination place. However, there seems to be no one-to-one correlation between any of these factors and the experience of travel but, instead, a very complex intersection of a variety of them.

Patriarchy has traditionally consigned women to the domestic space under the tutelage of their male relatives. For this reason, travel, whether in the form of tourism or even emigration, could be envisaged as a liberating experience. Ruth Hooley singles out, as a dominant theme in her anthology *The Female Line. Northern Irish Women Writers*, women's desire to escape in order to allow an independent self to emerge (1985: 2). One of the objectives of this article is to interrogate the common perception of travel as a liberating escape which gives rise to a sovereign, autonomous self and to inquire into other complex notions of relationship and interdependency. Hooley's observation could lead us to believe that the yearning for liberation through travel is, at least in part, a recent phenomenon related to the women's liberation movement of the 1970s and the consequent achievements in women's rights. However, the long history of emigration in Galicia and Ireland suggests that the perception of travel as liberating could be traced back to previous generations earlier in the twentieth century and may have been nourished by models of more advanced or progressive societies than Ireland or Galicia could be

---

2   I passed, in 2010, a set of questions about their perceptions of travel to a number of Irish and Galician women writers of different ages and genres. Their answers, whether reproduced literally or paraphrased, are included in this article with the writers' permission.

at the time. Heather Ingman's survey of the Irish short story, for instance, identifies several early twentieth-century narratives which portray emigration as a liberating experience for women who want either to escape paternal control or to avoid repeating their mothers' thwarted lives (2009: 100, 129).

Wanderlust has often been a sort of utopian counter-discourse that privileges the liberating benefits of travel over its challenges. Regarding women's passion for travel, we observe that it also manifested itself before the times of feminist self-affirmation in the 1970s, in spite of legislation hostile to women's mobility and restrictive social expectations about feminine behaviour. The Galician writer María do Carme Kruckenberg (1926), now in her eighties, has affirmed that, when young, her older female relatives gave her total freedom to travel as she wished. However, a younger writer, Teresa Moure (1969), has commented that her female relatives never encouraged her to visit new places. The age gap between these two writers exceeds forty years, which shows that the perception of women's travel has had a very uneven development throughout the twentieth century, as it is intertwined with complex factors such as social class, economic means and cultural background that forestall any simple one-to-one correlation. This passion for travel also runs counter to utilitarian discourses that view travel as a dispensable luxury. As Eva Moreda observes, "[F]or my aunts, travelling was not a priority, they would rather invest their money in something else; in fact, travels were seen as a sort of extravagance".[3]

When asked if the encounter with the foreigner features frequently in their writing, fiction writers are more likely than poets to answer yes, as poetry does not usually allow for the kind of character formation and plot development that this encounter implies. However, a close reading of Celia de Fréine's and Chus Pato's poems reveals various subtle manifestations of foreignness which will be discussed below and which show that poetry is a hospitable genre for the encounter with foreignness. A *caveat* to be born in mind is that writers often opt for an inclusive understanding of *foreignness* either as the Other within their own communities or as a trope. The latter is, for instance, the case when Chus Pato claims that "writing is always foreign".

---

3   These are the writers' answers to the question: Have you been encouraged by the women who surround you (in your family, school, social groups, etc.) to travel?

Celia de Fréine's Odyssey

Although Celia de Fréine maintains that her literary exploration of female mobility and her construction of alternative, non-hostile spaces for women are most often set in an Irish context, they have a concern with border-crossing which is understandable in a writer who claims: "All my life I've been travelling back and forth across the border".[4] De Fréine's family was in fact repeatedly divided by the North-South border as some of her relatives settled in Northern Ireland while others established themselves in the Republic. This continuous estrangement from part of her migrating family has motivated her to write: "My experience and that of my family is probably the driving force behind my writing —I write to find out who I am and where I'm from".[5] Her testimony "On the Border of Memory: Childhood in a Divided Ireland" (2004) tells of the hostility she experienced as a Catholic child when visiting her family in Northern Ireland.

Celia de Fréine's bilingual —Irish and English— poetry collection *imram: odyssey* (2010) was partly inspired by a one-month stay in Slovenia in 2006 funded by the programme "Literature across Frontiers". The collection is necessarily affected by the Yugoslav wars of the early 1990s and reflects on the artificiality of boundaries and the ravages of war, but also on the outsider's perspective, that of a foreign visitor in a post-war period. *Imram* is actually an Irish literary genre concerned with a voyage and the challenges that the traveller must face and overcome. As expected, this voyage becomes a metaphor for life, but de Fréine's adaptation of the genre also reveals a woman's wanderlust and yearning for adventure. The collection starts with the poem "Hope", which gives expression to the poetic persona's endless curiosity about the world as she sails to sea: "[The boat's] glass bottom a screen through which I glimpse / the fish and the crustaceans and the people who live / on the ocean bed [...]" (15). However, her voyage is soon frustrated by a storm, which serves as an anticipation that this *imram* will not be a placid one.

---

4   This is part of de Fréine's answer to the question: In your writings, have you explored places that are traditionally hostile to women?
5   This is part of de Fréine's answer to the question: Has your family's experience of emigration marked you in any particular way?

The following poem "Yeast" humorously delves into the contradictory desires of craving for adventure and diversity on the one hand but missing the security of home on the other. A similar tension between going and staying is deployed in the poem "Shade", where the poetic persona chooses to continue her journey, but her shadow refuses to follow her: "[My shade] grabs hold of the hotel door, growing / thinner and more morose as I continue on" (27).

A frequent concern among contemporary poets is the lack or unreliability of signposts in one's voyage through life. This is also the case in the poem "Dear Friend", where the poetic persona insists that we shall only know who and where we are after we incorporate foreignness into our self, an idea that recalls Julia Kristeva's claim that the foreigner is part and parcel of our subjectivity: "Strangely, the foreigner lives within us" (1991: 1). In the last poem of the collection, "Welcome", the lyrical I envisages the possibility of returning home, though not before visiting the dream realm of mermaids, whose singing is no longer a dangerous distraction —as in the classical narrative verse on the male hero's return home, *The Odyssey*— but a necessary port of call before the return trip can be undertaken.

Apart from delving into the purpose and challenges of the voyage, de Fréine's *imram* engages in the topic of frontier crossing. The poem "No Man's Land" compares the new frontiers established —probably within what used to be the state of Yugoslavia— with those that are progressively attenuated —probably in Ireland: "Have they not heard of that island where the border has / disappeared, where its people are no longer brigands / of each crossing, lovers of what they are forbidden?" (23). Frontiers actually trigger the desire to trespass them the way nature does, without any regard for these political divisions: "[B]irds have been known to carry / twigs and pieces of earth from one country to the other?" (23). However, De Fréine acknowledges her outsider's perspective, her *visitor* status and her incomplete vision of the political conflict that has raised these borders. History and the effects of war get intertwined with the contingencies of tourism in poems such as "Torment" and "Invitation", while any attempt at communication is hindered by language barriers, as in "Tongue": "across the net of understanding, each bringing / with it an extra jot of lint, a new layer of confusion" (53).

Chus Pato's Nomadic Subject

In her introduction to Chus Pato's *Hordes of Writing* (2011), Erín Moure highlights the importance of European migrations in this book and quotes Pato's discussion of the metaphorical scope of the term *horde*: "I wanted to write a book that did not derive its structural unity from free verse, but from a horde of words: a protective mechanism borne deep inside it, but with maximum freedom, and mobility" (7). Thus, Pato places the stress on the freedom of mobility and the protectiveness of the horde, aware as she is of the individual traveller's vulnerability. Hers is a call to a communal identity of all living beings, human and non-human, an identity that must incorporate the foreigner: "this strange adventuress who's welcomed as family" (2011:18).

There are some important gender considerations to be taken into account, because the horde is not defined through the usual stereotypes of male aggressiveness —it is protective "like the mother's womb"— and welcomes the female stranger who becomes the protagonist trickster figure of the book: Hrg, Mariana, Jekyll, I, the she-narrator, the she-author, the reader... Although the core of the horde is a feminine protective space, it is far from innocuous to others, as these hordes of writing aim to upset the conventions of lyrical poetry. The hordes become a fluid, persistent force similar to that of a volcano exploding: "Instead of letting the world into the poem, / the poet kicks writing out, like soft and transparent lava, muslin" (2011: 49). Nevertheless, the imagery employed is not that of violent destruction or havoc but that of a transparent veil gently covering the universe. Even when constricting notions such as the fatherland need to be dismantled, Pato opts for imagery of fluidity and polymorphism: "(my country —she continued— is a collapsible wall, a double river of alphabetic reading)" (2011: 53).

However, Pato does not allow the signified to attach itself to the signifier for more than just a passing encounter. Femininity, then, will not remain essentially tied to the image of the protective womb. There are other ways of construing femininity, as her provocative image of the pack of outlaw she-wolves shows: "outside the flock / outside the flag // in a pack of she-wolves (abandoned), of she-bandits who are meaning, a revolver in each voice" (2011: 58). Foreignness is here the female, the animal, the armed outlaw, but also poetic meaning and voice.

At times it seems that Pato embraces the utopian discourse of mobility as boundless freedom and bliss: "she greeted mobility as one facet of freedom and this made her a lucky protagonist" (2011: 23). However, freedom can also turn into a daunting and perilous plunge: "like the monstrous face of freedom, that slalom of abysses" (2011: 18). Besides, the protagonist has certain moments of weakness in which she resents the exposure that is concomitant of freedom and she yearns for home: "her ever growing need to go back or find a way to take cover" (2011: 23). Moving ahead is, then, counterbalanced with the desire of return in a pendulous motion not unlike the book's concern with the communal configuration of the future and the remembrance of the close and distant past. There is also, on occasion, a kind of circularity in the characters' itineraries, as is the case of Jekyll's or Mariana's promenades through streets and squares that are meticulously named, along with the buildings and monuments in which history is inscribed (2008: 33, 39-40) (2011: 33, 39).

Conclusion

In this article, we have seen how contemporary Irish and Galician women writers often construe the encounter with the unknown as liberating, although they are also aware of their dependence on both their familiar context —this is usually emotional dependence— and on the new foreign setting, as they need a substantial amount of information that only the foreigner can provide. Language barriers, differences in cultural codes and reciprocal ignorance of each other's culture increase the traveller's vulnerability.

The analysis of Celia de Fréine's collection *imram: odyssey* proves that poetry is a hospitable *locus* for the encounter with the foreigner. The following concerns in her poetry are relevant to the topic of women's mobility and her dialogue with foreignness: the choice of the Irish genre of the *imram*, the inquiry into the artificiality of boundaries, the personae's *visitor* status or outsider's perspective, the lack or unreliability of directions, and the divided self that tries to negotiate her craving for adventure and her nostalgia for home. Chus Pato's hybrid texts in *Hordes of Writing* combine the metaphorical import of notions such as foreignness and mobility with a more literal and historical concern with European migrations, Galician emigration, and the world's exiles and refugees. Her utopian discourse on mobility as freedom is counterbalanced with the fear of exposure, the pendulous yearning for advance and return, and the circularity in the itineraries of her protagonist trickster figure.

Bibliography

Butler, J. 2005. *Giving an Account of Oneself*, New York, Fordham UP.

De Fréine, C. 2010. *imram: odyssey*, Gaillimh, Arlen House.

—. 2004. "On the Border of Memory: Childhood in a Divided Ireland", *New Hibernia Review* 8: 1, 9-20.

Hooley, R. 1985. "Introduction", in R. Hooley (ed.), *The Female Line. Northern Irish Women Writers*, Belfast, Northern Ireland Women's Rights Movement, 1-2.

Ingman, H. 2009. *A History of the Irish Short Story*, Cambridge, Cambridge UP.

Kristeva, J. 1988. *Étrangers à nous-mêmes*, Paris, Fayard.

—. 1991. *Strangers to Ourselves*, L. S. Roudiez (trans.), New York, Columbia UP.

Moure, E. 2011. "Animality and Language", in Chus Pato, *Hordes of Writing*, Exeter, Shearsman, 7-8.

Pato, C. 2008. *Hordas de escritura*, Vigo, Xerais.

—. 2011. *Hordes of Writing*, E. Moure (trans.), Exeter, Shearsman.

Pedro Javier Pardo García

Representing the Foreign in the Quixotic Travelogue: August F. Jaccaci's *On the Trail of Don Quixote*

"An Americano in Argamasilla"

On page fifty eight of the British edition of August Florian Jaccaci's narrative of his travels in La Mancha, *On the Trail of Don Quixote* (1897), he referred to himself as "that most unusual sight —an Americano in Argamasilla". Whether he was the first American visiting Argamasilla or not, it is difficult —if not impossible— to decide, although we know for certain that he was not the first foreigner to travel there. Charles Bogue Luffmann recorded a similar visit only a couple of years earlier in his *A Vagabond in Spain* (1895), in which he similarly emphasised the strangeness of his presence in the Manchegan village, in this case by comparing it to that of a white elephant. And Jaccaci was certainly not the first foreign traveller to follow in the footsteps of Don Quixote: the subtitle of his work —"Being a Record of Rambles in the Ancient Province of La Mancha"— subtly alludes to the founding and paradigmatic example of literary travel in Spain, Henry David Inglis's *Rambles in the Footsteps of Don Quixote* (1837). The *Rambles* created the pattern of topographic reminiscence epitomised by the formula *this is the undoubted spot where Don Quixote...*, to be followed later by Jacacci, entailing a vision both of the literary work inspiring the pilgrimage and of the country that provides the setting for it, and thus giving rise to a representation of the foreign as encountered both in literature and in reality.

Although Jaccaci was not the founder of this kind of travelogue, despite a recent attempt to vindicate him as such by Esther Bautista (2010) in her very informative study and translation of the text (to which I am indebted for the factual data I am about to present), he is the indispensable disciple that any new species of writing requires in order to become a genre, playing *Guzmán* to Inglis's *Lazarillo*, so to speak. As a matter of fact, and as was also the case with the rise of the picaresque, the epigone writing half a century later was more decisive in the dissemination of the pattern first explored by Inglis, since he had a wider and more international reception. *On the Trail of Don Quixote* was first published in the *Scribner's Magazine* of New York (20.2, August-December 1896) and then in book form the same year by Scribner's. One year later, it was printed in London by Lawrence and Bullen and translated into French by Arsène Alexandre, a friend and collaborator of Jaccaci's. The translation, under the title *Au pays de Don Quichotte*, first appeared in instalments in a travel magazine, *Le Tour du Monde* (November, 45-48), and was subsequently published in book form by Hachette in 1901. Jaccaci's French origins and professional connections unquestionably had a lot to do with this early circulation of his work,[1] but it was also due to the 129 beautiful drawings by Daniel Vierge, one on the most reputed and acclaimed illustrators of the time, born in Spain but living and working in Paris.[2] His drawings, however, did not appear in the Spanish edition (published in 1915, reissued in 1916, 1917 and 1918), in which they were replaced by photographs taken by the translator, Ramón Jaén.

And yet the impact of the book in Spain was felt earlier in a less direct but more creative way with the publication in 1905 (the third centenary of *Don Quixote*) of two works following the same pattern of the quixotic trail, as Bautista has pointed out. The first one was Azorín's *La ruta de Don Quixote* (1905), although apparently his avowed predecessor was not Jaccaci but José Giménez Serrano's "Un paseo a la patria de

1   August Jaccaci was born in France in 1856, but he settled in the United States in the 1880s and there developed his career as a painter, art editor and writer for several American magazines and publishers, although he was also known in the artistic and literary circles of Europe, and particularly of France, where he died in 1930.

2   Vierge undertook this work in preparation for his set of illustrations of *Don Quixote*, which was left incomplete at his death in 1904 but was eventually printed both in English (1906) and French (1909) editions of the Spanish masterpiece. As a matter of fact, the drawings were possibly the initial motivation or stimulus for Jaccaci's book (a practice not at all unusual in the nineteenth century), as is suggested in the prologue (in which Jaccaci explains that Vierge travelled to La Mancha one year earlier than himself, probably in 1893) and by the presence of the name of the illustrator —but not of the writer— on the front cover of the book.

Don Quijote" (1848).[3] The second one was Rubén Darío's "En tierra de Don Quijote", published in *La Nación* (Buenos Aires), for which he seems to have got the idea while reading the French translation of *On the Trail of Don Quixote* (Bautista 2010: 99). Jaccaci, together with Inglis, was also frequently quoted in a later British exemplar of this kind of literary travel in Spain, Rupert Croft-Cooke's *The Quest for Quixote* (1959), which was immediately followed by D. B. Windham Lewis's *The Shadow of Cervantes* (1962), and, more recently, by Nicholas Wollaston and his *Tilting at Don Quixote* (1990). Finally, Miranda France has taken the genre into the twenty-first century with *Don Quixote's Delusions: Travels through Castilian Spain* (2002).

Although in these three latter examples the quixotic trail is blurred by other concerns (the biography of Cervantes, the authors' autobiography, or Spain in general, respectively), all these texts from Inglis to France can be grouped together in a species of travel narrative that I have explored elsewhere (forthcoming) and called the *quixotic travelogue*. This is a variant of the kind of travel writing that follows in the footsteps of a literary character, in this case the Spanish knight, which turns *Don Quixote* into a guidebook for the exploration of Spain and La Mancha in particular.[4] Whether the quixotic trail is strictly adhered to or not, the quixotic travelogue is always based on the coalescence or juxtaposition of topographic description and literary reminiscence, which creates an intimate fusion of present culture and past literature, country and book, as a result of a double and simultaneous act of reading: the book is seen —sanctioned— through the country, the country is seen —displaced—

3   Under this title, José Giménez Serrano published a collection of short chronicles of a tour of La Mancha in the *Semanario Pintoresco Español* in 1848. This is the same format in which Azorín, who mentioned Giménez Serrano's collection as his antecedent in later works, published the articles that make up *La ruta de Don Quijote* in *El Imparcial* (Bautista 2010: 32).

4   This purpose separates this kind of narratives from those of travellers passing through La Mancha and alluding to *Don Quixote*. Ortas (2006) has provided an exhaustive listing of these works in French and English. Among the latter, we can mention John Talbot Dillon's *Letters from an English Traveller in Spain in 1778* (1781), Edward Hawke Locker's *Views in Spain* (1813), and of course the best known travel books in Spain of their time, George Borrow's *The Bible in Spain* (1843) and Richard Ford's *A Handbook for Travellers in Spain* (1845). Chapters XI and XII of the already quoted *A Vagabond in Spain* are devoted to La Mancha, which also plays an important part in Walter Starkie's *Don Gipsy* (1936).

through the book. The quixotic travelogue turns on these two axes, the book and the place, which different authors relate and combine in different ways and with different emphases.

The Construction of the Foreign

On the Trail of Don Quixote cannot compare to Inglis's articulate discussion and interpretation of Cervantes's masterpiece, but it proves to be of far more interest in the representation of the foreign place, which it carries out in a fuller and more detailed fashion. This interest, as the recent constructivist trend in imagological studies has argued (Beller and Leerssen 2007), does not lie in the possible correspondence of the representation with reality, but in the means of representation. Establishing whether the image of foreign Spain constructed by Jaccaci was a true one or not is beyond the scope of literary scholarship (even of scholarship in general), but the strategies underlying his construction are certainly within its remit. As a matter of fact, Jaccaci's quixotic travelogue is exceptional for the way it makes vocal two strategies which underlie in a muted way most representations of the foreign, and thus highlights the process of cultural construction of all foreign images.

Literary Petrification

The image of La Mancha provided by Jaccaci in his *Trail* is significant because it is mediated through literature, but also because of the scope and centrality of this mediation. This is not limited to *Don Quixote*; it occasionally extends to the picaresque, particularly Quevedo's *Buscón*, and in so doing the author is following still a third literary model, Inglis, who is also an inspiration in his handling of the Spanish sources. Indeed, Inglis's Romantic interpretation of Cervantes's masterpiece underlies Jaccaci's references to the narrator's quixotic and sanchoesque sides; the companionship in travel with a native panzaic guide informing the *Rambles* is here echoed in the presence of Ezechiel [sic]; and so is the constant presence of Cervantism and Quixotism in Manchegan life, that is, of discussions on Cervantes as well as of characters and scenes similar to those in *Don Quixote*. Of course this permanence testifies to the validity of the novel as a historical record of Spain and La Mancha in particular: things are still as Cervantes represented them. And this has a twofold implication, concerning the book and the place, in accordance with the logic of dual reading we have formulated above as characteristic of the quixotic travelogue: on the one hand, Cervantes was a superior artist who produced an extraordinarily accurate and truthful account of Spanish reality; on the other, almost nothing has changed in La Mancha, which is petrified in the past. This *petrification*, a testimony to both the author's genius and the region's backwardness, is here the ruling principle in the representation of the foreign, as it was in the *Rambles*.

The strategy is clear from the first page, where La Mancha is described as "the most backward region in Spain" (1897: 3), and is reinforced subsequently by the recurring insistence on remoteness from civilization, poverty and savagery, on the aridity of the land and the sturdiness of the people, on the pervasiveness of ruins and traces of the past. The fact, however, that the governing idea and many of these motifs derive from the *Rambles* (written almost seventy years before), and ultimately from *Don Quixote* (almost three hundred), alerts us to the possibility that they are the product of myth as much as of reality; not just of empirical observation but also of literary imitation, since myth-making is based on the latter as well as the former. This suspicion seems to be confirmed by the way Jaccaci, at the end of his chronicle, counterpoints this myth of backwardness to that of Edenic Andalusia (as Inglis had also done), a region which he probably has not seen, but obviously has read about.[5] Of course it can be argued that the transtextual coincidences between the *Trail* and its sources were the result of real conditions, that La Mancha was in fact the most backward region in Spain; but, even so, it is difficult to believe that so little had changed since Cervantes's times. The pressure of the literary myth created by the combined action of

---

5   This points to a double *transtextuality*, since this is not just *hypertextual*, that is, comprising *Don Quixote* and the *Rambles* as *hypotexts* on which the *Trail* is modelled, one overt and the other covert; but it is also *intertextual*, since Jaccaci is certainly using in a more episodic or occasional way other travel books in Spain, such as Luffman's *A Vagabond in Spain*, which Jaccaci actually quotes (1897: 83), and of course other Spanish literary works such as the *Buscón*.

Cervantes and Inglis is undoubtedly at work in Jaccaci's mind, or rather, eyes.

The suspicion that literature is framing what is seen and how it is represented, and hence at least partly responsible for the petrification, seems to be corroborated by the manifest displeasure Inglis shows at finding signs of modernity that break the spell of the past he seems so eager to recover. This is clear in his negative impression on the buffet in Alcázar's railways station (1897: 138), his reluctance to travel by train (1897: 149 and 178), or his remarks on the modern-looking *bodegas* in Valdepeñas: "I suffered from the incongruity of seeing this blatant signature of civilization in so primitive a place, and found it particularly disagreeable to be so bluntly reminded from home" (1897: 179). These remarks leave room for speculation on how far the narrative is biased by this search of a literary past which evades *incongruities* (especially if they remind the traveller *from home* and the present), by a literarily motivated concentration on recovering the presence of the past rather than the present passing before his eyes. This is a feature of all literary travel: petrification is the condition that makes it worthwhile, it is travel in time as well as in space, a voyage to that most foreign of foreign lands: the past. But it is a subjective rather than an objective condition.

Cultural Estrangement

Literary petrification makes visible the process of construction of the foreign through explicit reference to and/or evident imitation of its literary sources. This process is also made visible by the second outstanding feature of Jaccaci's representation of the foreign, that is, the fact that it allows us to see the national standpoint informing it —in this case the narrator's condition as an American— in a very vivid way, a feature which separates him from the British and less transparent Inglis. I am not alluding here to the author's references, in different passages early in the narrative, to his origins, but to how the rationale of nationality, and not literature, can be discerned behind some of his anthropological or sociological observations regarding La Mancha. I am referring, for example, to (a) Jaccaci's outrage at the social and economic inequality in the distribution of property and work, at the patriarchal subjugation of women, or at the cruelty with which animals are treated, three observations that spring from a common concern for poverty and for different forms of oppression, exploitation or submission (social, sexual, animal), which is easy to understand in a citizen of North America, the land of plenty, equality and liberty; (b) his insistence on the all-pervading Arab or Moorish background (in landscape, language, habits, physical appearance), which exhibits a racial awareness not surprising for someone accustomed to Caucasian supremacy and race segregation (thus pointing to the contradictions and tensions conforming America), the opposite of the hybridisation he observes in Spain, where the alien racial inheritance has been integrated and has given shape to all aspects of life; (c) and his sensibility to history and its traces in literature and landscape (the ubiquity of ruins and medieval castles), to the weight of past and legend on the lives of the people, which is clearly related to a young nation with only recent history and, as he admits, "concerned mainly with the things of the immediate present" (1897: 103). There is here a certain awareness on the author's part of how his American way of life and its contrast with Spain's directs his gaze, and other similar instances of self-consciousness can be detected elsewhere, as when he contrasts Ciudad Real to New York (5), when he declares his reluctance to pronounce radical judgements on the people because they are "so far removed from us" (42-43), or when he admits that this is precisely what he is looking for, "the contrast […] to one's ordinary manner of life" (177). This statement amounts to an open confession that we construct the foreign through our own experience, through the process of estrangement resulting from such a contrast: what we see is determined by what we are.

That is how the *Trail* foregrounds a second shaping force in the representation of the foreign, the second filter in the bifocal lenses of image-building: cultural estrangement. It also evinces that any description of foreign character or *hetero-image* provides a *self-image*, in this case an implicit portrayal of American character: such description focuses on the traits that stand out against the backdrop of the traveller's cultural norms or habits because those traits are unusual, dissonant, deviant. By the same token, Jaccaci's irony in affirming the Spanish penchant for self-deprecation or his admiration for Manchegan courtesy and etiquette, as well as in spotting indolence and idleness, bespeaks the self-confidence, casualness, easy-going and hard-working manner ingrained in American identity; and his presentation of ridiculous Spanish regional nationalisms, of religious habits as either superficial or fanatical, and of the dirtiness in *posadas*, points to the modern habits, the tolerance or serious-mindedness in religious matters, and the belief in a strong national identity beyond cultural differences that all characterise American culture. All these observations draw a sketch of Spanish national character, but also allow us to glimpse one of the American character, as if containing a photographic negative waiting only for the chemistry of a counter-analysis to be developed into an image of the *Americano*, obverse and reverse of the same coin, of the same process of construction at work in the *Trail*.

Travel as Recognition

Two conclusions can be drawn from this brief examination of Jaccaci's *On the Trail of Don Quixote* regarding how it represents the foreign that are perfectly applicable to, if not all travel narratives, at least those belonging to what I have called the quixotic travelogue.

In the first place, the *Trail* demonstrates the dynamic nature of the construction of the foreign as a dialectics of conflicting forces, which we see at work at least on three levels. Firstly, the recurrence of a series of motifs and clichés in the literary representation of Spain suggests that they are founded on empirical observation and thus tends to validate them, but at the same time their literary and cultural roots point to their conventional nature and thus question them, thus becoming an oscillating index both of their reality and their fictionality. Secondly, there is a tension between estrangement and familiarisation, the first as a result of alienation by a different nationality or culture, the second of assimilation through previous literature or discourse. Finally, the representation of the Other is a simultaneous act of self-representation, which in turn gives shape to the former and thus pre-empts it. On all three levels, the cognition of the foreign is inextricably entwined with the recognition of the familiar in a never-ending interplay.

The second conclusion is that the *Trail* demonstrates how the literary determines the perception of the foreign, in the sense of shaping not just the itinerary but also the expectations, of directing not just the route but also the gaze, what is seen and not seen, again turning travel into recognition rather than cognition. Insofar as literary travel is travel oriented by discourse, —and ultimately all travel after the emergence of tourism in the nineteenth century is oriented by some form of discourse—, it lays bare the quixotic nature of image-construction in most travel writing: previous literary representation of place always frames later consumption of place, like the chivalric representation of reality frames Don Quixote's surrounding reality. By anchoring the traveller's expectations in a specific and identifiable transtextual net, in this case both overt and covert, the quixotic travelogue simply makes them visible and central. Literary travel makes explicit what is implicit in all travel as far as the representation or construction of the foreign is concerned. Quixotic literary travel reveals the quixotic nature of all travel.

Bibliography

Bautista Naranjo, E. 2010. *Un americano en La Mancha tras las huellas de don Quijote*, Ciudad Real, Centro de Estudios de Castilla-La Mancha, Universidad de Castilla-La Mancha.

Beller, M. & J. Leerssen (eds.). 2007. *Imagology: The Cultural Construction and Literary Representation of National Characters. A Critical Survey*, Amsterdam & New York, Rodopi.

Jaccaci, A. F. 1897. *On the Trail of Don Quixote*, London, Lawrence and Bullen.

Ortas Durand, E. 2006. *Leer el camino. Cervantes y el "Quijote" en los viajeros extranjeros por España* (1701-1846), Alcalá de Henares, Centro de Estudios Cervantinos.

Pardo, P. J. [forthcoming]. "Henry David Inglis, First Literary Tourist in Spain," in B. Colbert & J. Borm (eds.), *Foreign Correspondence*, Cambridge Scholars Press.

MIKEL PEREGRINA

El extranjero en la ciencia ficción: el alienígena

Introducción

Puede sorprender la aparición de este estudio en medio de un volumen centrado en las relaciones entre la literatura y el extranjero, pero, como se argumentará a continuación, otra forma de representar la alteridad se consigue por medio de la fantasía, instrumento básico de toda ficción literaria. Entre los géneros denominados no miméticos o proyectivos (Moreno 2010a: 95), el de la ciencia ficción es el que ofrece una mejor capacidad reflexiva sobre la naturaleza humana y su aversión ante lo desconocido. Así, para representar al Otro, este género literario, por mediación de la fantasía, convierte al extranjero en el extraterrestre o alienígena.

Definiendo la ciencia ficción

Primero debe entenderse cuál es la naturaleza de la ciencia ficción. Existen muchas definiciones y ningún consenso que haga predominar una sobre otra. Dada la variedad de temas que trata —*hard, space-opera*, distopía, ucronía—, resulta difícil establecer una explicación absolutamente satisfactoria sobre el término, el cual de por sí tampoco goza del entusiasmo de los aficionados. Una de las mejores definiciones del género que se han ofrecido, y que mejor viene para ilustrar este discurso, pertenece a Darko Suvin. En su libro *Metamorfosis de la ciencia ficción*, la definió como la literatura del "extrañamiento cognitivo" (1979: 26). Dos términos que deben destacarse: extrañamiento y cognición.

El primero de ambos, el extrañamiento, se refiere a que los mundos ficcionales que aparecen en la obras fictocientíficas no se corresponden con la realidad que nosotros conocemos, es decir, no reflejan nuestro mundo. Para conseguir este efecto, el escritor debe alejarse de la realidad empírica para crear un universo ficcional nuevo. No obstante, el segundo término, cognitivo, supone una paradoja con el primero, puesto que ese ejercicio imaginativo queda constreñido a un inviolable cumplimiento de las leyes naturales que rigen nuestro universo. Es decir, el mundo ficcional creado debe ser racional, debe mantener la ilusión de ser un mundo verificable, plausible para el lector. Para conseguir ese objetivo, el universo inventado debe basarse en la realidad empírica que conocemos. Este aspecto, la cognición, es la que aleja a la ciencia ficción de otros géneros no miméticos como la literatura fantástica y la literatura maravillosa.

Cognición también hace referencia al modo de trabajo de los autores del género, pues se trata de un método científico en el que el escritor fantacientífico establece una hipótesis a partir de un elemento que toma de su tiempo, después lo desarrolla hiperbolizado en la obra y así obtiene unas conclusiones. A ese elemento del que parte para construir el universo ficcional Suvin lo denominó *nóvum* o innovación cognoscitiva. El *nóvum* hace de mediador entre lo literario y lo extraliterario, entre lo ficticio y lo empírico. Puede presentar diferentes dimensiones: desde lo más básico, la invención discreta, como un aparato y sus consecuencias, hasta un nivel mayor, un ámbito espacio-temporal, un agente ajeno o nuevos tipos de relaciones.

Por lo tanto, un posible *nóvum*, y de por sí uno de los más frecuentes dentro del género, es la relación entre los seres humanos, el choque cultural o racial, que, mediante el proceso del extrañamiento, hiperbolizado, es el encuentro entre el ser humano y los extraterrestres. He aquí la relación y justificación para hablar ahora de la ciencia ficción, es decir, que su fuerza especulativa provoca que en un mundo distinto del nuestro se traten precisamente los problemas que nos conciernen.

De esta forma, el escritor fictocientífico es, como dice el hispanista Juan Ignacio Ferreras, un romántico hacia el futuro, un escritor capaz de plasmar un mundo diferente que se enfrenta de forma fragmentada con su propio universo, con su propia sociedad (1972: 200-204). En palabras de Fernando Moreno, uno de los principales investigadores del género en España:

La ciencia ficción, pese a que no se basa en la ciencia ni pretende romper con nuestra percepción de la realidad —como la narrativa fantástica— ni sugerir otra realidad autónoma —como la literatura maravillosa—, es un género que se articula mediante la tensión entre una mentalidad positivista moderna y los juegos disponibles en la literatura no mimética. Es decir, pese a su inexacto y desafortunado nombre, la ciencia ficción no trata de ciencia y literatura, sino de la relación retórica entre una visión materialista del mundo y las posibilidades de la narrativa especulativa (2010b: 14).

El alienígena como representación extrañada de la alteridad

De la misma manera que en las fábulas los animales adquieren rasgos de personalidad humanos para expresar moralejas o sentencias que sirvan para nuestro aprendizaje en la vida, para el alienígena, al margen de las especulaciones biológicas que representen su cuerpo, su carácter se construye a partir de rasgos humanos. Así, mediante la figura del extraterrestre, muchas obras de ciencia ficción reflexionan sobre la naturaleza humana en relación con lo desconocido.

Existen cuatro modelos de representación del extraterrestre, que aquí enumero en un proceso de extrañamiento creciente: a) el extranjero, es decir, el humano emigrado de la Tierra, habitante de otro planeta; b) con cuerpo humanoide, similar al nuestro, donde normalmente el choque es cultural; c) con cuerpo no humanoide, formado con elementos de la fauna y flora de nuestro planeta, o de animales fantásticos o mitológicos de culturas de la Tierra, cuyo choque, además de cultural, es de índole biológica; y d) sin forma definida, los más escasos, como puede ser una forma de vida gaseosa. Queda claro que cuanto mayor es la distancia, mayores son los problemas de comunicación y comprensión mutua.

Alienígenas no humanoides y sin forma definida

Una de las obras clave para el imaginario de extraterrestres pertenece a la pluma del escritor inglés Olaf Stapledon en *Hacedor de estrellas* (1937), donde un hombre que sube a una colina sufre un viaje místico por el cosmos y observa la vida del universo y de las razas que lo habitan, hasta encontrarse con el hacedor, una especie de ente divino. Son extrapolaciones de índole biológica que permiten mostrar otras estructuras sociales y que provienen de modelos basados en seres vivos presentes en nuestro planeta. La obra de Stapledon es relevante por el enorme elenco de criaturas que pululan por sus capítulos: una raza simbiótica de peces (ictioideos) y crustáceos (aracnoides), hombres planta, o los nautiloides, una especie de barcos vivientes.

Muchas veces han aparecido en la ciencia ficción, para representar el terror, los llamados BEM, abreviatura inglesa de *Bug Eyed Monster* (monstruo de ojos saltones, u ojos insectoides). Sin embargo, lo más interesante es la extrapolación de sus sociedades jerarquizadas y especializadas, como los insectos descritos por Robert A. Heinlein en *Tropas del espacio* (1959).

Una de las formas que más aparece en la ciencia ficción, y una de las más populares, consiste en la óptica de un primer encuentro. Un ejemplo a destacar sería *Solaris*, del escritor polaco Stanislaw Lem, donde se muestra la reacción humana ante lo incognoscible de una forma de vida distinta, un océano que ocupa todo el planeta y que parece funcionar como un único ente con consciencia propia. Es una forma de vida del cuarto tipo, sin forma definida. Por ello, a pesar de los múltiples esfuerzos, los humanos no llegan a entender a esta forma de vida, no la conciben dentro de sus esquemas mentales; el límite de nuestro entendimiento y el contacto fracasan. Así lo expresa uno de los personajes de la novela, Snaut, casi al final de la misma:

> No queremos conquistar el cosmos, sólo queremos extender la Tierra hasta los lindes del cosmos. Para nosotros, tal planeta es árido como el Sahara, tal otro glacial como el Polo Norte, un tercero lujurioso como la Amazonia. Somos humanitarios y caballerosos, no queremos someter a otras razas, queremos simplemente transmitirles nuestros valores y apoderarnos en cambio de un patrimonio ajeno. Nos consideramos los caballeros del Santo Contacto. Es otra mentira. No tenemos necesidad de otros mundos. Lo que necesitamos son espejos (Lem 1961: 87-88).

Alienígenas humanoides

Es el grupo que mejor refleja los problemas de las relaciones humanas, pues funciona como herramienta para expresar tabús actuales, los cuales aparecen personificados en la figura del extraterrestre, en ese encuentro con el Otro. Para muchos escritores, explorar la vida de los alienígenas se convierte en un ágil y efectivo modo de explorar sus propias posturas como individuos alienados. Por ello, muchos de los denominados discursos desde la marginalidad han analizado las potencialidades del género fantacientífico para tratar problemáticas que no son del aprecio del discurso establecido por el poder, como son la crítica feminista (Hollinger 2003: 125-36), la teoría crítica racial (Roberts 2000: 119-45) y la teoría *queer* (Pearson 2003: 149-60).

Los escritores tienden a tomar reivindicaciones que defienden estos movimientos y plasmarlos en la obra mediante una desfamiliarización, un distanciamiento, pero finalmente lo que están planteando es otra forma de entender conceptos como las relaciones humanas o la sexualidad. Un ejemplo puede encontrarse en *La mano izquierda de la oscuridad* (1969), de Ursula K. Le Guin. En esta novela, un diplomático acude al planeta Gueden, también llamado Invierno, para convencer a los dirigentes de las naciones que lo conforman para que se unan al Ekumen, una federación de planetas de fines comerciales. Pero los nativos de Gueden son seres ambisexuales, andróginos que solo se definen sexualmente en la época de celo. Esta naturaleza reproductiva tan peculiar influye totalmente en la vida del planeta y en la percepción que el diplomático Genly Ay tiene de ellos:

> Lo había intentado varias veces, pero mis esfuerzos concluían en un modo de mirar demasiado deliberado: un guedeniano me parecía entonces primero un hombre, y luego una mujer, y les asignaba así categorías del todo irrelevantes para ellos, y para mí fundamentales (Le Guin 1969: 589).

La autora parte de la presentación de una especie andrógina que ignore desigualdades de sexo, y con ello plantea un mundo donde las tensiones entre naciones no se resuelven mediante el conflicto bélico, al quedar eliminada la antinomia de los dos sexos. He aquí la reflexión sobre la naturaleza humana, el elemento especulativo de la autora. Le Guin se vale del alienígena como un símbolo con el que explorar la sexualidad y la identidad sexual, y las relaciones entre sexos.

Siguiendo con el tema de la sexualidad, es fácil encontrar obras donde se describen relaciones amorosas entre un humano y un extraterrestre que son repudiadas, como una alegoría del rechazo que puede tener en nuestra sociedad la relación de dos personas de distinta raza, o del mismo sexo. Un ejemplo lo constituye la novela del estadounidense Philip José Farmer, *Los amantes* (1952). La obra describe un mundo futuro gobernado por un estado teocrático totalitario que anula completamente los derechos y la libertad moral del individuo. El protagonista, Hal Yarrow, es un inadaptado que piensa de forma distinta a la que le imponen. Consigue formar parte de una expedición colonizadora a un nuevo planeta, que está habitado por alienígenas artrópodos. En este mundo Yarrow descubrirá una nueva forma de vida, una nueva moral e incluso un verdadero amor. Yarrow hallará en los extraterrestres todo lo que le negaban sus congéneres. Mediante el amor con Jeanette se liberará de sus prejuicios para convertirse en un hombre nuevo:

> Ella le alentaba a que los resaltase una y otra vez, hasta que conseguía librarse del peso del dolor, del odio y de la duda. Luego había siempre amor, un amor que él nunca había siquiera sospechado que existiese. Por primera vez, Hal supo que el hombre y la mujer podían ser una sola carne. Su mujer y él habían estado siempre fuera del círculo del otro, pero Jeannette conocía la geometría que le permitía a él ingresar en ella, y la química que le permitía mezclar su sustancia con la de ella (1952: 180).

Otro asunto que ha sido criticado diversas veces en la ciencia ficción es la colonización. El hombre acude a otro planeta con la intención de quedarse allí, aniquilar a sus habitantes o imponerles su forma de pensar y actuar. *Crónicas Marcianas* (1950), de Ray Bradbury, es un precioso ejemplo de este tipo. La obra está constituida por una serie de cuentos hilados cronológicamente que narran la llegada de los hombres al planeta Marte, los primeros contactos con los marcianos, el posterior exterminio de éstos y la repoblación con terráqueos. Desde luego, Bradbury nos presenta la colonización de Marte como una alegoría revisionista de la colonización americana: las expediciones de ultramar, los primeros asentamientos o la relación con los nativos.

El hombre como extraterrestre

Finalmente, el extraterrestre puede ser el propio hombre, es decir, los antiguos colonos que deciden independizarse o que han formado otro país con costumbres distintas. Ya no se sienten terráqueos, pertenecen a la nueva colonia. Un caso claro es la trilogía marciana (1993-1996) de Kim Stanley Robinson sobre la terraformación de Marte. En el último de los tomos, durante un viaje a la Tierra por parte de algunos colonos, sienten que ya no añoraban su planeta natal y todas las descripciones que hacen de nuestro planeta las realizan en comparación a lo que conocen, a la orografía marciana. Ya no son terráqueos.

En este punto debo destacar un clásico del género como es *Forastero en tierra extraña* (1961), de Robert A. Heinlein. En esta obra un humano, Valentin Michael Smith, que ha sido criado por marcianos, regresa a la Tierra, un mundo distinto al que le cuesta adaptarse, hasta el punto que termina por destruir las tradiciones éticas y morales de los terrícolas.

Cualquier conversación con Smith terminaba conduciendo a una particularidad de la conducta humana que no podía ser justificada de ninguna manera lógica, al menos en términos que Smith pudiera entender, y todos los intentos por conseguirlo resultaban infructuosos, una interminable pérdida de tiempo (Heinlein 1961: 287).

Conclusión

Como se ha podido observar, la ciencia ficción se caracteriza por una gran fuerza especulativa. En este ejercicio de la especulación, y mediante la herramienta del extrañamiento ya comentada, se convierte al alienígena en la representación de la alteridad, es decir, en una alegoría de las relaciones humanas. El extranjero es el extraterrestre, un ser venido de otros mundos, y la relación con nuestros congéneres produce un choque de culturas. Por eso, la ciencia ficción siempre habla de nuestra realidad y de nuestros problemas, pero a través de mundos inventados.

Bibliografía

Bradbury, R. 2007 [1950]. *Crónicas marcianas*, Barcelona, Minotauro,
Brown, F. 1982 [1955]. *Marciano, vete a casa*, Barcelona, Martínez Roca.
Farmer, P. J. 1982 [1952]. *Los amantes*, Barcelona, Acervo.

Ferreras, J. I. 1972. *La novela de ciencia ficción. Interpretación de una novela marginal*, Madrid, Siglo XXI.

Heinlein, R. A. 1989 [1959]. *Tropas del espacio*, Barcelona, Martínez Roca.

—. 1996 [1961]. *Forastero en tierra extraña*, Barcelona, Plaza & Janés.

Hollinger, V. 2003. "Feminist Theory and Science Fiction", in E. James & F. Mendleshon (eds.), *The Cambridge Companion to Science Fiction*, New York, Cambridge UP, 125-36.

Lem, S. 2008 [1961]. *Solaris*, Barcelona, Minotauro.

Le Guin, U. K. 2008 [1969]. *La mano izquierda de la oscuridad*, in *Los Mundos de Ursula K. Le Guin*, Barcelona, Minotauro, 575-872.

Moreno, F. A. 2010a. *Teoría de la Literatura de Ciencia Ficción. Poética y retórica de lo prospectivo*, Vitoria, Portal Editions.

—. 2010b. "Francotiradores de la literatura de la ciencia ficción en España (1980-2010)", *Ínsula* 765, 14-16.

Pearson, W. 2003. "Science Fiction and Queer Theory", in E. James & F. Mendleshon (eds.), *The Cambridge Companion to Science Fiction*, New York, Cambridge UP, 149-60.

Roberts, A. 2000. *Science Fiction*, London, Routledge.

Robinson, K. S. 2004-08 [1993-96]. *Marte Rojo, Marte Verde, Marte Azul*, 3 vols., Barcelona, Minotauro.

Rogan, A. M. D. 2004. "Alien Sex Acts in Feminist Science Fiction: Heuristic Models for Thinking a Feminist Future of Desire", *PMLA* 119: 3, 442-56.

Stapledon, O. 1985 [1937]. *Hacedor de estrellas*, Barcelona, Minotauro.

Suvin, D. 1984 [1979]. *Metamorfosis de la ciencia ficción. Sobre la poética y la historia de un género literario*, México, Fondo de Cultura Económica.

João Paulo Pereira da Silva

Ralph Fox and *Portugal Now* (1937): a Communist Militant's Vision of Salazar's Country during the Spanish Civil War

Although the number of travel narratives on Portugal by British authors who went to that country in the twentieth century is quite significant, these texts have been arguably disregarded by academics and researchers, despite the fact that they contain a crucial amount of information on specific historical periods, such as the First Republic (1910-1926), the military dictatorship (1926), Salazar's New State (1933-1968), as well as the democratic regime that followed the 1974 revolution. Their relative historical proximity has probably been the main cause for this oversight by the same historians and specialists who have thoroughly perused and studied similar texts from previous centuries (Silva 2009: 207-209).

However, in contradiction of this trend, in 2006 a Portuguese version of the travel narrative on Portugal by the British writer and communist militant Ralph Fox was issued by the publishing house Tinta-da-China. This travelogue was published for the first time in 1937 and the Portuguese translator curiously decided to keep its English title, *Portugal Now* (Fox 2006). This report was written by Fox in 1936 and dates precisely from the period when the author worked for the Spanish Republic, having previously joined the ranks of the International Brigades. Thus, during his stay in Portugal, Fox acted as a spy for the Spanish government, gathering information at the rear of the Nationalist army. His particular mission was actually to evaluate the extent of Portuguese intervention in the process of the Civil War, that is, to assess the amount of logistic, diplomatic, material and military support provided by Salazar's regime to the Burgos government.

Before proceeding to a brief analysis of this curious and unusual narrative it will be necessary to introduce its author. Ralph Winston Fox was born in 1900, in Halifax, Yorkshire, and came from a solid middle-class background. The author, who had always revealed a particular vo-

cation for a career as man of letters, went on to take a degree in Modern
Languages at Oxford University. At this time the choice of the life of
letters seemed to open before him. Nevertheless, in 1920, he decided to
leave Britain for the Soviet Union, where he worked with the Friends
Relief Mission, in Samara, a famine-hit area and one of the poorest regions in Russia. In 1925, he moved to Moscow where he started working
with the Communist International and was later appointed librarian at the
Marx-Engels Institute, in the Soviet capital. It is also known that he was
one of the co-founders of the Communist Party of Great Britain, established in 1920, and later became a distinguished member of the Comintern
(Fox 2006: 8; Silva 2009: 210).

In 1936, he joined the International Brigades with the assistance of
the French Communist Party. However, immediately before he left for
Spain, he travelled briefly through Portugal, in the service of the Spanish
Republic. By the end of 1936, he finally reached Spanish territory where
he fought on the side of the Republic together with thousands of other
European and American intellectuals, for whom the triumph of fascism
represented the suppression of freedom of speech, of literature and the
systematic destruction of humanist culture. After receiving military training in Albacete, he was assigned to the post of commander of the 14th
Brigade. He was immediately sent to the front in Andalusia (more precisely, to the village of Lopera in the province of Jaén), where he fell in
battle at the age of 36, on 27 September 1936 (Fox 2006: 11; Silva 2009:
210).

Fox's participation in the Spanish Civil War as well as his decision
to join the International Brigades should be perceived in the light of the
complex events of the 1930s, stirred up by the rise of totalitarian or authoritarian right-wing movements and regimes in several countries and
particularly the victory of the Nazi party in Germany. This process profoundly disturbed European intellectuals and gave rise to a strong ideological polarization. Intellectuals faced only two options: to oppose Fascism and Nazism, or to support them. Thus, among the intellectuals and
writers of the Western World there were few who did not take a political
stand during the hostilities (Fox 2006; Silva 2009).

Despite having died quite young, at the age of 36, Fox dedicated
much of his life to a brilliant literary career, leaving to posterity a vast
legacy covering a wide range of genres, including essays, novels, plays,
travel accounts and numerous newspaper articles. Among the sixteen

volumes published during his life or posthumously Fox's best-known
works are his travel reports, which record his impressions gathered during his stay in the Soviet Union as well as his numerous essays, encompassing biography, history, philosophy and political theory (Fox 2006;
Silva 2009).

Portugal Now is a work comprising eight chapters. The first part,
"European Journey", can be considered a prefatory chapter, containing
observations regarding the international political scene at a time when
Europe was already menaced by the growing fear of a new world conflict. In this brief introduction to his travel narrative, Fox describes his
passage through France and his short stay in Paris, where he waited
about a week for the ship that would transport him to Lisbon (Fox 1937:
8). Fox compares the situation in the Old Continent before the First
World War with the broad picture of Europe in the 1930s, clearly threatened by the rise of authoritarian and totalitarian regimes determined to
impose a "New Order". In the French capital the author catches a
glimpse of this new Europe, on the brink of destruction, describing how
the City of Light was then preparing itself to endure air raids and an organized attempt to destroy the very centre of European cultural heritage.
Thus, even in France, the heart of the Old Continent and one of the most
prominent bulwarks of Western Civilization (the true repository of the
Humanist tradition), was then under threat (Fox 1937: 21). The ideological tone which characterizes the first chapter remains unaltered in the
following section of the travelogue, entitled "Emigrant Ship", where the
author, adopting a strongly ironic register, describes his sea journey from
Boulogne to Lisbon, in the third class of a cargo ship, crowded with
emigrants, Jews and political refugees from Eastern Europe. The vessel
is figuratively transfigured into a true microcosm or a veritable allegory
of the Old Continent and "The New Europe", the monstrous form of
which was looming on the horizon.

The author, a well-read and educated traveller, possessing a vast
humanist culture and relatively well acquainted with the situation in Portugal, landed in Lisbon a few days later, without credentials and having
few contacts in the Lusitanian capital. During his stay in the Portuguese
capital, Fox, the communist militant and undercover spy, publicly assumed the identity of a writer interested in learning about New State
Portugal (*Estado Novo*) or even of the simple and innocent British tourist. After visiting the British Embassy and spending some time in the

seaside resort of Estoril (Fox 1937: 38-40), the author decides to put his plan into operation. Besides gathering information on the Nationalist Army's supply lines in Portuguese territory, Fox was actually determined to learn as much as he could about the country itself. Thus, having for such purpose obtained the address of the head of the National Propaganda Office, the author desperately tried to arrange an appointment with him, chasing him persistently for five consecutive days and nights. By the end of this farcical and fruitless pursuit, Fox definitely gives up trying to obtain the intelligence he sought from the Portuguese authorities (Fox 1937: 26-27).

Adopting an alternative course of action, the author promptly makes his way to Hotel Vitória, one of the favourite Nationalist meeting points in Lisbon, where thousands of Spanish refugees came together and also where the Nazi airmen stayed overnight when they called at the Portuguese capital, on their way to the Spanish front. Playing the role of the curious but innocent tourist, Fox decides to mix with the hotel guests and quickly starts chatting with the Spanish barman, an enthusiastic supporter of General Franco.

Particularly appealing is Fox's description of the perfectly free and unrestricted behaviour of the nationalist refugees living in Lisbon. The traveller illustrates to perfection the exuberant presence of Franco's supporters in the Portuguese capital, enjoying the tacit approval of the authorities. In this respect Fox's allegations are far from being the mere product of his fanciful imagination, being thoroughly confirmed by contemporary historical sources (Nogueira 2000: 177; Léonard 1996: 146-147). As a matter of fact, the Portuguese government's support of the Spanish Nationalists was not merely logistic, as it actually included the human and military fields. It is well known that thousands of Portuguese volunteers, namely members of the Portuguese Legion, fought with Franco's army against the Spanish Republic (Medina 2002: XII, 335). Fox provides details of this support to Franco:

> The story of intervention is a simple one. The government of Dr. Salazar, Europe's model dictator, looked upon itself as in military alliance with the Burgos government. Staff cars of the Burgos government, bearing official notice they had been requisitioned by the rebel military authorities, drove openly about Lisbon, from the hotel Aviz, their political headquarters, to the Victoria, their organizational centre, or to the Portuguese Government offices. [...] Moreover, by October, the rebels themselves were in a position to send armed merchantmen to Lisbon. [...]

Throughout August planes were being landed at Lisbon by German and Italian ships, mostly the former. They were assembled by German mechanics at the Lisbon airport and flown from there to Spain. The Junker bombers were fitted with bomb-racks and machine-gun turrets. The Germans have quite a number of mechanics le-gitimately in Lisbon, for it is a port of call for the Hindenburg and Graf Zeppelin and also a calling place for a seaplane line (Fox 1937: 32-33).

Despite the fact that, in September 1936, the Lisbon government was forced to join the neutrality pact by Great Britain and other Western powers, this agreement was never respected by the Portuguese authori-ties. However, as Fox naturally observes, this obvious disregard for the neutrality pact was common to several other Western European nations (Fox 1937: 32), such as the Netherlands, United Kingdom and France, where large companies and economic groups regularly sold weapons and airplanes to the Burgos government (Beevor 2007: 167-77; Léonard 1998: 147-48; Salvadó: 108-10). However, far more interesting than the previous sections of *Portugal Now* are chapters VI and VII, respectively entitled "A National Saviour" and "Dictatorship and Civilization," where Fox attempts to portray Salazar's Portugal, conveying to the reader his own impression of the "New State".

Unlike the majority of his fellow travellers who visited Portugal at the time, Fox clearly avoids reiterating the usual commonplaces about the Portuguese regime and the dictator's personality. Whilst the majority of his counterparts confined themselves to portraying Salazar as a messi-anic character, an honest, humble, merciful, but firm and divinely in-spired man (the benevolent and model dictator who managed to free Portugal from the social and political anarchy of the First Republic and succeeded in rescuing a ruined country from bankruptcy), Ralph Fox puts forward quite the opposite perspective —a realistic, blunt and caus-tic view of the Portugal of the time and of the dictator's character (Fox 1937: 46-47). In fact, the majority of British travellers who visited the country merely repeated *clichés* and reproduced uncritically hastily ab-sorbed arguments conveyed in the abundant propaganda materials issued by the Portuguese government. Fox's objective was precisely to decon-struct the idealized and immaculate image of the Portuguese dictator, who was treated with extreme benevolence by the foreign press. There-fore, he denounces with subtle irony all those (namely British journal-ists) who described Salazar as being a great statesman or a financial gen-ius:

As a spectacle Salazar has not got the first qualification for membership of the dictator's union. He never appears in public, nor speaks on the radio, nor reviews the army, nor wears a uniform, nor murders his enemies with his own hands, nor has his photograph hung up in every shop window. He himself explains his hermit life by the need for thought, and certainly the financial affairs of a Fascist state require some concentrated thinking [...] Not until 1933 did he even feel it necessary that a Salazar myth should be created to rival the Hitler or the Mussolini myth. But having made the decision, he has seen to it that his new propaganda department has created a very good variation in the dictator myths for home and foreign consumption. He is the modest and silent dictator, the philosopher ruler, the financial genius whose real-politik deals with first things first, and of course, the regeneration of the Portuguese national spirit (Fox 1937: 61-62).

The traveller quite ingeniously devises a way of redeeming the First Portuguese Republic from the deeply negative image so many had passed on, laying the blame on the disastrous economic recession into which the country had been plunged from 1910 to 1926, to the legacy of a corrupt and obscurantist monarchy, to Portugal's participation in the First World War and the subsequent economic crisis that shook the Western World:

The monarchy, in the persons of the members of the house of Braganza, was neither popular nor respected. As a country, Portugal has always been less priest-ridden than Spain, but the monarchy had the closest connections with the Church, that is to say with political and social reaction, with obscurantism, dirt, ignorance, and general unsavoriness. Administration was corrupt, the people overtaxed and wretched, the country bankrupt. [...] The important thing, is that the monarchy in Portugal left the new Republic with a heritage of debt and corruption (*Idem*: 47-49).

The closing chapter of the travelogue and final stage of Ralph Fox's journey to Portugal is doubtlessly one of the most captivating from a sociological viewpoint and proves to be of the utmost interest to specialists both in Anglo-Portuguese relations and in contemporary European history.

This particular section of *Portugal Now* can be considered fundamental as an historical document, since the traveller allegedly witnessed two events of relative importance occurred in Lisbon during his stay. The first of these was the Portuguese Navy's uprising that took place on 8 September 1936 (Fox 1937: 71), in which this section of the armed forces attempted to overthrow Salazar's dictatorship (Medina 2002: XII, 321-42; Serrão 2000: XIV, 90). Besides this allusion to the unsuccessful

"Sailor's Revolt", Fox witnessed the siege of the Spanish Embassy, organized by followers of the Burgos government with the support of the Portuguese authorities, and the subsequent invasion of the building, which took place after Portugal broke off diplomatic relations with the Spanish Republic. This tragic sequence of events occurred on the same day Ralph Fox intended to interview the Spanish ambassador, who had stuck by the Madrid government and would end by going into exile in France and Latin America (Fox 1937: 76-77; Medina 2002: XII, 334-35).

However, the most curious and fascinating aspect of this final section resides in its prophetic tone. The author's extensive knowledge of European politics and his understanding of international affairs deepen his acute awareness of the growing danger facing the Old Continent, once again on the eve of global war. Therefore, the author sees the Spanish civil conflict as a mere prelude to the disaster that was to follow and reveals his deep concern about Europe's future, in light of not only the expansionist policy of the Axis Powers, their intervention in Spain, but also their growing influence in Portugal. Ralph Fox was perfectly aware that Europe's future would be decided, at an early stage, in Iberia, revealing his obvious fear that Franco's victory and that of his staunch allies —Germany, Italy and Portugal— would seriously swing the balance of power in favour of the right-wing totalitarianism all over the Continent (Fox 1937: 78-79).

Whether we agree or disagree with the traveller's opinions, and the strong ideological and the occasional pamphletary tone of the text, this travelogue is arguably essential reading for anyone interested in contemporary history or who is committed to revealing the dark and obscure facet of Salazar's regime. The reader cannot fail to be impressed by Fox's candid and unaffected style, by his conviction and unwavering commitment to his principles. Although more than seven decades have elapsed since *Portugal Now* was first published in London and Ralph Fox fell in battle in the fields of Andalusia fighting for an ideal, this volume still deserves an attentive but objective perusal at the beginning of the twenty-first century.

Bibliography

Beevor, A. 2007 [1982]. *A Guerra Civil de Espanha*, Lisboa, Bertrand Editora.

Calado, A. I. N. 2005. *O Portugal de Salazar Visto de uma Janela Trasmontana*, Lisboa, CEAP, FCT.

Fox, R. 1937. *Portugal Now*, London, Lawrence and Wishart.

—. 2006. *Portugal Now, Um Espião Comunista no Estado Novo*, R. Lopes (trans.), J. Nunes (pref.), Lisboa, Tinta da China.

Léonard, Y. 1998 [1996]. *Salazarismo e Fascismo*, M. Soares (pref.), Mem-Martins, Editorial Inquérito.

Medina, J. (coord.). [2002]. *Historia de Portugal*, vol. 12, Madrid, S.A.P.E.

Nogueira, F. 2000 [1981]. *O Estado Novo (1933-1974)*, M. R. Sousa (pref.), Lisboa, Livraria Civilização Editora.

Rosas, F. & J. M. Brandão de Brito. 1996. *Dicionário de História do Estado Novo*, M. F. Rollo (coord.), 2 vols., Venda Nova, Bertrand Editora.

Salvadó, F. J. R. 2006 [2005]. *A Guerra Civil de Espanha, Origens Evolução e Consequências*, Mem-Martins, Publicações Europa-América.

Silva, J. P. P. 2009. "Ralph Fox e *Portugal Now*: a odisseia de um militante comunista à descoberta do país de Salazar", *Revista de Estudos Anglo-Portugueses* 18, 207-238.

Serrão, J. V. 2000. *História de Portugal (1935-1941)*, vol. 14, Lisboa, Verbo.

Vicente, A. P. 2003. *Espanha e Portugal, Um Olhar sobre as Relações Peninsulares no Século XX*, Lisboa, Tribuna da História.

MIQUEL POMAR AMER

Becoming the Other: Perceptions of the English in Nadeem Aslam's *Maps for Lost Lovers*

Nadeem Aslam was born in Pakistan but he moved to England when he was fourteen. He is now considered to be one of the most promising young British authors. Aslam represents English society from within even though his perspective is enriched with abundant references to his origins as well. Indeed, the characters in *Maps for Lost Lovers* belong to the close-knit Pakistani community in an unnamed English town. Obviously, the focus on the migrant community allows Aslam to approach the English from a defamiliarised point of view. For this reason, by "Becoming the other", the title refers to Aslam's intentional subversion of the roles assigned to local and migrant populations: he places white English society in an alien position, away from the central position it has used to occupy in English literature. Aslam acknowledges this intention in an interview with Michael O'Connor in which the latter states that "[t]here is no integration in the novel, England, as it were, is absent", only to be quickly corrected by Aslam, who says "only WHITE England is absent" (O'Connor 2005).

One of the most obvious results of the subversive technique that Aslam brings into play is that the dichotomy native versus non-native is questioned. For any reader of the novel this dichotomy might seem reinforced rather than blurred. Nevertheless, the apparent opposition between the host society and the migrant community is gradually softened. This relationship is summed up in a few lines in the opening chapter:

> It was a time in England when the white attitude towards the dark-skinned foreigners was just beginning to go from *I don't want to see them* to *I don't mind working next to them if I'm forced to, as long as I don't have to speak to them*, an attitude that would change again within the next ten years to *I don't mind speaking to them when I have to in the workplace, as long as I don't have to talk to them outside the working hours*, and then in another ten years to *I don't mind them socializing in the same place as me if they must, as long as I don't have to live next to them*. By then

it was 1970s and because the immigrant families had to live *somewhere* and were moving in next door to the whites, there were calls for a ban on immigration and the repatriation of the immigrants who were already here (11; emphasis in the original).

South Asian immigrants applied their strategies in order to turn England in a less hostile territory. One of the first measures is to rename the new environment according to their cultural inheritance as a way of accommodating themselves to the new space. Wittily, Aslam does not say in which English town the novel is set and the reader just knows of its existence through the new name given by the migrant community: Dasht-e-Tanhaii. However, this action is not homogeneous and each nationality in the neighbourhood —Indian, Pakistani, Bangladeshi or Sri Lankan— names the streets according to their homeland: "Only one name has been accepted by every group, remaining unchanged. It's the name of the town itself. Dasht-e-Tanhaii" (28-29).

However, this appropriation does not only affect urban place names. The English landscape is described in an exoticised way so that it is merely a pretext to describe the South Asian reality. For instance, by looking at the river in town, Shamas recalls the grandeur of the Indus:

This river is a recent stream compared to the rivers of the Indian Subcontinent: the Indus, its far bank wedded to the horizon, is an ocean-wide stretch of water that remembers thousands of years of history. And the river of his childhood —the Chenab— could rise by several metres during the monsoon (134).

The monsoon is yet another element that is missed by Shamas, who cannot avoid thinking about it at the sight of snow: "Among the innumerable other losses, to come to England was to lose a season, because, in the part of Pakistan that he is from, there are five seasons in a year [...] Winter, Spring, Summer, Monsoon, Autumn" (5). This scene, Moore claims, encompasses "motifs and references from the Pakistani to the northern English context in order to render the depressing urban landscape pastoral, even exotic" (2009: 7). Every experience is rooted in Pakistan, showing a balance between the absence and the presence.

In addition, apart from contributing to its exotic turn, the inclusion of certain alien elements in the English landscape opens up the possibility for hope: for instance, the existence of rose-ringed parakeets in the neighbourhood. This species has established feral populations worldwide, including urban areas of Europe and North America. Thus, parakeets are perceived as a representative of the homeland landscape and consequently welcomed:

> When she arrived in England all those years ago she had thought the reason this country lacked blossom-headed parakeets, lorikeets, mynahs and bee-eaters was that its inhabitants did not plant the correct trees and vines in their gardens (95).

However, the fear that the parakeets could expand their dominion over the town is also present: "they say there's a flock of them out here. And it's thriving. There is a fear that they'll soon be everywhere. Such a harsh voice" (172). However, following Phil Dewhurst's ideas, we should question the dichotomy between the native and the non-native: "The key question is 'at what point in time do we start with our taxonomy of native species?'" (qtd. in Tolia-Kelly 2008: 293). Thus, the inclusion of many South Asian aspects in the setting of the novel does not only give an exotic taste but also has more overarching consequences as it problematises purity and the notion of native versus alien.

In fact, longing for the homeland is a common aspect in the first-generation immigrants. Dasht-e-Tanhaii is translated as "The Wilderness of Solitude" or "The Desert of Loneliness". Obviously, this association is not free from its religious implications:

> [M]any improvements were made to the interiors which until then had been seen only as temporary accommodation in a country never thought of as home —the period in England was the equivalent of earthly suffering, the return one day to Pakistan entry into Paradise (96).

For this reason, it may not come as a surprise that there is a deep hatred for England while Pakistan is proudly celebrated. Nevertheless, this situation is the result of failed expectations. We can divide the diasporic experience of the first-generation members into three different phases.

Before departure, England is imagined as a land where everything is possible, close to a utopian state:

> Once, marvelling at the prosperity of England, a visitor from Pakistan had remarked that it was almost as though the Queen disguised herself every night and went out into the streets of her country to find out personally what her subjects most needed and desired in life, so she could arrange for their wishes to come true the next day (4-5).

Even though this fragment is hyperbolic, England is presented as a place where everybody wants to go because it means prosperity. The expectations are high enough to risk entering the country illegally, regardless of the difficulties they might find afterwards to get a job. An illegal immigrant berates another for supporting independence for Kashmir:

> You lot who have legal status in a rich country don't know how lucky you are. [...]
> Those bastard prime ministers and presidents and generals —both Indian and Paki-
> stani— they should see what people have to go through to reach a place where they
> can earn a decent living. They should ask those people whether they want freedom
> in Kashmir or a chance to live with safety and with food in our bellies in their own
> country (219-20).

This quote reveals that the migratory project is not such a dream because leaving their country is not a way of prospering as much as a way to escape from precariousness. Yet, such a project is a great investment both in economic and symbolic terms.

Consequently, the second phase comes out of the failure of such expectations. What they imagined before migrating does not coincide with the reality they must face: "A person can't do anything here that he can freely over there. A dog was asked why he was fleeing from a rich household where they fed him meat every day. 'They feed me meat, yes, but I am not allowed to bark'" (199). This frustration ends up in the third phase: hatred. Once they realise the social status they have in England, many migrants resign themselves to thinking that nothing will change and, ultimately, they turn that frustration into hatred towards the host country. Kaukab, the mother figure, represents this attitude in a very clear way: "Compared with England, Pakistan is a poor and humble country but she aches for it, because to be thirsty is to crave a glass of simple water and no amount of rich buttermilk will do" (70). All throughout the actual process of migration, though, there is the underlying idea of a future return. As Muhammad Anwar observes,

> For an average Pakistani, migration means that though he has had to come to Brit-
> ain for economic reasons he is never able to feel that he has come for good. Even if
> he thought he had come permanently there are kin and friends in Pakistan who can-
> not follow him because of the migration restrictions. By definition, then, the Paki-
> stani migrant is a person whose network of relations cannot be located in Britain
> alone (1979: 219).

The assumption that their stay in England is just temporary strengthens the boundaries between migrants and locals, not only because of strained attitudes of the locals but also because of migrants' reluctance to participate in the host society. However, characters as Kaukab also show a degree of ambivalence concerning the feasibility of the return because her offspring think of Britain as their country. Although her husband and she planned to go back to Pakistan after his retirement, she "has told him he would have to leave without her —she would remain in hated England because her children are here" (60). The return becomes a myth as it remains as an aim but it is very unlikely to ever happen. There is even the case of a woman who realizes she will never go back because "she has started monthly payments for funeral arrangements at her mosque near her house" (45).

In addition, England is despised because it is seen as an impure country and as an example of what Kaukab calls the Western decadence:

> England is a dirty country, an unsacred country full of people filthy with disgusting habits and practices, where, for all one knew, unclean dogs and cats, or unwashed people, or people who have not bathed after sexual congress, or drinks and people with invisible dried drops of alcohol on their shirts and trousers, or menstruating women, could very possibly have come into contact with the bus seat a good Muslim has just chosen to sit on, or touched an item in the shop that he or she has just picked up —and so most Muslim men and women of the neighbourhood have a few sets of clothing reserved solely for outdoors, taking them off the moment they get home to put on the ones they know to be clean (267).

Islam is considered the main source of purity. Consequently everything that goes against Islamic laws is considered impure. For this reason, prejudices do not apply only to white population but also to the non-Muslim South Asian communities. As Waterman says,

> Threats of contamination also exist between groups from different areas of the subcontinent, especially as regards Hindus and Sikhs in spite of their common bond as immigrants, leading one to the conclusion that such preoccupation with purity is based primarily on religion rather than race, wherein white skin in Britain is a marker of religious, rather than racial, difference (2010: 23).

The white English stand for the dangers of an open and free sexuality. For instance, there is a prostitute in the neighbourhood who undoubtedly is white because "had she been Indian or Pakistani, she would have been

assaulted and driven out of the area within days of moving in for bringing shame on her people" (16). Kaukab also accuses her daughter of
moving out to get "the freedom to do obscene things with white boys and
lead a sin-smeared life" (111). Her worries even extend to the future of
her grandson, "who would no doubt begin to chase girls as soon as he is
in his teens and be sexually active by the time he is fifteen, thinking dis-
play-of-wantonness and sex-before-marriage was the norm and not grave
sins!" (309).

In addition, the impurity of the whites turns them into the perfect
bogeyman to make children obey. A little girl is told to behave or

> she'll be given away to a white person who'll make her eat pork and drink alcohol
> and not wash her bottom after going to the toilet —forcing her to use only toilet pa-
> per. [...] I'll not only give you away to the whites, I'll give away your brother too.
> They'd make sure he doesn't learn to drive when he grows up and has to sit in the
> passenger while you drive. Do you want a eunuch like that for a brother? House-
> husbands, if you please! (220-21).

This threat, which is only used to prevent the girl from taking two lollies
at a shop, shows many of the prejudices and how they are passed on to
the next generation by stressing the differences in cultural practices.
Nonetheless, this critical approach is applicable not only to the Pakistani
community but also to English society as a whole: the intended white
English audience of the novel will recognise this representation as
stereotyping and it should make the reader question whether his/her
ideas about certain ethnic groups are not too simplistic, or even wrong.

Moreover, the English are also perceived as the enemy who does
everything to prevent Pakistanis from succeeding. Kaukab holds the art
teacher responsible for encouraging her son to become a painter instead
of working towards a position of influence (123). When her son also tells
her that he has undergone a vasectomy, she thinks of the operation as "a
Christian conspiracy to stop the number of Muslims from increasing"
(59). Yet, behind all these conspiracy theories there is another element of
the utmost importance: Pakistan's colonial past. Whites are considered
thieves because they "stole all [Pakistan's] wealth, beginning with the
Koh-i-Noor diamond" (45). However, these facts are relativized because
Pakistani immigrants also benefit from the English welfare state: "May
God keep the coffers of Queen Elizabeth filled to the brim, for she provides me and my daughter with food and housing. I don't care if she is

holding on to our Koh-i-Noor diamond so tightly her knuckles are white" (210).

Lemke considers that "the white population does not pose a tangible threat to the Pakistani community" (2008: 175). However, there appear many cases in the novel that show a high degree of intolerance. Although Lemke seems to be aware just of the bus abuse scene in which a white passenger insults the driver with a collection of prejudices and disturbing stereotypes summed up in one sentence —"Oi, Gupta, or whatever it is you call yourself, Abdul-Patel. Mr Illegal Immigrant-Asylum Seeker! Get back into your seat!" (178)— we can list some others like the pig head that appears in front of the mosque, several instances in which some characters say that they have been insulted —"she had been called a 'darkie bitch' by a white man in the town centre" (312)—, and the beating that Chanda's brothers receive in prison.

Yet, these negative perceptions are balanced with other rather positive descriptions. There is a certain inferiority complex that might be rooted into colonial ideology since it deals with questions of race and, even biological justifications. For instance, Kaukab feels tiny when she has to meet white people. On one occasion she has a white guest, and even though Kaukab has spent some time arranging herself before she arrives, she can only think of her ugliness compared to the guest's beauty, "she who no doubt had a perfectly made-up face framed by perfectly arranged hair" (36). Her self-hatred goes so far as to blame herself when she sees a defect in her white daughter-in-law: "she is ashamed when these marks appear on her own nails, yet another proof for the white people that the Pakistanis are unhealthy people, disease-riddled, filthy bearers of epidemics" (317). Certainly, her contact with white people is infrequent but she is never free from this inferiority complex, as when she goes to the doctor and he realises that it is her birthday, something that her husband had forgotten: "she's hot with shame at what the white doctor would now think of Pakistanis, of Muslims —they are like animals, not even remembering or celebrating birthdays. Dumb cattle"(65). Although these words are uttered by a Pakistani character, they reveal the trend of thought behind generalisations and stereotyping. It is even more striking that these are placed in the white doctor's mind, suggesting a critique of certain xenophobic attitudes.

To conclude, I would like to highlight that this novel has in mind an eminently white British audience. Consequently, this exercise of subverting the traditional roles and giving the chance of seeing the world from the Pakistani perspective will allow readers to question their own attitude towards the immigrants. In this case, whites are blamed for many things that they are not responsible for and it should encourage a white readership to think before freely accusing foreigners for what goes wrong in society. It is the evidence that an actual return is merely a myth that helps migrants to put up with their often precarious situation. The sooner both migrants and locals accept that they have come to stay and relations must be established in order to construct a cohesive society, the better. In fact, Kaukab and Shamas's children appear in the final chapters, leaving open the possibility of a generational change that goes for a higher degree of tolerance and coexistence regardless of one's origins or ethnicity.

Bibliography

Anwar, M. 1979. *The Myth of Return. Pakistanis in Britain*, London, Heinemann.

Aslam, N. 2004. *Maps for Lost Lovers*, London, Faber & Faber.

Lemke, C. 2008. "Racism in the Diaspora: Nadeem Aslam's *Maps for Lost Lovers* (2004)", in L. Eckstein et al. (eds.), *Multi-Ethnic Britain 2000+*, Amsterdam, Rodopi, 171-83.

Moore, L. 2009. "British Muslim Identities and Spectres of Terror in Nadeem Aslam's *Maps for Lost Lovers*" *Postcolonial Text* 5: 2, 1-18.

O'Connor, M. 2005. "Writing Against Terror–Nadeem Aslam", *Three Monkeys Online–The Free Current Affairs and Art Magazine*, <http://www.threemonkeysonline.com/als_page2/_nadeem_aslam_i nterview.html> [accessed 20 December 2010].

Tolia-Kelly, D. P. 2008. "Investigations into Diasporic 'Cosmopolitanism': Beyond Mythologies of the 'Non-native'", in C. Dwyer & C. Bressey (eds.), *New Geographies of Race and Racism*, Aldershot, Ashgate, 283-96.

Waterman, D. 2010. "Memory and Cultural Identity: Negotiating Modernity in Nadeem Aslam's *Maps for Lost Lovers*" *Pakistaniaat: A Journal of Pakistan Studies* 2: 2, 18-35.

BLANCA RIPOLL SINTES

"Extranjeros hasta en el nombre".
El rebautismo de los guerrilleros antifranquistas en
Las noches sin estrellas de Nino Quevedo

El Premio Nadal del año 1960 fue concedido a la faulkneriana novela de Ramiro Pinilla *Las ciegas hormigas* —hermosa novela reeditada en 2010 por Tusquets. Sin embargo, en un humilde tercer puesto, quedó, enmascarada por ciertos comentarios de la crítica contemporánea, una de las primeras novelas escritas en la España de la posguerra en torno a la vida del Maquis o guerrilla antifranquista: *Las noches sin estrellas*, de Nino Quevedo, que publicó editorial Destino en 1961.

Guerrilleros sin tregua, habitantes de la frontera, en tierra de nadie, condenados a vivir entre las sombras: entrar en el Maquis suponía perder la identidad propia —de ahí que se rebautizaran en función de un código particular—, cortar casi por lo sano toda raíz, ser considerado como traidor a la esencia española defendida por la ortodoxia del régimen franquista. Extranjeros, por tanto, personajes ajenos a la supuesta autenticidad esencial del país. Los guerrilleros del Maquis fueron temidos y a la vez idealizados, en tanto que héroes románticos, por los habitantes de las montañas del norte de España.

Reivindicar esta novela —sutil, de hermoso estilo, hábil dosificación de la intriga y trabada composición—, totalmente desconocida por el gran público, no solo es un deber para el investigador de la literatura sino una respuesta a un interés general hacia este fenómeno. No deja de ser significativo el hecho de que el Premio Nadal del año 2011 fuera concedido a la obra de Alicia Giménez Bartlett, *Donde nadie te encuentre*, basada en la vida de la "Pastora", la guerrillera maqui más buscada por la guardia civil; o que la obra de Almudena Grandes, *Inés o la alegría*, transcurra a lo largo de una fallida invasión del maquis en la Vall d'Aran, en el Pirineo leridano; o que en la última Bienal de Venecia, Lluís Galter llevara la película *Caracremada*, basada en la vida del guerrillero Ramon Vila. Sin duda, estas obras son testimonio de la vigencia de la que goza el tema del Maquis.

No obstante, las relaciones entre la guerrilla antifranquista y la literatura tienen un recorrido largo y complejo a sus espaldas. De 1997 es *Maquis*, la novela de Alfons Cervera, de 1994 *La agonía del búho chico*, de Justo Vila, y de 1985 la hermosa obra literaria *Luna de lobos* de Julio Llamazares. Piezas narrativas de distinta composición y diverso estilo que, no obstante, comparten un posicionamiento ideológico del autor que pretende reivindicar la existencia de los guerrilleros de los montes. Estas obras vienen a ser el eslabón perdido entre el boom editorial actual y cuatro novelas poco conocidas que durante la posguerra española trataron este fenómeno: *Víbora*, de Héctor Vázquez Azpiri; *Testamento en la montaña*, de Manuel Arce (ambas de 1956); *La paz empieza nunca*, de Emilio Romero (1958); y finalmente *Las noches sin estrellas*, de Nino Quevedo (1961).

Si bien ninguna de estas obras se sale de los márgenes prefijados por el régimen franquista, la actitud de los autores y el enfoque de cada uno de los narradores de las mismas son radicalmente distintos. La visión permitida y legitimada por el gobierno reducía dicho fenómeno a la sección de "Sucesos" en los periódicos de la época: crímenes, robos y secuestros. Es decir, lo establecido por el decreto-ley aprobado el 18 de abril de 1947 —después de dos años de intensa actividad guerrillera alrededor de la geografía española. Recordemos, además, que una Circular de la Dirección General de Seguridad (aprobada el 11 de marzo del mismo año de 1947) prohibía utilizar los términos "guerrilla" o "guerrillero" y ordenaba emplear los conceptos, enmascarados por la sesgada visión del régimen, "bandolerismo" o "bandolero" (Chaput 2003: 11). Como apunta Secundino Serrano: "Forma parte de la lógica política que el régimen franquista tejiera una red de silencios en torno a la guerrilla y estableciera un programa minucioso para hacerla invisible" (2001: 14).

No obstante, y como avanzábamos antes, existe una evidente gradación ideológica entre las tres novelas. En *Víbora*, de Vázquez Azpiri (1956), la acción de la novela transcurre en un pequeño pueblo asturiano cercano a los Picos de Europa, y en ella el narrador en tercera persona focaliza la acción, mayoritariamente, en la conciencia de Lin, un viejo campesino que trata de sobrevivir a la sequía y vive esperando que su hijo mayor Toño, regrese al pueblo. Lin, antiguo revolucionario en México, tiene un hijo menor, Juanco, que se echa al monte después de matar a su novia, Raquelina, debido a su adulterio y a sus burlas. En la línea ético-estética propia de la narrativa del realismo social de los años cincuenta, Vázquez Azpiri busca las raíces socio-antropológicas que configuran una patología criminal, ya que Juanco aparece en la novela como un "bandolero", es decir, un asesino. El determinismo familiar (una madre loca; un padre duro con sus hijos) provocará el carácter huraño de Juanco que, ante la traición y las burlas de Raquelina (adulterio y embarazo ilegítimo), se transforma en un ser animal, atávico, bestializado. Sus instintos criminales afloran de un modo similar a cómo se explica la violencia en el *Pascual Duarte* celiano o a cómo se explicaría, años más tarde, en *Las guerras de nuestros antepasados* (1975) de Miguel Delibes.

Por su parte, Manuel Arce situará también en territorio asturiano (Llanes) la acción de *Testamento en la montaña* (1970). En esta novela, los dos personajes escondidos en el monte, Enzo y El Bayona, desdoblan las dos facetas que Vázquez Azpiri aunaba en el personaje de Juanco: la patología criminal y la bestialidad atávica, irracional y desmedida. Enzo nos es descrito como un individuo imprevisible, con cambios repentinos de personalidad y una tendencia innata a la crueldad; por su parte, El Bayona es el brazo ejecutor del primero, para quien golpear o matar se ha convertido en una acción tan primaria como comer o dormir. No obstante, ambos personajes no son sino un pretexto para que se desarrolle la acción principal de la novela: la batalla interna que se libra en la conciencia de Nando Porrúa, entre el amor que ha sentido siempre por su mujer y la certeza —mayor a cada hora que transcurre en su secuestro en la montaña— de que su mujer nunca le ha querido.

Por el contrario, la novela de Emilio Romero *La paz empieza nunca* (1961), hace gala de una visión sin fisuras y totalmente adepta a la de la ortodoxia franquista. El personaje principal, López, falangista y miembro de la División Azul en Rusia, logrará infiltrarse, en una contrapartida, en la guerrilla antifranquista para aniquilarlos a todos mediante una treta final.

Frente a estas lecturas literarias de la historia, se nos proporciona un paso más en la evolución del tratamiento de este tema en la convocatoria del Premio Nadal de 1960. Aquel año recaería, como decíamos al principio, en Ramiro Pinilla; Gonzalo Torrente Malvido quedó como primer finalista con *Hombres varados* y en tercer lugar, hallamos la obra que va a centrar nuestro trabajo, la primera novela larga publicada por el escritor y cineasta santanderino, afincado en Madrid, Nino Quevedo, *Las noches sin estrellas*.

Quevedo —Nino o Benigno— había ya concurrido al Nadal anterior, concedido a Ana María Matute por *Primera memoria*, con la novela *La raya*; esta quedó entre los cinco primeros finalistas pero no contó con el premio de la publicación posterior, a cuyo texto nos ha sido imposible acceder. En cambio, sí vería la luz en la cuidada colección "Áncora y Delfín", su segundo intento de hacerse con el más codiciado galardón literario de la posguerra española,[1] el Eugenio Nadal de novela, convocado por Ediciones Destino.

Las noches sin estrellas es la primera novela escrita en territorio español —y durante la dictadura franquista— que focaliza la acción en la circunstancia de los guerrilleros del monte. La fábula que Nino Quevedo desgrana en los 47 capítulos de *Las noches sin estrellas*, a través de un enfoque narrativo multipolar, se centra en la historia de amor entre Bernardo y Zoila, que sirve a modo de foco principal alrededor del cual bailan los otros motivos —de un protagonismo similar en la novela—, como la dura existencia de los fugitivos en el monte, la miseria de la vida cotidiana en la España de la posguerra, o el abuso de poder de ciertos personajes al amparo del régimen, como el estraperlista y usurero Segundo García. Tras su primer encuentro en el baile dominical de Taces, Zoila y Bernardo empiezan una relación amorosa secreta, citándose por las noches en el pajar de la familia de Zoila, a las afueras de Villamayor. El narrador alterna la narración de esas noches sin estrellas —cubiertos por el tejado del pajar— con la de las acciones de los guerrilleros, las de Segundo García o las de la guardia civil. La pasión de Segundo por Zoila desencadena el trágico final: tras la delación de Segundo a la guardia civil, se produce la muerte de Bernardo, dejando a Zoila embarazada de pocos meses, y la de casi todos los guerrilleros del monte (a excepción de Zambrano y Manguán, que logran cruzar la frontera). Zoila, llena de

---

1   Hasta la creación, en 1959, del Premio Biblioteca Breve, en el seno del sello editorial Seix Barral, el Eugenio Nadal de novela, creado por los hombres de la revista *Destino* y de la casa editorial homónima en 1944 (concedido aquel año a la desconocida Carmen Laforet, por *Nada*), fue el premio narrativo más bien considerado. Hoy podemos afirmar que, con sus errores y aciertos, ofreció al panorama editorial español una nómina de novelistas que marcarían las décadas de la posguerra española: Laforet, Delibes, Matute, Suárez Carreño, Sánchez Ferlosio, Martín Gaite, Fernández Santos, etc. Para más información, véase Ripoll Sintes (2011: 50-71).

fría determinación, ultima la venganza final de la obra, matando a Segundo García y refugiándose en el único lugar seguro, amable, que queda: la cabaña de Brígido y Lucía, refugio habitual de los guerrilleros el cual permanece —en un final suspendido y abierto— como el único futuro posible para Zoila y su pequeño. La dosificación de la intriga, la contención poética del estilo y la estructura de tragedia clásica de la obra nos sitúan ante una novela de excelente trabazón interna, que gana en cada relectura nuevos simbolismos y matices.

La hábil estrategia que adoptó Nino Quevedo y que le permitió publicar dicha novela a pesar de la vigilancia de la censura fue de doble vía: en primer lugar, centró las actividades desarrolladas por el grupo de guerrilleros en cuestiones económicas, materiales, y no ideológicas (apenas insinuadas en la novela); en segundo lugar, se desvió de la Historia con mayúsculas y, siguiendo el binomio unamuniano, posó su mirada en la intrahistoria de los personajes. Son numerosos los elementos que traslucen una lectura ideológica, una actitud moral y reivindicativa del escritor frente al fenómeno en cuestión —elementos que desgranaremos a lo largo de este trabajo—, si bien el resultado final no ofrecía evidencias suficientes para que los censores de la época pudieran achacarle cualquier tipo de partidismo. El matiz y el silencio, aquello que se calla, aquello que se sugiere, son las herramientas con las que Nino Quevedo forjó el edificio de esta novela y, a su vez, son el escudo que la protegieron de los embates de la censura franquista.

Uno de los aspectos que más cuidadosamente ocultó el novelista fue el uso de los nombres propios y el de los alias de los guerrilleros. En todos los casos, el lector se halla ante nombres y apellidos (Bernardo, Manguán, Zambrano, Gallardo, Félix…), a excepción del Rojo, en cuya situación el narrador se apresura a precisar que es pelirrojo para evitar suspicacias: un evidente juego semiótico de doble sentido entre el color del pelo del personaje y la filiación ideológica que el lector adivina en él. A propósito de esta cuestión, explica Serrano:

> Los apodos eran obligatorios en la resistencia por cuestiones de seguridad. El nombre estaba relacionado con el que tenían en sus pueblos (en el medio rural era habitual que todas las familias fueran conocidas con algún sobrenombre). Cuando los maquis procedían de otras provincias, recibían como apodo el gentilicio correspondiente. También los atributos o defectos físicos, los oficios no habituales y la edad marcaban el nombre de los maquis, y proliferaban los "abuelos", "chavales", "prac-

ticantes", "zapateros", "rubios" y "mancos". [...] También se utilizaron alias de
héroes caídos en la lucha contra Franco (Durruti, Lenin, Carrillo) (2001: 209-10).

La seguridad y el temor por la vida propia y la de los allegados fue una
de las causas; otra, y no menos importante, fue su condición de estar
fuera de la realidad, de pertenecer casi a otro mundo regido por normas
distintas que transcurría a la luz de la luna en lugar de a la luz del sol. Un
mundo distinto que requería, en consecuencia, nombres distintos. Así, el
re-bautismo de cada uno de los guerrilleros abría la puerta de entrada a
esa otra "realidad" que, andando el tiempo, iba a ser uno de los distintos
factores que ayudaron a su aniquilación: el progresivo distanciamiento
entre la realidad de la guerrilla y la realidad cotidiana de los españoles
durante la posguerra. El extrañamiento de quienes antaño fueron héroes,
bien considerados por los habitantes de pequeños pueblos duramente
reprimidos por las fuerzas del orden, provocó que, cada vez más, sus
figuras fueran diluyéndose y pasaran la frontera de lo concreto a lo mítico y de lo mítico a lo innecesario cuando, ya a finales de los cincuenta,
no contaban con el apoyo del Partido Comunista Español en el exilio, ni
con la mayoría de sus enlaces en el llano, ni con la aprobación del pueblo
español que empezaba a salir paulatinamente de la miseria. Explica Serrano:

> Otro error fue que los guerrilleros no consiguieron identificarse como españoles y
> estigmatizar a Franco como invasor (ideológico). Por el contrario, el franquismo
> logró que los guerrilleros aparecieran como "extranjeros" hasta en el nombre: ma-
> quis (2001: 374).

La cuestión nominal, hábilmente disimulada por Nino Quevedo en *Las
noches sin estrellas*, sí ha sido tratada con detalle por las dos últimas
novelas que recientemente han focalizado su acción en torno a la guerrilla antifranquista. Almudena Grandes explica así la transformación de
uno de sus personajes principales, el príncipe azul de la novela, tornado
quijotescamente guerrillero del monte:

> El 2 de julio de 1944 me convertí en el capitán Galán. El hombre que salió de aquel
> pueblo era distinto del que había entrado en él, y necesitaba un nombre nuevo. Mis
> hombres sólo lo encontraron después de que el Lobo, al bajar del camión en el que
> había venido a felicitarnos con los franceses de la VI, se preguntara en voz alta si
> estaba viendo soldados o galanes de cine (2010: 143).

La capacidad metamorfoseadora del nombre propio, del apodo o alias, va a adquirir visos fisiológicos en la novela de Giménez Bartlett —basada en la obra de carácter histórico de José Calvo Segarra (2009)—, *Donde nadie te encuentre*. Tras toda una vida como mujer, Teresa Pla Messeguer logra vivir la identidad que ella-él decida. En una conversación con el guerrillero-jefe de su partida, Carlos el Catalán, la Pastora adquiere conciencia de que el carácter liberador de la guerrilla antifranquista no solamente va a tener un carácter social, general, sino que en su caso va a lograr liberarla de las cadenas físicas que la tuvieron toda su vida atada a unas faldas:

> -Yo te dije una vez que en la guerrilla cada uno es lo que quiere ser. ¿Tú te sientes un hombre, Pastora?
> -Sí –le dije, y bajé la vista para decirlo.
> - Pues un hombre serás. Esta noche te vienes conmigo a casa de mi hermana que es mujer, y del maquis, y ella te cortará los pelos y te buscará ropa de hombre. Y Teresa a la mierda, ¿comprendes? ¡A la mierda con ella! (2011: 250).

Como ya apuntábamos, Nino Quevedo apenas sugirió el carácter ideológico de lucha antifranquista de sus guerrilleros, pues eso contradecía las normas dictadas por la censura. No obstante, sí es evidente la condición de sus personajes de extranjeros, de parias en su propia tierra. Solo al transgredir las fronteras entre ambos mundos —la realidad de los montes, la del llano— se produce la tragedia, la muerte final de Bernardo: la normalidad aparente de las noches de amor en el pajar —sin estrellas— provoca que el guerrillero olvide su condición de apátrida, provoca que se abandone a la dulce cotidianidad de su relación conyugal a todos los efectos, a excepción de la oficialidad del rito. Al barajarse las normas que rigen ambos mundos, al traspasarse las fronteras, ni Bernardo ni Zoila logran sustraerse a las consecuencias de dicho choque, con lo que la realidad cruel contra la que luchaban acaba recayendo sobre ellos.

Únicamente se permite el autor dejar dos puertas abiertas al final de la novela: un futuro esperanzador para Zoila y su futuro bebé, y otra vida posible en el exilio para los dos únicos guerrilleros supervivientes, Zambrano y Manguán. Dos puertas abiertas que solo pueden acaecer en tierra de nadie, en espacios donde no rijan las mismas reglas que en su país.

Bibliografía

Arce, M. 1970. *Testamento en la montaña*, Barcelona, Planeta.

Calvo Segarra, J. 2009. *La Pastora. Del monte al mito*, Valencia, Antinea.

Chaput, M.-C. 2003. "La Guerrilla antifranquista en la prensa española (1944-1949)", *Quimera* 236 (noviembre), 11-15.

Giménez Bartlett, A. 2011. *Donde nadie te encuentre*, Barcelona, Destino.

Grandes, A. 2010. *Inés o la alegría*, Barcelona, Tusquets.

Ripoll Sintes, B. 2011. *La crítica de la literatura española en el semanario "Destino" (1939-1968). La novela*, Tesis doctoral. Universitat de Barcelona.

Romero, E. 1961. *La paz empieza nunca*, Barcelona, Planeta.

Serrano, S. 2001. *Maquis. Historia de la guerrilla antifranquista*, Madrid, Temas de Hoy.

Vázquez Azpiri, H. 1956. *Víbora*, Barcelona, Destino.

Ana Rueda

Episodios africanos (1897) de Nicolás Estévanez: viaje al pasado colonialista y al futuro de África

Nicolás Estévanez Murphy (1838-1914), escritor y militar nacido en Las Palmas de Gran Canaria, fue una figura señalada antes de caer en un olvido casi absoluto. Prestó sus servicios en la campaña de África de 1860, donde obtuvo méritos de guerra, así como en Santo Domingo y en Cuba, de donde acabaría expulsado del ejército por su oposición al fusilamiento de estudiantes independentistas. Rehusó los honores y pagas de su carrera militar y eventualmente pidió la licencia absoluta del ejército. Tomó parte activa en la revolución de 1868 y en el movimiento federal de 1869, que conducirían a la proclamación en 1873 de la Primera República Española. Integrado en el Partido Republicano Federal,[1] tuvo una intensa y turbulenta vida política en la que ejerció como ministro de guerra bajo Pi y Margall.[2] Con la Restauración, Estévanez hubo de partir al exilio, a Portugal, Cuba, EE.UU., México y París.

En cuanto a sus actividades literarias, fue un habitual colaborador de la prensa y en *El Imparcial* fue publicando sus *Memorias* (1899), que más tarde dio a la luz en forma de libro.[3] Publicó libros de tema militar y geográfico, así como compendios históricos. En París colaboró en la casa editora de los hermanos Garnier y tradujo numerosas obras, labor que se convertirá en su principal medio de subsistencia en su exilio. Allí publica también sus obras más imaginativas: *Las arañas* (1882), pieza de litera-

---

1   Según González, Estévanez defendió la autonomía para Cuba y Canarias, si bien integradas en una "República Federal Ibérica" (s.p.), y no bajo una monarquía española centralista, que se oponía a su concepto federalista del Estado.

2   Merecen mención sus actuaciones insurreccionales a través de su asociación con el anarquista Mateo Morral, quien atentó contra Alfonso XIII en 1906. Estévanez es descrito como "un anarquista de salón" (contraportada de Morral).

3   Para las diversas ediciones de sus memorias (1903; 1975; 1989) ver la bibliografía.

tura infantil; *Romances y cantares* (1891);[4] y dos obras sobre viajes, *La vuelta al mundo por un joven norte americano* (1891) y *Episodios africanos* (1897).[5]

Episodios africanos es un buen índice de su ideario, que conjuga la cuestión de Canarias como patria-isla y su visión de África y América como los continentes del futuro. Sus episodios radicalizan su ideología federalista ante la cuestión de la otredad africana, presentando una postura anticolonialista con respecto a las intervenciones europeas en África en el siglo XIX y también un africanismo utópico: en el siglo XXX África, un continente mejor y de clima más benigno, habrá formado pueblos que se gobernarán por sí mismos produciendo sociedades más perfectas sin confinamientos nacionales. Según su planteamiento, África habrá superado —y sobrevivido— a Europa. Estévanez despliega sobre los paisajes africanos una mirada sensible al Otro, acercándose más a la otredad humanista propuesta por un Lévinas o un Kapuściński que a la actuación de los militares africanistas coetáneos suyos que competían con otros países europeos en el reparto de África.

El complejo espíritu de la España finisecular que encarna Estévanez en su figura de hombre de estado, revolucionario irreductible y soldado viejo tiene un paralelo en su escritura. Tal como su postura política se va radicalizando —en lo social y lo político— al extremo opuesto del conservadurismo, *Episodios africanos* se distancia escrituralmente de los parámetros del regionalismo y del realismo decimonónico. El giro más innovador en esta obra proviene de la metáfora del viaje, que traslada al lector de la historia del colonialismo al campo de la ciencia ficción.

Episodios africanos es un "viaje" al pasado colonialista de África y a su prometedor futuro. Profetiza una Europa apocalíptica, que el autor pudo haber percibido en el ambiente pre-bélico de la guerra de 1914, y que proyecta al siglo XXX. La devastación de Europa abre paso a una visión utópica de África que funde las naciones:

---

4   *Romances y Cantares* incluye el poema "Canarias", que le ha valido a Estévanez la
    consideración de fundador de la Escuela Regionalista en el ámbito canario ("Cana-
    rias", en *Romances y cantares*, hppt://www.edicionesidea.com).
5   Se puede localizar un ejemplar de este raro libro en la Biblioteca Nacional de Fran-
    cia. El que la obra apareciera en la colección Biblioteca Selecta para la Juventud, tal
    como *La vuelta al mundo*, pudo haber influido en su didáctico y ameno diseño.

Cuando la vieja y deshabitada Europa esté completamente abandonada, no conteniendo más que ruinas denunciadoras de la barbarie presente, habrá desaparecido toda noción de frontera y toda idea de nacionalidad. Pero antes habrá un período de nacionalidades africanas que serán las actuales europeas [...]. Antes que llegue el día de su completa fusión, subsistirán las razas mucho tiempo con sus méritos y sus deméritos, con sus vicios y con sus virtudes [...]. Será un largo período de transición, en el cual se irán formando la noble humanidad del porvenir y la lengua universal. Pero ya en ese tiempo se podrá vivir y tendrán sentido positivo las palabras libertad, fraternidad, amor; ya no habrá dinastías por derecho propio ni por voluntad ajena que ensangrientan los valles y los montes; ya no existirá el vampiro de apariencia humana que se alimenta con la sangre y el llanto de su prójimo; ya no serán esclavas las mujeres ni habrá huérfanos y desheredados (183-84).

En conjunto, *Episodios africanos* deplora la ignorancia casi absoluta de los europeos sobre el continente africano, desmiente las falsas ideas geográficas y denuncia la colonización presumiblemente civilizadora por parte de los europeos. La obra adopta el concepto decimonónico del "episodio" como modalidad genérica para construir una interpretación ficcionalizada de la historia de España, como hiciera su paisano Galdós.[6] Sin embargo, *Episodios africanos* sitúa los intereses colonizadores en África en un ámbito internacional. La obra es un intento de entender la memoria histórica del continente africano a través de las exploraciones y colonizaciones que ha sufrido, desde el teatro de las guerras púnicas hasta la carrera de las potencias europeas por dominar Egipto, Argelia, Túnez, Trípoli y Marruecos. Estos episodios histórico-políticos, militares y de expansión geográfica están aderezados con una macedonia de textos y géneros dirigidos a avanzar la idea central de que África y América son "los continentes de lo porvenir" (179). En este sentido, la obra no se ajusta a una definición restringida de libro de viaje. Tal como señala Borm, la escritura de viajes se abre a "multiple crossing from one form of writing into another and, given the case, from one genre to another" (26).

Las aventuras de los intrépidos viajeros históricos se entretejen con las de viajeros imaginarios y quizá proféticos, como la del hombre que deja París buscando el calor del Senegal (itinerario que evoca el evento automovilístico París-Dakar) y la del africano que al final del libro visita una Europa en ruinas en el siglo XXX (sugerente de la devastación de

6   En "Voces en combate", bajo consideración en una colección de ensayos, contrasto
    Episodios africanos con el episodio nacional *Aita Tettauen*. Algunas observaciones
    se solapan forzosamente o se complementan con lo expuesto aquí.

Europa tras las guerras mundiales). Esta mezcla de viajes documentables y ficticios es una ingeniosa estrategia que pone en un primer plano el encontronazo entre la postura gubernamental europea de colonizar África y el creciente desagrado por parte de Estévanez de las tácticas coloniales: "Las naciones de Europa intentan apoderarse del África para civilizarla: tal es el pretexto. En realidad no buscan la conquista sino para enriquecerse, para abrir nuevos mercados a su creciente industria, para deshacerse de los desheredados" (8). Eventualmente, la conquista de África acabará reproduciendo "las crueldades, los crímenes, los horrores de las pasadas conquistas" (8). Los viajes colonizadores al continente africano se invierten geográficamente mediante el viaje "de la era de las comunicaciones siderales" (182) en que un africano va al norte a visitar las ruinas de Europa. Con ello, Estévanez da un giro de 180 grados al ímpetu colonizador a través de esta novedosa variante de la literatura de viajes en la España finisecular.

Al comienzo, el narrador de *Episodios africanos* se ve atraído por las condiciones agradables de la naturaleza y el clima de África, base para fundar una sociedad mejor. Siguiendo la idea de Homero de que "una tierra no es habitable si no produce vino, higos y aceite" (i), insiste en la necesidad de una naturaleza y un clima benignos para el hombre. A pesar de sus zonas tórridas, África —cuna de civilizaciones— es "uno de los continentes más habitables y de más admirable porvenir" (iii). Arguye que las repúblicas africanas, como Liberia, y no las monarquías, permiten la entrada de la civilización en África. Otro tanto ocurre con las islas, que "han sido siempre eminentemente civilizadoras" (17) ya que favorecen la navegación, las relaciones entre distintas razas, despiertan la afición al comercio y a los viajes. Desde las islas "penetrará la civilización en todo el continente africano" (18). En su ponderación incluye Canarias, que considera "africana" a pesar de constituir "por voluntad propia una provincia española" (18). Vaticina que "los canarienses" fundarán colonias prósperas en la costa de África (20) puesto que el canario "no amenaza ni promete ni ambiciona; encerrado en sí mismo, goza en la contemplación de todo un mundo ideal, sin cuidarse de externos convencionalismos" (22). El posicionamiento insular de Estévanez presta autoridad a su condición periférica frente al poder gubernamental central, a la vez que le permite deplorar el colonialismo en África, claramente incompatible con su humanismo.

Los viajes imaginarios de *Episodios africanos* operan como contrapunto de los viajes exploratorios y son una de las claves del pensamiento geográfico-político y humanista de la obra. Nos detendremos en el viajero que deja el frío de París por ir a África, para regresar muy brevemente al viajero africano que visita Europa. En el capítulo titulado "Aventuras de la costa", un hombre

> levantóse una mañana [...], y al abrir su ventana vió que estaba París envuelto en brumas y nieblas; el frío era todavía más penetrante que los días anteriores. Se acercó al termómetro, y vió que marcaba 12 grados bajo cero, temperatura no excesiva para los bárbaros del Norte, pero suficiente para congelar á un hombre del Mediodía y... de sentido común. Pero el termómetro mismo le indicó el remedio de sus males, pues contenía diversas y útiles indicaciones: á la altura del cero decía *hielo*, á la altura del 10 decía *naranjos*, y después de otras indicaciones á diferentes alturas, decía al nivel de los 50 centígrados: *temperatura del Senegal*.
> —¡Me voy al Senegal ahora mismo! Exclamó con su habitual buen sentido... (88).

Desoyendo a sus amigos, el personaje se embarca para Dakar, pensando en dedicarse a llevar la representación de varios editores parisinos. A la altura de Lisboa, "ya se sentía una temperatura más civilizada" (90); al pasar entre Tenerife y gran Canaria, el viajero puede estar sobre cubierta en mangas de camisa; y a los seis días de navegación llega a Dakar, donde "la columna mercurial no llegaba á los 40 grados, pero de todos modos ya se podía vivir; es más, se respiraba muy bien y era abundante la transpiración" (91). Como, aparte de la temperatura, no hay nada en Dakar que le complazca al viajero, decide trasladarse a la capital de la colonia, San Luis, pasando antes por la isla de Gorea.

En este punto, el narrador en tercera persona incorpora fragmentos del diario del viajero sobre la más antigua de las colonias francesas: Senegal. El diarista recoge los atropellos, las iniquidades y los crímenes que se cometieron en tiempos de esclavitud, "¡Cuántos barcos negreros han tomado allí su infame cargamento de carne humana!" (92). Pero considera que tanto Gorea como Dakar tienen porvenir por su ventajoso punto de escala para las líneas de navegación. El narrador que envuelve al diarista reflexiona que Francia ha tenido una positiva influencia en las cercanías de la colonia francesa, donde va desapareciendo "la odiosa esclavitud" (95). En este concepto, África le debe gratitud a Francia (96), aunque Francia ha sido incapaz de convertir Senegal en una colonia agrícola tras dos siglos de dominación. Lejos de fomentar la agricultura, ha

formado sus mejores tropas coloniales con soldados indígenas. Los tira-
dores senegaleses prestan servicios en las guerras tropicales de África, en
las que los soldados europeos sucumben debido a los rigores del clima,
tema sumamente sensible para Estévanez.

Los efectos de la colonización están directamente relacionados con
el viajero de París, quien antes de hacer una excursión pintoresca por el
río Senegal, quiere informarse de lo que puede hacerse en la colonia en
cuanto a la librería. Un negociante francés de San Luis le previene que
los únicos libros que se venderán son los de menos peso, porque "con
este calor no hay quien lea 50 páginas" (97). El viajero renuncia a su
proyecto de establecer un comercio y regresa a Francia. Desiste tanto de
la tentación de "civilizar" el Senegal como de colonizarlo. En suma,
renuncia a convertirse en un sujeto imperial y se contenta con los beneficios del clima. Antes de embarcarse de regreso, apunta que su excursión
por el Senegal lo ha curado por completo de los sabañones.

En los textos viajeros de la edad moderna, el viaje suele estar ligado
a las nociones de retorno al *oikos* (hogar), tal como señala van den Abbeele en *Travel as Metaphor*. En el prólogo analiza la economía de todo
viaje ("economía" deriva de *oikos*), en términos de pérdidas y ganancias,
sean económicas, físicas o educativas. En este sentido, el viaje *domestica*
o restituye al hogar la experiencia del viajero. En *Episodios africanos* el
concepto de la economía del viaje incluye consideraciones raciales, culturales, económicas y personales. El viajero ficticio de Estévanez no se
traslada a Senegal para establecer superioridad cultural, sino porque en
París simplemente pasa frío. Tampoco viaja allí para conceder o negar
valor al Otro. Al contrario, tras recoger en su diario las atrocidades que
los europeos han cometido con los pobladores de África, renuncia a establecer la influencia hegemónica que pudiera imponer mediante el establecimiento del negocio librero. Regresa sin ganancia económica, pero
con mejor salud, gracias al clima, y con una nueva valoración del papel
de Europa en África.

Mary Louise Pratt describe en *Imperial Eyes* los espacios de posible
encuentro con el Otro como "zonas de contacto", es decir, "social spaces
where disparate cultures meet, clash, and grapple with each other, often
in highly asymmetrical relations of domination and subordination —like
colonialism, slavery, or their aftermaths" (4). Las relaciones asimétricas
de dominación y subordinación sin duda se humanizan en la obra de
Estévanez. El texto mira con simpatía al Otro y se lamenta de las atroci-

dades que ha sufrido a manos del europeo. Lo hace sin describir en ningún momento a los africanos con la condescendencia que es habitual en el discurso colonial y que emerge en muchas obras de viajes (Mills 1991: 34, 155, 160).

Teniendo en cuenta la brutalidad de los encuentros entre europeos y africanos en el siglo XIX, la identificación que Estévanez traza entre el canario y el africano revela una identidad personal en *crisis* y una *crisis* de identidad nacional; ambas saltan a la superficie en la anécdota del viajero fugado de París que busca el calor del Senegal. Para Kapuściński, el viaje facilita que el viajero se sitúe en proximidad física con su Otro, lo cual pone en movimiento una dinámica intercultural, interracial e interpersonal: "to know ourselves we have to know Others, who act as the mirror in which we see ourselves reflected" (19). En términos escriturales, el viajero imaginario de Estévanez se convierte en el *autor* de un diario que a su vez *autoriza* el sentir intelectual y emocional que el primer narrador proyecta ante el Otro y su paisaje. El diario construye África como objeto de la narración y como fuente de experiencia viajera. De este modo, el viajero le sirve a Estévanez como autor para hablar etnográficamente de los senegaleses, evitando alardear de su superioridad como etnógrafo, como historiador y como escritor.

El movimiento europeo, explorador y colonial hacia África se invierte al final con el viaje del africano del siglo XXX que visita una Europa en ruinas, abandonada por su clima inhóspito y los efectos del colonialismo. Mientras Europa es "inhabitable", "diminuta" y "un antro de degradación y de miseria", el África futura camina hacia su perfecto desarrollo gracias a sus "campos vírgenes, brisas de libertad y un sol de fuego" (185).

El doble viaje, con ejes en el pasado y el futuro (colonialismo-utopismo), el sur y el norte (África-Europa), le sirve a Estévanez para cuestionar desde un federalismo transnacional y transcontinental el papel de España en "Europa" —término que le indignaba— y la intervención de España y de otras naciones en África, concepto que le acabó produciendo aversión. Debemos preguntarnos si en este texto el sueño europeo de un África superior logra sobreponerse al peso de la historia y a las atrocidades que los africanos han padecido a manos de los europeos. En última instancia, no, en tanto que en el momento de su formulación el africanismo de Estévanez pertenece a un espacio forzosamente utópico. No obstante, su sentimiento hacia los sometidos y su formulación visionaria despejan las barreras históricas y las fronteras nacionales sugiriendo nuevos cauces de comunicación futura. *Episodios africanos* es un texto clave para entender la fricción entre la rotundidad ideológica del pensamiento oficial y la del pensamiento liberal del siglo XIX español, en particular, la de un escritor que concibió África como un paisaje humano sin límites artificiales.

Bibliografía

Abbeele, G., van den. 1992. *Travel as Metaphor. From Montaigne to Rousseau*. Minneapolis, U of Minnesota P.

Borm, J. 2004. "Defining Travel: On the Travel Book, Travel Writing and Terminology", in G. Hooper & T. Youngs (eds.), *Perspectives on Travel Writing*, Aldershot, Ashgate, 13-26.

Estévanez, N. 1897. *Episodios africanos*. París, Garnier.

—. 1903, 2ª ed. *Fragmentos de mis memorias*, Madrid, Tipografía de los Hijos de R. Álvarez.

—. 1975. *Mis memorias*, Prólogo de José Luis Fernández-Rua, Madrid, Tebas.

—. 1989. *Fragmentos de mis memorias*, N. Reyes (ed.), Santa Cruz de Tenerife, Viceconsejería de Cultura y Deportes.

González, R. 2011. "Nicolás Estévanez y 'La sombra del almendro'" *Rincones del Atlántico* <http://rinconesdelatlantico.com-num2estevanez.htlm> [consultado el 12.VII.2011].

Kapuściński, R. 2008. *The Other*, New York, Verso.

Lévinas, E. 2003. *Humanism of the Other*, N. Poller (trad.), Chicago, U of Illinois P.

Mills, S. 1991. *Discourses of Difference. An Analysis of Women's Travel Writing and Colonialism*, London, Routledge.

Morral, M. 1978. *Pensamientos revolucionarios de Nicolás Estévanez*. Prólogo de Federico Urales. Barcelona/Palma de Mallorca, Olañeta.

Pratt, M. L. 1992. *Imperial Eyes: Travel Writing and Transculturation*, New York, Routledge.

Covadonga San Miguel Llorente

Desencuentros con la metrópolis y literatura de viajes: *Gleanings* (1837), de James F. Cooper, y *Viajes* (1849), de Domingo F. Sarmiento

La literatura de viajes constituye un extenso corpus literario que ha suscitado el interés de muchos autores. Diversos estudios me han llevado a la comparación de dos libros de literatura de viajes de la primera mitad del siglo XIX: *Gleanings in Europe: England* (1837) del estadounidense James Fenimore Cooper, y *Viajes por Europa, África y América* (1849) del argentino Domingo Faustino Sarmiento. Así pues, este trabajo se centra en los viajes de Cooper y Sarmiento por el continente europeo. *Gleanings* es una obra que está dedicada en su conjunto a la visita que Cooper hizo por Gran Bretaña, mientras que, en el caso de *Viajes* de Sarmiento, únicamente hay una pequeña parte que está dedicada a España.

En cuanto al contexto histórico de ambas obras, hay que señalar que muchas de las colonias americanas comenzaban entonces una nueva existencia que venía dada por su independencia con respecto a las potencias europeas. Tras la lectura y estudio de *Gleanings* y *Viajes* se observa claramente que la visión que de Gran Bretaña y España dan Cooper y Sarmiento, respectivamente, es negativa, como corroboran diferentes estudios sobre los autores y sus obras (Dekker y McWilliams 1973; Fanese 2002; Hozven 1993), así como otras obras sobre literatura estadounidense y británica en el caso de Cooper, e hispanoamericana y española en el de Sarmiento (Carr 1970; Martín y Martínez Shaw y Tusell 2005; Cunliffe 1991; Fernández 1997; Fernández y Millares y Becerra 1995; Madrigal 1993).

Ambos autores realizaron sendas giras por diferentes países europeos y lo hicieron desde la perspectiva de sus respectivas culturas. Desde siempre, cuando dos culturas entran en contacto, no permanecen en términos de igualdad. El Otro y su cultura, tradiciones, costumbres, en definitiva, todo lo que tiene que ver con él o le rodea, se ve y se trata como algo inferior o peor con respecto a lo relacionado con la que sería la cultura dominante. Este no saber ponerse en la piel del Otro y el no reconocer la riqueza que hay en la diferencia entre culturas es lo que Tom Burns Marañón ha llamado "desencuentro" en su libro *Hispano-manía* (2000: 25).

Una situación parecida se vivió en las experiencias de los primeros viajeros cuando dos culturas, la del propio viajero y la visitada, no estaban en el mismo nivel. No se veían como diferentes, sino que la del visitante quedaba establecida como la mejor y la visitada como inferior a la primera. No obstante con el tiempo esto ha ido cambiando. Ahora, en general, se respeta al Otro y se ve en la diferencia entre unos y otros una riqueza cultural que resitúa a todos en un nivel idéntico. Esta nueva forma de relación entre dos culturas, en la que sí hay un interés por el Otro, es lo que, siguiendo a Burns Marañón, sería un encuentro. Analizadas las obras de James Fenimore Cooper y de Domingo Faustino Sarmiento que son objeto de este estudio, uno no puede ver otra cosa en ellas que la expresión de un claro "desencuentro" entre la cultura norteamericana y la británica en el caso de Cooper, y la hispano-americana y la española en el de Sarmiento.

Centrándonos ya en el estudio de la imagen de la cultura, la sociedad y la política británica y española en dichas obras, se observa claramente que ambos autores hacen hincapié en los mismos asuntos. En cuanto a la cultura, tanto Cooper como Sarmiento estudian de manera crítica el lenguaje, inglés y español respectivamente, así como la prensa y la literatura de una y otra nación.

Cooper reflexiona y analiza la lengua "inglesa" en comparación con la "americana". Lo primero que le llama la atención es no haber encontrado demasiadas diferencias con respecto a la entonación o construcción de frases de uno y otro lado del Atlántico. Puede señalarse aquí una anécdota que él mismo cuenta. Estando en una reunión social, uno de los participantes alaba el buen inglés del autor:

> This young man amused me with the entire clones with which he complimented me on my English being as good as usual. These people are so accustomed to think of us as inferiors, that the bad taste of telling a man in society, "really, now, I do not see but you know how to speak, or to use a fork, or to drink your wine, or to go through the manual of polite life, quite as well as one of us," never appear to strike them (227).

No es de extrañar que Cooper diga que fue incapaz de entender dicho cumplido, ya que no hay nada más obvio para un estadounidense que hacer un uso correcto de la lengua inglesa. Quizás su interlocutor no era consciente de este hecho, pero probablemente Cooper intenta, con este ejemplo, ridiculizar a quien le dijo esto y, por ende, a todos los que en las Islas Británicas eran de esa opinión en la época.

Sarmiento por su parte se queja de las críticas que los españoles han lanzado contra el español americano. Para él, en España se traduce "mal lo malo" (8) y eso también es algo que saben y pueden hacer ellos en América. Si los propios españoles peninsulares no saben dar un uso apropiado y correcto del español, se pregunta el autor, ¿por qué deberían hacerlo quienes están al otro lado del Atlántico? Opina que se ha de reconocer el español americano como algo bueno y enriquecedor y no como meros errores del español peninsular. Según él, negando el español americano y sus aportaciones, tampoco se podría considerar aceptable la propia herencia que tiene la lengua española de otros pueblos y lenguas.

Por lo que respecta a la sociedad, quizás en su percepción de la británica es donde se produce un mayor "desencuentro" en el caso de Cooper, y lo mismo sucede en el de Sarmiento con respecto a la sociedad española. Respecto a esto, y en lo que se refiere a Cooper, no ve en la sociedad muchos puntos de disparidad entre estadounidenses y británicos en lo que al físico se refiere. Respecto a las costumbres, sí observa Cooper más diferencias, ya que nos dice que viven bajo sistemas totalmente diferentes. Los británicos muestran una cortesía extrema por parte de las clases bajas con respecto a las altas, mientras que los estadounidenses tienden a separarse precisamente de esta costumbre. Compara además a los británicos y estadounidenses de clases altas. Estos últimos se aferran a su sistema, conscientes de sus méritos y de sus fallos, pero siempre dispuestos a defenderlo en caso de ataque. En cambio, los primeros están acostumbrados a mofarse de la democracia que se ha instaurado en los Estados Unidos y tratan de exagerar en grado sumo cada problema o error que se les presenta. Cooper considera que ambas naciones han sido acusadas de ser arrogantes ya que tienden a compararse en todo momento con sus vecinos con un extremo sentimiento de superioridad. Cree que esto es así como resultado de la suma de vanidades individuales de ambos países; pero además explica que no es de extrañar si tenemos en cuenta que los pueblos en cuestión están mejor instruidos, son mayores en número y sus sentimientos forman más opiniones públicas que en cualquier otro lugar. Tal como Cooper indica:

> Both the Americans and the English are charged with being offensively boastful and arrogant, as nations, and too much disposed to compare themselves advantageously with their neighbors [...] The mass in both nations, are better instructed, and are of more account than the mass in other countries, and their sentiments form more of a public opinion than elsewhere (296).

Sarmiento, por su parte, estudia tipos sociales por separado, no haciendo una comparación global como es el caso de Cooper. El primero sería el del bandido. Con respecto a este personaje destaca el hecho de que siguiera existiendo en España, lo que para Sarmiento no deja de ser una muestra de la barbarie que subsiste en el país y de lo poco que ha avanzado el pueblo español como civilización. Otro de los personajes que menciona es el mendigo, también típico del país: "El viajero que busca el color local no reconoce la España sino cuando apercibe los mendigos apostados sobre cada uno de los rápidos ascensos" (18). Explica que en la época en que él visita la metrópoli los mendigos son perseguidos por ordenanzas reales. También habla de los ciegos que "en España forman una clase social, con fueros y ocupación peculiar" (19). Estos van juntos, en grupos, cantando con instrumentos típicos como guitarras y bandurrias. Igualmente dice, de manera irónica, que al ir en grupo es como si constituyeran una asociación industrial y artística. Finalmente habla de los alabarderos reales y los alguaciles, en referencia a lo que pudo observar durante una de las corridas de toros que se hicieron para festejar la boda de la reina. Están ahí para ejecutar las órdenes de la reina, y no tienen más defensa que la fuga, lo que en la visión de Sarmiento es parte del entretenimiento cuando señala que "aquella dispersión de los alguaciles, y su terror pánico cuando se ven atacados por el toro, forman la parte cómica del espectáculo" (30). Sarmiento pone de manifiesto el hecho de que algunos toreros acercan de manera voluntaria el toro a su posición con el único fin de que el público se ría.

En cuanto a los pueblos de España es de reseñar lo que dice de los vascos y catalanes. Comenta primero el origen de los vascos, que "descienden en línea recta y sin mezcla de romanos, godos, o árabes, de los vascos que habitaban los Pirineos ahora tres mil años" (15), para después hablarnos del empeño de los españoles en la supresión de sus fueros y la imposición de aduanas, gendarmes, estancos y de una Constitución, además de las "bestialidades" que, como señala Sarmiento, se cometieron con ellos en el desarrollo de las guerras carlistas. Por otro lado, menciona a los catalanes una vez se halla ya en Barcelona, al final de su viaje. Hay que señalar aquí que, para Sarmiento, el aspecto de la ciudad y de su gente es "enteramente europeo […] Aquí hay ómnibus, gas, vapor, seguros, tejidos, imprenta, humo y ruido; hay pues un pueblo europeo" (63). Se ve claramente por esta afirmación, y teniendo en cuenta todo lo anterior que sobre España y los españoles refiere en su obra, que para él el pueblo catalán es lo mejor que uno puede encontrar en la Península.

Finalmente, en cuanto a la política se refiere, hay que decir que Cooper estuvo toda su vida interesado en ella, pues la consideraba la base de cualquier sociedad. Fue capaz de utilizar a América y a Europa como puntos de partida desde los que podía criticar a ambas naciones mediante la comparación. En *Gleanings* analiza las instituciones británicas a la luz del experimento estadounidense. Lo que pretende es deshacer los prejuicios que los británicos tienen contra los estadounidenses y liberar la mentalidad norteamericana de su dependencia con respecto a la ex metrópolis (Schachterle 1982). Cooper considera que tanto las leyes como las instituciones británicas necesitan un cambo radical porque se han quedado ancladas en el pasado, y así lo explica en su texto:

> Were the people of England, free from the prejudices of their actual situation and absolutely without a political organization, assembled to select a polity for their future government, it is probable that the man who should propose the present system, would at once be set as a visionary, or a fool (145).

Opina que la monarquía,[1] tal y como está establecida en el momento de su estancia en el país, es una pura mitificación, al igual que muchas de las cosas que rodean la política británica, especialmente el Parlamento. Lo único favorable que Cooper ve en la forma actual de gobierno británico es "its admirable adaptation to the means necessary for keeping such an empire together" (258). Volviendo a la monarquía, explica que el rey tendría menos poder que el presidente de los Estados Unidos, dado que este último ejerce la autoridad que le confiere la Constitución, mientras que el monarca británico no ejercería el poder que le otorgan las

---

1   En 1828 era Jorge IV el rey que gobernaba Inglaterra. Considerado por muchos un rey extravagante y bastante terco, interfirió numerosas veces en la política del país.

leyes del país. Además, hace hincapié en el hecho de que un inglés ins-truido razonaría sobre las instituciones de su país como un británico, a la vez que su homólogo estadounidense razonaría sobre las suyas también como un británico; de ahí la importancia de conseguir no solamente la independencia material, sino también la intelectual con respecto a Gran Bretaña: "Of all burdens, that of the mental dependence created by colonial subserviency, appears to be the most difficult to remove" (233).

Sarmiento, a su vez, está en contra de la forma de gobierno que se ha establecido en Argentina: la dictadura de Rosas. Sin embargo, tam-bién rechazaba el gobierno colonial anterior que había establecido Espa-ña, porque no buscaba el bienestar del país y del pueblo, ni su completa libertad. A través de diversos comentarios en sus obras, se observa cómo rechaza el sistema francés, al que alabó en un principio, y no es de extra-ñar que, tras recorrer todos los países en formación (Italia, Alemania, Bélgica) o monarquías (España e Inglaterra), le quedase como único exponente de su ideario el sistema político de Estados Unidos, el modelo a seguir (Vizuela 2004: 44).

Cuando Sarmiento llega a España se van a celebrar las bodas de la reina Isabel II con Francisco de Asís y la de su hermana María Luisa Fernanda con el duque de Montpensier, matrimonios de conveniencia para mantener las alianzas establecidas por España. Sarmiento informa al lector de que los partidos políticos del momento tienen opiniones encon-tradas al respecto. Por un lado, la oposición sostenía que la nación entera estaba en contra del matrimonio entre una infanta española y un aristó-crata francés. Por otro, los políticos en el poder mantenían que el pueblo no podía estar más contento y entusiasmado con el enlace. Para el autor, la verdad es bien distinta, dado lo que pudo observar estando en Madrid: "el pueblo se ha mostrado pasablemente indiferente" (20). Esta lucha entre políticos ministeriales y oposición, en la que se manipula a la pren-sa, se le antoja a Sarmiento simplemente absurda: "nada ha quedado por decirse entre la oposición y los ministeriales, excepto la verdad" (20).

Ninguno de los dos autores es capaz de ponerse en el lugar del Otro, ni se plantean en ningún caso por qué se viven las situaciones que expli-can a lo largo de sus viajes, profundizando así en su conocimiento de las metrópolis. Quizás en el caso de Cooper se ven más ejemplos de "en-cuentro" entre ambas culturas cuando, por ejemplo, corrige el estereotipo que se tiene en Estados Unidos sobre la impuntualidad de los británicos, o cuando cuenta que hay británicos que consideran que sus leyes necesitan una reforma. Sin embargo, Sarmiento no se plantea que haya nada en España que pueda ser aprovechable para Hispanoamérica, puesto que todo lo español es malo y negativo a sus ojos. Para él, la nación española se halla sumida en un estado en decadencia y no ve soluciones a ese problema.

Finalmente hay que señalar que el grado de conciencia de alteridad presente en *Gleanings* y en *Viajes* difiere, y eso se debe posiblemente a la situación que los lugares de origen de los autores viven en esos momentos. Estados Unidos ha conseguido su independencia, tiene una constitución y está expandiéndose, además de ser el referente para otros muchos pueblos americanos que están en el inicio de esa independencia, mientras que Argentina vive bajo el mando de un dictador que no ha solucionado los problemas que, según Sarmiento, los españoles crearon allí en el pasado.

Así pues, se puede concluir que tanto *Gleanings* como *Viajes* constituyen un ejemplo de lo que fue el desencuentro —con respecto a Gran Bretaña y España— que ambos autores experimentaron a su manera y algunos de cuyos detalles he intentado exponer a lo largo de este trabajo.

Bibliografía

Burns Marañón, T. 2000. *Hispanomanía*, Barcelona, Plaza & Janés.

Carr, R. 1970. *España, 1808-1939*, Barcelona, Ariel.

Cooper, J. F. 1982 [1837]. *Gleanings in Europe: England,* Albany, State U of New York P.

Cunliffe, M. 1991. *The Literature of the United States*, London, Penguin.

Dekker, G. & J. P. McWilliams. 1973. *Fenimore Cooper. The Critical Heritage,* London, Routledge.

Fanese, G. 2002. "Imagen de España en *Viajes* y otros textos de Domingo Faustino Sarmiento", in E. Morillas (ed.), *España y Argentina en sus relaciones literarias*, Lleida, Universitat de Lleida, 105-18.

Fernández, T., S. Millares & E. Becerra. 1995. *Historia de la literatura Hispanoamericana*, Madrid, Universitas.

Fernández, T. 1997. *Teoría y crítica literaria de la emancipación Hispa-noamericana*, Alicante, Generalitat Valenciana y Diputación de Ali-cante.

Hozven, R. 1993. "Domingo Faustino Sarmiento", in L. I. Madrigal (co-ord.), *Historia de la Literatura Hispanoamericana,* Madrid, Cátedra, 427-45.

Martín, J. L., C. Martínez Shaw & J. Tusell. 2005. *Historia de España*, Madrid, Taurus.

Madrigal, L. I. (coord.). 1993. *Historia de la Literatura Hispano-americana*, Madrid, Cátedra,

Schachterle, L. 1982. "Cooper's Attitudes Towards England", *James Fenimore Cooper Society* <http://external.oneonta.edu/cooper/articles/suny/1982suny-schachterle.html> [consultado el 29.VI.2008]

Sarmiento, D. F. 1992 [1849]. *Viajes II: España e Italia*, Buenos Aires, Vaccaro.

Vizuela, G. E. 2001. *Viajes por Europa, Africa y América: su significado en la evolución del pensamiento político de Domingo Faustino Sar-miento*, Buenos Aires, Facultad de Filosofía, Humanidades y Artes.

CARMEN SERVÉN DÍEZ

La contribución de algunas escritoras españolas a la representación cultural de la mujer extranjera entre 1850 y 1936

El siglo XIX, en el que se produjeron numerosas y grandes expediciones, elaboró relaciones documentales de las mismas en forma de recuerdos, cartas, diarios y artículos de diversa índole, escritos por toda clase de viajeros: políticos o diplomáticos, periodistas, científicos... (Litvak 1984: 9). A través de las imágenes y noticias brindadas por los viajeros, así como de las representaciones plásticas o literarias que ofrece el arte de la época, se forja una galería de tipos de mujeres extranjeras en el imaginario cultural español. Mi propósito en el presente trabajo consiste en destacar la contribución de algunas escritoras españolas a esas construcciones culturales que dibujan la imagen de la extranjera entre 1850 y 1936.

Ya en los años sesenta del siglo XIX, doña Pilar Sinués de Marco ofrece una galería de mujeres occidentales en una revista que dirigía ella misma: *El Ángel del Hogar*. Esta revista se alinea con otras publicaciones femeninas que se multiplican en la España del siglo XIX, y que procuran "consejos del hogar, figurines de moda, relatos por entregas y ecos de sociedad", potencian "ternura, modestia, humildad y sumisión como ideales sociales y literarios" (Cantizano 2004: 295) y vienen sostenidas por las colaboraciones de las llamadas "escritoras virtuosas", según la afortunada denominación de Alda Blanco (2001). El conjunto de artículos de doña Pilar Sinués al que me refiero se incluye en el apartado dedicado a la moda, que el 31 de julio de 1866 se cierra con el siguiente anuncio:

> En mis próximos artículos os hablaré de la influencia que la moda tiene en la mujer española, en la inglesa y en la francesa, y del modo con que es considerada en estas tres naciones, donde verdaderamente tiene tres expléndidos (sic), sólidos y magníficos tronos (Sinués 1866: 219).

En los números siguientes aparecen descripciones de mujeres de distintos países, y en los textos se liga la actitud frente a la moda con el carácter nacional de que se trate. En un principio, la escritora se proponía expresamente hablar de la influencia que la moda tiene en España, en Inglaterra y en Francia, pero lo cierto es que más adelante también tratará de América y Alemania. E inicialmente se orienta a abordar el fenómeno de la moda, pero en números posteriores hace un texto híbrido que alberga reivindicaciones sociales y tópicos diversos. En su exposición la autora intercala exhortaciones a sus lectoras, empujándolas a mejorar su comportamiento y educación a imitación de las mujeres de otros países, y simultáneamente determina unos rasgos identitarios privativos de cada nacionalidad.

El pueblo francés, asegura Sinués, es industrioso y activo, "ganan más y gastan menos que nosotros; se ríen del excesivo culto que damos al lujo y de nuestro afán de imitarles" (1866: 249). De sus mujeres destaca "su amabilidad y perfecta cortesía de su lenguaje", lo que las convierte en "peligrosas"; además lucen una sabia elegancia hecha, no de lo que es moda, sino de lo que a ellas les sienta mejor en color y hechura. De todo lo dicho deduce que "las francesas tienen más cálculo, más inventiva, más ingenio, más templanza y una educación más esmerada que las españolas" (Sinués 1866: 250).

A la mujer inglesa dice conocerla de primera mano puesto que se refiere a su estancia personal en Londres. Y caracteriza a los ingleses en su conjunto: "pueblo adusto, grave, culto, que da lo mejor de su vida y de su caudal á los santos goces de la familia, y que ve en su casa el templo de la dicha". Así que la mujer inglesa "sabe cuidar y embellecer su casa", que es siempre un "conjunto de comodidades, un modelo de aseo, un delicioso asilo" (Sinués 1866: 257-58). Al revés que la española, asegura, la inglesa disfruta de gran independencia hasta que se casa, pero después se recluye en el hogar; y la autora se duele de la metamorfosis que se obra entonces en ella: pierde toda su belleza, aunque sigue siendo muy aseada. De ahí que los ingleses no se ocupen en absoluto de su esposa. En resumen: las inglesas "son laboriosas, modestas y cuidadosas de su casa; pero frías, severas, sistemáticas, calculadoras" (Sinués 1866: 265).

Por parecidos derroteros discurre la caracterización de las americanas y las alemanas, aunque a algunos de estos tipos declara no conocerlos de primera mano (Sinués 1866: 274). Frecuentemente intercala apreciaciones totalizadoras como las que ilustran los siguientes comentarios:

No hay que dudarlo: todos los países llevan el sello del carácter de la muger (sic).
Ved sino (sic) a nuestra España, católica, noble y severa: tales son sus mugeres (sic).
Ved á Francia, coqueta, superficial y llena de locos caprichos; ella refleja el carácter de sus hijas.
Ved a Inglaterra, helada, calculista y metódica: así son las inglesas.
América es bella como sus mujeres: entusiasta como sus mujeres: como ellas, hospitalaria y poética, porque la poesía reside en el alma de sus hijas (270).

Las colecciones costumbristas también contribuían a fijar identidades nacionales. Dejando aparte las colecciones ofrecidas por los escritores españoles,[1] vamos a atender ahora a la gran colección coordinada por Faustina Sáez de Melgar, *Las mujeres españolas, americanas y lusitanas pintadas por sí mismas,* que reúne textos de escritoras diversas ya en los años ochenta del siglo XIX. En la actualidad, la estudiosa María Ángeles Ayala destaca el afán didáctico y propagandista de esta colección; se trató de proporcionar modelos femeninos comentados y regidos por la determinación de reclamar una mejor educación para la mujer española de su tiempo.

Algunos de los dibujos contenidos en *Las mujeres españolas, americanas y lusitanas pintadas por sí mismas* están ligados al imaginario cultural construido por los viajeros de su época y difundido a través de lo que hoy llamaríamos reportajes periodísticos. Configuran, a su vez, identidades que tienen una proyección de largo alcance en la historia cultural española. Tal es el caso de los rasgos que Gregoria Urbina y Miranda atribuye a la mujer norteamericana en el artículo que preparó para dicha obra colectiva. Esta escritora, sin embargo, se refiere específicamente a la mujer californiana, puesto que, según explica al inicio de su texto, en el país del oro es donde ella misma nació y pasó su niñez (Urbina y Miranda [s.a.]: 706). Y comienza con una loa de la naturaleza californiana y

---

1   Entre las colecciones aparecidas en España durante la segunda mitad del siglo XIX, hallamos varias dedicadas por los escritores al estudio y dibujo de la mujer. En 1871 y 1872 se publicó, en dos volúmenes, *Las españolas pintadas por los españoles*. Al poco tiempo apareció *Las Mujeres Españolas, Portuguesas y Americanas*, que describe a las mujeres en función de su pertenencia geográfica y consta de tres volúmenes: los dos primeros, publicados en 1872-73, dedicados a las mujeres de cada una de las provincias españolas; el tercer tomo, de 1876, se dedica a las extranjeras, americanas o lusitanas. Sobre las colecciones costumbristas, véase el estudio de Ayala (1993).

sus aborígenes para continuar con un admirado elogio del "yankee" moderno. Después se detiene en la mujer californiana, que va "sola, tranquila, serena, segura de su propio valer y del respeto universal". Una mujer que conoce bien las leyes de su país, pero también la Biblia; que desde los dieciocho años es mayor de edad; que trabaja firme y esforzadamente para decidir por sí misma y casarse a su gusto; es un modelo de ilustración y libertad: "Sola se la ve en las universidades, en los vapores, en los ferrocarriles, por las calles y paseos, y nadie, absolutamente nadie, se atreve à faltarla (sic) al respeto" (Urbina y Miranda [s.a.]: 710-11). Además se refiere a la fortaleza moral de la norteamericana, su sumisión al marido cuando se casa, y a su capacidad para ocupar puestos del Estado en correos, telégrafos y juzgados, entre otros. Y la presenta como modelo a seguir por la mujer española.

Urbina y Miranda, en definitiva, dibuja a la norteamericana haciendo hincapié en que se trata de un modelo femenino avanzado, cuyas marcas distintivas son la amplia instrucción y la libertad. Precisamente, las mismas notas distintivas que los viajeros españoles comentaban en sus noticias sobre la sociedad y costumbres norteamericanas. Veámoslo a continuación.

En 1884, la *Revista Contemporánea*, una de las más acreditadas publicaciones culturales de su época, recoge en once fragmentos sucesivos un largo reportaje de José Jordana y Morera[2] titulado "Curiosidades naturales y carácter social de los Estados Unidos". Este texto es la historia de una expedición por diversos Estados de Norteamérica para conocer algunos fuertes en zonas aisladas y los principales grandes ríos, así como ciudades y casas de las gentes del país. Pretende dar noticia tanto de las bellezas naturales como de los hábitos sociales de los norteamericanos.

Uno de los aspectos que llaman la atención a Jordana y Morera es la libertad de que gozan las jóvenes norteamericanas, asunto al que dedica varias observaciones:

> Allí los hijos todos, sin distinción de sexos, reciben sus visitas con independencia de los demás miembros de la familia, si sólo ellos son los visitados. Con igual liber-

---

2   José Jordana y Morera (1836-1906), fue un ingeniero de montes que en 1876 formó parte de la comisión para el estudio de la producción forestal en los EE.UU. Además, fue comisario real de la Exposición Universal de Barcelona (1888), y publicó varios libros sobre su especialidad.

tad discurren por las calles las jóvenes solteras y aceptan la compañía de amigos y novios en paseos, teatros y excursiones (1884: LIII, 393-96).

El viajero se confiesa consciente del asombro que esa independencia femenina puede suscitar en sus lectores, así como de los inconvenientes que quizás acarrearía entre los pueblos latinos de Europa; pero asegura que en los Estados Unidos "contribuye a fortificar el carácter, ennoblecer el espíritu y dar más vuelos a la propia dignidad, realzando la natural independencia a medida que la razón se desarrolla". Los jóvenes, por este medio, se habitúan a "valerse de su propio juicio para decidir las cosas" y a "vencer los contratiempos sin auxilio extraño". Para defender el modo norteamericano de educar a las jóvenes en la independencia y responsabilidad, Jordana y Morera recurre a citas de Sor Juana Inés de la Cruz o Moratín, y explica que "no porque de esta libertad gocen, sufre menoscabo su virtud. La honestidad y el recato que tan bien sientan a las jóvenes, no han menester de oficiosos guardianes ni de hipócritas remilgos para conservarse incólumes (1884: LIII, 394-95). En otros pasajes de su trabajo, el autor se ha referido al hecho de que en la playa hombres y mujeres "se bañan juntos" con tranquilidad e "inocencia" (1884: LI, 64-65), o se ha extendido sobre el aspecto y conducta de las norteamericanas: visten "con pulcritud y atildada elegancia", andan "con desembarazo y firmeza"; tienen "el ánimo resuelto y festivo", la costumbre de madrugar, y una instrucción relativamente superior a la del hombre de su tierra; frecuentan las bibliotecas públicas y son "el alma de la vida intelectual" en su país. "Son sobrias de cumplidos y melindres" y "suelen tomar las cosas al pie de la letra [...] no comprendiendo como un hombre pueda [...] pintar con vivos colores una pasión mentida", pues ellas dan muestra permanente de su "franqueza" (1884: LI, 404-406).

A lo largo de su historia, otra importante revista nacida a fines de siglo, *La España Moderna*, fundada y dirigida por José Lázaro, reforzó las estimaciones ya mencionadas sobre la mujer norteamericana. Así, en 1897, Adolfo Posada, profesor de la Universidad de Oviedo, firma en ella un trabajo sobre "Progresos del feminismo", en el que se refiere a los avances e importancia del movimiento femenino como fenómeno social en diversos países occidentales, entre ellos los Estados Unidos; y anota la precocidad, fuerza y capacidad de irradiación del feminismo estadounidense, así como el destacado papel socio-político que juegan los clubs femeninos en ese país.

Años después, *La España Moderna* se refiere igualmente a la amplia instrucción, responsabilidad y libertad en que son educadas las jóvenes norteamericanas en sus *colleges*:

> La yanqui adora su vida de colegio y se desarrolla en él maravillosamente. Cada una tiene su cuarto, que adorna á su gusto, y es libre por completo, considerada como una mujer y responsable de sus actos. Allí asisten á conferencias, á experimentos y á excursiones, profundizan bastante en los estudios [...] y no desatienden los cuidados de su cuerpo, jugando a la pelota, remando y haciendo gimnasia (Araujo 1903: 174).

O comenta un artículo de Gina Lombrosi para el *Putnams' Magazine*, según el cual la cosa más interesante para toda europea que visite la América del Norte es la mujer americana, "la feliz y victoriosa heroína del feminismo moderno" (Araujo 1910: 198), sobre cuya independencia, amplia educación y fuerte personalidad se extiende Fernando Araujo en su sección "Revista de Revistas".

Es curioso constatar que todos estos cabos que sobre la figura de la norteamericana se tejen en las redes culturales del siglo XIX, se recogen y anudan en la literatura de inicios del siglo XX. Basta recordar cómo Margarita Nelken plantea la presencia e intervención de las mujeres norteamericanas en sus relatos cortos. A este respecto es paradigmático el caso de *La aventura de Roma* (1923), que narra la historia de una relación trabada fortuitamente en la Ciudad Eterna entre una joven estadounidense y un español; él es un andaluz de veintisiete años, mimado y desocupado, vulgar e inclinado a toda clase de tópicos para interpretar la conducta de las gentes. Se interesa enseguida por la joven americana, pasea con ella por la ciudad figurándose que será conquista fácil; al cabo recibe un chasco mayúsculo. Sobre el texto se proyecta el juego simbólico de la pertenencia nacional, y la figura de la joven norteamericana ha resultado un compendio de lo que en artículos decimonónicos nos aseguraban los viajeros: franca, directa, sincera, decidida, asombrosa e inesperada para el varón español medio.

Por tanto, la selección de rasgos atribuidos a la mujer norteamericana en la literatura y periodismo españoles entre 1850 y 1936, se corresponde con unas constantes, que se resumen en libertad y solidez, de tal forma que las estadounidenses aparecen como vanguardia del movimiento feminista mundial y sorprenden al varón español tradicional. Ecos de todo ello se recuperan en famosas novelas de otros autores décadas después de la guerra civil: recuérdese *La tesis de Nancy*, de Ramón J. Sender, en que las cualidades de la joven protagonista —el despejo y la amplia instrucción, la franqueza o falta de doblez, la rigurosa moral aunque puedan pensar lo contrario los espíritus pacatos— evocan un talante femenino ya cristalizado culturalmente años atrás. Por otra parte, la independencia y libertad que en el imaginario cultural español se atribuye a la mujer norteamericana es asunto que alcanza la actualidad: de ahí que en una novela de Elvira Lindo aparecida en 2005, un personaje femenino pueda decir a otro: "Hija, qué independiente eres, pareces americana" (2008: 132).

En conclusión: las escritoras españolas que trabajaron entre 1850 y 1936 contribuyeron en gran medida a forjar la imagen cultural que de la mujer extranjera se difundió por entonces en España. A este respecto es interesante anotar la progresiva consolidación de un determinado perfil para la mujer norteamericana, perfil que perdura a través de décadas incluso tras nuestra última guerra civil, y que se utiliza una y otra vez como contrapunto capaz de evidenciar los desequilibrios, contradicciones o sinsentidos del españolismo más rancio y estrecho. En general, el nacionalismo como principio articulador de la experiencia, factor identitario y proyecto de acción, opera en la cultura europea al menos durante los tres últimos siglos. Si, según señala Pérez Vejo (1999: 70), la "identidad nacional" aparece como la forma de representación colectiva por antonomasia y cobra radical importancia en el plano simbólico, la colaboración de algunas escritoras españolas en el diseño y difusión de ciertos parámetros y estereotipos nacionales vinculados a los roles de género merece ser tenida en cuenta.

Bibliografía

Araujo, F. 1903. "Revista de Revistas", *La España Moderna*, mayo, 156-194.

—.1910. "Revista de Revistas", *La España Moderna*, mayo, 177-205.

Ayala, M. A. 1993. *Las colecciones costumbristas (1870-1885)*, Alicante, Universidad de Alicante.

Blanco, A. 2001. *Escritoras virtuosas: narradoras de la domesticidad en la España isabelina,* Granada, Universidad de Granada.

Cantizano, B. 2004. "La mujer en la prensa femenina del XIX", *Ámbitos* 11-12, 281-298.

Jordana y Morera, J. 1884. "Curiosidades naturales y carácter social de los Estados Unidos", *Revista Contemporánea* LI (15 mayo, 48-66; 30 mayo, 129-152; 30 junio, 401-416), LII (15 julio, 47-64; 30 julio, 203-215; 15 agosto, 279-288; 30 agosto, 401-409) y LIII (15 sept., 43-60; 30 sept., 146-160; 15 oct., 270-284; 30 oct., 393-403).

Lindo, E. 2008. *Una palabra tuya,* Barcelona, Seix Barral.

Litvak, L. 1984. *Geografías mágicas. Viajeros españoles del siglo XIX por países exóticos (1800-1913),* Barcelona, Laertes.

Nelken, M. 1923. "La aventura de Roma", *La novela de Hoy* 40, 16 de febrero, sin paginar.

Pérez Vejo, T. 1999. *Nación, identidad nacional y otros mitos nacionalistas,* Oviedo, Nobel.

Posada, A. 1897. "Progresos del feminismo", *La España Moderna,* marzo, 1897, 91-138.

Sinués de Marco, P. 1866. *El ángel del hogar,* Madrid, Imprenta Española de Nieto y comp., vols. 28-38, de 31 de julio a 16 de octubre de 1866.

Urbina y Miranda, G. [s.a]. "La Mujer Norte-Americana", in F. Sáez de Melgar (coord.), *Las Mujeres Españolas, Americanas y Lusitanas pintadas por sí mismas,* Barcelona, Juan Pons, 706-713. Reproducción digital en http://www.cervantesvirtual.com/obra/las-mujeres-espanolas-americanas-y-lusitanas-pintadas-por-si-mismas--0/ [consultado el 14.1.2013].

GABRIELA STEINKE

Moving Between Worlds:
Foreignness in Diana Wynne Jones's Multiverse

It is a truth universally acknowledged that we are all foreigners some-where. The concept of the foreign, however, is notoriously difficult to pin down and, as Rebecca Saunders argues in the illuminating introduc-tory chapter of her eponymous book, it is always defined negatively: "to be foreign is *not* belonging to a group, *not* speaking a given language, *not* having the same customs; it is to be *un*familiar, *un*canny, *un*natural, *un*authorised, *in*comprehensible, *in*appropriate, *im*proper" (Saunders 2003: 3). Inherent in those very terms is an idea of hierarchy: that which is foreign is not merely other but lesser than what is regarded as the norm by those with the power to define the home standard. If we pursue this concept of the foreign beyond the tribe, the nation, the state (notions that are most often contrasted with "the foreign"), then it makes perfect sense to regard children as foreigners in an adult world. Unlike migrants, exiles, travellers and other adult foreigners who always remain foreign, children will (barring accidents) eventually grow out of this state; one could say their degree of foreignness lessens as they age (though teenag-ers as well as their parents might disagree), but during their childhood Saunders' list of attributes can undoubtedly be applied to them. And as far as hierarchies go, although our Western cultures may have moved on from notions of the child as an unfinished, lesser human being and chil-dren's rights may be enshrined in law, children have very little, if any actual power over their own lives and the conditions they find them-selves in. Adults order children's lives to fit in with what they consider the world should be like and there is very little children can do about it. This extends to their reading matter, which is moderated by a long line of adults, beginning with the authors of children's literature via agents, publishers, librarians, booksellers, parents, who produce, edit, distribute and buy these books before they are presented to child readers.

Good children's authors are aware of this and usually strive to empower their readers, if not entirely to take control of their lives, then at least to achieve a degree of agency by thinking through and making sense of this foreign world they find themselves in. One of the best modern writers for children is Diana Wynne Jones (1934-2011). She produced more than fifty books, mostly for children and young adults, all of them in the fantasy and science fiction genres and was one of the first writers for any age group to use the idea of parallel worlds and a multiverse, concepts with which we have since become much more familiar both in speculative fiction and in quantum physics. Jones's worlds can be ordered in parallel series, or they can cluster around a central point, or they can exist independently of one another in a multiverse and there is travel between these worlds —and what could be more foreign than a traveller to or from another world?

In Jones's work, however, nothing is ever straightforward. This paper will argue that Jones plays with concepts of foreignness in order to interrogate both what is perceived as foreign and what is perceived as familiar in ways that allow her readers to "think things through", as she puts it, in order not just to understand their world better but to understand that there can be a better world. This has nothing to do with escapism or the idea that a better world can only exist on another planet or indeed after death (as C. S. Lewis to a large extent suggests in his Narnia books); for Jones, using your imagination is the best way of trying to think in new, more fruitful ways about our lives and our world and perhaps effecting positive changes:

> Taking someone *away* from the pressures under which they live is much more valuable than grinding their noses into the fact that they are, say, of the wrong race or that their parents are divorcing, or both; particularly if, while they are away, this person is given a chance to use their imagination. Imagination doesn't just mean making things up. It means thinking things through, solving them, or hoping to do so, and being just distant enough to be able to laugh at things that are normally painful" (Jones 2012: 258).

Since it is impossible to do justice to Jones's large and endlessly inventive oeuvre in even a book-length study, I shall concentrate here on two books in particular, *The Lives of Christopher Chant* (first published in 1988) and *The Homeward Bounders* (first published in 1981). The latter, which Jones's eldest son Richard has called "the most tragic of her books" (Jones 2012: 286) is also one of the most obviously concerned with foreignness. Its narrator, Jamie, discovers that his world, along with the almost infinite number of other worlds in existence, is run by a race of demons who use the worlds and all the people living in them as counters in an endless, elaborate war game. Since the game relies on the "counters" not realising this, Jamie is "discarded" as a "random factor" and condemned to wander the boundaries between the worlds. He is promised he can return home and stay there, if he discovers the way back. He is hindered by the bounds, which jerk him from world to world at indeterminate intervals without being able to influence the time or direction of his moves.

Thus he becomes a "Homeward Bounder", caught in the bounds, bound for home, bounding between worlds, bound by the rules of an alien game,[1] and although he is initially alone and told that homeward bounders are not allowed to associate with one another (the bounds send them off to different worlds, if they meet), he realises that their number is large and that they do try to help one another (Jamie, for instance, is rescued from the ocean by the Flying Dutchman and receives advice from Ahasuerus, the Wandering Jew). Eventually, having lost all hope of returning home, he leads a rebellion against the demons and defeats them. He comes to the realisation, however, that he will have to patrol the bounds between the worlds for the rest of his life in order to prevent the remaining demons from returning. Jamie will, in effect, have to remain a foreigner forever to ensure a better world for everyone else.

It is possible to read this as a tale of adolescent alienation and feelings of helplessness in a confusingly complex adult world. The noted critic Maria Nikolajeva takes this approach when she asserts that

[i]n fantasy, especially, there are good reasons to interpret the events and happenings as a mindscape [...] Defamiliarization indicates the emotions of young people faced with new, unfamiliar, and disturbing phases in their lives. [...] In all Jones' novels, the young protagonists discover some form of superior —sometimes divine— authority that governs every single parallel world and has control and power over the fates of their inhabitants. The mysterious *They* in *The Homeward*

---

1   There are several other layers of meaning associated with the word "bound" and Jamie even meets Prometheus, both bound and unbound; intertextuality is a hallmark of Jones's work.

Bounders is perhaps the best example, representing the parental authority in an adolescent's life (Nikolajeva 2002: 27).

Apart from disputing that *all* Jones's novels contain such authorities, I
also consider this interpretation of the book rather reductive. What *The
Homeward Bounders* most certainly does display and plays with are
aspects of foreignness on several different levels.

Jamie's home is an ordinary city in our world; small details soon in-
dicate that the time is an industrialised but pre-motorised past. If (as L.P.
Hartley has it) the past is indeed a foreign country, then the reader is put
in the position of a foreign spectator, a distancing device that may be
very necessary for younger readers, given the tragic nature of the story to
come. We learn eventually that the year is eighteen seventy-nine (Jones
2000: 235), and in a neat inversion, Jamie returns to his own world in the
future, an even more foreign country than the past, so he does not recognise it. He has been on the bounds for what seems to him about a year of
his personal time (he now looks about thirteen), but over a hundred years
have passed in this world where the year is nineteen-eighty. Jones plays
with both Einstein's twins paradox, which proposes that a person travelling near the speed of light will age more slowly than a person remaining
at rest, and the much older motif found particularly in Celtic mythology
and folklore where the hero enters a fairy mound or other enchanted
place for what seems a short time, only to find many years have passed
in the world outside, which is now unfamiliar and in which he himself
has become a legend (cf. Mendlesohn 2005: 54 and Butler 2006: 103).

Jamie thus becomes a foreigner in his own city, believing it to be yet
another of the endless worlds he must visit. Realising the truth does not
alleviate his feeling of foreignness: this may be his world but it is no
longer his Home; the temporal dislocation has made it impossible for
him ever to reach Home again. Since this world is described as through
the eyes of a foreigner, the indigenous contemporary reader also experiences a distancing effect that provides a good deal of the humour which
makes bearable a tale that ends with the heartrending sentence: "But you
wouldn't believe how lonely you get" (Jones 2000: 267).

More conventional concepts of foreignness are introduced through
Jamie's sojourn on the different worlds he is forced to visit. He finds
unfamiliar landscapes, climates, languages, customs, political and social
structures and, unlike a voluntary traveller, who can choose to remain a

spectating outsider, Jamie must learn to adapt to these foreign environ-
ments in order to survive with his sanity, sense of personal identity and
purpose intact. Some of the worlds he experiences as pleasant, some as
dangerous and horrible, many are at war, and one has been emptied of all
life by what appears to have been a nuclear holocaust. It should be noted
here that there are no bug-eyed monsters on these other worlds; Jamie
encounters exclusively human societies and is thus able to acknowledge
that however strange and sometimes abhorrent they appear to him, they
are Home to the people who live there.[2] Since Jamie sees them as foreign
but is in turn regarded as a foreigner, specifically by the two friends from
two different worlds who he acquires along the way, and since all of
them are mostly helpless in the face of what is being done to them while
bringing different skills and knowledge to the task of surviving and de-
feating the demons, the notion of a hierarchy, whether in terms of power
or moral superiority, becomes redundant. Jamie and his world are certainly not set up as the standard against which to measure the foreign —
foreigners and foreign worlds are not inferior, merely different. Com-
monalities can be found quite easily, the most important being the desire
for self-determination. It is in order to safeguard the possibility of self-
determination for all the worlds that Jamie relinquishes any chance of
fashioning a new home for himself when he chooses to keep patrolling
the bounds; he is the perfect anti-colonialist.

The arrangement of worlds as well as representations of the foreign
are different in *The Lives of Christopher Chant*, one of several stories set
in the Chrestomanci universe, briefly described by Jones in a foreword:
"There are thousands of worlds, all different from ours. Chrestomanci's
world is the one next door to us, and the difference here is that magic is
as common as music is with us" (Jones 2001).[3] New worlds come into
existence all the time; this happens when a significant event can have
two contradictory outcomes —the world splits to accommodate both
possibilities. There are series of parallel worlds called "the Related
Worlds"; ours is 12b and gets only a brief, unfavourable mention. Chris-

---

2 The dead world, however, shows what will happen if the demons/people playing
   war games/stockpiling nuclear arsenals are not checked, one of the very few explicit morals to be found in Jone's work.
3 Chrestomanci is the title of a British government employee in charge of controlling
   the magic users so they do not mistreat ordinary people.

topher Chant, therefore, lives in a world that is almost identical with the reader's, except that it contains magic and its society runs along vaguely Edwardian lines. Everything else is familiar, the geography of London, the organisation of his boarding school, the game of cricket, and if the currency is pre-decimal, this is of a piece with the presence of household servants in a recognisable quasi-historical setting. Christopher and his immediate surroundings appear exceedingly English, though in an old-fashioned way.

Christopher's travelling between worlds and his reasons for doing so are fundamentally different from Jamie's. While Jamie was very much at home in his world and was torn from a loving family by force, Christopher is, to start with, much younger and knows very little of the world outside his nursery. He hardly sees his parents, who are estranged and try to use him to further their own ambitions, and so he travels to other worlds to escape his dismal and boring life, believing at first that he is dreaming, as does the reader. In the manner of small children, he simply accepts what he finds in the other worlds, uses them for relaxation and adventure, and never indicates that he finds them foreign or even strange. This only happens when he grows older and gains some more experience of his own world.

It is at this point that Jones begins to furnish some descriptions of the places Christopher visits, and while the boy seems completely comfortable in them, the reader can recognise foreignness in the sense of difference from England —other climates, other vegetation, other styles of building, other customs. Apart from containing a dragon and some mermaids, however, these worlds are remarkably like Earth. In one significant location, Christopher enters the temple of the Goddess Asheth (echoing the Babylonian Ishtar/Astarte) in a setting that could be Middle Eastern or Indian. Christopher thinks it "primitive and heathen-seeming" (Jones 2001: 376), obviously in comparison to the England he knows. On the other hand, when he encounters a young girl who is kept in the temple as "the Living Asheth", they get on perfectly well and over several visits develop an understanding that their situations are very similar: both are used by the adults around them without having a choice in the matter.

Their interaction emphasises familiarity on a deep level rather than the surface foreignness indicated by their living conditions. A good example is the Goddess's request for books, because the ones in the temple are "all educational or holy. And the Living Goddess isn't allowed to touch *anything* in this world outside the Temple. Anything in this *world*. Do you understand?" (Jones 2001: 320). Christopher understands "perfectly", not only the subterfuge employed by the Goddess but also, when he comes to choose books, that she would probably consider *The Arabian Nights* "educational". On the advice of a school friend with a sister, he buys her a series of school stories in the Angela Brazil or Enid Blyton mode, which prove to be a perfect choice. The girl from another world, living in a country very different from Christopher's England and containing aspects of a very foreign goddess, is thus shown to have the same thought processes and yearnings as a girl from Christopher's world. On the important personal level, therefore, she is not foreign.

This ability to relate, to understand and respect one another, extends to adults in the story, too. When the High Priestess of Asheth pays a visit to Christopher's by-then guardian, the current Chrestomanci, she makes it clear that her ideas of respectability, for instance, are very much the same as his (Jones 2001: 593-94). Chrestomanci, having previously decried some of her world's practices, like killing the Living Asheth when she grows too old, as vicious and uncivilised, nevertheless meets her as an equal: their powers are similar and their outlooks compatible. Both these adults have researched the other worlds, too, and are able to acknowledge the validity of other societal structures, consequently adopting a live-and-let-live attitude. Ideas of a hierarchy, therefore, may be expressed in theory but are not acted upon in practice.

Much more foreign, and indeed undesirable, are the inhabitants of the one world among the related worlds that cuts itself off from the rest, Series Eleven (a misnomer, as there is no series, only one world, in it). Jones has some fun playing with the notion that our idea of elves, often thought of, in the Tolkien tradition, as noble if remote, derives from this Series Eleven world, whose inhabitants are anything but noble. This rigidly class-ridden world is ruled by a tyrant and holds loyalty to him along with external display, haughtiness, and subterfuge in the highest regard. The other worlds are but objects of study and experiment, lab rats, if you will, and the tyrant aims to find ways to dominate them, too. It is interesting to note that the one thing the people of Eleven do not use is fire, and if we think of Prometheus again, this perhaps marks them out as less than human.

It seems clear that isolationist tendencies are detrimental and lead to a foreignness that means separation from humankind. In the parallel worlds of the Chrestomanci universe, there can be strangers and strangeness, but there is a possibility of understanding that precludes true foreignness. This is only found in a wilfully cut-off world like Eleven, where a meeting of minds cannot be achieved.

What I hope to have shown is that Jones uses the device of multiple worlds to refract human interaction and relationships at one remove in order to enable readers to think through ideas of foreignness and familiarity, standards and aberrations, and how valid are our understandings of "us" and "them". She comes down quite firmly on the side of recognising the common aspects of humanity rather than emphasising and overestimating the dividing ones. Foreignness, in Jones's work, need not be an immutable negative.

Bibliography

Butler, C. 2006. *Four British Fantasists. Place and Culture in the Children's Fantasies of Penelope Lively, Alan Garner, Diana Wynne Jones, and Susan Cooper*, Lanham, Maryland, Toronto, Oxford, Children's Literature Association and The Scarecrow Press.

Jones, D.W. 2000. *The Homeward Bounders*, London, Harper Collins Children's Books.

—. 2001. *The Chronicles of Chrestomanci*, Volume 1, London, Greenwillow.

—. 2012. *Reflections. On the Magic of Writing*, Oxford, David Fickling Books.

Mendlesohn, F. 2005. *Diana Wynne Jones: Children's Literature and the Fantastic Tradition*, New York & London, Routledge.

Nikolajeva, M. 2002. "Heterotopia as a Reflection of Postmodern Consciousness in the Work of Diana Wynne Jones", in T. Rosenberg, M. P. Hixon, S. M. Scapple & D. R. White (eds.), *Diana Wynne Jones. An Exciting and Exacting Wisdom*, New York, Peter Lang.

Saunders, R. 2003. *The Concept of the Foreign*, Oxford, Lexington Books.

AMILCAR TORRÃO FILHO

La ciudad en escombros. Imágenes del catolicismo luso-brasileño en los viajeros británicos

> Sí, de la ciudad has hecho un escombro,
> La ciudad fortificada está en ruinas.
>
> *Isaías, 25, 2.*

La literatura de viajes ha comportado un ejercicio de alteridad en el cual se busca la comprensión del mundo y su diversidad. Una de las formas privilegiadas de reconocimiento de la alteridad ha sido la observación de las prácticas religiosas de los pueblos visitados. En el caso del Brasil colonial, parece existir una relación entre las características del paisaje y las prácticas religiosas. Los viajeros británicos de los siglos XVIII y XIX identificaron las ciudades sobre colinas, tan del agrado de los portugueses, con el dominio de la idolatría y de la superstición. El Antiguo Testamento es revelador: "Deberéis destruir los lugares en donde las naciones que conquistareis hayan servido a sus dioses, sobre los altos montes, sobre las colinas y bajo todo árbol en su verdor" (Deuteronomio 12, 2). El Antiguo Testamento identifica la idolatría con las ofrendas y ritos realizados en lugares elevados en los que se realizaban ceremonias prohibidas. La Biblia, fuente privilegiada de imágenes en la literatura de viajes, forma parte de una "cultura compartida" entre el viajero y el lector, y entre viajeros, ya sean católicos o protestantes, e irrumpe en la narrativa "evocando el lugar fundamental que ocupa en su universo imaginario y el papel que desempeña en su lectura del mundo" (Payet-Meure 2005: 182). Las imágenes pintorescas y tan representativas de las ciudades luso-brasileñas, con torres de iglesias y conventos destacándose en el paisaje, sugirieron al viajero espacios de idolatría y paganismo.

El viaje, tradicionalmente, ha estado vinculado a la religión como itinerario de peregrinación, pero también ha significado un desplazamiento. Viajar significa separarse de los seres queridos, de la patria, presupone un duelo y también un regreso: en el "traslado que le fundamenta, en la distancia que se recorre, en el exilio que remata, reúne el otro y el mismo" (Lestringant 2005: 15). El viaje a países católicos, en el caso de los protestantes británicos, o a naciones poco desarrolladas y supersticiosas, en el caso de los católicos, obliga al viajero de antaño a dedicar una atención a la alteridad distinta de la que dedica cuando visita países islámicos o pueblos considerados "bárbaros" y "fetichistas" (Torrão Filho 2010; 2011). En dichos lugares la diferencia es evidente. En cambio, en las ciudades luso-brasileñas, la alteridad está dentro de un mismo esquema conceptual con representaciones muy cercanas. De ahí una extrañeza aún mayor por la proximidad de este universo simbólico que, no obstante, el viajero no reconoce como parte de su bagaje cultural.

La literatura "viática" tiene una estrecha relación con la idea de pasaje, que representa no solo el riesgo de viajar a otro mundo, sino el de transponerse a una realidad desconocida. El término *viático* viene del latín *viaticum*, derivado de camino, ruta, vía, "que traduce bien la idea de un recorrido" (Paquot 2005: 24). Significa tanto lo que es necesario para el trayecto (dinero, víveres, etc.) como también el sacramento administrado a los moribundos en su lecho de muerte. El viaje es un rito de pasaje que coloca al individuo en el umbral de dos mundos: el mundo del desplazamiento, donde se aleja de su espacio familiar y accede a lo desconocido, y el de la alteridad, donde transpone su cultura y, muchas veces, su religión, para acceder también a un conocimiento casi iniciático que le revela la forma del mundo y los fenómenos de la creación divina.

El relato anónimo de un miembro de la Missionary Society que estuvo en Rio de Janeiro en 1796 deja muy clara la incomodidad de los protestantes con los ritos católicos de Brasil. Su capital parece, para él, "exceder todos los locales papistas en materia de religión": en cada esquina se podía encontrar una figura de Nuestro Salvador y de la Virgen María "puesta en un nicho, o en una especie de armario, con una cortina y ventana de vidrio". Por la noche, había velas encendidas; y lo peor, al pasar delante de esas imágenes, "las personas se paran para rezar sus oraciones y durante toda la noche se puede oír la voz de sus cantos". Incluso el más pobre mendigo "hace negocio con la religión", ya que con un crucifijo en su pecho bendice a las personas que se le cruzan por el camino y "debe ser pagado por esa bendición así como el Papa" (1799: 33).[1] Lo que le llama más la atención y le indigna es la "idolatría" de los

---

1   Los textos en inglés en la versión original han sido traducidos por el autor.

católicos luso-brasileños. Recibidos en el palacio de gobierno, los miembros de la Missionary Society fueron atendidos por el coronel comandante con toda educación, y por su mujer, quien fue "especialmente atenta con nuestras esposas", señala el narrador. Sin embargo, añade, no pudieron agradecer las gentilezas,

> cuando vimos sus arraigadas supersticiones, sus rosarios y crucifijos pendiendo de sus cuellos; y la cruz y sus santos están en las esquinas de cada calle, y fuera de sus casas: a las que ellos se inclinan reverentes y se persignan cuando pasan. Ellos realmente parecen hundidos en la idolatría (1799: 35).

Ninguna demostración de cortesía puede compensar, para esos misioneros, los errores papales de los católicos portugueses en América; los consideran peores que los "salvajes" de los mares del Sur a los cuales pretendían convertir durante el mismo viaje.

Otra cosa que llamó la atención prácticamente a todo viajero que estuvo en las ciudades brasileñas fueron las procesiones. Los miembros de la Missionary Society asistieron a una de ellas, ciertamente importante, con sacerdotes, monjas y plañideras, "entrando en una de sus catedrales" en la que brillaban candelabros encendidos. Se rezaban oraciones y "cantaban los coros acompañados por una banda de músicos. La visión nos afligió al contemplar esta pompa externa de devoción y no descubrir ningún trazo de la inmaculada religión de Jesús" (1799: 36). Son estas, sin duda, descripciones muy parecidas a las de James Cook, cuya breve semblanza de Rio de Janeiro en su primer viaje de circunnavegación fue el punto de partida de casi todos los viajeros posteriores. Para él, las iglesias de la ciudad eran muy bonitas, pero había más "ostentación religiosa en ese lugar que en cualquiera de los países papistas de Europa". Se observan procesiones parroquiales todos los días, "con varias insignias, todas espléndidas y caras, de la más alta calidad". Y todavía se pide dinero y se rezan oraciones "en cada esquina de cada ciudad" (14).

Este será uno de los lugares comunes más frecuentes en la narrativa de viajes: la superficialidad de la fe brasileña, así como la de sus instituciones. Dicho tópico se incorporará a la historiografía de Brasil; será Sérgio Buarque de Holanda uno de los primeros en formular en su *Raízes do Brasil* (1936) la idea de "una religiosidad superficial, menos atenta al sentido íntimo de las ceremonias y más preocupada por el colorido y la pompa exterior" (1988: 111). En la descripción del catolicismo luso-brasileño lo material y lo moral se aproximan al promover una interpretación global de la sociedad.

No es la falta de devoción lo que molesta a los viajeros, sino una devoción mal orientada, inadecuada y muchas veces anacrónica. Watkin Tench, en 1787, también dirige su atención a los nichos con santos e imágenes de la Virgen en casi todas las esquinas. La excesiva devoción a esos lugares no puede dejar de causar "espanto al extranjero". La mayor parte de los habitantes, dice Tench, "parece no tener otra ocupación, a no ser la de devolver visitas e ir a la iglesia" (1789: 22-23). La administración de la ciudad se resentía de esas costumbres de devoción exterior que impedían el desempeño de otras actividades más ilustradas. Los oídos de los extranjeros eran "felicitados por el repique de las campanas de los conventos y sus ojos saludados por las procesiones de los devotos, cuya adoración y frivolidad parecen andar al mismo paso" (1789: 28).

John White, cirujano jefe de la armada del primer gobernador de Nueva Gales del Sur, describe una procesión en la ciudad de Río de Janeiro en 1787. Personas de todas las clases sociales, a pie, a caballo o en carroza, formaban una multitud que se dirigía a la Iglesia de la Gloria, frente a la cual se paraban para rezar y cantar himnos religiosos. En el camino, regresando de la procesión, White se fija en una pequeña iglesia en una calle secundaria, "ricamente ornamentada y elegantemente iluminada" en la que hombres, mujeres y niños se disputaban para entrar. Sin embargo, en dicha iglesia, la satisfacción que obtuvo al ser "exprimido y empujado", afirma con ironía, fue la de ver a los fieles cayendo de rodillas y rezando "con más fervor, en apariencia, que con verdadera devoción". Se distribuían rosarios bendecidos y las calles estaban llenas de vendedores ambulantes de artículos religiosos, además de muchos músicos y cantantes que se esforzaban por agradar a la audiencia. A las diez, los entretenimientos del día concluían con "fuegos artificiales y cohetes muy apreciados por los portugueses" (1790: 50-53). Desde el punto de vista del viajero, no es una fe fingida, sino una inadecuación incomprensible. No entiende la relación que se establece entre devoción, diversión y comercio; este sentimiento emana más de sus prejuicios que de la experiencia vivida en la ceremonia religiosa. Son, pues, los libros los que confieren a la religiosidad del catolicismo brasileño su carácter superficial, no un conocimiento adquirido por medio de la experiencia.

Observando en 1802 la procesión de Nuestra Señora de la Concepción de la Playa en Salvador, el contrabandista Thomas Lindley se sorprende también de la veneración que las imágenes "despiertan en el pueblo, que generalmente las adora de manera devota y abyecta, como si contuvieran la esencia de la misma Divinidad, descendida para la ocasión, *in propria persona*" (1805: 92). El día de Reyes, o cuando se conmemora el día en que "se supone" que los tres Reyes Magos visitaron y adoraron a Cristo, músicos ambulantes cruzan las calles en grupos, "yendo de casa en casa, sin ninguna ceremonia, y haciendo en cada una de ellas un bárbaro tumulto; y después de repetir las mismas tontas formalidades, siguen adelante para importunar al próximo habitante", lo que se repite durante la noche. La multitud participa de este "rudo regocijo y parece disfrutar de la escena". Mucho más que una celebración cristiana, le pareció al contrabandista "un carnaval italiano, con mucha confusión, pero sin el espíritu picante y el vivo interés que inspira esta fiesta" (1805: 123-24). Lindley no ve una relación entre la festividad y la forma tan curiosa de mantener la memoria de los Reyes; hay una inadecuación entre la festividad religiosa y la manera de celebrarla. Se trata, dice él, de "oscuros vestigios del siglo XIV que aún no han sido abolidos" (1805: 123-24). Se consolidan así otros dos elementos negativos de la religiosidad: desvirtúa la verdadera tradición y la hace atrasada y obscura.

En su breve estancia en Salvador, en 1800, John Turnbull, negociante y supuesto espía británico, muestra una actitud menos crítica con la religión católica en Brasil, aunque esa tolerancia revele, para él mismo, la superioridad de la fe reformada. Las iglesias de la ciudad le parecieron bastante bellas, bien decoradas y llenas de fieles de todas las dignidades. Juzgó la devoción tan sincera que, aun siendo protestante "y sin ninguna predilección por su santidad el Papa", no deja de experimentar una buena impresión (23). Asiste a una ceremonia en la catedral de la ciudad, un domingo de fiesta, con un sermón pronunciado por el obispo que él considera elocuente y vigoroso, aunque un poco exagerado, contra los "vicios e impiedades". Enseguida, la imagen de Nuestra Señora y la del príncipe de Brasil son llevadas en procesión por las calles de la ciudad, siendo reverenciadas por las mujeres desde los balcones: "un espectáculo teatral de ninguna manera desagradable, si la devoción de una religión equivocada puede admitirse como excusa por sus errores" (24-25). Turnbull no duda, contrariamente a otros viajeros, de la sinceridad de la fe católica de los luso-brasileños, aunque el gusto por la apariencia quede claro en la identificación de la festividad como espectáculo teatral.

John Luccock, negociante que vivió en Río de Janeiro de 1808 a 1818, también señaló aspectos de la religiosidad de los luso-brasileños y los perjuicios que ésta causaba a la misma organización de la sociedad, impidiéndoles, por ejemplo, una dieta más saludable. Observa que el pueblo suele alimentarse de carne de cerdo con mucha avidez, "como si le encantaran las oportunidades de demostrar que no son judíos ni mahometanos. Dudo, no obstante, de que tal como se cría en Brasil, sea una dieta ni deseable ni sana" (1820: 44). El cordero tampoco no se consume porque dicen que "no es comida propia de cristiano", por haber sido "el Cordero Divino que tomó consigo los pecados del mundo" (1820: 44). Estas creencias, vistas como costumbres atrasadas y religiosidad "superficial", le parecían a Luccock supersticiones que poco servían a la necesaria tarea de civilización de los luso-brasileños, no solo por lo que respecta a la fe cristiana sino sobre todo a la formación de buenos y útiles ciudadanos, una vez superado el estatuto colonial de la América portuguesa, ahora sede del Reino Unido de Portugal, Brasil y Algarves.

Esta incomprensión de los viajeros proviene de dos hechos: el anacronismo de las prácticas litúrgicas del catolicismo luso-brasileño y la dificultad para descifrar estas prácticas híbridas, situadas a caballo de lo profano, lo pagano y lo religioso. Eran acciones desubicadas en el universo simbólico del extranjero. William Gore Ouseley se horroriza con los exvotos que pedían protección para las naves en la capilla de Boa Viagem, en Rio de Janeiro, donde vivió entre 1832 y 1844. Le extraña la "adopción o modificación de costumbres paganas" que representan la absorción por el Catolicismo Romano de prácticas de la mitología griega, como los exvotos: "Por medio de una simple transición, el altar pagano fue reemplazado por el de Roma", afirma Ouseley. Si por un lado ofenden la doctrina, estas prácticas tienen el mérito de divertir, por lo pintoresco, y educar, al remitir a un pasado clásico y pagano, incorporado por el catolicismo. Es interesante, dice el autor, resaltar en estos ritos, "la distancia de tiempo y espacio que separan América del Sur del Olimpo" (Ouseley 1852: 24).

Tal como recuerda John Barrow, la religión subyace en la conquista de Brasil, en la conversión de los nativos a la religión cristiana, propiciando la enorme riqueza de las iglesias y conventos. Pero sin juzgar el celo del clero para llevar a cabo dicho proyecto, añade, "ese cuidado hace mucho tiempo que dio lugar a la indolencia y al lujo de la vida monástica". El celo del clero se transformó en prudencia para mantener "una imagen exterior de devoción en la que se observan, de una manera extraordinariamente puntual, las ceremonias religiosas que asombran la mirada del vulgo". Esta acomodación que acomete el clero luso-brasileño hace que este "afloje en su moral y en su conversión, y que no esté muy inclinado a la severidad con relación a los laicos" (131-32). Al ser el clero aún muy influyente, su laxitud de costumbres solamente puede tener una función dañina en la sociedad. Este relajamiento no influye por sí solo en la desagregación de una sociedad que se está formando. El ritual obsoleto y la riqueza inútil visibles en el lujo de las iglesias y en los ornamentos de las procesiones, con costosas joyas donadas por los habitantes más ricos, desagradan a Barrow. La mirada irónica de Barrow descubre que pocos de ellos eran "lo suficientemente impíos para que se rechazasen sus diamantes cuando se expone la Virgen a las miradas del público" (133). Ni el más contumaz pecador será lo suficientemente impío para no merecer el perdón, a cambio de oro o diamantes, de una Iglesia igualmente impía y codiciosa.

En las interpretaciones de los viajeros no importan las contradicciones ni las diferencias. De lo hasta aquí expuesto puede deducirse que el fanatismo y la indolencia son conceptos básicos para la comprensión de la sociedad formada en el Brasil colonial. Una sociedad cuya religiosidad de origen ibérico representa y explica el atraso de ésta y la distancia que existe entre la apariencia europea de sus ciudades e instituciones —como la monarquía o la Iglesia Católica— y la realidad de corrupción moral que se puede observar en ella. Una sociedad marcada por la superstición y por el anacronismo de formas religiosas teatralizadas, que no transmiten el verdadero espíritu de la religión. Esta idea, común a los viajeros protestantes y católicos, justificaría así la decadencia de este Edén tropical que es la América portuguesa.

Bibliografía

Anónimo. 1799. *A Missionary Voyage to the Southern Pacific Ocean*, London, Chapman.

Bíblia de Jerusalém. 2004. Gustavo da Silva Gorgulho et. al. (trads.), São Paulo, Paulus.

Barrow, J. 1807. *Voyage à la Cochinchine, par les îles de Madère, de Tenerife et du Cap Verd, le Brésil et l'île de Java*, vol. 1, Malte-Brun (trad.), Paris, Buisson.

Cook, J. 1862. *The Voyages of Captain James Cook*, vol. 1, London, William Smith.

Holanda, S. B. de. 1988. *Raízes do Brasil*, Rio de Janeiro, Olympio.

Lestringant, F. 2005. "Le voyage, une affaire de religion", in S. Linon-Chipon & J.-F. Guennoc (eds.), *Transhumances divines. Récits de voyage et religion*, Paris, Presses de l'Université de Paris-Sorbonne, 13-31.

Lindley, T. 1805. *Narrative of a Voyage to Brasil*, London, Johnson.

Luccock, J. 1820. *Notes on Rio de Janeiro, and the Southern Parts of Brazil*, London, Samuel Leigh.

Ouseley, W. G. 1852. *Descriptions of Views in South America*, London, Thomas McLean.

Paquot, T. 2005. "L'*autre* comme ailleurs", in P. Gras & C. Payen (dirs.), *Villes, voyages, voyageurs. Actes de la rencontre de Villeurbanne*, Paris & Budapest & Torino, L'Harmattan, 19-29.

Payet-Meure, C. 2005. "Robert Challe. La Bible à l'épreuve du voyage", in S. Linon-Chipon & J.-F. Guennoc (eds.), *Transhumances divines. Récits de voyage et religion*, Paris, Presses de l'Université de Paris-Sorbonne, 181-97.

Tench, W. 1789. *A Narrative of the Expedition to Botany Bay*, 2nd. Ed., London, Debrett.

Torrão Filho, A. 2010. "Cidade aberta, sem muralhas. A religião luso-brasileira na literatura de viagem", *História* 29: 1, 71-90. <http://www.scielo.br/scielo.php?script=sci_arttext&pid=S0101-90742010000100006&lng=en&nrm=iso> [consultado el 01.XII.2011].

—. 2011. "Le catholicisme luso-brésilien selon les voyageurs français du XIXe siècle", *Travaux de Littérature* 24, 207-17.

Turnbull, J. 1805. *A Voyage Round the World, in the Years 1800, 1801, 1802, and 1804*, vol. 1, London, Richard Phillips.

White, J. 1790. *Journal of a Voyage to New South Wales*, London, Debrett.

II

Exploring Otherness: Multiple Identities
in a Comparative Perspective

LEONARDO ROMERO TOBAR

Juan Valera: Visión de "grupos minoritarios" en países de Europa y América[1]

Introducción

Si en la Historia humana la construcción del grupo identificado como "propio" se verifica nítidamente desde la delimitación de los "otros" grupos, una forma de autodefinición que ha tenido y aún tiene potencia representativa es el contraste del grupo con los otros a los que se denomina "extranjeros". En la tradición de la Historia universal se ha visto, e incluso hoy día se sigue viendo al "extraño" o "extranjero" como una comunidad humana asentada en la noción de pertenencia, "es *extraño* todo lo que escapa al *orden* al que se pertenece" (Moureau 2007:12). El "extraño" o "extranjero" puede ser alguien físicamente próximo al observador pero ajeno a sus premisas vitales, premisas a las que, a partir del siglo XVIII, se suman las convenciones implicadas en el envoltorio político que constituye los Estados nacionales.

Un elocuentísimo registro escrito para la captación de estas variaciones de percepción reside en los escritos de los viajeros que se desplazan a lugares desconocidos para ellos, lugares cuyas características geográficas y, singularmente, lugares en los que el aspecto físico y el comportamiento de sus habitantes les descubren inéditas realidades culturales y humanas.[2]

---

1   En este texto las citas de la *Correspondencia* de Juan Valera se hacen sobre la edición de Leonardo Romero (dirección), María Ángeles Ezama y Enrique Serrano, Madrid, Castalia, 2002-2009, 8 volúmenes.

2   La peculiaridad española de *Pepita Jiménez* la señalaba el propio Valera en una carta a su hermana Sofía en la que afirmaba que "como es de cosas que ocurren en un lugar de Andalucía y tiene mucho color local y cierta originalidad española, los extranjeros que hay aquí, como Bauer, M. Layard y otros del cuerpo diplomático casi celebran más la novela que los españoles" (carta de 5-V-1874; V, 558).

280 Leonardo Romero Tobar

"Literatura de viajes" y "representación del extranjero" constituyen, desde la más remota Antigüedad mundos biunívocos sobre los que han aplicado sus intereses y desvelos los estudiosos de las más variadas disciplinas de las Ciencias Humanas. Testimonios radicales de la relación existente entre viajes y grado de conocimiento —de desconocimiento, en los ejemplos que aduzco— encontramos en la negación de la personalidad del propio viajero —el "Nadie" con que se nombra a sí mismo Ulises, en el conocido canto IX de la *Odisea*— o en la denominación privativa —"anywhere in the world"— con que el capitán Cook se refirió a la constelación de las islas.

Reduciendo el marco de este fenómeno universal a la literatura escrita en castellano recuérdese que, desde los textos medievales, la representación del "extranjero" tiene una presencia notable —judíos, musulmanes y francos en el *Cantar de Mio Cid*, habitantes del Oriente próximo en la *Embajada a Tamorlán*—, hasta el punto que llega a ser un rasgo clave en los textos de viaje que redactaron esforzados pasajeros del siglo XVI, que, procedentes de las coronas lusitana, castellana o catalano-aragonesa, llevaron a las páginas de manuscritos o primeros impresos sus impresiones de mundos orientales y occidentales absolutamente distintos a los que les resultaban familiares en las talasocracias peninsulares de las que procedían.

Vía distinta a las crónicas de los descubrimientos y conquistas son los textos redactados por los espías encubiertos o los embajadores oficiales que los monarcas destacaban a las cortes de otros reyes. Sin llegar al grado de sutil eficacia desplegada por los representantes de la república veneciana en otros Estados (Comisso 1985), no dejan de tener interés para el asunto que aquí nos convoca los despachos y correspondencias de diplomáticos españoles en las cortes europeas de los siglos XVI y XVII —conde de Gondomar en Londres (1613-1622), marqués de La Fuente en París (1659-1667)— función informativa que, una vez establecida la casa de Borbón al frente de la monarquía hispana experimentaría un impulso de modernización, como podemos leer en los informes del duque de Almodóvar en relación a su embajada en Rusia (1760-1763).

Valera en sus viajes

Un siglo después las cartas del viaje del joven Juan Valera a Rusia (1856-1857) lo convirtieron en un escritor público del que sus lectores quedaron fascinados; antes de esta correspondencia privada, que se publicó en el diario madrileño *La España*, el joven cordobés había comunicado a su familia e íntimos sus impresiones del reino de Nápoles y de Portugal y el Brasil de mediados del siglo, comunicaciones a las que seguirían millares de epístolas escritas en los varios países en los que residió. Don Juan Valera —el escritor cuya obra va a ser el laboratorio de prueba que en modo sintético ofreceré seguidamente— fue curioso viajero y diplomático de oficio, actividades ambas que le situaron en la circunstancia de ver y valorar tipos y paisajes muy variados y prácticamente desconocidos para los destinatarios de sus escritos que, en un primer alcance, fueron sus lectores de periódicos peninsulares y de sus cartas familiares y que, en un alcance posterior, para los informes, eran sus jefes administrativos en el Ministerio de Estado y para los problemas de actualidad en el "fin de siglo" sus lectores de periódicos editados en España, Buenos Aires o Nueva York.

La captación de fieles lectores fue para Valera, igual que para los muchos escritores de periódicos, el gran desafío que debía vencer, habida cuenta la escasa práctica de lectura en la España de su tiempo y el ínfimo nivel de intereses culturales mantenidos por los españoles de entonces. Una carencia que denunció y lamentó en muchísimas ocasiones, como en esta confidencia a su amigo diplomático, el belga Jules de Greindl: "Confieso que si yo tengo la desventaja de que en España se lee mil veces menos que en Francia, tengo sobre Vd. la ventaja de que en mi país hay más que enseñar y más que decir que parezca nuevo, por lo mismo que en España se sabe tan poco" (16-IV-1887; IV, 675). La carta prosigue con una expresiva consideración referida al estilo de su propia prosa, que reproducimos.[3] El propio Valera repite esta estimación en

---

3   "Creo que mi estilo es natural y no rebuscado, moderno y no arcaico, sencillo y no enrevesado. Si en Cabra o en Doña Mencía leyesen y se interesasen en el asunto, entenderían mis libros; pero la gente cursi de las capitales, que es la que lee en España, se ha fabricado en dicharachos periodísticos y frases hechas parlamentarias, neologismos franceses de salón y modismos de toreros y "cantaores [...]".

varias cartas dirigidas a otros corresponsales no españoles que no es el caso de recopilar aquí.

Juan Valera, hijo de familia aristocrática y acomodada, era andaluz de Cabra, circunstancias ambas que determinan su punto de vista en la percepción de los "otros" puesto que, como es bien sabido, en el siglo XIX la actitud social de la clase dominante y la de los meridionales eran harto diferentes a la de los españoles de clase media afincados en el interior de la Península, dado el tipo de comportamiento público que exhibían y que resultaba especialmente visible en Madrid. La capital de España ofrecía a los terratenientes y titulados del Sur un escenario multiforme en el que desplegar sus gestos de clase dominante —paseos públicos, plazas, iglesias, teatros, palacios—, lugares que en buena medida compartían con los andaluces populares que impregnaban la ciudad con sus pintorescas manifestaciones lingüísticas y festivas, cuando por la calle de Alcalá, como cantaba en unos caracoles el famoso Antonio Chacón, "suben y bajan los andaluces".

Juan Valera siempre se sintió hondamente arraigado en su tierra originaria; un deseo permanentemente insatisfecho era para él el poder retirarse a vivir en sus posesiones de Cabra y de Doña Mencía cuyos paisajes y tipos humanos tanto le atraían: los "tíos" del campo en sus tertulias y el espacio geográfico que él convirtió en una región entre real e imaginada, Villafría, el "lugar" de *Pepita Jiménez* —muchos años antes al invento faulkneriano del condado de Yoknapatawpha— (Romero Tobar 1997). Su visión de los "otros", entre risueña y escéptica, mucho tiene que ver con sus raíces cordobesas, y su mirada distanciada no podría explicarse sin su condición social de segundón nobiliario. A estas circunstancias han de sumarse las que con esfuerzo y determinación propia fueron tallando los perfiles de su personalidad, de las que destaco aquí la voracidad de lector y la voluntad de estilo que durante toda su vida caracterizó su actividad literaria.

Desde estos condicionantes de su visión del mundo hemos de explicar la percepción valeriana de la multitud de personajes y de fenómenos que fue observando a lo largo de sus viajes oficiales y privados y las relaciones humanas que fue estableciendo en su trama biográfica. Sus escritos de viajes se cifran en sus despachos oficiales (editados en su mayor parte y estudiados por Ana Navarro) y en su correspondencia familiar. Ahora bien, tanto el condicionante general de la percepción de los "otros" que antes he recordado como el marco habitual de las relaciones sociales de Valera —la "high life" a la que tantas veces se refiere[4]— limita sus percepciones y sus experiencias, punto de partida que delimita el contenido de mi intervención.

Sobre sus relaciones sociales las cartas dan toda la información que pudiéramos reclamar para nuestro análisis. Valga este testimonio de 1866, cuando desde Fránkfort hace partícipe a su amigo el profesor Gumersindo Laverde de su experiencia en las relaciones sociales, confesión que además del interés personal, merece la pena ser recordada para la Historia del krausismo español: "Los banqueros y comerciantes de esta ciudad y los diplomáticos, que es la gente con quien trato, son todos poco dados a las letras. Si preguntase aquí del filósofo Krause, que tanto ruido hace en España, nadie sabría darme razón; me dirían que ni siquiera habían oído mentar su nombre" (3-IV-1866; II, 254).

La posición de las personas y los grupos con los que se relacionaba Valera constituían los estratos más altos de la pirámide social: banqueros, comerciantes, políticos, militares superiores, escritores, aristócratas y familias reinantes; de estas últimas documenta interesantes informaciones directas relativas a la corte borbónica de Nápoles, la familia del Zar de Rusia y las cortes de Brasil, Portugal o Bélgica, de las que depara descripciones que no tienen nada que envidiar a las mejores páginas de los "esperpentos" de Valle-Inclán. Valga esta pintura de la corte de Bruselas en 1887:

> Los bailes de Palacio son brillantes; pero, sea dicho para inter nos y bajo sigilo muy firme, demasiado fantasmagóricos, pomposos, offenbáchicos y chirimbolescos. Hay en el gran salón un estrado o tarima, en anfiteatro, que se levanta del suelo una tercia. Esta tarima está cubierta de terciopelo y encima tiene sillas. En el centro se sientan el Rey, la Reina y los condes de Flanes; detrás la servidumbre de Palacio; a la derecha los del cuerpo diplomático extranjero, hechos unos alfajores dorados; y a la izquierda los ministros de la Corona, los altos dignatarios y sus damas (carta a Alfredo Weil de 21-II-1887; IV, 638-9).

En cualquier caso, la desautomatización que le traían usos y comportamientos para él inusitados es una de las pistas de información más esti-

---

4   Enuncia esta situación en el curso de su viaje a Rusia cuando escribe a su jefe Leopoldo Augusto de Cueto: "A todo esto, sin embargo, no conocemos más que la alta sociedad de Rusia, que indispensablemente se asemeja a la de otros pueblos e ignoramos lo que este es, a no llevarnos de ligero o guiarnos por lo que dicen los libros" (carta de 20-I-1857; I, 389).

mulantes que ofrece su *Correspondencia*. Por ejemplo, en un don Juan consumado como fue nuestro don Juan Valera, la percepción de las mujeres es uno de los terrenos más atractivos para la lectura y el análisis crítico de sus textos y, si esa percepción del sexo femenino venía proyectada desde modelos femeninos —mujeres cultas y lectoras, mujeres que tomaban la iniciativa en los escarceos amatorios, mujeres que fuman...— el mensaje transcrito por Valera cobra singular atractivo. Recordemos cómo describe a una mujer fumadora a la que observa en su trayecto ferroviario desde San Petersburgo a Moscú en el año 1857:

> Mucho me sorprendió ver que había vagón para los fumadores, donde entré por instinto [...] donde hallé fumando a todo bicho viviente y a no pocas, al parecer, damas. Una mujer fumando despierta en mi alma, o si se quiere en mi cuerpo, sentimientos pecaminosos. No sé por qué, mas ello es que imagino que, pues tan sensible a un placer tan vaporoso que ni en público puede privarse de él, debe serlo más en secreto a otros más serios placeres, si es que placer alguno puede tenerse por cosa seria en este valle de lágrimas que habitamos (carta de Cueto de 18-V-1857; I, 531).

Una mínima atención a la constelación de observaciones curiosas sobre los países y las sociedades foráneas con los que Valera tuvo alguna relación daría lugar a una extensa antología de textos, y el estudio de estos fragmentos de cartas y de artículos periodísticos habría de desarrollarse con la técnica del análisis de contenido que sistematizaría una recopilación de asertos —todo lo ingeniosos que se quiera— referidos a las ideas establecidas sobre los "caracteres nacionales". Teniendo en cuenta estos condicionantes, en mi contribución a la cuestión que aquí nos convoca he considerado más pertinente limitarme a la visión que tiene Valera de los grupos minoritarios de los lugares en los que residió por algún tiempo, tanto en Europa como en América. Dejo, pues, fuera de mi exposición cómo tipificaba con generalidades tópicas a los distintos nacionales de los países que conoció, del mismo modo que tampoco me detengo en sus escarceos costumbristas sobre los tipos regionales españoles, a los que también prestó una atención de descriptor antropológico.

Tipología de grupos observados

La sola atención a los grupos minoritarios que he recopilado plantea, de entrada, la dificultad inicial de la frecuente mixtura que nuestro autor realiza al entrelazar grupos étnicos con marginados sociales, conjuntos culturalmente homogéneos con agentes profesionales. Solamente sus consideraciones sobre las minorías raciales afincadas en los lugares en los que prestó servicios diplomáticos —Rusia, Brasil, Estados Unidos, imperio austríaco— podrían dar lugar a una extensa monografía. Precisamente su última estancia diplomática, la que vivió en la corte de Viena, le lleva a valorar el papel histórico y social del Imperio austro-húngaro como una eficaz fuerza de contención del variado mosaico de razas y religiones que aquel Estado cobijaba. Lo sintetizaba en un párrafo de carta a Tamayo y Baus: "Todas estas castas de húngaros, tudescos, bohemios, eslovenos, rutenos, bosniacos, polacos, serbios, rumanos, y croatas, se combinan aquí amorosamente, con mucho de semita a menudo, a pesar del antisemitismo, y da la combinación excelentes resultados sobre todo en el mejoramiento del sexo femenino" (carta 12-X-1893; V, 596). Una perspectiva integradora opuesta por el vértice a la impresión que le produce el "melting-pot" que conforma la heterogénea mezcla racial y social que advierte en los Estados Unidos al escribir a su hermana Sofía Valera en 1884:

> La gente de aquí más high life se parece a los señores de la Alameda de Málaga; los politicians de aquí son como Morenito el menciano, por lo judas y tunantes; y luego, como pueblo, muchos negros, muchos irlandeses escapados, muchos alemanes hambrientos de lo peor, que inmigran aquí; y por último toda la hez y escoria de China, de Cuba y de las repúblicas hispanoamericanas. Todo esto, mal amalgamado, constituye los elementos de esta gran República (carta de 26-V-1884; IV, 127).

La estimación del "melting pot" norteamericano debió de impresionarle más de lo común ya que aparece en varios momentos de las cartas escritas en Estados Unidos; valga como otra muestra este testimonio:

> Mi admiración y entusiasmo por la prosperidad de esta gran República no han sido nunca notables, y cada día disminuyen. Siempre me ha pasmado bastante el que los pensadores se hayan quebrado y aún se quiebren tanto la cabeza para explicar las causas de la grandeza de las naciones. ¿Para qué alambicar? Aquí, por ejemplo, todo es claro. Como hay mucha tierra y mucha gente, la nación es grande, sin que lo

que evite que lo que ha venido aquí sea la escoria o los desperdicios de Europa. Hay que tener en cuenta también que han traído aquí los mejores negros de África, robustos, guapetones e inteligentes. Con lo peor de Europa y lo mejor de África se va componiendo aquí una imponente y activa combinación que da resultados, plausibles a veces, movida siempre por el afán de allegar dineros (carta a Greindl de 27-IV-1885; IV, 303).

Con todo y antes de centrarme en las minorías más definidas en los textos de Valera, expondré brevemente un selectivo catálogo de grupos minoritarios sobre los que nuestro autor realizó algún tipo de consideración en sus escritos.

1. Sirve la primera categoría la clasificación sexual de los tipos humanos, un campo en el que el punto de vista de nuestro autor se fija casi exclusivamente en la dicotomía masculino/femenino, ya que la consideración sobre los grupos sexuales marginales solo la manifiesta desde la broma homófoba cuando insiste en brutalidades acaecidas a personajes notoriamente homosexuales como era el caso de Emilio Castelar.[5] Sobre las mujeres —como no era menos de esperar en don Juan— las impresiones son abundantísimas, tanto sobre las distintas edades de las mismas como sobre su origen nacional y formas de comportamiento. Ahora bien, la atención a los diversos comportamientos de hombres y de mujeres cobra un relieve especial en el curso de su permanencia en los Estados Unidos donde los varones a los que trata —políticos por modo fundamental— le resultan muy dispares a sus equivalentes de los países europeos. Del presidente Cleveland —sobre cuya toma de posesión de la más alta magistratura del Estado da noticia en breves crónicas de un enorme interés— llega a afirmar que "es hombre de cortas luces, y además le acusan de haber ahorcado a tres o cuatro personas con su propia mano, cuando fue *sheriff,* para ahorrarse los 12 ó 15 duros de verdugo" (carta a su hijo Carlos de 3-XI-1884; IV, 212). Sobre los varones en general Valera formula el inevitable juicio comparativo con los que él mejor conocía como prototipos de la zafiedad, sus paisanos de Cabra y Doña Mencía:

5   Escribe a Narciso Campillo "No me maravilla eso que cuenta usted de Castelar. Supongo que él será la *fembra*; y envidio la pujanza y el valor y el estómago del Sr. Alvarado, al par que abomino del empleo que les da. Odio el delito, y en vez de compadecer, envidio al delincuente. ¡Qué brío, qué turgencia, qué virilidad semidivina no tendrá el Sr. Alvarado para que no se afloje y marchite la lanza [...]!" (carta de 20-IX-1887; IV, 732).

La sociedad de aquí es muy rara. A veces quieren tener su high life y a veces hacen cosas de la mayor franqueza y rusticidad, que ni en la propia Doña Mencía. Las mujeres son las que presumen más de finas; los hombres suelen ser más toscos que los cabreños, y haciendo cosas feas, que los cabreños no hacen, como por ejemplo, mascar tabaco, echar los pies por alto, cuando se sientan y sonarse los mocos poniendo el dedo en la nariz y disparando lo que de allí sale (carta a su esposa de 28-IV-1885; IV, 306).

En el mismo terreno de observación norteamericano le llama la atención el papel social que tienen las mujeres: "Soy poco admirador de los yankees, dicho sea entre nosotros —confía a Narciso Campillo—, pero celebro y aplaudo la elevación, la libertad, la independencia de la mujer de aquí; lo cual no sería posible sin un respeto altísimo, casi religioso, a su pudor" (carta de 27-XI-1884; IV, 221). Las mujeres que conoce y trata en Norteamérica son lectoras cultas ("licurgas" las llama en algún momento y, en contraste con ellas, "los hombres, en cambio, apenas se ocupan de más ciencia ni arte que de procurarse dinero" (carta a su hija Carmen de 14-IV-1885; V, 296), llegando a la desenvoltura que las mujeres jóvenes despliegan en las reuniones familiares con unas formas de relación amorosa que revisten un aire de espontaneidad muy llamativas para él; en esos "parties", por ejemplo, "hay al empezar cada escalera, seis o cinco parejas amorosas o *flirteadoras*. Y se sientan con arte y previsión" (carta a su hermana Sofía, 3-VI-1884; V, 131).

Impresiones opuestas por el vértice sobre los comportamientos eróticos acostumbraba a recoger en sus estancias de las capitales europeas, donde el comercio erótico de ciudades como París o Viena le suscitan páginas de una expresividad intensa y, en ocasiones de un refinamiento literario de altura; sirva de muestra este apunte sobre el ambiente callejero del gran París del segundo Imperio:

Entre tanto, en estas calles, y sobre todo en los bulevares, claustro pleno de la Universidad de Amor, se queda uno embobado viendo pasar a las doctoras; y como ellas son tomistas y los hombres escotistas, según afirma ya de su época el discreto Jacinto Polo, se arman discusiones muy instructivas y profundas, e imita uno a Cristo, que también discutió con los doctores, aunque de esta imitación no habla Kempis (carta a Cueto de 23-VI-1857; I, 557).

O esta viñeta estadística sobre la Viena del "fin de siglo": "Esos paseos, jardines pastelerías calles y plazas están cuajados, hierven en mujeres guapas, impetuosas, lozanas, bien vestidas, generosas y que van pidiendo guerra y dándola" (carta a su pariente José Alcalá Galiano, 2-IX-1894; V, 751).

2. Los grupos profesionales suscitan en Valera anotaciones de paso que él mismo remite a sus experiencias vividas con los profesionales de otros lugares. De los clérigos, por ejemplo, pergeña esbozos muy gráficos en sus novelas, desde *Pepita Jiménez* (1874) hasta *Morsamor* (1899). Pero la proximidad humana de personajes inventados contrasta con la visión áspera que da de los tonsurados italianos, a los que describe en las ciudades del rey de Nápoles como una "caterva de inmundos frailes de todos colores, gordos y cebones, con camisa y descamisados, holgazanes y bellacos, que pululan como un enjambre de zánganos por todos sus dominios" (carta de abril de 1847 a su hermano José Freuller; I, 44), o con la caracterización de los clérigos ortodoxos rusos, en los que "lo raído y sucio del traje, lo mal peinado de las greñas, el aire poco inteligente y muy aguardentoso de la fisonomía y la rudeza de los modales no los distinguen de los mujiks, antes bien muchos de estos clérigos o curas de aldea parecen y deben ser más rudos que los mujiks mismos" (carta a Cueto de 8-V-1857; I, 533). Y, sin abandonar su recorrido eslavo, merece la pena tener en cuenta cómo dibuja a los cosacos tanto en su presencia física como en su función militar que él compara, en asociación de lector de crónicas medievales, con los "antiguos almogávares":

> [El príncipe Gorchakov] venía en coche abierto y escoltado por ocho cosacos, de los colonos militares del Cáucaso, vestidos de extraña manera, con muchos puñales y gumías y pistolas de plata prolijamente cinceladas, gorras circasianas, lanzas larguísimas y rocines pequeñuelos, peludos y feos que galopaban sobre la nieve como si tuviesen el diablo en el cuerpo. Esta gente, aunque vestidos con gran lujo, se parecen en las costumbres y en la organización a nuestros antiguos almogávares, y así como aquellos combatían de continuo con los moros fronterizos, combaten estos con las tribus guerreras de las montañas donde Prometeo estuvo encadenado (carta de 30-XI-1856 dirigida a Cueto desde Varsovia; I, 334).

El recurso de la comparación automática con los trabajadores subalternos —empleados, sirvientes, etc.— conocidos en España por Valera era inevitable, teniendo en cuenta que su percepción de estas capas de la sociedad era la del señor situado en un plano superior. En las novelas y en alguno de sus escasos artículos costumbristas intervienen personajes que sirven en las casas de los señores y que están caracterizados con rasgos de cordial humanidad: la Antoñona de *Pepita Jiménez*, la criada Rafaela de *El Comendador Mendoza*, la señora Petra en *Doña Luz*, el Respetilla de *Las ilusiones del Doctor Faustino*, y tantos otros.

Esta perspectiva de directa simpatía no le resultaba un recurso de "verosimilitud" artística cuando se refería a los criados auténticos que le servían en sus estancias extranjeras, por lo que tiende a referirse a ellos con pinceladas rápidas y de chafarrinón en las que el elemento económico tiene un papel fundamental, tal como subraya especialmente en las advertencias sobre la instalación doméstica que hace a su esposa, en Viena: "Los criados son aquí carísimos y no me parecen más ágiles, ni menos flojos, ni menos sisones que los criados españoles", "aquí todos los criados son muy humildes. Encajan mil excelencias por minuto y besan la mano cuando les da uno dinero", observaciones que traslada a su visión sobre los caracteres "nacionales" cuando escribe, por ejemplo, que "aquí hay una disciplina social que raya en el servilismo. A cada instante, pero más que nunca cuando da uno dinero, le agarran a uno la mano y se la besan; pero es feroz el afán de besar la mano con ese motivo y el desventurado que es pobre y que está en cierta posición que aquí se considera elevada tiene que estar muy sobre aviso para que no le besen la mano demasiado y se la dejen seca y vacía la faltriquera".[6]

Los profesionales de las Letras, en fin, interesan a Valera en todos sus desplazamientos tanto por la comunicación que mantuvo con quienes compartían con él afanes y trabajos como por la valiosa relación profesional y personal que podía establecer con ellos. En sus primeras estancias de Alemania se asombra de no coincidir con grandes intelectuales, como comunica a diversos corresponsales que se dedicaban a la docencia o la literatura: su sobrino Salvador Valera y Gumersindo Laverde, ambos catedráticos, su jefe el erudito Cueto o su protegido y admirado Marcelino Menéndez Pelayo. Estas noticias, además de servir de nudo de relación en la red profesional, no eran otra cosa que la aplicación de una vetusta norma del arte epistolar cual es la de que el asunto que se trata en la carta ha de estar vinculado con la cualificación e intereses del receptor de la misma.

Por ejemplo, escribe a su sobrino Salvador en 1865 desde Fráncfort: "No veo ni trato a ningún filósofo. En esta tierra clásica de la filosofía, los filósofos andan metidos por los zaquizamíes y camaranchones; quie-

---

6   Las citas corresponden respectivamente a cartas enviadas a Dolores Delavat desde Viena en 6-III-1893, 17-III-1893 (V, 481, 498), y a Vega Armijo en 28-III-1893 (V, 515).

nes figuran y viven en grande son los profanos e ignorantes que se dedican al comercio, a la industria, a las putas y al juego" (carta de 22-IX-1865; II, 244). Y según va avanzando en las relaciones con sabios dedicados a estudiar temas relacionados con España, es decir, con el mundo profesional de los "hispanistas", sus noticias y comentarios son cada vez más amplios y ajustados. En el viaje a Rusia habla de Sobolewsky y de Kratnokutski, desde el mundo germano aparecen Ferdinand Wolf, Friedrich von Schack, Rudolf Beer, Arturo Farinelli, en Francia Alfred Morel-Fatio, los Merimée, y así otros muchos.

3. Las razas marcan, en fin, una línea de percepción de los "otros" que el novelista cordobés se limita a mencionar sin fijar características que las definan. No debió de sostener trato directo con los originarios de América, ya que en sus estancias brasileña y norteamericana se limita a citar a los indios aborígenes con breves observaciones, posiblemente recibidas de fuentes informativas ajenas. En Río de Janeiro observa que "los indios bravos, que aún andan errantes por los bosques, no quieren someterse a la vida laboriosa y sedentaria y prefieren la muerte" (carta a Estébanez Calderón de 10-III-1852; I, 184). De las tribus de Norteamérica no dice nada aunque sí alude a los traslados forzosos de mano de obra china o hispana, sin entrar en más detalles.

Con todo, sobre las gentes de color es más explícito en la medida que los trabajos domésticos que le resolvían en sus viviendas americanas eran obra de estas personas. El respeto por esta comunidad racial dejaba mucho que desear en la época, a pesar de las proclamas igualitarias; recuérdese cómo pone en boca de su jefe de la embajada brasileña estos asertos suscitados por el comportamiento lascivo de un mulato del servicio:

El bardo, que es peor que los negros, pues es mulato, hace perder la paciencia a D. José; y el otro día llegó a tal extremo de maldad, que les enseñó a las negras sus vergüenzas en la cocina y en ocasión en que la hija de D. José estaba presente. Supo D. José el negocio, se amoscó como era natural, dijo que pasaba de castaño oscuro (lo cual yo creo sin haberle visto) y mandó dar al culpable tres docenas de vergajazos para que fuese castigado con un instrumento semejante al de su delito. Cuando yo subí al comedor, estaban acabando de dar la tunda al bardo, y D. José exclamaba: "¡Quisiera yo ver aquí a Mrs. Stowe y preguntarle qué haría en tales circunstancias! Añade D. José que lo que trae tan alborotado y lascivo al bardo son los cantares, y más aún la danza llamada fado, que por lo mímica y afrodisíaca sobrepuja al vito de nuestros gitanos y a la timorodea de los isleños de Otaiti" (carta de 8-IV-1853 a Estébanez Calderón; I, 209).[7]

La etapa de Río Janeiro es la más fecunda en observaciones sobre el deplorable estado de los esclavos en aquel país, el número abrumador de los mismos y los terribles efectos que podría generar una sublevación. Contrasta esta despierta atención hacia la gente de color con la mucho más reducida que ofrece durante su permanencia en Washington; los años que cargaban sobre él y las circunstancias familiares que desde España entonces le aquejaban explicarían la parva información que ofrece al respecto como también podrían ser motivos de atenuación informativa sobre la reciente guerra de Secesión que había decidido la situación jurídica de los esclavos norteamericanos.[8] Sí señala la presencia de hispanos en las ciudades que visita, aunque para él la palabra que a todos engloba es la de "españoles", ya que en Nueva York escribe a su mujer lo siguiente: "He conocido aquí a muchos cubanos, españoles establecidos y gentes de las repúblicas españolas, que han venido a visitarme, y algunos me han obsequiado" (23-IX-1885; IV, 379).

Quizás la tradición literaria hispana —el negro del Lazarillo y los que intervienen en entremeses y comedias de costumbres del siglo XVII— unida a la sexualidad atribuida a las gentes de color serían las motivaciones inmediatas para las anécdotas chistosas o salaces que nuestro autor atribuye a distintos servidores negros. Todavía en su estancia en Viena, lugar en el que no era muy abundante el número de personas de tales características, refiere algún suceso en los que la vertiente erótica queda puesta de manifiesto, como este caso en el que la directora de escena es una noble dama austriaca:

> La broma era con un atezado negro de la Nubia, mahometano, que tiene Wiedmann de criado. La condesa (Taaffe) le hallaba tan joven, tan guapo y tan curioso y fuera de lo común, que le decía que él debía tener en Viena, viele Geliebten. El negro, con mucha modestia, dijo que no tenía más que una. La condesa entonces contó cómo una comedianta de aquí vivía con su madre y que, cuando preguntaban a la

7   Ver también las cartas dirigidas al mismo destinatario de fechas 10-III-1852 (I, 184-185); 8-IX-1852 (I, 206).

8   No deja de reconocer la agilidad mental de individuos de color con los que tiene algún contacto: "Tengo, además de Víctor (un criado hispano), que me parece cada día más idiota, un criado negro que tiene más talento que Víctor y que habla inglés, pero que acabará por entenderse con Víctor en castellano" (carta a su hijo Carlos de 12-III-1884; IV, 74).

madre cuantos amigos tenía su hija, decía que nada más que uno, pero muy generoso. ¿Y cómo se llama? —continuaban preguntando—. Y la mamá respondía: Se
llama Jockey-Club. Por el estilo será tu única Geliebte, decía la condesa al negro, y
el negro se ruborizaba. Esta condesa Taafe le echa la zancadilla a la marquesa de La
Laguna en punto a desvergüenza (carta a su hija Carmen de 25-VI-1895; VI, 60).

Las minorías con arraigo español

El rápido repaso que acabo de hacer de la visión que tuvo Juan Valera de
las minorías sexuales, raciales o culturales de lugares diversos de Europa
y América, nos explica, como he ido sugiriendo, la relación más o menos
directa que pudo tener con ellas y la capacidad de distorsión expresiva
que el escritor sabía dar a observaciones condicionadas por los estereotipos que él compartía. Por supuesto que su mejor comprensión de estos
grupos reposa en las semejanzas que él establecía con otros grupos
humanos que le resultaban más familiares (campesinos andaluces, criados peninsulares, mujeres del pueblo...) o con los que poseían o habían
poseído mayor arraigo en el ámbito español. Con esta percepción Juan
Valera reiteraba el inevitable recurso analógico que los viajeros de todos
los tiempos han empleado y emplean a la hora de asimilar las personas y
lugares desconocidos que se les van apareciendo durante sus recorridos.
Juan Valera en el curso de sus viajes mantuvo contactos con dos grupos
minoritarios de los que ya poseía experiencia de trato en España y que,
además, contaban con sendas trayectorias de individualización caracteri-
zadora en la tradición hispana: los judíos y los gitanos. En lo que sigue
me referiré a estos dos grupos, tan especialmente significativos en el
ámbito de la historia y la cultura españolas.

Judíos

La expulsión de los judíos de la monarquía hispana había producido la
desaparición de esta comunidad en la Península hasta el punto que,
cuando en la segunda mitad del siglo XIX, diversas propuestas de políticos liberales o progresistas propugnaron su admisión en la sociedad es-

pañola de 1877 el censo oficial cifraba su número en 406 personas.[9] Valera percibió, pues, a los grupos judíos fuera de su patria aunque en ella mantuviera estrecha amistad con algunas familias de notables. Al regreso del viaje a Rusia evoca para su jefe Leopoldo Augusto de Cueto sus últimas impresiones de Alemania entre las que anota a los "judíos ricos de Fráncfort, con sus tiendas y almacenes bien surtidos y sin temer que los quemen o les corten las orejas" (carta de 23-VI-1857; I, 557). La misma ciudad genera un efecto similar unos años después, cuando el diplomático representa a España ante la Dieta Germánica: "Aún no he visto aquí sabio ni filósofo alguno, sino mucho judío comerciante y cuantos vagos hay en Europa en la clase alta" (carta a Laverde de 29-VIII-1865; II, 241). Pinceladas rápidas que pasan a la denominación ultrajante cuando ha de aludir a un viaje por el curso del Rhin en la compañía de varias familias de judíos ricos, al escribir a Greindl desde Spa: "Hemos tenido aquí a los Bauer de Madrid y a los Cahen d'Anvers de París, y no sé por qué d'Anvers, sus parientes y correligionarios. Con esta judería, que por nuestra amistad con Mme Bauer nos cercaba de continuo hemos hecho una divertidísima expedición al Rhin y por el Rhin" (carta de 26 VIII-1887; IV, 716-717).

Los Bauer a los que acabo de citar constituyen una familia con la que Valera y los suyos mantuvieron amistosísimas relaciones desde los años sesenta. La confianza con Ignacio Bauer y su esposa Ida Marupurgo y con sus hijos es paralela a la que cultivó también con los Weil, familias ambas que representaban en España los intereses de los Rothschild y afortunados empresarios de obras ferroviarias y otros cometidos. Valera elogia la generosidad y buena pasta de Ignacio Bauer, las habilidades sociales de Ida —a la que dedicó su novela *El Comendador Mendoza*— sin dejar de subrayar los buenos servicios que esta familia podía prestarle; la confianza es de tal grado que no duda en llamar a Ignacio "el gran Rabino", a Ida la "gran Rabina" y a la brillante tertulia que reunían en su casa, "la Sinagoga". Las bromas cariñosas no dejan de ocultar el interés que en ocasiones mueve al escritor egabrense, confiado en obtener "turrones" de un grupo económicamente tan poderoso y próximo a otro

---

9   Sagasta garantizaba al judío sefardita Henry Guedalla que el artículo XI de la Constitución de 1876 significaba de hecho la revocación del edicto de Expulsión de 1492 (De Vidas 2005: 327; véase también Manrique Escudero 2009 y López-Morell & O'Kean Alonso 2008).

294 Leonardo Romero Tobar

notable judío luso, Moisés Camondo, con quien tenía contraídas deudas de préstamos.

La denominación judaica que aplica a los Bauer es tanto broma amistosa como guiño cultural que entrelaza con otras referencias en las que llama a sus amigas con nombres prestigiosos de la cultura grecolatina; valga este párrafo sintético de una carta a Menéndez Pelayo escrita en Doña Mencía: "Aquí no hay Hipatias, ni Lydias, ni judías elegantes con quien tratar. No hay más que cristianas católicas, feas por lo común y poco aseadas" (14-X-1880; III, 218).

El toque de afecto personal y un fondo de motivaciones interesadas son las manifestaciones más llamativas en la representación que hace Valera de sus amigos judíos, un grupo reducidísimo y encajado en el "Madrid elegante" y que por esas características le sirve para justificar la inexistencia de sentimientos antisemitas en la España coetánea. Escribe a este propósito en 1898:

> Lo que es en el día, en que más de media España es racionalista, casi nadie comprende por aquí el antisemitismo. Acaso no había en toda España más judía soltera que la hija de D. Ignacio Bauer, y ésta se ha casado nada menos que con el futuro duque de Baena, de la histórica y gloriosa casa de Altamira, y ya es marquesa y pronto será duquesa, sin que a nadie le choque (carta a Greindl de 18-II-898; VI, 364).

Por ello su disponibilidad hacia las iniciativas del Dr. Pulido en favor de los judíos sefarditas no tiene nada de extraño[10] y explica el que escriba al diplomático y escritor Antonio de Zayas en 1904 sobre las campañas emprendidas por este médico y sus propuestas para la difusión de libros españoles entre los judíos del oriente de Europa:

> Muchos escritores, y yo entre ellos, hemos dado algunos libros. La Academia Española, solicitada por el Sr. Pulido, trata de coadyuvar a su propósito, enviando libros también y nombrando académicos correspondientes a dos ilustres rabinos, uno de Bucarest y otro no sé si de Constantinopla o de Salónica (carta de 6-VI-1904; VII, 481).

Hay un punto en las cartas de Valera en el que coinciden personas de los dos grupos minoritarios que ahora estoy considerando; se trata del mo-

---

10   En su primera etapa de la embajada en Lisboa Valera conoció al Dr. Ángel Pulido, aunque no le aplicó entonces un calificativo estimulante ya que dice de él que "es también tonto, lo que no quita que su alegría y buen humor me diviertan" (carta a Sofía Valera, 21-IX-1850; I, 116).

mento en el que Ida Bauer, acompañada de nuestro autor, presencia en Sevilla un espectáculo de danza gitana:

> En Sevilla estaba Mme Bauer con otra judía, su hermana, que habrá tenido buenos bigotes y que aún está bien, aunque jamona. Yo estuve muy amable con ellas y las acompañé a ver a los gitanos y entramos en una tienda de ellos y les hice bailar para que lo vieran, de lo que ellas quedaron muy divertidas (carta a su hermana Sofía de 21-IV-1880; III, 198).

Gitanos

No se puede afirmar que para un español los gitanos fueran "extranjeros" en sentido estricto, aunque las características del grupo se los presentasen como un prototipo de los "ajenos", por muy próximos que estuviesen a ellos desde un punto de vista geográfico. La contrapuesta estimación de admiración y rechazo hacia los gitanos que se documenta desde textos medievales siguió vigente en el siglo XIX. Sintetizando lo conocido sobre la relación entre "payos" y gitanos en esta centuria he escrito en otro lugar que existen suficientes testimonios de la desconfianza que estos últimos suscitaban entre los primeros así como de las abrumadoras pruebas de aceptación que sus comportamientos artísticos generaban (Romero Tobar 2010: 335-36).

Para un cordobés como Valera que se había educado en Andalucía y que pasaba muchas temporadas en los pueblos de su provincia natal, los gitanos formaban parte del paisaje natural y por ello en sus novelas cruzan personajes de esta etnia, cuyo universo cultural le servía para documentar testimonios léxicos.[11] Cabe destacar palabras como "pepla" o el topónimo de el "Olen del Oclaye", maldiciones —los "malos chuqueles te tagelen el drupo de Antoñona"— y anécdotas expresivas recogidas de la tradición oral y que él mismo incluyó en el libro folclórico firmado

---

11   Precioso testimonio en este párrafo de un artículo de tema lingüístico publicado en 1900: "Y no sólo en comedias, sainetes, novelas y cuentos hay vocablos de la jerga de chulos, rufianes y bandidos, sino también del extraño idioma de los gitanos. Así, verbigracia, *camelar* y *camelo*, cuyo noble origen se halla en el idioma de los Vedas. Y así también *chachipé, churi, diquelar, jamar, tajelar, chusquel, churumbel, cocal* y otros términos de que se sirve el vulgo en Andalucía y en otras comarcas, y que los escritores trasladan a los diálogos de sus obras de pasatiempo" ("Nuevas cartas americanas", in *Obras Completas*, Madrid, Aguilar, 1947, III, 555a).

con seudónimo y en unión de dos amigos bajo el título de *Cuentos y chascarrillos andaluces* (1896).

Tanto en artículos periodísticos como en sus obras de ficción Valera introduce la referencia a la presencia del mundo de los gitanos desde la doble perspectiva a la que me he referido y que responde al doble esquema de percepción estandarizado con el que esta minoría era considerada en Europa: el esquema "predador" (ladrones y mentirosos) y el esquema "trovador" (fascinantes en sus cantes y en sus bailes) (Gritti 1982: 48). Antonio Gómez Alfaro ha trazado un útil recamado de textos de nuestro autor en los que esta doble y antitética percepción está presente, desde sus primeros escritos hasta su última novela *Morsamor*, en la que dos figuras de gitanillas —una hispana y otra hindú— enmarcan la fantástica aventura marítima del protagonista.

Con todo, una visión entusiasmada del arte de los gitanos vistos por él fuera de España es la que comunica a Cueto en una de sus cartas desde Rusia en la que le da noticia de un extraordinario espectáculo de danzas y canciones dirigidas por un gitano llamado Iván Vasílievich:

> Este gran artista y glorioso patriarca tiene bajo sus órdenes, jurisdicción y protección, por lo menos una docena de ninfas cantadoras y seis o siete guitarristas y cantores de lo más inspirados de todo el Egipto o la Bohemia o como quiera llamarse a la patria misteriosa e incógnita de esta raza singular y vagabunda. En parte alguna hay más gitanos que en Rusia [...]. Alguna de las sirenas que componen esta compañía del gran Iván Vasílievich alcanza tanta fama como la Alboni, al menos en Rusia, y causa más entusiasmo que aquella célebre contralto italiana. Y verdaderamente merecen tanta fama y tanto rendimiento, porque por la voz, el alma y el primor con que cantan no tienen quien en el mundo se les iguale. Sus canciones son preciosas; las más andan en estampa y yo tengo ejemplar de ellas; mas el chic verdadero, el arte y forma y manera especialísima de estas canciones es incomunicable por escrito y es menester oír a estas sirenas para comprender hasta qué extremo llega la magia de su canto y de sus salidas de tono, que adquieren más singularidad aún por los gestos, chillidos, suspiros, meneos, danzas y palmadas con que suelen acompañarlos. Sólo los gitanos de España pueden dar una idea de lo que son los gitanos de Rusia (carta de 18-V-1857; I, 544).

El parangón de lo recién conocido en el extranjero con lo familiar de la patria vuelve a imponerse en la percepción de la minoría gitana. Y encontraríamos nuevos recursos a la representación de lo "otro" a partir de las analogías si yo abusase de vuestra probada paciencia durante mucho más tiempo del que me ha sido concedido.

Conclusión

Para concluir mi intervención creo que, después del tiempo que he empleado en la cosecha y edición de las cartas de don Juan Valera, estoy autorizado para resumir su visión de los grupos minoritarios con los que se fue topando en el curso de sus viajes subrayando cómo las ideas establecidas condicionaban su percepción inicial, si bien el ágil sistema asociativo de nuestro autor y la habilidad con la que manejaba los recursos de la retórica epistolar y la escritura literaria le permitían trazar brillantes esbozos de los variados grupos humanos en textos que, en unas ocasiones, nos conducen a la hilaridad y, en otras, producen nuestra admiración ante unas páginas llenas de vida y color.

Bibliografía

Comisso, G. 1985. *Gli Ambasciatori veneti (1525-1792)*, Milano, Longanesi.

De Vidas, A. 2005. "El Dr. Ángel Pulido y el redescubrimiento de los sefardíes a final del s. XX", *Aragón Sefarad* 1, 321-38.

Gómez Alfaro, A. 2005. "Don Juan Valera y los gitanos", in *I Tchatchipen* 52 (Octubre-Diciembre), 39-54.

Gritti, J. 1982. *Déraciner les racismes*, Paris, Editions SOS.

López-Morell, M. A. & J. M. O'Kean Alonso. 2008. "La red de negocios de la casa Rothschild en España como una estructura de toma de decisiones y de gestión empresarial", *Revista de la historia de la economía y de la empresa* 2, 41-64.

Manrique Escudero, M. 2009. "Los judíos y la Revolución de 1868", *Hesperia* 12, 209-220.

Moureau, F. 2007. "Descubrimiento y redescubrimiento: Estado actual de los estudios sobre la literatura de viajes", in J. M. Oliver, C. Curell, C. G. Uriarte & B. Pico (eds.), *Escrituras y reescrituras del viaje. Miradas plurales a través del tiempo y de las culturas*, Bern, Peter Lang, 11-19.

Navarro, A. 2006. "Don Juan Valera diplomático", in R. Bonilla, A. Costa & E. Sánchez (eds.), *Juan Valera (1905-2005). Actas del II Congreso Internacional celebrado en Cabra, 2005*, Cabra, Ayuntamiento de Cabra, 151-76.

Romero Tobar, L. 1997. "Recursos de la ficción en los relatos de Valera", in M. Galera (ed.), *Actas del primer Congreso Internacional sobre don Juan Valera*, Cabra, Ayuntamiento de Cabra, 75-88.

—. 2010. "Los gitanos en la narrativa romántica española", in *La lira de ébano. Escritos sobre el Romanticismo español*, Málaga, Publicaciones de la Universidad de Málaga, 333-49.

Valera, J. 1896. *Cuentos y chascarrillos andaluces tomados de la boca del vulgo*, Madrid, Librería de Fernando Fe.

—. 1947. *Cartas Americanas* y *Nuevas Cartas Americanas*, in *Obras Completas*, vol. 3, Madrid, Aguilar, 211-590.

—. 2002-2009. *Correspondencia,* 8 vols., L. Romero Tobar (dir), Mª A. Ezama & E. Serrano (eds.), Madrid, Castalia.

ELOY MARTÍN CORRALES

Del esclavo al vecino inmigrante: la imagen del negro en España[1]

Lo primero que llama la atención a la hora de abordar el tema de la presencia de los negros en España entre la Alta Edad Media y la actualidad, es que son muy conocidos los siglos XVI y XVII, por un lado, y el último tercio del siglo XX y lo que llevamos del XXI, por el otro. En efecto, la bibliografía sobre la esclavitud negra en la España peninsular es oceánica, casi tanto como la relativa a la presencia de los inmigrantes subsaharianos en los últimos cuarenta años.[2] Por el contrario, desde la segunda mitad del siglo XVII, cuando el número de esclavos negros, y por consiguiente el de los libertos, disminuyó bruscamente, y hasta la década de los ochenta del siglo XX, cuando la inmigración de origen subsahariano comenzó a ser visible, apenas hay nada publicado.

Entre la esclavitud y el Rey Mago: los negros en la España de los siglos XVI y XVII

Es sobradamente conocida la presencia de esclavos negros en la Península Ibérica en los siglos medievales. Habitualmente fueron traídos a estas tierras por los musulmanes, los únicos con capacidad entonces para capturar a los citados esclavos e introducirlos en la Península. Formaban parte de lo más selecto del ejército que protegía a califas, sultanes y emi-

---

1   Esta investigación se inscribe en el marco del proyecto "Transiciones imperiales, cambio institucional y divergencias. Un análisis de la trayectoria colonial y postcolonial de las posesiones españolas en América, Asia y África (1500-1914)", financiado por el Ministerio de Ciencia e Innovación (referencia HAR2009-14099-C02-01).

2   Dada la oceánica bibliografía disponible renuncio a ocuparme de ella, limitándome a señalar las obras más adecuadas para la elaboración de este texto.

res, o como criados domésticos y trabajadores en diversas ocupaciones (Cortés López 1986). Con las vicisitudes de la Reconquista, secular lucha entre cristianos y musulmanes, no pocos de estos esclavos fueron incorporados por los primeros como botín de guerra en su lento, pero implacable avance hacia el sur. El interés en la mano de obra esclava se puso de relieve cuando los reinos cristianos, en especial Portugal, dispusieron de puertos, y por tanto de flotas, desde los cuales comenzaron a organizar expediciones para procurarse directamente los esclavos del Sudán o África Negra. En todo caso, antes de que finalizara la Reconquista, los esclavos negros ya tenían cierta importancia en España, como demuestran los casos de Sevilla (ciudad en la que los negros esclavos y libertos alcanzaron el 10% de la población) y otras localidades (Franco Silva 1992).

La decisión, tras una viva polémica, de descartar el convertir en esclavos a los habitantes ("indios") de la recién "descubierta" América, tuvo una trágica repercusión para los africanos. Se optó por utilizar esclavos africanos para disponer de la mano de obra necesaria en las nuevas colonias americanas. En los cuatro siglos siguientes, millones de habitantes de África fueron arrancados de sus tierras para utilizarlos como esclavos en las plantaciones americanas; esta práctica fue común a todas las potencias europeas que tuvieron colonias en el ámbito americano. En el caso de las colonias españolas, se concedió el monopolio de la introducción de africanos en sus colonias (el Asiento de Negros) a los portugueses, quienes se habían garantizado el dominio del Golfo de Guinea y costas situadas al sur que a partir de entonces se convirtieron en el auténtico vivero del que se sacaron miles y miles de esclavos hacia Europa, primero, y América, después.

No todos los africanos capturados, intercambiados o comprados, fueron enviados a las nacientes colonias americanas. Un número importante pasó a formar parte de la población de numerosas ciudades españolas, especialmente de la Baja Andalucía. Fruto de esa realidad, es la frecuente aparición de los negros en la literatura. Decenas de comedias incluyeron personajes negros e, incluso, en un número importante de ellas, fueron los protagonistas principales. En buena parte de las piezas fueron presentados como individuos torpes e ignorantes y se hacía mofa de ellos por medio de la utilización del "habla de negros", figurando entre los autores que se ocuparon de estos personajes Lope de Vega, Lope de Rueda, Andrés de Claramonte, Diego Sánchez de Badajoz, Juan

Bautista Diamante, Eugenio de Salazar, Francisco de Avellaneda, Luis de Góngora, Miguel de Cervantes y muchos autores más (Fra Molinero 1995).

También la huella de los negros, esclavos o libertos, en la profusa iconografía de los siglos XVI y XVII, fue importante, en especial en la pintura. Normalmente, aparecían en los márgenes de los cuadros como figuras secundarias. En concreto, aparecían en numerosas escenas de la vida cotidiana. Sirvan de ejemplo los personajes que aparecen en *Vista de Sevilla desde Triana* (s. XVI) y *Vista de Sevilla* (1640). En buena parte de las obras figuraban como fieles servidores que realzaban con su atuendo el poder y el prestigio de sus amos. También aparecen en la obra de importantes pintores, como en el caso de Juan de Roelas (*Inmaculada*), Cristóbal de Morales (*Retrato de Juana de Austria acompañada de un paje negro*), Bartolomé Esteban Murillo (*Los tres niños* y *Martirio de San Andrés*), Diego Velázquez (*La Mulata* y *Escena de cocina con la cena de Emaús*), José de Ribera (*Martirio de San Bartolomé*) y Luca Giordano (*Episodio de la historia de Job. Job recibe la noticia de sus desgracias*).

En paralelo, se popularizó aun más si cabe la figura del Rey Negro y su séquito, que supuso hasta cierto punto la imagen del negro en una infinidad de cuadros expuestos a la vista de la totalidad de los fieles (es imposible ocuparse en este texto de esta ingente producción). Este proceso coincidió en la práctica con la evangelización de la mayoría de los negros (por poco o mucho superficial que fuese) y su inclusión en las principales festividades religiosas, en especial en las procesiones del Corpus Christi. En diversas ciudades españolas los negros llegaron a formar cofradías y desfilar en procesión con sus imágenes sagradas en Sevilla, Cádiz, El Puerto de Santa María, Jerez, Huelva, Jaén, Badajoz, Valencia, Barcelona y Palma de Mallorca (Moreno 1997).

Posiblemente, esta aculturación religiosa, favorecida por cierta predisposición de los negros a integrarse en la sociedad que los oprimía (a diferencia de lo que sucedía con la gran mayoría de los esclavos musulmanes) posibilitó el que una selecta minoría de negros (o sus directos descendientes) lograra escapar del estigma de la esclavitud y alcanzar un estatus prestigioso en la sociedad española del momento. Así, en los siglos XVI y XVII destacaron algunos pintores como Juan de Güéjar, quien había trabajado con Alejo Fernández. En el siglo siguiente, Sebastián Gómez, mulato adquirido por Bartolomé Esteban Murillo, también se inició como pintor. Más importancia alcanzó Juan de Pareja, esclavo al que Velázquez concedió la libertad y también retrató (1650), y quien a su vez se autorretrató en 1661 en La *Conversión de San Mateo* (Méndez Rodríguez 2011). También hay que citar a licenciados como Juan Latino, o Juan de Sesa, que impartió docencia en la universidad de Granada en la segunda mitad del siglo XVI, o una de las más famosas comediantas del siglo XVII, la mulata Maria de Cordova y de la Vega, Amarilis. Otros alcanzaron la santidad, como Santa Ifigenia de Etiopía, San Benito de Palermo y San Martín de Porres. Fueron venerados en capillas de iglesias españolas, aunque sus vidas transcurrieron fuera de la Península.

Sin que sepamos a ciencia cierta qué sucedió en realidad, a partir de la segunda mitad del siglo XVII, la presencia de esclavos y libertos en España disminuyó drásticamente. Sin duda alguna, los terribles efectos de las epidemias de peste, especialmente las de 1648-1652, golpearon con especial intensidad a los esclavos, población marginal y con menos recursos para hacer frente a tales calamidades. También es posible que el extraordinario crecimiento de la demanda de mano de obra esclava en la América colonial explique de una u otra manera un trasvase de buena parte de los esclavos (cuyo valor de cambio era indudable) que estaban en España hacia las colonias.

Un siglo de oscuridad: presencia residual del negro en el siglo XVIII

Sea como fuere, el número y la importancia de los esclavos negros y de los libertos disminuyeron de forma importante en la segunda mitad del Seiscientos. Buena parte de las referencias a los negros se referían a los esclavos de las colonias americanas. Es lo que sucedió con la producción iconográfica que hacía alusión a los descendientes de matrimonios mixtos o mestizos, entre españoles, criollos, indios y negros. Fue mucho más conocida en el ámbito colonial que en la metrópolis.

Mientras tanto, en la Península buena parte de las imágenes del negro quedaba casi reducida a los numerosos cuadros de la Adoración de los Reyes Magos, y en menor medida a otros cuadros de carácter religioso en los que aparecía un personaje negro, tal como hemos visto en los dos siglos anteriores. Aparecían, además, en los cada vez más populares belenes, en los que el Rey Negro y su séquito, más numerosos que en las pinturas, destacaban por su exotismo o en ocasiones por su reproducción exacta de la realidad. Sirvan de ejemplo las figuras de barro cocido que aparecen en el belén del escultor murciano Francisco Salzillo, quien las comenzó a elaborar en 1776. Y las del elaborado belén del convento de Santa María de Jesús, en Sevilla, igualmente del siglo XVIII.

Contamos con algunos magníficos ejemplos de la presencia de los negros en la vida cotidiana en el Setecientos. Sirva de ejemplo la obra de Domingo Martínez, *Carro del Fuego, Carro del Aire, Carro del Pregón y Carro del Víctor y del Parnaso* (1747), en celebración de la exaltación al trono de Fernando VI, en la que aparecen diferentes personajes negros. En la primera de las piezas figura un grupo de nueve, dos de ellos con guitarra, bailando. También, ejercitándose con la música, aparecen dos negros con instrumentos de viento, en el zócalo del monasterio de la Encarnación de Osuna que representa la Alameda de Hércules sevillana hacia 1780. Tampoco no debe de extrañarnos que Fernando de Castro y Ramón de la Cruz hicieran intervenir en sendos entremeses a un "coro de negritas".

Asimismo cabe destacar el zócalo de azulejos de Manises, *Escena de cocina*, donde se nos presenta una doméstica negra y su señora; la pieza está depositada en el Museo de Artes Decorativas de Madrid y está datada en el siglo XVIII. A Francisco de Goya debemos el interesante dibujo *La Duquesa de Alba teniendo a la niña negra María de la Luz sobre sus rodillas* (1796-97). No menos importante resulta la aparición de dos grupos de negros, uno de ellos con el estandarte de la Cofradía de los Negritos, en la ilustración del *Corpus Christi* sevillano de 1780.

A fines del siglo XVIII, y gracias a la aparición de la prensa en diversas ciudades españolas, sabemos que mientras continuaba la compra y venta de esclavos negros, especialmente niños, un grupo de libertos ofrecía sus servicios profesionales (coser, cocinar, planchar, peinar y otras ocupaciones similares).[3] Un buen ejemplo nos lo proporciona el aguador que aparece en *El ciego de la guitarra* (1778) de Francisco de

---

3   Para el caso de Cataluña, véase mi artículo "La esclavitud en la Cataluña de fines del siglo XVIII y primera mitad del XIX: Los amados sirvientes de indianos y negreros" (1999).

Goya. Lo anterior evidencia que el reducido número de negros se estaba integrando lenta, pero definitiva y totalmente, en los sectores más marginales de la capas populares españolas.

Lenta emergencia del negro libre en la España liberal. Siglo XIX.

A comienzos del siglo XIX soplaban vientos favorables a la abolición de la esclavitud y a la persecución de la trata negrera. El impacto de la Revolución Francesa y la abolición de la esclavitud por parte de Inglaterra favorecieron el que se impusiera la persecución de la trata. En el caso español hay que registrar un doble proceder. Mientras que en la metrópolis se prohibió la trata en 1817 y se impuso la necesidad de acabar definitivamente con la esclavitud, en las colonias americanas (reducidas a Cuba y Puerto Rico), esta práctica conoció un período de apogeo debido a la expansión de los ingenios de azúcar, demandadores y devoradores de una creciente mano de obra esclava.

En 1820 los Capitanes Generales de las distintas regiones españolas fueron consultados acerca del número de esclavos existentes en cada territorio, de cara a decidir la oportunidad de abolir la esclavitud. Aunque no se sabe con exactitud cuándo se decretó, todo parece indicar que fue entre la citada fecha y la promulgación de la primera constitución liberal a mediados de los años treinta. Como es sabido, la esclavitud continuó existiendo en los dominios coloniales, en los cuales se favoreció clandestinamente la trata negrera, en la que numerosas empresas y capitanes de barco españoles participaron activamente. Esa doble legislación, según los territorios, dio lugar a paradojas como la consistente en que un esclavo que llegara a la Península acompañando a su amo, alcanzara la calidad de libre en el momento de desembarcar; pero si regresaba a América, "recuperaba" su condición de esclavo.

Lo anterior explica que buena parte de las imágenes referidas a la esclavitud se deban a los cada vez más numerosos defensores de la abolición de la esclavitud en las colonias americanas. La prensa satírica de la época está llena de ilustraciones condenando tajantemente la permanencia de la esclavitud y en la que los esclavos se presentan como víctimas de unos odiosos amos, usualmente presentados como militares, nobles y clérigos. Esta imagen del negro comenzó a cambiar a raíz de las guerras independentistas cubanas, cuando la prensa satírica, las ilustraciones de romances y alguna que otra colección de cromos presentaron a los negros como monos, salvajes, crueles y lascivos.

Mientras tanto, las imágenes de los negros en España se referían, en parte de los casos conocidos, a antiguos esclavos reconvertidos en fieles sirvientes, casi parientes en algunos casos de sus antiguos amos. Entre otros indianos que regresaron a España acompañados de sirvientes negros hay que destacar a Pedro Blanco, "el Negrero", y al naviero Antonio López. Pero la mayoría de los negros que vivían en la España decimonónica pasaron a engrosar las capas más marginales de la sociedad española. Sirva de ejemplo el cuadro que nos presenta una cola de pobres madrileños, entre ellos un negro, esperando la sopa boba.

Sin ningún género de dudas, lo más importante por lo que a la imagen del negro se refiere fue su creciente importancia y visibilidad en el mundo del espectáculo. Está perfectamente atestiguada su presencia en plazas de toros, teatros y, especialmente, en el ámbito musical. Esto último lo ejemplifica perfectamente la creciente popularización de los ritmos africanos en la España de la época: tangos (de los Negros, del Cucoyé, del Sangá, Cangú y otros), cumbé y otros (Martín Corrales 2000).

Entre el negro libre y el negro colonizado: siglo XX

Desde fines del siglo XIX, asistimos a otro cambio importante en la imagen del negro, favorecida por la consolidación del dominio colonial español en el Golfo de Guinea, en Fernando Poo (actual Malabo) y Río Muni (actual Bata). La emergencia de la figura del negro colonizado, del guineano, fue posible por la consolidación del dominio colonial español en Malabo y Bata. Se hizo hincapié en la figura del negro civilizado y cristianizado gracias a —se argumentaba— la abnegada ayuda de los misioneros españoles. En paralelo, se explotaba la imagen del negro exótico, para lo que se hicieron viajar a la Península algunos grupos.

Destacaron la exhibición en 1897, en Madrid y Barcelona, de un grupo de ashantis, de los que se vendieron postales. Lo mismo ocurrió con el grupo guineano llevado a la Exposición Iberoamericana de Sevilla de 1929. No hay que olvidar, por otra parte, la exposición de un jefe tribal de Botsuana, cuyos restos expuestos en un museo de la localidad catalana de Banyoles durante un siglo, fueron, tras una agria polémica pública, definitivamente enterrados en África no hace muchos años (Muñoz Torreblanca 2010; Sánchez Gómez 2006).

En este período se multiplicó la utilización del negro en la publicidad de productos tropicales: cacao o chocolate (Amatller, Caobanía, Cola-Cao, Elgorriaga, La Negrita y Popular), café (Kenya), caucho (General Compañía Española de Neumáticos) y otros. También sirvió de soporte a la publicidad de productos que no tenían nada que ver con Guinea en particular, o con África en general. Es el caso de los Guisantes Francisco Moreno, de Calahorra; de los Azafranes El Negrito, de Novelda; de los vinos Francisco Caballero, de Jerez; y de las Galletas Nanuk. Pero también los hubo muy denigrantes. Siguiendo la moda impuesta por los jabones de Marsella (que llegaba hasta a "blanquear" a los hombres no blancos), la Lejía Higiénica El Negrito, de Flix (Tarragona), mostraba cómo un negro se iba convirtiendo en blanco gracias a su lavado con la citada lejía. La Lejía de los Tres Ramos, valenciana, incluía una escena en la que un negrito regaba con la citada lejía a otro que se convertía en blanco ("¡Qué gracia!¡Queda blanco!"). Sin tanta agresividad, pero vinculado de alguna manera con los ejemplos anteriores, hay que citar el hecho de que los jabones Heno de Pravia utilizaran una sirvienta negra en su publicidad. Por su parte, la Tintura Instantánea Zeugidor era publicitada por un negro que afirmaba que su "resultado es de un negro inalterable como mi piel". Más tarde, lámparas Z nos presentaba a un negro, un blanco y una lampara Z que daba una luz blanca, en un canto clarísimo a la labor civilizadora, o "iluminadora", que el hombre blanco cumplía acerca del negro. En paralelo, el cinematógrafo incidía en los mismos estereotipos en las escasas películas españolas que abordaban el tema de África en general y el de Guinea española en particular (Arnalte 1995; Elena 2010; Ortín y Pereiro 2006).

La inmigración del último tercio del siglo XX. El negro, nuestro vecino, nuestro conciudadano

En 1968, la ex-Guinea española se convirtió en la República de Guinea Ecuatorial: el colonialismo ha finalizado. Un número creciente, aunque no muy importante de guineanos, se trasladó a la Península sobre todo por motivos políticos, huyendo de la represión que se desencadenó en aquel país. En paralelo comenzaron a llegar a España africanos de diversos países: futbolistas que se integran en los equipos españoles, inmigrantes que se dedican a diferentes ocupaciones (venta ambulante, construcción y otras actividades), casi siempre en calidad de mano de obra barata.

Esta inmigración, en buena parte inesperada, vino a coincidir con la transición política española y la instauración de un régimen democrático que supuso la adopción mayoritaria de una ideología respetuosa, o más respetuosa que en los períodos precedentes, para con los inmigrantes en general, y con los inmigrantes de color en particular. La sociedad española, al menos en las tribunas públicas (prensa, radios, cátedras, foros, televisiones y demás), alababa el pluralismo de todo tipo y hacía hincapié en la riqueza que suponía ese pluralismo. Los medios de comunicación y los partidos políticos impusieron un discurso políticamente correcto en lo que se refería a los inmigrantes. Los sindicatos y organizaciones políticas se dotaron de organizaciones específicas para atender las necesidades de los inmigrantes (CITE de CC.OO.), mientras que los mismos inmigrantes crearon sus propias organizaciones y surgieron otras dedicadas a combatir el racismo (S.O.S. Racismo). Las publicaciones de ayuntamientos, sindicatos, partidos políticos, asociaciones de vecinos y otras instituciones incluían fotografías o ilustraciones caracterizadas por la mezcla de etnias, culturas, colores, lenguas, saberes y demás. La idea del puzzle se impuso al tiempo que se generalizaban las denuncias en los medios de comunicación contra los abusos a que son sometidos los inmigrantes.

Sin embargo, los inmigrantes, además de ser vecinos y compañeros de trabajo y de sindicato, se convirtieron poco a poco en clientes. Diversas empresas de atención sanitaria, de seguros, de transportes, grandes almacenes y demás utilizan en sus carteles reclamos a embarazadas, niños y adultos de color (El Corte Inglés, Iberia, Capio Sanidad, Assistència Sanitària Col·legial, DirectSeguros y otras muchas más). Se destaca la capacidad atlética o la belleza de hombres y mujeres de color, ideales para anuncios de marcas deportivas y para presentarlos como modelos (El Corte Inglés, TurGalicia, Pirelli, Telefónica y SportArea, entre otras). Con todo, es en el ámbito de la música (que incluye desde el jazz hasta los ritmos caribeños y africanos) donde la figura del negro ha gozado de más fortuna hasta la fecha.[4]

A pesar de todo lo expuesto, no toda la sociedad española comparte esa imagen revalorizada del negro. Una parte, de la que es difícil calcular su importancia —dado que, al menos de momento, están condenados a la marginalidad en el debate público— continúa comulgando con una visión racista o excluyente de los inmigrantes. Eso explica que algunas tendencias heredadas del período anterior sigan estando presentes, aunque adaptadas a los nuevos tiempos. Persiste la publicidad que relaciona el color de la piel con el origen de los productos, como puede verse en el caso de los cafés Saimaza y San Lorenzo. Otro tipo de publicidad va más lejos y enfatiza el potencial sexual de los negros. Abundan los negros entre los musculados individuos que "prestigian" discotecas y lugares dedicados a las despedidas de solteras. La imagen del semental negro se utiliza tanto por estudiantes Erasmus en Barcelona, como por bares de ambiente gay de la misma ciudad. Añadamos, para finalizar, que la marca Conguitos promueve su conocido producto de chocolate caracterizándolo como un negro salvaje aunque de aspecto risueño.

Bibliografía

Arnalte, A. 1995. "La imagen del negro en cómics y tebeos. Feos, torpes, caníbales y sexualmente superdotados", *El Viejo Topo* 86, 73-76.

Cortés López, J. L. 1986. *Los orígenes de la esclavitud negra en España*, Madrid, Mundo Negro.

---

4   Me he ocupado del tratamiento de la imagen de los inmigrantes en el último capítulo de mi libro *La imagen de los magrebíes en España. Siglos XVI-XX: una perspectiva histórica* (2001).

Elena, A. 2010. *La llamada de África. Estudios sobre el cine colonial español*, Barcelona, Edicions Bellaterra.

Fra Molinero, B. 1995. *La imagen de los negros en el teatro de los Siglos de Oro*, Madrid, Siglo XXI.

Franco Silva, A. 1992. *La esclavitud en Andalucía, 1450-1550*, Granada, Universidad de Granada.

Méndez Rodríguez, L. 2011. *Esclavos en la pintura sevillana de los Siglos de Oro*, Sevilla, Universidad de Sevilla-Ateneo de Sevilla.

Martín Corrales, E. 1999. "La esclavitud en la Cataluña de fines del siglo XVIII y primera mitad del XIX: Los amados sirvientes de indianos y negreros", in C. Martínez Shaw (ed.), *Historia Moderna, historia en construcción*, Lleida, Milenio, vol. 1, 133-50.

—. 2000. "Los sones negros del Flamenco: sus orígenes africanos", *La Factoría* 12, 89-107.

—. 2001. *La imagen de los magrebíes en España. Siglos XVI-XX: una perspectiva histórica*, Barcelona, Edicions Bellaterra.

Moreno, I. 1997. *La Antigua Hermandad de los Negros de Sevilla. Etnicidad, poder y sociedad en 600 años de historia,* Sevilla, Universidad de Sevilla.

Muñoz Torreblanca, M. 2010. "La recepción de lo 'primitivo' en las exposiciones celebradas en España hasta 1929". Tesis doctoral, Universitat Pompeu Fabra.

Ortín, P. & V. Pereiro. 2006. *Mbini. Cazadores de imágenes en la Guinea colonial*, Barcelona, Altaïr/We Are Here Films

Sánchez Gómez, L. A. 2006. "África en Sevilla: la exhibición colonial en la Exposición Iberoamericana de 1929", *Hispania* 224, 1045-82.

MARGARITA ALFARO AMIEIRO

El pensamiento social y la representación literaria de la otredad desde la perspectiva de la experiencia vivida. Mujeres escritoras: Chahdortt Djavann y Ayaah Hirsi Ali

Alain Touraine, figura de referencia en los estudios de sociología intercultural, cuestiona el determinismo del discurso dominante asumido a lo largo del siglo XX en el mundo occidental. Con su primera obra publicada en 1992 bajo el título de *Critique de la modernité*, seguida de *Qu'est-ce que la démocratie?* (1994), *Pourrons-nous vivre ensemble?* (1997) y *Comment sortir du libéralisme?* (1999), por citar sus obras más relevantes, profundiza en una línea novedosa de comprensión del mundo contemporáneo en relación al pensamiento social como medio de lucha contra los instrumentos que apoyan la ideología de los grupos y las fuerzas en el poder (Touraine 2006: 196). Touraine argumenta la posibilidad de alcanzar un nuevo paradigma integrador en el que cada individuo adquiera la responsabilidad de su trayectoria al margen de los diferentes modos de integración social. Según el autor, las conductas sociales no deben ser impuestas por la sociedad o la cultura sino por el propio sujeto que es en sí mismo portador de situaciones sociales y culturales singulares. Sus obras más recientes, *Pour comprendre le monde d'aujourd'hui* (2005), *Le monde des femmes* (2006), y en especial su ensayo *Penser autrement* (2007), exponen que el único modo de llevar a cabo la aceptación y la integración del *otro* ha de producirse a través del reconocimiento de los derechos políticos, sociales y culturales de todos los hombres y mujeres en tanto que sujetos responsables. Considera que la dependencia histórica de las mujeres, el rechazo de las minorías y la situación de la generación actual de jóvenes, frecuentemente margina-dos, son los ámbitos en los que el pensamiento social debe actuar desde una perspectiva en la que el individuo sea creador de sí mismo frente a las reglas sociales impuestas y asumidas tradicionalmente.

Mujeres escritoras: Chahdortt Djavann y Ayaan Hirsi Ali

En este marco teórico, nuestro análisis parte de la premisa reflexiva en relación con el pensamiento social y su enfoque del individuo como actor de la integración social. Asimismo, y desde una óptica distinta, el estudio de la literatura intercultural[1] en Europa nos permite acercarnos al conocimiento de un corpus de escritoras marcadas por la experiencia del exilio político que introducen nuevos elementos de reflexión desde múltiples perspectivas, en particular desde la óptica del pensamiento social y la representación del *otro* (Cossée 2000). Así pues, centraremos nuestra atención en las aportaciones de dos escritoras extranjeras que llegan a Europa como lugar de acogida en el umbral del siglo XXI.

De un lado, Chahdortt Djavann (1967), de origen iraní, y de otro lado, Ayaan Hirsi Ali (1969), de origen somalí, nos permiten señalar los efectos más relevantes en relación al hecho de la desterritorialización: el exilio, la integración cultural, el cambio de lengua y la búsqueda de una nueva identidad literaria y cívica. Ambas autoras con sus ensayos y sus escritos autobiográficos aportan un nuevo enfoque sociocultural y literario enriquecedor de los estudios de la representación de los extranjeros de origen islamista en el seno de la nueva idea de Europa. Tanto una autora como otra se sienten en la actualidad muy cercanas en sus fundamentos, si bien ambas inician sus trayectorias alejadas una de otra debido a la cultura de adopción. Las dos han planteado, desde la vertiente del sujeto femenino que ha vivido el sometimiento, la humillación y el desgarro del exilio ideológico, cultural y geográfico, un fuerte debate en torno al potencial de la experiencia vivida en sus países de origen y su proyección en el marco europeo actual. El paralelismo entre ambas autoras, extranjeras y comprometidas socialmente, nos permitirá realizar un planteamiento desde el cual podremos observar el nacimiento de un nuevo proyecto tanto de representación como de integración de la figura femenina extranjera en el seno de la identidad social y literaria europea.

---

1   Entendemos literatura intercultural como el estudio de relaciones interactivas, al menos, entre dos culturas, dos literaturas, dos lenguas que ofrecen un nuevo ámbito literario diferente al de las literaturas nacionales de origen o de adopción.

Chahdortt Djavann

Nace en Irán (1967) en el seno de la familia de Pacha Khan, figura notable iraní, privado de libertad por el *sha* en 1979 a consecuencia de la revolución. De esta experiencia familiar surge su deseo de alcanzar la libertad personal. En 1993, a la edad de 26 años, Djavann se exilia a consecuencia del régimen dictatorial islamista de su país, implantado desde la llegada de Khomeyni en 1979. Pasa unos meses en Estambul y ese mismo año se instala en París sin conocer la lengua francesa. Se enfrenta a la integración cultural y lingüística. Lleva a cabo estudios de antropología en la Escuela de *Hautes Études en Sciences Sociales* y dedica su trabajo de investigación al carácter manipulador en materia de formación religiosa de los manuales escolares de su país de origen. En 2002 obtiene la nacionalidad francesa. Actualmente es una figura relevante en el ámbito intelectual francófono, galardonada con el *Grand prix de la Laïcité* (2003) y el de *Chevalier des arts et des lettres* (2004).

Se hizo conocer ante el gran público con el ensayo *Bas les voiles!* (2003), traducido al castellano en 2004. El 18 de febrero de 2008 escribió un artículo comprometido en *Le Figaro* en apoyo a Ayaan Hirsi Ali, amenazada de muerte en Holanda. Su compromiso con la libertad se manifiesta en su crítica a los dogmatismos religiosos y exige que la Unión Europea castigue *la fatwa*[2] como acto criminal. Sus obras de ficción publicadas hasta el momento son ya numerosas. *Je viens d'ailleurs* (2002) es la primera novela de la autora y en ella la narradora cuenta de forma fragmentaria la vida de una joven iraní que se rebela contra las injusticias del régimen político de Khomeyni en 1979. Sigue *Autoportrait de l'autre* (2004), novela que narra en primera persona la crónica de la guerra vivida por un personaje femenino hasta el punto de perturbar su identidad. En 2006 Djavann publica *Comment peut-on être français?*. Se trata de una novedosa reescritura de *Les Lettres persanes* de Montesquieu a través de Roxane, personaje de origen iraní, que se exilia en París y se ve en la situación de enfrentarse a una nueva vida donde lo más importante es la integración cultural y la adquisición de una lengua en la que la protagonista se siente una invitada (Alfaro 2012: 43-60). *La*

---

2   Término árabe que indica juicio o valoración de índole diversa (religiosa, ciudadana, personal) emitido por un juez con el fin de evitar un problema no explicitado en la normativa islámica.

muette (2008) introduce el diario íntimo de una adolescente que escribe desde la prisión en el contexto del Irán de los mulás; para la protagonista la escritura se convierte en una forma de vida que la aparta del miedo ante la muerte. Recientemente Djavann ha publicado *Je ne suis pas celle que je suis* (2011), relato en primera persona de una mujer iraní exiliada en París que cuenta de manera retrospectiva su vida en el pasado, en Oriente, y su vida en el presente, en Occidente. La autora escenifica la desintegración del individuo que vive desgarrado entre dos mundos y dos identidades.

Hasta el momento ha publicado diferentes ensayos que amplían y explican su posición intelectual: *Bas les voiles!* (2003), *Que pense Allah de l'Europe?* (2004), *À mon corps défendant l'Occident* (2007) y *Ne négociez pas avec le régime iranien. Lettre ouverte aux dirigeants occidentaux* (2009). De un ensayo a otro, la autora plantea ante la opinión pública occidental, y francesa en particular, el dogmatismo de la religión islámica y sus consecuencias para las mujeres, no solo en los países islámicos sino también en Europa. Considera que Francia es una sociedad laica que no debe ofrecer ningún tipo de apoyo institucional que propicie el desarrollo del integrismo.

Ayaan Hirsi Ali

Nace en Somalia (1969) en el seno de una comunidad musulmana. Su padre tuvo que exiliarse a Kenia debido a enfrentamientos políticos y ella recibe una formación islámica ortodoxa. A la edad de veinte años se exilia. Antes de llegar a Europa vivió en Arabia Saudí, en Etiopía y finalmente llega a Holanda para huir de una boda concertada por su familia. Su vida como refugiada política en Holanda fue muy dura; se enfrenta a una nueva realidad cultural y lingüística que supera gracias a su empeño personal por no caer en la marginalización. Realiza estudios de Ciencias Políticas en la universidad de Leiden donde toma contacto con las teorías de los filósofos liberales y se hace seguidora del *Manifiesto ateo* de Herman Philipse. En los años 90 se convierte en una activista de referencia por trabajar en defensa de los derechos de la mujer en el ámbito musulmán y criticar los aspectos ligados a la tradición y la jerarquía que ella considera las causas más graves de la opresión de las mujeres musulmanas. Entre 2003 y 2006 llega a ser diputada al Parlamento por el

Partido Popular por la Libertad y Democracia (VVD) y es reconocida como una de las políticas más respetadas en el ámbito internacional. En 2006 vive un nuevo exilio debido a las numerosas amenazas de muerte que recibe. Se instala en EEUU y trabaja en el *American Enterprise Institute* desarrollando políticas de inmigración favorables a los inmigrantes musulmanes. En 2007 crea la *Fundación Ayaan Hirsi Ali* que propicia la instrucción de los ciudadanos inmigrantes y el impulso del pensamiento crítico. Entre los reconocimientos recibidos destacan el *Premio a la Tolerancia* por la Comunidad de Madrid en 2005 y el Premio *Simone de Beauvoir* en 2008. En 2006 fue nominada para el Premio Nobel de la Paz.

Hasta el momento, Ayaan Hirsi Ali ha publicado varios ensayos, dos obras autobiográficas y relatos de ficción en inglés, traducidos al castellano, que han tenido una gran repercusión social e intelectual. En 2006 publicó *Yo acuso. Defensa de la emancipación de las mujeres musulmanas* y *Mi vida, mi libertad*. La primera obra es un ensayo en el que la autora expone, desde su experiencia, su visión del Islam y apuesta por establecer un equilibrio coherente entre la razón y la religión. Critica asimismo las políticas holandesas multiculturales que durante varias décadas no permitieron avanzar en la integración de los inmigrantes debido a que seguían manteniendo sus hábitos culturales. *Mi vida, mi libertad* es una lúcida autobiografía en la que recorre los momentos esenciales de su vida marcada por el drama de la imposición de la religión así como por la revolución personal que lleva a cabo para alcanzar la libertad. A consecuencia de su denuncia, Ayaan Hirsi se verá duramente amenazada por su lucha en defensa de las mujeres islámicas y su crítica contra el Islam. Su exilio en los EEUU se debe al hecho de haber incorporado en su obra la referencia al guión cinematográfico de *Submission Part*, del cineasta holandés Theo Van Gogh, asesinado en 2004 por denunciar la situación de las mujeres musulmanas. En 2008 publica el relato *Adán y Eva* en el que pone en escena a dos adolescentes que viven en Amsterdam, cada uno de origen diferente, marroquí y judío; descubren juntos que el mundo en el que viven puede ser interpretado de modo distinto a como se lo han transmitido en sus propias familias. En 2011 ha publicado *Nómada*, relato híbrido entre la autobiografía, la ficción y el ensayo, en el que lanza un llamamiento a Occidente para que no ceda ante los ideales islamistas y defienda mediante la acción los derechos de las mujeres del Islam.

Experiencia vivida: las mujeres musulmanas. Propuestas.

La vida y la obra de ambas autoras nos permiten establecer algunos principios en común en relación con la representación y la integración de la figura femenina extranjera en el seno de la identidad literaria europea actual. Observamos dos orientaciones complementarias, el discurso crítico y la denuncia, de un lado, y la elaboración de propuestas con repercusión social, de otro. En el primer caso, la denuncia se realiza por ambas autoras con dureza debido al compromiso que sienten en relación con sus vivencias personales. Una y otra recrean personajes que han vivido el desarraigo y la superación personal. En cuanto al segundo, ambas autoras van más allá del discurso crítico y hacen propuestas sociales de integración en sus respectivas sociedades de acogida que están siendo valoradas muy favorablemente en el debate social y aplicadas en centros destinados a inmigrantes de origen musulmán.

Así pues, las propuestas, tanto de Djavann como de Hirsi Ali, están contribuyendo a remodelar el edificio social en Europa. Especialmente en Francia, lugar donde reside Djavann, y en Holanda, donde vivió Ayaan Hirsi Ali, se está tratando desde hace varios años la integración de la mujer de origen extranjero desde una perspectiva que va más allá de lo normativo y jurídico. En Madrid, el *Centro Ayaan Hirsi Ali*, creado en 2005, ofrece formación a las mujeres de origen musulmán de todas las edades. Ambas figuras están haciendo posible que se rompa con las instituciones autoritarias y jerárquicas y que se propicie la transición hacia un mundo moderno en el que el individuo, hombre o mujer, puede gozar de derechos y libertades.

Chahdortt Djavann fundamenta su denuncia teniendo como referente su experiencia personal de haber llevado el velo durante diez años. Considera que la situación en Francia no es justa y realiza un análisis incisivo sobre una realidad que va más allá de la defensa de la laicidad de una sociedad. Señala en *Bas les voiles!*, la desvalorización jurídica y social de la mujer musulmana en Occidente. Con el ensayo *À mon corps défendant l'Occident* pretende alertar a la opinión pública occidental sobre el dogmatismo de la religión islámica y cuestiona la tolerancia de los dirigentes franceses. Considera que el apoyo institucional recibido por las mezquitas en Francia propicia la presencia del islamismo a largo plazo. Asimismo, en *Ne négociez pas avec le régime iranien* lanza un llamamiento a los dirigentes occidentales para que no negocien ningún tipo de acuerdo con los reformadores del régimen iraní debido a su ideología y a la propia organización que sostienen. Finalmente, en el ensayo *Que pense Allah de l'Europe?*, plantea el modo que tienen los islamistas de ir penetrando en el tejido del mundo occidental y en particular de Europa. Las respuestas que apunta se encaminan hacia la búsqueda de la pluralidad de un pensamiento donde la religión no ocupe un lugar preponderante.

Hirsi Ali, a su vez, afronta la crítica al islamismo desde la misoginia que impera en el mundo musulmán y con la cual experimenta la necesidad de comprometerse para liberar a las mujeres del sometimiento en relación con la tradición del Islam. Reconoce que "la justicia social empieza en un individuo libre y digno" (2006b: 14) debido a su desacuerdo con la idea de considerar a los extranjeros en Europa como grupo de minorías y no como individuos. Tanto cuando vivía en Europa como ahora en Estados Unidos, lucha por la integración y la emancipación de las mujeres extranjeras para ofrecerles lo que en su propia cultura no han podido encontrar. Hirsi Ali reclama un periodo similar al de la Ilustración para el islamismo y solicita al mundo occidental que se les permita tener un Voltaire que propicie con urgencia el equilibrio entre la razón y la religión.

Conclusión

Chahdortt Djavann y Ayaan Hirsi Ali son dos ejemplos de intelectuales y escritoras exiliadas que están impulsando en Europa transformaciones sociales desde la perspectiva de la integración y en especial del tratamiento de la realidad musulmana de las mujeres. Las dos autoras convergen en sus propuestas de defender la libertad individual por encima de la tradición cultural o el grupo social (Touraine 2006: 159-79). Asimismo, argumentan la necesidad de hacer evolucionar la sociedad europea, no solo desde posiciones económicas o militares, sino desde una posición firme por parte de los dirigentes que impida el desarrollo de un nuevo capítulo totalitario de la historia de Europa vinculado a la imposición del dogmatismo religioso. En ambos casos la reconstrucción de la experiencia personal tiene, además de un valor testimonial, una dimensión intelectual favorecedora de una interacción positiva entre los individuos y los grupos sociales. Finalmente, ambas autoras plantean con sus escritos de ficción y de reflexión la dualidad de la identidad subjetiva y la identidad cultural así como el acceso a la cultura del *otro*. El desafío que propugnan es, no solamente la integración y la aceptación de la lengua y los valores culturales de la sociedad de acogida para los extranjeros, sino también dejar un espacio de auto-pertenencia, un vacío, por medio del cual cada ser humano se pertenezca a sí mismo con independencia de la cultura, la religión, la lengua y el género.

Bibliografía

Alfaro, M. 2012. "Chahdortt Djavann", in *Paseos literarios por la Europa intercultural*, M. Alfaro & al. (eds.), Madrid, Calambur, 43-60.

Cossée, C., E. Lada & I. Rigoni (eds.). 2000. *Faire figure d'étranger. Regards croisés sur la production de l'altérité*, Paris, Armand Colin.

Djavann, C. 2002. *Je viens d'ailleurs*, Paris, Folio.

—. 2003. *Bas les voiles!*, Paris, Folio.

—. 2004. *¡Abajo el velo!*, Barcelona, El Aleph.

—. 2004. *Autoportrait de l'autre*, Paris, Folio.

—. 2004. *Que pense Allah de l'Europe?*, Paris, Flammarion.

—. 2006. *Comment peut-on être français?*, Paris, Folio.

—. 2007. *À mon corps défendant l'Occident*, Paris, Flammarion.

—. 2008. *La muette*, Paris, Folio.

—. 2009. *Ne négociez pas avec le régime iranien. Lettre ouverte aux dirigeants occidentaux*, Paris, Flammarion.

—. 2011. *Je ne suis pas celle que je suis*, Paris, Flammarion.

Hirsi Ali, A. 2006a. *Mi vida, mi libertad*, Barcelona, Galaxia Gutenberg.

—. 2006b. *Yo acuso. Defensa de la emancipación de las mujeres musulmanas*, Barcelona, Galaxia Gutenberg.

—. 2008. *Adán y Eva*, Barcelona, Galaxia Gutenberg.

—. 2011. *Nómada*, Barcelona, Galaxia Gutenberg.

Touraine, A. 2006. *Le Monde des femmes*, Paris, Fayard.

—. 2007. *Penser autrement*, Paris, Fayard.

Begoña Alonso Monedero

Metaficción *con una esquina rota* (sobre "Exilio" de Clara Obligado)

La experiencia del exilio es un tema consustancial de la literatura latinoamericana y, más en particular, de la literatura argentina (De Diego 2000: 431). En relación a esta última, observa Francisca Noguerol, subyace en muchas ocasiones la necesidad de contar la historia desde la ficción; pero también se trasluce la consideración de la novela como documento histórico, pues, como sostiene Tomás Eloy Martínez, "las mejores novelas argentinas del último medio siglo pueden ser leídas como respuestas a las censuras y a los silencios de la historiografía" (1996: 91). A las estrategias de representación de la historia en la narrativa de la diáspora argentina que estudia Noguerol (las tramas policíacas, o de violencia, la literatura del "trauma" basada en los testimonios de los supervivientes, el discurso alegórico, etc.), quisiera añadir la que despliega técnicas narrativas autorreferenciales, como hace la argentina Clara Obligado en "Exilio". La autora remitía a este cuento al responder en una entrevista a la pregunta de si alguna vez había escrito sobre su experiencia del exilio; confesaba que en él había tratado de "contar lo que la historia *no contaba bien*" (Cortés 2011). "Exilio" es el último de los cuentos de *Las otras vidas*, publicado en España en 2005 y con posterioridad, en 2009, en México, en el primer volumen de la revista *Sólo cuento* (2009).

En este relato, la autora indaga en las formas de contar la experiencia del exilio no como literatura confesional, sino como materia de ficción que construye, más allá de lo personal, una verdad poética extensa, de alcance universal. Merced a la técnica metaficcional se arrastra al lector a leer el relato por encima de lo autobiográfico. Más allá del testimonio, la metaficción, paradójicamente, restaura el valor de la voz enunciadora del texto literario, mediante un lenguaje también trasterrado, trasnacional, para un lector de "cualquier parte". Es lo que he querido señalar, utilizando palabras de Mario Benedetti, como "metaficción con una esquina rota", la sabia y originalísima combinación en que aparecen el tema del exilio y la estrategia metaficcional.

"Exilio" se construye a partir de distintos fragmentos yuxtapuestos que van refiriendo una y otra vez el inicio de ese viaje al exilio, la llegada a Madrid y los avatares de un periodo de tiempo que llega hasta el presente desde el que se cuenta, transcurridos seis años, cuando ya es posible el regreso a Argentina. El relato arranca en primera persona —y en un pretérito definido— con este vuelo hacia lo desconocido, "hacia lo ignoto" (epígrafe bajo el que aparece en la edición de la UNAM):

> El 5 de diciembre de 1976 llegué a Madrid, procedente de Argentina. Lo hice en un avión de Iberia, que tomé en Montevideo, por el temor que me producían las constantes desapariciones en la frontera. Salí vestida de verano, como si fuera una turista que se dirige a las playas del Uruguay y, dos o tres días más tarde, subí al avión que me llevaría a España, donde era invierno. Me despidieron mi padre y mi hermana. Tardé seis años —los que duró la dictadura— en poder regresar al país (119).

Este primer párrafo es el núcleo germinal del que arranca el resto de los fragmentos y de las historias que componen el cuento. En principio, los hechos aparecen presentados sucintamente y coinciden con los que perfilan parte de la biografía conocida de esta escritora a través de entrevistas o artículos sobre su obra (Rebollo 2006). El lector, en un primer momento, si conoce a la autora, puede pensar que está ante una narración con visos de autobiografía. Además, algunos de los acontecimientos aludidos —los desaparecidos o las madres de mayo— son también reconocibles como verdad histórica. Otros forman parte de la imagen literaria del exilio, como la soledad, los problemas de idioma, la incertidumbre, la incomunicación, elementos que se integran en un relato que no está exento de humor y de ironía.

No obstante, en la entrevista citada, su autora comenta que en "Exilio" cuenta la historia de "*un personaje* [que] llega el día que yo llegué a España y va teniendo múltiples vidas". Parece clara la voluntad de marcar distancia con esa primera persona, ese *yo* que no lleva el nombre de Clara Obligado, pero que refiere experiencias del exilio que, por qué no, podrían pertenecerle. Se resitúa, por tanto, el relato en un marco posible de narración autoficcional, al introducir al lector en el terreno de la indeterminación y de la ambigüedad referencial e interpretativa, marcas de este género según Manuel Alberca (1999: 59). En la autoficción hay ambigüedad en cuanto a si el pacto establecido con el lector es autobiográfico o es un pacto novelesco. En el primer caso, el compromiso implica que "quien dice *yo* en el texto es la misma persona que firma en la portada y, por lo tanto, se responsabiliza de lo que ese *yo* dice", mientras que en el pacto novelesco, el autor "pide implícitamente a su lector que imagine *como verdadero o posible* lo que va a contar". Y continúa Alberca:

> El narrador cuenta *sin decirnos que se trata de algo inventado o falso*, al contrario cuenta *como si hubiese acaecido realmente* [...] se comporta como si se tratase de un relato real y exige al relato verosimilitud, suspendiendo mientras lee su principio de incredulidad. (los subrayados son míos) (1999: 59).

El cuento de Obligado contrasta tanto en esta cuestión de la verosimilitud, como en que en él no predomina el tono lírico narrativo más frecuente en la autoficción hispanoamericana de las últimas décadas, con una función retrospectiva, de rememoración de la infancia (Alberca 2006: 11).

No parece irrelevante el hecho de que Obligado haya elegido una primera persona narrativa anónima. A pesar de ello, e incluso así, el inicio de la narración propicia el llamado "principio de identidad", de forma que el pacto autoficcional se mantiene activo, pues si bien la primera persona no aparece con el nombre explícito de la autora (como se reclama a menudo para la autoficción), de forma *implícita* sí se puede verificar la identificación propuesta por Lejeune (1994: 64) para las autoficciones (autor = narrador = personaje), al menos para algunas partes de la narración. También puede considerarse autoficción, según Vicent Colonna, al darse en el relato "una especie de ficcionalización de la sustancia misma de la experiencia vivida" (cit. en Alberca 1999: 57). La elección del anonimato del yo protagonista puede adquirir todavía más significado. Si la coincidencia del nombre de autor y personaje es tan significativa para la autoficción, el hecho de que la autora renuncie a ello también debe serlo. Según Alberca, más que contribuir a dotar al texto de mayor verosimilitud o "aura de verdad", la coincidencia señalada proporciona al lector "un primer desconcierto, por inusual o antinovelesco, y al mismo tiempo un complejo escepticismo" hacia la verdad del texto literario (1999: 66). La autora parece alejarse voluntariamente de esa sombra de escepticismo, al haber dejado sin cumplir "la ficcionalización del nombre propio, la conversión de la propia persona del autor en personaje novelesco" (1999: 67), y, de resultas, el yo de la ficción o de la autoficción no va a permanecer en la ambigüedad narrativa.

Por otra parte, si la narrativa de corte testimonial, como dice De Diego, "tiende a acentuar la verosimilitud de lo narrado como un modo de contrarrestar lo inverosímil que resulta el relato de la experiencia del horror vivido" (2000: 445), "Exilio" se coloca en el extremo opuesto. La estructura narrativa no solo avanza superando la verdad biográfica, sino que lo hace con un desconcertante desapego de la verosimilitud de la historia, o quizá mejor, de las historias contadas. Mientras el lector se debate entre el relato biográfico y el autoficcional, la secuencia narrativa va desenvolviéndose (no necesariamente avanza) en una estructura cíclica —y con el único enlace de la aparentemente misma primera persona narrativa como elemento de cohesión— a lo largo de los 16 fragmentos que siguen al párrafo inicial; estos vuelven al mismo punto de origen, una y otra vez, en una repetición cíclica de hechos. Para ello, utiliza elementos de repetición discursiva como los siguientes: "El 5 de diciembre llegué a Madrid", "Llegué a Madrid en un avión de Iberia", "Llegué a España como si fuera una turista". En otras ocasiones, varía alguna de las vicisitudes del relato.

Hasta la mitad del cuento, la breve extensión de los primeros fragmentos va creciendo, aunque, en principio, cada uno de ellos pretende resumir el mismo periodo de tiempo de seis años, con absoluto predominio de los tiempos de pretérito y de la acción externa. A medida que avanza el relato, las secciones se alargan en detalles y dan cabida a más comentarios valorativos expresados desde el presente, o se establecen analogías entre un fragmento y otro, subrayando una obsesión en la narración. El relato se repite, se desdobla, se bifurca, se contradice y se corrige en una estructura en abismo (Ricardou 1973: 47, 73). Parece un solo relato, por efecto de la voz narrativa y de las recurrencias, pero al mismo tiempo son distintos y contradictorios. Una y otra vez una primera persona se presenta con apariencia de ser la misma y de vivir, sin embargo, vidas distintas, "otras vidas". Lo individual, lo personal y lo autobiográfico se vuelven incompatibles dentro de la coherencia de un único relato (no ha ocurrido una vez: se sugiere la idea de que ocurre una y otra vez, constantemente), y por ello el mecanismo autoficcional queda absorbido por la estructura en abismo, y ésta atenta contra la coherencia y la verosimilitud. El lector percibe como imposible una lectura autobiográfica, y parece que tampoco se le invita a entrar en el juego autoficcional, pues no se pretende trazar una línea ambigua en la frontera entre la realidad y la ficción:[1] es a través del mecanismo metaficcional como se quiere contar una historia, otras historias y también *la historia* de otra manera, y evitar los riesgos de una lectura en clave autobiográfica de los que habla Alberca, que ignora o desatiende la elaboración ficticia de lo "real" (2006: 15).

Se puede decir, pues, que se altera el pacto autobiográfico e incluso el novelesco, ya que los hechos no se presentan *como si hubiesen podido suceder*, ni se pretende tampoco que así lo parezca. El recurso narrativo de la repetición con variaciones conduce a la sensación de una ficción imposible, inverosímil y claustrofóbica, de la que parece imposible salir, que representa, eso sí, con exactitud poética, la sensación de "encerrados afuera" del trasterrado: fuera del tiempo, al menos del tiempo lineal, y una progresión de quien no sufre desarraigo. "Los hechos graves están fuera del tiempo", afirma Clara Obligado, recordando a Borges, quien fuera su maestro. Y el exilio transcurre en un tiempo sin tiempo, "no termina nunca, ni con el regreso" (dice la escritora en otro de sus cuentos, "El cazador"). En el exilio, también observa Wittlin, "la palabra sólo se recuerda, sin oírla, no es la voz directa de la vida, sino su eco, y el desterrado vive simultáneamente en varios niveles de temporalidad, presentes y pretéritos, sin distinguirlos siempre bien" (Guillén 1998: 88-89).

Y, sin embargo, la circularidad describe en cada fragmento un movimiento más amplio y una mirada más detallada y modificada sobre los mismos objetos. Esto es muy patente en la visión de la ciudad de Madrid que presenta la protagonista en los distintos fragmentos narrativos: a la llegada, es una ciudad detenida en el tiempo: aparece simplemente aburrida o deprimente, tras el atentado de los abogados laboralistas de Atocha en 1977. Al final, en la última de estas vidas posibles, sin embargo, declara: "Me gusta Madrid, tengo amigos, estoy incorporada" (2005: 129). La mirada no es constante, no puede serlo en la narración, como tampoco lo es en la autobiografía. El yo (biográfico o narrativo) no se

1   Señala Pozuelo Yvancos, a propósito de Philip Roth, que éste "parece interesado en visitar la frontera autobiográfica entre realidad y ficción y en pasar constantemente de un lado a otro de ella. ¿Con qué objeto? [...]: la idea central de todo este juego es la inevitable literaturización de la escritura autobiográfica y el imposible salto a la verdad de los hechos" (2006: 202).

constituye desde un único presente, sino desde las distancias cambiantes que va formando cada nuevo presente con el pasado narrado, en "la diferencia de tiempos en cada tiempo". Esta idea que Paul Ricoeur expone en *Soi-même comme un autre* es crucial, como señala Pozuelo Yvancos (2006: 238), tanto para la autobiografía como para la biografía, pues muestra una identidad ya no únicamente fragmentada o contradictoria, sino también dispersa en el tiempo, lo que creemos que afecta al planteamiento poético del cuento de Clara Obligado.

La puesta en abismo de los destinos de este yo ficcional que se remite una y otra vez a distintos *yoes* mediante la autorreferencialidad anafórica, está identificando en su posición de equivalencia a todas esas identidades, cambiantes en la sucesión, idénticas en la simultaneidad. Lo que afirma el texto, al dar un paso más en la autoficción hacia la estrategia metaficcional, podría formularse como *yo soy yo y también el de los otros que pude haber sido, o los que he ido siendo con el paso del tiempo*. El principio de identidad aparece problematizado. Y la identidad del yo no solo aparece dispersa a lo largo del espacio y del tiempo, fragmentada, sino también desdoblada por efecto de la *mise en abîme* (Ricardou, 1973: 73). Es la identidad del yo traspasada por la alteridad. La sucesión de imágenes va constituyendo una nueva realidad poliédrica, la verdadera referencia del trasterrado en otro nivel de simbolización, que no es de referencia testimonial sino de representación simbólica.

Frente a otros tipos de literatura testimonial del exilio, la autorreferencialidad del texto, como recuerda Ródenas, "atenta contra la implicación patética del lector en el mundo ficcional por el procedimiento de desviar el referente desde el mundo representado al discurso lingüístico que lo crea y transmite" (1995: 335). La diégesis que acaba transformando la ficción en metaficción exige del lector una lectura *meta* en busca de la coherencia y la cohesión textual. La mirada del lector se dirige hacia el sujeto que sostiene la enunciación, en busca de la cohesión y la unidad del texto. Esto ocurre una vez desautomatizada la posibilidad de una lectura verosímil o en pos de la comprobación de hechos factuales que son imposibles para un mismo sujeto, lectura que realizaría un lector autobiográfico, de por sí bastante reacio a cualquier tipo de innovación (Alberca 1999: 74).

La autoficción, reconfigurada como metaficción, declara con "sinceridad enunciativa" el modo en que el lector debe leer el texto, *sólo un cuento que trata de contar la verdad sobre el exilio*, pero cuyo valor de verdad no se asienta en lo testimonial sino en su fuerza poética y en su verdad moral, la verdad de la literatura, como afirma Javier Cercas (2011: 33). En él, el lector encuentra toda la variedad referencial que adquiere en nuestro tiempo la palabra "exilio", según Wittlin, o "los grados diferentes de realidad que lleva implícitos, entre la metáfora pura y la experiencia directa" (cit. en Guillén 1998: 85), incluido el que lo señala como el lugar descentrado desde el que el escritor mira el mundo y lo escribe. Una forma de narrar que Obligado consolida y refrenda en la estructura narrativa de su siguiente libro, *El libro de los viajes equivocados* (2011), donde el tiempo y el espacio novelescos reproducen esa misma espiral de la escritura y la memoria.

Que "la experiencia del exilio modifica la escritura" (De Diego 2000: 445) es algo comprobado a uno y otro lado del Atlántico. Pérez Bowie (2005: 21-22) ha señalado que, en los escritores exiliados españoles —frente a los que permanecieron— se puede constatar "una más firme voluntad de renovación formal", con rasgos como "la indefinición del sujeto narrador", "las dislocaciones espacio-temporales" y "la ruptura de la coherencia por la que se regía la narración tradicional". "Una nueva manera de mirar", concluye, que "nos muestra una realidad más compleja y problemática". Es, como ha dicho Clara Obligado, a propósito de la obra de Roberto Bolaño, "la expresión de un mundo roto" (Cortés 2011), o al menos, parafraseando de nuevo a Mario Benedetti, con muchas de *sus esquinas rotas*.

Bibliografía

Alberca, M. 1999. "En las fronteras de la autobiografía", in M. Ledesma Pedraz (coord.), *Escritura autobiográfica y géneros literarios*, II, *Escritura autobiografía*, Universidad de Jaén, 53-75.

—. 2005-2006. "¿Existe la autoficción hispanoamericana?", *Cuadernos del CILHA: Revista del Centro Interdisciplinario de Literatura Hispanoamericana* 7-8, 5-17.

Cercas, J. 2011. "La tercera verdad", *El País, Babelia* (25 de junio), 32-33.

Cortés, A. 2011. "La escritura al margen (Entrevista a Clara Obligado)", *La jornada semanal* 832 (13 de febrero),

<http://www.jornada.unam.mx/2011/02/13/sem-adriana.html> [consultado el 2.IX.2011].

De Diego, J. L. 2000. "Relatos atravesados por los exilios", in E. Drucaroff (dir.), *La narración gana la partida. Historia crítica de la literatura argentina*, vol. 11, Buenos Aires, Emecé, 431-58.

Guillén, C. 1998. *Múltiples moradas. Ensayo de literatura comparada*, Barcelona, Tusquets.

Lejeune, P. 1994. *El pacto autobiográfico y otros estudios*, A. Torrent (trad.), Madrid, Endimión.

Martínez, T. E. 1996. "Historia y Ficción: dos paralelas que se tocan", in K. Kohot (ed.), *Literaturas del Río de la Plata hoy: de las utopías al desencanto,* Frankfurt, Centro de Estudio Latinoamericano de la Universidad Católica de Eichstatt.

Noguerol, F. 2007. "Contar la historia sin morir en el intento: versiones al margen", in *Conferencias de la Profesora Noguerol en la Universidad de Salamanca* [consultado el 13.V.2011] <http://www.ffzg.unizg.hr/khk/Conferencias%20prof%20F.Noguerol.doc>

Obligado, C. 2005. *Las otras vidas*, Madrid, Páginas de Espuma.

—. 2009. "Exilio", in *Sólo cuento* 1: 1 (selección y notas de Alberto Arriaga), México, UNAM, 119-32.

—. 2011. *El libro de los viajes equivocados*, Madrid. Páginas de Espuma.

Pérez Bowie, J. A. 2005. "La modernidad de la narrativa breve del exilio", *Quimera* 252, 21-25.

Pozuelo Yvancos, J. M. 2006. *De la autobiografía. Teoría y estilos,* Barcelona, Crítica.

Rebollo, M. 2006. "Entrevista a Clara Obligado", *Periódico Diagonal* 25 (5 de junio), <http://www.diagonalperiodico.net/Clara-Obligado-La-palabra-patria.html> [consultado el 2.IX.2011].

Ricardou, J. 1973. *Le nouveau roman*, Paris, Éditions du Seuil.

Ródenas de Moya, D. 1994-1995. "Metaficción y metaficciones: del concepto y las tipologías", *Tropelías* 5-6, 323-35.

DAVID ARES MANSO

Las masas como arma de destrucción aristocrática. El judío, el catalán y el caballero español en *Adán, Eva y yo* (1939)

Introducción

Como observa José Carlos Mainer en su artículo "La retórica de la obviedad: ideología e intimidad en algunas novelas de guerra", las novelas escritas en contacto con los acontecimientos bélicos utilizan "una retórica reconocible y fácil" (141) y están muy apegadas a las vivencias personales de los autores, por lo que la distancia y reelaboración de los elementos novelescos es muy pobre. Estas características se pueden encontrar en *Adán, Eva y yo,* novela publicada en 1939 por el entonces exitoso novelista Rafael López de Haro. El presente trabajo no trata de ser el rescate de un autor olvidado sino que busca responder a la demanda de Ignacio Soldevila acerca del estudio de una obra que él consideraba "fundamental para entender la mentalidad colectiva de las derechas radicales de los años treinta" (24).

Para Mainer es habitual que estas novelas se centren en un proceso de conversión del autor-personaje que trata de convencerse y de convencer al lector de su identificación con un cierto campo ideológico. En la novela se cuenta de modo cronológico y en primera persona las vivencias del protagonista desde sus primeros recuerdos hasta su fusilamiento durante la guerra civil. La vida sentimental de Miguel es uno de los temas principales. En lugar de casarse con Moncha Noreda, que le habría dado una selecta descendencia, el protagonista va a dejarse llevar por la tentación de la carne y emprenderá una relación apasionada con Tamara Benamán, una judía perversa y casada que intentará convencer a Miguel de la superioridad de la raza judía. Miguel, en sus momentos de lucidez, va a reprocharse su comportamiento y se considera digno de emprender la misión de desenmascarar el oculto poder judío. La guerra civil sorprende a Miguel en Barcelona y no duda en unirse a los rebeldes causando numerosas bajas entre los republicanos. Aunque Tamara inicialmente le protege, los celos de esta van a ser la principal causa de su posterior fusilamiento.

Razas y castas en *Adán, Eva y yo*

López de Haro está muy influido por las doctrinas racistas de su época que se confunden con la tradición casticista española de la limpieza de sangre. Stallaert define etimológicamente el término "casta" atendiendo a su sentido hispánico como "un grupo social cuya afiliación se determina por nacimiento e implica la noción común de descendencia (linaje)". La casta supone una ascendencia común, real o ficticia, simbolizada por la sangre. Además "la religión es un marcador étnico privilegiado debido a la frecuente vinculación entre los mitos de orígenes del grupo y el mito de la creación" (4). Siguiendo estas reflexiones podemos constatar que López de Haro clasifica a los personajes en tres grupos en función de su linaje. Por una parte, está el grupo étnico judío, al que López de Haro, como tantos en su época, denomina "raza". Por otra parte, un grupo de españoles que no aceptan el dinamismo del grupo étnico al que pertenecen y buscan distinguirse y formar una nueva casta superior. Frente a ellos, la sociedad española de la República se ve considerada como un conjunto de masas o de "infrahombres" que reniega de su pasado religioso e ideológico creando una república de trabajadores laica.

Todos los personajes están determinados por su herencia biológica puesto que, como indica el narrador al principio de la novela, "cada uno es hijo de sus padres, de su estirpe, de su nación y de su raza" (12). El judío y el elemento de la masa republicana ("el infrahombre") se oponen por lo tanto al modelo de Miguel. Esta confrontación se pretende manifestar del modo más científico y más aparente: la anatomía, el comportamiento, la sensibilidad de cada uno de estos grupos son distintos, y por tanto, no poseen las mismas aptitudes ni el mismo grado de humanidad (Gilman 1996: 163). El determinismo de raza y linaje resultan, así pues, absolutos e inevitables y se definen como agentes motores de una historia que se entiende como conflicto entre herencias biológicas que son antagónicas: arios frente a judíos, "gente bien", como dice el novelista, frente a los mestizos degenerados.

El caballero español

El protagonista, Miguel, no podía dejar de ser un español de casta: "Por línea paterna soy, pues, ario, noble y radicalmente español. He comprobado algunos detalles de herencia biológica: por ejemplo, la forma y volumen del cráneo, invariables a través de las generaciones" (13). Miguel es dolicocéfalo, tiene el pie pequeño, es hermoso y elegante. Pero su principal superioridad es intelectual, lo que también atribuye al linaje:

> Yo pude nacer anormal, imbécil, loco, sordomudo, epiléptico, pero yo no hubiese nacido jamás estúpido. La estupidez, es hereditaria, viene de siglos. Un Lobo de Carpio puede ser cualquier cosa menos hombre masa. Hay clases, hay castas. "Miguel –dije a mi hombre-, hay castas y tú perteneces a la superior" (1939: 453).

Sus orígenes nobles están documentados: visigodo por parte de padre, astur por parte de madre, y con voluntad de superación que también se justifica por el determinismo biológico.

Judíos

Frente al tipo del caballero español, encontramos la aristocracia judía representada por los Benamán o los Heimann, también modelos arquetípicos de la "raza" como se señala en la propia novela (332). Se trata de familias aún más preocupadas por el linaje y que practican conscientemente la endogamia con el objetivo de la dominación universal. Sin embargo, esto no se manifiesta en una particular apostura física, al menos, en el caso de los varones.

En la descripción del padre de Tamara se combinan las imágenes del judío capitalista, proverbialmente obeso, cuya nariz y manos evocan las de un ave de presa, y del judío del gueto, sucio y ladrón. Sin embargo, el señor Benamán no se mostrará avaro a lo largo del relato, sino que, al contrario, hará gala de prodigalidad. Este derroche anormal, no obstante, únicamente sirve para subrayar el verdadero carácter del sefardita: "es incapaz de gastar un franco que no le pueda reportar cien" (80). Cada semita está marcado por los estigmas que son propios a su grupo y que a un observador atento no se le escapan. En el fondo, la operación que realiza el observador antisemita, como es en este caso el narrador, es ver aquello que desea ver.

Tamara aparece descrita en numerosas ocasiones a lo largo de la novela, lo que nos permite seguir sus transformaciones desde su adolescencia hasta su espléndida madurez, pero en estos retratos se busca sobre todo presentar el tipo femenino de belleza, elegancia y desenvoltura que causaría solaz a los lectores de las novelas eróticas de López de Haro. Los autores de la Promoción del Cuento Semanal, como indica García de Nora (1973: 400), prefiguran la novela rosa, en la que uno de los ingredientes fundamentales es la profusa descripción de suntuosos ambientes y vestidos, particularmente femeninos. Onsurbe, médico antropólogo amigo de Miguel, celebra a Tamara como un ejemplar perfecto de su raza.

En la novela Tamara tiene el pelo negro pero su marido y la señora Cohen son rubios. Jonás Heimann es alto pero Elías Benamán es de pequeña estatura. Los hijos de Zacarías Benamán tienen la piel atezada pero su madre es muy pálida. Se podría afirmar, por lo tanto, que a pesar de la concurrencia de ciertos rasgos estereotípicos, el judío es esencialmente indefinible. El joven Miguel lo plantea así: "Si me dicen: 'Ese es un inglés', ya sé que es un inglés; 'ése es un francés', ya sé que es un francés. Pero si me dicen: 'Este es un judío', me parece que no me han dicho nada; no sé dónde situarlo" (1939: 99). Y, sin embargo, las descripciones juegan un papel muy importante. Con frecuencia recurren a un discurso antropométrico pero su resultado no es constante dado que los judíos suponen, sobre todo a partir de los años veinte, un enigma para los métodos de identificación de la antropología física. Así que, junto a los síntomas físicos, son las actitudes, la psicología "de judío" (avaricia, traición, lascivia), las que hacen que estos se transformen en estigmas.

Si la descripción física es un rasgo recurrente de la literatura antisemita es porque para combatir al judío, primero hay que ser capaz de reconocerlo. Solamente reconociendo al enemigo, podemos defendernos de sus maquinaciones. Así se nos busca mostrar que el judío puede estar en cualquier parte, puede ser cualquiera. Se crea una imagen difuminada que pretende mantener al lector en permanente estado de alerta ante algo que denuncie el origen judío. Este algo, que no se define con claridad pero que siempre está presente, que basta solo con mencionar, es reconocido tanto por el autor como por el lector, ya que disponen del mismo código. López de Haro es consciente de estar escribiendo para "gente 'bien', señores, [...] subscriptor[es] de *La Época* o *El Debate*" (448) con los que comparte la misma visión del mundo. Esta obra manifiesta la cultura conspiracionista de cierta burguesía de la que el autor forma parte, que necesita atribuir a alguien a la vez concreto y fantástico la crisis de la que es víctima. La judía hermosa que conduce al hombre a su perdición o el judío adinerado no parten de la observación, sino que son invariantes de la tradición literaria antisemita.

Las masas catalanas

Según el darwinista Gustave Le Bon existe una analogía entre razas y clases sociales. Las razas inferiores se caracterizan por su incapacidad de razonar, su gran credulidad, su falta de previsión y de autocontrol, mientras que las razas superiores poseen todas las aptitudes intelectuales y de carácter. Las capas inferiores de las naciones civilizadas, equivalentes a los pueblos primitivos, supondrían una amenaza interior para la civilización, al no ser capaces sus componentes de adaptarse al ritmo del progreso (41-2). Estas posturas aparecen también en los escritos de eugenistas franceses tales como Vacher de Lapouge o Alexis Carrel.

Le Bon consideraba que, cuanto más se desciende en la escala social, mayor es la uniformización entre individuos mientras que, por el contrario "l'inégalité entre divers individus d'une race est d'autant plus grande que cette race est plus élevée" (48). De ahí que la gran atención que le dedica la novela de modo individualizado al protagonista y a su rival, seres excepcionales los dos, solo tenga parangón con el interés que despierta en los últimos capítulos, no un personaje en concreto, sino toda la clase obrera republicana como personaje colectivo.

Los judíos han logrado desestabilizar el país gracias al control sobre los medios de comunicación y la masonería que les ha permitido difundir ideas opuestas a la cosmovisión aristocrática del caballero español. El honor, la religión y la familia se ven atacados de manera sistemática por el marxismo, el sicoanálisis o el nudismo, todo esto responsabilidad directa de los judíos. Los elementos sobresalientes del país, en lugar de establecer enlaces solamente entre sí, se ven incitados por la propaganda judía al libertinaje y a la indiferenciación social, que conduce irremediablemente a la decadencia y a la pérdida de la identidad. Por eso las descripciones de los republicanos nos los presentan como grotescas fieras horripilantes:

> Frentes estrechas, deprimidas, ojos hundidos que miran torvos y turbios; quijada enorme, angulosa; orejas separadas del cráneo, que yo creo que las mueven; bocas con belfo, grandes manos con dedos porrudos, grandes pies, muchas arrugas en el cuello de reptil. Son de otra raza (1939: 393).

Son, para Gobineau (173) y sus seguidores, un producto espurio y desequilibrado, fruto de una unión que no es natural y que produce la degeneración de la raza, la pérdida de sus esencias. El aumento del número de mestizos en las sociedades contemporáneas es el responsable de estos movimientos de voluntad incontrolada movida por el resentimiento.

De ahí que sea precisamente en Cataluña, debido a que, según Tamara, la mezcla racial y el elemento semita es mayor, donde la fidelidad a la República es más intensa. Tamara le explica a Miguel que, en realidad, Fernando de Aragón permitió que se quedaran los judíos en su reino pero estos se cruzaron con otros pueblos dando lugar a una "ensalada de razas" caracterizada fundamentalmente por "un judaísmo mestizo y vergonzante cuyo carácter racial más típico es el odio a Castilla" (356). Esta presencia de sangre judía degenerada en España permite al autor una interpretación en clave racial de la historia. El fruto del mestizaje de conversos y de la confusión racial característica del mediterráneo son los "infrahombres", proclives por naturaleza a los movimientos revolucionarios.

El conjunto de las naciones de Occidente se halla sumido en una crisis precisamente desde que, tras la Revolución Francesa, el igualitarismo y la democracia vinieron a sustituir a una sociedad jerárquica y aristocrática: "La civilización occidental [...] parece enemiga de las razas blancas y tiende a nivelar las clases, a cruzarlas" (212). De este caos se aprovecha la minoría judía para su propio beneficio. Dado que es vista como extrajera, en todas partes se mantiene al margen de los conflictos interclasistas, que azuza, pero absteniéndose de participar directa y abiertamente en ellos. Su superioridad, preservada gracias a sus prácticas racistas y eugénicas, hace que se imponga sin dificultad en las sociedades controladas —o mejor dicho, descontroladas— por las masas.

> La aristocracia judía sabe muy bien que la fuerza de un pueblo no radica en el número sino en la calidad; sabe muy bien que privándola de sus clases selectas, cualquier nación por poderosa que sea, se derrumba. Las masas ni construyen ni conservan. Por eso los judíos impulsan a las masas al exterminio de sus aristocracias, de todas (1939: 332).

Conclusión

Como hemos visto, tanto Rafael López de Haro como Miguel Lobo del Carpio, el protagonista de la novela, pertenecen a familias de abolengo venidas a menos. Ambos ejercen profesiones vinculadas con el derecho y se sienten frustrados puesto que consideran que ocupan una plaza en la sociedad que no es la que les corresponde; el linaje y la inteligencia deberían haber hecho de Miguel un personaje excepcional destinado a ejercer, junto a los de su casta, las tareas rectoras de la sociedad pero los avances del igualitarismo y de la corrupción moral no lo permitirán. Esta visión del mundo parece nacer de una frustración pequeño-burguesa que le lleva a reivindicarse a sí mismo. En palabras de Muñoz Olivares, nos encontramos ante un

> señor de la clase media española, hijo de segundones, nostálgica de su pasado, víctima del presente y positivamente dueña de su porvenir porque de ella salieron, salen y saldrán los hombres cumbres, como depositaria que es del genio nacional y de su historia; la aristocracia de la sangre, que no degenera porque estudia y trabaja (2000: 165).

Este miembro de la clase media española pero con ínfulas de grandeza, necesitaba marcar las diferencias con la clase obrera, cada vez más próxima y reivindicativa. En la novela, Miguel, también de una familia venida a menos, aspira a recuperar una posición social perdida desde hace siglos y, para ello, se convierte en el portavoz acérrimo de los valores de la aristocracia. De ahí, las continuas muestras de desprecio por las clases desfavorecidas: la posible confusión con ellas resulta insoportable. El simple hecho de compartir la nacionalidad o la condición de ser humano con estos individuos es inaceptable para el autor y el personaje, y tiene que acuñar una explicación mítica: la conspiración judía.

Bibliografía

García de Nora, E. 1973. *La novela española contemporánea. 1898-1919*, Madrid, Gredos.

Gilman, S. L. 1996. *L'Autre et le Moi. Stéréotypes occidentaux de la Race, de la Sexualité et de la Maladie*, Paris, PUF.

Gobineau, A. 1983. *Œuvres*, vol. I, Paris, Gallimard.

Le Bon, G. 1919. *Lois psychologiques de l'évolution des peuples*, Paris, Alcan.

López de Haro, R. 1939. *Adán, Eva y yo*, Barcelona, Araluce.

Mainer, J. C. 1989. "La retórica de la obviedad: ideología e intimidad en algunas novelas de guerra", in *La corona hecha trizas*, Barcelona, PPU.

Muñoz Olivares, C. 2001. *Rafael López de Haro en la literatura española de principios del siglo XX*, Cuenca, Diputación Provincial.

Soldevila Durante, I. 1980. *La novela desde 1936*, Madrid, Alhambra.

Stallaert, C. 2003. "La cuestión conversa y la limpieza de sangre a la luz de las conceptualizaciones antropológicas actuales sobre la etnicidad", in P. Joan i Tous & H. Nottebaum (eds.), *El olivo y la espada. Estudios sobre el antisemitismo en España (siglos XVI-XX)*, Tübingen, Max Niemeyer, 1-27.

Taguieff, P-A. 1999. *L'antisémitisme de plume*, Paris, Berg.

—. 2002. *La couleur et le sang. Doctrines racistes à la française*, Paris, Mille et une nuits.

FREDERIC BARBERÀ

Writing in Catalan in French Catalonia. From Marginalisation at Home to Literary Success across the Border. The Example of Joan Daniel Bezsonoff

Joan Daniel Bezsonoff (Perpignan, 1963) has recently stirred the debate on cultural identity on the Spanish side of the Catalan border as a result of the publication of *Una educació francesa* (Bezsonoff 2009; hereafter *FE*), where he explores his French cultural legacy, and also *Un país de butxaca* (Bezsonoff 2010; hereafter *PB*), where his Catalan identity is discussed from a perspective quite unfamiliar to his compatriots in *Southern* Catalonia. In fact he had already consolidated his literary career on both sides of the Pyrenees after the critical acclaim attained by novels like *La guerra dels cornuts* (2004), on the presence of *Southern* Catalan volunteers in the Great War. His subsequent novel in 2005, *Les amnèsies de Déu*, which won three prestigious critical awards in Barcelona, is set during World War II, at a time when the sexual exploits of a priest between French Catalonia and Béziers are used to portray a time when France started losing its multilingual identity. Bezsonoff's idiosyncratic narrative tone, half way between cynical and nostalgic, was already present in *La presonera d'Alger* (2002), where he continues to assess from his complex perspective the last days of the French colonial presence in Algeria, as he had already done in *Les lletres d'amor no serveixen de res* (1997), and previously in *Les rambles de Saigon* (1996), on the end of French colonial rule in Indochina.

Gilbert Larochelle lucidly explains the two polarised outcomes of cultural globalisation, *integration* and *fragmentation* (155-56). In this context, in which fragmentation often acquires a multifaceted nature, involving language, culture (and hence identity) and politics, the case of Joan Daniel Bezsonoff is of real interest, particularly given the high quality of his literary production and the debate on identity prompted on the other side of the Catalan border by the two aforementioned essays.

The example of Bezsonoff becomes even more paradigmatic in the wider context of those nation-states like Spain and France (and their cultural production) that over a decade, particularly since the new wave of political Americanisation after 9/11 2001, have felt threatened by globalisation and have formulated various responses in the field of cultural politics, all intended to re-assert the identity and culture of the nation-state. Here, half way between a France which has issued hyperprotective linguistic policies for the French language and where Catalans are to be found in an aseptic *Département des Pyrénées Orientales* and a Spain of seventeen watered-down autonomous communities where a new wave of *patriotismo constitucional* has made itself present for over a decade, Bezsonoff constitutes an unusual paradigm of how interdependence between cultures (he openly acknowledges the importance of his French legacy) and marginalisation of Catalan in French Catalonia can however result in intellectual and literary success on the other side of the border, where Barcelona has become a new centre in the context of that dialectic struggle between the global and the local. This success has been possible in the context of, or perhaps because of, the political limitations and market restrictions faced by the non-state-sponsored nations, where often new and imaginative channels of communication open up for cultural production, sometimes reaching a high degree of quality based on a broad intercultural content that is successfully transformed into cultural innovation. This innovation is indeed to be found in Bezsonoff's alternative voice in his literary creation, where a convincing narrative approach often in the first person is poised between the elegiac tone prompted by a rich but fading Catalan identity and the sharp cynicism of someone imbued with the *grandeur* of colonial France.

The confluence of this explosive duality is presented to the (mostly *Spanish*) Catalan reader, and hence to our reflection in this academic paper, with an earlier essay (2009), *Una educació francesa* (*EF*), where the author openly incorporates his French legacy as an integral part of his identity and hence as an inspiring platform for his literary creation. The very title of his subsequent essay (2010), *País de butxaca* (*PB*) also openly acknowledges the *smallness* or *"portability"* of his Catalan identity in late twentieth-century France. Our reflection in this paper will find an ideal counterpart in some of the ideas put to us by another *North* Catalan author, Joan-Lluís Lluís, in his rather caustic pamphlet published in 2002 *Conversa amb el meu gos sobre França i els francesos* (Lluís 2002; hereafter *CMG*).

If we track the cultural and linguistic evolution from the loss of the Roussillon to France (1659) to the present day in that region, for Bezsonoff, as is the case for his contemporary J.-L. Lluís, an early start can be seen in the outcome of the Peace of the Pyrenees in 1659, which would have launched a subsequent process of what linguists call "bastardisation", where most new words entering the Catalan language on either side of the border have come respectively from French and Spanish. *Bezso* ironically accepts the exception of *entrepà* (sandwich) and *cap de setmana* (weekend) (*EF* 35), neologisms which would have been generated from within the language. Yet historical processes that run parallel to each other on both sides of the border were those responsible for a further broadening of the divide between North and South. This process can be clearly observed at the beginning of the twentieth century, particularly between 1914 and 1939, when the Spanish Civil War was totally alien to Bezsonoff's grandmother, for whom the bombings of Barcelona in 1938 where so distant as would later be the bombings of Hiroshima. In fact, J.-L. Lluís reminds us that the little village of Orellà had the strange privilege of being the French municipality that proportionally had provided France with the highest number of dead in the battlefield: one third of the whole population at the end of World War I, a conflict so emotionally distant for many Southern Catalans (*CMG* 38). And yet, if we are to believe historian Rovira i Virgili, when he crossed the border into exile at the beginning of 1939 and their coach stopped at Perpignan, at the time this town was as Catalan-speaking as Granollers, in Southern Catalonia (Rovira i Virgili 2001). A reality that, as witnessed by Bezsonoff, was to continue until the 1970s, when "el català era la llengua del país, la llengua de l'amor, de la mort, de la política, dels jocs, de les penes i de les alegries. La llengua que parlaven a casa, a les botigues, pels carrers, a l'autobús, amb els desconeguts" (*EF* 35). But despite this long-lasting normality, it was only after World War II that a new generation of children ceased to learn the language as a matter of course. Our author personalises this process in his own mother, who ceased to be a Catalan speaker at the age of 6 (in 1949), when she joined a religious boarding school in Perpignan where "[l]es monges li van ensenyar el llatí, l'anglès, el castellà i li van fer oblidar la seua llengua" (*PB* 26). This oblivion was part of what the writer has known to be "la mort d'una llengua. Un assassinat programat amb milers d'assassins i còmplices" (*PB* 9). And yet for Bezsonoff a whole community cannot be blamed for interrupting the transmission of their language and speaking the language of the state to their children; nobody can blame them for willing them-selves to be French, Spanish, Andorran or Italian (*PB* 65). In fact, when this process of interruption started taking place in France, it also started occurring in Spain (the city of Alicante is a good example), Italy or even Louisiana, at a time when even T. S. Eliot in his *Notes towards the Defi-nition of Culture*, first published in 1948, in a brief essay entitled "Unity and Diversity: The Region" (1962: 50-66), saw cultures disposed in con-stellations (in which the stars would have been state-sponsored cultures), with a copious presence of "satellite cultures" (he gives the examples of Wales, Ireland and Scotland in the British context; and that of Brittany in the French context), obviously dependent on "stars" like English or French culture respectively (1962: 54-58). However neither metaphorical concept ("satellite" or "constellation") seems fit to fully explain relation-ships or hierarchies in our globalised postmodern world because it denies the possibility of intercultural exchange, indeed a crucial feature at the core of Bezsonoff's originality.

But for us to further understand that distant concept of culture in the recent post World War II period, we must also remind ourselves of "the three senses of culture" that Eliot saw in another brief essay in the same book (1962: 21-34). Here class, religion and common culture would have operated as fixed references. But then again, focusing only on the class category, there is clearly an abyss between the unchallenged American "melting pot" of Eliot's day and the politically correct "multi-culturalism" of our day. Indeed the cultural assimilation that the genera-tion of Bezsonoff's mother suffered was to be politically challenged half a century later, when it clearly seemed to be a *fait accompli* to quite an extent for many North Catalans of a certain age. Thus our author epito-mises the effects of globalisation in present-day Roussillon through the objective correlative of a summer party taking place opposite the church of Pontellà, a village nearby, where late at night tourists get drunk to the sound of awful American music and where the language of Ramon Mun-taner has vanished like mist on a summer morning (*PB* 16). Not even the reciprocal discovery of other Catalan speakers that took place in Roussillon as of 1962, also witnessed by our writer (*PB* 36), when many *potes negres* (*pieds noirs* in French) of a Valencian descent coming from

Oran settled in the area, was to discontinue a well advanced process of linguistic replacement.

Our author is therefore an anomaly within the process of linguistic interruption analysed above. It was his grandfather who spoke Catalan to him despite the sociolinguistic trend imposed across the region: "-Parlez-lui en français ou vous n'en ferez qu'un con de paysan" (*PB* 28), was the grandfather warned by his son-in-law. It was also through his grandfather's trips to Southern Catalonia that Bezsonoff gained an understanding of the linguistic unity across the border. Thus Bezsonoff was told about the Barcelona of 1929, when his grandfather visited the *Exposició Universal*, and that of 1952 when the *Congrés Eucarístic* took place. On the third trip that his grandfather took to Barcelona in 1978, in which he acted as a guide for his family, he was also joined by the teenage Bezsonoff, who could see through his grandfather's perplexity a transformed Barcelona with many people who only spoke Spanish from Andalusia (*PB* 53). It was also his grandfather who introduced him to Joan Cayrol, the butcher from Espirà de l'Aglí that composed monologues, poems and songs who for our writer best represented the spirit of North Catalans (*PB* 56). Although young Bezsonoff soon shared his grandfather's admiration for Cayrol and didn't even dare answering back in Catalan to the artist when he met him at a concert, the writer-to-be soon experienced an identity crisis during which Cayrol did not set the expected example. How could one be French and Catalan, as suggested by Cayrol? (*PB* 63). Bezsonoff didn't find Cayrol's explanation satisfactory. In fact Bezsonoff's contemporary, Joan-Lluís Lluís puts it in blunt terms: for him, Francophile Catalanism is "una aberració intel·lectual. És com un xai que volgués assistir a l'aplec anual dels llops" (*CMG* 97).

Again, looking back at Eliot's collection of essays on the concept of culture can assist us in seeing how unsettled the relationships between the various factors involved have become since the late 1940s. If above it was demonstrated how dysfunctional the metaphors "constellation" and "satellite" had become vis-à-vis the relationship of interdependence between cultures in our postmodern world, now to grasp the scope of the big leap that there was from Cayrol to young Bezsonoff in the late 1970s in how our writer came to gradually conceive his cultural identity, we must also understand that the relationship between culture and politics has also become very unsettled since Eliot's day. Indeed for Eliot in his other brief essay "A Note on Culture and Politics" (1962: 83-94), culture was just a "department of politics" (1962: 83). In this way, culture in the reduced sense of the word was everything that is picturesque, harmless and separable from politics, paradoxically the corner reserved by the French state to cultures like that of the Catalans, which to this day has been considered folkloric and provincial. Since Eliot's day, in the 1990s Larochelle (155-156) noted another dimension of this politics-culture relationship in that globalisation entailed a spiritual impoverishment running parallel to the materialisation of world relationships in which objects have now acquired a predominant status. And despite this process, France has remained aware of the importance of state intervention in the promotion of culture, hence, as implicitly suggested by Barral i Altet (36), Chirac's urge to increase state intervention in the management of French culture at the turn of the new millennium would be out of place with the needs of a new world in which the traditional role of the state in cultural affairs has often become dysfunctional. Dysfunctional or not, for Joan-Lluís Lluís the state-sponsored promotion of French culture with a very specific political goal has continued to this day:

> Francia sabe explotar su legado intelectual —de Voltaire a Sartre— como un instrumento de identidad y cohesión que ni siquiera requiere lectura previa. Y esa utilización del escritor como símbolo sin contenido intelectual es un gran hallazgo patriótico (Amiguet 2009).

In this context, for the same author (and the same can be applied to Bezsonoff), the very fact of not writing in French turns you into a regionalist restricted to folklore:

> El hecho de no escribir en francés en Francia te convierte ipso facto en un actor regionalista que está obligado y restringido al folklorismo, las estampas típicas y el color local. Recuerdo cuando la literatura catalana fue invitada en Frankfurt: muchos intelectuales franceses se lamentaron de cómo los alemanes, en principio serios, habían sido engañados por "una cultura provinciana" (Amiguet 2009).

Bezsonoff too is indeed uncomfortable with this proactive marginalisation of Catalan writers. And if his personal evolution has gone far enough for him to realise the extent of this marginalisation and detach himself from an unquestioned love for the French *patrie* (he ironically acknowledges that from the day when he felt hurt at seeing the burning of a French flag in 1985 at the Universitat Catalana d'Estiu, "he has since evolved" (*PB* 65), he has however continued to this very day to hold a political agenda based on common sense (some might dare say that it is somewhat naïve) consisting of expecting that the *other* languages of France be treated equally. In this light, at the very moment of my finalising this piece (18 May 2012), I've been copied a series of e-mails between Catalan writers and publishers in which they refer to the letter that Bezsonoff has addressed to the new Catalan-born Home Minister of France, Manuel Valls, in which after acknowledging his love for the French language and praising the high quality of education granted by France he asks for the same treatment for the other languages. He does so in these terms:

> M'hauria agradat, però, que la dolça França respectés i estimés les seves germanetes catalana, occitana, basca, corsa, arpitana, bretona, flamenca, alsaciana. Ja no som al segle XIX. Europa s'està construint. Les fronteres han caigut i potser seria hora que la república no se sentís amenaçada per la seva diversitat i reconegués la seva riquesa lingüística (Bezsonoff 2012).

Bezsonoff's approach to Catalan identity is rather different from what might be expected from those Catalans on the other side of the Pyrenees. Given Roussillon's sociolinguistic parameters in which our writer has been reared, here Bezsonoff openly accepts that French is his mother tongue; a condition of which he is even proud, for it provides him with a precious cultural tool and, as we saw above, nobody is to blame for having taught their children the language of the state. And yet Catalan constitutes an essential pillar of his personality (*PB* 65); and only through this chosen Catalan identity can those who have chosen it attain a fulfilment of their identity that allows them to read their own landscape, establishing a link with their forebears and opening themselves to the other Catalans across the border (*PB* 65). Ultimately Bezsonoff wants to avoid his Roussillon becoming pure Catalan archaeology, as happened with German identity in Eastern Prussia after World War II (*PB* 66).

Bezsonoff knows that for the rest of his life he will continue to be asked why he writes in Catalan rather than in French or Russian (*PB* 47); as stated above, he's aware of the provincial niche reserved in France for those who do not write in French. It was in that context that he felt the need to continue to publish in Barcelona, a new centre springing from the dialectic struggle from the global and the local. A centre that has provided Bezsonoff with reputable publishing houses in Catalan, substantial literary prizes, newspapers and magazines in which to publish his articles, and TV and radio stations where to publicise his new books. It is all sustained by a few million speakers at least potentially interested in an impressive literary production in which he has turned his personal approach at intercultural exchange and cultural innovation into one of the most promising literary careers in the Catalan language, where even the painful chronicle of a dying world has attained a high literary status by means of a moving elegiac evocation like this:

> Els anys passen. Els catalans es moren. Arriben gent del nord de França, d'Àfrica, de Rússia. Com els senegalesos i els russos podrien aprendre una llengua vergonyosa que es parla només entre amics i parents? Els darrers catalans llegeixen *L'indépendant* cada dia, segueixen els partits de la USAP i desapareixen, un per un, com els sons i les paraules de la nostra llengua (*EF* 35).

Bibliography

Amiguet, L. 2009. "Hay en Perpiñán mucho deseo de lengua catalana" [interview to Joan-Lluís Lluís], *La Vanguardia*, August 11.

Barral i Altet, X. 2002 [28 May]. "Reflexions de política cultural (2)", *Avui,* Barcelona, 36.

Bezsonoff, J. D. 2012. "Carta a Manuel Valls", *E-Notícies*, <http://opinio.e-noticies.cat/la-punteta/carta-a-manuel-valls-64690.html> [Accessed May 18, 2012]

—. 2010. *Un país de butxaca*, Barcelona, Empúries.

—. 2009. *Una educació francesa*, Barcelona, L'Avenç.

Eliot, T. S. 1962 [1948]. *Notes Towards the Definition of Culture*, London, Faber & Faber.

Larochelle, G. 1992. "Interdependence, Globalization and Fragmentation", in Z. Mlinar (ed.), *Globalization and Territorial Identities*, Newcastle-upon-Tyne, Athenaeum Press.

Lluís, J.-L. 2002. *Conversa amb el meu gos sobre França i els francesos*, Barcelona, La Magrana.

Rovira i Virgili, A. 2001 [1940]. *Darrers dies de la Catalunya republicana*, Barcelona, Curial.

ISABEL CAMPELO

A Sense of "Otherness":
The Use of the English Language
in the Construction of Portuguese Pop-Rock

In a TED lecture about language loss and the globalization of the English language which took place in Dubai in December 2010, English teacher Patricia Ryan stated that the existing 6,000 languages in the world will turn to 600 in ninety years' time. The prevalence of the English language —the "undisputed global language" (Ryan 2010)— along the processes of globalization is becoming an increasingly debated issue. My article aims to focus on what has happened in the music domain, particularly with popular music and specifically pop-rock in Portugal, where English has been engaged in a territorial struggle with Portuguese over the last five decades, bipolarizing the mediated soundscape language-wise, and creating what I consider to be a sense of "otherness" towards the Portuguese language.

Some of my main operative concepts may be worthy of clarification. Popular music has been a much contested concept in ethnomusicology, particularly in popular music studies, mainly due to its difficult translation. In this essay, the term will be used to refer to the genres, sub-genres and musical practices of Anglophone origin which invaded the soundscape from the 1950s onwards both in Europe and in the United States, which were mass-disseminated through radio, records, television and cinema (Cidra 2010). The notion of "soundscape" is acknowledged to R. Murray Schafer (Cox 2004: 29). Despite the embracing character of the term, involving the everyday environmental sounds that allow us to construct our notion of space, I use it referring to the mediated musical soundscape that became prevalent through mass-dissemination from the 1960s onwards. Pop-rock is generally considered a sub-genre of rock. This term will be used to signify "the assemblage of musical styles formed in the USA and in Great Britain from the 1950s onwards, which had a global diffusion associated to the mass media, specially the record industry" (Cidra 2010: 1035).[1]

Portugal lived under a dictatorship for forty-eight years (1928-1974). Salazar, the most prominent political figure of this period until 1968 believed that a closed, culturally limited society was the best way of exercising power. In a letter to the Coca-Cola European division's director, he wrote: "Portugal is a conservative, paternalistic and —thank God— 'retarded' country, a term I consider appreciative rather than pejorative". He also claimed to fear the introduction in Portugal of what he detested, above all —"modernism and the famous 'efficiency'" (Hatton 2011: 149, my translation). Before the appearance of pop-rock, *música ligeira* ("light music"), a generic term covering a variety of musical styles, involving compositions with orchestral or piano arrangements occupied a considerable space in the musical production and dissemination, both through the radio and records (Moreira 2010). The *canção* (Portuguese word for song) was its main genre, performed by national and international artists regularly disseminated through the radio in Portuguese, French, Spanish, Italian as well as English. Yet, around the 1960s, when pop-rock was becoming increasingly popular both in the USA and in Europe, a group of middle-class Portuguese musicians identified themselves with the image of modernity, emancipation and consumption associated to rock and roll and to the life style of the North-American [and British] youth (Cidra 2010). Due to the political situation, the representation of "modernity", generally speaking, and of a certain cosmopolitanism came together with an attempt to reject anything remotely Portuguese, as far as language was concerned (see Appadurai 1996: 3; Torino 2008: 119). As Carlos Mendes —singer and song-writer of *The Sheiks*— observed in a recent interview, "Portuguese was very much associated with Fado and the corny songs of light music;[2] it was something considered very grey and weird". He notes that his group "wanted to do what the young people abroad did and in Portuguese that didn't work; besides, it was "cooler" to speak in English, so everything

1   The translations of the Portuguese texts cited in this essay are mine.
2   Fado is an urban popular musical practice, generally considered the most representative of the country. Fado songs are usually performed by a solo singer and accompanied by a wire-strung acoustic guitar and the Portuguese *guitarra*. Fado was inscribed in the UNESCO list of world's Intangible Cultural Heritage in 2011.

was in English" (Carlos Mendes, interview, April 2011).[3] *The Sheiks,* a pop-rock group that started its career in the 60`s, included songs in English, French and Portuguese in their *repertoire.* But their major hits were sung in English. Having The Beatles as a clear inspiration, the group split in 1968 (Tilly 2010). However, in 1980 they released a record sung completely in Portuguese: the political revolution of April 1974 had placed the use of the Portuguese language in a different symbolic space.

The revolution of 25 April 1974 put an end to the forty-eight years' dictatorship. It generated a type of music conceived as a means of social and political action, represented by the *canção de intervenção* ("intervention song"), a type of composition characterized by politically loaded lyrics, usually accompanied by an acoustic guitar. As a consequence, the pop-rock styles that had been implemented in the sixties, declined in importance. However, by the end of the decade, patterns of change were noticeable in the new styles of pop-rock (Cidra 2010). The Portuguese language reacquired a new value, once questions of national identity became a major topic in society. Singing in a foreign language was no longer "cool". Portuguese was "the thing". *Ar de Roque*, the first album of Rui Veloso, one of the most well-known singer/songwriters of the country, took shape from this historical background. *Ar de Roque* was released in 1980, selling over 20,000 copies. It labeled Veloso as "the father of *Português* rock". The lyrics of the songs, written by Veloso's lyricist and music companion Carlos Tê, were inspired in the profound social developments of a rapidly changing society. The demo-tape shown to the record company was all sung in English, except for one song sung in Portuguese. This song —"Chico Fininho"— determined the record contract, with the express demand for both musicians to write and compose all of the songs in Portuguese (Campelo 2010). A whole new process of organizing musical sounds through very sonically distinctive words —the Portuguese— originated what later became known as *rock*

---

3   I passed a set of questions to a number of Portuguese musicians asking their opinions about language use and music. Their answers, reproduced literally or paraphrased, are included in this article with the writers' permission. The interviews were as follows: Rui Veloso (Vale de Lobo, December 2003); Carlos Tê (Oporto, September 2008); David Fonseca (Lisbon, April 2011); Carlos Mendes (Lisbon, April 2011); Tó Zé Brito (Lisbon, July 2011); Fernando Martins (Lisbon, September 2011).

Português ("Portuguese rock"). Rui Veloso and Carlos Te have made the following observations regarding language use:

> The Portuguese language "flavors" the music; generally speaking, the Portuguese singers who sing in English tend to use *clichés* [...] the English language "pushes" you to the universe of the English-speaking people, very different from our own. So, for me, it is a contradiction that a Portuguese person wants to communicate a world which is not his own (Rui Veloso, interview, December 2003).

> The issue around Portuguese has to do with the enormous exposure which is to write in our own language [...]. The English and the Americans learn to express themselves artistically with the same words that they learn to live with —their artistic language is their utilitarian language In Portugal: there is a utilitarian language— Portuguese, but... our artistic expression finds an obstacle there as far as expressing our emotions (Carlos Tê, interview, September 2008).

"Portuguese rock" gave rise to a generalized investment on the part of recording labels towards many emergent groups and solo artists singing in Portuguese, polarizing the attraction of media such as radio and TV. However, and quoting Tó Zé Brito, well-known musician and composer, "this is a cyclical business; if in the 80's Portuguese music had an incredible peak, by the 90's it began to fall; singing in English became fashionable again" (Brito, interview, July 2011). Therefore, in the late 1990s, "pop-rock ceased to show local specificity and several groups had substantial public impact singing in English" (Cidra 2010). Such was the case of Silence Four, the group that launched the solo career of David Fonseca. In 1998, "A Little Respect" (a cover version of a song by the British band Erasure) was recorded by this recently formed group (of which David was the lead singer) and included in a collection sponsored by a radio station. It became a major hit. Before this, the group had already sent English-sung demo-tapes to a few record labels, without success, on account of "the language issue":

> The constraint of living in a very small place —Leiria— where things happened occasionally was deep, and I perceived in music a way out of everything the world around me represented. By singing in English, I felt I left that world where I lived (Fonseca, interview, April 2011).

David and his band kept faithful to their choice of language until 2001. However, in spite of the decline that Portuguese rock endured, discourse around the national language was still an issue. "The Radio Law" (*Lei da Radio*), which made it compulsory for radio stations to disseminate a pre-determined quota of Portuguese music, was approved in the Parliament by this time (February 23, 2001). Another issue that contributed for the debate was the success of other musicians who established an international career singing exclusively in their mother tongue —Dulce Pontes and Madredeus, for example. This led some press to emphasize the fact by judging Fonseca's choice of language in deprecatory terms:

> We were described [by the press as]: "a band who wanted to go to the Wembley Stadium, and therefore sang in English, dreaming of an international career"; we were the opposite of that! We were ambitious, but not in the sense of wanting to colonize the world with our songs sung in English (Fonseca, interview, April 2011).

The band split in 2001, but David Fonseca has followed a solo career from 2003 until today, always composing and singing in English. His language choice seems to follow the quest for some sort of "otherness" that is only possible through the language of others:

> Writing in English distances me from the universe around me […] and puts me in a slightly different space, away from my everyday life. Singing in Portuguese is the opposite: it brings me closer to each moment, each gesture of my day-to-day routine (Fonseca, interview, April 2011).

Portuguese has become the preferred language of many groups and solo artists in the last five years and nowadays it is difficult to say where the predominance lies. It seems, at this point, that Self and the Other co-exist in the same musical arena.

"Le Portugais, c'est du velours" ("the Portuguese language is like velvet"), the French singer/song-writer Carla Bruni said once in a TV show. This is not a consensual opinion, though: Portuguese is often considered —by Portuguese singers and song-writers— difficult and harsh as opposed to English, which is considered to be easier and sweet. Brito, being the lyricist of many songs written in Portuguese, agrees: "We have much longer words, unlike English, which is loaded with monosyllables and disyllables. Therefore, the musical sentences are shorter. In Portuguese, the musical sentences have to be longer, you have to compose in a different way" (Brito, interview, July 2011). The concept of Otherness is a cultural representation of difference usually evaluated according to certain dichotomies related to race (black/white), power (power-ful/powerless), civilization (East/West), gender (male/female) and, I would add, language. In this particular case, I consider Otherness to be an attitude towards a native language that generates a distance with it, appropriating one Other's language and its representation, and creating, eventually, a new one which is neither. Although the language appropri-ated does belong to an Other whose difference does not lie in terms of race or gender, questions of power are involved. This "othering" of the language involves a transformation in the musical sound, the lyric con-tent and the language that results from this hybridization process.

Several plausible causes for this attitude may include the symbolic value of the language appropriated, the cyclical changes of the music industry, the features of the language itself —considering, as a premise, English to be an easier language to work with— and also the idea that, by singing in English, the possibility of reaching the international main-stream record market will be larger.[4] In terms of lyric content, the sub-mission to the musical models of the early pop-rock in the 1960s limited the use of Portuguese to the available one and two-syllable words that could "fit" in the pattern, since the music was composed before the lyr-ics. This compositional model yielded only superficial lyrics, once the lexical options were limited. Also, the conceptual universe present in the lyrics written in both languages raises questions of authenticity: can we really speak about ourselves when we use a different language? Accord-ing to the aforementioned Carlos Tê, we cannot. There is also the issue of credibility for an English-speaking person: some of the texts written in English by Portuguese lyricists were described by an English citizen (also an English teacher) I showed them to as "not being English", as "an English person doesn't write like that". This leads me to argue for the idea of a third language involved in this process, a sort of neutral territo-ry constructed to represent my Self, based on one Other's language, but being neither. Timothy Dean Taylor offers interesting contributions to these questions, proposing the concept of *exoticisms*, that is, "manifesta-tions of an awareness of racial, ethnic and cultural Others captured in sound" (2007: 2), to which I would add the linguistic Others. The same

---

4   The concept of mainstream refers, generally speaking, to "the kind of music most accessible to and considered very appealing by a very diverse audience" (Elicker 1997: 46).

critic believes that "the ideologies produced by the three main systems of domination and exploitation —colonialism, imperialism and globalization— that foster appropriations of music and representations of non-Western Others" (2007: 1). The notion of ideologies produced in certain historical backgrounds resonates with another idea presented by Kathryn A. Woolard and Bambi B. Schieffelin: language ideologies —"groups of ideas within a given society about the meanings associated to particular languages [which] tie language choice in popular music" (Berger 2003: xv). Following the path traced by Taylor, post-colonial literature may offer other possibilities of theoretical framing. Boaventura de Sousa Santos considers Portuguese colonialism "subaltern, itself colonized in its peripheral condition". This particular colonialism generates a complex identity where traces of colonizer combine with those of the colonized (Santos 2002).

On The Voice of Portugal, a TV show in which I recently took part as vocal coach, eighty per cent of the songs chosen for the candidates to sing were in English. Fernando Martins, the show's music producer, stated that according to media audits, when a Portuguese song is heard, people switch channel (Martins, interview, September 2011). From what has been stated so far, I believe Portugal may constitute a singular case-study regarding the two other southern European countries —Spain and Italy—, which share a similar historical, cultural and linguistic background —in "othering" the native language in the pop-rock mainstream. This hypothesis, arguably, goes far beyond the music domain and resonates with the country's historical distrust in its values. It merits further systematic exploration. When facing the issue of language loss, we face other losses as well: each language has a particular way of expressing and representing internal and external realities. And, as Patricia Ryan wisely stated, "when a language dies, we don't know what dies with it" (Ryan 2010).

Bibliography

Appadurai, A. 1996. *Modernity at Large: Cultural Dimensions of Globalization*, Minneapolis, U of Minnesota P.

Berger, H. M. & M. T. Carroll (eds.). 2003. *Global Pop Local Language*, Oxford, Miss., U P of Mississippi.

Campelo, I. 2010. "Na Estrada com Rui Veloso: A Construção da Performance", M. A. Thesis, Universidade Nova de Lisboa.

Cidra, R. & P. Félix. 2010. "Pop-Rock", in S. Castelo-Branco. (dir.), *Enciclopédia da Música Portuguesa do Século XX*, vol. 2, Lisboa, Círculo de Leitores, 1035-56.

Cox, C. & D.Warner. 2004. *Audio Culture: Readings in Modern Music*, New York, Continuum.

Elicker, M. 1997. *Semiotics of Popular Music: the Theme of Loneliness in Mainstream Pop and Rock Songs*, Tübingen, Gunter Narr.

"Fado, Urban Popular Song of Portugal", *UNESCO, Intangible Cultural Heritage* <http://www.unesco.org/culture/ich/index.php?lg=en&pg=00011&RL=00563> [accessed May 19, 2012]

Hatton, B. 2011. *Os Portugueses,* Lisboa, Clube do Autor.

Moreira, P., R. Cidra & S. Castelo-Branco. 2010. "Música Ligeira", in S. Castelo-Branco (dir.), *Enciclopédia da Música Portuguesa do Século XX*, vol. 2, Lisboa, Círculo de Leitores, 872-75.

Ryan, P. 2010. "Don't Insist on English!", in TEDxDubai, Dec. 2010, <http://www.ted.com/talks/patricia_ryan_ideas_in_all_languages_not_just_english.html> [accessed July 15, 2011]

Santos, B. S. 2002. "Between Prospero and Caliban: Colonialism, Postcolonialism and Inter-Identity*", Luso-Brasilian Review* 39: 2, 9-43.

Taylor, T. 2007. *Beyond Exoticism: Western Music and the World*, Durham, Duke UP.

Tilly, A. & J. C. Calixto. 2010. "The Sheiks", in S. Castelo-Branco (dir.), *Enciclopédia da Música Portuguesa do Século XX*, vol. 3, Lisboa, Círculo de Leitores, 1207-08.

Torino, T. 2008. *Music as Social Life*, Chicago, U of Chicago P.

LUISA SHU-YING CHANG

¿Quién mira a quién? Imaginación, invención o inversión en *Cartas de relación* de Hernán Cortés

Introducción

García Márquez en su discurso "La soledad de América Latina" se refirió al libro de viajes de Antonio Pigafetta publicado en 1524 mencionando lo siguiente:

> Antonio Pigafetta, un navegante florentino que acompañó a Magallanes en el primer viaje alrededor del mundo, escribió a su paso por nuestra América meridional una crónica rigurosa que sin embargo parece una aventura de la imaginación. Contó que había visto cerdos con el ombligo en el lomo, y unos pájaros sin patas cuyas hembras empollaban en las espaldas del macho, y otros como alcatraces sin lengua cuyos picos parecían una cuchara. Contó que había visto un engendro animal con cabeza y orejas de mula, cuerpo de camello, patas de ciervo y relincho de caballo. Contó que al primer nativo que encontraron en la Patagonia le pusieron enfrente un espejo, y que aquel gigante enardecido perdió el uso de la razón por el pavor de su propia imagen. (2011: s.p.)

Estos comentarios sobre el *Primer viaje en torno del globo*, titulado originalmente *Relazione del primo viaggio intorno al mondo* (y también conocido como *Relación de Pigafetta*), reflejan la mirada e imaginación de los viajeros europeos frente al mundo desconocido, como la que Colón manifestó en sus diarios repitiendo el ideologema "maravilla" al ver la tierra del Nuevo Mundo.[1] Tanto Pigafetta como Colón parten de una exageración de lo visto y lo descubierto frente a lo raro, lo extraño o lo maravilloso del nuevo continente. Hernán Cortés, que dirigió las *Cartas de relación* al emperador Carlos V desde 1519 hasta 1526, describe

---

1   Hablan de ello, entre otras, las entradas de los diarios de los días 16 de octubre (103), 18 de noviembre (138), 24 de diciembre (193), 26 de diciembre (199), 29 de diciembre (204) y 31 de diciembre (206).

en ellas su viaje a Nueva España, su llegada a la capital azteca, Tenoch-titlán, y algunos acontecimientos acaecidos en la conquista de México, manifestando asimismo una mirada de asombro semejante a la de Colón y Pigafetta.

Cortés, al tiempo que se ocupa en sus descripciones de revelar el misterio y la maravilla de las tierras que visita, incluye en *Cartas de relación* matices egocéntricos que revelan la psicología de superioridad de las élites europeas frente a las colonias conquistadas. Las *Cartas*, a su vez, intentan mostrar la "re-presencia" o "re-invención" de todo lo europeo en el nuevo continente, denominando los territorios descubiertos "el resto del mundo". En el presente trabajo, abordaremos primero la "representación" del aspecto cultural-intelectual del imperio español en la Nueva España y luego el poder colonial y la actividad conquistadora frente a los indígenas.

Las mil caras de la imaginación e invención: de España a Nueva España

Hernán Cortés, personaje polifacético y polémico, que suscitó adhesiones y antipatías, es el primer cronista que relata la conquista de México. En sus *Cartas* se ven descripciones minuciosas de la "épica cortesiana" donde resalta su valor y talento en la conquista que realizó en nombre del rey de España, no sin engrandecer al mismo tiempo su propia figura para que el monarca le admirase y tuviese confianza en él. Al hilo de la lectura de las cartas, se percibe que él es el arquetipo de conquistador español cuando muestra el entusiasmo que siente al cumplir su deber de servir a Dios y al emperador y llevar la verdad y la civilización a ultramar.

Cortés es uno de los pocos conquistadores españoles "cultos" y su lenguaje es formal, cargado de "un espíritu mesiánico de reconquista" y con plena mentalidad áurea del Siglo de Oro (Charnay y Alcalá 2010: i-xxiii). Es bien sabido que los conquistadores veían a los indígenas como seres inferiores. Cortés no sería la excepción. Mary Louise Pratt argumenta que la literatura de viajes europea alcanzó una expansión imperial y llegó a ser significativa y deseable para las poblaciones del imperio, dándole a su público lector un sentido de propiedad, derecho y familiaridad respecto al remoto mundo de la otra orilla (Pratt 2010: 19-24). Además, los escritos de viajes se convirtieron en un arma clave para que el pueblo colonizador sintiera el expansionismo europeo como creación del "sujeto doméstico" del imperio (24). Esta observación de Pratt se puede aplicar a la mayoría de los libros de viaje redactados por gentes del Viejo Continente que recorren el Nuevo. En las *Cartas* de Cortés se advierte una reproducción o representación de la España europea y de sus múltiples facetas en la tierra americana conquistada.

En la primera carta, Cortés cuenta los primeros descubrimientos de la Tierra Firme, los hechos ocurridos en Cuba y otras tierras visitadas. La parte interesante es la descripción de centenares de ejemplares de la fauna y la flora equiparados con los de la tierra ibérica:

> Hay en esta tierra todo género de caza y animales y aves conforme a los de nuestra naturaleza, así como ciervos, corzos, gamos, lobos, zorros, perdices, palomas, tórtolas de dos o tres maneras, codornices, liebres, conejos; por manera que en aves y animales no hay diferencia de esta tierra a España (24).

Luego, en la segunda carta, se nos revela la primera conquista de Cortés y su victoria en varios sitios, incluso la masacre violenta y cruel de la Matanza de Cholula, tomándola como una acción preventiva. Hace hincapié en los maravillosos edificios de la provincia de Culúa, la ciudad de Tenustitlán y el rey Moctezuma, con los ritos y ceremonias aztecas. Allí empezó Cortés a paladear el sabor del triunfo, transformándose "de un hidalgo español a dios azteca" (Madariaga 2009: 128), y así empezó su ambiciosa empresa colonial:

> Hay hombres como los que llaman en Castilla ganapanes, para traer cargas. [...] Hay todas las maneras de verduras que se hallan, especialmente cebollas, puerros, ajos, mastuerzo, berros, borrajas, acederas y cardos y tagarninas. Hay frutas de muchas maneras, en que hay cerezas y ciruelas, que son semejables a las de España. [...] Venden colores para pintores, cuanto se pueden hallar en España, y de tan excelentes matices cuanto pueden ver (78).

Esta segunda carta, según Désiré Charnay y Manuel Alcalá, es "la más interesante" y "la más dramática" (2010: xvi). También es la carta que manifiesta más la mentalidad y la raíz cultural de Cortés como conquistador de la tierra hallada, etiquetándola como tierra española. Fue entonces cuando solicitó a Carlos V la autorización oficial de poner a esos territorios de la conquista el nombre de "Nueva España":

> Por lo que yo he visto y comprendido cerca de la similitud que toda esta tierra tiene a España, así en la fertilidad como en la grandeza y fríos que en ella hace, y en otras muchas cosas que la equiparan a ella, me pareció que el más conveniente nombre para esta dicha tierra era llamarse la Nueva España del mar Océano; y así, en nombre de vuestra majestad se le puso aqueste nombre. Humildemente suplico a vuestra alteza lo tenga por bien y mande que se nombre así (120).

Cortés destaca los recursos y bellezas naturales del nuevo mundo para equiparar lo español y lo mexicano. También justifica la masacre de indígenas como necesaria e inevitable para la conquista posterior, lo que se corresponde con la concepción de Benedict Anderson respecto a la nación y el nacionalismo. "Se imagina la nación como una comunidad, a pesar de que internamente existe la explotación e injusticia, la nación es considerada como una entidad del amor filial, de profunda fraternidad y hermandad, de igual a igual", afirma el historiador en *Imagined Communities*, concluyendo que "[a] consecuencia de esto, dentro del marco limitado de la imaginación común, se empuja a millones de gente que luchan y matan sin paliativo por el nacionalismo" (7).

Otra evidencia será un fragmento de esta segunda carta en la que Cortés clasifica la categoría social desde la situación de superioridad del noble y con la intención de educar a los naturales de Nueva España:

> Hermanos y amigos míos, ya sabéis que de mucho tiempo acá vosotros y vuestros padres y abuelos habéis sido y sois súbditos y vasallos de mis antecesores y míos, y siempre de ellos y de mí habéis sido muy bien tratados y honrados, y vosotros asimismo habéis hecho lo que buenos y leales vasallos son obligados a sus naturales señores; y también creo que de vuestros antecesores tenéis memoria cómo nosotros no somos naturales de esta tierra, y que vinieron a ella de muy lejos tierra, y los trajo un señor que en ella los dejó, cuyos vasallos todos eran (74).

En este discurso de Cortés, pese a que tiene un sentimiento de hermandad, subyace un tono triunfador y una noción de poder autoritario. Lo mismo vemos en la tercera carta, donde dice "pero siempre, loores a Nuestro Señor, hemos sido vencedores" (163). Cortés marcó una frontera colonial que revela una perspectiva europea expansionista. Este expansionismo, sin embargo, lo matiza Pratt con el concepto de la llamada "zona de contacto", que define así:

El término *contacto* pone en primer plano las dimensiones interactivas e imprevistas de los encuentros coloniales, tan fácilmente dejadas de lado o hasta suprimidas por los relatos de conquista y dominación contados desde el punto de vista del invasor. [...] Además, trata de las relaciones entre colonizadores y colonizados, o de viajeros y "viajados", no en términos de separación sino en término de presencia simultánea, de interacción, de conceptos y prácticas entrelazadas (34).

Pratt emplea "zona de contacto" como una nueva mirada para interpretar las distintas culturas, así como las posibilidades de nuevas competencias y conocimientos. Se trata de unos espacios socio-culturales donde las culturas se encuentran, chocan y luchan entre sí, en contextos de relaciones muy asimétricas de poder, de dialéctica o contraste de dos polos opuestos, como el colonialismo y el esclavismo, el nacionalismo y el indigenismo, lo que se debate hoy día en el marco de la globalización y el localismo.

La mirada y la representación de la otredad

Homi K. Bhabha, en *El lugar de la cultura*, se pregunta sobre el "modo de representación de la otredad" (93), es decir, la construcción del sujeto colonial y el ejercicio del poder a través del discurso exigen una articulación de formas de diferencia racial y sexual. El origen y la diferencia cultural-nacional parecen ser elementos contradictorios y a la vez unitarios para entender y aceptar la condición de extranjero. Cortés, desde la perspectiva de un intruso europeo, para representarse a sí mismo y a la otredad, construye y articula el discurso de la identidad nacional como aparato de poder. Dicho de otra forma, el discurso europeo sobre el territorio y las razas de América "desterritorializa" a los autóctonos del territorio que habían dominado y en el que siguen sobreviviendo para que los dominadores puedan "territorializarse" a sí mismos y convertirse en sujetos.

Estas premisas proyectan la ambición de Cortés en las últimas tres cartas. En la tercera carta detalla la conquista de Tenochtitlan y la distribución de fuerzas militares bajo su liderazgo en esta zona, además de preocuparse por la construcción y reorganización del cerco de la ciudad de Otumba, sede del poder de México y Temixtitan (140). A medida que va conquistando el territorio, Cortés va enalteciendo su superioridad: "Y otro día tres principales de aquellos pueblos vinieron a pedirme perdón por lo pasado, y rogáronme que no los destruyese más, y que ellos me prometían de no recibir más en sus pueblos a ninguno de los de Temixtitan", dice Cortés. "Y porque éstas no eran personas de mucho caso, y eran vasallos de don Fernando, yo les perdoné en nombre de vuestra majestad" (144).

En una carta fechada el mismo día que la cuarta, 15 de octubre de 1524, en donde trata de la estrategia de sus capitanes y de unos conatos de amotinamiento, Cortés, una vez más, manifiesta la hegemonía del imperio español y su declaración del poder sobre los nativos:

> Y junto con este capítulo, muy poderoso Señor, se sigue otro en la instrucción de vuestra majestad por el cual manda que a los naturales de estas partes se les haga entender el dominio que vuestra celsitud sobre ellos tiene, como supremo señor, y el servicio que ellos a vuestra excelencia son obligados, como súbditos y vasallos; y manda así mismo que en reconocimiento de esto se tenga forma con ellos como den y contribuyan a vuestra majestad *certum quid* en cada un año (267).

Cabe notar que las cartas de Cortés son una voz lateral, subjetiva, cerrada, sin diálogos. Spivak, en "¿Puede hablar el sujeto subalterno?", reveló su visión de lo subalterno referida a los grupos oprimidos sin voz. El sujeto subalterno no puede hablar porque no tiene un lugar de enunciación que lo permita. El discurso dominante hace que el colonizado o subalterno sea incapaz de razonar por sí mismo, necesitando siempre de la mediación y la representación de "el intelectual del primer mundo" (294). Cortés mira a los subalternos y éstos no se ven ni se dejan ver en su situación marginada. Cuando los marginados son visibles y audibles, el propósito de la representación del sujeto subalterno es político e ideológico. El sujeto dominante "habla por" aquellos que piensan sin voz, porque si no, serán ignorados totalmente (295).

En la quinta carta Cortés ensalza cómo él mismo ha encabezado una expedición a Hibueras para someter la rebelión. Habla de su encuentro pacífico con los mayas, cuya convivencia y despedida marcan un episodio memorable de esta carta. Sin embargo, el conquistador resulta perjudicado por su propia conquista. La expedición a Hibueras le hizo al altivo Cortés perder México (Madariaga 2009: 471). Además, durante su ausencia, se le acusó a Cortés de una posible traición y él, confiado, confiesa a Carlos V:

> acusarme ante vuestra potencia de *crimine lesae majestatis*, diciendo que yo no tengo esta tierra en su poderoso nombre, sino en tiránica e inefable forma [...] si las verdaderas obras miraran, y justos jueces fueran, muy a lo contrario lo debieran significar; porque hasta hoy no se ha visto ni se verá en cuanto yo viviere, que ante mí o a mi noticia haya venido carta u otro mandamiento de vuestra majestad, que no haya sido, es y sea obedecido y cumplido (349-50).

Cortés tiene voz y arma (la escritura) y puede presentar su apelación para su autodefensa, cosa que nunca se permitiría a los subalternos. Como afirma Pratt (35, 83), la conciencia de *anticonquista* que la burguesía europea tuvo a partir del siglo XVIII —y que sustituyó a la imperialista de épocas anteriores, según la cual la labor colonizadora era beneficiosa para los nativos— muestra la inocencia de la conquista al considerarla encuentro de civilizaciones pero mostrando de forma encubierta la superioridad de la nación invasora.

Conclusión

La identidad cultural-nacional ha sido un tema candente de la época poscolonial que induce a rastrear la vena étnica, la ruta de la evolución histórica y la búsqueda de la raíz cultural a la que uno pertenece. Se trata de estudiar el doble de uno mismo bajo la doble perspectiva del mirar y el ser mirado. ¿Quién mira a quién? y ¿con qué lupa o lente? Carmen R. Rabell enuncia que "[e]n 1492, los españoles no descubrieron América sino que comenzaron a inventarla. Colón y los primeros conquistadores atribuyeron sus propias leyendas e ideas a las nuevas tierras descubiertas" (102). Concluimos así con otro comentario de García Márquez, en respuesta a una pregunta de Plinio Apuleyo Mendoza (1993: 19), donde se revela la conciencia de los pueblos latinoamericanos:

> Seguramente porque su racionalismo les impide ver que la realidad no termina en el precio de los tomates o de los huevos. La vida cotidiana en América Latina nos de-

muestra que la realidad está llena de cosas extraordinarias [...] pues al fin y al cabo no les cuento nada que no se parezca a la vida que ellos viven (1993: 19)

Esto es una parodia que hace el Nobel para responder a la mirada de los europeos del siglo XVI y a la negación de los mismos del siglo XX. Sea imaginación, invención o inversión, lo que importa es reconocer una cultura de mestizaje, un espacio de conjunción de lo heterogéneo, aceptando la variedad de los hechos sin despreciar a ninguno.

Bibliografía

Anderson, B. 2006. *Imagined Communities*, New York, Verso.

Bhabha, H. K. 2002. *El lugar de la cultura*, Buenos Aires, Manantial.

Colón, C. 2006. *Diario de a bordo*, Madrid, Edaf.

Cortés, H. 2010. *Cartas de relación*, México, Porrúa.

Charnay, D. & M. Alcalá. 2010. "Introducción", in H. Cortés, *Cartas de relación*, México, Porrúa.

García Márquez, G. 2011. "La soledad de América Latina", in <http://www.nobelprize.org/nobel_prizes/literature/laureates/1982/marquez-lecture-sp.html> [consultado el 28. XI. 2011]

—. 1993. *El olor de la guayaba*, Buenos Aires, Sudamericana.

Madariaga, S. de. 2009. *Hernán Cortés*, Madrid, Espasa-Calpe.

Pigafetta, A. 2004. *Primer viaje en torno del globo*, Madrid, Espasa-Calpe.

Pratt, M. L. 2010. *Ojos imperiales,* México, Fondo de Cultura Económica.

Rabell, C. R. 1987. "De los documentos de Colón a *Cien años de soledad*: el paso de la invención a la inversión", *Cincinnati Romance Review* 6, 102-14.

Spivak, G. C. 1988. "Can the Subaltern Speak?", in *Marxism and the Interpretation of Culture*, London, Macmillan, 271-313.

DANIEL ESCANDELL MONTIEL

Argentina en la memoria. Cómo *Más respeto, que soy tu madre* abrazó España en la hoja impresa

Introducción

La blogonovela, como género narrativo dependiente del formato de publicación, se desarrolla encorsetada dentro de los preceptos que definen en la red el concepto de *blog*. Establecemos así una clara oposición entre una obra publicada en un blog, que no sería sino una publicación por entregas, y una blogoficción, en la que narración y formato se retroalimentan de acuerdo a unas reglas formales que son impuestas por el aparato crítico-bitacórico. El blog nace como la traslación a la red del diario personal o incluso la epístola, donde la autoexposición pública de la privacidad se normaliza en el proceso psicológico conocido como *extimidad* (Sibilia 2008: 35), que se traslada también a la creación literaria. La blogonovela es, entre las blogoficciones, la narración en la que se aprovecha el formato y la intencionalidad clásica de la bitácora para componer obras fictivas donde el autor encarna el papel del bloguero (que coincide casi exclusivamente con el del personaje protagónico). El escritor se apropia de esos entes para que, según lo establecido por Lejeune (1991: 47-62), el lector parta del supuesto de que está ante una obra autobiográfica. La exhibición de la vida propia fictiva se maquilla de realidad para proyectar una imagen en la que el blog actúa como un espejo deformante en una feria por la que pasan sus lectores. Así, el autor proyecta su personaje desde el escenario digital en el que se convierte la bitácora a través de la pantalla.

En este contexto sociológico y tecnológico Hernán Casciari desarrolla la blogonovela nacida como *Weblog de una mujer gorda* (y conocida en la actualidad como *Más respeto, que soy tu madre*). Se trata de una blogonovela (autodiegética y publicada por entregas en tiempo real durante un extenso periodo de 2003 a 2004) en la que adopta el papel de una mujer de mediana edad originaria de Mercedes, en la provincia de Buenos Aires, y que de manera nada casual es también la ciudad natal del autor.

La blogonovela y su paso al papel

Partiendo de la obra en línea *Weblog de una mujer gorda* se edita en España por Plaza & Janés la primera adaptación impresa, cambiando el nombre a *Más respeto, que soy tu madre* (2005), seguida de una edición de bolsillo (2006b). De esta edición surgirá la mexicana, publicada en 2006 con el mismo título por la editorial Grijalbo, aunque presenta leves modificaciones léxicas de las que hablaremos posteriormente. Estas dos ediciones constituyen, en resumidas cuentas, un único texto. Por otro lado, en Argentina se publica un año más tarde la primera edición de la novela bajo el nombre *Diario de una mujer gorda* (2006a). Es posterior a la española, pero tiene un título similar al de la bitácora original (se sustituye únicamente el término *blog* por *diario*) y mantiene una estructura mucho más parecida a la que nos encontramos en internet, algo lógico dado el éxito en Argentina del texto digital original. Sin cambios en la propia novela, en 2009 se publicó en Argentina una nueva edición en la que destaca la adopción del título, ya internacional, *Más respeto, que soy tu madre* en detrimento del original (y que se ha empleado en las traducciones al francés, italiano y portugués). De hecho, ese año se cambió el nombre del blog y se dio a conocer la obra teatral, de gran éxito comercial.[1] Asimismo, se incorpora en esa edición un epílogo en el que la proteica protagonista, Mirta, cuenta cómo ha sido su vida en los cinco años posteriores a la finalización del blog, cómo el libro ha sido un éxito editorial y cómo "Gasalla se va a disfrazar de mí en el teatro y va a contar otra vez la historia, nuestra historia" (Casciari 2009: 316).

La blogonovela fue escrita como resultado de una nostalgia tras asentarse Casciari en Barcelona, coincidiendo en el tiempo su nueva situación vital y su aproximación a la bitácora como formato de publicación. Es, en cierto sentido, una novela de un espíritu emigrado que mira

---

1 Protagonizada por Antonio Gasalla en el papel de Mirta.

atrás en su vida y se llena de regionalismos, usos lingüísticos propios del lunfardo y expresiones poco habituales para el lector español, pero propias de la cotidianidad de la vida bonaerense. La lejanía del hogar impacta en Casciari al tiempo que el choque cultural lo neutraliza como autor literario, al sentirse sin la capacidad de dominar con destreza suficiente el español peninsular en el que se hallaba inmerso, provocándole incluso dos años de parón creativo (Toledo 2005). Como extranjero, Casciari busca el contacto de sus amistades próximas, retratando a una mujer mercedina que soporta a una familia de lo más peculiar. Lo hace retratando los devenires de una vida humorística asentada en el retrato deformado de la realidad de esa región, un recuerdo infantil reflejado en las dedicatorias de las ediciones argentinas, pero no en la española (dedicada a su pareja, Cristina, durante el embarazo), al tiempo que en la edición impresa en Argentina de 2009 afirmaba que es "un documento de la vida cotidiana [...] escrito de puño y letra por una señora de mi pueblo que bien podría haber sido mi madre" (12).

Más allá de estas alteraciones en el ámbito paratextual, se dan cambios notables en el paso a la página impresa que en algunos casos han sido atribuidos específicamente a una dislocación de la historia para, precisamente, localizarla en el mercado español. Claudia García atribuye los cambios a esa traslación del público inicialmente previsto al receptor español (2010). Sin embargo, el análisis de García de la obra excluye la edición mexicana que, como dijimos, es virtualmente idéntica a la española. Igualmente, atribuye también muchos cambios a elementos idiosincrásicos españoles, incidiendo especialmente en lo que ella considera una visión negativa de la inmigración, como la sustitución de una mujer paraguaya en la original (la Negra Cabeza) por una guineana, un cambio que, afirma, se produce para reflejar "el malestar que provoca el tema inmigratorio en el tejido social español" (García 2010), sustentándose también en el retrato que se hace de la mendicidad puerta a puerta que, señala, se asocia en la versión española a inmigrantes, lo que "subraya la ilegalidad y el rasgo fenotípico, identificándolos con la pobreza" (2010). Estos y otros cambios los atribuye García a una "voluntad editorial de evitar cuestiones socialmente sensibles" (2010), pero eso justificaría *de facto* la omisión total de la novelización del blog, dada su voluntad continua de transgredir la cándida imagen prototípica de la familia, considerando incluso que la inmigración y su representación son el motor principal de la obra y que estas alteraciones se dan, en la edición española, con una "complacencia [que] no sólo traiciona el sentido de tolerancia frente a la inmigración que anima el blog [...] sino que es curiosamente ambigua en un autor que es, él mismo, un inmigrante en España" (2010). Sin embargo, como hemos visto, Casciari nos habla de la morriña (que habitualmente conlleva nostalgia positiva y crítica en la distancia) como motivación para la blogonovela, sin que la inmigración sea su fuerza motriz: en todo caso lo sería la emigración.

Traslación intercultural en la edición impresa

Una lectura de la novela impresa en España muestra que, en efecto, se adaptó y se produjeron modificaciones que en algunos casos surgieron directamente de propuestas de la editorial (Casciari 2008). El cambio muestra cierta voluntad por evitar la expresión "mujer gorda" que bautizó el blog en su concepción original (y la primera edición argentina). La blogonovela original cumplía con el objetivo de, mediante su espíritu transgresor, retratar paródicamente el carácter autoexploratorio del bloguero, pero su modificación no puede ser atribuible a una inferencia esencialmente española. Esta pérdida del título original es un claro movimiento de mercadotecnia: responde a la necesidad de no ofender al público femenino que desconozca el carácter satírico de la obra, evitando que, por su título, se generen prejuicios negativos ante el libro, recurriendo con el nuevo nombre a la búsqueda de una empatía maternal. Entre los cambios en la edición española, en esa misma línea, encontramos que el hijo pequeño, Caio, pasa a llamarse Toño; a Zacarías, el marido, ya no lo despiden de Plastivida, sino de unos astilleros; y Mirta Bertotti se transforma en Lola B., con reducción del apellido a la mera inicial, entre otros cambios en los nombres y en algunos rasgos lingüísticos específicos de determinados personajes. Ya no están en Argentina, sino en España, pero son historias coetáneas de un mundo globalizado. La vida de Mirta/Lola es prácticamente idéntica, pese a que el libro impreso introduce alteraciones y, sobre todo, supresiones: muchas son las cosas que se quedan en el blog y que no llegan a formar parte de la obra impresa en la edición española. Esos cambios son relevantes, pues implican alteraciones que van más allá de que los vulgarismos, los giros y expresiones sean sustituidos por otros mucho más familiares para el lector español (pese a que se mantienen italianismos en el idiolecto del abuelo Américo, llamado cariñosamente Nonno, que en el *blog* empleaba el cocoliche). Por lo tanto, la transfiguración en hoja impresa se divide en dos resultados diferenciados derivados de la cultura objetivo: la versión argentina mantiene esa identidad, pero para España se produce un reajuste para introducir referentes próximos a los históricos y culturales (alteración que fue revisada para México).

La edición de México se diferencia de la española en unos pocos rasgos anecdóticos vinculados a la variedad dialectal y a algunos matices culturales. Una lectura atenta a estas ediciones muestra que los rasgos diferenciales son poco trascendentales y ausentes por completo en la macroestructura de la narración. La composición y contenido de los capítulos de esta edición es idéntica, pero se han realizado cambios léxicos de referentes culturales, como el uso de *Papá Noel* (Casciari 2006b: 111) y *Santa Claus* (Casciari 2006c: 114) o de expresiones populares, sobre todo disfemismos: *pánfilo* (Casciari 2006b: 111) y *zoquete* (Casciari 2006c: 114). Los cambios en la edición mexicana con respecto a la española no introducen alteraciones en el significado ni orientación de la obra, pero sí la acercan al lenguaje cotidiano previsible de los personajes: no se trata de un caso de enculturación ni de aculturación para defender la existencia de una edición específica peninsular, como se desprende del análisis de García. En el blog, por su parte, nos encontramos con un uso extensivo de argentinismos, pero ese vocabulario se apoya en un sistema de breves definiciones emergentes (*pop-ups*) al pasar el cursor sobre esas palabras. Un mecanismo parecido se usa para ofrecer una pantalla emergente con información esencial sobre quién es cada personaje de la historia, aportando fotografía y descripción (Escandell 2010: 131).

En el capítulo titulado "Uno que pide", se nos presenta en la versión española un retrato de la mendicidad puerta a puerta, refiriéndose a esas personas como "inmigrantes que piden algo" (Casciari 2006b: 20-23), lo que no sucede en el blog, donde son "gente que pide" (<http://mujergorda.bitacoras.com/cap/000117.php>). En el mismo capítulo del blog se da también el retrato fenotípico ("el turco que vende alfombras") mientras el retrato social no está, en realidad, diferenciado entre las versiones. La principal alteración, de hecho, se da en Carnecruda, mendigo que proviene, en la versión española, de un país del Este y es descrito como "un mendigo de esos que antes, en sus países, eran profesionales, y que después se les ha ido de las manos, o sus países han desaparecido del mapa" (Casciari 2006b: 21), una visión asociada al mapa político tras la caída del telón de acero. En el blog, en ese mismo capítulo, es un mendigo local, "de esos que antes eran profesionales, y que después la vida se le fue de las manos", lo que tiene sentido en el contexto de la crisis de principios de milenio que experimentó el país. Las descripciones físicas responden a realidades socioculturales diferentes, pero el retrato de fondo que se hace del extranjero es compartido tanto por Mirta como por Lola sin que eso implique una demonización del inmigrante en ninguno de los casos.

Si, como apunta García, esos cambios se motivan en parte para evitar cuestiones sensibles en la sociedad española, deberían haberse eliminado o alterado sustancialmente los muchos pasajes sexuales que nos encontramos a lo largo de la obra. Sí se percibe, en cambio, una reducción de los episodios próximos a la violencia familiar, aunque queda patente una notable homofobia que el padre, Zacarías, proyecta sobre su hijo mayor, Nacho; un abuelo que consume estupefacientes; una hija, Sofi, ligera de cascos; y un hijo menor, Caio/Toño, cuya mayor habilidad reside en hacer estatuas con sus heces. Las omisiones y cambios responden, más bien, al cambio transmediático del paso del blog a la hoja impresa, concibiendo la novela no como una traslación textual sino como una adaptación al formato libro. Un ejemplo destacado lo encontramos en la eliminación de una serie de capítulos centrados en la hija en la novelización española. En todas las versiones Sofía, apenas adolescente, recibe reprimendas de su madre por su extensa experiencia sexual y mantiene sin alteraciones muchas de sus conductas e intervenciones. Sin embargo, sí que se elimina en la edición española una subtrama en torno al uso de una webcam para realizar espectáculos eróticos en línea. La supresión no puede justificarse por preocupaciones sociales o decorosas de la editorial para con el público español, sino por una preocupación acerca de la comprensión y recepción de la obra fuera de su contexto electrónico.

Otras omisiones en las ediciones impresas las encontramos en el uso de estructuras y referentes extraídos de otros blogs, como en el caso de la bitácora *Las cinco del viernes*, popular en 2003. Casciari lo integra en su blogonovela (cap. 26, 34, 57 y 72), pero no aparecen en ninguna de las ediciones impresas. Además de los capítulos interblogosferos, se pierde también la encuesta con la que Mirta quiere decidir si le es infiel a su marido (cap. 71 del blog), entre otros elementos nativamente digitales, como los comentarios de los lectores.

La blogonovela (y su traslación directa al papel para Argentina) es rica en digresiones, algo previsible en su concepción blogonovelística, dado el fuerte carácter atomista de las creaciones en línea, donde se espera que se interactúe con los lectores a través de los comentarios (Escandell 2010: 128), pero también que el carácter de baja ilación de las entradas facilite la incorporación de nuevos lectores en cualquier momento. Se trata, por tanto, de una estructura caótica donde el hilo narrativo queda en segundo plano, o incluso desaparece temporalmente, para luego retornar. Este factor se atenúa en la edición española, donde no solo desaparecen las fechas de los capítulos, sino que también se centra en las tramas del núcleo familiar, descubriéndose finalmente a Zacarías, el padre de familia, como el eje de la trama: la historia concluye cuando, tras lo acaecido con el hijo mayor, éste finalmente le convierte en abuelo y se enfrenta a la anagnórisis de su nuevo rol familiar. En la edición argentina, como en el blog, esto también sucede, pero en el cénit narrativo la historia no se cierra y se dilata un poco más, diluyéndose el efecto de clímax novelístico, fruto de una reducción de tramas y digresiones que concentra el núcleo de la obra.

Conclusión

No consideramos que el prejuicio social, étnico o moral que se pueda dar en la sociedad española sea la clave real de las alteraciones de la obra, pues al fin y al cabo la trasposición de nombres y usos lingüísticos no deja de ser puramente anecdótica. El auténtico elemento diferencial, es decir, lo que convierte a Lola en el reverso del retrato cubista de Mirta, es que emerge como un personaje novelístico, no blogonovelístico. Casciari reinscribe a Mirta en la transfiguración de Lola como reencarnación de la blogonovela en novela que es resultado de una reescritura casi completa del original. Mirta, por tanto, se mantiene viva en el blog y en el libro para Argentina, pero Lola es su otra cara, la novela que hubiera sido –que fue, de hecho– la creación literaria digital que, en su destino

libresco español, se amolda al devenir de su circunstancia y abraza, finalmente, a España para despedirse de la Argentina en la que cobró vida su
encarnación original.

Bibliografía

Casciari,   H.   2003.   *Más   respeto,   que   soy   tu   madre.*
  <http://mujergorda.bitacoras.com/> [consultado el 12.V.2012].
—. 2005. *Más respeto, que soy tu madre*, Barcelona, Plaza & Janés.
—. 2006a. *Diario de una mujer gorda,* Argentina, Debolsillo.
—. 2006b. *Más respeto, que soy tu madre,* Barcelona, Debolsillo.
—. 2006c. *Más respeto, que soy tu madre*, México, Grijalbo.
—. 2008. "Cómo se construyó *Más respeto, que soy tu madre*", *Clarin.com*
  <http://edant.clarin.com/diario/2008/08/06/um/m-01730811.htm>
  [consultado el 12.V.2012].
—. 2009. *Más respeto, que soy tu madre,* Argentina, Plaza & Janés.
Escandell Montiel, D. 2010. "The Writer Seeking Vengeance:
  Blognovelism and its Relationship with Literary Critics", in S. C.
  Bibb & D. Escandell (eds.), *Best Served Cold: Studies on Revenge*,
  Oxford, ID-Press, 127-34.
García, C. 2010. "Mirta Berttoti se transforma en Lola B. Re-
  inscripciones textuales y representación social en *Más respeto que
  soy tu madre*, de Hernán Casciari", *Espéculo. Revista de estudios
  literarios* 46, <http://www.ucm.es/info/especulo/numero46/ mas-
  respe.html> [consultado el 12.V.2012].
Lejeune, P. 1991. "El pacto autobiográfico", *Anthropos: Boletín de in-
  formación y documentación* 29, 47-62.
Sibilia, P. 2008. *La intimidad como espectáculo*, El Salvador, Fondo de
  Cultura Económica.
Toledo, B. 2005. "El ama de casa más leída de Internet se llama Hernán
  Casciari", Informativos Telecinco.com, <http://www.informativos.
  telecinco.es/entrevista/casciari/mujer-gorda/dn_9367.htm>
  [consultado el 12.V.2012].

Mireya Fernández Merino

Miradas de reconocimiento: El Yo y el Otro en *Praisesong for the Widow* de Paule Marshall

La búsqueda de los orígenes es uno de los temas que alimenta la creación literaria. La narrativa que nace en el seno de las distintas diásporas caribeñas no escapa a esta tendencia, de tal modo que los escritores circunscritos a este ámbito geográfico frecuentemente enfatizan la necesidad de identificación que tiene el ser humano con un espacio y un territorio, la vuelta a casa y el reconocerse en la semejanza. El desplazamiento corresponde en muchos de los relatos con una búsqueda de sí mismo, una toma de conciencia que se despliega a partir de la diferencia entre el Yo y el Otro.

La escritura de la novelista afroamericana Paule Marshall, nacida en Brooklyn en 1929, es un buen ejemplo de ello. La autora de familia barbadiense dibuja con su pluma el retrato de esta comunidad antillana que, desde finales del siglo XIX, comenzó a emigrar a los Estados Unidos. En sus novelas, se reconstruye el desplazamiento, la lucha por labrarse un camino, el olvido de una identidad colectiva y la necesidad de rescatar y reivindicar la huella de las diásporas africanas. La creación literaria representa el movimiento pendular entre la contingencia del presente y la genealogía del pasado, es decir, un vivir entre dos tiempos, el de la acción y el de la memoria, y también entre dos lugares, el del espacio habitado y aquel que se ha dejado atrás (Boyarín y Boyarín 2002; Santos 2000). La conciencia de una identidad colectiva se refuerza o se debilita en función de las fuerzas moldeadoras del momento y de la herencia remota, del estatus que arrastran estos legados y la posición relativa de los grupos respecto a su entorno: en resumen, las circunstancias políticas, sociales y económicas que condicionan la personalidad del individuo y el peso de su comunidad (Isaac 1989). Son estos aspectos sobre los que se dibuja el fresco ficcional, la representación del "nosotros-ellos", el poder o la debilidad de cada colectivo, la forma cómo se celebran o rechazan los valores propios y ajenos.

Una mirada a la obra de Marshall —desde su primera y reconocida novela *Brown Girl, Brownstones* (1959) hasta el reciente libro de memorias *Triangular Road* (2009)— muestra su interés por recrear el conflicto que anida en el seno de estas comunidades: la fuerza que los impulsa a sobrevivir, a adaptarse a la sociedad receptora, y aquella que se sustenta en la reacción contraria, es decir, el apego y la defensa de su cultura. A esto se suma el tema racial, pues los antillanos sufren, por el color de la piel, los mismos prejuicios que la colectividad negra de los Estados Unidos, ya que se intensifica la diferencia entre el modo de vida de la sociedad norteamericana y el de los caribeños. Su empeño no queda en marcar estos contrastes. La autora establece además los puntos de contacto y de alejamiento entre los dos colectivos negros cuyo origen común no borra la distancia que los separa. La representación del Yo y del Otro se enriquece y despliega el complejo entramado que la sustenta. Marshall traspasa los relatos maniqueos y penetra el oscuro laberinto de la identidad, ilumina las diferentes aristas. Su tercera novela, *Praisesong for the Widow*, por la cual fue galardonada con el premio Before Columbus Foundation American Book Award, es un ejemplo de esta afirmación.

El extravío espiritual es el tema central de dicha novela, publicada en el año 1983. El discurso narrativo asume la forma de viaje iniciático. El personaje de Avey Johnson, una viuda de setenta años, sufre una crisis existencial, mientras realiza un crucero por el Caribe. La travesía se transforma en una búsqueda interior, un reencuentro consigo misma y con sus raíces africanas. Marshall hace uso de la estructura arquetipal para construir la historia. Las partes de la novela —"Runagate", "Sleeper's Wake", "Lave Tête" y "The Beg Pardon"— simbolizan una etapa del viaje físico y espiritual del personaje.

La síntesis de la historia ayuda al lector a comprender el desarrollo de la trama y el valor metafórico de su contenido. Un extraño malestar ataca a la protagonista. Su decisión de abandonar el barco y regresar en un vuelo a Nueva York se ve frustrada, pues la mujer debe permanecer en Grenada a la espera de un vuelo el día siguiente. El rumbo del relato hace que la mujer conozca a un anciano, Lebert Joseph, quien le propone que lo acompañe en la peregrinación que cada año hacen los inmigrantes de Carriacou a su isla natal. La travesía se convierte en el nudo dramático de los acontecimientos. Avey Johnson atraviesa las aguas turbulentas del mar que separa las dos ínsulas y se incorpora a la celebración.

El lector es testigo del drama privado. La mujer negra ha asimilado los valores que imperan en la sociedad estadounidense, asumido el statu quo y olvidado las tradiciones y costumbres de las comunidades de origen africano. Es este el nudo del conflicto. Sin hacer uso de clichés o discursos altisonantes, Marshall describe la herida psíquica del personaje. El contraste entre un sector de esa sociedad y otro se estructura mediante un conjunto de símbolos. La contraposición trasciende, sin embargo, la diferencia entre blancos y negros para focalizar aquella que se alza entre afroamericanos y antillanos. Avey Johnson representa a los primeros mientras que el anciano y los habitantes de Carriacou, a los segundos; la imagen de un nos-otros entre los descendientes de África.

El título de la primera parte del relato, "Runagate", revela su contenido y el rol que desempeña el personaje en la historia; Avey es la oveja perdida que ha abandonado el redil. La descripción de la protagonista, el número de maletas con que viaja, la elegancia de sus trajes y joyas son la muestra de su nivel de vida. El crucero se convierte en símbolo de su posición. El nombre de éste, Bianca Pride, no deja lugar a dudas. Todo en la nave reluce como una joya y sorprende a los pasajeros: "All that dazzling white steel!" (Marshall 1983: 15). El brillo refuerza la capacidad de deslumbrar y enceguecer. Es esto lo que le ha ocurrido al personaje.

El conflicto de Avey Johnson se desata en medio del evento más importante del crucero, la tradicional cena del capitán, en el gran salón, con su decoración Luis XIV, plata y cristal en todas las mesas. La indisposición física que experimenta tiene un culpable, el *Peach Parfait à la Versailles*, rodajas y sorbete de melocotón bajo capas de suculenta nata. La descripción de la nave, del comedor y del postre brinda un *crescendo* de luminosidad y blancura que desata la batalla. El simbolismo apela a un orden social determinado, el modo opulento de lujo y riqueza material (Fernández 2007). El personaje ha abrazado el sueño americano y sufre las molestias de su "indigestión psíquica", la revulsión interna ante ese mundo de lujos y comodidades que hacen de ella una mujer diferente a lo que era en su infancia y juventud. "Pieles negras, máscaras blancas": el título de la obra de Frantz Fanon (1952) sin duda resulta aquí apropiado para describir la condición del personaje. La escena en el comedor, la imposibilidad que siente de reconocer a la mujer vestida de crepé de china y perlas, revela su extrañeza ante la imagen de la mujer alta y de piel oscura que no es otra que ella misma reflejada en el espejo. Comienza así el periplo que conduce a Avey Johnson a desenterrar su otro yo hundido en las profundidades de la psique.

El revulsivo físico se acompaña de uno interior. Marshall enriquece el viaje iniciático del personaje con otro de los elementos recurrentes en este tipo de narración: los sueños. Su contenido muestra las fuerzas que combaten en la mente de la protagonista. Las imágenes recuperan pasajes de la infancia: la presencia de la tía abuela Cuney, los paseos junto a ella por la isla de Tatem en Carolina del Sur, la leyenda que le contaba sobre los antiguos indígenas Ibos. Otras imágenes anuncian la desintegración del mundo que se ha construido: el servicio de plata, la fina vajilla y cristalería, la gran lámpara de cristal, todo convertido en cenizas. En síntesis, el choque entre el mundo de la infancia y el de la madurez, entre las costumbres familiares y aquellas que ha asimilado en su ascenso social.

A estas imágenes oníricas se suma la figura del marido, Jerome Johnson, que surge ante ella como una aparición para recriminarle el abandono del crucero. El contraste entre los primeros años de matrimonio cuando la pareja habitaba un humilde apartamento en Brooklyn y los últimos tiempos en su residencia en North White Plains, después de que Jerome Johnson se hubiera convertido en un próspero hombre de negocios, revela el antes y el después en la vida de la pareja. El personaje del esposo se convierte en el eje central de la segunda parte del relato. La metamorfosis que sufre es el antecedente de la transformación que experimenta la mujer. El prejuicio racial que enfrenta la sociedad norteamericana lo asimila cuando logra el éxito económico. Las palabras son el eco de estereotipos y prejuicios: "That's the trouble with half these Negroes you see out here. Always looking for the white man to give them something instead of getting out and doing for themselves" (Marshall 1983: 131). El proceso de blanqueamiento lo aleja de sus semejantes al asumir como propios los criterios simplistas y encasillados sobre los negros. El joven Jay da paso al respetable y exitoso Jerome. El cambio de nombre tipifica la escisión del personaje. Lo mismo ocurre con Avey Johnson: su nombre, Avatara, ha quedado en el olvido. Como en los cuentos de hadas, los protagonistas han sido víctimas de un encantamiento. En este relato se produce la asimilación de los valores del WASP, es decir, del hombre blanco, anglosajón y protestante.

Marshall da forma narrativa a los postulados que explican el proceso de blanqueamiento de la raza. La autora convierte en trama novelesca la necesidad del hombre negro de mimetizarse en un mundo de blancos.

Pero esta actitud de "ser como el otro", en lugar de transformarse en un arma de resistencia (Bhabha 1994), abre paso a la alienación. El conflicto nace cuando la metamorfosis se hace de manera inconsciente, cuando las falsas creencias sobre el Otro, en este caso la población negra, se asumen como verdaderas y alejan a los sujetos de su cultura. La autora recrea la posesión por la máscara; el precio que pagan los personajes tras su éxito social. Por ello, el tema del viaje adquiere especial relevancia en la tercera parte de la novela.

El encuentro con Lebert Joseph y la travesía a la isla de Carriacou son las secuencias centrales. La figura del anciano adopta en el relato la función del ayudante que guía con su sabiduría a Avey Johnson en las diferentes pruebas. Las palabras del viejo enfatizan la importancia de mantener vivas las tradiciones, las razones que impulsan a los carriacouenses a volver año tras año a su lugar de origen: la visita a la familia, el reencuentro con la tierra, pero, sobre todo, el culto a los antepasados, "The Old Parents, The Long-Time People". Su discurso señala también el alto precio que se paga cuando se les arroja al olvido. Los argumentos convencen a la mujer. La alteridad cobra así forma en el relato.

La secuencia del desplazamiento se llena de connotaciones. En la embarcación, el sonido del viento y la charla en *patois* de las mujeres que la rodean activan los recuerdos. Avey Johnson rememora los días de la niñez, el paseo anual junto a sus padres y otras familias negras por el río Hudson, a bordo de otra nave, el Robert Fulton. Recuerda la sensación de estar unida a todos ellos a través de un cordón invisible: "she would feel what seemed to be hundreds of slender threads steaming out from her navel and from the place where her heart was to enter those around her" (Marshall 1983: 190). La evocación revive los sentimientos de pertenencia al grupo.

Marshall establece un paralelismo entre el pasado y el presente del personaje para enfatizar la proximidad entre los negros de Estados Unidos y los de las islas del Caribe. La experiencia de los isleños se convierte en recordatorio de los ritos que mantenían unida a la comunidad negra en la ciudad de Nueva York. La peregrinación anual actúa como un espejo en el que el personaje comienza a reconocer la semejanza con esos Otros a quienes había marcado, en un primer momento, con el signo de la diferencia. El Otro no es el blanco; es el negro antillano cuya presencia despierta la conciencia dormida de la protagonista.

La autora enfatiza la importancia de la integración en el grupo cuando introduce en la historia el elemento religioso: la reunión en la iglesia durante el tiempo de Pascua, las palabras del reverendo, el sermón sobre la resurrección de Cristo, todo ello una alegoría que la autora emplea para representar la identidad del colectivo y la posibilidad de reconocerse en el Otro. La escena funciona como bisagra narrativa. La náusea que siente el personaje durante la ceremonia se repite mientras navega hacia la pequeña isla. La expulsión de la materia descompuesta que arroja Avey Johnson en el plano físico simboliza, en el espiritual, la liberación de los demonios que anidan en el personaje. Al llegar a la isla, su cuerpo es lavado y ungido en aceites. El ritual de purificación prepara a la mujer para participar en la ceremonia que se describe en el episodio final (Fernández 2007).

"The Beg Pardon", título de la última parte de la novela, es el nombre de la festividad y el estado que alcanza el personaje cuando participa junto a los isleños en el rito anual. La mujer, a semejanza de las heroínas de los cuentos, ha cumplido las tareas y logrado cruzar el umbral de los iniciados. El baile alrededor del círculo la convierte en un miembro más de la comunidad de Carriacou. La experiencia la lleva a rememorar otra danza, el Ring Shout, en la que participaba su tía abuela en Carolina del Sur. El deseo de ser parte de aquel ritual se hace realidad en ese momento, cuando logra compartir con los isleños y rendir honores a los antepasados. La escena en el patio de la vieja casa de Lebert Joseph conduce finalmente a Avey Johnson al reencuentro con sus raíces:

And for the time since she was a girl, she felt the threads, that myriad of shiny, silken, brightly colored threads (like the kind used in embroidery) which were thin to the point of invisibility yet as strong as the ropes at Coney Island. Looking outside the church in Tatem, standing waiting for the Robert Fulton on the crowded pier at 125th Street, she used to feel them streaming out of everyone there to enter her, making her part of what seemed a far-reaching, wide-ranging confraternity.

Now, suddenly, as if she were that girl again, with her entire life yet to live, she felt the threads streaming out from the old people around her in Lebert Joseph's yard. From their seared eyes. From their navels and their cast-iron hearts. And their brightness as they entered her spoke of possibilities and becoming even in the face of their bared bones and their burnt-out ends (Marshall 1983: 249).

Paule Marshall crea una historia de reconciliación. La autora se vale del personaje para mostrar que el camino de la reivindicación social no está reñido con el homenaje a las costumbres y tradiciones heredadas de los antiguos esclavos. La representación del Yo y del Otro trasciende los lugares comunes y las historias trilladas. Su experiencia como mujer negra de familia antillana, nacida en los Estados Unidos amplía y enriquece su perspectiva. La diferencia no está únicamente en el color de la piel. La alteridad se tiñe con los colores del ébano.

La novela revela la vigencia de un tópico en la literatura de todos los tiempos: el viaje. La repetición temática evidencia, sin embargo, su continuidad y su diferencia. El lector podría anticipar que, en ese rescate de las tradiciones y costumbres, Marshall conduciría a sus personajes hacia las costas africanas. El viaje a ese continente ha sido tema recurrente de los escritores de las diásporas. No obstante, la autora rompe el molde y sitúa el reencuentro en un espacio cercano, en una isla del Caribe. Sus raíces familiares sellan el cambio de rumbo. A semejanza de lo que acaece al personaje principal al final de la novela, la escritora neoyorquina de familia barbadiense preserva sus propias raíces. Escoger la isla como espacio de reencuentro con su herencia cultural no es una decisión arbitraria. Durante su infancia, aprendió el arte de contar historias (Marshall 2001). Las charlas de su madre y de las otras mujeres de la isla alrededor de la cocina fueron entretenimiento y legado: una tradición oral que preserva y a la que rinde honor con sus escritos. La historia de Avey Johnson es su canto personal, su *praise song* para alumbrar el camino de regreso de aquellos que se han perdido y quieren volver, como el hijo pródigo, a casa.

Bibliografía

Bhabha, H. 1994. *The Location of Culture*, London & New York, Routledge.

Boyarin, J. & D. Boyarin. 2002. *Powers of Diaspora. Two Essays on the Relevance of Jewish Culture*, Minneapolis, U of Minnesota P.

Fanon, F. 1952. *Peau noire, masques blancs*, Paris, Editions du Seuil.

Fernández, M. 2007. "El viaje a la isla. *Praisesong for the Widow* de Paule Marshall", *Actualidades* 18-19, 87-108.

Isaac, H. 1989. *Idols of the Tribe*, Cambridge, Cambridge UP.

Marshall, P. 2001. "From the Poets in the Kitchen", *Callaloo* 24: 2, 627-33.

—. 1983. *Praisesong for the Widow*, New York, Plume.

Santos, M. 2000. *La naturaleza del espacio. Técnica y tiempo. Razón y emoción*, Barcelona, Ariel.

MARIA FERRER-LIGHTNER

"Moneda de regne estrany": Veus i identitats

Un dels elements més atractius del teatre ibèric del Renaixement és la presència, no majoritària, de la figura de l'estranger o de l'Altre com a personatge preferentment secundari. En termes generals, algunes mostres de teatre en castellà, en portuguès o en català de la primera meitat del segle XVI, on hi trobem aquest tipus, el fan servir com un element dramàtic que aporta comicitat. És a dir, la representació dels gitanos, de l'home i la dona subsaharians, la de l'àrab, el francès i el luterà, es converteix en un recurs escènic que complementa la teatralitat de l'obra. En el cas d'alguns *autos viejos* o drames sacres, però, hi trobem una intenció molt més senyalada: la presència d'una càrrega ideològica, social i religiosa, creada, per una banda, per la reafirmació del castellà com a llengua oficial de les Corones unificades i, per l'altra, pels nous preceptes catòlics, sortits del Concili, que pretengueren fer front a la Reforma luterana estesa ja per Europa. Aquest càrrega ideològica, dèiem, converteix els personatges estrangers o de fora de la cultura local en víctimes de llur existència.

Els estrangers, o fins i tot la població ibèrica, parlen en cada cas en un "argot" que barreja paraules del castellà i paraules de les seves llengües. El Luterà no parla alemany, sinó un italià corrupte. En general, tots els tipus estan parodiats. En la literatura ibèrica, les figures del Biscaí, el Bobo i el Moro ja eren tipus còmics permanents; a més a més, en aquesta ocasió i en aquests personatges, s'afegeix el tret de pecador a la ja adjudicada estrangeria. En la parla del Moro observem les característiques del seu argot, un ús excessiu del parlar papissot (és a dir, el *ceceo* castellà), la falta de conjugació de verbs, la confusió entre ser i estar, la barreja de pronoms personals i l'intercanvi entre oclusives labials: l'ús de *b* en comptes de *p* (*tenbrano* per "temprano", *becado* per "pecado" i *boder* per "poder"). Finalment, veiem que l'estructura sintàctica no s'adapta sempre a la castellana. Quant al Biscaí, s'aprecia de seguida el seu to sever i distant, també el fet que el propi personatge es refereix a sí ma-

teix en segona persona i fins i tot en tercera persona quan el sentim respondre al personatge Amor ("vizcayno has granjeado"). També l'ús excessiu d'infinitius en comptes de la conjugació corresponent i, en general, la falta bàsica de concordança gramatical.

En aquest treball ens agradaria aprofundir en algunes obres que in-
clouen alguns dels personatges esmentats. Endevinem un doble joc. Per
una banda, la *deficiència* lingüística dels personatges es converteix en
una arma contra ells. Són estrangers i com a tals no dominen el castellà,
que és la llengua vehicular (social) de l'obra. El domini i l'ús de la llengua es converteix en un element clau que determina el personatge. Per
altra banda, la seva qualitat de foraster els condemna moralment: són
"moneda de regne estrany", tal com ens mostra la *Farsa sacramental de
la Moneda* (Rouanet 1901). La influència de tot el que ve de fora és considerada dolenta perquè és diferent i suposa un canvi del que està establert; així doncs, és socialment negativa i moralment perjudicial. L'ús de
llengües variades, del galimaties i de l'argot, en gran part del teatre del
segle XVI, reflecteix la representació i les actituds lingüístiques que
acaben esdevenint, en algunes obres d'aquest teatre religiós, elements
d'inclusió o exclusió moral i social. Segons Enrique Rull, no es pot explicar l'origen d'aquestes peces religioses només apel·lant a motivacions
antiprotestants; aquest crític conclou que, malgrat no ser contrareformis-
ta en els seus orígens, l'*auto* a la llarga fa més palès i explícit el seu con-
trareformisme (Rull 1986).[1] Llengua i religió també en aquest moment
històric han assolit una qualitat de complement i d'equivalència on la
força d'una alimenta a l'altra i viceversa.

Les obres es troben recollides en els volums que va publicar Léo
Rouanet el 1901, amb el títol *Autos, Farsas y Coloquios del siglo XVI*
(96 peces). Mercedes de los Reyes Peña va publicar-ne una edició nova
l'any 1988, que s'afegeix a l'estudi d'una part del *corpus* que ja havia
realitzat Pérez Priego (1988). Són obres quasi bé totes anònimes, que
presenten segons cada crític una classificació temàtica variada: un grup
ampli sense referències eucarístiques i un altre, més reduït, subdividit en
les que fan o no referències al Santíssim Sagrament (Hermenegildo
2001: 116-17). En general, se suposa que van ser escrites a la segona
meitat del segle XVI. Són obres d'elevada concentració dogmàtica, sentit

---

1   Sobre aquesta polèmica mantinguda entre Eduardo González Pedroso (1864) i
     Marcel Bataillon (1940), vegeu Poppenberg (2000).

figurat i gran militarisme. Els seus personatges són força variats, com ja hem indicat. Les farses dels sagraments fan servir una nova fórmula, l'al·legoria, amb referents a la realitat contemporània o a successos de la vida diària (Pérez Priego 1998: 37). A la *Farsa sacramental de la Moneda* aquesta realitat es percep mitjançant al·lusions a disposicions de l'època sobre l'encunyació de moneda. També es reconeix el personatge de Concilio, en relació al Concili de Trento (1545 i 1563) i la referència a la Pragmàtica reial de 1566.

La representació literària de l'Altre, en l'àmbit del teatre occidental, es fa palesa ja en obres dramàtiques clàssiques gregues, on un personatge de fora de la comunitat es presenta parlant en una varietat lingüística diferent o en una altra llengua, fins i tot inventada (Coulter 1934: 137). Entre els seus objectius s'endevina el de voler crear intencionadament comicitat a l'obra teatral, sempre tan necessària. El Renaixement va traslladar la presència de l'Altre al teatre europeu en part també amb el mateix objectiu. Però seria enganyar-nos el pensar que aquesta presència es degué només a l'afany de fer riure. A continuació insinuem tres punts que alhora que es presenten com elements independents, són necessaris: les actituds i representacions sociolingüístiques, els espais socials on succeeixen les interaccions, i els agents que hi participen.

Segons Ralph Fasold (1984), la definició de l'actitud lingüística en general es limita als estudis de les actituds cap a la llengua per sí mateixa; reconeix, però, que la majoria dels estudis amplien la definició per incloure-hi actituds cap als parlants d'una llengua o dialecte (148). La llengua acaba funcionant com un símbol de pertinença a una comunitat social o religiosa. Segons Angela L. Di Tullio (2003), les actituds i representacions lingüístiques d'una comunitat expliquen els comportaments, els quals l'estudiosa classifica en dues categories segons la seva naturalesa: com esquemes conceptuals que configuren "el imaginario social" i com esquemes afectius que formen la ideologia (37). Pep Subirós (2010) recull la idea quan fa referència a les diferències culturals com a pretext. Parla de situacions estructurals, profundament enquistades, que es retroalimenten contínuament (30-31). Aquests comportaments es desenvolupen en els espais lingüístic i religiós quan s'assumeixen veritats històriques originades en mites i tradicions. Les obres teatrals escollides ens permeten descobrir, a partir del comportament de personatges, el conjunt dels factors que defineixen les seves actituds vers els altres, en la forma del desconeixement que hi ha entre ells, les pors, les amenaces que senten, la llengua que parlen, que actua com un mur que els separa i es converteix en una amenaça per la comunitat, l'ús de codis lingüístics que els permet l'entrada a la comunitat d'acollida i, en ocasions, la seva pròpia invisibilitat.

En un primer exemple de les actituds i comportaments s'observa ja la mala relació que hi ha entre alguns personatges a la *Farsa del sacramento llamada de los Lenguajes*, on els comentaris del Bobo sobre alguns dels individus que desfilen davant d'Amor Divino el dia del Judici Final, enfilen els ànims. Així el sentim comentar en contra del Luterà i la seva parla: "Pesi a mi con el sinson, / Y su lengua de estropajo!" (275).[2] Per la seva banda, el Portuguès, molt d´acord amb el seu caràcter orgullós, no estalvia una resposta tallant al Bobo: "N´abra un pase su merçe, / Castejao mal mirado!" (209). Evidentment, les baralles entre ells són aprofitades per Amor Divino per demostrar amb cert esperit ecumènic que s'han d'unir tots sota un mateix codi religiós. Cadascun d'ells és acusat d'alguna cosa (orgull, mala fe, amor propi, heretgia) a la qual intenten respondre sense massa èxit. Al final de l'obra tots es penedeixen i així ho expressen:

> BOBO: Digo que yo me arrepiento / de cuanto a Dios [e] ofendido (365-66).
> MORO: A, mi xonior, yo te pido / que me dax batiçamiento (367-68).
> VYZCAINO: Juras a Dios, Vizcayno / lloras culpas y pecados (370-71).
> PORTUGUÉS: Juro por consagraçon / en fazer repentimento" (377-78).
> LUTERANO: Dichi que tu esta, ti adovero / e biasfemo de Lutero" (388-89).

A manera d'exemple que mostra els estereotips, hi ha les crítiques que el Bobo de l'*Aucto de la Huida de Egipto* fa a les dones gitanes quan una de elles es nega a donar alberg a la Verge, a Josep i al nen Jesús que fugen d'Herodes. El Bobo diu: "Aquestos del gitanaje, / soncas, no tienen pelaje" (232-33). I malgrat que una d'elles, la segona gitana, els dóna acollida —"Mira que zomos prezonaz" (272) —, el Bobo insisteix: "Mi fee, no soys, si ladronas / que nos venis a hurtar" (275). Un cop els ànims es calmen, les gitanes llegeixen la bonaventura a la Verge. En aquesta escena, es produeix un d'aquells moments en els quals els personatges que no pertanyen a la comunitat religiosa demostren un nivell d'assimilació important. En aquest cas, són les gitanes les encarregades

---

2   Totes les cites són de l'edició de Rouanet (1901) i la numeració es refereix als versos.

d'explicar al públic la Història Sagrada. És una clara ruptura del principi d'adequació estilística (lingüística i moral), segons el qual el personatge de fora del cercle religiós és l'encarregat d'explicar la doctrina cristiana. El sincretisme religiós es fa present.

Quant als espais socials de les interaccions, distingim d'una banda el lingüístic i de l'altra el religiós. Pep Subirós els inclou dins els prejudicis bioculturals amb la raça i l'ètnia, com a elements que constitueixen el "racisme de baixa intensitat" (34). En relació al primer espai —el lingüístic—, des de finals del segle XV i durant tot el segle XVI, Europa ha experimentat un moviment filològic clau, recolzat per l'aparició en l'esfera política de l'estat modern, en el qual les llengües romàniques s'han posat a l'altura social i intel·lectual que els pertoca, rellevant el llatí en matèries oficials. L'estat modern, amb la monarquia autoritària, va necessitar la fortalesa i seguretat d'una llengua nacional que el recolzés i que l'ajudés en el propòsit de la unificació que perseguia. Per altra banda, els descobriments, els viatges, la curiositat intel·lectual i l'economia són factors que exposen una societat a la diversitat; així mateix, si l'àmbit geogràfic és extens i s'amplia (Amèrica), cal trobar una sèrie d'elements unificadors. Amb la reunificació de les corones Castellana i Catalano-Aragonesa, el castellà a la Península es converteix en la llengua hereva del llatí. Ofereix així una fortalesa, un pedigrí cultural i un espai demogràfic important, entre altres factors, que l'eleven a ser la llengua del futur imperi espanyol. La monarquia ha de cohesionar la societat. La llengua i el seu ús es converteixen en elements determinants d'identitat comunitària. Cal afegir també un altre factor, un cop la llengua oficial ha estat reconeguda: el grau de puresa de la mateixa. El concepte de puresa de la llengua té dues vessants, tal com es dedueix irònicament de les paraules de Nebrija en el pròleg de la seva *Gramática Castellana*: unificar i "reduzir en artificio este nuestro lenguaje castellano" (fol. 2v.), és a dir, eliminar el que és incorrecte i estranger. Com comenta Di Tullio, "Para preservar la identidad e integridad nacionales, se impone contrarrestar el cambio y las interferencias de otras lenguas" (31). L'ascens de la llengua castellana a la Península —i a fora— fa que aquesta *deficiència* lingüística sigui molt més significativa. És amb aquest contrast lingüístic que es posa tot al descobert, i és amb el comportament social i espiritual dels que la pateixen que es reforça la fermesa de l'estructura de la llengua. Hi ha un fet rellevant que recolza les estrictes actituds lingüístiques de l'Espanya del moment: la poca producció de gramàtiques d'altres llengües, en contra del gran augment de gramàtiques del castellà publicades fora d'Espanya (Lope Blanch 1986).

L'altre espai social és el de la religió. El destí de la llengua s'associarà al destí de l'imperi i, fent-ne un ús ideològic, s'associarà també al dogma catòlic com a instrument de conquesta, conversió i imitació. També caldria afegir-hi la influència del providencialisme i així queda reflectit en la literatura mitjançant personatges de diferents estaments o que poden pertànyer al món espiritual o al terrenal, i que també parlen diverses llengües o variants lingüístiques (Ferrer 2010: 383). La reposició dels valors catòlics del Concili de Trento (1545-1562) com a reacció a la Reforma protestant es va manifestar en el teatre a través d'aquests *autos* i farses així com en els posteriors *autos sacramentales* barrocs. La defensa de l'espai religiós es tradueix en l'obra dramàtica en un contrast exagerat i còmic de personatges de fora de la comunitat que s'han de justificar constantment i demanar perdó per no formar-ne part. Les paraules de la segona gitana vistes anteriorment així ho confirmen. També les de l'àrab de la *Farsa del sacramento llamada de los Lenguajes*, que diu: "Xenpre yo estar ben creado, / mi no hurtar, ni matar, / ni hacer otro becado" (122-24). Les diferències lingüístiques funcionen com la clau que obre l'abisme entre personatges. La figura de l'Altre presenta la incorrecció lingüística o una ridícula imitació d'una llengua estrangera en un to en ocasions innocent i defensiu. El seu missatge expressa la incomprensió que rep; innocentment revela la seva filiació no catòlica, circumstància que fa que en ocasions se'l condemni sense cap explicació.

El contingut ideològic es fa palès. El llenguatge mixt en forma d'argot o mala imitació de llengua estrangera representa les influències herètiques que vénen de fora. A l'al·legòrica *Farsa sacramental de la Moneda* (LXXXIV), Jesucrist mateix no només es fa ressò del moviment de la Reforma protestant que amenaçava Europa, sinó que proposa més endavant reencarnar-se ell mateix en un metall nou. Les seves paraules reflecteixen la presència perniciosa de tot allò que ve de fora. L'obra està escrita en un to de crida militar en el qual apel·la els seus "oficiales" i altres subordinats a "tomar tarea". Al final de l'obra, hi ha la venjança esperada: un Luterà que estava pres és condemnat a morir a la foguera.

No tots els dramaturgs de l'època feren servir l'estranger o la figura de l'Altre, però a la llarga s'acabaren convertint en personatges estereotipats. Socialment, el món oficial se separa del món no-oficial, com ja hem pogut comprovar amb l'ús de la llengua i la religió. En general se'ls tracta com a personatges que pertanyen a un grup indefinit d'infidels o gent deslleial. No aporten res de bo a la societat que els acull i aquesta els mira amb recel i por. En ocasions utilitzen un llenguatge específic que els serveix de codi d'entrada per accedir al món oficial. En altres ocasions, és tant patent la seva invisibilitat que fins i tot no tenen nom, tal com observem en les obres esmentades. Se'ls reconeix quan parlen pel gentilici que fan servir o pel grup ètnic o raça a la qual pertanyen: la dona negra, la gitana, el moro, etc. En els casos més extrems, perden el seu nom en veure'l canviat per un altre que els assimila i els fa invisibles socialment; en aquests casos, el bescanvi que han fet per guanyar la inclusió els porta a una pèrdua d'identitat social. Aquest fenomen es repeteix al llarg de la història de la literatura en tots els seus gèneres. A *La aurora en Copacabana* (1661) de Calderón de la Barca, la verge inca Guacolda passa a ser María i el seu company Iupangui, Francisco, un cop han abandonat Idolatria. Més proper a nosaltres, a *L'últim patriarca* de Najat El Hachmi, llegim un veredicte semblant respecte a Mimoun quan aconsegueix una feina: "Per cert, li havia dit l'oncle, com que li costa molt de dir el teu nom, diu que a partir d'ara et diràs Manel" (83). En definitiva, és el món no oficial desposseït de cultura i identitat, que s'ha vist superat per l'oficial que paradoxalment el necessita.

El teatre del Renaixement peninsular està encara molt lligat al seu teatre medieval i es limita a dos àmbits socials claus, el cortesà i el religiós. El teatre religiós va seguir sent el més assequible a la massa popular. A partir de la segona meitat de segle, les obres es van posar a càrrec de grups de professionals, la qual cosa va portar canvis de qualitat i quantitat a les festes religioses del Corpus. Un element que va donar volum i personalitat a alguns personatges va ser el donar-los una llengua o una particularitat lingüística diferent. Aquest ús es convertí, a parer nostre, en un mecanisme escènic d'una teatralitat inesperada, que omplia la manca d'altres elements dramàtics en un teatre encara primitiu.

Per acabar, aquest petit grup d'*autos* i farses vells no van constituir un fenomen aïllat. El teatre ibèric de la primera meitat del segle XVI, des del castellà Juan del Encina al portuguès Gil Vicente, ja havia recollit la figura de l'Altre i l'apropava al seu públic. Tot i que un dels objectius més clars va ser el de fer riure, l'objectiu religiós de difondre les "veritats eternes" del moment també es va materialitzar en alguns d'aquests *autos viejos*, en textos de certa dificultat al·legòrica, amb finalitat propagandística i un militarisme exigent, on la figura de l'Altre es mou entre la despossessió i l'assimilació total.

Bibliografia

Coulter, C. 1934. "The Speech of Foreigners in Greek and Latin Comedies", *Philological Quarterly* 13, 135-39.

Di Tullio, A. L. 2003. *Políticas lingüísticas e inmigración. El caso argentino,* Buenos Aires, Eudeba.

El Hachmi, N. 2001. *L'últim patriarca,* Barcelona, Planeta.

Fasold, R. 1984. *The Sociolinguistics of Society,* New York, Blackwell.

Ferrer Agell, M. J. 2010. "El lenguaje mixto en el teatro peninsular y en castellano de finales del siglo XV a mediados del siglo XVI". Tesis doctoral, Madrid, UNED.

Hermenegildo, A. 2001. *El teatro del siglo XVI,* Madrid, Júcar.

Lope Blanch, J. M. 1986. "La lingüística española del Siglo de Oro", in D. Kosoff et al. (coords.), *Actas del VIII Congreso de la Asociación Internacional de Hispanistas,* vol. 1, Madrid, Istmo, 37-58.

Nebrija, E. A. 1909 [1492]. *Gramatica castellana: reproduction photo-typique de l'édition princeps.* Tübingen, Niemeyer.

Pérez Priego, M. A. 1998. *Estudios sobre el teatro del Renacimiento,* Madrid, UNED.

Poppenberg, G. 2000. "Religión y política en algunos autos sacramentales de Calderón", in K. Reichenberger & T. Reichenberger (eds.). *Calderón: Protagonista eminente del Barroco europeo,* vol. 1, Kassel, Reichenberger.

Rouanet, L. (ed.). 1901. *Colección de Autos, Farsas y Coloquios del siglo XVI,* 4 vols., Barcelona, L'Avenç.

Subirós, P. 2010. *Ser immigrant a Catalunya,* Barcelona, Edicions 62.

Rull, E. 1986. "Introducción", in E. Rull (ed.), *Autos sacramentales del siglo de Oro,* Plaza & Janés, 13-112.

RICARDO GIL SOEIRO

Figuring Figures: Otherness and Trauma in the Painting of Samuel Bak

A survivor of the Holocaust, Samuel Bak (born in 1933) has always been engaged with an acute traumatic approach to history. His paintings are peopled by the displaced, the dismembered, refugees, and wanderers. In this essay, I will try to come to an understanding of the plurality of meanings that characterizes Bak's representation of these figures by drawing on the theoretical framework provided by a "prophetic post-structuralist" approach (John Caputo's incandescent phrase), namely Derrida's notion of "unconditional hospitality", as well as Lévinas's idea of the absolute alterity of the Other.

In his moving testimony "What, How, and When: On My Art and Myself", included in the book *Representing the Irreparable: The Shoah, the Bible, and the Art of Samuel Bak*, Samuel Bak, addressing an all too personal path of a life of grim survival and flourishing creativity, states that his paintings do not harbor any answers, only questions. Indeed, one could easily argue that Bak's paintings constitute a privileged stage where multiple meanings in motion thrive, irrevocably drawing the viewer into the complex and living landscape of dreams the painter seeks to convey. Bak's work departs from the painful truth of memory in order to deconstruct it by precariously making an attempt at what he calls *tikkun olam*, a repair of the world. Out of a multifaceted visual grammar across which Magritte's shadow flits (and in which, rather paradoxically, the chromatic exuberance contrasts with the bleakness of themes portrayed) an enigmatic voice is born: it is the voice of a painter of unremitting questioning inhabited by the harsh and unforgiving breath of memory and forgetfulness. It is precisely this mnemonic dimension, tied up with the interrogative tone of Bak's painting, which polarizes the reflection of a critic such as Lawrence Langer who, in *Preempting the Holocaust* (1998), asserts:

> Although all art requires active involvement, Holocaust art is especially demanding. Memory is a crucial catalyst in this process. The lack of human figures in most of Bak's forsaken landscapes will be a mystery only to those who ignore the incandescent shimmer that so often ripples through their atmosphere or the sinister smoke-stacks that rise like accusing fingers from a barren terrain. An unholy glow is all that lingers from millions of bodies consumed by fire. Among other possibilities, these paintings are dramatic bulwarks against amnesia (Langer 1998: 81).

Bak's paintings arise from a deeply personal imagetic discourse which is then enriched by several symbols of a waste land made perceptible by a post-Holocaust era (Bak himself admits that "Being an artist, I tried to depict my own mental images, metaphorical visions of a terrain transformed by the Shoah", 2002a: 95): blindfolded chess pieces scattered on a fractured chess board (*Auspicious Moon*, 2001), pears symbolizing the frailty of the human condition (*Contemporary*, 2002) or the haunting presence of music, namely in *For the End of Time* (1996) which, quite explicitly, draws inspiration from *Quatuor pour la fin du temps*, by Olivier Messiaen, which was composed in 1941 at a Nazi concentration camp. It is a whole lexicon acutely rooted in the Jewish experience (the shattered Tablets of the Law, buried cities painted in the shape of the Star of David) which is then re-examined in the dark light of Auschwitz, "an event without response" in Blanchot's poignant phrase. Hence the obsessive presence of smoke rising from the crematoria, as well as the ragged clothes of the concentration camps prisoners.

The Genesis narratives portrayed by the masters (Michelangelo, Rembrandt or Mantegna) are now re-read through a Bakian lens, raising the endless and poignant question of the silence of God:[1] the creation of Adam, the banishment from the Garden of Eden, Jacob's dream, the Flood or Akedah. Undoubtedly, the viewers are compelled to assume their role as compulsory witnesses: powerless bystanders before a world in perpetual loss in which the Fall emerges as one of the most imposing metaphoric-conceptual instruments. In *Creation in Time of War III* (1999) and in *Creation* (1999), despite the appropriation of the Christian representation of creation by Michelangelo as seen in the Sistine Chapel, it is no longer the demiurgic trust that is made manifest in the lightness of that frozen moment where God's finger is reaching to touch Adam's;

---

1   For an informed analysis of the topic of *Hester Panim* in Samuel Bak's painting and Paul Celan's poetry, see Kimberly Socha (2010).

rather, what is being questioned here is the very legitimacy of the cove-nant between creator and creature, between divinity and humanity. In both of these pressing paintings one's attention is almost unwillingly drawn to the accusatory tone implied by the gesture of the human figure, either dressed in garments of a belligerent soldier or an exhausted pris-oner. Either way, God is only an imperceptible and barely noticeable silhouette, formed by the agglomeration of large blocks of stone that hang in the air. What is more: the only element that remains as a trait of the anthropomorphic representation of God is the hand but, in Bak's rendering, the hand is no longer able to be creative, it is merely suspend-ed by a rope. In *Creation*, one human hand is wrapped in bandages while a second one (a mere prosthesis?) is supported by a crutch.

In the series *Remembering Angels* (2007), the way in which cultural memory is re-worked by Bak is particularly poignant. As always echoing the *magna opera* of the great masters, in this particular series Bak choos-es to draw upon Dürer's famous engraving *Melencolia I* (1514). Dürer's angel is here dismembered and re-shaped according to different meta-morphoses. The divine order that was still tangible in Dürer's Renais-sance concerning the nature of human creativity, aspirations, and limits, is placed in a catastrophic time, giving way to a world of chaos and arbi-trariness where stones and trees float through the air (*With Other Rem-nants*), building blocks become dice (*Guardian of Suspended Warnings*), feathers outweigh cannon shells (*On the Other Hand*), and right is left and left is upside-down (*Between Right and Wrong*). Even though *Melencolia*'s emblems of a radiant rationality are still there, they are no longer illuminated by a promising rainbow and a dazzling comet, but rather reinscribed as pitiless insignia of a site of brokenness and of in-congruity. It is a work of mourning Bak is painting, a kind of counter-*Melencolia*, a skeptical counter-*Aufklärung* narrative, if you will, of which the famous lines "These fragments I have shored against my ru-ins", by T. S. Eliot, are a fitting literary echo. Even if the melancholic facet still holds true, it is undisputable that in Bak's new configuration the gesture of inner retreat and attentiveness yields to a traumatic gesture of contemplating the heap of ruins brought about by the wreck of the dream of reason —in a way echoing Goya's ambiguous etching *El sueño de la razón produce monstruos* (1797-1799).

One is instantly reminded of Walter Benjamin's prescient text *Über den Begriff der Geschichte* where he alludes to Paul Klee's *Angelus*

Novus (1920) in order to put into question the very notion of historical progress as a cruel illusion, a kind of a false idol —in the Nietzschean sense it acquires in *Götzen-Dämmerung* (1889). Interestingly enough, Benjamin himself perceives in Dürer's engraving a sort of deadening of the emotions, an intense degree of sadness, so much so that the instruments of mathematics and science are of no use to the disconsolate angel who stares at the surroundings deprived of meaning. However, through the window of her study, a gleaming light fills the scene: Benjamin believes that an enigmatic wisdom dwells in every object, made accessible by the very sorrow that contemplates a disenchanted world. Such a cheerful stance is absent from Bak's understanding. The angel herself is but a work in progress: a sculpture, a machine, a cutout, a collage, or even a refugee as in, for example, *Boarding the Saint Louis* (2006). The wings of the manifold angels are torn apart, shredded, dismantled, partially removed, under repair, affixed to trees, or cast in stone. Sometimes they are even supported by nails or crutches (as in *Testimonials*, 2006, and *On the other hand*, 2007 —in both these works the darkness is made visible through the background from whence the crematorium smoke rises). Peopled with precarious ladders about to crumble, rainbows merely supported by ropes (as in *Ongoing elegy*, 2006, and *Covenants*, 2007), or blindfolded angels as in *Six Wings for One* or in *Guardian of Sleep*, the series *Remembering Angels* sets the stage for an endless elegy on a world gone awry.

We will now turn our attention to the series "Figuring Figures" where the *topos* of the foreigner is explicitly displayed. However, as I hope to have argued so far, I am convinced that Bak's work as a whole deepens the need to think about questions of displacement, exile, migration, foreignness, and alterity. In one way or another, Bak's figures always remain foreigners either to themselves or to transcendence. And as always in Bak, symbols, objects, and motifs are more than meets the eye. In this series, in particular, worthy of specific mention is *Definition of Self* (2009), where the outline of a desolate human face is made up of heaps of fragments and debris, and *Instrospection* (2008) and *Self Questioning* (2009), where the abyss of self-reflexivity of the self is taken to its utmost extreme. In addition, take also notice of the suitcase or the baggage as prominent symbols of the migrant, refugee, drifter, wanderer, traveler, or nomad (cf. *Revelation*, 2009, and *Accidental Music*, 2007), as well as the obsessive presence of boots (cf. *Forthcoming Change*, 2008, and *As Clear As It Gets*, 2009), coexisting in complex ways with elements of hope and redemption, featured in the bird —as in *Forthcoming Change*, and in the balloons (as in *As Clear As It Gets*). *The Art of Reading* (2009) presents the reader as a refugee: he is here depicted as a solitary figure in a refugee camp. The books are burning in the distance, but the reader keeps on reading. By being utterly absorbed in his spellbinding task (the art of the reader is the art of the survivor), he seems to have found a home in the midst of a devastated landscape, a world in flames. In *Historian* (2009), the historian bears witness to the trauma, yet is immobilized by it: he, too, is a refugee.

The new series *Adam and Eve*, completed in 2011, presents us with the first couple in the aftermath of the Holocaust as solitary survivors, travellers in the void. God becomes just another one of the relics that displaced people carry around with them on their exilic odyssey to nowhere. It seems to me, however, that despite the blatant biblical echoes here at play, the depicted couple is to be read in a more apposite framework: as a metonymy for the experiences of displacement and migration that impinge upon the lives of an ever-increasing number of people worldwide. This is particularly evident in paintings such as: *Adam and Eve and the Road Taken* (2011), *Adam and Eve and the Passports* (2011), and *Adam and Eve and Dissent* (2011).

For what remains of the present analysis, I would like to draw, however briefly, upon what John Caputo has called a prophetic postmodernism (inspired by Kierkegaard), which he opposes to a Dionysian postmodernism (inspired by Nietzsche). Most of the objections made against postmodernism have in mind the Dionysian version of *différance* as violence: relativism, subjectivism, skepticism, and nihilism. In Caputo's view, however, there is another line of thought at work within postmodernism: a more Lévinasian theorization of *différance* as alterity. It is this direction that I now wish to explore. In formulating his confrontation with Heidegger in terms of Heidegger's exclusion of the *jewgreek*, Caputo uses the expression Derrida has borrowed from James Joyce. And he explains further:

> By "jew" I mean above all what Lyotard calls *les juifs*, so that the expression "jewgreek" results from running together Derrida and Lyotard, Lévinas and James Joyce, meaning everyone who is out, outside, silenced, deprived of an idiom or a home or both [...], everyone who is Abrahamic, driven from native land (1993: 7).

To Heidegger's myth of Being Caputo opposes a myth of justice anchored in the work of Lyotard, but particularly in the thinking of Derrida and Lévinas for they are the philosophers of concrete obligation and of responsibility as a reciprocal asymmetry, choosing to respond not to the call of Being but to the call of the concrete singularity of the one in need, to the "widow, orphan, and stranger", a biblical discourse, states Caputo, that Lévinas has infused into post-structuralist thought.

The influence of Lévinas's philosophy is evident in Derrida's later writings (on themes such as law, justice, responsibility, gift, and friendship) where he increasingly emphasized a Lévinasian ethics as being at the heart of deconstruction. Lévinas's work is based on the ethics of the Other, an ethics as first philosophy, or, to put it differently, philosophy as the "wisdom of love": in any case, the primacy of his ethics clearly derives from the experience of the encounter with the Other —made manifest in the epiphany which takes place in the face-to-face encounter with the absolutely Other. For the author of *Totality and Infinity*, coming face to face with the Other is a non-symmetrical relationship. Longing for a retreat from the straightjacket of ontological metaphysics, he writes in *Otherwise than Being or Beyond Essence*: "The subject is hostage" (Lévinas 1981: 112). Picking up this thread, Derrida offers his own musings on the concept of hospitality. In *Of Hospitality* (2000), he asks us if hospitality is not an interruption of the self. In accordance to his reasoning, in order to occur, pure or absolute hospitality must entail an absolute surprise, a true gift. To be truly hospitable, the host should accept the foreigner as the messianic surprise. In order to get closer to unconditional hospitality, we must be willing to surrender ourselves to ambiguity, to uncertainty, to aporetic openings, to the experience of the impossible, in short, "the exercise of impossible hospitality", as Derrida puts it in the book *Acts of Religion* (2002: 364). In Derridean terms, to wait without waiting, awaiting absolute surprise, the unexpected visitor, awaited without a horizon of expectation —such is the madness of the concept of hospitality. In *Deconstruction in a Nutshell* (1997), Caputo concurs with Derrida in the sense that hospitality is always to come, it is an enigmatic experience beyond knowledge in which we set out for the stranger, for the Other, for the unknown, where we cannot go. "Hospitality really starts to happen when I push against this limit, this threshold, this paralysis, inviting hospitality to cross its own threshold and limit, its own self-limitation, to become a gift beyond hospitality", he says. "Thus, for hospitality to occur, it is necessary for hospitality to go beyond hospitality" (Caputo 1997: 111). Caputo is well aware of the fact that the demands placed upon us by the singularity of the wholly Other are, indeed, tremendous and that is why he speaks of a hyperbolical justice.

I do believe that Bak's work calls for a hyperbolic ethics of this order, one that, on the one hand, seeks to sever ties with the enclosed self-onto-logical mechanism of Western narcissism (a journey against the sovereign power of metaphysics on which Derrida will be only too glad to embark); and, on the other hand, is keen to respond to the calls of otherness. If we think about "Bak's astounding visionary surrealism" (Cynthia Ozick's phrase), if we think about the figures which crowd Bak's canvases (and to do so we must not shy away from tackling the complex question of the presence and absence of the human and the divine in his paintings), it is clear that, whilst speaking about the unspeakable, he nevertheless succeeds in, in Lévinasian terms, calling us to be available to the face of the Other who, in its infinite and irreducible alterity, is foreign to us and, by doing so, be more able to say *Here I am*.

The viewer, or more truthfully the reader, of Bak's paintings is always faced with the challenge of endless interpretation. In this respect, Danna Fewell persuasively argues that "[l]ike complex literary texts, Bak's works impose on his audience the responsibility of interpretation. The outcome of this venture is always uncertain, because more often than not we are left with the burden of afflicted consciousness rather than the satisfaction of having found easy meanings" (Fewell 2008: xi). One should not be surprised, then, by the constant presence of keys in Bak's work: colossal keys, broken keys, hidden locks (as in *The Hidden Question*, 1994, *Interpretation*, 2003, or *Remnants*, 2002). The labyrinth of ambiguity which sets the tone for the hermeneutical quest offers us a chiaroscuro of uncertainty that oscillates between the total devastation of the *forma mentis* which permeates all of his paintings and construction of a meaning (*Tikkum Olam*), precarious as it may be.

In the face of total devastation, or "absolute tragedy" (in George Steiner's terminology) how can the tablets be repaired? In the introduction of the magnificent book *Representing the Irreparable: the Shoah, the Bible, and the Art of Samuel Bak*, Danna Nolan Fewell tries to come to an understanding of such disconcerting perplexity. She argues that Bak's art "entrances" and at the same time "disquiets", being characterized by a series of elements that she describes with the following terms:

Dismembered human figures of flesh, metal, wood, and stone. Broken pottery and rusted keys, petrified teddy bears and discarded children's shoes, floating rocks, and uprooted trees. Broken chess pieces. Fractured rainbows. Books turned buildings, tablets turned tombstones, memorial candles turned crematoria. Soundless musical instruments, flightless doves, mechanized, immobile angels, crucified children. And yet: pears and paradise, new growth on broken branches, sunrises in sunsets. Color and catastrophe. Genesis and genocide. Exodus and expulsion. Ruins and remnants. Michelangelo, Rembrandt, Mantegna, Dürer, de Chirico echoed and subverted. Paradoxes. Contradictions. Ambiguities. Excesses. All ingredients of a survivor's post-Holocaust landscape (Fewell 2008: xi).

Like Lévinas's philosophy, or even Paul Celan's poetry, Bak's paintings make us more alert to the cry of the Other, to its irreplaceable singularity. By choosing to walk that path, we, too, may feel a little bit more human. And with Ithaca always in our mind, as in Cavafy's poem, we are only asked to wish for the road to be long.

Bibliography

Bak, S. 2002a. *Painted in Words: A Memoir*, Bloomington, Indiana UP.
—. 2002b. "Dürer and I", in I. Tayler (ed.). *Between Worlds: The Paintings and Drawings of Samuel Bak from 1946 to 2001*, Boston, Pucker Art Publications, 271-72.
Caputo, J. 1993. *Demythologizing Heidegger*, Bloomington, Indiana UP.
—. 1997. *Deconstruction in a Nutshell: A Conversation with Jacques Derrida*, New York, Fordham UP.
Derrida, J. 2002. *Acts of Religion*, G. Anidjar (ed.), New York, Routledge.
Fewell, D. N., G. A. Phillips & Y. Sherwood (eds.). 2008. *Representing the Irreparable: The Shoah, the Bible, and the Art of Samuel Bak*, Boston, Pucker Art Publications.
Langer, L. 1998. "Landscapes of Jewish Experience: The Holocaust Art of Samuel Bak", in *Preempting the Holocaust*, New Haven, Yale UP, 80-120.
Lévinas, E. 1981. *Otherwise than Being or Beyond Essence*, A. Lingis (trans.), The Hague, Martinus Nijhoff.
Socha, K. 2010. "Outside the Reign of Logic, Outside the Reach of God: Hester Panim in the Surreal Art of Paul Celan and Samuel Bak", *War, Literature & the Arts: An International Journal of the Humanities* 22, 1-15.

Marta Gómez Garrido

Voces olvidadas de la Edad de Plata: la otredad en la sexualidad

La identidad sexual ha representado uno de los mayores motivos de marginación a lo largo de la historia. Este rasgo identitario ha sido motivo de exclusión social, ya sea en la vida ordinaria o en el ámbito literario, donde muchos autores y autoras se han visto relegados al olvido histórico y literario por razones de género e incluso, en algunos casos, se han visto obligados a esconderse por miedo a las represalias. En el presente artículo pretendemos analizar cómo se refleja esa marginación en los textos de los que han vivido y desarrollado su obra en los márgenes de la sociedad, centrándonos en algunas poetas de la Edad de Plata.

Las mujeres españolas consiguieron avanzar de forma visible en los primeros años del siglo XX, avance en el cual la irrupción del psicoanálisis y la eclosión de las vanguardias, dos elementos estrechamente ligados entre sí, influyeron notablemente. No obstante, el primer intento de destruir el discurso sexual dominante se puede establecer en la aparición decimonónica de un discurso protofeminista que se iría consolidando a lo largo del siglo XX. El cuestionamiento que hizo la crítica feminista de género, estableciéndolo como categoría social y sexual, permitió el análisis de la sexualidad como un hecho social y cultural nacido de una necesidad ideológica y no como un atributo inherente a la persona (Mandrell 1999: 212). Fue Simone de Beauvoir, en *El segundo sexo*, quien expresó esta dialéctica con la mítica frase: "una no nace mujer, se hace" [on ne naît pas femme, on le devient] (1983: 13). En dicha obra la autora concluía que cada individuo se veía obligado a adoptar un género a través de la coacción de la sociedad, que exigía a sus ciudadanos que se sintiesen identificados con uno de los dos, pero aseguraba que esta elección no tenía nada que ver con el sexo. La autora fue incluso más allá y subrayó la determinación de lo femenino por contraposición a lo masculino, defendiendo que la identidad femenina se construía, no en sí misma sino en relación con la alteridad del hombre. Aparece así la lucha entre la concepción esencialista y la constructivista del sexo.

Michel Foucault analizó en *Historia de la sexualidad* el papel que esta juega en la sociedad, llegando a la conclusión de que lo considerado "normal" desde una perspectiva sexual varía sobremanera de unas sociedades a otras (2005: 51). Por su parte, Linda McDowell, partiendo del principio de que las prácticas sexuales aceptadas cambian con cada periodo histórico, sostiene en *Género, identidad y lugar* que "la larga historia de la política sexual del siglo XX constituye un intento de destruir tanto el poder de esos discursos dominantes como los tópicos" (2000: 81). El esfuerzo de las feministas será aprovechado años más tarde para las reivindicaciones homosexuales, canalizadas parcialmente a través de la *gender theory*.

A pesar de las modernas transformaciones que experimentó el concepto de identidad sexual a principios del siglo XX en España, después de la contienda civil, la consideración de la mujer entró en una fase regresiva. José Luis Ferris apunta en la biografía de Maruja Mallo que "tras la guerra civil parecía casi un deber borrar las huellas de todas aquellas modernas que habían perturbado el orden establecido" (2004: 21). Aunque en los años anteriores al Franquismo la mujer consiguió avanzar posiciones en el contexto social, lo cierto es que esos logros no se vieron de forma positiva desde algunos sectores del país. Tal como señala José Carlos Mainer, "la derecha más berroqueña vio con mucha aprensión el fenómeno de la emancipación femenina y, en su marco, la dedicación de la mujer a la escritura" (1990: 15).

El estudio de Mainer cita, entre otras, tres de las escritoras que nos ocupan aquí por su supuesta relación afectiva y sexual con personas del mismo sexo: Lucía Sánchez Saornil, Ana María Martínez Sagi y Carmen Conde. Todas ellas han sido relacionadas por la crítica con otras mujeres; pero lo que más nos interesa es subrayar la presencia de fuertes rasgos de indeterminación sexual en sus textos, sean o no ciertas las relaciones evocadas. Una aproximación literaria a estos rasgos, enmarcada dentro de los estudios culturales, cobra relevancia en la actualidad porque ayuda a iluminar aspectos de unos textos y de la tradición que habían permanecido ocultos hasta ahora, renovando así, mediante nuevas interpretaciones, la visión tradicional de la literatura. Por todo ello, es importante acercarse a los textos sin caer en apriorismos ni en simplificaciones sobre la presunta homosexualidad de sus autoras. Se trata de sacar a la luz la historia de aquellas que fueron marginadas en el canon ya que tenían la necesidad de expresarse con un código distinto; así lo señala Mary E. Galvin al afirmar que "una mente que puede imaginar otras sexualidades e identidades de género debe ser capaz también de imaginar otras maneras de hablar" (1999: xii). En este contexto de invisibilidad, se hace especialmente necesario entender el tipo de represión al cual se han visto sujetas las mujeres, ya que esta ha sido más silenciada que la de los hombres. ¿Se encuentran rasgos de esa identidad y de su marginación en su obra? Una de las respuestas la encontramos en el momento histórico que vivieron, fuertemente influido por corrientes ideológicas conservadoras y por la toma de conciencia de lo reprimido en el inconsciente.

A principios del siglo XX surge una nueva comprensión del ser humano a raíz de las publicaciones de los trabajos de Sigmund Freud, de cuyas teorías psicoanalíticas nos interesan especialmente dos. Por un lado, aquellas que inciden en la ambigüedad sexual existente en el ser humano, con las que se rompe la dicotomía rígida del binomio hombre/mujer. Por otro lado, el poder de lo inconsciente, de enormes posibilidades para la creación artística. Julia Kristeva dio un paso más en las teorías enunciadas por Freud; elabora en *Poderes de la perversión* (1988) una teoría sobre aquellos elementos que conforman la identidad, pero que han de reprimirse para entrar en contacto con la sociedad. A estos elementos los denomina "abyección". Esta forma de represión se plantea como un elemento singular que tienta y repugna a la vez al sujeto. La investigadora Elizabeth Wright apunta en la misma dirección al afirmar que "los instintos del Yo, preocupados por la autopreservación y la necesidad de relacionarse con otros, están en conflicto con los instintos sexuales" (1985: 37). La necesaria socialización pone en una encrucijada con sus propios deseos a aquellos individuos que no encajan en lo que la sociedad considera el entorno social establecido.

Aunque la corriente psicoanalítica ya había llegado a España antes, a través del contacto de algunos intelectuales que conocían el francés y el alemán, fue el filósofo Ortega y Gasset quien pidió a José Ruiz-Castillo, editor de Biblioteca Nueva, que tradujese al castellano las obras completas de Freud, prologando él mismo el primer volumen en 1922 (Sánchez-Barranco 2005: 133). A la luz de estos datos, la cuestión es discernir en qué manera esas pulsiones se podrían haber reflejado en los textos de la literatura del momento. Los filósofos y psicólogos que teorizaron sobre el psicoanálisis coinciden en recalcar la importancia del inconsciente en los procesos de creación. Para Freud, el psicoanálisis arroja luz al proceso de creación; de hecho, en su discurso LXXV asegura que "las fuerzas impulsoras del arte son aquellos mismos conflictos que conducen a otros individuos a la neurosis y han movido a la sociedad a la creación de sus instituciones" (2003: 1865). El padre del psicoanálisis señala también que las fuerzas destinadas a la creación cultural provienen de la represión de los elementos de excitación sexual; sobre este material, de origen sexual aunque reprimido, actúa el mecanismo de la sublimación, mediante el cual el artista transforma en cultura, es decir, en material socialmente aceptable, aquello que intenta reprimir (1979: 168). Por su parte, el psicoanalista e historiador del arte austriaconorteamericano Ernst Kris, abundando en las tesis de Freud, llegó a establecer que la personalidad del artista era preconsciente —aquello que es capaz de volverse consciente fácilmente y en situaciones usuales— dado que "el que habla no es el sujeto, sino una voz que sale de él. Lo que dicha voz, que surge de él, proclama, le era desconocido antes del estado de inspiración" (1964: 125).

Una vez considerada como normal la presencia de ese conflicto identitario en los textos de las autoras aquí estudiadas, podremos buscar en sus obras el rastro de ese deseo vedado y de la exclusión social que ha conllevado. Tal como veremos más adelante, al analizar dichas obras hemos encontrado indefinición sexual tanto en la autoría como en el propio texto.

Rasgos de ambigüedad en la autoría y en el texto

En algunos casos de ambigüedad genérica, el autor se escuda tras un pseudónimo; este es el caso de Lucía Sánchez Saornil, que utilizaba el nombre de Luciano de San-Saor para firmar la mayor parte de sus textos. Al firmar como hombre, la autora podía permitirse dirigir sus poemas de amor a un sujeto femenino, recurso que podría explicarse bien como una manifestación de una tendencia homosexual o bien como una mera excusa poética. A este respecto, Dolores Romero señala, al referirse a este grupo de autoras, que "las razones que les impulsaron a sustituir su nombre civil son múltiples y variadas, pero se percibe una necesidad de huir de un destino social impuesto en virtud de su identidad como mujeres" (2011: 153). En otros casos, el conflicto de género se muestra a través de la indeterminación sexual —ya sea en el yo lírico, ya sea en el ser amado— de la asexualidad del alma y de la presencia de un código común metafórico.

Indeterminación sexual

La homosexualidad a principios del siglo XX se consideraba una cuestión innombrable y no es sino hasta los años 60 o 70 cuando comienza a hacerse visible (Villena 2002: 21). En este contexto cronológico, se entiende que los primeros signos de una orientación sexual no aceptada se manifestaran en las poesías de la época a través de la ambigüedad que se escondía tras la ausencia de signos sexuales en la gran mayoría de casos.

La indeterminación sexual aparece en la ausencia de género en el yo lírico. Por ejemplo, Ana María Martínez Sagi pide en la poesía "Invéntame" (2000: 571) derribar las murallas del cuerpo y el nombre, relacionados con el género, para poder seguir viviendo. Carmen Conde, por su parte, presenta en varias de sus composiciones un yo lírico ambiguo e incluso abstracto. El poema "Sino" habla del yo del poeta como "[e]ste ser" e indica que "[e]l contacto con este ser es para tu cuerpo lo que la lumbre para la plata" (2007: 148). También existe cierta ambigüedad en el poema "Motivos galantes" en el que Sánchez Saornil escribe sobre una conversación entre amantes: el ser amado parece ser una mujer, por sus "labios ardientes y rojos", mientras que se establece cierto paralelismo entre el yo lírico y la luna, de rasgos femeninos (1996: 54).

Un efecto parecido consigue Ana María Martínez Sagi en el poema "Lo imborrable" a través de la ausencia de género en el ser amado. Escribe dicha autora: "Fue verdad / el deseo. / La ofrenda generosa / de mi cuerpo a tu cuerpo" (1969: 135). Habla así de un deseo concreto, aunque en toda la composición no se encuentra una sola mención al género de aquellos cuerpos. En otras ocasiones, no solo no se menciona el género del ser amado o se le esconde tras el "tú" sino que además se le transfigura como un ser no humano. En "Fusión", Martínez Sagi identifica al ser amado con una sombra: "Me persigues ¡oh sombra!" (1969: 149). Esta transfiguración queda todavía más clara en el poema de Sánchez Saornil "Crepúsculo sensual", donde se identifica al amante con un jardín sensual lleno de "perfumes" con el cual se establece un contacto "de carne y espíritu" (1996: 67). Carmen Conde, a su vez, confunde en "Paisaje" a la persona amada con un paisaje, para después concluir que "[s]ólo en la vida se halla un rostro que es la suma de todos los paisajes" (2007: 148). La indeterminación sexual también se observa en la utilización de pronombres personales. El ejemplo más representativo de este encubrimiento de la persona amada se encuentra en el poema "La despedida" de Martínez Sagi donde escribe: "Tú y Yo en el albo sendero, / dos sombras blancas / perdidas en la noche de los sueños / sin esperanza" (1932: 81). La utilización de los pronombres en mayúsculas, como nombres propios, indica una sustitución consciente.

El alma asexuada. Metáforas de la ambigüedad

La identificación de la persona con su alma, por encima de etiquetas sexuales, es uno de los rasgos característicos en varios de los poemas de las autoras. La que mejor define esta ambigüedad en el género es Elisabeth Mulder en el poema que le dedica a Ana María Martínez Sagi en la introducción de su obra *Inquietud* (1932): "Pero el alma no sabe de locuras. / Pero el alma, insexuada, es siempre buena" (1932:13).

El crítico Daniel Eisenberg afirma que en el siglo XX hubo poca discusión pública sobre el tema de la homosexualidad, pero sí gran cantidad de "alusiones codificadas" (1999:13). Los sujetos que se han visto excluidos de la sociedad únicamente pueden romper esa marginación a través de un nuevo lenguaje cuya creación no solo encuentra su fundamento en la ruptura de la marginación, sino también en la necesidad de expresar unos sentimientos que son diferentes a los de la mayoría. Así lo defiende Alicia Redondo Goicoechea en *Mujeres y narrativa: otra historia de la literatura* (2009).

Las metáforas que componen el código de la ambigüedad en las obras de las tres autoras se pueden resumir en dos grandes grupos: punición y deseo. Esta división nos muestra la esencia del problema homosexual, es decir, el deseo que lo caracteriza y su prohibición. Por un lado, tenemos las metáforas negativas de la punición que marcan un amor y un deseo vedados: la oscuridad, la sombra, la amargura, la ceniza y el desierto, el silencio y el espejo. Por otro, las metáforas positivas del deseo físico y espiritual: las partes del cuerpo, los sueños, el agua, las flores y la luna. Las metáforas se sitúan así como opuestos, pero también se interrelacionan en una relación causal, ya que es el deseo vedado por la sociedad del momento el que provoca la punición. Frente a la oposición de los dos grupos hay un punto en común. Todas ellas hacen referencia a una experiencia sensitiva que se traduce a través de la figura literaria en un elemento emocional. Con esta división podemos constituir una ontología metafórica de la ambigüedad, en la que las metáforas, utilizadas en infinidad de movimientos literarios con otras connotaciones, adquieren un nuevo significado en este contexto de deseos vedados.

Tras este rápido repaso, podemos concluir que existe cierta ambigüedad en la poesía amorosa de estas tres autoras de la Edad de Plata. No se suele mostrar el género del ser amado y se tiende a utilizar un código común relacionado con el deseo y la punición. El hecho de que estas experiencias se reflejen de forma ambigua se debe tanto a la necesidad de ocultar esos sentimientos como a que, según observa James Mandrell, "las experiencias de los gays y lesbianas, como es el caso de muchos de los marginados, suelen ser siempre ambiguas" (225). La indefinición es, así, no solamente un refugio, sino también una cualidad del ser humano inteligente, que piensa por sí mismo y no se limita a las etiquetas impuestas por la sociedad.

Bibliografía

Beauvoir, S. de. 1983. *El segundo sexo. La experiencia vivida,* Buenos Aires, Siglo XX.
Conde, C. 2007. *Poesía completa*, E. Miró (ed.), Madrid, Castalia.
Eisenberg, D. 1999. "La escondida senda. Homosexuality in Spanish History and Culture", in D. W. Foster (ed.), *Spanish Writers on Gay and Lesbian Themes: A Bio-Critical Sourcebook*, Westport, CT, Greenwood, 1-21.
Ferris, J. L. 2004. *Maruja Mallo. La gran transgresora del 27*, Madrid, Temas de Hoy.
Foucault, M. 2005. *Historia de la sexualidad 1: La voluntad del saber*, México, Siglo XXI.

Freud, S. 1979 [1908]. *La moral sexual cultural y la nerviosidad moderna*, in *Obras Completas*, vol. IX, Buenos Aires, Amorrortu, 159-81.
—. 2003. *Obras completas. Tomo II, Ensayos XXVI al XCVII: (1905-1915[1917])*, Madrid, Biblioteca Nueva.
Galvin, M. E. 1999. *Queer Poetics. Five Modernist Women Writers*, Westport, CT, Greenwood.
Kris, E. 1964. *Psicoanálisis del arte y del artista*, Buenos Aires, Paidós.
Kristeva, J. 1988. *Poderes de la perversión*, Buenos Aires, Catálogos Editora & Siglo XXI.
Mainer, J. C. 1990. "Las escritoras del 27 (con María Teresa León al fondo)", in *Homenaje a María Teresa León: Cursos de Verano en El Escorial (1989)*, Madrid, Universidad Complutense, 13-40.
Mandrell, J. 1999. "Estudios gay y lesbianos. La revelación del cuerpo masculino: una mirada gay", in F. la Rubia Prado & J. M. del Pino (eds.), *El hispanismo en los Estados Unidos*, Madrid, Visor, 211-30.
Martínez Sagi, A. M. 1932. *Inquietud*, Barcelona, [s. e.]
—. 1969. *Laberinto de presencias*, León, [s. e.]
—. 2000. "La voz sola", in J. M. de Prada (ed.), *Las esquinas del aire. En busca de Ana María Martínez Sagi*, Barcelona, Planeta, 541-78.
McDowell, L. & P. Linares. 2000. *Género, identidad y lugar: un estudio de las geografías feministas*, Madrid, Cátedra.
Redondo Goicoechea, A. 2009. *Mujeres y narrativa: otra historia de la literatura*, Madrid, Siglo XXI.
Romero López, D. 2011 "La identidad velada: el uso del seudónimo en algunas literatas de la Edad de Plata", in J. Álvarez Barrientos (ed.), *Imposturas literarias españolas*, Salamanca, Universidad de Salamanca, 151-70.
Sánchez-Barranco, A. & R. Vallejo. 2005. "Ortega y Gasset, la psicología y el psicoanálisis", *Revista de la Asociación Española de Neuropsiquiatría* 25 (julio/septiembre), 121-37.
Sánchez Saornil, L. 1996. *Poesía*, R. M. Martín Casamitjana (ed.), Valencia, Pre-Textos.
Villena, L. A. de 2002. *Amores iguales. Antología de la poesía gay y lésbica*, Madrid, Esfera de los Libros.
Wright, E. 1985. *Psicoanálisis y crítica cultural*, Buenos Aires, Editorial Per Abbat.

María Pilar González de la Rosa

"You are Memsahib on a cycle?":
la visión recíproca del Otro en Bettina Selby

La creciente irrupción de obras, escritores y críticos en torno al género de viajes y la escritura viajera de las últimas décadas del siglo XX evidencia, sin duda, el momento extraordinariamente decisivo por el que atraviesa la literatura de viajes, materializado en la producción de antologías, monografías y ensayos de diversa índole que son, en nuestra opinión, muy oportunos y vitales para su consolidación como género, en tanto que han abordado los textos como el contexto en el que se han venido produciendo desde un enfoque interdisciplinar, y han intentado definir los cambios estéticos más representativos del panorama reciente. De la creatividad, carácter distintivo, complejidad en algunos casos y renovación del género, vienen dando buena cuenta los variadísimos enfoques. Entre estos, la categoría de la otredad y los conflictos de identidad que se derivan de su representación y análisis en el discurso crítico y literario contemporáneo, son algunos de los que han suscitado más interés. En este sentido, el concepto de alteridad, enriquecido en las últimas décadas con interpretaciones ajenas al canon establecido, postuladas desde el postmodernismo, el feminismo, los estudios culturales, la teoría postcolonial o los estudios de género, ha tenido mucho que ver con la atención que el viaje femenino ha recibido por parte de la crítica, después de haber sido obviado en numerosas investigaciones.

La presencia de la mujer —tantas veces ese Otro silenciado— y la construcción de la identidad del sujeto femenino son objeto de análisis en antologías y estudios distintos (Middleton 1965; Stevenson 1982; Strobel 1987; Mills 1991; Robinson 1994; Bohls 1995; Korte 2000; Siegel 2004), entre los que destacamos el de Susan Bassnett (2002), quien reivindica el papel de la mujer y su capacidad para asimilar y saber mediar en la relación entre la percepción del yo y la consciencia del Otro y del entorno en procesos de alteridad e hibridación:

Travel writers today are producing texts for an age characterised by increasing interest in concepts of hybridity, an age in which theories of race and ethnicity, once used as a means of dividing peoples, are starting to crumble [...] Once the gaze of the traveller reflected the singularity of a dominant culture; today, the gaze is more likely to be multi-focal, reflecting the demise of a world-view that separated us from them, and the role of women in adjusting perspectives is immense (2002: 240).

Dentro de la narrativa de viajes femenina de los últimos tiempos queremos destacar a Bettina Selby, que cuenta con nueve libros publicados en los que narra sus distintos periplos en bicicleta por España, Turquía, Oriente Medio, Sudán, Egipto, Pakistán, parte de la India, Nepal y su país natal, el Reino Unido. En esta ocasión nos centraremos en el subcontinente asiático, destino de su viaje en *Riding the Mountains Down* (1984), a la vez que la obra con la que irrumpe en el panorama literario.

En este primer viaje, Selby se adentra en el Himalaya a través de los territorios de Pakistán, la India y Nepal. Es el atlas geográfico que ha hojeado tantas veces desde niña el acicate que la pone en movimiento. No se trata de satisfacer una inquietud interna que la mera consulta bibliográfica pueda satisfacer. La evocación de las montañas del Himalaya a través de la visión de una postal, un documental, o las experiencias narradas por otros viajeros tampoco bastarán para cumplir sus aspiraciones. El ímpetu que incita a nuestra viajera a emprender el viaje al Himalaya en su primer periplo es satisfacer un anhelo, el reto que para ella significa poder disfrutar de plena libertad de movimiento; posiblemente, la libertad de movimiento que vio frustrada la autora en sus años de adolescencia y juventud después de la contienda de la Segunda Guerra Mundial, que condicionó entonces las oportunidades que le habría procurado tener una familia y vivir en un contexto distinto al de la postguerra en Gran Bretaña. Selby consuma este ferviente deseo hasta entonces insatisfecho pedaleando hasta allí en su bicicleta y constatándolo por sí misma. Como ocurriera a otras viajeras, ha estado esperando el momento oportuno para, una vez desentendida de restricciones de tipo familiar, terminados sus estudios universitarios ya adulta y aprovechando su buena condición física para un viaje de estas características, escapar y satisfacer sus aletargadas ilusiones a punto de cumplir medio siglo.

En el tránsito de la esfera privada a la pública de nuestra viajera, vamos a analizar las perspectivas recíprocas que Selby y los habitantes de estas latitudes tienen, respectivamente, a lo largo de este periplo. No en vano, tal como señala Trinh T. Minh-ha: "In travelling, one is a being-for-other, but also a being-with-other. The seer is seen while s/he sees. To see and to be seen constitute the double approach of identity" (23). Lo primero que podemos constatar acerca de la visión que tienen los otros de Selby, no escapa de lo que Robinson (xv) cataloga como "greater disincentives" que la mujer ha tenido que soportar a través de los siglos y que aún tiene que sobrellevar en mayor medida en determinadas zonas geográficas como las que abarca su viaje. La persecución de la chiquillería, que en alguna ocasión le tira piedras, la persigue o le recrimina que no lleve velo, son algunas de las reacciones a su presencia, no en vano poco edificantes al comienzo de su singladura. Las cuestiones que un periodista le formula en Karachi a propósito de su entrevista constatan la visión de la mujer y el planteamiento de la emancipación femenina en la sociedad que visita. Asimismo, son relativamente frecuentes las situaciones que ignoran y/o cuestionan su presencia y su paso por algunas zonas. Selby, irónicamente, argumenta que ello puede deberse a que no hablan inglés, son sordos o resulta ser que ella es invisible, ya que siendo una mujer su respetabilidad queda en entredicho en una sociedad que no permite que la mujer pueda invadir la esfera de dominio masculino.

Otro detalle que prueba el choque de mentalidades puede observarse en el poco respeto que muestran a Selby, cuya reputación se pone en duda por viajar sola. En algún momento puntual, incluso, serán los propios hombres quienes la alertan del peligro que comporta, provocando que casi llegue a convencerse de que va a necesitar protección masculina, la misma que, como señala Strobel (7), experimentaron otras viajeras en décadas anteriores ante el temor de ser asaltadas por los indígenas, práctica habitual de la ideología imperial y sexista entonces. Asimismo, como sucediera a otras mujeres británicas en el siglo XIX, para dirigirse a ella algunos la llaman Memsahib, término que en absoluto parece agradarle.

Todos sus periplos en bicicleta constituyen una prueba de rendimiento físico en una época en que la disponibilidad y oferta de medios de transporte es más que sobresaliente. El motivo que parece llevar a nuestra viajera a desplazarse en este medio, cualquiera que sea el destino, es que la bicicleta proporciona oportunidades que parecen de alguna forma olvidadas en la vorágine de vida en la que nos movemos hoy y que Selby no quiere desdeñar definitivamente. Entre otras cuestiones, viajar en bicicleta, según ella misma manifiesta, evita males mayores

como el tráfico, estimula el reencuentro con uno mismo y con los demás
—especialmente en zonas que resultan singularmente conflictivas o bien
resultan casi impracticables en la actualidad— y facilita el contacto con
la naturaleza.

A pesar de las complicaciones que le deparará este viaje, Selby va
ajustando su itinerario a las peculiares características que el contexto, las
costumbres de estos lugares y la excepcionalidad que la bicicleta como
medio de transporte imponen a su ritmo. Ello mismo explicará que nuestra viajera, al igual que lo hicieran otras anteriormente, tenga que adaptar
su atuendo, *disfrazarse* en algunas áreas y servirse de ciertas estrategias
para poder proseguir su periplo. Una de ellas será la de las "cartas de
presentación o recomendación", práctica habitual, recogida por Casson
(319-21) al referirse a los viajeros en la antigüedad. Su movilidad en este
viaje, tantas veces amenazada por un sistema burocrático lento, atrasado
y corrupto como el que encuentra en estos países, se satisface gracias a
ellas. Además de presentar al futuro huésped, facilitan su alojamiento
cuando los lugares por los que transita no ofrecen ninguna seguridad, o
bien, como en el caso de Selby, cuando la socorrida tienda para pernoctar no es en absoluto recomendable, propiciando un recibimiento sin
mayores altercados, alojamiento relativamente seguro y numerosos encuentros con los lugareños.

Si en determinadas zonas geográficas en la antigüedad era menester
portar una identificación que distinguiera a los viajeros cristianos del
resto de transeúntes, en Paquistán, a finales del siglo XX, las cartas de
presentación son la contraseña recomendada por las autoridades británicas y locales para la consecución del itinerario marcado. Al igual que la
viajera victoriana Marianne North, Selby es huésped de un Obispo y de
otros cargos de la jerarquía eclesiástica, pernocta en casas de descanso,
en hostales de la Young Women's Christian Association (YWCA), en
granjas y casas muy humildes. No le preocupa tanto la comodidad —de
la que huye en alguna ocasión— como la seguridad de sentirse protegida
y todavía más, si cabe, aceptada, en lugares donde la hostilidad es públi-
camente manifiesta. Siempre que tiene que pernoctar en una aldea donde
las cartas no tengan validez alguna, la consigna que recibe de los propios
habitantes es hacerlo donde haya mujeres, entre quienes siempre, a lo
largo de toda su expedición, va a encontrar complicidad y solidaridad.
Esta circunstancia corrobora la visión que tienen del rol de la mujer y la
mentalidad de los habitantes, profundamente marcada por tabúes cultura-

les y religiosos. Por otra parte, la imagen lasciva de los hombres hindúes, que la sorprende muy negativamente, no parece haber variado mucho, según explica Strobel (1991), del estereotipo que de ellos tenían las británicas en el siglo XIX. Frente a esto, lejos de acobardarse, Selby recurre en múltiples ocasiones a su característico sentido del humor.

El humor profundiza aún más la perspectiva crítica y el sentido que da a sus viajes. Un humor sutil que nos descubre a Selby riéndose de sí misma, desvelando su ingenio, enorme curiosidad e interés por comprender a las gentes y los lugares a través de múltiples anécdotas. Sintiéndose la única representante de su sexo en un mundo masculino, es lógico que una de sus quejas en este viaje sea la de la poca privacidad de la que disfruta ante la enorme curiosidad que provoca —para bien, o para mal. De esta forma, despierta la mirada del Otro convirtiéndose en lo que ella cataloga como "a tantalizing sex-object" (41) en una sociedad en la que el trato discriminatorio a la mujer es patente. En este sentido, sobre la percepción recíproca entre el yo que observa y el yo que es observado, Minh-ha subraya: "To travel can consist in operating a profoundly unsettling inversion of one's identity: I become me via an other. Depending on who is looking, the exotic is the other, or it is me" (23). Resulta curioso comprobar, además, cómo nuestra viajera, como occidental y británica, se convierte en algunas zonas remotas en una especie de objetivo a alcanzar por aquellos que han tenido algún tipo de contacto con la civilización occidental, y más concretamente con la anglosajona. Al igual que en la época imperial, Selby "[becomes] a source of information about European culture and society" (Strobel 1991: 35).

Ya se trate de barreras religiosas o sociales, su escritura se debate entre dos estados fronterizos: ser libre para desplazarse por cualquier lugar en una época en que la movilidad es casi completa, y afrontar los obstáculos de una realidad y cultura nuevas, distantes y diferentes, que no van a facilitar el viaje, ni geográfica ni socialmente, y requerirán de su progresiva adaptación y aceptación. Es precisamente ésta una de las aptitudes deseables del buen viajero, como apunta Crossley-Holland (xxvi), y de Selby, como así lo corroboran multitud de ejemplos a lo largo de esta obra y del resto de su producción. Su progresiva adaptabilidad queda patente en su capacidad para poder soportar y superar las barreras sociales, políticas y religiosas del sudeste asiático. De esta forma, las circunstancias y las particularidades históricas de estas zonas tradicionalmente consideradas exóticas y tan diferentes no son óbice para que

Selby haya elegido otro destino más accesible. Las montañas del Himalaya se presentan como símbolo de la pureza primaria del país y una de las mayores bellezas naturales del planeta, y nuestra escritora no ceja en su empeño, dispuesta a verificarlo.

Otro de los rasgos característicos de la naturaleza selbyana que conocemos a través de este viaje y será una constante a lo largo de toda su producción, es su necesidad de comunicarse con la gente. El viaje en bicicleta le permite profundizar mucho más en la experiencia y complejidad que caracterizan al ser humano. A medida que avanza parece entablar una relación de solidaridad, favorecida por el hecho de moverse en bicicleta, solidaridad que se puede entender como valor decisivo para la identificación con estas personas. En su estudio sobre la relación entre las viajeras y el medio de locomoción utilizado en sus desplazamientos, Smith sostiene:

> In the twentieth and twenty-first centuries, the desire to pursue defining mobility at modernity's edges renders the terms of mobility every bit as critical to the project as the destination. Travel by foot or by animal attaches the traveler bodily to the ground. An intimate of the ground, she imagines herself an intimate of the people of the land (xvi-xvii).

La bicicleta facilita la proximidad de Selby, al igual que la cercanía del Otro respecto a ella. Como ha señalado Smith (2001) y recoge Youngs (2004), los avances en los medios de transporte y los modos de desplazamiento —atípicos o convencionales— han afectado notablemente la percepción de los viajeros. A pesar de todas las precauciones que tiene que tomar, nuestra autora se congratula de haber podido disfrutar de la oportunidad de compartir mucho más de cerca las vidas de las gentes que la han acogido a lo largo del viaje, especialmente cuando en estas zonas el contacto con los occidentales ha sido escaso y entiende que tiene que mirar con otros ojos el mundo que descubre. Llega a alcanzar tal grado de compenetración con algunas de las personas que conoce más de cerca, que logra transmitir al lector el entusiasmo que experimenta cuando se involucra en estas latitudes.

Al principio del libro la autora percibe un medio muy hostil, nada halagüeño y extraño a cualquier occidental, no solo a la hora de viajar, también para poder vivir y convivir. Las ciudades atestadas de gente, la miseria, el tráfico infernal, los rudimentarios medios de transporte, las

inclemencias del tiempo, el peligro de derrumbamientos, el comportamiento de los habitantes, los sentimientos de impotencia y frustración,
los trances en los que se encuentra, los peligros que sortea y sobrelleva,
la deshidratación, los problemas técnicos de la bicicleta y las privaciones
de una singladura tan larga que jalonan la narración, a la par que le permiten explorar sus propios límites y nos revelan algunos de sus puntos
débiles, nos hacen pensar en que van a mediatizar su actitud y punto de
vista. Tal y como sostiene Minh-ha: "Every voyage can be said to involve a re-siting of boundaries" (9). Efectivamente, aunque su empresa
no sea nada fácil, la salud y fortaleza física de las que goza, las múltiples
medidas profilácticas, el *sofisticado* medio de transporte, su habilidad
con la bicicleta, la adaptación de su ritmo al entorno que le rodea, la
comunión con el Otro y con el paisaje, pero, sobre todo, su temperamento, perspicacia, fuerza de voluntad y determinación, serán sus armas de
supervivencia en éste y sus sucesivos viajes, así como los baluartes de su
éxito.

Selby transgrede las expectativas de los orientales porque es mujer,
extranjera, viaja sola y, además, lo hace en bicicleta. Y viceversa, sus
expectativas sobre el sudeste asiático despiertan en ella un instinto de
comprensión y tolerancia que contraviene lo que, a priori, desde Gran
Bretaña y sobre el terreno, parecía un viaje casi imposible de llevar a
cabo por la cantidad de obstáculos que tiene que negociar. El éxtasis que
le provoca la contemplación y la supervivencia de este enclave privilegiado de la Tierra —el Himalaya— y el mapa de emociones, no el to-
pográfico —las miradas, los gestos y las palabras muchas veces incom-
prensibles que resuenan en sus oídos—, justifican sus palabras finales: "a
deep sense of triumph and achievement" (393). En efecto, el medio de
transporte utilizado y como bien señala Minh-ha, la ruta resultado del
viaje —no la organizada de los viajes turísticos, sino la improvisada en
aras de avanzar— reconfigura la identidad de la viajera, enriqueciéndola,
transformándola en una experiencia plural, de sí misma y del mundo que
atraviesa, de modo tal, que la identidad se construye en el sentido de la
aceptación de la diferencia y la pertenencia:

> The itinerary displaces the foundation, the background of my identity, and what it
> incessantly unfolds is the very encounter of self with the other —other than myself
> and, my other self [...] Travelling allows one to see things differently from what
> they are, differently from how one has seen them, and differently from what one is

[...] Travelling can thus turn out to be a process whereby the self loses its fixed boundaries —a disturbing yet potentially empowering practice of difference (1994: 23).

Bibliografía

Bassnett, S. 2002. "Travel and Gender", in P. Hulme & T. Youngs (eds.), *The Cambridge Companion to Travel Writing*, Cambridge, Cambridge UP, 225-41.

Bohls, E. A. *Women Travel Writers and the Language of Aesthetics, 1716-1818*, Cambridge, Cambridge UP.

Casson, L. 1994. *Travel in the Ancient World*, Baltimore, Johns Hopkins UP.

Crossley-Holland, K. (ed.). 1989 [1986]. *The Oxford Book of Travel Verse*, Oxford, Oxford UP.

Korte, B. 2000. *English Travel Writing*. Basingstoke, Macmillan.

Middleton, D. 1965. *Victorian Lady Travellers*, London, Routledge.

Mills, S. 1991. *Discourses of Difference*. London & New York, Routledge.

Minh-ha, T. T. 1994. "Other than myself/my other self", in G. Robertson, M. Mash et al. (eds.), *Travellers' Tales. Narratives of Home and Displacement*, London & New York, Routledge, 9-26.

Robinson, J. 1994. *Unsuitable for Ladies. An Anthology of Women Travellers*, Oxford & New York, Oxford UP.

Selby, B. 1985 [1984]. *Riding the Mountains Down*, London, Gollancz.

Siegel, K. (ed.). 2004. *Gender, Genre and Identity in Women's Travel Writing*. New York, Peter Lang.

Smith, S. 2001. *Moving Lives. Twentieth-Century Women's Travel Writing*, Minneapolis, U of Minnesota P.

Stevenson, C. B. 1982. *Victorian Women Travel Writers in Africa*, Boston, Twayne.

Strobel, M. 1991. *European Women and the Second British Empire*, Bloomington, Indiana UP.

Youngs, T. 2004. "Where Are We Going? Cross-border Approaches to Travel Writing", in G. Hooper & T. Youngs (eds.), *Perspectives on Travel Writing*, Aldershot, Ashgate, 167-80.

SANDRA HURTADO ESCOBAR

Entre páginas y bytes: *Entre Ville* de J. R. Carpenter y la literatura de viajes digital

La flexibilidad de la literatura de viajes

El ser humano, desde la antigüedad clásica a nuestros días, ha tenido siempre la necesidad de explicar y describir los nuevos territorios explorados, las experiencias viajeras, ya sean reales o imaginadas. La literatura de viajes, a lo largo de la historia, se ha adaptado a los distintos géneros, sin casarse con uno solo. Desde sus orígenes lleva implícita la necesidad de redefinirse. Su carácter maleable le ha permitido aparecer bajo distintas perspectivas y formatos. Quizá por ello, hoy en día, siga disfrutando de una revitalización constante. Y ahora, en pleno siglo XXI, cuando la presencia de las tecnologías es cada vez más frecuente en diferentes ámbitos, incluso culturales y artísticos, no sorprende que la literatura de viajes se adapte también al formato digital en sus varias versiones y con distintas utilidades. La combinación de tecnología y literatura ha posibilitado el desarrollo de proyectos en los que el GPS y los dispositivos de iphone y android juegan un papel fundamental. La literatura de viajes está dispuesta a traspasar fronteras, incluso a acabar con ellas y romper con todos los tópicos hasta ahora encorsetados a este género. Jorge Carrión, autor de varios libros de viajes, confiesa:

> Para empezar a mí lo que me interesa es la literatura de viajes en su sentido más amplio, es decir, en el sentido más literario: escrita como poesía, con conciencia del lenguaje propia de la literatura. [...] De modo que con esa perspectiva más amplia te das cuenta de que no hay límites, que puedes escribir lo que te da la gana a partir del viaje tal como tú lo consideras. Por otro lado en mis libros nunca me limito sólo al relato del viaje, sino que ensayo en el sentido más básico del término, del ensayo como prueba, experimento, divagación de ideas. Intento darle una tensión no solamente lingüística sino también narrativa, con el ideal de encontrar una sintonía entre la forma del texto y la forma del espacio (citado en Tocco 2009: s. p.).

En esta línea, pues, Internet ofrece un conjunto de posibilidades que están siendo exploradas, en general, por artistas y también por escritores. Así autores de obras digitales se atreven también con este género híbrido que no deja de reinventarse. Obras como *Senghor on the Rocks* de Christoph Benda (2008) o *Voyage Into the Unknown* (2008) de Roderick Coover presentan características tan propias de la literatura de viajes como el discurrir y explorar nuevos lugares o la experiencia personal del viajero, pero en este caso sirviéndose de imágenes de satélite, del *Google maps*, del video, *mashups*, fotos y gráficos. En su caso, sin duda, se producen cambios y transformaciones que afectan a todos los niveles, no solamente de creación sino también de recepción, dado que, según afirma el propio Jorge Carrión:

> [s]u influencia en las artes y los saberes de nuestra era, como no se le escapa a nadie, es brutal. Tanto las experiencias físicas como las intelectuales pasan hoy día por el filtro o la frontera de la pantalla: viajar, conducir, consumir, investigar, escribir, leer […]. Cada computadora es, simultáneamente, el lugar de la preproducción, de la creación y de la expansión. Por eso Internet y su forma, *Google*, están siendo mucho más importantes en el arte del siglo XXI de lo que fueron otros medios, herramientas o canales en los siglos precedentes. En tanto que medio, inocula mensaje (2009: s. p.)

Hacia los *bytes*

Un ejemplo más de esta nueva literatura de viajes en formato digital es *Entre Ville* (2006), de J. R. Carpenter, obra recogida en el segundo volumen de la Electronic Literature Collection.[1] Su autora, que ha confesado en varias ocasiones que escribe sobre lo que ve, oye y escucha, se traslada desde la provincia de Nueva Escocia a Montreal con tan solo

---

1   Para celebrar el 50 aniversario del "Conseil des Arts de Montréal", OBORO (un centro dedicado a la producción y a la presentación del arte, las prácticas contemporáneas y los nuevos medios de comunicación), encargó a Carpenter una obra de creación. El resultado fue *Entre Ville*. La colección donde apareció está promovida por la Electronic Literature Organization, un ente que promueve la literatura digital. Para más información, véase el portal de dicha organización en <http://eliterature.org/> [consultado el 12.VIII.2011].

doce años. Se instala en el barrio de Mille End, concretamente en Saint Urbain Street, calle que conoce gracias a Mordecai Richler quien describió el barrio en muchas de sus novelas. Carpenter es pues una extranjera más en un barrio multicultural. Ella misma señala que:

> I spent the next fifteen years learning the vocabulary of the neighbourhood. I don't mean French, English, Italian, Greek, Portuguese, Yiddish or any of the other languages spoken in the Mile End. I refer rather to the cumulative vocabulary of neighbourhood: the aural, audio, visual, spatial, tactile, aromatic and climatic vocabulary of community (Carpenter 2006: s. p.).

La autora observa desde la ventana de su estudio y recorre, siempre acompañada de su perro, el barrio, bajo la mirada atenta del Otro, pero con la peculiaridad de formar parte de un auténtico *collage* integrado por muchos Otros. Se comparten los mismos sentimientos, se estrechan vínculos y todos ellos constituyen materia prima de la obra, al mismo tiempo que en cierto modo se convierten también en autores. Precisamente de ahí surge su título: "*Entre* is the French word for 'between', as in: *entre nous*, 'between us'. *Ville* is the French word for city", dice la autora, quien además añade:

> *Entre Ville* is a text of walking, and a walk through texts. There are many authors of our neighbourhood. Some are famous, some less so. This paper gives fictional, poetic and philosophical voices equal credence. And the neighbours get a say. It's a shared city, after all, this city entre nous (2006: s. p.)

Durante años, Carpenter ha ido recopilando toda una serie de materiales con el que compone la obra. Por una parte, los dibujos que ella misma realiza en 1992 en la libreta que la acompaña en sus paseos por el barrio. Por otra, el poema "Sant-Urbain Street Heat" que escribe en 2004 y que publica un año más tarde en la revista *online Nthposition*. Con una especial sensibilidad y sencillez es capaz de dotar a su obra de una inusual unidad, al mismo tiempo que los materiales que la componen no pierden su fuerza e independencia. Es precisamente este poema el eje vertebrador de toda la obra. De hecho, Carpenter confiesa que "all of the Web projects start with a piece of writing; it's not about technology, for me" (Carpenter 2006: s. p.). Este *modus operandi* es muy frecuente entre la mayoría de los autores digitales. En ningún caso se produce una fascinación injustificada ni deslumbramiento por las herramientas tecnológicas.

La autora es sumamente consciente de que su obra sería quizá más atractiva estéticamente y más compleja desde el punto de vista de la creación
si la hubiera hecho con Flash; señala, sin embargo, que "I like the idea
that the internet is all made out of text. I'm a writer so I want my texts to
be text in internet terms" (Carpenter 2006: s. p.). No se trata pues de
destacar por la forma sino por su contenido, por la calidad literaria en sí
misma.

Entre Ville se nos presenta bajo un formato sencillo y tradicional:
una libreta con el poema de "Sant-Urbain Street Heat" acompañado por
unos dibujos de edificios hechos a mano con poco esmero. Alrededor de
la libreta, algunas pequeñas imágenes: números de distintas casas, grafi-
tis, sellos, flores y el perro, cuya presencia es fundamental. Sin duda, la
estampa recoge la esencia de la literatura de viajes, donde el viajero anota en su libreta experiencias, impresiones y sensaciones. En este caso, sin
embargo, el texto adquiere una nueva forma y la amplificación se da a
través de varios elementos. El inventario de los materiales que conforman la obra la convierte en un "todo" enriquecido. Por una parte el texto,
sin un lugar fijo, desparramado por toda la obra, se encuentra acompañado por el dibujo, la imagen estática. Por otra, los vídeos pausados, rela-
jados, acompañados por los sonidos característicos del barrio. El vaivén
entre la quietud y el movimiento de los distintos lenguajes nos sumerge
en un recorrido en el que todos los sentidos se ven involucrados.

Las distintas ventanas y puertas de los edificios nos permiten acceder a esa amalgama de lenguajes expresivos con los que la autora reseña
el barrio. El tratamiento perfeccionista al que se someten los elementos
es quizá unos de los rasgos más distintivos y singulares de esta obra.
Realmente, sorprende la forma en la que la autora redescubre el barrio en
cada uno de sus paseos. Los tendederos de los que cuelgan las ropas de
los vecinos, las músicas que se escapan por las ventanas abiertas, las
flores y plantas que se enredan en los postes, las conversaciones más
privadas en varios idiomas que traspasan las paredes, los olores de las
cocinas que se cuelan por las ventanas… El calor asfixiante hace que las
casas se abran al exterior a través de balcones donde los vecinos hacen
vida y se convierten en auténticos escaparates. Todo ello hace que la
frontera entre lo privado y lo público se desdibuje en *Entre Ville*. Se trata
de una obra en la que el concepto de frontera a niveles distintos se confunde e, incluso, desaparece.

Así, tampoco existen fronteras lingüísticas, según demuestra la presencia de lenguas como el francés, inglés o griego. Ni siquiera las fronteras entre los diversos géneros literarios están bien delimitadas. Se da, por tanto, una redefinición o más bien transformación del género poético. Se parte de un poema, "Sant-Urbain Street Heat", pero se incorpora también otro poema, "Sniffing for Stories". Ambos recogen la experiencia y visión más personal de la autora y quizá son los textos más significativos puesto que condensan lo que después Carpenter amplifica con distintos recursos. Pero en el momento en el que el texto poético se somete al formato digital sufre una curiosa e interesante transformación. Ahora ya no se lee como poesía sino como una narración que nada tiene de convencional. Estamos ante una narración de estructura rizomática donde la organización de los materiales heterogéneos que la componen no se presenta bajo un orden jerárquico preestablecido, sino como un cúmulo de materiales interconectados entre sí que configuran un posible mapa, un itinerario totalmente alterable.

"The intimacies born of our proximity" (*Entre Ville*)

La aparición de la literatura digital ha provocado un cambio sustancial no solo en la obra en sí misma sino también en todo el sistema literario, en general. Se pregunta Espen Aarseth si "[e]l hipertexto, que es sin lugar a dudas, una nueva manera de escribir (mediante enlaces activos), ¿podría considerarse como una manera totalmente nueva de leer?" (2006: 86). Sin duda, el crítico tiene clara la respuesta. El papel del lector experimenta también una notable transformación. El lector del hipertexto crea su propia ruta de navegación y asume la responsabilidad de adentrarse por una senda u otra ya que "el hipertexto debe recorrerse como se visita una exposición de pintura o una ciudad extranjera. Su régimen de lectura favorito es el paseo." (2006: 85-86). El paseo es precisamente el *leitmotiv* de nuestra obra. El formato digital permite al lector vagar de un lugar a otro de forma laberíntica, dejándose llevar por ese afán de explorador/descubridor que impulsa a cualquier viajero. El lector decide, toca, lee, ve, observa con determinación y escucha. La implicación de todos los sentidos está más que garantizada gracias al formato digital. Ahora el lector es más viajero que nunca. Sin embargo, citando a Carpenter, no hay que olvidar que "the intimacies [are] born of our proximity", por lo cual, es a través de la mirada subjetiva de la autora desde la que observamos y nos adentramos en el barrio. Así, la libertad que siente el lector es en cierto modo una falacia, una quimera inalcanzable. La autora ha diseñado y creado la obra teniendo muy presente cuáles son los posibles caminos.

Partiendo de la idea de Bolter (1991) sobre la técnica de la repetición al hablar del hipertexto, el lector de *Entre Ville*, con frecuencia, recorre los mismos lugares, accede repetidamente a los vídeos, a las mismas imágenes. En definitiva, lleva a cabo un proceso de relectura apasionado e intenso. Y así sucede, en primer lugar, porque el lector, consciente o inconscientemente, se deja llevar por el deseo de querer captar y sentir todos y cada uno de los detalles. Y, en segundo lugar, por deseo expreso de la autora quien ha configurado su obra con un recorrido que puede llegar a ser finito, aspecto poco frecuente en las textualidades electrónicas. El lector en su papel activo es quien decide cuándo, cómo y dónde acabar con su lectura y asume que aventurarse por ciertos caminos quizá lo excluya de poder transitar otros. Sin embargo, el riesgo, la duda o incluso el miedo forman parte de la ficción, despuntando así lo que tiene de juego esta literatura. En realidad *Entre Ville* tiene de lúdico sobre todo el ofrecer un viaje dentro de un viaje, como si de unas muñecas rusas se tratase. El lector es viajero por partida doble: por la temática del texto en sí misma y por la forma en la que el texto se presenta. Es un todo completo en sí mismo como lo es cualquier libro de literatura de viajes impreso.

Bajo el estigma de la Otra

A medida que se profundiza en el análisis de la literatura digital y la literatura de viajes como dos vías paralelas que se entrecruzan, como por ejemplo ocurre en *Entre Ville*, se observan puntos en común que en un primer momento podrían pasar desapercibidos. Lo que caracteriza a ambas literaturas, como ya se apuntaba al inicio, es una sorprendente flexibilidad y gran capacidad de adaptación. Estas literaturas viven en los márgenes y en ellas no existen las fronteras. Son cajones de sastre en los que la tradición y la innovación se mezclan sin caer en ningún tipo de contradicción. Por otra parte, ambas aparecen de un modo u otro bajo el estigma de la Otra. A pesar de la larga tradición de la literatura de viajes y del importante corpus que ésta ha generado, no ha sido considerada unánimemente por la crítica como un género propio. Algo similar le ocurre a la literatura digital, en este caso provocado sobre todo por su carácter novedoso.

Todavía en la actualidad, a pesar de que vivimos rodeados de pantallas, la unión entre literatura y tecnología resulta cuanto menos sorprendente y chocante, como si de dos realidades antagónicas se tratase. Clément, sin embargo, afirma que "asistimos sin duda al nacimiento de un nuevo género pero nadie puede predecir cuál será su futuro, pues nos falta el distanciamiento que permitiría abordar un corpus ya consolidado de obras lo suficientemente numerosas y variadas" (2006: 78). Las textualidades electrónicas se nos presentan como medios perfectos para amplificar los significados y la naturaleza dinámica de la lectura. Obras como *Entre Ville* son un claro ejemplo de ello.

Afortunadamente, la presencia de la literatura digital es cada vez menos extraña y se está abriendo camino como demuestra la presencia de autores nacionales e internacionales, estudios y tesis doctorales, artículos, simposios y congresos. Por otra parte, surgen recopilaciones como los de la Electronic Literature Collection de la Electronic Literature Organization. Además, se cuenta con interesantes proyectos como el de la Electronic Literature as a Model of Creativity and Innovation in Practice (ELMCIP) (<http://elmcip.net/>) o bien con grupos de investigación como Hermeneia (<http://www.hermeneia.net/>), pionero en esta disciplina en el estado español con más de diez años de experiencia investigando la confluencia entre las tecnologías digitales y la literatura en un sentido amplio de creación y de reflexión.

El elenco de posibilidades y la potencialidad de la literatura digital es realmente increíble y demostrable si se presta atención al análisis de estas obras. Podríamos decir que es todavía una cuestión de tiempo el poderse desprender de la etiqueta "otra" y/o "nueva". A la luz de todo lo expuesto aquí, parece que nos adentramos en el buen camino.

Bibliografía

Aarseth, E. 2006. "Sin sensación de final: la estética hipertextual", in M. T. Vilariño & A. Abuín (eds.), *Teoría del hipertexto. La literatura en la era electrónica*, Madrid, Arco/Libros.

Benda, Ch. 2008. *Senghor on the Rocks*, <www.senghorontherocks.net/ [consultado el 12.I.2013]

Bolter, J. D. 1991. *Writing Space: The Computer, Hypertext, and the History of Writing*, Boston, Houghton Mifflin.

Carpenter, J. R. 2006. *Entre Ville: This City Between Us.* <http://luckysoap.com/entreville/thiscitybetweenus/index.html> *Entre Ville. HTML, DHTML, javascript, Quicktime*, in <http://www.narrabase.net/> [consultado el 20.VII.2011]

Carrión, J. 2009. "Google o la Divinidad", in *Suplemento Ñ, del diario Clarín*, <http://jorgecarrion.com/2009/05/14/google-o-la-divinidad/> [consultado el 28.VII.2011]

Clément, J. 2006. "Hipertexto de ficción: ¿nacimiento de un nuevo género?", in M. T. Vilariño & A. Abuín (eds.), *Teoría del hipertexto. La literatura en la era electrónica*, Madrid, Arco/Libros, 77-91.

Coover, R. 2008. *Voyage into the Unknown*, <http://collection.eliterature.org/2/works/coover_voyage/VoyageInt oTheUnknown/index.html> [consultado el 12.I.2013]

Tocco, F. 2009. "Entrevista a Jorge Carrión{2" <http://www.criptahda.matiasf.com.ar/2009/08/entrevista-a-jorge-carrion-2/> [consultado el 12.I.2013].

ALBERT JORNET SOMOZA

Identidades desbordadas: espacio y sujeto en la narrativa breve de Dino Buzzati

Se ha dicho muchas veces que la narrativa occidental del siglo XX se caracteriza por su capacidad de ficcionalizar la "crisis del sujeto moderno": un sujeto cuya creencia en su esencia dada se ha difuminado, un sujeto radicalmente contingente y muchas veces preso de un solipsismo endémico, fruto de una ruptura epistemológica con el mundo de las cosas creadas y de su caída en el pozo de la incertidumbre ontológica. Quisiera analizar la plasmación de esta experiencia, presente en gran parte de la literatura contemporánea (Kafka, Borges, Camus, Beckett), en la narrativa breve de Dino Buzzati. Más concretamente, en el libro que reúne los cuentos que escribió hasta 1958, es decir, sus *Sessanta racconti*. Y me interesan estos relatos en la medida en que logran situar en el centro del conflicto narrativo la tensión del sujeto en su condición de constructor de una identidad.

Para ello, quisiera poner atención, en primer lugar, en un par de aspectos narrativos que encontramos casi invariablemente a lo largo de los cuentos compilados en este volumen. El primero de ellos trata de la condición de los personajes que generalmente se sitúan en el foco de la acción: los protagonistas buzzatianos aparecen habitualmente como seres pasivos, contempladores, a quienes les sucede algo a menudo dado desde el exterior, y ante lo cual ellos deben reaccionar. Son personajes que nunca se mueven por convicciones propias sino que asisten a los sucesos dentro de una lógica del cambio de sus parámetros habituales.

El segundo aspecto responde a un procedimiento narrativo que afecta a la estructura de muchos de sus relatos: se trata de la elipsis del desenlace final de la trama. A mi modo de ver, este recurso no persigue solamente una voluntad efectista de suspense o de polisemia, sino que, escamoteándonos el final explícito del relato, Buzzati está descentrando la importancia de la acción, está desviando la atención respecto a la secuencialidad de los hechos narrados para enfatizar que el núcleo del cuento, la tensión propia de sus narraciones, no se halla en los fenómenos sino en la condición de los sujetos que los transitan y su relación con lo sucedido.

El relato "Una goccia" (142-44) ejemplifica a la perfección estos dos aspectos. En éste, el habitante del sexto piso de un bloque de casas narra el descubrimiento de una gota de agua que cada noche sube por las escaleras del edificio. El extraño acontecimiento es negado en un primer momento por su casera pero, tras algunos días, todo el vecindario está al corriente y, pese a que el silencio impera entre ellos, cada uno interpreta el fenómeno a su manera: "Ora molte orecchie restano tese nel buio, quando la notte è scesa a opprimere il genere umano. E chi pensa a una cosa, chi a un'altra" (143). Efectivamente los personajes, incluso el narrador homodiegético, permanecen pasivos contemplando el misterio de la gota de agua y el relato acaba sin dar cuenta de qué sucede con ella. En su lugar, el discurso termina plasmando los intentos de interpretación del vecindario y la respuesta aplastante del narrador:

> Ma che cosa sarebbe poi questa goccia: —domandano con esasperante buona fede— un topo forse? Un rospetto uscito dalle cantine? No davvero.
>
> E allora —insistono— sarebbe per caso una allegoria? Si vorrebbe, così per dire, simboleggiare la morte? o qualche pericolo? o gli anni che passano? [...]
>
> O più sottilmente si intende raffigurare i sogni e le chimere? Le terre vagheggiate e lontane dove si presume la felicità? Qualcosa di poetico insomma?
>
> [...] Ma no, vi dico, non è uno scherzo, non ci sono doppi sensi, trattasi ahimè di una goccia d'acqua, a quanto è dato presumere, che di notte viene su per le scale. Tic, tic, misteriosamente, di gradino in gradino. E perciò si ha paura (144).

El relato, pues, no termina con el final del nudo narrativo —no sabemos qué sucede con esta gota—, sino con el inquietante y fallido intento por comprender el fenómeno. Como decíamos, el hecho de no saber qué sucede desvía la atención de la trama: el relato no está simplemente recreando un elemento fantástico como es la posibilidad de que una gota de agua suba cada noche por unas escaleras, sino que está expresando la necesidad del sujeto, de todo sujeto, de interpretar la realidad que le rodea. El cuento plasma, a la vez, la imposibilidad última del propio intento en el momento en que los fenómenos se salen de las normas de interpretación convencionales. Los personajes buzzatianos son, por consiguiente, ante todo *intérpretes de sus realidades*, y es precisamente esta tarea hermenéutica, sus causas y consecuencias, sus límites y aporías, lo que tematizan los propios relatos. A través de este procedimiento, pues, nuestra lectura se convierte en una interpretación de la interpretación, en una hermenéutica de segundo grado.

Visto esto, hay que resaltar cómo, en algunos de los cuentos, este retrato de los personajes como hermeneutas de su entorno incide especialmente en el proceso de resignificación de la propia identidad. Al fin y al cabo, ¿qué es la identidad sino el resultado de la acción hermenéutica de un sujeto sobre sí mismo, es decir, de la búsqueda de un significado para el significante que supone el propio individuo?

Efectivamente, el punto de máxima tensión narrativa de muchos de los textos de Buzzati se halla en el hecho de que sus protagonistas ven alterada, siempre involuntariamente, su propia condición. Como podemos encontrar en relatos como "L'assalto al convoglio" (8-23) o "Il borghese stregato" (135-42), el acto interpretador de los personajes va ligado al desajuste respecto a su antigua identidad. En el primero, un capo de la mafia vuelve al centro de operaciones de su banda tras pasar tres años en la cárcel, pero cuando constata que sus hombres ya no lo reconocen y que su puesto ha sido suplantado por el actual capo, éste decide no revelar su identidad, porque interpreta que ya no le pertenece. "Il borghese stregato", por su parte, muestra la inmersión de un hombre adulto paseando en un bosque en el que descubre a unos niños jugueteando. La fantasiosa travesía con ellos le hará descubrir la vulgaridad en la que se ha sumido su vida y el regreso supondrá para él una misteriosa pero casi placentera muerte.

Como vemos, se repite la estructura narrativa de un sujeto en tránsito, que al observar cómo cambian sus circunstancias también sufre una alteración profunda de su condición; una muerte, como la del burgués encantado, de su antigua identidad. El elemento esencial que inicia la narración es siempre el desplazamiento del individuo, tanto a nivel espacial como temporal, que a medida que avanza el texto debemos entender como correlato del descentramiento del sujeto. La extrañeza, la tensión y el misterio que transpiran estos textos radican en el nunca explícito proceso de interpretación al que se ven forzados sus protagonistas para aceptar que no son *lo que creían ser*, que *ya* no lo son. Si Bajtín (1989), al ejemplificar su célebre concepto de cronotopo, descubría que en la novela griega antigua dominaba una "lógica del suceso", que convertía en abstracto el tiempo externo de la novela pero en fortuito e inesperado el tiempo interno de las aventuras, podemos convenir que lo que existe en los relatos de Buzzati es una "lógica del cambio". En esta lógica encontramos siempre la tensión entre la aparente continuidad de las circunstancias y la novedad, pero una novedad que tarda en ser desvelada porque solamente es comprensible desde el sujeto interpretador de la realidad y su consuetudinaria resistencia al cambio. De ahí que la tensión sea siempre gradual y difícil de asumir. El tiempo y el espacio buzzatiano aparecen, pues, como subjetivos, porque únicamente a través de la acción hermenéutica del sujeto cobran sentido en el relato en la medida en que denuncian una alteración de su identidad. Esta característica la encontramos en su dimensión más trágica en el relato "Sette piani" (24-40): en él, un hombre acude a un hospital para tratarse una dolencia común y no muy complicada de sanar. Pero el hospital tiene la particularidad de dividir a los pacientes según el grado de gravedad, de manera que cuanto más bajo es el piso, más preocupante resulta ser la enfermedad. El relato no es otra cosa que la renuencia de Giuseppe Corte, nuestro protagonista, en aceptar su particular descenso a los infiernos, desde el plácido séptimo piso al primero, ante las constantes excusas extraterapéuticas por parte de los doctores para justificar el ingreso en la planta inferior. Corte se niega a interpretar la realidad del desplazamiento, la pérdida de su salud, su condición de enfermo grave, hasta que ve cerrarse por última vez las persianas de su última habitación.

En los relatos de Buzzati, pues, se tematiza el desplazamiento de sus personajes, crucial para la tarea hermenéutica de interpretación de sí mismos. Contrariamente a la novela de aventuras, en la que por lo general el héroe, movido por un ideal o por una necesidad, no ve alterada su identidad pese a los viajes y tribulaciones que pueda llevar a cabo, y por eso puede volver a casa victorioso e inalterado, el espacio buzzatiano está marcado por una ley implícita que dicta que un desplazamiento supone también una pérdida de la propia condición, a la cual ya no se puede volver. No es la aventura lo que prevale en éste, sino la capacidad de asumir el movimiento, exterior e interior, del personaje. La identidad, como vemos, se muestra susceptible al movimiento, y por tanto lleva implícita en su condición dos presupuestos: 1) que la identidad es una construcción semiótica *del* y *sobre* el sujeto —consciente o inconsciente, individual o colectiva— y 2) que una identidad estable solo está a salvo en el aislamiento abstracto del sujeto ante el contacto con *el otro*, con *lo otro*. Los relatos de Buzzati acaban mostrando la relación de extrañeza que mantiene el sujeto con su propia identidad, es decir, denuncian la ilusión de una identidad invariable a través de la representación de identidades desbordadas.

Ahora bien, si por un lado vemos que la identidad es móvil y variable, a la vez también tenemos que constatar que ésta es, para los personajes, única e individual, ya que configura la peculiar manera de interpretación de cada personaje. En este sentido, podemos aplicar al concepto de identidad la frase que, referida a la lengua, Derrida (1997: 39) extrae del poeta Abdelkebir Khatibi, en un texto sobre "el monolingüismo del otro" que reza así: "no tengo más que una lengua, y no es la mía". Los personajes de Buzzati se caracterizan por pasar un proceso que les hace tomar consciencia de que "no tienen más que una identidad, y no es la suya". Únicamente pueden interpretar la realidad desde lo que son, pero a la vez eso les muestra que ya no son aquello con lo que estaban habituados a identificarse.

La paradoja de la identidad, pues, acaba instaurando en el sujeto una angustiosa contradicción: si por un lado se plasma en él un instinto de conservación e inmovilismo, por otro lado la consciencia de su descentramiento, del frágil espejismo de la identidad, también lo lleva a una búsqueda hacia *lo otro*, a una expansión de sus fronteras. En este sentido hay dos relatos muy interesantes del escritor italiano, que articulan más que ningún otro una "voluntad de horizonte" (Prado Biezma 2009: 302), y que ponen en juego narrativamente tanto la representación de un espacio físico subjetivizado como la apertura de las fronteras identitarias hacia *el otro*. A través de estos dos relatos *el otro* será descrito como aporía, por una parte, y como deseo, por la otra, ambos como consecuencia de las dos caras de la paradójica moneda de la identidad. Los cuentos son "I sette messaggeri" (3-7) y "Ombra del sud" (41-6), respectivamente.

En el primero de ellos, Buzzati narra la empresa del hijo de un rey, cuya geografía, época y nombre desconocemos, que emprende un viaje hacia la frontera meridional de su reino para encontrar sus confines. El narrador explica que lleva ocho años viajando hacia el sur, a caballo, y que para emprender la expedición se dotó de siete mensajeros que irían llevando noticias a y desde la capital del reino, a los cuales, como regla nemotécnica les otorga nombres ordenados alfabéticamente: Alessandro, Bartolomeo, Caio, Domenico, etc. El protagonista no tarda en darse cuenta de que el tiempo que necesitan los mensajeros para ir y volver de la capital es cinco veces el número de días que llevan viajando (Geerts 1976). El presente de enunciación del relato se sitúa en el momento en el que el narrador despedirá al último mensajero, Domenico, pues éste tardaría treinta y cuatro años en regresar y él tendría ya setenta y dos años, pero, según dice, se siente ya muy cansado de viajar remotamente hacia el sur. De esta manera, Buzzati representa la aporía que supone llegar al *otro*: por mucho que ande hacia la frontera, solo encuentra gente que habla su lengua, que es de su mismo reino, y por ello el narrador llega a reconocer que: "quanto più procedo, più vado convincendomi che non esiste frontiera" (6). Pero, a la vez, la imposibilidad misma de llegar a la frontera, el desplazamiento infinito hacia este *otro*, lo desvincula de su origen, de su identidad, al mismo ritmo que va perdiendo poco a poco esos lazos en forma de mensajeros: "Mi portavano curiose lettere ingiallite dal tempo, e in esse trovavo nomi dimenticati, modi di dire a me insoliti, sentimenti che non riuscivo a capire" (5). El pensamiento, el lenguaje y los sentimientos de su ciudad natal se han vuelto extraños al narrador, y ve cómo mengua paulatinamente su capacidad de interpretar las cartas que le llegan de su casa. Pese a ser incapaz de llegar al *otro*, el sujeto en tránsito ha perdido toda identidad, todo reconocimiento con su origen, en un laberinto donde la infinitud espacial del reino no es más que el símbolo del paradigma del sujeto, cuyas barreras no puede llegar a traspasar sencillamente porque no es capaz ni de llegar a verlas.

¿Está, entonces, el sujeto, según la representación que vemos en Buzzati, abocado al fracaso del encuentro del *otro* en la aporía de la identidad, que por un lado no lo deja salir de su propio paradigma, pero por otro lado al desplazarse pierde la ilusión de un centro estable y tranquilizador? Hay un segundo elemento, en esta búsqueda aparentemente frustrada del *otro*, que en los relatos del italiano parecen salvaguardar la posibilidad del encuentro: la voluntad, el deseo, la esperanza. "I sette messaggeri" toma un aire inesperado y poético cuando, al finalizar, toda la angustia y la fatiga del narrador se ven trocadas por la esperanza de encontrar el *otro*: "Un ansia inconsueta da qualche tempo si accende in me alla sera [...]: è l'impazienza di conoscere le terre ignote a cui mi dirigo" (7). El lenguaje objetivo y despeinado que abunda en el relato se convierte ahora en una encendida estética de la evocación de lo desconocido: "Una speranza nuova mi trarrà domattina ancora più avanti, verso quelle montagne inesplorate che le ombre della notte stanno occultando" (7).

Si la búsqueda del *otro* resulta ser una aporía desde la realidad cerrada del pensamiento y del lenguaje que definen la identidad, parece que la dimensión que da sentido a la propia búsqueda acaba siendo la del *deseo* y la *voluntad* del encuentro. El *otro*, como deseo innato del sujeto, abre una fisura que, si bien no parece resolver la situación de nuestro narrador, sí le da una explicación por sí misma: le hace ver la realidad de una manera *otra*, no contemplable ni en los propios sueños —"neppure nei sogni"—, procurándole un placer vivificador y epifánico. Se nos insinúa, entonces, que la pulsión del encuentro con el *otro* justifica por sí mismo la búsqueda, pues aunque no sea posible alcanzar al *otro*, sí se logra modificar la interpretación de la realidad y por tanto escapar, aunque sea por momentos, de la inexorable cerrazón del sujeto. La apertura hacia el misterio del *otro*, hacia lo desconocido, permite el sueño de cancelar la desolada finitud del sujeto (Coriasso 2009: 47).

El otro relato en el que podemos constatar esta doble condición del *otro* como aporístico y deseado, es "Ombra del sud". En éste, se nos presenta un turista occidental en Egipto que, para su sorpresa, se encuentra en varios puntos de su ruta a una misma persona, un hombre árabe que anda bamboleándose en la lejanía. Asistimos a la evolución del pensamiento del personaje que rápidamente se percata de que él es el único que puede verlo: no sabe si es "di carne ed ossa o miraggio", "un effetto di luce" o "un'illusione banale degli occhi" (43). Los esfuerzos por entender qué sucede con aquel hombre, se van alternando con sucesivas interpretaciones: "quell'essere mi risultava adesso come una personificazione, racchiudente il segreto stesso dell'Africa" (44). Igualmente, los estados del propio personaje son analizados por él mismo, desde la "inquietudine" y la "paura" iniciales hasta que estas sensaciones dan paso a "sentirsi deboli, inferiori a ciò che ci aspetta" (45). El narrador se da cuenta de la incapacidad del lenguaje para explicar aquello: "le parole mi si ingorgavano in bocca" (43). Finalmente hallamos la interpretación del protagonista: "mi pare di avere capito che tu vorresti condurmi più in là, ogni volta più in là, sempre più nel centro, fino alle frontiere del tuo incognito regno" (46).

Los elementos son los mismos que los que hemos estado viendo: la llamada del sujeto hacia la frontera de un espacio infinito, el intento de interpretación de la realidad, la incapacidad del lenguaje y el pensamiento por entenderlo, y la resuelta voluntad final hacia el confín desconocido, hacia el *otro*, en este caso personificado en la figura misteriosa del árabe, que empuja al protagonista del cuento a tomar la decisión de acudir a la intrigante llamada de éste:

Questa sera mi sento veramente bene, sebbene i pensieri ondeggino un poco, e ho preso la decisione di partire (Ma sarò poi capace? Non farà storie poi la mia anima, al momento buono non si metterà a tremare, non nasconderà la testa tra le pavide ali dicendo di non andare più avanti?) (46).

De nuevo el pensamiento —"pensieri"— es de lo que se sirve el instinto de conservación de la propia identidad —"la mia anima"— y lo que debe sortear el *deseo del otro* para acudir a su encuentro. De esta forma, haciendo prevalecer el deseo a la razón, y la voluntad al logocentrismo, Buzzati huye de posibles determinismos y de dinámicas de dominación, apostando por el acercamiento al *otro* desde la apertura y la puesta en solfa de la propia identidad, entregando el sujeto desprejuiciado a la aventura que supone el encuentro con el *otro*.

Bibliografía

Bajtín, M. 1989 [1937-38]. "Las formas del tiempo y del cronotopo en la novela", in *Teoría y estética de la novela*, Madrid, Taurus, 237-409.
Buzzati, D. 1994 [1958]. *Sessanta racconti*, Milano, Mondadori.
Coriasso, C. 2009. "El laberinto como símbolo del referente inexistente: una comparación entre Borges y Buzzati", *Amaltea. Revista de mitocrítica* 1, 43-47.
Derrida, J. 1997. *El monolingüismo del otro o la prótesis de origen*, Buenos Aires, Manantial.
Geerts, W. 1976. "Il nucleo narrativo-pragmatico nei racconti di Buzzati", *Bulletin of the American Association of Teachers of Italian* 53: 1, 3-7.
Prado Biezma, J. del. 2009. "Fronteras estancas, fronteras porosas: del *triangolo* y la *striscia* de Buzzati a las *orillas en bruma* y *follaje* de Gracq", *Revista de Filología Alemana*, anejo I, 299-321.

MIRIAM LÓPEZ SANTOS

"Ese otro que soy yo". Transferencia y transgresión en la novela gótica española

La historia de la supervivencia del horror gótico es la historia de la progresiva interiorización y reconocimiento del miedo como generado por uno mismo, al margen de espíritus fantasmales y seres de ultratumba, porque el terror más espantoso, el verdadero horror, proviene, a no dudar, del ser humano, de su propia naturaleza. Los góticos ingleses, en una segunda etapa de confirmación del género, insistieron en la otredad vinculada a lo humano, a los hombres de siniestra naturaleza y a sus prácticas terribles. Es cierto que esta visión irrumpe impetuosa con Anne Radcliffe y su novela *El Italiano*, aunque se radicaliza de la mano de Matthew Lewis, a finales de la década de 1790, y su máxima utilización coincide con el apogeo del género hacia 1810, momento en que triunfa el horror gótico cultivado por figuras como Charles Maturin o William Henry Ireland. El lugar del mal vacilaba entre los individuos perturbados y las prácticas vinculadas a los mismos, aunque siempre latiendo en el fondo un fuerte carácter nacionalista, una revalorización de los elementos que hacen a un pueblo diferente; de ahí que lo malvado, lo extraño, en las novelas de esta época, viniera generalmente desde fuera y sobre todo desde España e Italia. Es comúnmente aceptado que el sur de Europa, y en especial estos dos países, atrajeron la imaginación occidental durante las últimas décadas de finales del siglo XVIII y principios de XIX.

La fascinación romántica por la cultura del sur que sintieron artistas y escritores americanos, británicos y franceses del siglo XIX comienza con los viajeros ingleses del siglo XVIII que buscaban lo pintoresco en rutas turísticas inexploradas. Sin embargo, la representación del sur en la novela gótica, aunque debe mucho a estos viajeros ingleses en cuanto a su imagen visual, no responde solo al placer por lo pintoresco, sino al contexto cultural británico, mediatizado por circunstancias históricas políticas y religiosas. El gótico encuentra en el sur un caldo de cultivo

para introducir una temática cultural, latente y prohibida por la maquina-
ria represora protestante, especialmente en lo referido a las escenas
sexuales que se vuelven particularmente explícitas cuando se producen
en conventos y monasterios o involucran de manera directa a la iglesia
católica. Se caracteriza, entonces, un Sur antagónico en lo político (España y Francia) y en lo religioso (España e Italia).[1]

La novela gótica nació, según hemos observado, como una expresión nacionalista artística, una revalorización de los elementos que hacen
a un pueblo diferente; de ahí que lo malvado, lo extraño en las novelas
de esta época viniera generalmente desde fuera y sobre todo desde España e Italia, como hemos apuntado. La ficción gótica, en cuanto forma
ficcional distintivamente británica, conlleva un componente nacionalista,
opuesto a lo continental y a lo católico, pues esta versión nacionalista
radical de la novela gótica criticaba la opresión aristocrática (cuyos más
poderosos representantes eran el feudalismo y la iglesia católica romana)
y sugería una libertad ancestral de todo lo inglés, amenazada por los
poderes alienantes colonizadores del sur del continente. Además de
provocar la sublimación en los sentimientos de sus lectores y exaltarlos,
el subgénero gótico servía, al mismo tiempo, de propaganda política
contra el despotismo francés, el papismo italiano y el medievalismo absolutista español, con su cultura de la superstición, su pervivencia del
poder católico y su aterradora política inquisitorial.

La mirada de estos escritores es preconcebida y recogen en sus novelas aquellos rasgos culturales que les permiten expresar de forma más
explícita su visión civilizada o incivilizada del "otro", anclado en un
modo de vivir arcaico, conservador y supersticioso. Una sociedad feudal
y oscurantista en su comportamiento frente a un mundo racional y moderno, el inglés, en el que el concepto de civilización se anteponía al que
representaban los países absolutistas del sur de Europa, especialmente
España. De esta manera, el escenario latino sirve a los intereses de esta
nueva novela gótica en su doble sentido de aspiración nacionalista y de
fuerza enfrentada a lo extraño, a lo diferente, a lo "otro", en definitiva. Y
pocas instituciones eran capaces de ensalzar mejor estos sentimientos
nacionalistas como la iglesia católica, gracias a una visión ocultista y

---

1   García Iborra así lo sostiene al afirmar que "el universo mediterráneo forma parte
     de lo gótico como fuente de una serie de temas políticos y culturales pertinentes en
     la época en que esta surge" (2007: 192).

esotérica,[2] denostada por la iglesia anglicana desde el siglo XVII y que suponía una reafirmación protestante y como consecuencia una reafirmación nacionalista del pueblo inglés.

En efecto, a un nivel puramente temático, la supremacía del país inglés sobre España quedó así plasmada en la visión que estas novelas ofrecían de la religión católica, uno de los temas primordiales del género gótico. De hecho, en muchas de las novelas la misma se emplea como fuente principal generadora de atmósferas góticas y sublimes. Aunque fuera Horace Walpole el impulsor del género, el potencial del catolicismo como medio de infundir terror se exaltaría durante la evolución del gótico, cuando la actitud negativa hacia este se hizo más que presente, se tornó protagonista; desde Lewis y su *Monje* a Radcliffe, con *El italiano*, o Maturin y su novela *Melmoth el errabundo,* la novela gótica, en su ansia de buscar temas y situaciones opuestas a las de su predecesora, la novela sentimental, explotó el catolicismo para conmover y excitar los sentimientos de los lectores. Los escritores góticos, sin embargo, se concentraban como motivo y fuente de lo sublime en aspectos como la vida monástica y la Inquisición, más que en aspectos teológicos, con el fin de dejar a un lado posibles debates religiosos, que no interesaban, y centrar los esfuerzos narratológicos en producir más que terror, horror en el lector. Así pues, pocas instituciones eran capaces de suscitar mayor terror en la mente inglesa como el catolicismo de Roma con sus ansias de poder, la oscuridad de sus ritos, la recreación en la tortura, pero también a través de la vida monástica, la reclusión femenina, la represión de impulsos sexuales y la ignorancia y superstición de monjes y clérigos.

Esta visión de la España católica afectaba al paisaje, a los personajes, a los comportamientos asociados a estos y a una de las instituciones más terribles, que durante el reinado de Fernando VII se había reactivado y gozaba de pleno auge, la Santa Inquisición. El paisaje establece la dualidad cultural igualdad/otredad, al pintar escenarios reconocibles pero amenazantes desde la perspectiva de lo diferente, de lo extraño. El castillo inglés deja paso a conventos, abadías, monasterios en ruinas, aislados y abandonados a la depravación y la lujuria de unos personajes que dejan de ser tan predecibles como aquellos emplazados en escenarios del norte de Europa. En el dibujo de los personajes la otredad cultural aparece

---

2   Norman (1968) y Sage (1988) han estudiado en profundidad el anticatolicismo de la tradición protestante.

representada en la identidad no civilizada, en contraposición con la superior civilización inglesa. La encarnación de la identidad nacional es representada en la heroína mientras que el proceder del villano, que será sustituido por este personaje religioso, monje o clérigo, representa de forma conjunta la otredad. Un ser satánico, malvado y maquiavélico, movido por unos deseos sexuales que ha visto reprimidos, que a medida que avanza el género y de la mano de Radcliffe va adquiriendo forma más humana, víctima de los sufrimientos internos motivados por sus actos depravados y su naturaleza siniestra. Junto a este, nuevos personajes femeninos, monjas o abadesas que, frente a aquel, no son presentados de forma tan terrorífica como los masculinos pues su comportamiento indecoroso está motivado por amor, envidia o crueldad y no por maldad inherente al personaje.

En cuanto a la Inquisición aparece vinculada al catolicismo más salvaje e ignorante, y en estrecha dependencia de la nación española. No olvidemos que estaba aún vigente en España cuando el género alcanzaba su mayor apogeo y es un tema clave en el desarrollo del anti-catolicismo del gótico y en la tradición protestante y nacionalista inglesa. Si el catolicismo se asociaba a lo sublime, la Inquisición era fuente de terror y horror, pues se la suponía desde fuera, y desde dentro, capaz de las mayores atrocidades. De hecho, desde tiempos remotos, pertenecía al ideario inglés: el espionaje, las estancias laberínticas, la captura silenciosa y nocturna de las víctimas, la cámara de torturas, los enormes candelabros. ¿Cómo no iba la novela gótica a volver sus ojos a esta institución en su búsqueda constante de nuevos terrores?

En esta pretensión, sus autores exaltaron todo el entramado del proceso inquisitorial, desde el reo encarcelado: la confesión, la deliberación del tribunal, el entorno que rodea el juicio, hasta la sentencia, en la absoluta soledad primera y en el proceso final, terriblemente sublime, aunque tampoco olvidaron los excesos y horrores de la misma, que no se limitaban a las actuaciones del tribunal en su corte, sino que trascendían a toda la sociedad, desde el monarca hasta el pueblo llano. Y todo ello con la sola intención de recrear un arma medieval, terrible y espeluznante, de efectos sublimes y símbolo del poder absoluto.

El anticlericalismo de la novela gótica inglesa, en definitiva, acabó por revelar dos mundos opuestos: el que representa la otredad (villanos, comportamientos extranjeros según la experiencia inglesa, escenario exótico y sublime, monasterios, conventos, prisiones y la Inquisición) y el que representa lo inglés, lo doméstico, lo cercano, ejemplificado en la burguesía, lo femenino, los valores y las convicciones políticas conservadoras.

Ahora bien, ¿cómo adaptar un género extranjero, profundamente nacionalista y anticlerical a un país católico, conservador y receloso de lo foráneo? Ríos de tinta han corrido en torno a la inexistencia de la novela gótica en España (López Santos 2010). Cierto es que la experimentación con el terror exigía un cierto grado de trasgresión, un tránsito por los laberintos más oscuros de la conciencia humana y cierto es también que la literatura española no estaba preparada para la tal trasgresión, sobre todo en lo que se refiere al tratamiento de lo sobrenatural. El principal problema de la trasgresión, sin embargo, no era solo que se subvirtieran ideas, es decir, que se desarrollaran ampliamente y en toda su riqueza de matices los temas tabú o se diera rienda suelta a la irracionalidad. El verdadero conflicto de la adaptación del género viene principalmente determinado por este fuerte carácter nacionalista del mismo y los componentes que derivan de su aplicación. Lo gótico trataba de insertar de algún modo, como hemos visto, un manifiesto cultural, del que se mostraba tajantemente en contra, en una cultura ya desarrollada y que deseaba encontrar otras oportunidades lúdicas conforme a su línea de pensamiento político. No obstante, estas nociones trasladadas a otras culturas, precisamente a aquellas con las que entraba en conflicto, resultaban imposibles de sostener. Los ideales anticatólicos que impulsaba la Ilustración penetraron ampliamente en Inglaterra y Francia y, añadidos estos a la propaganda inglesa protestante anticatólica, influyeron en la Ilustración española, aunque con signo diferente.

La Ilustración en España no podía de ninguna manera decantarse por una oposición manifiesta al catolicismo, como había sucedido en Inglaterra, país protestante, o en Francia, con ideas liberales. Ni tan siquiera aquella parcela de ilustrados españoles, con principios menos conservadores, que criticaba abiertamente el férreo sometimiento a la fe de Roma o, al menos, a algunos de sus principios o instituciones por suponer un retroceso en la modernización del país, estaba preparada para asumir una literatura que atacara a los principios básicos en los que se sustentaba el sistema, pues pretendían tan solo, y lejos de suprimir la doctrina, un catolicismo menos apegado a Roma y más españolizado que reflejara lo pintoresco y nacional del mismo. En España, el catolicismo era considerado algo más que una institución, un verdadero sello identificador, y la novela gótica debía perder o suavizar, en la transferencia genérica, aquella carga subversiva que suponía un ataque directo a la cultura española en la pretensión de encontrar un lugar definitivo entre autores y público.

Sin embargo, los prejuicios de la novela gótica iban más lejos, pues no solo el punto de mira se dirigía a la Iglesia católica y a su forma de gobierno absolutista, sino que se hacían extensibles a todo aquello que remitiera de alguna forma a lo español, a su cultura ancestral extremadamente supersticiosa y anclada en períodos oscuros. Aquella profunda aversión hacia todo lo latino es la primera de las dificultades de entre tantas con las que se topó la ficción gótica en su transferencia a la literatura española. Los escritores españoles se vieron obligados, y ello de acuerdo con las exigencias novelescas de adecuación a las costumbres nacionales, a una adaptación que no condujera al rechazo, pues aunque pueda entenderse como actitud crítica, la censura tampoco iba a permitir este ataque feroz y directo a las instituciones fundamentales en las que se sustentaba la sociedad y, en definitiva, a lo más hondo del alma hispánica, y además en un momento en el que el nacionalismo era algo más que un movimiento incipiente. Esta complicación hubo de solventarse entonces en pro de la censura, pero sobre todo del movimiento lector al que iba dirigido y que la reclamaba. Los autores debían acudir a infinidad de artificios literarios, la presentación de vicios o comportamientos exaltados como medida aleccionadora, el ataque a determinadas facciones de la Iglesia, o justificaciones de diversa índole, en prólogos y advertencias iniciales, para solventar estos problemas, si pretendían recoger éxitos similares a los obtenidos en otros países europeos. Y aunque es cierto que determinados motivos, como la condena a la Inquisición y sus métodos, se aprovecharon para el desarrollo de las tramas de terror y de hecho fueron algunos de los más prolíficos, en obras como *Cornelia Bororquia*, *Vargas* o *Viaje al mundo subterráneo*, así como en las traducciones de *La abades* o de *El monje* no lo serían, sin embargo, en los mismos términos ni con idénticas motivaciones que los ingleses. Estas novelas son un perfecto ejemplo de la novela gótica anticatólica, donde la religión no es solo un confinamiento mental, sino que supone también un elemento político patente y al mismo tiempo filosófico. Si el catolicismo en la cultura inglesa inducía horror frente a la práctica protestante, desde su interior, el horror resulta evidente, respondiendo también a motivos políticos. El material anticatólico incrementa el aura siniestra y melodramática de la novela cuando esta mira hacia dentro. Mientras los escritores góticos ingleses pretendían usar el catolicismo, lejos de comprenderlo o al menos intentarlo, como un legado histórico y cultural para sus fines góticos, estas novelas españolas van más lejos, pues se plantean como una crítica directa a las estructuras, pretendiendo una reforma de las mismas, no solo una muestra de sus atrocidades.

Dependiendo del grado de terror que pretendan reflejar, se emplazarán en un momento histórico pasado y oscuro, para ahondar en las épocas terribles del Tribunal y sus torturas, o en el presente, más apoyado en el terror psicológico de la desesperación humana, un entorno reciente igualmente plagado de pánico y desesperación, para ahondar en esa idea de realismo y verosimilitud, para acercar al lector la experiencia vital del texto y para asegurar las dosis necesarias de terror que precisa una novela para calificarse de gótica.

Buscan un cambio, pero amparados en una intención propagandística de raíz diferente al origen. Los elementos formales del género gótico se adaptan en España a las necesidades que implican unos presupuestos ideológicos mucho más definidos y menos eclécticos. La novela gótica encontró en el argumento anticlerical, a medida que el género evolucionaba y abría horizontes a otras realidades literarias, una fuente de expresión nueva que enriqueció su fija estructura formularia, pero que debía tratarse con cautela para no atentar directamente contra los presupuestos de un país demasiado conservador. No se trataba solo de poner en tela de juicio una institución ambivalente, de carácter político y religioso a un tiempo, ni de presentar una institución absolutamente carente de humanidad. El trasfondo aterrador y la falta de límites en la presentación de la crueldad del ser humano revelan la intención de los autores de jugar con el terror sublime. La realidad aparece desvirtuada al servicio de la ficción literaria, del entretenimiento del público, aunque los personajes fueran tomados de la realidad o basados en ella, como el caso de Cornelia Bororquia. Se elimina la crítica directa, arbitraria y atroz, realizada desde la superioridad cultural, religiosa y moral, aunque se continúa presentando la perversa tiranía de ciertos representantes de la Iglesia, el hondo sufrimiento moral que padecen los personajes, héroes o villanos, sometidos a su rigidez, y la inevitable fijación con el espacio físico cerrado y opresor del subterráneo o del calabozo. La imagen de la España ancestral, supersticiosa, pero también oscura, tétrica, injusta y opresiva que reflejaba aquella novela gótica inglesa se desdibuja en estas narraciones españolas. Por el contrario, irá más allá en el ambiente opresivo y

asfixiante, en la cercanía con la realidad, en los personajes, en la crueldad de las descripciones, en la maldad del ser humano, en la crudeza de
un mundo sin esperanza.

En estas novelas encontramos, en definitiva, todo el ambiente anticlerical que iniciara *El Monje* y culminara *Melmoth el errabundo*, pero
sin pretender un ataque directo a la cultura española. Presentan su pre-
tendido carácter anticlerical desde una ideología liberal, una decidida
pretensión histórica y un marcado carácter político y declamatorio, pero
se ha eliminado la mirada censora a una religión que no dudaba en es-
conder la ideología y los intereses económicos imperialistas y liberales
ingleses, frente a un mundo atrasado y absolutista, el español, situado en
la otredad cultural, política y religiosa.

Bibliografía

García Iborra, J. 2007. "La representación cultural del sur en la novela
    gótica inglesa (1764-1820): otredad política y religiosa", Tesis doc-
    toral, Bellaterra, Universidad Autónoma de Barcelona.
López Santos, M. 2010. *La novela gótica en España (1788-1833)*, Vigo,
    Academia del Hispanismo.
Muñoz Sempere, D. 2002. "Represión política y literatura inquisitorial",
    Cuadernos de Ilustración y Romanticismo 10, 77-87.
—. 2008. *La Inquisición española como tema literario: política, historia
    y ficción en la crisis del antiguo régimen*, Woodbridge, Tamesis Books.
Norman, E. 1968. *Anti-Catholicism in Victorian England*, London, Allen
    & Unwin.
Sage, V. 1988. *Horror Fiction in the Protestant Tradition*, Basingstoke,
    Macmillan.

Eva March

Presencia y ausencia de Velázquez en la literatura inglesa de viajes del siglo XVIII

En 1623, Carlos de Inglaterra, siendo todavía príncipe de Gales, era inmortalizado por Diego Velázquez durante una breve visita por España, iniciándose, de este modo, la fructífera relación que los británicos establecerían con el pintor. No muchos años después, a finales de 1638 y por gentileza de su majestad Felipe IV de España, llegaban a Inglaterra las tres primeras copias de las obras de Velázquez: los retratos de Felipe IV, Isabel de Borbón y el Príncipe Baltasar Carlos (las tres en The Royal Collection, Hampton Court), mientras que ya en la primera mitad del siglo XVIII, las copias, en aquel momento casi tan estimadas como los originales, estaban presentes tanto en el mercado artístico londinense como en las residencias de británicos ilustres. Sirva de ejemplo la copia del *Retrato de Juan de Pareja* que hacia 1750 colgaba de las paredes de Castle Howard, propiedad de Lord Carlisle, o las diversas copias de Velázquez, entre ellas la de las *Meninas*, que estaban en posesión de Lord Grantham, el mismo Lord de la mano del cual llegó a Inglaterra, en 1784, el primer Velázquez original, esto si dejamos de lado el mencionado *Retrato de Carlos I,* perdido o no identificado todavía, y la *Lección de equitación del Príncipe Baltasar Carlos* (hoy en la colección del duque de Westminster).

Desde este momento hasta la afirmación suscrita en 1855 por el escocés Sir William Stirling-Maxwell en la monografía que inicia los estudios modernos sobre Velázquez —Gran Bretaña albergaba, en aquel momento, el conjunto de obras más importantes del pintor fuera del Museo del Prado— hay un largo trecho. Un largo trecho durante el cual la pintura del Siglo de Oro español, y más concretamente la de Velázquez, fue admirada y conocida gracias, ciertamente, a los incipientes coleccionistas, a versados eruditos o a insignes pintores británicos que pronunciaron al respecto fervientes elogios. No obstante, la valoración del arte de Velázquez tuvo su punto de inflexión más determinante en el testimonio que proporcionaron los que pueden considerarse sus verdaderos descubridores: los viajeros ingleses del siglo XVIII, unos viajeros llegados a España no en las primeras décadas del setecientos sino posteriormente, cuando las reformas introducidas por Fernando VI y sobre todo por Carlos III hicieron que el país fuera visto como un destino asequible. Los viajeros británicos del siglo XVII, pese a que comentaron aspectos artísticos del arte español, especialmente la arquitectura, no escribieron palabra alguna sobre Velázquez, como tampoco lo hicieron los grandes tratadistas y biógrafos europeos que pasaron por España.

Los relatos de Edward Clarke, Henry Swinburne, Richard Twiss, Richard Cumberland y los del resto de viajeros que repasaremos se anticiparán pues a los producidos por los viajeros de cualquier otro país europeo en lo que a Velázquez se refiere. Por este motivo no podemos esperar discursos sistematizados ni visiones estructuradas de Velázquez. Son, más bien, percepciones aisladas y puntuales, juicios personales, que merecen ser destacados, justamente, por su carácter innovador, el cual sitúa a los viajeros ingleses del siglo XVIII como los legítimos iniciadores de la fortuna crítica velazqueña dentro de la literatura de viajes. Como acabamos de decir, no contaron con relatos previos de viajes que les sirvieran de apoyo; sí que dispusieron en cambio de tratados artísticos españoles de los siglos XVII y XVIII de los que se sirvieron. Unos tratados que fueron ampliamente difundidos en Inglaterra, donde se publicaron no pocas traducciones y versiones reducidas de buena parte de ellos.

Sin duda, la principal fuente de información que tenían respecto a la pintura barroca española en general y sobre Velázquez en particular, era la obra de Antonio Palomino *El Parnaso Español Pintoresco Laureado* (1724). Parcialmente traducida al inglés en 1739, fue también publicada —resumidamente— en castellano, en Londres, el año 1742 y, todavía, en 1746. También en castellano, salió a la luz un tercer libro que es la suma de la obra de Palomino y la descripción de las obras que se encontraban en El Escorial realizada por Francisco de los Santos (1657). De esta obra se hicieron sendas traducciones inglesas: una, abreviada, en 1671 y otra en 1760.

Igual de influyente fue el *Viaje de España* (1772-1794) de Antonio Ponz, una de las personalidades más significativas de la Ilustración española. Relacionada con Ponz está la importante contribución del pintor y teórico neoclásico Anton Raphael Mengs. La larga carta que el pintor del rey le escribe relatándole el estado de las Bellas Artes en España y añadiendo una descripción de las pinturas del Palacio Real —incluida en el sexto tomo del *Viaje de España* (1776)—, fue un texto de referencia, como demuestran no solo las reiteradas citas que tuvo sino el hecho de que en 1782 fuera traducida al inglés.

El primero de los viajeros ingleses del siglo XVIII que escribió sobre pintura española fue el reverendo Edward Clarke, quien publicó sus *Letters Concerning the Spanish Nation* (1763) tres años después de haber recalado en España, donde llegó en 1760 para ser capellán del embajador británico. Desde este año hasta el viaje a España realizado en 1787 por William Beckford median pues casi treinta años, durante los cuales se sucedieron los viajes —que también adoptaron forma de libro— de Joseph Baretti, Richard Twiss, Henry Swinburne, John Talbot Dillon, Alexander Jardine, Richard Cumberland y Joseph Townsend. A ellos nos referiremos en las siguientes líneas.

La primera advertencia que cabe hacer respecto a cómo estos viajeros juzgaron el arte de Velázquez está relacionada con los lugares donde podían contemplarlo. A diferencia de los demás pintores españoles del siglo XVII cuyas obras estaban dispersas en iglesias, entornos monásticos y residencias particulares, el caso de Velázquez, pintor de Felipe IV desde 1623 hasta su muerte, es sensiblemente diferente. La mayor parte de su producción estaba custodiada en los Sitios Reales: el monasterio de San Lorenzo de El Escorial, pero sobre todo, el Palacio Real de Madrid. Únicamente una reducida parte de las obras del pintor sevillano se encontraban en colecciones particulares madrileñas o sevillanas y en alguna que otra iglesia capitalina. Por tanto, la visita al Palacio Real era paso obligado para poder hacerse una debida idea de la capacidad de Velázquez, un palacio que, durante los meses en los que el monarca lo ocupaba (de noviembre a Semana Santa) podía tener restringido su acceso, al menos parcialmente.

Pese a este eventual contratiempo, todos los autores de los libros de viajes pasaron por el Palacio Real, incluidos Clarke y Baretti, quienes lo visitaron en mayo y en octubre de 1760 respectivamente, cuando la ilustre residencia todavía estaba inacabada. También todos ellos —a excepción de Baretti— dejaron por escrito sus impresiones acerca de El Escorial. Además, Twiss, Jardine y Townsend mencionan algunas pinturas de Velázquez presentes en colecciones particulares del entorno sevillano — el *Retrato de Quevedo* y la *Adoración de los Magos* en la colección de Francisco de Bruna—. Townsend también se detiene, igual que Swinburne, en la madrileña colección del duque de Alba, donde se hallaba expuesta la *Venus del espejo* que hoy cuelga de las paredes de la National Gallery. Tal vez los comentarios suscritos por el político irlandés Sir John Talbot Dillon constituyen la excepción a lo dicho puesto que, aunque afirma haber visitado el palacio madrileño, solamente se refiere a Velázquez en relación al Buen Retiro.

Para poder valorar en su justa medida los juicios emitidos con respecto a Velázquez es necesario recalcar que, a menudo, los elogios hacia el pintor se formulan de manera velada. En más de una ocasión, dichos viajeros son parcos al referirse a Velázquez, pero en comparación con las inexistentes menciones a cualquier otro pintor, son, en realidad, muy generosos con él. Este sería el caso, por ejemplo, del mencionado Talbot Dillon, en cuya obra no aparece referido el nombre de ningún pintor español exceptuando a Velázquez, a quien por otro lado, únicamente cita para precisar, siguiendo fielmente a Ponz, que la escultura de Felipe IV de Pietro Tacca del Palacio del Buen Retiro fue realizada según un cuadro del pintor (Talbot Dillon 1780: 79).

Algo parecido podría decirse de Clarke, quien, como colofón a su visita a El Escorial, remarca cuáles eran los grandes pintores españoles: *El Españoleto*, Murillo, Navarrete el Mudo y Velázquez. De los cuatro, solo del pintor sevillano no se limita a proporcionar lacónicos datos biográficos sino que apostilla, en referencia a la *Túnica de José*: "he was the most astonishing master of the art, in design and expression, as may be seen in that picture of his in the Escurial" (1763: 154). Pese a su brevedad, lo que Clarke dijo de Velázquez fue mucho más de lo que nunca escribiera sobre cualquier otro pintor, español o italiano. En cuanto a Townsend, también la lectura de su relato deja ver la gran consideración que le merecía la pintura de Velázquez, especialmente el Velázquez que vio en el Palacio Real, donde menciona, como obras debidas a su mano, los retratos ecuestres de Felipe III, Felipe IV y los de sus esposas, el *Retrato ecuestre del Conde Duque de Olivares,* la *Fragua de Vulcano*, *Mercurio y Argos*, un *Paisaje con dos eremitas* (San Antonio Abad y san Pablo) y las *Meninas*. Todas estas pinturas, junto a las demás presentes en el Palacio, aparecen mencionadas en un listado que solamente rompe esta condición en dos ocasiones: una, al referirse a las copias que Rubens hizo de Tiziano, y la otra al contemplar los cinco mencionados retratos ecuestres de Velázquez, de los que duda "que nunca hayan sido vistos juntos cinco caballos más perfectos y llenos de vida" (Townsend 1988:

107). Estas vehementes palabras van a la par con la conclusión de lo visto en la colección real. Un párrafo muy significativo pues solamente aparece en él un nombre propio, el de Diego Velázquez, a quien sitúa, además, por encima de cualquier pintor italiano o flamenco en lo concerniente a la construcción de la perspectiva aérea (Townsend 1988: 110).

En cuanto a las opiniones suscritas por Cumberland y Beckford, éstas constituyen un capítulo aparte, pues en ambos casos dirigen elocuentes y emotivos elogios a Velázquez —"the great luminary of the Spanish School"— o a la *Túnica de José*, de la que el primero dice que aunque fuera la única obra conservada del pintor sería suficiente "to rank him the highest in his art" (Cumberland 1806: 248-49). El segundo apostilla que es "la más conmovedora pintura que conozco [...] la prueba más contundente del genio estupendo de Velázquez plasmada en las más noble obra que ha producido el arte" (Beckford 1966: 104). Así, el nombre de Velázquez queda singularmente emparejado con el de los más celebrados pintores del Renacimiento italiano. A Beckford la impresión que le causó la contemplación de la *Túnica de José* velazqueña y las rafaelistas *Virgen de la Perla* y *Virgen del Pez* le dificultaron poder admirar ninguna otra gran obra de las que se hallaban en El Escorial. Cumberland también pone en paralelo el arte de Velázquez al de Rafael y Tiziano, aunque haciendo relucir en el mismo plano a Rubens y Claudio Coello.

Respecto a Twiss, además de aportar datos biográficos sobre Velázquez, de referenciar más de una docena de obras del pintor, y de considerarle (junto a Murillo) el mejor pintor de España, su testimonio es especialmente relevante porque transcribe un manuscrito en el que su autor —un inglés que había visitado El Escorial en 1754— defendía la autoría de *la Virgen del pez* de Rafael. En este manuscrito, ya publicado por Ponz, como Twiss sabe, se elogia el nombre de Velázquez y, más concretamente, su *Retrato ecuestre del Conde Duque de Olivares* se presenta como paradigma de la perfección en cuanto al equilibrio que deben mantener las figuras en un cuadro. En este texto se mencionan como pinturas de referencia diversas composiciones debidas a pintores italianos (Leonardo, Tintoretto o Correggio), pero curiosamente no se cita ningún otro cuadro de un pintor español contemporáneo ni se considera que estos puedan servir como un ejemplo a seguir.

De manera similar a Twiss, en el sentido que también cita un buen número de obras de Velázquez y que maneja con saber datos y descrip-

ciones relativas a pinturas debidas a otros artistas, el viajero Henry
Swinburne —especialmente en el ámbito del Palacio Real— es claramente positivo con Velázquez. A éste dedica prácticamente el doble de
espacio que a cualquier otro pintor de entre "my favorites", es decir,
Correggio, Rubens, Murillo, Van Dyck, Ribera, Mengs y Tiziano. Comentarios como "the best portrait I ever beheld" (Swinburne 1787: 174)
referido al *Retrato ecuestre del Conde Duque de Olivares* —aunque
copiado literalmente del citado manuscrito publicado por Ponz— no
dejan lugar a dudas sobre la estimación que le merecía el pintor.

De todo lo dicho hasta ahora, se puede confirmar que, como ya ad-
vertíamos al principio, los viajeros ingleses del siglo XVIII tuvieron muy
en cuenta las fuentes artístico-literarias españolas para emitir sus propios
juicios artísticos —lo que en absoluto quiere decir que en ocasiones no
fueran absolutamente originales, como también se ha visto— pero
además, lejos de mantener respecto a ellas una actitud pasiva, pudieron
llegar, incluso, a rectificar las informaciones de las que partían, lo que
sin duda les convierte en unos muy atentos lectores. En este sentido tal
vez el caso más relevante sea el de Clarke quien, no contentándose con
advertir las imprecisiones que había detectado en la transcripción de las
inscripciones de El Escorial contenidas en la traducción inglesa de 1760
de la *Descripción breve del Monasterio*, referencia como obras debidas a
Velázquez, además de la *Túnica de José*, el *Retrato de Felipe IV* (*Felipe
IV con vestido marrón bordado en plata,* actualmente en la National
Gallery londinense), una obra que no aparece en la mencionada traducción ni tampoco en la edición castellana original.

Además de esto, lo que también se deduce de una lectura cronoló-
gica de los relatos que han dejado los viajeros ingleses del XVIII es que,
paradójicamente, no se copian entre ellos, lo que significa, por un lado,
que no dejan que las opiniones de sus compatriotas intervengan o modi-
fiquen las suyas propias, que sus comentarios sean más genuinos, pero
también que, en ocasiones, desaprovechen la oportunidad de incorporar
noticias o descripciones que les hubieran sido muy provechosas. A este
respecto cabe mencionar, sobre todo, las dos obras publicadas por Cumberland en 1782 y 1787: la primera, una especie de extracto de *El Parnaso* de Palomino, con aportaciones personales de Cumberland, y la segunda el *Catálogo de pinturas del Palacio Real*. Estas obras, pese a no ser
libros de viajes y a que su autor, en realidad, no sea más que el co-autor
de las mismas, contienen un sinfín de apreciaciones sobre determinadas

obras de Velázquez —los *Borrachos* o la *Fragua de Vulcano* sin ir más lejos— absolutamente inéditas hasta aquel momento.

Otro ejemplo que ilustraría este desconocimiento acerca de lo que habían publicado sus compatriotas lo encontramos en Swinburne, quien ignoraba que Twiss había publicado el manuscrito referente a la autoría de la *Virgen del Pez* de Rafael. Cabe recordar que Swinburne llega a España en 1775, el mismo año que Twiss había publicado en Londres su obra, pero también que él no publicó la suya hasta 1779, lo que le daba cierto margen de tiempo para incorporar lo que otros hubieran dicho al respecto. Señalar también la "originalidad" de Townsend al considerar que las dos obras más valiosas de El Escorial eran la *Virgen de la Perla* de Rafael y la *Última Cena* de Tiziano y en cambio, no decir ni media palabra de la *Túnica de José*, de mención obligada para todos los viajeros ingleses que habían pasado por el monasterio jerónimo antes que él.

Por tanto, podemos concluir que, exceptuando a Baretti, más interesado en dar noticia y resaltar a los pintores del siglo XVIII, y también si se quiere a Jardine —quien, pese a no mencionar en todo su libro una sola obra de ningún pintor, valora el arte de Velázquez y el de Murillo bajo una óptica italiana—, los viajeros ingleses dieciochescos enaltecieron el arte de Velázquez como nadie había hecho hasta aquel momento. Así, contribuyeron decisivamente no solo a construir la imagen de Velázquez en Gran Bretaña sino también a proyectar internacionalmente al pintor, máxime cuando los otros mecanismos que pudieran haber ayudado a difundir su obra, como los grabados, fueron muy infrecuentes en España hasta los primeros años del siglo XIX.

Bibliografía

Baretti, J. 1770. *A Journey from London to Genova, through England, Portugal, Spain, and France*, vol. 2, London, Davies.

Beckford, W. 1966 [1834]. *Un inglés en la España de Godoy*, J. Pardo (trad.), Madrid, Taurus.

Clarke, E. 1763. *Letters Concerning the Spanish Nation*, Londres, T. Becket & P. A. De Hondt.

Cumberland, R. 1806. *Memoirs of Richard Cumberland*, New York, Brisban and Brannan.

Jardine, A. 2001 [1788]. *Cartas de España*, J. F. Pérez Berenguel (trad.), Alicante, Publicaciones de la Universidad de Alicante.

Palomino, A. 1724. "El Parnaso Español Pintoresco Laureado", in *Museo pictórico y escala óptica,* vol. 2, Madrid, Lucas Antonio de Bedmar, 231-498.

Ponz, A. 1988 [1772-1794]. *Viaje de España,* vol. 1 (tomos I-IV), vol. 2 (tomos V-VIII), Madrid, Aguilar.

Santos, F. de los. 1657. *Descripción breve del Monasterio de S. Lorenzo El Real del Escorial*, Madrid, Imprenta Real.

Swinburne, H. 1787 [1779], *Travels through Spain in the Years 1775 and 1776*, vol. 2, London, Davis.

Talbot Dillon, J. 1780. *Travels through Spain*, London, Robinson.

Townsend, J. 1988 [1791]. *Viaje por España en la época de Carlos III (1786-1787),* J. Portús (trad.), Madrid, Turner.

Twiss, R. 1999 [1775]. *Viaje por España en 1773*, M. Delgado (trad.), Madrid, Cátedra.

Luigi Marfè

Palabra y otredad en la literatura de viajes contemporánea[1]

Durante siglos, los libros de viajes fueron un instrumento para compartir, según las palabras de Walter Benjamin, la "sabiduría de lo lejano" ofrecida por los países extranjeros. En su ensayo sobre el arte de narrar (1936: 16-33), el filósofo alemán escribió que los primeros narradores fueron viajeros que, después de haber regresado a su país, comenzaron a relatar lo que habían visto y oído en sus itinerarios. Para Benjamin, el arte de narrar nació como manera de compartir historias e imágenes de la otredad, y el viaje fue la previa condición de esta participación.

Desde los primeros relatos de la antigüedad clásica, la confianza en el poder narrativo de los viajes estimuló obras que dieron a la cultura occidental su imagen del mundo (Todorov 1989). Sin embargo, a finales del siglo XIX, esta misma confianza quebró. De repente, los mapas perdieron sus últimas tierras incógnitas y la literatura de viajes se vio privada de su significado original. Desde entonces, la experiencia de la otredad se ha convertido en encuentros cada vez más raros, incluso en las antípodas. La cultura occidental entró en lo que el antropólogo Claude Lévi-Strauss (1955: 38) ha llamado la era del "fin de los viajes": no en el sentido que no se viaje más, sino, por el contrario, que se viaja demasiado y mal, porque ya no se sabe confiar en la capacidad de los lugares de ser espacios de experiencias identitarias.

Para reafirmarse como género literario, la narrativa de viajes tuvo que transformarse profundamente. Entre sus temas más persistentes, hay preguntas como estas: ¿cómo reactivar una posible relación entre las personas y los lugares? ¿de qué manera pensar de nuevo el viaje como una oportunidad para descubrir el yo y el "otro"? Este trabajo describe algunos pasos de esta metamorfosis, con particular referencia a la "re-

---

1   Para una discusión más amplia sobre estos mismos temas, véase mi monografía *Oltre la fine dei viaggi. I resoconti dell'altrove nella letteratura contemporanea* (2009).

tórica de la otredad" (Hartog 1980: 225) propia de la escritura de viajes contemporánea.

1. En 1899, Joseph Conrad representó el agotamiento del sentido cognitivo del viaje en *Heart of Darkness*, una novela que, entre múltiples significados, cuenta las contradicciones del mundo colonial europeo frente al descubrimiento de la otredad africana. En las primeras páginas del libro, un personaje, Marlow, explica las razones de su pasión por los viajes, recordando cuando era niño y vio por vez primera un mapa. Instintivamente, Marlow puso el dedo sobre la mayor área vacía de África y dijo: "when I'll grow up, I will go there", cuando crezca, iré allí. Este episodio describe vivamente el circulo dialéctico sobre el que se basa toda la historia de los relatos de viajes, como subrayó Michel de Certeau (1977): un viajero lee un libro de viajes; la lectura lo estimula a ver lo que su antecesor no pudo ver; cuando regresa del viaje escribe un nuevo libro sobre las tierras que ha visitado; este libro despierta el interés de un nuevo viajero; a su vez, este viajero decide ir más allá de su antecesor; y así hasta el infinito.

En realidad, este infinito pareció haberse acabado precisamente en el tiempo de Conrad, cuando el planeta se encontró de repente completamente visto, caminado, narrado. Desde entonces, nuevos medios de comunicación han propagado una enorme cantidad de imágenes de lugares lejanos: primero la fotografía, luego la televisión, ahora internet. ¿Por qué razones escribir libros de viajes si podemos pasear por Manhattan a través de google.maps? ¿Qué sentido tiene compartir la sabiduría de lo lejano cuando ya está al alcance de un clic?

Convirtiéndose en práctica común, los viajes han modificado radicalmente nuestra manera de percibir la otredad. Al describir su estancia en Brasil, Lévi-Strauss argumentó que los viajes verdaderos ya se acabaron y los relatos de viajes resultaban inútiles. En 1935, Brasil ya tenía todas las señales de la futura globalización:

> Je comprends alors la passion, la folie, la duperie des récits de voyage. Ils apportent l'illusion de ce qui n'existe plus et qui devrait être encore, pour que nous échappions à l'accablante évidence que vingt mille ans d'histoire sont joués. Il n'y a plus rien à faire: […] l'humanité s'installe dans la monoculture; elle s'apprête à produire la civilisation en masse, comme la betterave (Lévi-Strauss 1955: 39).

Hoy es habitual resumir los procesos de empobrecimiento cultural del espacio con una expresión de éxito, aunque muy ambigua, de Marc Augé (1992). Este antropólogo afirmó que el mundo se está reduciendo a "no-lugares", espacios que han perdido su vocación territorial y no permiten ningún tipo de identificación. Los "no-lugares" serían espacios de multitudes, anónimos y homologados, y se caracterizarían por una completa confusión entre realidad y ficción. No hace mucho, argumentó Augé, eran las postales las que representaban los lugares: ahora son éstos que las imitan, persiguiendo una belleza abstracta, como la de los folletos turísticos, y vendiendo su propia identidad para ser económicamente más atractivos (Augé 1997).

2. Muchos años antes de Lévi-Strauss y de Augé, el peligro de la homologación cultural de los lugares fue profetizado por Victor Segalen, un escritor viajero cuya "estética de la diversidad" (Forsdick 2000) debería considerarse como la base de las teorías contemporáneas de la otredad. Después de haber viajado por Extremo Oriente, Segalen describió el gradual enrarecimiento de la otredad, incluso en Tahití. En su polémica con Pierre Loti, él creía que no son exóticas las raras extravagancias, sino la experiencia de la diversidad cultural. Toda su obra aspira a "dépouiller l'exotisme de ce qu'il a de *géographique*", es decir, se puede ir a miles de kilómetros de casa y no ver nada; dar un paseo y hacer un viaje. La distancia es una oportunidad, pero lo que produce lo lejano es un choque cognitivo que renueva las ideas del viajero sobre sí mismo a partir del encuentro con el "otro". El exotismo, escribió Segalen, "n'est autre que la notion du différent; la perception du Divers; la connaissance que quelque chose n'est pas soi-même; et le pouvoir d'exotisme [...] n'est que le pouvoir de concevoir autre" (Segalen 1908: 23).

El íntimo vínculo entre viaje, identidad y otredad fue sondeado también por otro autor de la modernidad que es probablemente el maestro de la narrativa viajera reciente. Me refiero a Arthur Rimbaud, que se fue a Abisinia para vender armas a los etíopes, convencido de que solamente yendo tan lejos, solamente desplazándose en un camino infinito, habría podido quedarse solo consigo mismo. En una de sus cartas (*Lettre aux siens*, Aden 5 mai 1884), Rimbaud se interrogó sobre el sentido de su viaje, preguntándose: "que fais-je ici, moi?" (377), o sea: "¿qué hago aquí?". De esta manera, implícitamente, se preguntó también: "¿quién soy yo?", "¿quiénes son los otros?". Y probó cómo, incluso en un momento histórico en el que los discursos sobre la subjetividad se iban complicando, la otredad podría ser una oportunidad oblicua para pensar en nuevas formas de la identidad personal, porque, como decía Rimbaud, "Je est un autre" (254).

Durante la primera mitad del siglo XX, los escritores viajeros capaces de seguir una "estética de la diversidad" como aquella de Rimbaud y de Segalen fueron muy pocos: me refiero a Henri Michaux en *Ecuador* (1929), a Osip Mandelshtam en el *Putešestvie v Armeniju* (1933), a Robert Byron en *The Road to Oxiana* (1937) y a otros que supieron apostar por el significado existencial y poiético del viaje. Sin embargo, gran parte de la narrativa de viajes del momento, como bien explicó Paul Fussell (1980), era muy diferente: después de años forzosamente sedentarios por la Gran Guerra, la oportunidad de ir por todas partes ensombreció los procesos antropológicos antedichos. En aquellos años, fueron sin duda más problemáticas las representaciones del viaje de novelas como *Amerika* (1927) de Franz Kafka y el *Voyage au bout de la nuit* (1932) de Louis-Ferdinand Céline. En estas obras, la sabiduría de lo lejano volvió a ofrecer imágenes del "otro" porque a los viajes geográficos se superpusieron rutas textuales de gran perspicacia metaliteraria. De esta manera, la desorientación en el espacio se abrió a un profundo desplazamiento cognitivo e identitario: cada uno a su manera, personajes como Rossmann y Bardamu están *verschollen*, o sea desaparecidos, en palabras de Kafka, porque viajar es para ellos como perderse en las diferencias de la otredad.

3. "¿Qué hago aquí?" es el pasaporte de toda la narrativa de viajes más reciente. Esta pregunta se puede encontrar en muchas obras de todos los *travel writers* contemporáneos que han reflexionado sobre el sentido de la experiencia del viaje y la necesidad de continuar narrándola: me refiero por ejemplo a las obras del escritor inglés Bruce Chatwin, del poeta suizo Nicolas Bouvier, del antropólogo italiano Fosco Maraini, del reportero polaco Ryszard Kapuściński. Tras las huellas de la revolución modernista del viaje de Rimbaud, autores como ellos han demostrado que dar voz a lo lejano significa inventar nuevas estrategias textuales con el fin de capturar el choque cognitivo del viaje. Si el viajero sabe buscar una perspectiva original desde donde ver su ineludible otredad, como dijo el americano Paul Theroux, también "nowhere is a place" (Chatwin y Theroux 1985: 17): también un no-lugar puede volver a ser un lugar.

En las últimas generaciones de escritores viajeros, Chatwin es el autor más renombrado precisamente por esta razón. Casi despedido de la revista en donde trabajaba, en 1974 se fue a Sudamérica con el pretexto de encontrar un raro objeto que soñaba desde niño. De hecho, esta investigación le importaba poco, y el fracaso de la búsqueda prueba cómo el objetivo de su viaje nunca fue un destino exacto, sino la indefinida vagancia. Andando por Patagonia, Chatwin encontró continuos rastros de todo lo que no debería estar en las antípodas: mineros alemanes, aristócratas rusas, agricultores galeses. *In Patagonia* (1977) representa un mundo entero de desterrados europeos, cuyas historias improbables se tejen sobre un espacio textual antes que geográfico. Una mezcla de historias reunidas por una condición existencial idéntica, que era la misma de Chatwin: la de sentirse en casa sólo encontrándose lejos de casa, con la convicción de que el viaje sea algo más que un momento temporal de la existencia.

"Travel does not merely broaden the mind. It makes the mind", escribió Chatwin (1996: 101). La obstinada investigación de una otredad ajena a cualquier presunción etnocéntrica caracterizó también las vidas itinerantes de Fosco Maraini y de Nicolas Bouvier, dos autores que como él se han preguntado "¿qué hago aquí?" en rincones olvidados del mundo. Entre los pocos europeos que se fueron al Tíbet en los años treinta, Maraini empezó a viajar como fotógrafo. Su amor por las culturas de Asia provenía de una reverente curiosidad por la diferencia cultural. Después de muchos años en Japón, Maraini solía decir que viajar era indispensable para él porque le permitía ampliar el *endocosmo* (el cosmos interior) alimentándolo de *esocosmo* (el cosmos externo). La otredad de las culturas que estudió durante toda la vida —la japonesa, la tibetana, la indostánica— ha sido para Maraini una especie de *mandala* para comprenderse a sí mismo: un secreto mapa de la subjetividad, una brújula itinerante de orientación interior.

La misma confianza en el valor formativo de la otredad se encuentra en los relatos de viaje de Nicolas Bouvier. Después de viajar por toda Asia, durante más de cuatro años, en un Fiat Topolino de Ginebra a Japón, Bouvier se convenció de que si el *dehors* (lo de afuera) es tan indispensable para el *dedans* (lo de adentro), no es por las nociones que cada viajero piensa que podrá acumular día tras día. Al contrario, los viajes auténticos eran para él recorridos de una formación que despeja la mente de sus hábitos. Bouvier creía que el viaje es un mapa de la identi-

dad porque, a través del agotamiento, libera el espacio mental hacia lo
que realmente importa: la posibilidad de encontrar al "otro", de entregar-
se a su diferencia y de dejarse impregnar por ella. "Un pas vers le moins
est un pas vers le mieux", le gustaba decir (Bouvier 1981: 40): cada paso
hacia lo mínimo, es un paso hacia lo mejor, porque libera de las barreras
que impiden ver y escuchar la otredad.

Perseguir la voz del "otro" ha sido también la tarea del último
auténtico escritor viajero europeo. Durante su vida entre Asia, Sudamérica y África, Ryszard Kapuściński vio y narró más de cuarenta guerras de
pobres. Apostando por el método herodotiano de autopsia, él creía que,
para ser algo más que turismo intelectual, la literatura de viajes debía
convertirse en una forma de traducción: no de una lengua a otra, sino de
una cultura a otra. La obra de Kapuściński enseña que, en el tiempo del
fin de los viajes, este género literario necesita una fuerte connotación
testimonial. Delante del corazón de las tinieblas de África, Kapuściński
descubrió, como Conrad, que los hombres se parecen más de lo que qui-
sieran confesar. Pero esta verdad no fue para él motivo de horror, sino de
empatía, y lo convenció para tratar de derrocar el muro de indiferencia
que separa cada individuo de los demás. Kapuściński se sentía el testigo
de las personas que había visto y oído: el testigo del "otro" y de sus infinitas voces y razones (Kapuściński 2004).

4. En un mundo que mezcla y confunde sin cesar centros y perife-
rias, extranjeros e indígenas, ¿cómo pensar de manera eficaz la dialéctica
entre el "otro" y uno mismo? En una edad que homologa la diferencia
cultural, ¿cómo encontrar y representar la otredad? Para reencontrar su
antiguo papel cognitivo, la narrativa de viajes contemporánea ha ido
buscando nuevas estrategias. Acerca del nivel geográfico de sus rutas,
Chatwin, Maraini, Bouvier y Kapuściński han añadido espacios imagina-
tivos de reinvención poética, con la convicción que cruzar las fronteras
de la otredad significa aprestarse a la intima relación entre los lugares y
la palabra, el espacio y el lenguaje.

Durante muchos siglos, las acusaciones de fingir historias e inventar
mentiras han sido la gran debilidad de la narrativa de viajes. Tomando en
serio la paronomasia del alemán entre la palabra (*Wort*) y el lugar (*Ort*),
estos autores han convertido esta debilidad en una nueva oportunidad
para encontrar la sabiduría de lo lejano. Desde esta perspectiva, viaje y
literatura son dimensiones que se necesitan recíprocamente. Por un lado,
el viaje es literalmente el *pre-texto* en el que la escritura encuentra la

materia de sus historias. Por otro, la escritura es el palimpsesto donde se van a recoger las variantes del mundo. Algunos años después de Patagonia, Chatwin se fue al desierto australiano, y encontró una leyenda aborigen que explicaba vivamente esta poética. De hecho, el mito tribal de las *dreamlines* relata que el mundo ha sido creado por los antepasados que le dieron forma caminando, a través de sus cantos. De manera similar, Chatwin creía que contar el viaje significaba pedirle a la otredad sus historias y a cambio salvaguardarlas para que no mueran en el olvido. "An unsung land is a dead land. If the songs are forgotten, the land itself will die", escribió a este respecto: sin cuentos que la narren, una tierra está muerta (Chatwin 1987: 52).

En un tiempo sin *blanks* o lagunas cartográficas en los mapas, son todavía muchas las lagunas imaginativas que hacen que la otredad del espacio contemporáneo sea representada según estereotipos etnocéntricos (Kapuściński 2004). Desde siempre, los intentos de representar lo lejano coincidieron, para los escritores viajeros, con la dificultad de explicar su diferencia en términos comprensibles (Hartog 1980). La solución tradicional al problema, como explicó Tzvetan Todorov, fue una retórica de la otredad que devolvía la diferencia de lo lejano al esquema mental de "nosotros y los otros". Para los autores antedichos, contar el viaje significaba derribar esta dialéctica, y pensar en la literatura como en una oportunidad de traducción, que continuamente redefine la frontera entre "nosotros" y los "otros" como espacio autónomo. Solamente de esta manera las fronteras de la otredad se podrían abrir a un "tercer espacio", un *in-between*, en donde el dialogo intercultural pueda convertirse en un palimpsesto de nuevas contaminaciones (Bhabha 1994).

"Everything forgotten returns to the circling winds" (Heat-Moon 1982: 412): todo lo que se olvida, deja de existir. En *Blue Highways*, libro paradigmático en la narrativa de viajes contemporánea, el escritor americano William Least Heat-Moon escribió que la tarea más urgente de este género literario consiste en la recuperación del nexo entre la "curiosidad" (*curiositas*) del viajero y la "curación" (*cura*) de los lugares. Por "curación", Heat-Moon hace referencia al antiguo sentido latín de "cuidado" y "atención": el cuidado y la atención de los viajeros que se interesan por el destino de la otredad y, a través de la escritura, se encargan de darle espacio y duración.

Bibliografía

Augé, M. 1992. *Non-lieux. Introduction à une anthropologie de la sur-modernité*, Paris, Seuil.

—. 1997. *L'Impossible voyage. Le tourisme et ses images*, Paris, Payot-Rivages.

Benjamin, W. 1936. "Der Erzähler. Betrachtungen zum Werk Nikolai Lesskows", in *Orient und Occident*, NF 3, 16-33.

Bhabha, H. 1994. *The Location of Culture*, London, Routledge.

Bouvier, N. 1981, *Le Poisson-Scorpion*, Vevey, Galland.

—. 1997. *Le Dehors et le dedans*, Paris, Zoé.

Byron, R. 1937. *The Road to Oxiana*, London, Cape.

Céline, L.F. 1932. *Voyage au bout de la nuit*, Paris, Denoël-Steele.

Certeau, M. de. 1977, *Écrire la mer*, in J. Verne, *Les Grands Navigateurs du XVIII siècle* (1879), Paris, Ramsay.

Chatwin, B. 1977. *In Patagonia*, London, Picador.

—. 1987. *The Songlines*, London, Picador-Cape.

—. 1996. *Anatomy of Restlessness: Selected Writings*, London, Cape.

— & P. Theroux. 1985. *Patagonia Revisited*, London, Cape.

Conrad, J. 1990. *Heart of Darkness*, C. Watts (ed.), Oxford, Oxford UP.

Forsdick, C. 2000. *Victor Segalen and the Aesthetics of Diversity*, Oxford, Oxford UP.

Fussell, P. 1980. *Abroad: British Literary Traveling between the Wars*, Oxford, Oxford UP.

Hartog, F. 1980. *Le Miroir d'Hérodote*, Paris, Gallimard.

Heat-Moon, W. L. 1982. *Blue Highways*, New York, Fawcett.

Kafka, F. 1927. *Amerika*, München, Wolff.

Kapuściński, R. 2004. *Podróze z Herodotem*, Kraków, Znak.

Lévi-Strauss, C. 1955. *Tristes tropiques*, Paris, Plon.

Mandel'štam, O.E. 1933. "Putešestvie v Armeniju", *Zvezda* 5, 103-125.

Maraini, F. 1997. *Gli ultimi pagani. Appunti di viaggio di un etnologo poeta*, Como, Red.

Marfè, L. 2009. *Oltre la fine dei viaggi*, Firenze, Olschki.

Michaux, H. 1929. *Ecuador. Journal de voyage*, Paris, NFR.

Rimbaud, A. 1946. *Œuvres complètes*, Paris, Gallimard.

Segalen, V. 1978 [1908]. *Essai sur l'exotisme. Une esthétique du divers*, Montpellier, Fata Morgana.

Todorov, T. 1989. *Nous et les autres. La réflexion française sur la diversité humaine*, Paris, Seuil.

Rafael M. Mérida Jiménez

Alteridad y género en la Barcelona china[1]

Un caso emblemático de la transformación de Barcelona —incluso me atrevería a denominar de "alterización" de Barcelona— tanto desde una perspectiva urbana como desde un análisis de su imaginario literario y cultural, interior y exterior, a lo largo del siglo pasado, sería el del antiguo "Distrito Quinto", parte del cual acabó conociéndose popularmente como "Barrio Chino" desde la década de los años 20 y que en la actualidad se engloba en el "Raval" ("Arrabal", en castellano). Según consta Villar:

> En 1925 el periodista Francisco Madrid bautizaría una zona del Raval con el ocurrente nombre de Barrio Chino. En el semanario *El Escándalo* apareció una serie de dos reportajes titulados "Los Bajos Fondos de Barcelona", en los que por primera vez se mencionaba el topónimo Barrio Chino. La denominación alcanzó una aceptación total. Comenzaba así una etapa de asfixiante peregrinaje al Barrio Chino encabezada por todo tipo de periodistas y escritores. El Barrio Chino fue rastreado palmo a palmo; descubierto y redescubierto; falseado y adulterado; encumbrado y censurado. Era el Barrio Chino de La Criolla, del Sacristà, de Villa Rosa, de Madame Petit, de Cal Manco, de las calles Cid, Migdia, Cirés, Arc del Teatre... El Barrio Chino se convirtió en una ruta turística de primer orden (1996: 155).

Se trata del mismo barrio por el que han paseado tantos autores canónicos o marginales y tantos personajes imborrables de las letras del siglo XX;[2] el mismo que patearon Jean Genet (1910-1986, *Journal du voleur*, 1949), Claude Simon (1913-2005, *Le Palace*, 1962), Henry-François

---

1   Este trabajo se inscribe en el Proyecto de Investigación FEM 2011-24064 del Ministerio de Ciencia e Innovación.
2   Mucho antes y mucho después de que Don Quijote la elogiara en la segunda parte de sus aventuras (1615), la capital catalana se incorporó al universo de incontables autores. La nómina resulta extensa y ha sido analizada por distintos investigadores: Elke Sturm (1996), Carles Carreras (2003), Julià Guillamon (2001) y Joan Ramon Resina (2008), o los que figuran en el volumen coordinado por Margarida Casacuberta y Marina Gustà (2008), entre otros de consulta aconsejable.

Rey (1920-1987, *Les pianos mécaniques*, 1962) y André Pieyre de Man-
diargues (1909-1991, *La marge*, 1967), por citar solo a algunos narradores franceses que escribieron durante la dictadura franquista (Broch
1991), o al alemán Wolfgang Koeppen (1906-1996), quien en 1956 ani-
maba nada menos que a la estatua de Cristóbal Colón a bajar de su columna y adentrarse en el bullicio de sus calles (Strausfeld 2005: 148).

Sin embargo, en un estudio sobre las representaciones literarias de
esta zona de la Ciudad Condal en las letras catalanas del primer tercio
del siglo XX, Jordi Castellanos (2008: 93) analizó diversos autores y
obras que habían logrado previamente convertir el Distrito Quinto en un
espacio de denuncia contra la literatura burguesa: sería el caso emblemático de Juli Vallmitjana (1873-1937). Puede sugerirse, por consiguiente,
que, en primera instancia, la imagen literaria de este micro-barrio barcelonés empezó a desarrollarse a principio del siglo XX como topografía
de una alteridad social, pero que, a partir de 1925, esta alteridad —que
participaba de unos principios ideológicos de denuncia política muy
próximos al anarquismo— se vio desplazada y empezó a sufrir un cambio de enorme envergadura.

La introducción de la denominación periodística "Barrio Chino", si
bien por razones obvias no pudo sustituir la administrativa de "Distrito
Quinto", representó el triunfo de una alteridad interesada, nacida al calor
de la prensa sensacionalista de la época, cuyo exotismo orientalizante y
canalla inventó las puertas que facilitaron la apertura de un nuevo paisaje
—metafórico y simbólico, a un tiempo— que fue describiéndose y re-
creándose de muy diversas maneras y con objetivos antagónicos. Un
paisaje que se sobrepuso a la realidad urbana —recuérdese que la presencia en aquel entonces de una comunidad de procedencia china en
Barcelona era nula— y que fue criticada desde muy diversas instancias
coetáneas. Por ejemplo, en la exposición gráfica "La Nova Barcelona"
(1934) realizada por el GATCPAC ["Grupo de Arquitectos y Técnicos
Catalanes para el Progreso de la Arquitectura Contemporánea" creado en
1929 por Josep Lluís Sert y Josep Torres-Clavé], a partir de fotografías
de Margaret Michaelis (1902-1985), en donde bajo un plafón que mostraba las interioridades menos amables de escaleras y patios de vecinos
del Distrito, podía leerse la siguiente leyenda: "La literatura sobre els

barris baixos i l'afany de convertir aquests en centre d'interès turístic és un signe característic d'una civilització decadent".[3]

Aquel "Barrio Chino" era una zona tan céntrica como proletaria, tan transitada como humilde, en cuyas oscuras calles de habitaciones arracimadas vivían trabajadores autóctonos e inmigrantes junto a quienes representaban lo que por entonces se denominó "bajos fondos", esas "gentes de mal vivir" que, como las prostitutas y las artistas de los garitos ubicados por la zona, iban ganándose la vida "fuera de las murallas de la ciudad" (que se empezaron a derribar a partir de 1854): la zona que, en definitiva, designa la palabra "raval". El periodista y narrador ruso Iliá Erenburg (1891-1967) lo describió, a la altura de 1932, de manera realista (Permanyer 2007: 397-99), aunque la suya sea una acerada sátira contra aquellos periodistas y escritores franceses atraídos por el exotismo del sur, al fin y al cabo, con precios más baratos que en el norte y con una aureola posromántica que combinaba dosis de criminalidad, sexualidad y peligrosidad para potenciar su alteridad.[4] Una descripción interesada que bien puede relacionarse con el retrato que pintó Jean Genet de su estancia en Barcelona, hacia 1934 (pero escrito en la década de los 40 y publicado en 1949).

Y es que su *Journal du voleur* ofrece un puñado de excelentes anécdotas sobre la vida cotidiana de aquellas calles en la Barcelona republicana. Por un lado, las escenas que contempló a lo largo y ancho del "Barrio Chino", "parmi les mendiants, les voleurs, les tapettes et les filles" (29). Por otro lado, cuando intenta prostituirse, travestido, en una sala de fiestas tan famosa como precisamente "La Criolla" (68-70). Por tan poderosa razón, no resulta sorprendente que de esta pieza autobiográfica de Genet pueda llegar a afirmarse que constituye un verdadero manifiesto a favor de la marginalidad y de la delincuencia, abiertamente homosexual (Carreras 2003: 145-46).

Es en este contexto que me interesa introducir la representación literaria de otra modalidad de alteridad, vinculada a la sexualidad, pero no la de la sexualidad más común y recreada, como es la de la prostitución

---

3   Véase el catálogo *Margaret Michaelis: fotografía, vanguardia y política en la Barcelona de la República* (Barcelona: Centro de Cultura Contemporánea de Barcelona, 1998). He obtenido esta información en el trabajo de Mendelson (2004: 42-43), en donde se recoge este montaje fotográfico.

4   Véase (en Permanyer 2004: 386) la descripción del barrio en la novela titulada *Mademoiselle Bambù*, de 1930, del escritor francés Pierre Mac Orlan (1883-1970).

femenina, sino la vinculada a la prostitución masculina y al travestismo, y, por extensión al espacio de sociabilidad "homosexual" en la Barcelona de aquellos años.

Uno de los episodios más pertinentes para mis propósitos, justamente, sería el rememorado por Jean Genet en *Journal du voleur*, a propósito de un singular cortejo fúnebre de travestis:

> Celles, que l'une d'entre elles appelle les Carolines, sur l'emplacement d'une ves-pasienne détruite se rendirent processionnellement. Les révoltés, lors des émeutes de 1933, arrachèrent l'une des tasses les plus sales, mais des plus chères. Elle était près du port et de la caserne, et c'est l'urine chaude de milliers de soldats qui en avait corrodé la tôle. Quand sa mort définitive fut constatée, en châles, en mantilles, en robes de soie, en vestons cintrés, les carolines —non toutes mais choisies en dé-légation solennelle— vinrent sur son emplacement déposer une gerbe de roses rouges nouée d'un voile de crêpe. Le cortège partit du Parallelo, traversa la calle Sao Paulo, descendit les Ramblas de las Florès jusqu'à la statue de Colomb. Les ta-pettes étaient peut-être une trentaine, à huit heures du matin, au soleil levant. Je les vis passer. Je les accompagnai de loin. Je savais que ma place était au milieu d'elles, non à cause que j'étais l'une d'elles, mais leurs voix aigres, leurs cris, leurs gestes outrés, n'avaient, me semblait-il, d'autre but que vouloir percer la couche de mépris du monde. Les Carolines étaient grandes. Elles étaient les Filles de la Honte. Arrivées au port elles tournèrent à droite, vers la caserne, et sur la tôle rouillée et puante de la pissotière abattue sur le tas de ferrailles mortes elles déposèrent les fleurs (Genet 1982: 72-73).

Por supuesto, nos topamos con el mismo espacio urbano marginal que retrataron tantos escritores en lengua catalana del primer tercio del siglo XX. Así, Josep Maria de Sagarra (1894-1961), por citar solo uno de los autores más reconocidos, en *Vida privada*, novela ambientada entre 1927 y 1931 —durante la dictadura del general Primo de Rivera y el inicio de la República, por tanto—, se explaya en la siguiente escena con un punto de vista narrativo absolutamente antitético al de Jean Genet:

> Enfilaren altre cop el carrer Perecamps, que estava desert, i de la taverna que en diuen *Cal Sagristà* va sortir un homenot que començà a seguir-los. Aquell homenot era horrible; deuria tenir uns quaranta anys, anava emmascarat de vermell i portava els cabells impregnats d'oli de coco; se'ls plantà al davant i bellugant les anques de la manera més trista, començà dient, amb una veu de mascaró que vol imitar la d'una dona i fent aquell ploriqueig assossegat i llepissós dels invertits professionals: *"¿No tenéis un cigarrillo para la Lolita?"* A les dones els causà una impressió es-tranya, d'un absurd que no haurien pogut definir; en canvi, els homes, més que sen-sació d'angúnia i de fàstic, van sentir un pànic veritable. Aquell homenot inofensiu

els feia por, una por que els privava de donar-li una empenta, de contestar-li res. L'homenot insistia demanant *"un cigarrillo para la Lolita"*; ells intentaren apartar-se i apretar el pas. L'homenot els seguia ploriquejant, i fent uns "ais" inaguantables a l'orella dels quatre homes que fugien; uns "ais" com si volguessin imitar l'orgasme femení.

—Davant d'una cosa com aquesta —va fer Emili Borràs— un no sap què dir; se't nua la gola, et sents tan avergonyit, que et vénen ganes de plorar... (Sagarra 2010: 181).

Frente a la dignidad solemne del luto de "las Carolinas" de Genet, el horror bienpensante del narrador y de los personajes de la novela de Sagarra ante los "invertits professionals". Frente a la mirada que me atrevería a calificar de queer, *avant la lettre*, del yo narrativo autobiográfico francés del *Diario del ladrón*, el distanciamiento burgués que contempla la decadencia de la aristocracia catalana en *Vida privada*. Frente a la fascinación y el comunitarismo del uno, la abyección de un abismo tan atractivo como repulsivo. Un abismo que, no debe olvidarse, estaba reflejando las diferencias sociales y económicas que cobijaba la *floreciente* ciudad. Un abismo que, en el caso de Sagarra también refleja una alteridad lingüística antitética, pues Genet escribe en francés, pero Sagarra hace hablar en español a "Lolita".

¿Quién es Lolita? Tal vez sea uno de aquellos "hombres afeminados con la cara pintada y las manos pulidas como si fuesen damiselas" que frecuentaban "La Criolla", según los describe el periodista francés Gui Befesse en su crónica de 1933 titulada *Las profesionales del amor* (en Permanyer 2007: 412). O tal vez fuera amigo de Pedro, una de las dos "mariconas" —en español y en femenino en el original francés—, a quien se enfrenta Genet, según narra un episodio de su *Diario*, gracias al cual descubre la existencia de pestañas postizas.[5]

Tal vez Lolita fuera un transformista venido a menos, vecina de aquel joven travestido que Georges Bataille (1897-1962) describía en *Le*

5 "Les Ramblas, à mon époque, étaient parcourues par deux jeunes *mariconas* qui portaient sur l'épaule un petit singe apprivoisé. C'était un facile prétexte pour aborder les clients: le singe sautait sur l'homme qu'on lui montrait. L'une de ces *mariconas* s'appelait Pedro. Il était pâle et mince. Sa taille était très souple, sa démarche rapide. Ses yeux surtout étaient admirables, ses cils immenses et recourbés. Lui ayant, par jeu, demandé quel était le singe, lui ou l'animal qu'il portait à l'épaule, nous nous querellâmes. Je lui donnai un coup de poing: ses cils restèrent collés à mes phalanges, ils étaient faux. Je venais d'apprendre l'existence des truquages" (Genet 1982: 69-70).

bleu du ciel, quien interpretaba una danza española en el escenario de
"La Criolla", hacia 1935, con un traje de noche escotado hasta las nalgas
(Bataille 2008: 109). Quizá simplemente fuera uno de los "dos mil maricones" de Barcelona a quienes conoce el protagonista de *Printemps en
Espagne* (1931), en donde Francis Carco (1886-1958) narra su viaje por
la España de 1929 (en Héron 2003: 207-8). En el "Barrio Chino" se
"concentraba la diversión *non-sancta* de la ciudad", y en uno de sus límites, la avenida del Paralelo, abierta en 1894, "se alineaban cafés, teatros,
barracones, subastas, atracciones y tabernas [...] los espectáculos que
ofrecían aquellos chamizos pestilentes, sórdidos y tenebrosos [...] eran
todo lo perverso, grosero y salaz que se puede ser", según describen
Cristina y Eduardo Mendoza (1991: 153, 156), desde finales del siglo
XIX, pero que obtuvieron un renovado éxito de transeúntes en la Barcelona de los *alocados años 20* y de la Segunda República.[6]

El Barrio Chino fue forjando una topografía a la manera de una encrucijada cultural para propios y extraños, nacionales y extranjeros, que
casaba bien con el diseño de un laberinto sexual que fue rito de paso para
tantos, sobre todo varones heterosexuales. Esta realidad aparecerá retra-
tada en obras posteriores, como muy bien constatan, por citar dos ejemplos, desde *Años de penitencia*, el primer volumen de memorias de Carlos Barral (1990: 173-93) hasta *Caligrafía de los sueños*, la novela más
reciente de Juan Marsé (2011: 231-67), en donde en un diálogo entre el
joven protagonista y su padre, éste le rememora los años 30 de aquellas
calles para explicarle qué significa la palabra "purgaciones":

–Es una enfermedad infecciosa en la minga que se coge yendo de burilla con mujeres del Barrio Chino. [...] Furcias. ¿Sabes lo que es eso? Claro que furcias las hay
en todas partes, no sólo en el Chino, que conste... Además —añade con gesto lasti-
mero—, hoy ese distrito ya no es lo que era, ni mucho menos. Tenías que haber visto aquello hace quince años, cuando íbamos a La Criolla en la calle del Cid... Bue-

---

6   La moda de los transformistas o "imitadores de estrellas" alcanzó su apogeo durante los años de la República. Todos los cabarets del Barrio Chino presentaban en su
programa la actuación de un transformista. En el *Wu-Li-Ghang*, en *La Criolla* o en
el *Gran Kursaal*, alternaban números con las artistas, y en muchos casos eran la
principal atracción del local. Algunos eran excelentes artistas, cantaban y bailaban
bien, y sus chistes hacían reír. Otros, en cambio, no imitaban a estrellas, sino a mujeres" (Villar 1996: 205). Sobre la presencia de los "imitadores de estrellas" en la
Barcelona de aquellos años, véase Mérida Jiménez (2011).

no, yo sólo fui una vez. Callejuelas miserables llenas de tascas, con fulanas y maricones y chulos de la peor calaña... (Marsé 2011: 198).

No cabe duda de que las callejuelas del Barrio Chino igualmente facilitaron la existencia de otras alteridades, entre las que no conviene olvidar la de los varones "homosexuales", catalanes, españoles y extranjeros, en las décadas de los años 10, 20 y 30 del siglo XX, como callan tantas obras literarias, pero ilustran explícitamente no pocos archivos fotográficos.[7] Resulta fascinante constatar cómo una realidad histórica tan específica y un espacio urbano tan reducido propiciaron esta multiplicación de alteridades: una alteridad tan china como ficticia, una alteridad lingüística que se integra o que se distancia, una alteridad social que se disfraza de moral. Y también debe subrayarse que propiciaron una pluralidad de registros discursivos verdaderamente explosiva: de la autobiografía a la crónica periodística, pasando por la novela y la poesía, el ensayo, el libro de viajes o el relato breve. Y es que en la "Barcelona china" de hacia 1931 se acrisolaron y exportaron *genders* y *genres* de toda suerte.

Bibliografía

Barral, C. 1990. *Años de penitencia. Memorias I*, Barcelona, Tusquets.

Bataille, G. 2008. *El azul del cielo*, Barcelona, Tusquets.

Broch, A. 1991. "La mirada estrangera", *Barcelona metrópolis mediterránea* 20, 116-20.

Carreras, C. 2003. *La Barcelona literària. Una introducció geogràfica*, Barcelona, Proa.

Casacuberta, M. & M. Gustà, (eds.) 2008. *Narrativas urbanas. La construcción literaria de Barcelona*, Barcelona, Fundació Antoni Tàpies-Arxiu Històric de la Ciutat.

Castellanos, J. 2008. "El descubrimiento literario del Distrito Quinto", in M. Casacuberta & M. Gustà (eds.), *Narrativas urbanas. La cons-*

---

7 Véanse, a modo de ejemplo, el encarte fotográfico final de Villar (1996) y algunas imágenes reproducidas en el catálogo de la exposición *Guía secreta de la Rambla*, que se presentó en el barcelonés Palau de la Virreina en 2010.

trucción literaria de Barcelona, Barcelona, Fundació Antoni Tàpies-Arxiu Històric de la Ciutat, 89-118.

Genet, J. 1982. *Journal du voleur*, Paris, Gallimard.

Guillamon, J. 2001. *La ciutat interrompuda*, Barcelona, La Magrana.

Héron, P. M. 2003. *Pierre-Marie Héron présente "Journal du Voleur" de Jean Genet*, Paris, Gallimard.

Marsé, J. 2011. *Caligrafía de los sueños*, Barcelona, Lumen.

Mendelson, J. 2004. "Presencia imperceptible: el fotógrafo como folklorista", in D. Balsells & J. Ribalta (eds.), *Joan Colom. Fotografías de Barcelona, 1958-1964*, Barcelona, Lunwerg, 37-44.

Mendoza, C. & E. Mendoza. 1991. *Barcelona modernista*, Barcelona, Planeta.

Mérida Jiménez, R. M. (2011). "El ensayismo tardío de Álvaro Retana: producciones discursivas en *Historia del arte frívolo*", in D. Falconí & N. Acedo (eds.), *El cuerpo del significante. La literatura contemporánea desde las teorías corporales*, Barcelona, EdiUOC, 93-103.

Permanyer, L. 2007. *1000 testimonis sobre Barcelona*, Barcelona, La Campana.

Resina, J. R. 2008. *La vocació de modernitat de Barcelona. Auge i declivi d'una imatge urbana*, Barcelona, Galàxia Gutenberg.

Sagarra, J. M. de. 2010. *Vida privada*, Barcelona, Edicions 62.

Strausfeld, M. 2005. "Das kommt rir Spanisch vor", *Granta* 4, 139-48.

Sturm-Trigonakis, E. 1996. *Barcelona: la novel·la urbana (1944-1988)*, Kassel, Reichenberger.

Villar, P. 1996. *Historia y leyenda del Barrio Chino. Crónica y documentos de los bajos fondos de Barcelona (1900-1992)*, Barcelona, La Campana.

JULIA OERI

Conflicto entre Occidente y Oriente: Endre Ady en París y la creación de un mito

"El sol, la humanidad y la historia avanza del Este al Oeste" (Ignotus 1908),[1] escribe el redactor jefe de la revista húngara *Nyugat* [en español *Occidente*], en el primer número de la misma. El sol simboliza el recorrido del pueblo *magiar* que vino del Este hace más de mil años hasta el actual territorio de Hungría y que no dejó de querer pertenecer, religiosa, intelectual y socialmente, al que ahora llamamos mundo occidental.

La revista *Nyugat* fue la realización por excelencia de la voluntad de progreso de los húngaros a principios del siglo XX. El nombre de la revista ya contiene en sí todo un programa: el término *Occidente* llama la atención hacia el entorno cultural al que la revista desea pertenecer. Los redactores intentaron, a lo largo de los treinta y tres años de publicación de la revista, entre 1908 y 1941, realizar el sueño de los intelectuales húngaros "d'une littérature nouvelle, digne des grandes littératures occidentales" (Karátson 1969: 60).

Endre Ady (1877-1919) fue el primer gran poeta de esta nueva generación y el símbolo mismo de la voluntad de renovación por la vía de la cultura occidental. El Occidente para Ady se encarnó en la capital literaria de Europa, es decir, en París. La ciudad se convirtió, a principios del siglo XX, en lugar común, en dos sentidos: un lugar cuya visita era casi "obligatoria" para un escritor y un *topos* en la literatura misma. Además, para los húngaros, París suponía un contrapunto a la hegemonía de la cultura y la lengua alemanas. Después de Ady, las generaciones siguientes no solo peregrinaban allí por su espíritu occidental, sino que "les intellectuels hongrois n'ont cessé de rechercher l'écho des pas d'Ady au long du Boulevard Saint-Michel" (Nagy 1986: 406).

Ady tenía una compleja y a veces ambigua relación con la capital francesa que sin duda determinó su carrera literaria. A continuación pre-

---

1   Las traducciones de los textos húngaros son nuestras, excepto los poemas.

sentaremos el París de Ady. En primer lugar, en el apartado que llama-
remos "De Oriente a Occidente", resumiremos el recorrido del poeta
desde sus comienzos hasta su llegada a París y la representación de esta
ciudad en sus primeros poemas. En segundo lugar, en el apartado que
denominamos "De Occidente a Oriente", se tratará del cambio del concepto de París en la poesía de Ady, sus últimos viajes y la vuelta definitiva a Hungría.

De Oriente a Occidente

Tras sus estudios, Ady vivió tres años en Nagyvárad, una pequeña ciudad que, no obstante, contaba con una vida cultural animada. Trabajó
como periodista, lo que le permitió conocer a fondo la actualidad política. Muy pronto empezó a interesarse por Francia, escribía artículos sobre
l'*Affaire Dreyfus* en los que se comprometía en favor de los derechos
humanos y "de la nación de la *gloire*" (Ady 1999: 168). Durante toda su
carrera periodística, que llevó a cabo con más o menos intensidad hasta
el final de su vida, analizaba los asuntos con una sorprendente perspicacia y con un pensamiento enteramente moderno sobre temas tan polémi-
cos como la situación de la mujer, las injusticias sociales, el nacionalismo o la Iglesia, entre otros.

En 1903 conoció a Adél Brüll, quien aparecerá como Léda en su poesía, el gran amor de su vida y la persona por la que se decidió a emprender su viaje a París. Su primera estancia empezó en 1904 y duró un
año. Tal como las siguientes líneas reflejan, escribe sobre París lleno de
admiración y de exaltación, como un enamorado hablaría a su amante:

> Vago por tus calles, grande y santa ciudad maravillosa a la que con deseos llenos de
> besos quiero acercarme desde hace unas semanas de delirio. Vago y quiero que seas
> mía. No puede amarte, entenderte, ni sentirte en tu magnificencia nadie más que yo
> (Ady 1999: 1195).

Se llevaba consigo desde Hungría la imagen idealizada de París que continuó viendo igual durante sus primeros viajes. Según su amigo György
Bölöni, Ady utilizó de la ciudad únicamente lo que necesitaba y ni si-

quiera quiso intentar ser francés porque le hubiera parecido una impostura y un esnobismo. Además Bölöni reconoce que

[s]u amor propio de escritor y su dignidad humana no le permitieron aceptar que en la sociedad francesa de escritores le hubieran mirado por encima del hombro, al húngaro, al "balcánico", al oriental, al escritor de una nación pequeña y desconocida, cuando se consideraba él mismo mucho más extraordinario que la gran parte de los escritores (1966: 140).

Además de la influencia de la vida política y cultural de París, las lecturas de Ady también jugaron un rol esencial en la evolución de su poesía. Léda le descubrió Baudelaire y Verlaine cuyos poemas traducidos incorporó a una nueva publicación, con los de Jehan Rictus. A partir de los *Versos nuevos* de 1906, consideramos a Ady como el poeta simbolista por excelencia de Hungría. Sus complejas metáforas de doble sentido, las variaciones entre la alegoría y el símbolo, el amor maldito y la tentación de Dios y del Diablo, le acercan más al simbolismo romántico de Baudelaire que al simbolismo de Mallarmé:

Il bouleversait la quiétude intellectuelle par son langage complexe, par ses hardiesses d'associations d'idées, par son symbolisme si nouveau en Hongrie. Il bouleversait la quiétude morale par sa nouvelle conception de l'amour qu'il évoquait sous la forme des 'noces d'éperviers', comme une lutte meurtrière des sexes (Karátson 1969: 69).

En los *Versos nuevos*, Ady consagró un capítulo entero a los poemas de inspiración directa en París, que se titula "Cantarín París". En este primer poemario la ciudad se representa en general bajo dos formas: de manera personal mediante la personificación y, en comparación con las tierras húngaras, como el símbolo de Occidente.

La personificación de París, cuyo canto refleja la felicidad del poeta y su representación lírica, aparece en muchas ocasiones en los poemas de Endre Ady. París es un ser animado al que el poeta interpela como a un viejo amigo. Por ejemplo, en "Leda va a París", el poeta pide a la ciudad que le devuelva su amante: "Alguien tengo que es mi todo, / todo lo deja y se va: / París, París, tú ponte firme, / si puedes, devuélvemela" (2008: 55). También en el poema "En la Gare de l'Est", el poeta se representa diciendo adiós a su París, pidiéndole un último canto: "París, gigante cantarín, / cántame ebriedad" (2008: 107). El poeta se declara el único ser capaz de entender esa ciudad, el único que puede dialogar con ella. Se otorga un rol mesiánico, con lo que se acerca a la concepción romántica del poeta que guía a su pueblo.

Este papel de guía aparece también en los poemas en los que trata el carácter simbólico de París. En el poema "En un alba parisina", el contraste de cultura y de barbarie entre Francia y Hungría se manifiesta en la oposición entre la luz y la oscuridad. El poeta observa el París alumbrado por los primeros rayos de sol y se presenta como el sacerdote del Sol-Dios que adora la luz y el calor. Así reúne a la vez en sí mismo la religión pagana de "su sangre oriental" y la luz, la metáfora de la cultura: "¿Pálido yo? Rojo as asiome. / Mi feliz Ady-antecesor antepasado / mozo era, ¿no?, siendo tu acólito. / Mil años ha que palidezco" (2008: 97). El sol, además, también simboliza el recorrido desde Oriente a Occidente, con lo que hace evidente la referencia a la división vertical del mundo según el nivel de cultura: "Mártir soy yo del santo oriente / que en occidente descanso busca" (2008: 99).

Estos poemas que transmiten una dura crítica hacia Hungría se clasifican en el grupo de los poemas llamados *azotantes*. El país de Ady se denomina "yermo húngaro", término que evoca la esterilidad de la llanura, incapaz de acoger la modernidad. Francia y Hungría se enfrentan en las imágenes de vida y muerte, acción e inacción, creación y esterilidad.

"En la Gare de l'Est" relata el adiós del poeta a París. Todavía está en su ciudad adorada, "ciudad santa", pero sus pensamientos ya se proyectan hacia su patria (el nombre de la estación indica también su situación entre dos países). En este poema, Ady compara Hungría a un cementerio: "Mañana seré yo más blanco, / del panteón me llega invernal viento, / son besos que me envía / el camposanto húngaro" (2008: 105). Estas imágenes evocan la esterilidad y la muerte: muerte intelectual, política y física.

"A orillas del Sena" es un poema que compara Francia y Hungría mediante las imágenes del Sena y del Danubio. Estos dos ríos, que tienen mucho en común si consideramos su relevancia en las dos ciudades, se diferencian por los lugares que cruzan. El Sena se caracteriza por los dulces sueños, el amor virgen —imágenes de la delicadeza—, mientras que el Danubio no puede dar más que felicidad ruda, mujeres fáciles y vino: es el lugar de la barbarie. El poeta esquizofrénico que se asimila a su entorno pero se considera más noble, se divide en dos *yoes* que viven en dos sitios. Sin embargo, ninguno puede darle una verdadera vida:

"Vive a orillas del Sena el otro, / y ése también soy yo, soy yo, / vive dos vidas en dos formas / un muerto" (2008: 111).

En el poemario *Sangre y oro* (1907) Ady continúa su papel de poeta vidente que azota a su pueblo, pero su concepción de París se matiza. En el poema "Otoño estuvo en París", la presencia de la muerte es palpable: aunque todavía es verano en París, el poeta ya se da cuenta de que "se deslizó el otoño por París en el auge del verano" (1987: 31), como si el viento de la muerte soplase ya en la juventud. En "París es mi Bakony". Ady establece una correspondencia sorprendente entre la capital francesa y la montaña húngara donde se escondían sus compatriotas durante la guerra de liberación en el siglo XVIII. París, que tiene bosques formados por la multitud de gente que vive allí, esconde igual, o mejor, al poeta que la montaña. Pero Ady invierte las relaciones: los húngaros se escondían de los extranjeros en Hungría, mientras que él se esconde de los húngaros en el extranjero. Los antiguos todavía tenían una patria por la que luchar, pero él es extranjero en todos los sitios.

En resumen, en la primera etapa de su poesía, Ady relaciona París sobre todo con experiencias positivas y Hungría con imágenes negativas. Esta dualidad es el resultado de la idealización de la capital francesa y de la preocupación por su país. Pero, después del primer poemario, el contraste disminuye y los poemas se caracterizarán sobre todo por la nostalgia. Este sentimiento se refuerza a partir de 1909 cuando empieza su segunda etapa en París.

De Occidente a Oriente

Entre 1904 y 1911, Ady fue siete veces a la capital francesa, pero con el tiempo pasó estancias menos largas allí. La ciudad francesa poco a poco perdió algo de su magnetismo para él. Sus discusiones con Léda, su vida nocturna autodestructiva, la escasez de dinero y su decepción ante la Tercera República francesa le desengañaron de su amor incondicional hacia París. Su desilusión resultó de la decepción de la vida misma, de la pérdida de la juventud, del cambio —no de París— sino de sí mismo. El propio autor lamenta dicha situación con las siguientes palabras:

No puedo engañar, porque el engañado soy yo, el antiguo París no existe, porque yo
no he vuelto a ser ni nuevo, ni antiguo: por lo tanto, ave París que hoy no conozco y
que hoy ni siquiera me sorprende, te saludo, París a quién no recuerdo (1999: 241).

En los poemarios de Ady a partir de 1909, París aparece menos y, cuando surge, se conecta con imágenes negativas o nostálgicas. En "Dedos en
el Sena", las olas del Sena torturado reflejan el estado de ánimo del poeta
que se siente como si grandes dedos arañasen su alma. El sufrimiento
físico insoportable corresponde al sufrimiento psicológico. Los dedos
que arañan el río evocan a los hombres que enturbian las olas y que no
dejan al poeta en paz. El río y el puente también hacen referencia a las
ganas de morir: el vacío y la profundidad del río llaman al poeta.

El poema "De nuevo en camino a París" representa un viaje inverso
al de "En la Gare de l'Est": en este último el poeta expresaba su tristeza
a causa de su partida de París, y en cambio, en el otro, avanza en dirección de París, pero ya no puede alegrarse por ello. Está otra vez triste,
pero en este caso es su falta de interés hacia la ciudad que le apesadum-
bra. París había significado el único sitio donde se sentía feliz, pero ahora había perdido definitivamente este último refugio: todo parece negativo y todos los países carecen de sentido cuando uno envejece.

El tema de la pérdida de París también se evoca en "París me huye".
El poeta intenta volver a encontrarse con la antigua ciudad, pero ésta se
ríe de él. La pérdida se metaforiza en la desorientación en las calles y en
la falta de equilibrio. Finalmente, consigue reunirse con París, pero ya
nada es como antes: en todo el poema dominan imágenes frías: niebla,
nieve, hielo. El sentimiento de la muerte prevalece y ante el poeta se
abren grandes tumbas rojas y muy profundas.

El resentimiento inicial hacia su pueblo, expresado en los primeros
poemarios, deja paso, en las siguientes publicaciones, a una especie de
vuelta a la patria: el poeta se siente extranjero en París y confiesa su imposibilidad de dejar Hungría. Esta necesidad de volver se expresa en el
poema "Como la piedra que se arroja a lo alto", donde la piedra es el
mismo poeta que "va buscando las más lejanas torres", a saber, Occidente y la cultura de París, pero cuando llega a lo más alto no puede evitar la
caída en "el polvo mismo de donde escapara", a Hungría. Se declara
definitivamente hijo de su país: "Como la piedra que se arroja a lo alto, /
Tu hijo vuelve, pobre país mío, / Siempre a casa, al tacto de tu mano"

(1987: 18). Finalmente asume su rol de poeta mesiánico-romántico cuya idea ya le había tentado antes, y decide sacrificarse, simbólicamente, por su pueblo.

Endre Ady se sentía extranjero en todas partes. En su pueblo añoraba París y en París añoraba su pueblo. Su amigo György Bölöni resume así este sentimiento:

> Ady —ahora por primera vez— no se encuentra a él mismo en París. Pero no tiene casa en ningún sitio. Érdmintszent, el pueblo, sólo puede ocuparlo, atraerlo y guardarlo durante algunos días. En el París cosmopolita, el silencio, el polvo, el barro del pueblo húngaro, la acacia, la campanada y el ladrido: recuerdo quimérico. Pero en la realidad, aburrido e insoportable (1966: 265).

Ady siempre estuvo entre dos ciudades, dos países y dos culturas: la primera parecía ideal o por lo menos mejor que la otra; la segunda era su patria. Se sentía extranjero en todas partes porque se sentía extranjero en la vida misma.

La relación compleja de Ady con la capital francesa, que se mueve de la exaltación al desinterés, se manifiesta en sus poemas, sus artículos y sus cartas, de los que hemos intentado presentar la gama más variada posible. La escritura del poeta sobre París nos ha conducido al descubrimiento de un universo de ensoñación, compuesto de dos itinerarios complementarios: de Oriente a Occidente y de Occidente a Oriente.

Después de Ady, un gran número de destacados escritores húngaros fueron a pasar algún tiempo en París: por ejemplo Jenő Heltai, András Hevesi, Gyula Illyés, Attila József, Miklós Radnóti y Sándor Márai. Los escritores y los viajeros húngaros intentaron buscar las huellas de Ady en París, siguiendo los topónimos aparecidos en los poemas. András Hevesi, escritor y traductor que murió en 1940 en la segunda guerra mundial como soldado voluntario francés, describió el fenómeno de la siguiente manera:

> A Ady las tradiciones francesas le aburrían, pero independientemente de la guía turística, creó de unas calles, parques y monumentos parisinos una tradición húngara, cuyos signos gráficos abrían de manera milagrosa las cerraduras de la nostalgia húngara. Desde que estuvo en París, Hungría empieza en la Gare de l'Est. Goethe regaló Roma a los alemanes, Maurras regaló Atenas a los franceses, a nosotros, a los húngaros, el poeta nos regaló una estación de trenes de París (Hevesi 2000: 325).

El poeta creó un verdadero mito, el mito de París o, quizá mejor dicho, el mito de Endre Ady en París.

Bibliografía

Ady, E. 1983. *Ady Endre levelei*, G. Belia (ed.), Budapest, Szépirodalmi Könyvkiadó, <http://mek.oszk.hu/06000/06054> [consultado el 09.V.2012].

—. 1987. *Antología*, J. Pardo & J. Villán (trads.), Madrid, Torre Manrique.

—. 1999. *Ady Endre összes prózai művei*, Budapest, Arcanum Adatbázis, <http://mek.oszk.hu/00500/00583> [consultado el 05.V.2012].

—. 2008. *Versos nuevos; Los últimos barcos*, J. Pardo (trad.), Barcelona, La Poesía Señor Hidalgo.

Bölöni, G. 1966. *Az igazi Ady*, Budapest, Szépirodalmi könyvkiadó.

Hevesi, A. 2000. "A Gare de l'Est-en", in *Párizs, isten hozzád ! Magyar írók párizsi novellái és feljegyzései*, Budapest, Noran, 323-333.

Ignotus. 1908. "Kelet népe", *Nyugat* 1, <http://epa.oszk.hu/00000/00022/nyugat.htm> [consultado el 05.V.2012].

Karátson, A. 1969. *Le symbolisme en Hongrie*, Paris, PUF.

Nagy, P. 1986. "Paris-Budapest, relations rationnelles et passionnelles", in *Paris et le phénomène des capitales littéraires: carrefour ou dialogue des cultures. Actes du premier Congrès international du Centre de recherche en littérature comparée*, Université de Paris-Sorbonne (Paris IV), 22-26 mai 1984, vol. 1, Paris, Université de Paris IV, 401-407.

MARTA PUXAN-OLIVA

Gènere narratiu i alteritat imperial a *Lord Jim* de Joseph Conrad

Al prefaci d'*Almayer's Folly* Joseph Conrad comenta que una lletrada distingida criticava la literatura que parla de "strange people and prowls in far-off countries, under the shade of palms, in the unsheltered glare of sunbeaten beaches, amongst honest cannibals and the more sophisticated pioneers of our glorious virtues", tot desaprovant aquestes històries d'aventures per "descivilitzadores". Conrad infereix que no només les històries s'entenen com a descivilitzadores, sinó els mateixos individus, "who are finally condemned in a veredict of contemptous dislike" (1927: ix). Conrad se sent molest pel comentari dirigit a la novel·la d'aventures i a la literatura de viatges en voga durant la segona meitat —i especialment a finals— del segle XIX. S'hi sent perquè, com a autor, ha viatjat realment als llocs dels quals parla i vol parlar de persones, no del que anomena "the charming and graceful phantoms that move about in our mud and smoke and are sofly luminous with the radiance of all our virtues" (1927: x).

Com s'aprecia en aquest comentari, Conrad admirava les aportacions intel·lectuals del gènere de la novel·la d'aventures del seu temps. Aquest gènere es desenvolupà frec a frec amb la literatura de viatges durant tot el segle XIX fins a tal punt que la línia entre els dos gèneres esdevingué molt borrosa. Tal i com explica Andrea White:

> So closely allied with travel writing, a genre that aspired to fact, after all, adventure fiction came to be viewed as a special case, demanding more credibility than other fictions. That both appeared not only in such an important publication as *Blackwoods* [...] but also side by side in such popular periodicals as *The Graphic*, the *Illustrated London News*, *Cassel's*, *Cosmopolis*, *Cornhill*, *Fraser's*, *Longman's*, and *T.P.'s Weekly*, earned for both a special status, marking them as part of the factual, workday world of newsprint, not fanciful but part of the informational machinery of the day (1993: 41).

La literatura de viatges narrava els esdeveniments èpicament per tal d'entretenir el lector amb un gènere que, essent de no ficció, podia resultar avorrit per a una part del públic lector; contràriament, la novel·la d'aventures d'autors tan coneguts com el H. Rider Haggard de *The Salomon Mines* es documentava i incorporava notes a peu de plana per tal de donar un flaire històric i documentalista a les novel·les. Com qui llegeix avui novel·la històrica, el lector de novel·la d'aventures, altrament dita novel·la imperial (*imperial romance*), llegia per conèixer els territoris desconeguts en què l'Imperi Britànic posava el peu primer i després s'hi establia, en els confins més remots per al públic anglès. I és així com la situació de les primeres novel·les de Conrad en el context malai, que coneixia de primera mà, li valgué l'atribut del "Kipling de l'Arxipèl·lag Malai" en una ressenya a *The Spectator* (Sherry 1973: 61).

No obstant això, Conrad no s'identifica a si mateix com a escriptor de novel·la d'aventures. Més aviat se'n distancia, ja que se sent fent una novel·la molt més moderna i, sobretot, molt menys comercial. El distanciament del gènere del qual beu és patent fins i tot en aquelles novel·les que li van valdre aquesta categorització. Si *Heart of Darkness* n'és un cas exemplar, *Lord Jim* excel·leix en aquest sentit. Certament, *Lord Jim* és un experiment genèric que desafia qualsevol adscripció a un gènere en concret, com Jakob Lothe ha demostrat. Si bé la crítica ha aclamat la primera part de la novel·la com a pròpia de la novel·la moderna, també n'ha menystingut la segona part per una clara derivació en els paràmetres novel·lístics de la novel·la d'aventures. Conseqüentment, sovint s'ha concebut *Lord Jim* com una novel·la fallida a causa d'una derivació massa depenent dels *clixés* propis d'aquest gènere popular. Molt particularment, la representació estereotipada de l'Altre, en aquest cas dels malais de Patusan, indueix a aquesta interpretació de la novel·la, una interpretació que demana una revisió que ens ajudaria a comprendre millor l'eficàcia de l'experiment genèric de *Lord Jim*.

Publicada l'any 1900, *Lord Jim* explica la història de Jim, un *gentleman* anglès i oficial de la Marina Mercant Britànica, qui abandona amb la resta de la tripulació blanca el vaixell de vapor *Patna* amb vuit-cents pelegrins musulmans a bord quan el vaixell comença a enfonsar-se després d'un xoc. Perduda l'acreditació, Jim vaga d'un lloc a l'altre sota la tutela del capità narrador, Marlow, i acaba com a administrador a Patusan, un lloc remot històricament situat a l'illa de Borneo, on allibera la població de les urpes del Rajah i d'uns àrabs, acollit per un grup malai i reconegut com a futur governant. Marlow pretén difondre la història de Jim, de qui en dubta la condició de *gentleman* colonial britànic i la dignitat moral.

Narrada per diverses veus narratives, la novel·la introdueix un canvi brusc en les convencions genèriques que adopta. La primera part de *Lord Jim* explica la carrera de Jim com a mariner britànic i la seva negligència del codi de comportament establert quan salta del vaixell, tot abandonant les responsabilitats assignades. La narració és una crítica subtil i audaç de la figura del *gentleman* que l'Imperi Britànic utilitza com a model per a la colonització i que configura un ideal d'individu molt estereotipat que finalment no concorda amb Jim.[1] Teixida a partir de la narració de múltiples veus i amb un marcat escepticisme, fragmentació, i treball de la subjectivitat i de la pèrdua de coordenades del món modern, la primera part de *Lord Jim* és genuïnament moderna i s'expressa en els termes en què ho fan els transformadors de la novel·la contemporanis, com Henry James o Thomas Hardy. Però el canvi d'escenari a Patusan marca clarament un canvi genèric. Fora del microcosmos del mar que ha servit des de Melville com a experiment de la tècnica novel·lística, l'espai colonial condueix el narrador Marlow a adoptar conscientment el gènere de la novel·la d'aventures, com per exemple suggerint que els malais "are like people in a book, aren't they?" (156). L'espai colonial, doncs, genera el llenguatge de l'Exòtic i la representació de l'Altre a partir dels estereotips racials (fenotípics i culturals) com a manera d'explicar les virtuts radiants que Conrad esmenta, les glòries de la civilització que justifica l'acció colonitzadora.

Precisament. En contradicció amb la resposta de Conrad a la desconsideració de la novel·la d'aventures, Hugh Clifford, un oficial de l'administració imperial als estats malais, qui publicava episodis autobiogràfics a la revista *Blackwoods'* simultàniament a la publicació seriada de *Lord Jim*, criticava *Almayer's Folly* d'una "complete ignorance of Malays and their habits and customs" i del recurs fàcil a l'estereotip (Hampson 2002: 72). La segona part de *Lord Jim* no és gaire diferent

---

1   La crítica de l'*English Gentleman* s'emmarca dins de la crisi de lideratge que pateix l'Imperi Britànic a finals del s. XIX a la qual aquest respon amb una marcada propaganda imperialista. Sobre la figura de l'*English Gentleman*, vegeu sobretot Gilmour (1981); Castronovo (1987); Berberich (2007). Pel que fa a les crisis dels anys 1880-1900, vegeu Eldridge (1996) i Mackenzie (1984).

d'aquesta novel·la primerenca. Conrad es defensa observant que ha obtingut la informació de llibres seriosos i històrics —i té una experiència personal del lloc— però el fet és que les narracions incorporen els estereotips directament i no ofereixen la crítica que rep el món propi i metropolità en la primera part de *Lord Jim*. En poques paraules, la crítica del *gentleman* blanc dirigent de les operacions colonials britàniques articulada en una complexa primera part de la novel·la esdevé una glorificació de Jim en la segona, produïda pel contrast clàssic amb la població malaia i àrab colonitzada, de manera que l'acció imperial, al cap i a la fi, queda restablerta al final de la novel·la.

Si bé Conrad introdueix alguns detalls d'ordre històric, els personatges no tenen altra funció en la història narrada que reeixir la figura de Jim, marginada de la societat que l'ha educat per un incompliment del deure. El lector de la novel·la imperial no se sorprèn quan troba detalls històrics com les referències als dominis portuguès i holandès, o a les distincions dels grups presents a Borneo, d'àrabs, malais i bugis, per les referències als productes comercials, toponímia de l'arxipèlag malai, vocabulari propi del context, o models històrics com James Brooke.[2] Però l'autoritat que la novel·la d'aventures basteix a partir d'aquests elements es veu fortament malmesa per la representació dels personatges, ja que aquests es construeixen a partir dels contrastos que situen els extrems contraposats del "món civilitzat" i el "món no civilitzat".[3] Marlow representa els personatges malais així:

> But as to what I was leaving behind, I cannot imagine any alteration. The immense and magnanimous Doramin and his little motherly witch of a wife, gazing together upon the land and nursing secretly their dreams of parental ambition; Tunku Allang, wizened and greatly perplexed; Dain Waris, intelligent and brave, with his faith in Jim, with his firm glance and his ironic friendliness; the girl, absorbed in her frightened, suspicious adoration; Tamb' Itam, surly and faithful; Cornelius, leaning his forehead against the fence under the moonlight —I am certain of them. They exist as under an enchanter's wand (Conrad 1998: 196).

Si els malais són com figures de cera, immòbils en el temps i perfectament clares en la ment de Marlow, Jim —"the figure round which all

2   Per a la documentació històrica del món malai vegeu Hampson (2002) i Sherry (1966).
3   Sobre el discurs colonial a Patusan vegeu Darras (1982), Parry (1983) i Collits (2005).

these are grouped— that one lives, and I am not certain of him. No magician's wand can immobilize him under my eyes. He is one of us" (196). Certament, per a Marlow, Jim és una figura multidimensional que evoluciona, es mou, creix; mentre que els malais li semblem talment extrets d'una pintura, persones sense més fons. Aquesta diferència essencial distingeix no només els personatges sinó els dos modes amb què es narra la història de Jim. Marlow recorre al qüestionament i l'escepticisme propis de la novel·la moderna per llegir Jim i això li pren la novel·la sencera. El dubte sobre qui és Jim i l'esforç per copsar aquest personatge és immens i irresoluble. Així, la novel·la acaba amb el dubte: "And that's the end. He passes away under a cloud, inscrutable at heart, forgotten, unforgiven, and excessively romantic" (246). És la perspectiva de Jim com a personatge complex el que justifica aquest mode de narrar. Contràriament, la concepció dels personatges malais com a simples justifica l'adopció d'un mode de narrar absent de matisos i satisfet amb l'adopció planera dels estereotips racials, perfectament definits per la novel·la d'aventures i la literatura de viatges.[4]

Els malais, doncs, apareixen com a ignorants de la mentida i de la imatge falsa de Jim, com a infants que no saben resoldre les contínues baralles fruit de la manca d'ordre social, i com a innocents en l'admiració cega per Jim. Tant és així que els malais inventen llegendes sobre la força de Jim que acaben justificant el seu futur govern com a successor del cap Bugi, Doramin, desplaçant el seu fill, Dain Waris. Dain respon a la figura establerta de l'amic fidel amb qualitats gairebé europees de l'heroi colonial. Els mestissos adopten igualment les funcions convencionalment fixades per la literatura i l'art: una dona exòtica que serà abandonada en un final tràgic i un posat melancòlic, i un mestís amb mala fe que és a punt de matar Jim i que coneix bé les dues cultures però en constitueix una amenaça.

Les virtuts heroiques del colonitzador, per contra, no només en consoliden la imatge sinó que en són la clau del poder. Així ho apuntava James Brooke, Rajah de Sarawak a Borneo entre 1842 i 1868 i model històric de Conrad per a Jim, quan reflexiona en els seus exitosos diaris arran els bugis: "The more virtuous, the more civilized, the more educated a people, the more turbulent, indolent, and sullen, when reduced to a state of subjection" (Keppel 1991: 128). El que complau James Brooke

---

4   Dryden (2000) i White (1993) han analitzat la novel·la d'aventures a Conrad.

dels bugis és el que complau Jim i Marlow: la docilitat i la salvatgia com a circumstàncies òptimes de domini. Però aquests dos estatus són, com molt bé es dedueix de les reflexions tant de Brooke com de Marlow, una imatge de com convé veure els pobles colonitzats més que no pas una descripció de la realitat que troben.

D'aquesta manera, tant les narratives de viatges històriques com la novel·la d'aventures filtren selectivament en el text la realitat per tal d'exaltar-ne narrativament l'ideal. Si els bugis a *Lord Jim* apareixen tal i com els vol veure James Brooke, la mateixa estratègia retratista del poble malai modela la imatge que Brooke i Jim volen oferir de si mateixos. És a dir, l'estereotip modela l'estereotip. I és aquí on rau la paradoxa de *Lord Jim*. A la segona part, l'adopció de la novel·la d'aventures i dels estereotips racials que descriuen els malais sense sotmetre'ls a revisió repassen les línies que ha dibuixat Jim, no per fer-lo més complex i més viu, ans al contrari, per essencialitzar-lo i apropar-lo altra vegada a l'estereotip. I és aquí on Marlow, observador de la complexitat humana, opta contràriament per retornar-la a uns motlles estables que no desperten les inquietuds sobre el subjecte i la seva existència que destorbaven els artífexs de la novel·la moderna. Amb la fal·laç pretensió de distingir l'individu complex de l'individu primari, el gènere de la novel·la d'aventures essencialitza tant la descripció de l'un com de l'altre, tot restablint la figura del *gentleman* anglès com a figura central no qüestionada del discurs racial i imperialista de finals del segle XIX, i esborrant els contorns humans de Jim que havien propiciat la crítica de l'estereotip.

Amb tot, però, la subtilesa tècnica de Conrad no ens deixa caure en el parany temptador d'identificar la submissió genèrica de *Lord Jim* a la novel·la d'aventures i a la literatura de viatges. És Marlow, el narrador d'històries, qui genera aquests dos modes de narrar. Al capdavall, Marlow admet la fal·làcia del discurs colonial quan afirma que "For a moment, I had a view of a world that seemed to wear a vast and dismal aspect of disorder, while, in truth, thanks to our unwearied efforts, it is as sunny an arrangement of small conveniences as the mind of man can conceive. But still —it was only a moment: I went back into my shell directly" (186). És precisament la por a enfrontar una realitat que contradiu el discurs imperialista farcit d'estereotips que defineixen idealment els uns i pejorativament els altres, el que frena Marlow en un relat perillosament escèptic de la història de Jim. Però Marlow és escèptic per naturalesa i fins i tot aquesta reproducció mimètica de la novel·la d'aventures, que resitua Jim com a digne exemple colonitzador, es veu destorbada per un punt paròdic. Aquesta perspectiva paròdica és possible per la insistència del narrador sobre l'adopció d'aquest gènere i per la reaparició intermitent del dubte. Conscient de l'esforç ficcionalitzador que embelleix i ennobleix el relat de Jim, la novel·la d'aventures a Patusan esdevé gairebé una paròdia del gènere mateix perquè, si bé els malais no coneixen el passat de Jim, l'audiència de Marlow sí el coneix i Jim esdevé una mena d'heroi a qui se li tapen les vergonyes. A això s'afegeix que Marlow clou el relat recuperant el dubte sobre Jim, convidant a una relectura que consideri críticament l'orientació ideològica de la narració de Marlow.

És en la combinació genèrica on s'estableix la posició de la novel·la en la tradició narrativa i en relació a l'imperialisme britànic. En ambdós casos la posició és crítica i ambivalent. La combinació de gèneres fa que la novel·la avanci de l'escepticisme del que Daphna Erdinast-Vulcan ha anomenat el "Modern temper", a la fe ideològica que basteix la literatura de viatges i la novel·la d'aventures britànica de finals del segle XIX. Però és també aquesta combinació la que defineix la crítica de les fal·làcies ideològiques de l'Imperi britànic, fent aparèixer l'ombra del dubte al final. D'aquesta manera, Conrad força ambdós gèneres narratius, el de la novel·la moderna i el de la novel·la d'aventures i de viatges, a una revisió. La novel·la moderna rep el fort impacte del tractament històric del subjecte, que es troba immers en les dinàmiques històriques i atrapat per la força dels discursos ideològics que fonamenten les empreses econòmiques imperials. La novel·la d'aventures i la literatura de viatges, per la seva banda, reben la dignificació del tractament històric però pateixen les restriccions ideològiques fortament ancorades en la reproducció acrítica dels *clixés* i en el pes de la seva funció propagandística. Aquesta treballada combinació il·lumina tant les ironies dels gèneres adoptats com n'explica l'adequació. I és així com aquesta novel·la híbrida aconsegueix a la vegada pronunciar-se críticament sobre la tipologia de gèneres vigent i adoptar una forma narrativa que encarna la confusió ideològica i un sentiment d'inquietud que alguns fets crítics succeïts durant el segle XIX havien generat al si de l'Imperi britànic.

Bibliografia

Berberich, C. 2007. *The Image of the English Gentleman in Twentieth-Century Literature*, Hampshire and Burlington, Ashgate.

Castronovo, D. 1987. *The English Gentleman: Images and Ideals in Literature and Society*, New York, Ungar.

Collits, T. 2005. *Postcolonial Conrad: Paradoxes of Empire*, London & New York, Routledge.

Conrad, J. 1927 [1895]. *Almayer's Folly*, New York, Doubleday, Page & Company.

—. 1996 [1900]. *Lord Jim. A Norton Critical Edition*, T. S. Moser (ed.), NewYork, W. W. Norton.

Darras, J. 1982. *Joseph Conrad and the West: Signs of Empire*, London, Macmillan.

Dryden, L. 2000. *Joseph Conrad and the Imperial Romance*, London, Macmillan; New York, St. Martin's.

Eldridge, C. C. 1996. *The Imperial Experience: From Carlyle to Forster*, London, Macmillan.

Erdinast-Vulcan, D. 1991. *Joseph Conrad and the Modern Temper*, Oxford, Clarendon Press.

Gilmour, R. 1981. *The Idea of the Gentleman in the Victorian Novel*, London, Allen & Unwin.

Hampson, R. 2002. *Cross-Cultural Encounters in Joseph Conrad's Malay Fiction*, Houndmills, Basingstoke, Palgrave.

Keppel, H. 1991 [1846]. *The Expedition to Borneo of H. M. S. Dido for the Suppression of Piracy*, R. W. Reece (ed.), Singapur, Oxford UP.

Lothe, J. 2008. "Conrad's *Lord Jim*: Narrative and Genre", in J. Lothe, J. Hawthorn & J. Phelan (eds.), *Joseph Conrad. Voice, Sequence, History, Genre*, Columbus, Ohio State UP, 236-253.

Mackenzie, J. 1984. *Propaganda and Empire: The Manipulation of British Public Opinion, 1880-1960*, Manchester, Manchester UP.

Parry, B. 1983. *Conrad and Imperialism: Ideological Boundaries and Visionary Frontiers*, London, Macmillan.

Sherry, N. 1966. *Conrad's Eastern World*, Cambridge, Cambridge UP.

—. 1973. *Conrad: The Critical Heritage*, London, Routledge.

White, A. 1993. *Joseph Conrad and the Adventure Tradition*, Cambridge, Cambridge UP.

HÉLÈNE RUFAT

¿Qué extrañeidad para la "literatura-mundo"?

Desde que se publicó, el 16 de marzo de 2007, en el diario *Le Monde*, el Manifiesto de los 44, parece que la fortuna del término "littérature-monde" se va afirmando. Con el fin de llegar más allá de los límites geopolíticos y nacionales, esta literatura representaría la realización, o incluso el reconocimiento de las múltiples identidades interculturales nacidas en todo el mundo que se expresan en francés. Aun así, conviene tener presente que estas identidades se han construido necesariamente a partir de sus diversos contactos con el Otro y el Extranjero, en el sentido más amplio posible. Así pues, ¿cómo se representan estas relaciones interculturales en estas literaturas? ¿La extrañeidad sigue conservando sus características de alteridad? ¿En qué aspectos se ha podido modificar? Partiendo de un trabajo sobre las representaciones de la alteridad mediterránea (Rufat 2002), queremos presentar unos esquemas de estudio que revelen la alteridad como la otra cara necesaria de la identidad, sin por ello necesitar la figura del Extranjero-Otro. Este hecho anuncia una alteridad que podría describirse sin tener que recurrir a las características de la extrañeidad. Tratada de este modo, la alteridad se acepta más fácilmente como otra parte de un "yo" a través del cual el camino de aceptación del extraño-extranjero aparece más despejado. Mediante textos de Le Clézio, Ben Jelloun o de Orsenna (tres de los firmantes del Manifiesto), buscaremos ejemplos de esta extrañeidad desvanecida y de las implicaciones que ello conlleva. Por último veremos que al estar asociada a los movimientos migratorios y a su literatura, esta imagen del Otro aparece como un nuevo camino hacia el personaje extranjero.

Por lo que atañe a la literatura francófona que emerge en torno al Mediterráneo, las imágenes del Otro que puede presentar vienen marcadas por siglos de tradición y de relación entre Francia y Oriente. Efectivamente, el exotismo que suponía para un francés cualquier persona o personaje que viniera de "más allá de los Pirineos" es una fuente de referencias para la cuestión de la alteridad. Rápidamente, se puede mencionar que, en el caso de Montesquieu en sus *Cartas persas* (y para remontarnos hasta el siglo XVIII), el extranjero era asimilable al "Otro desconocido" que, por ser tal, representaba una amenaza para la colectividad. Montesquieu hace un esfuerzo por presentar a un persa sabio, culto y pacífico, pero aun así este personaje intercultural finalmente regresa a su casa, en Persia.

Adoptando un punto de vista más socio-histórico, se puede observar que ya desde el Renacimiento, se tiende, por lo que respecta a la valorización del Mediterráneo y sus habitantes, a reconocer una deuda de la cultura europea con la tradición greco-romana.[1] Por el contrario, la herencia fenicia queda relegada en el olvido. Del mismo modo, se potencian y ensalzan las raíces judeocristianas de nuestra cultura mediterránea, pero se reduce y se disimula todo el legado musulmán. Y estas tendencias han condicionado la construcción de la alteridad mediterránea, incluso hasta el siglo XX: se instaura un sistema de valores binario y a su vez antagónico entre los países del norte y los del sur del Mediterráneo. De hecho, una subjetividad similar, pero invirtiendo estos juicios de valor se aprecia en los textos de los escritores francófonos que consiguen ser publicados a principios del siglo XX: para ellos, el norte, y especialmente las ciudades del norte del Mediterráneo, se ven grises, sucias, ruidosas. En ellas, las personas enferman enseguida, las diferencias sociales son más marcadas y los ritmos de vida carecen de naturalidad y espontaneidad.[2] Las imágenes antagónicas así creadas son persistentes, y se ha llegado a forjar una doble oposición entre Francia y "sus" países francófonos: entre el Norte y el Sur, pero también entre Occidente y Oriente.

Sin embargo, los movimientos migratorios postcoloniales han ido relativizando este enfrentamiento, y esta evolución ha quedado reflejada

---

1 La construcción de las alteridades mediterráneas fue analizada durante los años 2000-2002 en el proyecto de investigación "Imaginario y alteridad: arquetipologia general de la dinámica transcultural", dirigido por Alain Verjat (Universidad de Barcelona). Algunos de los resultados de dicho estudio se publicaron posteriormente en mi artículo "Constructions des altérités méditerranéennes" (Rufat 2002).

2 La enfermedad a la que se alude puede ser física (y los autores tienden a observar el tono pálido y enfermizo, de los franceses de Francia) o moral (puesto que se comprueba sobre todo que los franceses carecen de moralidad, e incluso pueden ser "pervertidos" cuando no siguen ninguna religión).

en la literatura.[3] Pero como el término "francófono" implica una diferencia entre la literatura producida en la metrópolis y la producida en "Outre
France", miraremos aquí qué matices su definición puede aportar al concepto "littérature-monde" propuesto por los cuarenta y cuatro firmantes
del Manifiesto. En el año 2006, se otorgaron prestigiosos premios literarios franceses a escritores francófonos.[4] Por esta razón, los firmantes del
Manifiesto evocan en el mismo una "revolución copernicana" en lo que
se refiere a la literatura francesa, puesto que les parece que justifica el
"fin de la francofonía": ya no se apreciarían diferencias (ni en los temas
ni en las formas) entre los textos de "Outre France" y los de la metrópolis, y por lo tanto ya no es necesario utilizar un término diferenciador
como el de "francofonía". En la publicación del Manifiesto que salió
unos meses más tarde, en mayo de 2007, editado por Gallimard, con
veintisiete contribuciones pertenecientes a los firmantes de éste, la mayoría de los escritores expresan su malestar al tener que escribir en una
lengua que parece discriminarlos cuando empiezan a utilizarla. Y lo que
reivindican es la posibilidad de tratar libremente cualquier tema relacionado con el ser humano, sin tener que limitarse a las "otras culturas". Se
puede decir que estos escritores ya no quieren que se les relacione con
una noción que evoca otra época. En este sentido, cabe destacar la opinión de Fazia Aitel quien, al hablar de la resistencia del mundo francófono a las teorías postcoloniales, afirma que esta se debe en parte a "the
state of colonial memory in France for France refuses to recognize its
postcolonial status as we are continually reminded" (2009: s. p.). En
efecto, en Francia una reivindicación de la memoria todavía está pen-
diente en lo que se refiere a sus relaciones coloniales y postcoloniales.

Si consideramos la relación mantenida con el estado-nación, podemos comprobar que este siempre ha sido reconocido como un poder
central; sin embargo, la aparición de numerosos gobiernos autónomos ha
ido modificando esta relación paternalista que ya no tiene por qué ser así.
Cabe entonces advertir que la francofonía institucional sigue viva cuando

---

3   Según Hélé Béji, estos desplazamientos humanos son más obligatorios que volun-
      tarios; por lo tanto, a estos francófonos no se les puede llamar propiamente "viaje-
      ros", ya que "ils sont pour toujours des 'immigrés'" (2008: 187, 197).
4   El premio Goncourt y el Grand prix du Roman de l'Académie Française fueron
      otorgados a *Les Bienveillantes* de Jonathan Littell, el premio Renaudot a *Mémoires
      de porc-épic* d'Alain Mabanckou, y el premio Femina destacó el texto *Lignes de
      faille* de Nancy Huston.

va acompañada del recuerdo de los valores humanos iniciales que la han justificado.[5] Pero justamente, debido a los movimientos sociales, el Otro cada vez se ve menos diferente: la lengua que habla el francés de Francia es prácticamente idéntica a la del francés de *Outre France* (y ya se sabe lo importante que resulta para un francés la identificación entre lengua y nación). Además, gracias a la normalización lingüística, los valores sociales y humanos también se han generalizado; así, la francofonía puede verse como una "lumière d'étoile morte" (Ben Jelloun 2007: 118).

En un estudio comparativo, Véronique Porra identifica las diferencias entre la francofonía (institucional y literaria) y la "littérature-monde". Un primer criterio diferenciador sería la relación de identidad entre el hecho político y el literario: la "littérature-monde" defiende una libertad que se aleja de la tradicional dependencia, puesto que ya no se ve obligada a respetar el pacto establecido con la nación. Un segundo criterio se referiría a la percepción multicultural, y pondría en evidencia que la francofonía favorece una valorización de las culturas locales, acentuando por lo tanto las diferencias. En cambio, para la "littérature-monde", si existen diferencias culturales, estas pueden mezclarse, de lo que resulta una interculturalidad presentada como una riqueza para todos. En estas condiciones, se entiende que los rasgos estético-culturales diferenciadores —tercer criterio de identificación—, no pueden estar activos en la "littérature-monde", mientras que en la francofonía se valorizan los "colores locales", tanto por lo que se refiere a sus argumentos como a sus descripciones. Finalmente, esta comparación demuestra bien que la "littérature-monde" exige un espacio de libertad estética para producir una literatura que cada vez responde menos a las expectativas de la francofonía más institucional. De hecho, a finales del siglo XX estos cambios eran suficientemente visibles como para que Jean-Marc Moura dijera que estábamos entrando en el "troisième âge de la littérature post-coloniale" (1999: 395).

Así pues, debido a la menor importancia atribuida al hecho identitario, se puede prever en la "littérature-monde" una percepción relativizada del extranjero. Y, si integramos la definición de Julia Kristeva, podemos afirmar que el sentimiento de extrañeidad es a su vez subjetivo y

---

5   Michel Guillou recuerda que en noviembre de 1962, en la revista *Esprit*, Léopold
     Sédar Senghor escribía esta definición: "La Francophonie, c'est cet Humanisme
     intégral, qui se tisse autour de la terre" (2005: 13).

colectivo; podemos hablar también de "aquellos otros que me hacen ser yo" (Kristeva 1998: 9). Por lo tanto, un personaje quedará identificado a partir de las alteridades que lo rodean así como a partir de sus alienaciones. En principio, las alteridades que rodean a un individuo participarán de su comunidad, pero, tal como observa Hélé Béji, estos referentes culturales no siempre son claros.[6] Y cuando esta geografía paradójica se vive mal porque la comunicación resulta deficiente, suele generar unos análisis reductores de las identidades.[7]

Este último ejemplo puede ayudar a entender que cuando un escritor francófono analiza su identidad como francófono, la percibe a menudo como una estigmatización. Este sería el caso de Tahar Ben Jelloun que denuncia el hecho de que "est considéré comme francophone l'écrivain métèque, celui qui vient d'ailleurs et qui est prié de s'en tenir à son statut légèrement décalé par rapport aux écrivains français de souche" (2007: 117).[8] Pero Hélé Béji quizá sea la escritora que lleva más lejos sus reflexiones sobre las implicaciones de la francofonía. Según ella, ya no se trata de un problema de lengua ni de identidad, sino que se cuestiona el mismísimo principio de libertad:

> "'D'où êtes-vous?' voilà la question qu'on entend partout. Les hommes ne se soucient plus de 'naître libres'. Ils veulent, dès leur naissance, être prédéterminés; ils réclament les liens de la mémoire, la religion de leurs pères. Cette parenté primitive est devenue leur désir le plus profond" (Béji 2008: 157).

Sin duda esta es una gran paradoja. El beneficio de la libertad se impone. La libertad de la identidad crea obligaciones cuando se escoge una identidad colectiva para reconocerse, para apoyarse sobre una memoria co-

---

6   "La terre où je me contemple est l'Orient, le lieu où je m'exprime est l'Occident. La bizarrerie de cette posture ne m'échappe pas, car je m'éprouve d'abord sous la forme d'une géographie paradoxale, dans laquelle rien ne correspond mais où tout communique" (Béji 1997: 13).

7   Este ha sido el caso de Romain Gary, tal como recuerda Nancy Huston: "Il est désolant de voir un écrivain de l'envergure de Romain Gary […] réduit par certains à son identité juive, par d'autres à son identité russe, par d'autres encore à son identité de diplomate" (2007: 155).

8   Anna Moï comparte este mismo sentimiento de *décalage*: "Je publiai. On m'étiqueta écrivain francophone. J'étais encore *l'autre*. […] Ma lettre ouverte est une invitation à être *l'autre*" (citado in Le Bris & Rouaud 2007: 249).

lectiva.[9] En los textos de ficción escritos por artistas francófonos que en su día firmaron el Manifiesto para una "littérature-monde", podemos observar estas nuevas identidades poco definidas, siempre cambiantes. Por ejemplo, en *La nuit sacrée* de Ben Jelloun, la identidad del protagonista está constantemente cuestionada, ya sea su identidad sexual, social, cultural o religiosa: este héroe precisamente es el elemento "extranjero" de las diferentes comunidades que lo acogen; de hecho, este sentimiento de extrañeidad es el que reconoce el propio narrador. Sin embargo, al final de la novela, la imagen del extranjero o la extranjera se difumina en un paisaje de ensueño, como si este sentimiento de extrañeidad ya no tuviera ningún sentido al lado de la sabiduría que sus vivencias le han proporcionado. En el caso de *Madame Bâ*, una novela de Erik Orsenna, el lector descubre a una mujer africana muy occidentalizada que escribe una carta al presidente de la República Francesa, otorgando a este último todas las características del Otro (opuesto a ella, en relación con sus creencias y sus tradiciones). Sin embargo, la propia Madame Bâ se reconoce extranjera ante los franceses pero también con "los suyos", puesto que según ella, solo los antepasados son considerados como personas no-extranjeras. Con este personaje, Orsenna ilustra un sentimiento de extrañeidad que puede relativizarse puesto que si todo el mundo es considerado extranjero, esto significa que este sentimiento ya no se refiere solo a una alteridad social o cultural concreta sino que se está evocando una tradición moral e incluso histórica. Por último, mencionar que la imagen del extranjero que presenta J. M. G. Le Clézio en su novela *L'Africain* también resulta poco convencional: este sentimiento de extrañeidad lo experimenta aquí un niño de ocho años por partida doble. Por un lado, él mismo se siente extranjero cuando llega a África, pero durante mucho tiempo el representante del extranjero, para él, ha sido su propio padre que vivía en África, antes que el resto de su familia se reuniera con él. La alteridad que aquí interviene también es generacional y altamente psicológica; sin embargo, debemos fijarnos en la originalidad que comparten estas tres obras en cuanto a los nuevos criterios utilizados para evocar la figura y el sentimiento de extrañeidad.

---

9   Quizás este sea el "nuevo humanismo" evocado por Claude Lévi-Strauss en tantas
      ocasiones a lo largo del siglo XX. Y un valor fundamental de este humanismo sería
      la tolerancia, en el sentido que Voltaire prestaba ya a su mandarín en el *Traité sur
      la tolérance* ("commencez par n'être ni intolérants ni intolérables").

Parece que los escritores franceses, en el caso que nos ocupa, tienen por tarea presentar nuevas maneras de encontrar una identidad partiendo, justamente, de las vivencias transculturales o interculturales, y este objetivo también les obliga a definir las imágenes asociadas al extranjero y al sentimiento de extrañeidad. Y todos los firmantes del Manifiesto entienden claramente la necesidad de modificar los vínculos tradicionales entre lo extranjero y la lengua, e incluso entre lo extranjero y la cultura. Sin duda podemos nuevamente seguir la reflexión de Fazia Aitel cuando dice que "to free francophone literature from the power of the French state is still a troubled work in progress" (2009: s.p.). Pero podemos afirmar que ya se ha progresado mucho al reconocer la falta de antagonismo en los "nuevos sentimientos de extrañeidad" que existen entre el Uno y el Otro. Ya lo indicaba Julia Kristeva a finales del siglo XX: "En France, en cette fin de XXe siècle, chacun est destiné à rester le même *et* l'autre" (1998: 288). Le Bris prefiere hablar de una "occidentalización del mundo" para expresar la disminución del sentimiento de extrañeidad. Así se puede añadir un nivel ético a los niveles institucionales, ideológicos y estéticos para poder situar una nueva imagen del "extranjero intercultural". De este modo, las nuevas imágenes del sentimiento de ser extranjero, presentadas a través de la "littérature-monde" en francés, parecen anunciar el final de un determinismo persistente, gracias a una ética compartida. Más que seguir un camino, los escritores francófonos están haciendo camino, un camino sinuoso para contribuir a las creaciones de esta "littérature-monde" en la que el sentimiento de extrañeidad ya no participa de un sistema dualista sino que pertenece a un conjunto de valores éticos.

Bibliografía

Aitel, F. 2009. "'Littérature-Monde' and 'World Literature': A Comparison in the Tracks of Colonialism", in "Littérature-monde: New Wave or New Hype?" (abstract), Florida State University, 2009 <http://www.icffs.fsu.edu/conferences/Litterature_mond/littmonde_abstracts.cfm?id=117> [consultado el 5.II.2013]

Béji, H. 1997. *L'imposture culturelle*, Paris, Stock.

—. 2008. *Nous, décolonisés*, Paris, Arléa.

Ben Jelloun, T. 2007. "La cave de ma mémoire, le toit de ma maison sont des mots français", in M. Le Bris & J. Rouaud (dir.), *Pour une littérature monde*, Paris, Gallimard, 113-24.

Elenga, Y. C. 2003. "Identités postcoloniales et temps des incertitudes" in M.-A. Somdah (dir.), *Identités postcoloniales et discours dans les cultures francophones*, Paris, L'Harmattan, 23-40.

Guillou, M. 2005. *Francophonie-Puissance*, Paris, Ellipses.

Huston, N. 2007. "Traduttore non è traditore", in M. Le Bris & J. Rouaud (dir.), *Pour une littérature monde*, Paris, Gallimard, 151-60.

Kristeva, J. 1998. *Étrangers à nous-mêmes*, Paris, Fayard.

Le Bris, M. & J. Rouaud (dir.) 2007. *Pour une littérature monde*, Paris, Gallimard.

Mbassi Atéba, R. 2008. *Identité et fluidité dans l'œuvre de Jean-Marie Gustave Le Clézio. Une poétique de la mondialité*, Paris, L'Harmattan.

Molina Romero, C. 2004. "Double langue et création littéraire", *L'esprit du temps* 14, 189-204.

Moura, J.-M. 2007. *Littératures francophones et théorie postcoloniale*, Paris, PUF.

Navarro, J. 2005. *La extrañeza de sí mismo*, Madrid, Fénix Editora.

Porra, V. 2008. "'Pour une littérature-monde en français': Les limites d'un discours utopique", *Intercâmbio* 1, 2ª série, 33-54.

—. 2011. *Langue française, langue d'adoption. Une littérature "invitee" entre création, stratégies et contraintes (1946-2000)*, Hildesheim-Zürich-New York, Georg Olms Verlag.

Rufat, H. 2002. "Constructions des altérités méditerranéennes", *Anuari de Filologia (Secció G)* 24: 12, 71-82.

JORDI SALA-LLEAL

Alteridad y xenofobia en las versiones cinematográficas de *Enrique V* (y sus doblajes)

La controversia hermenéutica

Obra central en el segmento histórico del canon shakespeariano, *Enrique V* es, fuera del mundo anglosajón, una de las obras más ignoradas del bardo, lo que es de lamentar dada su riqueza hermenéutica: en *Enrique V* se dan cita como en ningún otro lugar de ese canon la amalgama de discursos sobre la identidad nacional, la pertenencia al clan, la fidelidad a la patria y las tensiones, a medio camino entre la aversión y la atracción, con lo extranjero y los extranjeros. En las últimas décadas, se ha convertido ya en un tópico en el seno de la erudición shakespeariana señalar la flagrante ambivalencia de la obra: esta se puede interpretar tanto en un sentido patriótico como en uno diametralmente opuesto. Y, contra lo que cabría esperar, la lectura "antipatriótica" no es tan reciente frente a la lectura supuestamente tradicional: son llamativos los comentarios de insignes lectores como Hazlitt, Yeats y Bernard Shaw, como ha explicado Emma Smith (2002: 21) en un ejemplar estudio de la suerte escénica de la obra. Los pasajes controvertidos que se suelen destacar son tres: la tendenciosa conspiración de los religiosos en la interpretación de la ley sálica (I.1 y I.2), la brutalidad de las amenazas contenidas en el discurso del rey antes de la batalla de Harfleur (III.3) y las alusiones a la traición de Falstaff por parte del rey (*"the king has killed his heart"*, II.1). Pero la brutalidad del rey se manifiesta también en el pasaje de la ejecución de los traidores (II.2), el de la orden de matar a los prisioneros y el de la ejecución de Bardolph (IV.7). Y además, y a ello iremos luego, está el papel de Catalina: tanto en la escena de la clase de inglés (III.4) como en la escena del cortejo (V.2).

Así pues, *Enrique V* es una obra de una extraordinaria riqueza de significados que derivan de su ambigüedad intrínseca en lo referente al discurso sobre la sumisión a los deberes colectivos y el derecho latente a una insumisión que es fruto de un sentido profundo de la justicia. Esa ambigüedad es llevada hasta el extremo en lo referente a los supuestos derechos de una nación sobre otra (los de Inglaterra sobre Francia, en este caso) y a las guerras "justas" (y las manipulaciones para que lo parezcan), y al objetivo último de anular la diferencia del extranjero para la consecución de una plena posesión. Las versiones cinematográficas de la obra (y sus doblajes españoles) constituyen lecturas tendenciosas en el seno de esa ambigüedad. Todas ellas, como no podría ser de otro modo, releen a Shakespeare para hablar de su tiempo; de igual modo la crítica, estas páginas incluidas, releen esas versiones y esos doblajes para hablar, también, de nuestro tiempo.

La versión de Olivier, de 1944, fue en parte propaganda de guerra, y de ahí la controvertida cuestión del patriotismo del film; Anthony Davies (2007) ha repasado la extensa bibliografía sobre el tema. A pesar de ello, sir Laurence optó por dedicar la primera media hora del metraje a la reconstrucción de una puesta en escena en el Globe histórico, aunque más bien rindiera tributo a las escenificaciones de los siglos XVIII y XIX (Davies 1988: 26). De ahí la unanimidad de la crítica en su parecer de que el film tiene un gran alcance artístico. Graham Holderness (1992: 186-87, 190) incluso opina que la opción de Olivier tiene unas consecuencias ideológicamente subversivas, y no le falta razón, a pesar de que no se nos debería escapar que la reconstrucción cinematográfica de ese legado glorioso que fue el teatro isabelino también tiene mucho de patriótico, aunque se trate de una forma más culta, más tolerable de servicio a la nación. De hecho, el carácter patriótico del film curiosamente se constata más en lo que omite que en lo que muestra: Olivier nos birla la ejecución de los traidores, las amenazas del rey ante las puertas de Harfleur, la orden de matar a los prisioneros y la ejecución de Bardolph, aunque en su descargo deben recordarse la fecha y las circunstancias del rodaje.[1]

---

1   Además, es obvio que Olivier no llegó nunca al extremo de una Riefenstahl o de un Veith Harlan. A propósito de este, Kenneth S. Rothwell (1999: 51) compara la representación de la figura de Enrique con la manera en que Harlan dibujó a Federico de Prusia en la guerra de los Siete Años en *Der Grosse König*, un film de propaganda nazi del año 1944.

La otra gran versión cinematográfica de *Enrique V* es la dirigida por Kenneth Branagh, de 1989, film ampliamente elogiado por su inteligencia y habilidad técnica. No obstante, y aunque se constate en él la voluntad de mostrar algunos recodos oscuros de la pieza, resulta ideológicamente engañoso. Valga el siguiente ejemplo. Branagh pretende apuntar una crítica al rey al echar mano de *Enrique IV Primera Parte* para, antes de dar paso a la monstruosa ejecución de Bardolph, insertar un *flashback* donde asistimos a la cariñosa amistad entre ambos. Pero cuidado: durante la ejecución, por el rostro del rey discurre una lágrima, reflejo de una emoción que no es acorde con el personaje que podemos imaginar en la lectura del texto. La controversia hermenéutica también aquí está servida: Peter Donaldson (1991: 61) la considera ambivalente desde el punto de vista ideológico, y más taxativo es Holderness (1992: 201, 205). Mireia Aragay (1999: 14) subraya que el énfasis del film se encuentra en la emoción personal de Enrique, de modo que la pretendida identificación del espectador con el héroe se tiñe de unas connotaciones peligrosas. La tesis es irrefutable, sobre todo si no olvidamos que la película es de 1989, cuando el recuerdo de la guerra de las Malvinas/Falklands aún estaba fresco.

Quizás un desaforado patriotismo posterior a la segunda guerra mundial explica por qué la BBC produjo la obra para la televisión cuatro veces en la década de los cincuenta, amén de más ocasiones posteriores. Aquí no trataremos de ellas: nos ocupamos de la gran pantalla. Y, en esta, únicamente hay que contar las dos producciones de Olivier y Branagh, aunque también cabe mencionar un par de filmes norteamericanos prácticamente amateurs, uno de Neil J. Gauger de 2003 y otro de Peter Babakitis de 2007.

Franceses extranjeros, ingleses extrañados

En estas arenas movedizas que son *Enrique V* y aún más sus versiones cinematográficas, el concepto de alteridad constituye un elemento central. De hecho se trata de dos piezas: la visión de los franceses como la otredad, como lo extranjero, y la mirada irónica sobre sí mismos de los ingleses, que son objeto de un lúdico extrañamiento.

Los franceses aparecen en trece escenas, y en algunas de ellas
(III.5, III.7, IV.2 y IV.5) Shakespeare introdujo algunas frases o expresiones en francés, a modo de nota puramente colorista. En IV.4 aparece
un soldado francés, obligado a pagar a Pistol para salvar su vida, que
solo habla su lengua materna, y es traducido por un paje inglés; también
hay III.4, la clase de inglés, y V.2, el cortejo, escenas de las que hablaremos luego. A lo largo del texto shakespeariano, es manifiesta y delibe-
rada la oposición entre la afectación de los militares franceses y la ga-
llardía de los ingleses, sobre todo de su rey, que, sin que obste a la mag-
nificencia de sus discursos, hace gala de una cierta tosquedad de maneras
derivada de su sentido práctico de la vida. Los franceses están sobre todo
representados por un estol de nobles jactanciosos con el arrogante Delfín
al frente, mientras que entre los ingleses se realza la parte cómica del
elenco, gente extraída de los estratos bajos de la sociedad por la que es
inevitable sentir una corriente de simpatía.

En la versión de Laurence Olivier, la puesta en escena en lo tocante
a lo francés enfatiza esa sensación xenófoba (formada antes de hostilidad
y burla que de sentimientos más ruines) que desprende el texto. En la
corte francesa, cuya representación resulta irrisoria porque salta a la vista
que es un decorado, los nobles parecen espantapájaros, todos ellos vani-
dosamente disfrazados y ridículamente ociosos, el rey inclusive. Jack J.
Jorgens (1977: 123-24) apunta que Francia se nos presenta en el film
como un país decadente a causa de un exceso de civilización. Sí: y precisamente por eso no hay parangón posible entre esa caricatura de Francia
y la malherida y salvaje Alemania nazi, de modo que el ensañamiento de
Olivier para con lo francés no deja de resultar sorprendente tratándose de
un país por entonces aliado... a no ser que la patética corte de la película
sea una velada referencia al gobierno de Vichy. Por su parte, en la versión de Branagh, y como es lógico por la fecha, hay algo más de come-
dimiento en la sátira de los franceses. Aun así, frente al rey, hombre serio y responsable, el Delfín transpira arrogancia, como en general lo
hacen los otros nobles, que van extremadamente bien peinados y vestidos para ir a la guerra, frente a una lograda naturalidad de los guerreros
ingleses.

Pero no solamente lo francés es objeto de sátira en *Enrique V*. En un
ejercicio sumamente curioso con unos ciertos tintes auto-xenófobos,
valga la paradoja, Shakespeare, siempre proclive a dar la palabra a todos,
la da a los franceses para que expresen la opinión que les merecen los

ingleses. Ello sucede sobre todo en III.5, donde se presenta a la nación inglesa como un pueblo bárbaro formado por bastardos descendientes de los normandos del norte de Francia (*"The emptying of our fathers' luxury"*, afirma el Delfín) que sufren un clima y una bebida pésimos; y en el final de III.7, donde son tildados de descerebrados y cobardes.[2] Es probable que Shakespeare se divirtiera con esas pullas contra su propia gente; en cambio, cuando los apelativos resultan más insultantes, como en IV.2, lo que se produce más bien es un reflejo de la bravuconería de los franceses a través de sus discursos. Ahí radica lo más sustancial de la visión de lo francés como extranjero en la obra: no en lo que se dice de él, sino en lo que ellos dicen y cómo lo dicen.

La princesa extranjera no sabe inglés

En III.4 y V.2, que se dirían escenas que Shakespeare introdujera como con calzador, aparece la princesa Catalina, y la lengua francesa adquiere un protagonismo determinante. La escena III.4 es un diálogo monolingüe entre Catalina y su asistenta Alicia; esta enseña algunas palabras en inglés a la joven, quien comete errores grotescos, como confundir *foot* con *foutre* y *gown* con *con*. A pesar de su comicidad, no debemos olvidar que la clase de inglés versa sobre la anatomía de la princesa (mano, dedos, uñas, brazo, codo, cuello, mentón, pie), y es que, en efecto, Catalina será el trofeo de guerra de la victoria de Enrique sobre la Francia sometida. El extranjero es, ante todo, alguien a quien someter, empezando por el idioma; si la extranjera es mujer, se le exigirá además que pague la derrota con su cuerpo. Por eso Catalina paga por adelantado (la deuda no vence hasta que los ingleses ganen la batalla final), y paga doble: debe aprender inglés y empieza por las palabras que designan las partes de su

---

2   En la auto-xenófoba descripción de los ingleses de III.7, Luis Astrana Marín traduce *"Foolish curs, that run winking into the mouth of a Russian bear"* por "¡Tontos perruchos, que vienen a arrojarse ciegos en la bocaza del oso de Rusia!" (W. Shakespeare, *Obras completas. Tragedias*, Madrid, Aguilar, 2003, 715): un simple cambio de determinante que quizás encierra una proclama antiliberal y anticomunista. La traducción se hizo durante el régimen de Primo de Rivera.

cuerpo, como si se tratara de la primera víctima tendida en el campo de batalla de Agincourt.

En su versión, Laurence Olivier omite toda la escena y la sustituye por una breve secuencia muda en la que la princesa pasa por delante de los nobles franceses, quienes al parecer la encuentran apetitosa; de ahí se deduce su condición de botín sexual, según Ace G. Pilkington (1991: 125-26). En el film de Kenneth Branagh, el inicio y el final le dan a la escena, como ha apuntado José Ramón Díaz Fernández (2001: 15), un tinte irónico, que subraya la inconsciencia de Catalina ante los sucesos. Aun así, es dudoso que en la intención de Branagh haya censura alguna: ¿no será que el director también peca de inconsciencia al presentarnos a la joven tan alegremente excitada en su condición de botín de guerra y ante un futuro que le depara ser reina... de Inglaterra?

Si la escena de la clase de inglés es lingüísticamente compleja de por sí, el doblaje español del film de Branagh la conduce a lo absurdo. Mientras que en la versión original se mantiene en francés con subtítulos en inglés, en el doblaje la princesa habla un español deliberadamente defectuoso que roza el ridículo —solo se detecta un rotacismo dislálico en un acento genuinamente español—, lo que convierte en paradójico que el resto de personajes franceses de la película manejen un español perfecto. Pero es que, además, con ese doblaje la comicidad de la escena se desmorona: a pesar de que se permite introducir *vulvo* por *elbow* en un juego que no se da en el original y que anticipa las procacidades posteriores, en castellano no se entienden las chanzas con *foot* y *gown*.

La escena V.2 es un episodio bilingüe en que Enrique, habiendo ya conquistado el reino de Francia, pretende asimismo salir airoso de su empeño de hacerse con el corazón de la hija del monarca francés... como si le hiciera falta. Al no mediar conocimientos lingüísticos compartidos, la escena del cortejo de la extranjera termina por resultar hilarante, pero a un tiempo subraya implícitamente una reflexión sobre el mismo concepto de alteridad. Olivier rodó y protagonizó la escena con mucha dulzura: Enrique y Catalina sonríen permanentemente, no hay sensación alguna de forcejeo ni imposición, y ella incluso parece enamorada, a juzgar por sus ojos y la placidez de su rostro, y hasta se adivina un coqueteo divertido por su parte que sugiere que está disfrutando de la situación. (Sobre estos aspectos, es destacable el trabajo de Donaldson 1990, que detalla el tratamiento del género en la película.) En fin: el espectador casi llega a creer que la mujer tiene derecho a decidir. El final del cortejo, aparentemente gracioso, es revelador. Cuando Enrique arrebata el beso a Catalina son sorprendidos por los nobles que entran, y Borgoña pregunta si estaban dando clase de inglés. Es decir: si el poder se materializa en la imposición de la lengua, enseñarla es someter al "otro", al extranjero, como somete a su cuerpo un beso hurtado. El doblaje español de la película mantiene con buen tino las frases en francés que pronuncia Catalina, y cuando intenta hablar en inglés se la reviste de una cierta tosquedad jugando con el rotacismo y con un acento francés en general bastante verosímil.

La tendenciosidad de Branagh en la escena del cortejo es notoria, como ha subrayado la crítica; da cuenta de ello Kathy M. Howlett (2000: 110). Robert Lane (1994: 44) equipara la escena con una conquista militar, ya visible en el texto, y describe la forma en que la conduce Branagh para que el espectador la apruebe. Lo cierto es que la princesa parece resistirse: al principio está enfurruñada, lo que resulta paradójico respecto a la clase de inglés, y Enrique se siente incómodo, pero al poco ella empieza a mejorar el semblante, sobre todo cuando entra el tema musical, de tono marcadamente romántico. En general, la muchacha se mantiene seria, como con un cierto aire responsable, hasta que el rey intenta hablar en francés. Entonces se relaja: quien tiene la lengua tiene el poder, y en ese lance ella tiene un poder momentáneo. De hecho, es precisamente cuando el rey, por así decirlo, se rebaja a hablar en francés cuando conquista su corazón. Branagh filma e interpreta sagazmente el pasaje, pero no nos advierte de la perversidad que encierra: se trata de un paréntesis en una relación en que, por descontado, quien deberá aprender un idioma extranjero es la mujer, una forma de violación que parece aceptar de buen grado la princesa de su film.

La escasa credibilidad que le quedaba al doblaje español del film de Branagh se va al traste en esta escena. De golpe y porrazo, Catalina empieza a hablar en un francés recién adquirido, aunque luego lo pierde y recupera el español: un desbarajuste. Y lo que es peor, la pobre Catalina de la versión doblada es ultrajada tres veces: por estar obligada a aprender una lengua extranjera, por tener que ceder su cuerpo y su vida al rey extranjero, y porque ni tan solo sabe su lengua materna y apenas acierta a hablar ridículamente el español, para ella otra lengua extranjera.

486

Bibliografía

Aragay, M. 1999. "A little touch of Branagh: *Henry V*", *Links & Letters* 6, 11-22.

Davies, A. 1988. *Filming Shakespeare's Plays: The Adaptations of Laurence Olivier, Orson Welles, Peter Brook and Akira Kurosawa,* Cambridge, Cambridge UP.

—. 2007. "The Shakespeare films of Laurence Olivier", in R. Jackson (ed.), *The Cambridge Companion to Shakespeare on Film,* Cambridge, Cambridge UP, 167-75.

Díaz Fernández, J. R. 2001. "Harry el sucio: *Enrique V* de Kenneth Branagh", *Contrastes* 16, 8-16.

Donaldson, P. S. 1990. "'Claiming from the Female': Gender and Representation in Laurence Olivier's *Henry V*", in *Shakespearean Films/Shakespearean Directors,* Winchester, Unwin Hyman, 1-30.

—. 1991. "Taking on Shakespeare: Kenneth Branagh's *Henry V*", *Shakespeare Quarterly* 42, 60-71.

Holderness, G. 1992. *Shakespeare Recycled: The Making of Historical Drama,* Hatfield, Harvester Wheatsheaf.

Howlett, K. M. 2000. "Framing Ambiguity: Kenneth Branagh's *Henry V*", in *Framing Shakespeare on Film,* Athens, Ohio UP, 92-114.

Jorgens, J. 1991 [1977]. *Shakespeare on Film,* Lanham, Maryland, UP of America.

Lane, R. 1994. "*When Blood is their Argument*: Class, Character, and Historymaking in Shakespeare's and Branagh's *Henry V*", *English Literary History* 61: 1, 27-52.

Pilkington, A. G. 1991. "The BBC Henry V", "Laurence Olivier's Henry V", in *Screening Shakespeare from* Richard II *to* Henry V, Newark, U of Delaware P, 87-129.

Rothwell, K. S. 2004 [1999]. "Henry V (1944) and "Henry V (1989)", in *A History of Shakespeare on Screen: A Century of Film and Television,* Cambridge, Cambridge UP, 50-54, 234-38.

Smith, E. 2002. "Introduction", in W. Shakespeare, *Henry V,* Cambridge, Cambridge UP, 1-79.

Nuria Sánchez Villadangos

El padecimiento de la otredad en la narrativa de Lourdes Ortiz

Como establece Paul Ricoeur "lo Otro no es solo la contrapartida de lo Mismo, sino que pertenece a la constitución íntima de su sentido" (1996: 365). Es preciso remarcar que lo Otro no existiría o no tendría razón de ser sin lo Mismo. Por lo tanto, la otredad se conectaría inevitablemente con la mismidad, de igual manera que se relacionaría con la identidad a la cual hay que ver como una categoría compleja que "puede interpretarse como un compendio de discursos, creencias, suposiciones culturales e interpelaciones ideológicas, entre otras" (Pacheco 2009: 354). A decir verdad, cada uno de nosotros tenemos una identidad que nos singulariza o, mejor dicho, somos el compendio de varias identidades: sexual, histórica, personal, cultural, política y nacional. Además, según Gilda Pacheco, glosando las teorías del sociólogo británico Richard Dyer:

> Esta identidad es la construcción del ser dentro de su grupo social. Así, vemos cómo se define el ser, el individuo dentro de la sociedad en donde la identidad se vislumbra como un proceso que fluye, un proceso permanente de construcción y reconstrucción [...] [donde] el ser está inmerso en las colectividades de clase, raza, etnicidad, religión, ideología, región, nación, sexualidad y género, entre otras (Pacheco 2009: 354).

A propósito de todo ello, sería preciso señalar una serie de marcadores o señas de identidad: unos claramente visuales, "como el color de la piel o los rasgos propios del género", y otros menos evidentes o visibles, como "las creencias y los valores", que serían partes fundamentales de las personas y que contribuirían a determinar su subjetividad intransferible. Con todo, parece obvio que "en la construcción de la identidad es indispensable tanto la alteridad como la otredad", tal como afirma Gilda Pacheco, "pues se necesita el proceso del descubrimiento del otro desde el yo y la yuxtaposición con el otro, es decir, la condición o estado de ser el otro, para definir el ser" (2009: 354). Cabe observar que, según Iris Zavala, "el tema de la *alteridad* (*alterité, autrui*) constituye uno de los puntos de vista privilegiados por muchas teorías lingüísticas postestructuralistas, en particular la deconstrucción y el psicoanálisis" (1991: 175).

En realidad, en las sociedades actuales donde las identidades individuales parecen diluidas, o incluso llegan a asemejarse unas a otras, y donde la sanción más dura es la de no saber cuál es la verdadera identificación, es necesario —casi vital— abogar por la tenencia de una clara identidad, pues el poseerla implica tener conciencia, es decir, ocasiona la creencia en uno mismo y el ser capaz de crear y de realizar sueños e ideas para superarse y vivir de un modo acorde a las posibilidades personales. El portal de internet "Redesearte paz" incluye en su diccionario la definición de "Otredad", que define bajo los siguientes términos: "los otros son otros en la medida en que son diferentes de nosotros; la otredad es entonces esa posibilidad de reconocer, respetar y convivir con la diferencia" (<www.redeseartepaz.org/2009/07/diccionario/>).

Ahora bien, en ciertas ocasiones, es necesario vivir la pérdida de lo que somos o fuimos, el extravío de nuestra propia identidad, y experimentar el dolor que ello causa para poder reflexionar sobre el porqué de la angustia y el desconsuelo. Sin duda, la literatura está llena de relatos de gentes que se sienten intrusas en sus propias vidas o que padecen las adversidades que causa el creerse extranjero en el propio país o en el ajeno. En relación con ello, Lourdes Ortiz en su magistral libro de cuentos titulado *Fátima de los naufragios. Relatos de tierra y mar* (1998), así como en los relatos agrupados en *Ojos de gato* (2011), expresa como nadie las ausencias, las muertes anónimas, los amores épicos y los anhelos incumplidos de una serie de personajes inmersos en historias con sentimientos viscerales, hondos e insospechados, en los que los retazos de la existencia cotidiana, desprovistos de los encajes de la retórica, palpitan con una intensidad desgarradora. En definitiva, estaríamos ante relatos unidos por el común denominador de la angustiosa soledad de sus protagonistas, los cuales, en su búsqueda del ignoto y utópico paraíso, se han extraviado sin remedio y sin retorno, sorprendidos por el sentimiento de la otredad como un espejismo sórdido y caprichoso.

A decir verdad, la autora madrileña, con hondo dramatismo, consigue presentar a lo largo de estos relatos una exploración lúcida y sincera de las aflicciones y los sinsentidos de la ambición humana, contraponiendo identidad y otredad a lo largo de todo el discurso literario. De esta manera, el cuento que abre y que da título a la antología de relatos, "Fátima de los naufragios", expresa el drama de la inmigración en pateras por la temida posibilidad de caer en las garras de la muerte al intentar cruzar el mar que separa España de los países africanos. La protagonista, Fátima, vive en la playa a la espera de la llegada de su hijo, el cual murió ahogado en una noche oscura cuando la embarcación en la que viajaba naufragó. La desconsolada madre hace guardia frente al mar, suplicándole que le devuelva el cuerpo ya sin vida de su joven hijo. Las gentes del lugar ven a Fátima como la Otra, la mujer exótica, y recibe calificativos como "la muda", "estatua de dolor", "la loca de la playa", "la mendiga africana", "una pobre mujer", "una chiflada", "la santa mora silenciosa", "la moreneta", "fantasma, aparición o santa o virgen morena" y "la Virgen de las pateras, nuestra señora de los naufragios" (1998: 7, 8, 10, 18, 22), epítetos que reflejan la indefinición para caracterizarla; en definitiva, para identificarla. Tal y como establece Ricoeur, "identificar algo es poder dar a conocer a los demás, dentro de una gama de cosas particulares del mismo tipo, aquello de lo que tenemos intención de hablar". Pero, además, él mismo añade que "la individualización puede caracterizarse, en líneas generales, como el proceso inverso al de la clasificación, que elimina las singularidades en provecho del concepto" (1996: 1, 2).

Otro de los relatos de Ortiz recogido en la misma antología y que también habla del drama de la inmigración cuando se le dan tintes de sobreexplotación humana es el titulado "La piel de Marcelinda", siguiendo la línea de Lourdes Ortiz de colocar a una mujer como protagonista clara de una narración para mostrar los recovecos del ser y del sentir femeninos, así como los diversos puntos de vista desde los que son vislumbradas, haciendo hincapié en los falsos mitos femeninos y en la reivindicación de la figura de la mujer. En este caso, Marcelinda es una atractiva mujer inmigrante, menor de edad, que se ve obligada a ejercer la prostitución para pagar el visado que la ha traído a España, pues, en ciertas ocasiones, ser "la otra" puede implicar o llevar aparejado el tener que desempeñar trabajos tan denigrantes como es el vender por obligación el propio cuerpo en el país de destino donde las mujeres son tratadas, además, como "lote guay de negratas", o "mercancía", o "negocio" o "material de trabajo" (1998: 25, 28). Asimismo, estas mismas mujeres inmigrantes han de soportar vejaciones verbales y físicas por parte de aquellos que requieren de sus servicios sexuales, que las usan para luego tirarlas como si fueran despojos y que se muestran odiosamente xenófobos con ellas: "Hay muchos que los pone a cien llamarlas negras y decir-les que se vayan pa'su tierra, tratarlas como esclavas, que eso forma parte de la cuestión" (1998: 38).

Por otro lado, esa otredad que sentimos en lo ajeno a nosotros mismos la podemos notar ya en las impresiones que nos causan las ropas, los gestos, o las respuestas de los desconocidos a los que nos enfrentamos cada día, si bien, hay instantes en los que resulta más interesante indagar acerca de en qué momentos el Otro puede ser uno mismo, tal y como se ve en el relato titulado "El vuelo de la mariposa". La narración invita a una reflexión acerca de nuestros prejuicios y nuestra forma de juzgar a los demás por las apariencias: "Había cuatro mesas vacías y dos ocupadas. En una, una pareja de alemanes —o eso me parecieron— [...]. En la otra, una mujer mayor, con pinta también de extranjera —¿o no?— leía un libro" (1998: 55). En otra ocasión no se prejuzga a los extranjeros sino a las mujeres solteras: "Solterona es lo que es; las conozco con sólo mirarlas. Y si me equivoco tampoco importa" (1998: 65).

El relato es una reflexión acerca de cómo, en un minuto, nos puede cambiar la vida, dependiendo de con quién nos podamos encontrar o qué decisiones o qué actos llevemos a cabo en ciertos instantes de nuestra vida cotidiana. Estamos, en suma, ante una calculada deliberación acerca de cuándo uno mismo se convierte en el Otro, en un forastero, hasta el punto de no llegar a reconocerse, tal y como confiesa el protagonista del relato del que no sabemos ni su nombre: "Me veía a mí mismo y apenas me reconocía en aquel hombre que de pronto se mostraba altanero y seguro" (1998: 76). A decir verdad, todo el cuento sería, además, una calculada meditación sobre las eventualidades de la vida y una reflexión sobre las incertidumbres del día a día, pues la existencia es imprevisible y efímera ya que "cuando una mariposa mueve sus alas en un punto cualquiera de la tierra, en el extremo más opuesto, en las antípodas, algo sucede. El vuelo repercute" (1998: 80). Nada ni nadie puede evitarlo.

Por su parte, la novela titulada *La fuente de la vida* también destaca por el compromiso social que mana en cada palabra con la intención de narrar, con una gran plasticidad, el devenir cotidiano de unos personajes que acusan grandes traumas e insuperables tragedias personales. Estas les impiden continuar con sus vidas normales, acuciados como están, además, por una sociedad que les empuja a cometer actos impuros, delic-tivos y viles sin tener opción o sin ni siquiera poder plantearse la negati-va a perpetrarlos, y con el miedo siempre helador a ser descubiertos y condenados sin remedio. Ahora bien, quizás lo más curioso de la obra sea que el lector no sienta rabia (o no pueda sentirla) hacia esos personajes sino que, más bien, llega a experimentar una tímida compasión y una agónica pena por cómo (sobre)viven y qué les lleva a plantear sus existencias al margen de la ley, abocando sus vidas a un precipicio donde la caída es mortal e irreversible, y sin tener ni una mínima oportunidad para el arrepentimiento o para el cambio hacia el lado del bien.

Asimismo, también en *La fuente de la vida* es destacable el poder que ostentan las mujeres a lo largo de toda la narración. Únicamente ellas, frente a los fríos y, a veces, impasibles y pusilánimes hombres, son capaces de aglutinar todos los buenos y malos sentimientos. Solamente ellas son valientes para actuar con decisión, para cometer los hechos más viles y reconocerlos, y para intentar sin remedio enmendar los errores y recuperar el orden y el tiempo perdidos. De esta manera, María, Nelly, Esther, Ródika y Lisa, como protagonistas de la obra, son diversos modelos de mujer, todas diferentes y en nada complementarias. Son rivales ya por el mero hecho de pertenecer a países y culturas diferentes que parecen impedir un acercamiento real y un entendimiento sincero entre ellas. Así, la norteamericana Nelly, "sensual y desconocida" como una "diosa antigua, una de esas sacerdotisas sagradas" de cabellos rojos — símbolo tradicional de la mujer perversa o del demonio disfrazado de mujer capaz de atrapar a los hombres y disponer de ellos a capricho—, queda definida por oposición a la embarazada María, mujer de Ramiro, a la que se caracteriza como una "Madonna", una "Virgencita barroca [...] enorme vientre generador, un vientre rosado y terso" (1995: 104-105).

Por su parte, Esther, la novia de Esteban, se define como un alma libre, libidinosa y pasional. En cambio, su contrario, Ródika, la chica rumana por la que Esteban llega a sentir algo entre la compasión y el asco, queda caracterizada como una mujer de treinta y siete años ya con "canas que brotaban sobre una frente arrugada; [...] para revelar el cadáver inerte, alerta, que yacía bajo la piel, todavía suave, todavía acariciable" (1995: 77). Ahora bien, tal vez, el contraste entre la Esther de clase media, segura, altiva y arrogante y la Ródika mísera, insegura, tímida, y al mismo tiempo, lujuriosa —"hembra del infierno" (1995: 192); "mujer vampiro, cochambrosa y tersa", (1995: 240)— se vea mejor en las comparaciones que realiza el propio Esteban entre las dos mujeres, donde muestra una exagerada atracción por Esther —"una mujer perfecta, una esposa espléndida, guapa, rozagante"— (1995: 183), y una manifiesta y

declarada repulsión por Ródika —"una mujer desvalida y algo asustada"— (1995: 185).

Por otro lado, la narración también nos descubre una mujer especial,
frágil, no hecha para el mundo cruel, inocente e inexperta: Lisa, una
joven chica rumana enamorada de Esteban y que le sirve de guía por
Rumanía. También ella queda definida por oposición a las otras dos mujeres: "Ródika, Esther, Lisa. Le daba pena utilizar a la muchacha dulce
[…] y sabía que ella y Ródika seguramente no iban a entenderse, pero…,
y en Esther prefería no pensar por ahora" (1995: 225).

Con todo, María y Esther y sus respectivas parejas, Ramiro y Esteban, son seres del Primer Mundo que han tenido todo a su alcance para
progresar en la vida. Aunque con existencias aburridas o poco aprove-
chadas, han disfrutado de los placeres y sinsabores del día a día llenos de
problemas pero también de beneficios, tristezas y sobradas alegrías. Nelly, igualmente ciudadana del que tal vez sea el país más poderoso del
mundo, no ha sabido medir las consecuencias de sus actos y ha pagado
con su propia vida el haber traspasado la fina línea entre lo correcto y lo
horrendo. Por su parte, Ródika y Lisa son hijas de unos tiempos duros en
un país frío y casi aún dictatorial como es Rumanía. Por lo tanto, a través
de las vivencias de los personajes son visibles las diferencias que en los
noventa, y quizás también ahora, se daban entre países como España y
Estados Unidos frente a Perú y Rumanía donde los viejos rencores parecen imposibles de olvidar.

En la línea de los libros hasta ahora analizados, el último volumen
de relatos de Lourdes Ortiz, la antología de cuentos *Ojos de gato*, responde al momento de crisis económica, pero también moral, que se vive
en pleno siglo XXI. Para la autora es preciso seguir escribiendo sobre las
miserias humanas, la pobreza, las guerras, las amenazas terroristas, la
inmigración, la desconexión entre hombres y mujeres, entre otra serie de
males, que oprimen al mundo. El volumen supone una compilación de
doce relatos, que habían permanecido inéditos, distribuidos en dos apar-
tados. El primero, titulado "Cruces", destaca por sus protagonistas masculinos y está más centrado en captar esa falta de integración social de
los inmigrantes llegados a España con la idea de una vida mejor. En el
segundo, "Ellas", las protagonistas son unas mujeres que están al límite y
que no parecen tener un futuro satisfactorio sino, más bien, un porvenir
lleno de frustraciones y pérdidas. Ambas partes se hallan unidas por la
común mirada irónica, preocupada, melancólica y, a veces, humorística

de la autora. En suma, *Ojos de gato* es una antología de cuentos sobre la soledad y la marginalidad y sobre la capacidad que tenemos los seres humanos para sobrevivir en situaciones hostiles y caóticas.

En conclusión, Lourdes Ortiz ha sabido reflejar en los relatos y en la novela analizados en este trabajo que el Otro no es objeto de pensamiento sino que, al igual que uno mismo, es sujeto de pensamiento. Un sujeto de pensamiento que, en palabras de Paul Ricoeur "me percibe a mí mismo como otro distinto de él mismo; que, juntos, miramos el mundo como una naturaleza común" (1996: 369). Ahora bien, el tema de la otredad de los demás o de la alteridad del sujeto no conoce un fin definitivo y aclarador sino todo lo contrario. Se renueva en cada ser y en cada escritor que reflexiona sobre ello, como un padecimiento, una dolencia o un problema difícil de resolver ya que, tal como afirma Ociel Flores, "la otredad es un sentimiento de extrañeza que asalta al hombre tarde o temprano, porque tarde o temprano toma, necesariamente, conciencia de su individualidad". Queda claro, por consiguiente, que el hombre "en algún momento cae en la cuenta de que vive separado de los demás; de que existe aquél que no es él; de que están los otros y de que hay algo más allá de lo que él percibe o imagina" (1999: [s.p.]). Tal vez, siguiendo planteamientos de Derrida, la otredad es un devenir, un "soy y no soy". Con todo, a modo de final abierto para nuevas reflexiones, resulta interesante el siguiente fragmento extraído de la novela *Rayuela* de Julio Cortázar:

> Así, paradójicamente, el colmo de soledad conducía [...] a la gran ilusión de la compañía ajena, al hombre solo en la sala de los espejos y los ecos. Pero gentes como él y tantos otros, que se aceptaban a sí mismos (o que se rechazaban pero conociéndose de cerca) entraban en la peor paradoja, la de estar quizá al borde de la otredad y no poder franquearlo. La verdadera otredad hecha de delicados contactos, de maravillosos ajustes con el mundo, no podía cumplirse desde un solo término, a la mano tendida debía responder otra mano desde el afuera, desde lo otro (1980: 120-21).

Este fragmento, aclaratorio a la par que confuso de lo que implica la otredad, nos la presenta como un sentimiento incómodo y curioso, enriquecedor e inquietante. Es este mismo sentimiento que late bajo la narrativa de Lourdes Ortiz.

Bibliografía

Cortázar, J. 1980. *Rayuela*, Barcelona, Edhasa.

Flores, O. 1999. "Octavio Paz: la otredad, el amor y la poesía", *Razón y palabra* 15, s.p. <www.razonypalabra.org.mx/anteriores/n15/ oflores15.html> [consultado el 27.IX.2011].

"Otredad". 2009. *Redesearte paz*, <www.redeseartepaz.org/2009/07/ diccionario/> [consultado el 13.VII.2011].

Ortiz, L. 1995. *La fuente de la vida*, Barcelona, Planeta.

—. 1998. *Fátima de los naufragios. Relatos de tierra y mar*, Barcelona, Planeta.

—. 2011. *Ojos de gato*, Madrid, Ediciones Irreverentes.

Pacheco, G. 2009. "De la otredad a la identidad: perspectivas de teoría feminista de fines del siglo XX", *Revista de Lenguas Modernas* 10, 353-59.

Ricoeur, P. 1996. *Sí mismo como otro*, Madrid, Siglo XXI.

Zavala, I. 1991. *La Posmodernidad y Mijail Bajtín. Una poética dialógica*, Madrid, Espasa Calpe.

MARÍA DEL PINO SANTANA QUINTANA

"La promesa de la alteridad": otredad e hibridismo en el libro de viajes contemporáneo

En los mapas de nuestro siglo apenas existen espacios en blanco: el avance de la tecnología y los medios de comunicación nos acercan a cualquier rincón del mundo y a los más remotos modelos de sociedades; pero la alteridad proporcionada por un país distinto al de nuestro origen no ha desaparecido. La figura del Otro continúa erigiéndose como uno de los mayores elementos de atracción en la literatura de viajes contemporánea. Las representaciones del mundo que llevan a cabo los viajeros se caracterizan, especialmente, por la diversidad geográfica, la novedad paisajística, el contraste cultural y los distintos modelos de vida; la presencia del Otro anima sus recorridos y les facilita el camino hacia la composición del relato. El Otro implica lo extraño, lo distinto a nuestro entorno cotidiano, lo que es opuesto al yo y a su mundo dialogal. El viajero natural de una nación que acomete la empresa de aventurarse en otra es el único extraño en un entorno que es común a sus habitantes nativos; es él, y no el indígena, el que está fuera de una homogeneidad étnica, religiosa, lingüística o cultural, y el que debe esforzarse en comprender lo que le rodea. No existe, en palabras de Robert Louis Stevenson, una tierra extraña; es el viajero el que es extranjero porque solo él la desconoce (2000: 33).

La complicación del conocimiento del Otro no es únicamente un problema lingüístico; existe, además, todo un entramado de mecanismos culturales externos e internos que afectan de igual forma al entendimiento entre sociedades diferentes. Estos mecanismos son perceptibles desde el primer contacto con la cultura extranjera. La diversidad cultural que ofrece la tierra desconocida en el momento de la llegada se sitúa fuera del alcance, pues se desconoce y no presenta rasgos afines al lugar de procedencia del viajero. Tal y como sostiene el sociólogo Georges Balandier, en la distancia que nos facilita el desplazamiento se establece la "diferencia exterior" o "exótica" bajo la que el viajero observa al Otro

(1993: 37). El exotismo, como construcción imaginaria del sujeto extranjero, alimenta esta diversidad; aporta una imagen fantaseada del Otro que no tiene por qué coincidir con la real, puesto que no se basa en una observación reflexionada, sino en una impresión provocada por la alteridad excesiva que el viajero encuentra a su llegada. La súbita extrañeza que ocasiona el primer contacto con la geografía del Otro provoca una confusión, en ocasiones, un sentimiento de marginación personal que, unido a la fatiga, el esfuerzo, la soledad y la duda, pueden acabar en un estado de decepción. Le ocurre a Edith Wharton (*In Morocco*, 1920) cuando descubre los oasis y harenes de Marruecos, espacios que suelen ser imaginados como el súmmum del exotismo en la mente occidental; y también cuando se adentra en los zocos de Marrakech y Fez y, en vez de multitudes con ropajes coloridos que portan manjares suculentos, lo que Wharton encuentra es un enjambre de mendigos que transitan por callejuelas en penumbra o sobre burros malolientes. Redmond O'Hanlon, un viajero y geógrafo de nuestro tiempo, viaja a Borneo persiguiendo una idea romántica y preconcebida de los habitantes de la selva como gente incorrupta y de costumbres ancestrales. Los primeros encuentros con la tribu Ukit, sin embargo, se tornan decepcionantes. En su libro de viajes *Into the Heart of Borneo* (1984), O'Hanlon nos cuenta, bajo el tono hostil y apesadumbrado del desencanto, que algunos de los miembros de la tribu Ukit hablan inglés y, para peor suerte, tienen conocimiento de la música disco.

El primer encuentro con la alteridad, la no pertenencia a un determinado círculo espacial, puede asimismo ocasionar trastornos emocionales y psicológicos. Paul Theroux, un viajero que no precisa presentación, aficionado a recorridos difíciles y remotos, no duda en asemejar la experiencia del extraño en un país extranjero a una forma de locura. A este propósito, en su colección de ensayos *The Tao of Travel* (2011), Theroux sostiene:

> Otherness can be like an illness; being a stranger can be analogous to experiencing a form of madness —those same intimations of the unreal and the irrational, when everything that has been familiar is stripped away. It is hard to be a stranger. A traveler may have no power, no influence, no known identity. That is why a traveler needs optimism and heart, because without confidence travel is misery. Generally, the traveler is anonymous, ignorant, easy to deceive, at the mercy of the people he or she travels among (2011: 123).

La desubicación geográfica, que en la narrativa de viajes siempre corre paralela a la emocional, no solo aísla al viajero, sino que también lo debilita ante el Otro. Como sugiere Theroux en la cita anterior, el viajero debe emprender su recorrido con un talante optimista, empaparse de confianza ante la ausencia de códigos familiares y confiar en que ese estado de irrealidad febril al que conduce el primer encuentro con la gente nativa es pasajero.

Y es que el desorden psicológico que puede llegar a provocar lo profundamente diferente, ya sea con respecto a lo familiar, como con respecto a las expectativas previas a la partida, puede dar origen a una experiencia fluida y satisfactoria una vez que el viajero se familiariza con lo que le rodea. Afincado fuera de su entorno habitual, el viajero advierte y participa de cualidades y estilos de vida inherentes al país extranjero, alcanzando, en ocasiones, a conocer lo que se siente como ciudadano de esa otra cultura. Es en estos casos, tan recurrentes en los libros de viajes, cuando el viajero aprende a asimilar la diferencia; el Otro deja de ser cuestionado desde la distancia, pasando a revelarse desde la proximidad. De acuerdo con Georges Balandier, estas diferencias que se observan en la cercanía son de tipo "intrasocial" e "intracultural" (1993: 37), es decir, que conciernen a la pertenencia a un grupo social, a una religión o a una generación concretas, pero son discrepancias que no sobrepasan los márgenes de la sociedad.

Mediante este tipo de alteridad próxima, la diferencia del extranjero con respecto a los demás se reduce a aspectos internos de la cultura y la identidad del país anfitrión. Lejos de preservar esa sensación de alteridad absoluta que se percibe tras su primera toma de contacto con el país, el viajero se adapta al entorno, su perspectiva como extranjero queda atenuada. Y, dado que cuanto más profundiza en lo distinto, menor es su extrañeza, su visión exótica del Otro —y también de su entorno— es reconstruida; es decir, paulatinamente, el extranjero adopta el punto de vista del nativo y se amolda a los nuevos códigos culturales. De esta forma, todos aquellos elementos que por su condición de novedad llamaban la atención del viajero se despojan de su valor inicial, pierden el aura de lo desconocido, pasando así a formar parte de la realidad circundante. En su descubrimiento personal de la alteridad, el viajero reconstruye el exotismo, lo raro y lo pintoresco, hasta tornarlo familiar y parte de lo cotidiano. El viajero, finalmente, lleva a cabo la transfiguración de lo exótico a lo cotidiano.

La función del viajero no es otra que la de franquear fronteras, bien hacia lo distinto, bien hacia el espacio de pertenencia, el punto de partida o, si se prefiere, el hogar. Si bien es cierto que la noción habitual de frontera es la de unos límites naturales —nacionales, territoriales y geográficos—, en un sentido metafórico, la frontera representa ese pasaje abismal cuyo cruce supone dejar de ser nativo para convertirse en extranjero. Traspasarla constituye una forma de abandono de la identidad, pues lo que le espera al viajero al otro lado de la frontera no es la pertenencia a un lugar, sino la inmersión en un mundo diverso e inexplorado. Pero es también en los límites y en las fronteras donde los extraños se encuentran, se conocen y, consciente o inconscientemente, se influyen.

El viajero, como el emigrante, se mueve contra corriente, en la vía opuesta a lo que Iain Chambers define como los límites de nuestra herencia (2001: 115). En el momento de la llegada a un entorno desconocido, el viajero tiene que confrontar la diferencia y negociar entre lo poco que lleva consigo —lo propio— y lo mucho que tiene de ajeno el territorio que acaba de alcanzar. Su identidad queda, entonces, suspendida en el vacío hasta el momento de la elección. En una primera opción, el recuerdo del hogar y las lazos culturales que lo vinculan a su tierra pueden mantenerse vigentes, de modo que todo lo que concierne al Otro permanezca en la oscuridad; se trata, en consecuencia, de una tendencia enfocada hacia el mantenimiento y la protección de la cultura originaria del extranjero. Otra opción posible en el proceso de construcción del viajero en un espacio foráneo es la de adaptarse al nuevo ambiente que le ofrece la sociedad de acogida, sin cuestionarse su identidad territorial; se trata, en este caso, de una tendencia que se dirige hacia la asimilación y la integración dentro de la cultura dominante. Estas dos modalidades se corresponden con la acción de acercamiento o alejamiento que Todorov plantea en su obra *La conquista de América. El problema del otro* (1982), y que viene a significar para el extranjero un ejercicio de selección entre lo que Todorov considera "la sumisión al otro y la sumisión del otro" (1989: 195). Pero, existe también una tercera opción en la que se aúnan las dos anteriores, de modo que el extranjero asimila y preserva a un mismo tiempo aquello que más le conviene de ambas sociedades. De igual forma lo plantea Chan Kwok Bun, en cuyo artículo "Sobre la condición de extranjero" (2005) nos advierte de la posibilidad del migrante moderno de "mantenerse aferrado a ambas culturas —la de partida y la de llegada—, oscilando entre una y otra" (2005: 55). Esta última alternativa es la que conduce al viajero a la condición de hibridismo, un concepto que alude a la fusión paulatina de elementos de procedencias diversas y a su repercusión en la formación de la identidad. Cuando el contacto con una sociedad extranjera deriva en intercambio mediante la proliferación de la cultura propia y la influencia de la cultura ajena, surge lo que Chan Kwok Bun define como "una forma de implicación mutua entre el yo y el otro" (2005: 58).

En este sentido, la problemática de la alteridad se plantea cuando no existe comprensión —o "implicación"— entre el yo y el Otro. El sentimiento de extrañeza puede surgir tanto del propio extranjero hacia el nativo como del mismo nativo hacia el extranjero, a quien mira con curiosidad y cierta incomprensión por encontrarse en una tierra que no es la suya. Cuando la condición de extranjería opera en esta última dirección, el viajero experimenta esa cualidad de extrañeza que suscita el extranjero entre quienes lo han acogido, y que puede traducirse tanto en animosidad, como en una curiosidad irrefrenable. El nativo, al observar al extranjero, se muestra inquisitivo acerca de los motivos que lo traen a su tierra, se pregunta qué hace ahí, en un espacio que no es su lugar. El viajero norteamericano William Least Heat-Moon, en su libro *Blue Highways* (1983), deja constancia de esta cualidad de intruso que despierta el viajero en la mirada del Otro. Paseando por algunas pequeñas ciudades del norte de Estados Unidos, solo y ansioso de entablar conversación con algún nativo, Heat-Moon escribe: "people, wondering who the outsider was, would look at me; but as soon as I nodded they looked down, up, left, right, or turned around as if summoned by an invisible caller" (1984: 289). En su libro *The Wrong Way Home* (1999), el escritor de viajes australiano Peter Moore refleja lo risiblemente incómodo que puede resultar la presencia de un extraño en el territorio de la alteridad. Moore, que viaja desde Londres hasta Sydney en una amalgama de medios de transporte —desde desplazamientos en autobús de veintidós horas y trenes nauseabundos, hasta interminables marchas a pie y embarcaciones familiares—, cuenta cómo, a su paso por Isfahán, se convierte en la atracción absoluta de la ciudad:

Everywhere I went I seemed to cause a civil disturbance. If I stopped to look at the map in my guidebook, a gaggle of men would gather and peer over my shoulder. When I bought a felafel or a Coke from a stall, a group of Iranians would rush over and buy them too, as if I had given the place my official stamp of approval. As I walked down a street, black-shawled women would giggle and point and cry out "Hello Mister" (1999: 150).

En el encuentro del viajero con la alteridad, observamos situaciones en las que la mentalidad, la cultura o la expresión lingüística del nativo no encajan con la del extranjero. Es algo que siempre surge de forma inevitable y que ejemplifica ese mundo complejo e ignoto que constituye para el viajero las anomalías del país visitado. En su transitar por otros mundos y otras realidades, el escritor de viajes se enfrenta una y otra vez a situaciones que convierten la experiencia del periplo en una narración puramente cómica. Los libros de viajes cuentan con un nutrido repertorio de equivocaciones, malentendidos y suposiciones que el viajero tiende a narrar con un acertado sentido del humor. El escritor británico Peter Mayle, afincado en Provenza durante décadas, es uno de esos extranjeros que se esfuerzan en contemplarse a sí mismos desde el punto de vista del Otro, y es justamente ese esfuerzo lo que genera en su obra situaciones propias de la comedia. Como Mayle, el escritor de viajes norteamericano Bill Bryson es un claro ejemplo del extranjero que se enfrenta a un espacio foráneo recurriendo al humor como mecanismo de defensa. Una buena parte de sus encontronazos con la alteridad nos son relatados con ese estilo hilarante que caracteriza su obra y que le ha reportado una fama notable en el género. Bryson, pese a llevar más de dos décadas viviendo en Inglaterra, acaso por esa sensación de invasión del espacio del Otro, emplea el humor para reflejar la falta de conexión entre su propia cultura y la del país anfitrión. Su libro *Notes from a Small Island* (1995), un recorrido sentimental a lo largo y ancho de Gran Bretaña, expone los primeros casos del inglés nativo que plantea cuestiones ridículas sobre Norteamérica. A su paso por la ciudad de Bournemouth, por ejemplo, Bryson evoca sus dos años de trabajo como redactor en un periódico local. Recordando a uno de sus compañeros, el autor relata una situación absurda e insólita:

> Every time our gazes locked he would ask me some mystifying question to do with America. "Tell me", he would say, "is it true that Mickey Rooney never consummated his marriage with Ava Gardner, as I've read?" or "I've often wondered, and perhaps you can tell me, why is it that the nua-nua bird of Hawaii subsists only on pink-shelled molluscs when white-shelled molluscs are more numerous and of equal nutritive value, or so I've read" (1998: 93-4).

Estas preguntas del nativo hacia el extranjero sorprenden por su formulación insospechada y por el hecho mismo de que las respuestas que se esperan del autor resultan imposibles de atinar. Mientras su compañero asume que, por ser norteamericano, Bryson debe conocer aspectos raramente penetrables de su propia cultura, el viajero, por el contrario, se siente desconcertado ante la idea de que su nacionalidad tan solo alcance a suscitar este tipo de cuestiones.

Otras veces, en el transcurso de su periplo por Gran Bretaña, Bryson se inclina por un tono no tan humorístico y sí más autocompasivo. En Ludlow, una pequeña ciudad al oeste de Inglaterra, el viajero se describe a sí mismo como un paria. La situación que nos narra no deja de ser común a cualquier sujeto extranjero: Bryson entra en un restaurante de la ciudad y, viendo que está totalmente vacío, se decide por una mesa para cuatro personas. Minutos más tarde, el establecimiento se llena y muchos de los clientes comienzan a mirarlo despectivamente por ocupar un espacio del comedor que no estaba designado para un solo comensal:

> As I sat there, trying to eat quickly and be obscure, a man from two tables away came and asked me in a pointed tone if I was using one of the chairs, and took it without waiting my reply. I finished my food and slunk from the place in shame (1998: 266).

Inmediatamente después de abandonar este espacio de hostilidad, Bryson toma un tren atestado de pasajeros y encuentra un sitio libre justo en medio de cuatro personas que viajan juntas, plácidamente, y que miran con desdén al viajero inoportuno y despistado. Bryson, abrumado por la continua contrariedad de sentirse extranjero y fuera de lugar, vierte una imagen de sí mismo anti-heroica y vulnerable. No en vano, exclama: "more enemies! What a day I was having!" (1998: 266)

Cuando el viajero no encaja en el sistema de convenciones compartidas, cuando desconoce las reglas sociales y de conducta bajo las que opera el indígena en su propio entorno, recurre a la autocompasión. No obstante, y pese a los ejemplos mencionados, la experiencia de la alteridad no ha de implicar consecuencias negativas para el viajero. De ser así, no encontraríamos el entusiasmo que derrochan los libros de viajes y que nos viene dado en gran medida por la extraordinaria capacidad de integración del viajero contemporáneo. Avanzar hacia otros espacios invita al extranjero a un sinfín de posibilidades: la construcción de una identidad más acorde con la mentalidad y los valores del país visitado, la hibridación cultural y, sobre todo, lo que Carlos García Gual considera "el mejor reclamo del viaje". Tal como afirma el eminente helenista, "[e]l afán de conocer puede influir en el motivo del viaje, un viaje puede aportar conocimientos, pero lo mejor es ese avanzar hacia el encuentro con lo diverso, lo otro. La promesa de la alteridad es el mejor reclamo del viaje" (1999: 90).

Bibliografía

Balandier, G. 1993. "La aprehensión del otro: antropología desde fuera y antropología desde dentro", *Revista de Occidente* 140, 35-42.

Beriain, J. 1996. "La construcción de la identidad colectiva en las socie-dades modernas", in J. Beriain & P. Lanceros (comps.), *Identidades culturales*, Bilbao, Universidad de Deusto, 13-43.

Bryson, B. 1998. *Notes from a Small Island*, London, Black Swan.

Bun, Ch. K. 2005. "Sobre la condición de extranjero", *Revista de Occi-dente* 286, 45-61.

Chambers, I. 2001. *Migrancy, Culture, and Identity,* London, Routledge.

García Gual, C. 1999. "Viajes y libros", *Revista de Occidente* 218-219, 81-91.

Heat-Moon, W. L. 1984. *Blue Highways*: *A Journey into America*, New York, Fawcett.

Moore, P. 1999. *The Wrong Way Home*, London, Bantam.

O'Hanlon, R. 1985 [1984]. *Into the Heart of Borneo*: *An Account of a Journey Made in 1983 to the Mountains of Batu Tiban with James Fenton*, London, Penguin.

Stevenson, R. L. 2000 [1883]. *The Silverado Squatters*, Sandy, UT, Quiet Vision Publishing.

Theroux, P. 2011. *The Tao of Travel*: *Enlightments from Lives on the Road*, New York, Houghton Mifflin Harcourt.

Todorov, T. 1989. *La conquista de América. El problema del otro*, México, Siglo Veintiuno.

Wharton, E. 2009 [1920]. *In Morocco*, Oxford, Stanfords Travel Clas-sics, John Beaufoy Publishing.

Diego Santos Sánchez

"*Verboten!*" La censura del teatro extranjero durante el Franquismo: el caso de Bertolt Brecht

La censura teatral franquista y el teatro extranjero

Tras el final de la Guerra Civil, el general Franco se ponía al frente de una nueva España que habría de basar su discurso ideológico en dos pilares básicos: la Nación y el Catolicismo. Este nuevo dogma, el Nacional-Catolicismo, se le imponía a una sociedad dividida con el ánimo de generar una nueva España unida en torno al protagonismo indiscutible de la religión y el concepto de Patria. Con el fin de supervisar esta ortodoxia, el régimen forjó una serie de mecanismos de control que podrían definirse como "aparatos ideológicos de estado" (Althusser 1976), de entre los que la censura contó con un papel destacado. En el terreno teatral, su existencia durante los casi cuarenta años de la dictadura da fe de este férreo control impuesto en nombre de la religión y la patria. La tinta censora cercenó la producción teatral y prestó especial atención a todo aquello "que atent[ara] de alguna manera contra nuestras instituciones o ceremonias" (norma 14ª/2ª) o contra "la dignidad nacional"[1] (norma 17ª/2ª).

El régimen entendía esta nueva España como estandarte del Catolicismo frente a una corrupta e impía Europa. Esta dicotomía convertía en sinónimos lo extranjero y lo peligroso, al tiempo que buscaba preservar lo específicamente español como rasgo de autenticidad. Esta tendencia se observa incluso a la hora de interpretar los textos de los autores españoles, muchas veces *corruptos* por modas foráneas. Así, la obra *De tren a tren*, de Julia Maura, merece las siguientes palabras de un censor en 1952: "su lenguaje está muy influido por otras obras, principalmente

---

1   *Boletín Oficial del Estado*, "Orden de 9 de febrero de 1963 por la que se aprueban las 'Normas de censura cinematográfica', 9/2/1963, 3930.

anglosajonas; se halla, por lo tanto, carente de significación y tradición católica y española".[2] Estas palabras del censor, que esconden un anhelo por impulsar la dramaturgia española y un desdén hacia todo lo foráneo, podrían llevarnos a pensar que el régimen fue totalmente hermético hacia el teatro extranjero. Sin embargo esta hipótesis debería ser matizada: este trabajo ilustrará la presencia que tuvo el teatro de Brecht en la España de Franco, así como las asunciones que sobre su dramaturgia hizo la poderosa censura. Como se observará en las páginas siguientes, el aislacionismo cultural del primer Franquismo fue dejando paso a una mayor permeabilidad, en una etapa en que la defensa del público español frente a las herejías del teatro extranjero se convirtió en la mayor prioridad de la censura.

Ha sido señalado cómo durante los primeros años de la dictadura el régimen no permitía sino triunfalismo y escapismo (Blanco Aguinaga et al. 1984: 116). Podría por tanto suponerse que, *a priori*, el teatro extranjero satisfaría esta necesidad al ofrecerle al espectador un alejamiento de su cotidianidad y una puerta a nuevas realidades; sin embargo, el mero contacto con lo extranjero planteaba un conflicto con la agenda extremadamente nacionalista de Franco y la presencia de teatro no español fue mínima durante los primeros años del Franquismo. Sin embargo, hubo un género que gozó de una especial difusión por aquel tiempo. Por su finura y su carácter políticamente aséptico, las revistas fueron las obras extranjeras que disfrutaron de mayor presencia en las tablas españolas de aquellos años. Otros géneros del teatro extranjero fueron vistos con demasiados reparos por parte del régimen: si el teatro americano se mostraba excesivamente realista en sus planteamientos morales-sexuales, la vanguardia parisina resultaba demasiado experimental para la escena española (London 1997: 88, 115). De este modo la dramaturgia que cosechaba grandes éxitos en los escenarios de medio mundo brilló por su ausencia en la España de los años cuarenta y cincuenta.

Sin embargo, en los primeros sesenta, el régimen llevó a cabo lo que se ha venido en denominar proceso de *apertura* (Muñoz Cáliz 2005: 25-

---

2   Archivo General de la Administración (en citas siguientes, AGA), expediente O-46/54 (*De tren a tren*, Julia Maura). Los expedientes de censura constan de una serie de documentos sin paginar, por lo que no se ofrecerá paginación de estas referencias. Del mismo modo, las citas sin referencia pertenecen al expediente citado anteriormente, a menos que se indique lo contrario.

29). El Franquismo necesitaba legitimarse en la cada vez más necesaria escena internacional y, para ello, llevó a cabo una serie de políticas que le otorgaban una ficticia apariencia de democratización. El proceso, impulsado por el Ministro de Información y Turismo, Manuel Fraga, tuvo su reflejo en la abolición de la censura previa para publicaciones y en la aplicación al teatro en 1964 de las reglas de censura cinematográfica del año anterior, que ofrecía a los autores un listado de elementos a evitar.[3] De esta época datan los primeros estrenos de autores hasta entonces proscritos, como Lorca y Valle-Inclán, pero también de las voces del exilio y de los grandes nombres del teatro contemporáneo, como Brecht, Sartre o Camus.

Sin embargo, algunos autores españoles como Sastre (traductor al español de la mayoría de obras de Sartre) hablan de una "liberalización de fachada" (Sastre 1971: 129) para las importaciones culturales, que le permitía al régimen hacer propaganda de su tolerancia en el exterior y así granjearse socios en la esfera internacional. Se trató, en efecto, de autorizaciones que escondían grandes mutilaciones y un impacto muy marginal.

El teatro de Bertolt Brecht

La censura del teatro de Bertolt Brecht ilustra a la perfección este proceso. Si bien en el Archivo General de la Administración (AGA) constan hasta 106 expedientes censores de versiones de sus obras, la gran mayoría de ellas datan de la última parte del Franquismo, a partir de finales de la década de los sesenta. Este hecho es significativo *per se* y revela cómo los directores de escena no se aventuraron a solicitar autorización para el montaje de textos del autor comunista en los años más duros del régimen y esperaron a que la política de apertura se desarrollara para lanzarse a una empresa sin duda alguna arriesgada.

Terror y miseria en el III Reich, obra sobre los horrores de la Alemania nazi, es un excelente ejemplo del tratamiento que recibió el autor alemán por parte de las autoridades censoras franquistas. El texto fue

3 *Boletín Oficial del Estado*, "Orden de 9 de febrero de 1963 por la que se aprueban las 'Normas de censura cinematográfica'", 9/2/1963.

prohibido en 1968 en la primera solicitud a censura.[4] Uno de los lectores interpretaba que el único fin de poner en escena esta obra, calificada de "texto panfletario", era la celebración de un mitin, ya que "solo una intención extrateatral justifica[ba] su presencia hoy en un escenario español". La censura incidió en que "la crítica al nazismo y la acusación a Hitler, estan [sic] hechas de manera que resucitar estos textos ahora, donde se habla de represión policiaca, de ausencia de libertad y de opinion [sic], de la religion [sic] sometida al poder, de trabajos forzado[s], etc, traerá más quebraderos de cabeza, que ilustración y enseñanza teatrales". En base a estos criterios, la obra fue prohibida.

En dos nuevas solicitudes de 1970 y 1971, sin embargo, el texto se autorizó para sesiones únicas en un pequeño teatro de Madrid, aunque no sin nuevas objeciones: los acontecimientos que se representaban estaban para los censores "vistos desde una mentalidad y proyección netamente comunistas" y, además, se resaltaba la peligrosidad que podía derivarse del texto por "el mayor o menor mimetismo con estructuras, métodos y actuaciones políticas españolas".[5] A pesar de estos supuestos peligros y blandiéndose el argumento de que el texto estaba sujeto a la historicidad de los hechos,[6] las autorizaciones se produjeron con cortes y siempre que la acción se situase "en la Alemania nazi, sin dar lugar a actualización alguna" (exp. 201/71). En 1971 una nueva solicitud para teatros comerciales fue denegada, quedando el texto restringido al reducido circuito de cámara.

Los dictámenes encontrados para el resto de obras siguen una tónica muy similar. En *El círculo de tiza caucasiano*, por ejemplo, se indicaba que "la acción de esta obra ha de situarse en su época, sin que haya actualizaciones que la desvirtúen".[7] Los censores, acostumbrados ya a las lecturas contemporaneizadoras de las obras históricas de la generación realista, ponían especial atención en textos que hablasen de represión y que pudiesen ser extrapolados a la España de Franco. El visado del ensayo general, en virtud del cual funcionarios de la censura comprobaban que el montaje no violaba la ambientación de la obra, se convirtió de este modo en una necesidad para el régimen y en una traba más para los di-

---

4   AGA, exp. 163/68 (*Terror y miseria en el III Reich*).
5   AGA, exp. 201/71 (*Terror y miseria en el III Reich*).
6   AGA, exp. 300/70 (*Terror y miseria en el III Reich*)
7   AGA, exp. 418/69 (*El círculo de tiza caucasiano*).

rectores que intentaban vehicular con sus puestas en escena un mensaje crítico al Franquismo.

Conviene aquí destacar la naturaleza de la infraestructura legal que permitió los primeros estrenos de autores extranjeros en la España franquista. En 1955 la censura reguló la actividad de teatros de cámara y compañías no profesionales. Este nuevo régimen teatral permitía representaciones en función única y con un público reducido (los socios del teatro) para obras no comerciales, abriendo así una válvula de escape para el estrangulado repertorio de aquellos años. Esta diferenciación entre el régimen comercial y el de cámara ofrecía una nueva plataforma para un público minoritario y urbano, interesado en un teatro más intelectual del que hasta entonces se había intentado proteger al gran público por su supuesta peligrosidad. A su vez, este resorte le permitía al régimen contentar a los reducidos círculos intelectuales y hacer propaganda de democratización en el exterior, al tiempo que el teatro comercial seguía blindado frente a la heterodoxia y mostrando la supuesta pureza de las letras españolas.

A pesar de la marginalidad y del limitado impacto de este tipo de salas, gracias a ellas dramaturgias como la de Brecht comenzaron a irrumpir en las tablas españolas. Sin embargo, los censores no siempre entendieron la estrategia propagandística del régimen y con frecuencia protestaron ante la presencia de ciertos autores en el circuito teatral español. Un caso destacado es el intento de llevar a escena *El círculo de tiza caucasiano* por parte de los Teatros Nacionales, en un claro ejemplo de la herramienta propagandística comentada más arriba. Con este estreno, el Estado buscaba legitimar su política cultural siempre que el espectáculo estuviese "absolutamente limpio de toda expresión o intención marsista [sic]".[8] El censor López Rubio, encargado de dictaminar la oportunidad de aquel estreno, reaccionó contundentemente ante la propuesta:

> si el comunismo y sus compañeros de viaje quieren hacer su propaganda y se les complace, que al menos no sea con el dinero de nuestros contribuyentes. Por lo menos, que sea con el oro de nuestras reservas, que hoy nos vendrían tan al pelo, que se llevaron hace unos años.

8   AGA, exp. O-7/68 (*El círculo de tiza caucasiano*).

También hubo voces que advirtieron que, a sabiendas de que habría que censurar partes del texto para poderlo autorizar, se produciría un "reproche exterior [...] por haber 'censurado' al dramático santón del comunismo", conscientes de que la estrategia propagandística del régimen podría finalmente volverse en su propia contra. En cualquier caso, los censores manifestaron su discrepancia al intento de estrenar la obra de un icono comunista en un teatro oficial, hecho que ilustra las contradicciones internas de una censura que busca ser garante en moral y política a la vez que oportuna y ficticiamente liberal.

Al margen de sus textos, el nombre de Brecht se asoció sistemáticamente en los informes de los censores al comunismo: "el *gran* dramaturgo Brecht fue también un *gran* comunista";[9] "el único autor viable que el marxismo ha podido ofrecer en cincuenta años, por lo cual ha habido que abrumar con él al mundo, por obvias razones de propaganda".[10] Abundan los comentarios molestos con las solicitudes de obras del autor alemán. Es frecuente encontrar desde expresiones del tipo "otra vez Brecht" hasta quejas por el deseo de "alancear de nuevo al moro muerto", que suponen ejemplos del desagrado de los censores ante la insistencia de los directores por llevar a escena el teatro brechtiano.

A la problemática política que ofrecía un autor como Brecht se sumaba la de orden religioso, que se observa de manera magistral en la obra *Galileo Galilei*. El contenido de este texto se oponía frontalmente al dogma católico y, por ende, entraba en colisión con el estrecho margen de permisividad de la censura, que había legislado para prohibir cualquier atentado contra "la Iglesia Católica, su dogma, su moral y su culto".[11] En su solicitud de 1965, la obra fue sometida a cortes en fragmentos como los siguientes: "ha quedado en descubierto que las bóvedas celestes están vacías" o "¿de qué servirían las Sagradas Escrituras [...] si ahora se encontraran llenas de errores?".[12] Los censores criticaron la actitud impía de la obra y su carácter propagandístico "contra la Iglesia y la Biblia y a favor de la ética de situación, de la que se hace padre a Galileo". Denunciaron que el texto imponía ciencia a religión, que presenta-

---

9   AGA, exp. 201/71 (*Terror y miseria en el III Reich*). Subrayado en el original.
10   AGA, exp. 0-7/68 (*El círculo de tiza caucasiano*).
11   *Boletín Oficial del Estado*, "Orden de 9 de febrero de 1963 por la que se aprueban las 'Normas de censura cinematográfica', 9/2/1963, 3930.
12   AGA, exp. 156/65 (*Galileo Galilei*).

ba a la Iglesia como opresora y contraria al progreso y que hacía del protagonista "una especie de proto-héroe del marxismo". A estos ataques contra el dogma había que sumar el hecho de "que presenta[ra] a unos monjes, frailes, cardenales y Papa estúpidos y entregados a la ignorancia más crasa". Así las cosas, el texto se prohibió para representaciones comerciales en 1965 y quedó autorizado para sesiones de cámara hasta su aprobación para el gran público en 1976, ya después de la muerte de Franco. No en vano, como se ha señalado, el Franquismo entendía España como estandarte del Catolicismo en la moralmente decrépita Europa.

Existía, sin embargo, un deseo manifiesto por parte del régimen de demostrarle a sus detractores que podía tolerar obras impías. Esta dualidad se observa en el carácter heterogéneo de los censores de la Junta, entre los que había quienes alababan la calidad de los autores heterodoxos y sugerían su autorización amparándose en su presentación rigurosa de los hechos históricos o en lo innovador de su lenguaje. Uno de los censores partidarios de autorizar *Galileo Galilei* decía, en referencia a los aspectos religiosos incómodos de la obra: "puede representarse. Y debe serlo con el texto íntegro. Evitémonos ser, una vez más, los católicos españoles más papistas que el Papa". Este tipo de lecturas, más abiertas a la innovación teatral, fue ganando terreno y determinó que finalmente la mayoría de las obras fuesen autorizadas, si bien con cortes y restringidas a funciones de cámara y ensayo.

Conclusión

El caso de Brecht es paradigmático para entender la recepción por parte de la censura del teatro extranjero. Los procesos observados a través de los expedientes de sus obras se repiten en las de otros autores como Sartre y Camus. Así sucede, por ejemplo, con la tendencia general de los censores a juzgar viables las representaciones siempre que se vieran despojadas de ambigüedades que pudiesen propiciar una lectura en *clave española*; es decir, siempre que los contextos históricos ofrecidos en las obras inhabilitasen cualquier lectura metafórica y crítica de la España de Franco. Para ello se impusieron férreos visados de ensayo general, encargados de supervisar que la ambientación y el vestuario se adhiriesen estrictamente a lo dispuesto originalmente en el texto, de manera que no cupiese ambigüedad alguna.

Esta permisividad se debe a dos razones. La primera es el anhelo del régimen por demostrar su carácter de liberalización en los sesenta, necesitado como estaba de establecer vínculos en la escena internacional. La actividad del minoritario y aislado régimen de cámara, con los propios Teatros Nacionales a la cabeza, hacía posibles portadas de diarios internacionales en que se leía que el régimen de Franco autorizaba a autores comunistas, mientras que el impacto de dichos estrenos tanto en el público como en la sociedad era marginal. Se entendía, además, que el espectador culto relativizaría las cuestiones espinosas, que habrían sido más nocivas para el espectador medio de los grandes teatros. Por tanto, el salto al régimen comercial, como se ha ilustrado, fue muy escaso y, cuando se produjo, no estuvo exento de dificultades. La segunda razón para la presencia de este tipo de obras en la escena de los sesenta fue, sin duda, la calidad de los textos y la vehemente defensa de un núcleo menos reaccionario de censores. Pese a estar en desacuerdo con su tratamiento moral, las alabanzas a las obras citadas son lugar común en buena parte de los juicios.

En 1962, un censor veía problemas en el hecho de que un sacerdote pretendiese al personaje de Madre Coraje: "teniendo en cuenta la sensibilidad del público español ante escenas de esta índole […] sugeriría la supresión de ese pasaje".[13] En efecto, la censura asumió que existía una *sensibilidad del público español* y que ésta contaba con umbrales más tímidos que los de otros países europeos. Por ende, existía una asunción tácita según la cual las obras que venían de fuera incluían elementos que podían dañar dicha sensibilidad, tanto en su aspecto político como en el religioso-moral. Sin embargo, en los años sesenta se produjo una serie de fenómenos derivados de la *apertura*: por un lado, el régimen cobró conciencia de que debía suavizar su imagen totalitaria para salir del aislacionismo imperante en el primer Franquismo; por otro, se generó un público intelectual y urbano que demandaba el teatro que llevaba años triunfando en Europa. El régimen de teatro de cámara, cuyas características ya se han desgranado, supuso una vía de escape para este nuevo espectador, al tiempo que ofrecía un lavado de cara para el Franquismo.

---

13   AGA, exp. 227/62 (*Madre Coraje*).

A través de los informes de censura se observan los miedos ante lo foráneo, que es sistemáticamente corrupto y decadente. Miedos que derivan de una concepción anacrónica de España como estandarte de la virtud y del Catolicismo en el marasmo moral europeo. Este trabajo ilustra cómo esta concepción obsoleta se vio obligada a claudicar, haciendo quebrar un aislacionismo cultural insostenible y permitiendo la tímida entrada de teatros como el de Brecht en las tablas españolas.

Bibliografía

Althusser, L. 1976. "Idéologie et appareils idéologiques d'État. (Notes pour une recherche)", in L. Althusser, *Positions (1964-1975)*, Paris, Éditions Sociales.

Blanco Aguinaga, C., J. Rodríguez Puértolas & I. Zavala. 1984. *Historia social de la literatura española (en lengua castellana)*, vol. 3, Madrid, Castalia.

London, J. 1997. *Reception and Renewal in Modern Spanish Theatre: 1939-1963*, Leeds, Maney & Son.

Muñoz Cáliz, B. 2005. *El teatro crítico español durante el franquismo, visto por sus censores*, Madrid, Fundación Universitaria Española.

Sastre, A. 1971. *La revolución y la crítica de la cultura*, Barcelona, Grijalbo.

ANGELINA SAULE

Scenes of Fantasy: Desiring the Oriental Other in the Persian Poems of Velimir Khlebnikov

In 1921, one of Russia's foremost Futurist poets, Velimir Khlebnikov (1885-1922), born in the multicultural city of Astrakhan, near the Caspian Sea, fulfilled his dream of "going East". He followed the Red Army to the Gilan province of Iran, where the Soviets meant to back up the local rebels who were fighting to establish a socialist republic. There, in the city of Rasht —the Persian "gate of Europe" on the shores of the Caspian Sea— Khlebnikov had time to wander and write a lot, often disregarding his army-related duties. Even though his stay was brief (the Red Army withdrew in September 1921), his Iranian experiences left an imprint in his poetry that we will attempt to explore here. Drawing on the poet's highly experimental notion of poetry, this paper will contend that the conception of the East in Khlebnikov's Persian poems is allocated a space which is represented by the notion of *zaum* ("trans-sense" or "beyond-sense" language), a term coined by his fellow poet Aleksei Kruchenykh in 1913. This space, the East, reinforces yet also breaks with certain traditions within Russian literature regarding how the East is represented, and what the East itself should come to represent.

Before discussing Khlebnikov's texts, however, it will help to outline briefly how *zaum* is connected with this imagined space of the East. *Zaum* is depicted by Khlebnikov as a model of language which is material, emptied of meaning, thus coming to represent the decentered rhizome of meaning and how the meaning of a word is an endless depository of multiplicity waiting to be made. In other words, *zaum* is the idea that alternative word formation could create a universal language full of meaning (Khlebnikov 2005: 167-76), and that by confronting the materiality of the word and the letter, one could strip language of its semantic conditioning. Hence signata (from signatum, that is, meaning) are arbitrary and can be created and applied by and for the poem, as for example in the private word symbolism in Lewis Carroll's nonsense text *The*

Hunting of the Snark (1876). Carroll's narrative poem is held hostage to the neologism "snark", which everyone is seeking in the poem yet are unaware of what exactly a "snark" is, and it is this private wor(l)d symbolism that generates the language and action of the poem itself —in this case, a parallel must be made with Beckett's *Waiting for Godot* (1953) and Khlebnikov's laugh that generates the neologisms in the famous poem, "The Incantation of Laughter" (Khlebnikov 1986: 54).

The East, and in the case of the Persian poems, Iran, is a space denoted by a myriad of Oriental religious, mythological, and historical figures which are used to recreate a world cleansed of static and unnatural references by reanimating and repositioning these figures — displacing them as one has displaced the word itself as defined by Khlebnikov in his programmatic essay, "Our Foundation" [Nasha osnova] (Khlebnikov 2005: 167). In this well-known essay it is stated that something which is "always third" is harbouring within a word: *slovotvorchestvo* ("word-creation") and *zaum* were a means to free and liberate the word from the perils of common sense, that is to say, from the standard and conservative usage of a word that denied the possibility of other meanings being created. As the materiality of the word has become displaced by *slovotrorchestvo*, the word is reduced to a pre-linguistic sign that is distinguished by the fact that it does not represent standard Russian, and it is these very elements of language that generate poetic language, a language of the unconscious similar to notions of automatic writing that preoccupied the Surrealists. Yet, the technique of *zaum* was more systematic in the approach to language as form and content simultaneously.

An interesting example of *zaum* displacing the scene of fantasy is evident in Khlebnikov's poem, "Reed of the Rose-Mullah". The speaker is reconfigured by this word-play of language to create the scene of fantasy, yet it is this scene of fantasy that generates such an image of the self —that is, of the speaker of the poem:

> This prophet
> Descended from the snowy peaks
> Descended from the mountains
> To meet the progeny,
> Khlebnikov,
> Rejoicing!

Saul, Adam
The belief of the north.
Thanks to you
For your star –
Many prophets have sung
Their glory to you.
Present —silence— everything is good.
"Ours!" said the holy mountain.
"Ours!" sang out the flowers.
On the green tablecloth
Clumsily spilled with spring (Khlebnikov 1986: 349)

The dervish presented in this poem is a metaphor of the possibilities within *zaum*, as he —based on the author— is a Russian dervish addressed as "Adam", the first man in the Biblical tradition far removed from the Persia of the Rose-Mullah referred to in the Islamic-inspired title of the poem. As a dervish exists outside the religious hierarchy, the scene is confused further by the prophets who have sung in praise of him, thanking him in the local Azeri dialect ("Saul"), which also has the heightened Judeo-Christian connotations of King Saul, the first king of Israel. Thus, by means of *zaum* the East is depicted as a drama, a movement away from its source, deviating from fixity, as the language experiments of *zaum* demonstrate. It is sanctified by the foreign usages; the projection as the East makes it holy, a place for dervishes to inhabit. In short, the "Russian dervish" —a term the Iranian people of Gilan often employed to refer to Khlebnikov— cannot articulate the East: his articulation is assigned a kind of decodification. As a poetic system, then, *zaum* does not allow for the complete digestion of a space —of a word, nor of a world— and therefore the East cannot be rudimentarily classified.

This approach to language is one of displacement that establishes meaning as a technique that reveals unknown norms that inhabit the known word, thus becoming foreign to itself in the process of poetic creation, following a tradition in line with Aristotle's conception that poetic speech is a foreign tongued speech (Aristotle 1981: 60-62). The unfamiliar, the unknown, or "beyond-sense" (as the Futurists coined it) that resides within the innards of language begot itself; that is, the potential possibilities of signification projected within language. The rhizome, as defined in this essay, is a metaphor of Khlebnikov's displacement as poetics which is envisioned as a series of connections, lines and flights of multiplicity. This particular displacement as poetics central to the word is also central to the conception of the world of Iran as envisioned, generated and displaced in Khlebnikov's Persian poems.

The attempt to embody the East in these poems is also subject to displacement and in consequence is fashioned to become a crucial constituent of *zaum*. Khlebnikov treats Iran as a form and substance combined as in a letter of the alphabet. This idea is described in the essay "Our Foundation": it is empty, as the East it can be "spacepainted" and open to arbitrary and overlocking networks of "Easternness" that may or may not refer to Iran (Khlebnikov 2005: 167). Thus, through the poetic language of Khlebnikov, Iran becomes a mythopoeia in its own right and is reduced to a scene of fantasy of what Iran could be in Khlebnikov's search for the Other. As a representative of the Russian Avant-Garde, Khlebnikov's search for the Other is the search for the scene of the fantasy which has been designated as Iran by the Persian poems, the poems generated by the desire for the Other, regulated by a "production of an image of identity and the transformation of the subject in assuming that image" (Bhabha 2008: 64).[1]

As the Persian poems are metonymical representations of the East, and according to Khlebnikov's mythopoeia the East is made up of and united by such diverse nations as China, India, Persia, Russia, Siam and Afghanistan, the East is perceived of as a language of signs, an alphabet of relations. This is what Khlebnikov states in his well-known essay "Indo-Russian Union" (2005: V, 271), where he reflects, among other issues, on the confluence of three worlds: Islam, Christianity, and Buddhism. For Khlebnikov the East is *zaum*, as the language of the Other is *zaum*, a blur of countries and sounds that are heard but not understood by the onlooker, credibly coming to signify anything and everything, as it

---

1   In the chapter titled "Interrogating Identity", Bhabha sets out to redefine Frantz Fanon's language of identity by focusing on the Lacanian model of the subject's signification in language and society. Bhabha, like Khlebnikov, focuses on the materiality of the letter —in this instance, the letter "er" which is the first vowel in Hindi— to reinforce the notion that there is always something "supplementary" in the process of signification, and that the letter "er" in a poem by Jussawalla, occupies a different location of culture, something that is supplementary, yet redefines, the Indo-European "a".

does in Khlebnikov's poems and essays. His Orientalism is not only a discourse, but a culture of fetishism that exists as a sublime key of expression within the poet's system of *zaum* in the search for this desired self-generated Other. It is a quest for a representation of the Other that has become joined to that which it is supposed to cover, seeking this "holy island" of representation as Khlebnikov envisions it in his manifesto "Asiaunion" (2005: V, 299). The East is reduced to a system of contingency based on the gaze which is "imagined by me in the field of the Other" (Lacan 1998: 84). The Other is a field (or island) that is constituted by the effects of speech on the subject, an effect which is always one and multiple in Khlebnikov's East. The Other is the possibility of change and hope, a location where the principles of Futurism —the destruction of syntax, word-creation, and the breaking with tradition— can be realized. The Other in the form of the East is necessary as the lyrical narrator in the Russian tongue has to appear in the field of the Other. In the light of this, the East as reconfigured by Khlebnikov is created by desire; consequently this essay will suggest that there is no Other in the configuration of the East in the Persian poems of Khlebnikov as envisioned by him.

The vision of Iran is a fantasy constituted by the structure of relations that depend on the preservation of the use of synecdoches and other tropes structured as ellipses which convey Iran. These inner relations between tropes impart the idea of the East, usages and coinages such as parallelisms, inversions, or exchanges which displace the East as a historical and geographic space. If the substance of the East is in some parts irreplaceable, then this strange stage setting of Iran could be envisioned easily as a place of Heaven or Hell, or of the Christian world and Islamic world being depicted simultaneously, as in the following extract from the narrative poem, "The Reed of the Rose-Mullah". The use of such tropes constructs a new vision; the image of Iran as the prerogative East is displaced by Khlebnikov's hyper usage of images and *zvukopis*, by referring to a world beyond Iran, as the poem below shows. The world that is projected in this poem is created by the many worlds of the East, as well as by elements of Western civilization and not necessarily Iran: it is a proposed or a desired Iran that displaces any real understanding of what Iran is or should be:

A country, where all men are Adams,
The bared roots of sky's heaven.
Where money is "pul",
And in a mountain cave,
Under a roaring waterfall
Khans walk about in white gowns
To haul salmon
With long nets on poles.
And everything is with a "sha": "Shah", "Shai", "Shira"[2]
Where that calling name—
"Ai"
Has been given to the quiet moon.
In this country is I! (Khlebnikov 2005: III, 310, my translation)

Where the Farsi word "Adam" (meaning "man") is used to suspend attention on the fact that if man is expressed as "Adam", surely that location of culture, which is Iran, should be one of a Garden of Eden. The fact that "man" also means the "First Man" in Aramaic and Hebrew (although it also means "red" and "earth" in both Semitic languages, meanings that appeal to the notion of a displaced origin of multiplicity), applies to the setting of the poem which is visualized as a potential heaven on earth created by these "first men" who are in opposition to the roots of heaven hanging above. These men, simultaneously depicted as being both Khans and fishermen, toil as tirelessly in this space of paradise as described in the Book of Ezekiel as "a place for spreading of the nets", which is to fulfill the doomed prophecies of the future (26: 5, 14), much in the same way as Khlebnikov's narrative poem, "The Crane".

Khlebnikov superimposition of the image of the fishermen on the Khans obviously problematizes the scene, as these "Men" come to represent the "first men", the "everymen" (in the guise of the fishermen), and holy men (these men are Khans, and like the Quranic fishermen are connected with the transgression of the Sabbath in the Sura "The Heights" [7:163-64]). Conclusively, the Khan may or may not be participating in an act of transgression similar to the Quranic transgression, as they are still in their religious robes and are fishing.

The fact that the Khans as lords or local chieftains are fishing is an element of cultural fetishism desired: the Adams here are split by the

2   "Shai" means little things in Farsi (and in Arabic), while "Shira" is the end of an
     opium butt.

desire of the speaker to create the Other, and who has unwittingly made them partial: "neither is sufficient unto itself" (Bhabha 2008: 72). The desire for the Self and Other has created a stage of splitting, which is reinforced by the fixation on the sound "Sh" in Farsi to denote both sacred ideas ("Shah") and simultaneously the profane (small things, "shai"; opium, "shira"). Khlebnikov accentuates the displacement of the letter's associations to emphasize that these sounds are connected, yet these sounds in Farsi which are to be foreign in the Russian poem are not sounds or words foreign to Russian. "Shah" possesses the same meaning, while "Shai" and "Shira" could be mere deformations of the Russian words "tea" (chai) and "wider" (shir'e), further displacing the Russian word by means of *zaum*, and consequently not sufficiently expert at identifying the image of the Oriental Other, which is always a theatre of actors limited by mimicry and the limits of language —even if Khlebnikov's word games attempt to demonstrate otherwise.

This displacement of language is manipulated for aesthetic and philological purposes, a dissection of sounds that are to signify the foreignness of the scene for the narrator. Yet, this word-game is further refined by the end of the poem, since the "Ai" (which means the "first month" in Farsi) is given to the moon. Meanwhile, we are reminded that this is unfolding around the all-important "I" of the poem, who is standing in this foreign landscape, and it is on this letter (which is also the last letter of the Russian alphabet) that the poem decisively ends on. The desired East is evidently perceived and suspended on this exuberant "I", and through the effects of the "I" —that is, "ya" (Я) the last letter of the alphabet— the subject has finally realized himself in the dominion of the Other. It is due to this very letter that the lyrical voice of the poem, in the field of the Other, has been unable to eject himself and is "ever more divided, pulverized, in the circumscribable metonymy of speech" (Lacan 1998: 188). The "I" of the poem is produced by the desire for the East, whereby the Other subscribed to Persia in the poems has created a lyrical subject consisting of faulty lines running between these productions and representations in the quest to have the hero's desire realized. Summing up, the East has become the only playing field where the "I" of the poem, in the field of the Other, can speak.

Bibliography

Aristotle. 1981. "On the Art of Poetry", in T. S. Dorsch (trans.), *Classical Literary Criticism,* Ringwood, Victoria, Penguin.

Bhabha, H. 2008. *The Location of Culture*, London, Routledge.

Khlebnikov, V. 1986, *Creative Works*, Moscow, Soviet Writer.

—. 2005. *Collected Writings*, vols. 1-6, Moscow, The Institute of World Literature of The Russian Academy of Sciences.

The Holy Bible. King James Version. 1953. Sydney, Collins.

The Koran (with Parallel Arabic Text). 2000. N. J. Dawood (trans.), Camberwell, Victoria, Penguin.

Lacan, J. 1998. "Anamorphosis", in J. E. Miller (ed.), *The Four Fundamental Concepts of Psychoanalysis*, A. Sheridan (trans.), New York, Norton, 79-90.

—. 1998. "From Love to the Libido", in J. E. Miller (ed.), *The Four Fundamental Concepts of Psychoanalysis*, A. Sheridan (trans.), New York, Norton, 187-200.

Notes on Contributors

MARGARITA ALFARO AMIEIRO is a Lecturer in French Literature and the French-speaking world at the Autonomous University of Madrid. She has published numerous articles on twentieth-century women's autobiographical writing. Her current research focuses on representations of mobility (travellers, exiles, migrants and expatriates).

BEGOÑA ALONSO MONEDERO holds a PhD in Literary Theory from the University of Salamanca, Spain. She has published articles on intertextuality and metafiction in contemporary narrative. She has also published essays on the ancient and medieval metaphor of "life as a river" and other topics in medieval sermons.

DAVID ARES MANSO has taught at the University of Lyon II and at Laval University (Québec). He is currently completing a PhD thesis on anti-Semitism and Spanish literature around the 1930s, jointly supervised by the universities of Valladolid and Paris III. He has published articles on Spanish Fascist literature and racism.

FREDERIC BARBERÀ is Senior Lecturer in Spanish and Catalan Studies at Lancaster University. He has written on Spanish and Catalan narratives and cultural history, including the books *Gabriel Miró and Catalan Culture* and *Baltasar Porcel o l'òptica aberrant sobre el món*. He has also produced a critical edition of Gabriel Miró's *Epistolario*.

MIQUEL BERGA BAGUÉ is a Senior Lecturer in English literature at Pompeu Fabra University in Barcelona. He has published extensively on George Orwell and other British writers involved in the Spanish Civil War, including a biography of John Langdon-Davies.

ISABELLE BES HOGHTON is a Lecturer in French at the University of the Balearic Islands in Palma de Mallorca. She has published articles on nineteenth-century travel literature and also on the topic of the island in travel writing.

EDUARD CAIROL holds PhD in Philosophy from the University of Barcelona. He has taught at Eina Escola de Disseny i Art, and currently lectures in Art History at Pompeu Fabra University in Barcelona. He is author of the book *Maragall i Novalis: poesia i experiència mística*, and has translated poems of Novalis and Rilke into Catalan.

CATERINA CALAFAT is a Lecturer in French at the University of the Balearic Islands in Palma de Mallorca. She has extensive experience as a conference interpreter and literary translator, and has researched in the fields of translation, FLT, and transculturality in the English- and French-speaking worlds.

ISABEL CAMPELO is a singer and a researcher in Musical Sciences, and currently teaches vocal practices in various Performing Arts schools. She is developing her doctoral thesis around record production in Portugal after the 1974 political revolution. Some of her research has been recently published in the *Journal on the Art of Record Production*.

MARIA ZULMIRA CASTANHEIRA is a Lecturer at the New University of Lisbon. She is also coordinator of the Lisbon branch of the Centre for English, Translation and Anglo-Portuguese Studies (CETAPS). She has written on British travel writing on Portugal and on the reception of British culture in the periodical press of Portuguese Romanticism.

ROSA CERAROLS is a Lecturer in Geography in the Humanities Department at Pompeu Fabra University in Barcelona. She is also a member of the Geography and Gender Research Group at the Autonomous University of Barcelona. Her research links gender geography with cultural and historical studies.

LUISA SHU-YING CHANG is Professor of Spanish Literature at Taiwan National University. She has published articles on travel writing, the Picaresque novel, film and literature, as well as on Orientalism in Latin American Modernism. She also has translated more than ten Hispanic novels into Chinese.

AGUSTÍN COLETES BLANCO is Professor of English at the University of Oviedo. He is also an honorary Visiting Professor at the University of Hull. He has published widely on literary and cultural reception and on British travellers in northern Spain. He is also the editor and Spanish translator of works by Johnson, Byron and other British Romantic poets.

MONTSERRAT COTS is Professor of French Literature at Pompeu Fabra University in Barcelona and President of the Spanish Comparative Literature Association. Her publications have focused above all on different aspects of French literature and the relationship between literatures through translation. She is member of an international research team that studies the links between humour and literature.

TOM DICKINS is a Senior Lecturer and Course Leader for Linguistics in the School of Law, Social Sciences and Communications at the University of Wolverhampton. His publications relate primarily to applied Slavonic linguistics: in particular, Czech lexicology, language variation and change, linguistic purism and loanwords, and language and political discourse.

DANIEL ESCANDELL MONTIEL has a PhD in Spanish Literature from the University of Salamanca, Spain. His research explores digital literature and new literary forms. He is the founder of the journal *Caracteres. Estudios culturales y críticos de la esfera digital* and has published several articles on blognovelism and the avatar.

MIREYA FERNÁNDEZ MERINO is Professor of Comparative Literature at the Central University of Venezuela. Her field of study is the narrative of the Spanish and British Caribbean. She is author of the book *Escrituras híbridas. Juego intertextual y ficción en García Márquez y Jean Rhys*.

MARIA J. FERRER-LIGHTNER is Assistant Professor of Hispanic Studies at Pacific Lutheran University in Tacoma, Washington (USA). She has published articles on early modern Spanish theatre and has translated into Spanish *Los juegos del amor y del lenguaje en la obra de Antón de Montoro, Rodrigo de Cota y Fernando de Rojas*.

MARGARITA GARBISU is a Lecturer in Literature at Madrid Open University. Her main line of research is the reception of Spanish culture of the twenties and thirties in Europe, specifically in Italy and the United Kingdom. She has published several papers on this topic, including "*The Criterion:* su trayectoria y su vínculo europeo con la *Revista de Occidente*" or "Jorge Guillén y John B. Trend, una amistad marcada por el exilio".

PERE GIFRA-ADROHER is a Senior Lecturer in English and American literature at Pompeu Fabra University in Barcelona. He is author of *Between History and Romance: Travel Writing on Spain in the Early Nineteenth-Century United States* and has edited a bilingual edition of Bayard Taylor's account of his journey to Andorra in 1867. His current research focuses on British and American women travellers in Catalonia.

RICARDO GIL SOEIRO is a Professor of Literature at ISLA Campus Lisbon–Laureate International Universities, and also a researcher at the Research Centre for Comparative Studies at the University of Lisbon. His publications include *Gramática da Esperança, Iminência do Encontro*, and the edited volumes *O Pensamento tornado dança: estudos em torno de George Steiner* and *The Wounds of Possibility*.

MARTA GÓMEZ GARRIDO has a degree in Journalism and is completing a PhD in Spanish Literature at the Complutense University of Madrid. Her current research focuses on sexuality and sexual indeterminacy in the poetry of the Spanish Silver Age. She has also published two novels and two books of poetry.

MARÍA DEL PILAR GONZÁLEZ DE LA ROSA is Lecturer at the University of Las Palmas de Gran Canaria, and is currently completing a PhD on stance-taking in an early modern English text on instructions for travellers. She has published articles on postcolonial literature, contemporary travel writing and specialised discourse.

HELENA GONZÁLEZ-VAQUERIZO teaches Greek language and literature at the Autonomous University of Madrid. Her areas of research include the Classical tradition and its reception into the twentieth and twenty-first centuries, modern Greek literature and comparative literature. She has published articles on Nikos Kazantzakis's work.

GLYN HAMBROOK is Co-Director of the Centre for Transnational and Transcultural Research at the University of Wolverhampton (UK). He is co-editor of the British Comparative Literature Association's journal, *Comparative Critical Studies*, and he also serves on the editorial board of the *Revue de Littérature Comparée*. His research focuses on the European Fin de Siècle.

RICHARD HITCHCOCK is Emeritus Professor of Hispano-Arabic Studies at the University of Exeter. His extensive research comprises many articles on the Arabs on Spain, nineteenth-century Hispano-Arabic historiography, and Golden Age Spanish literature, including Góngora and Cervantes. His recent books are *Mozarabs in Medieval and Early Modern Spain* (2008) and *Muslim Spain Reconsidered* (2013)

SANDRA HURTADO ESCOBAR has a Master's degree in Literature in the Digital era from the University of Barcelona. She is member of *Hermeneia*, a research group on Literary Studies and Digital Technologies, and co-founder of Kuiri, cultural association dedicated to promoting education and e-learning.

ALBERT JORNET SOMOZA is completing a PhD in Humanities at Pompeu Fabra University in Barcelona. His research focuses on lyrical discourses from the seventeenth to the twentieth century in Hispanic literature, and his articles on poetry and literary theory have been published in several journals as well as in edited volumes.

BEGOÑA LASA ÁLVAREZ has a PhD in English Studies and has been working as a researcher and secondary-school teacher. She currently belongs to a funded research group at the University of A Coruña. She has published extensively on eighteenth-century British and Irish women writers and on the reception of British and Irish literature and culture in Spain.

MIRIAM LÓPEZ SANTOS completed her PhD in Hispanic Studies at the University of León in 2009. She currently teaches both in secondary education and at the university. Her research focuses on the Gothic novel and the links between literature and film. She is author of *La novela gótica en España (1788-1833)*, and has recently edited *La urna sangrienta o el panteón de Scianella* by Pérez y Rodríguez.

ANTONIO LUNA-GARCÍA is a Senior Lecturer in Geography at Pompeu Fabra University in Barcelona, where he also is the Head of the Humanities Department. He is currently working in two different areas: on the relationship between Orientalism and Nationalism in the travel narratives of Catalan authors, and the relation between the symbolic economies of cities and the urban renewal policies.

EVA MARCH is a Lecturer in Art History in the Department of Humanities at Pompeu Fabra University in Barcelona. Her research and publications have been centred on museums and collecting in Barcelona during the first third of the twentieth century.

LUIGI MARFÈ is post-doctoral research fellow at the University of Torino. He works on travel writing and literary theory. He is the author of *Oltre la fine dei viaggi* (2009) and *Introduzione alle teorie narrative* (2011). He has recently translated Nicolas Bouvier's poems into Italian.

ELOY MARTÍN CORRALES has taught at the University of Seville and at the Autonomous University of Barcelona, and he is now Senior Lecturer in History at Pompeu Fabra University (Barcelona). His extensive research comprises many articles focusing above all on Spain's presence in Morocco. He is author of *Comercio de Cataluña con el Mediterráneo musulmán* and *La imagen del magrebí en España*, and also editor of *La conferencia de Algeciras en 1906* and *Marruecos y el colonialismo español (1859-1912)*.

RAFAEL M. MÉRIDA JIMÉNEZ is Senior Lecturer in Hispanic and Gender Studies at the University of Lleida. He has published numerous articles, editions and books on Spanish and Catalan literatures that include *Women in Medieval Iberia* (2002), *El gran libro de las brujas* (2004) and *Damas, santas y pecadoras. Hijas medievales de Eva* (2008).

VLADIMIR MONTAÑA MESTIZO is completing a joint PhD in Anthropology at the EHESS (Paris) and the University of São Paulo. His current research explores the anthropological thought that had developed up until the time of the postcolonial transition in Colombia and northern South America. He has published articles on representations by European travellers of the different social categories in eighteenth- and nineteenth-century Colombia.

EDUARD MOYÀ completed his PhD in Comparative Cultural Studies at the University of Queensland (Australia) in 2012. He is now Lecturer in English and Literature at the University of the Balearic Islands in Palma de Mallorca. He has published articles on the representation of Spain and the Mediterranean by twentieth-century British travel writers.

PAULINA NALEWAJKO teaches Latin American Literature and Spanish at the University of Warsaw. She has published articles on eroticism and sensuality in literature. Her current research explores the representation of sensuality in Gabriel García Márquez's short stories.

JULIA OERI is completing a PhD in French studies at the Complutense University of Madrid with a scholarship awarded by the Spanish Ministry of Education. Her principal area of research is bilingualism in literature, especially in the work of the Franco-Hungarian writers.

ISABEL OLIVEIRA MARTINS is Lecturer in American Literature at the Faculty of Social and Human Sciences, New University of Lisbon. She is the co-author of *Mark Twain in Portugal* (2010) and has published numerous articles on Anglo-Portuguese studies (mainly British and American travellers in Portugal), Portuguese-American studies, North American literature and literary translation since 1983.

MANUELA PALACIOS is Senior Lecturer in English Literature at the University of Santiago de Compostela, Spain. She coordinates a research project on contemporary Irish and Galician women writers which has resulted in several collections of essays and anthologies of poetry. Other interests include English Modernism and translation studies.

PEDRO JAVIER PARDO is a Senior Lecturer at the University of Sala-manca. He has published *La tradición cervantina en la novela inglesa del siglo XVIII* (1997) as well as numerous articles on the reception of *Don Quixote* and on film adaptation. He has also edited two mono-graphic issues in *1616* (2011) and *Comparative Critical Studies* (2012) on the representation of the foreign.

MIKEL PEREGRINA is completing a PhD in Spanish Literature at the Complutense University of Madrid. His current research focuses on the study of the Spanish science-fiction short story. He has published on the relation between science fiction and the representation of urban spaces.

JOÃO PAULO PEREIRA DA SILVA is a Lecturer in the Faculty of Human and Social Sciences at the New University of Lisbon, where he has been teaching English culture, eighteenth- and nineteenth-century English literature and Anglo-Portuguese studies, since 1992. His main research fields are Anglo-Portuguese literary and cultural relations and British travel writing on Portugal.

MIQUEL POMAR AMER is completing a PhD in Spanish at the University of Manchester. His research establishes a comparison between the repre-sentations of diasporic individuals in a selection of works by authors of Pakistani descent in England and Moroccan descent in Catalonia. He has published articles on questions of identity.

MARTA PUXAN-OLIVA is a postdoctoral fellow in the Department of Comparative Literature at Harvard University. Her current work explores the relationship between narrative reliability and racial conflicts in the Modernist novel. She has published articles on William Faulkner, Joseph Conrad, unreliability, and the cultural practice of "passing".

BLANCA RIPOLL SINTES is a Lecturer in Spanish Literature at the Uni-versity of Barcelona. She has published *"Destino" y la novela española de posguerra (1939-1949)* as well as articles and chapters in collective volumes on post-war Spanish literature and journalism.

LEONARDO ROMERO TOBAR is Emeritus Professor of Spanish Literature at the University of Zaragoza. His research has focused on nineteenth-century Spanish literature, particularly on the work of Juan Valera. His main publications are *La novela popular española del siglo XIX* (1976), *Panorama crítico del Romanicismo español* (1994), *La literatura en su historia* (2006) and *La lira de Ébano* (2010). He has also directed the edition of Juan Valera's *Correspondencia* (8 volumes, 2002-2009).

ANA RUEDA is Professor of Spanish Literature and Chair of Hispanic Studies at the University of Kentucky. She works on the modern and contemporary Spanish narrative (eighteenth to twentieth centuries). Her publications use interdisciplinary approaches and focus on the short story, the novel, epistolarity, war literature, and travel writing.

HÉLÈNE RUFAT is a Senior Lecturer in French and literary research at Pompeu Fabra University in Barcelona. Her current study explores representations of human values in French literature from the sixteenth to twentieth centuries, particularly in relation to Otherness. She has published articles on French writers and world literature.

JORDI SALA LLEAL is a Lecturer in Literary Theory and Comparative Literature at the University of Girona, Spain. He has published books and articles on literary theory and criticism, drama, poetry, and translation. His current work deals with the relationship between theatre and film.

COVADONGA SAN MIGUEL LLORENTE is completing a PhD in Travel Writing at the University of Oviedo, Spain. Her current research explores the representation of Spaniards in American, British and Australian women travellers in Spain during the Franco regime.

NURIA SÁNCHEZ VILLADANGOS is completing a PhD in Hispanic Philology at the University of León, Spain. Her current research explores women's writing, comparative literature, detective fiction and fantastic literature. She is a member of the research groups "Literary Theory and Comparatism" and "Fantastic Literature in Spanish".

MARÍA DEL PINO SANTANA QUINTANA lectures in English and British narrative at the University of Las Palmas de Gran Canaria, Spain. She has published *Cosmopolitismo e identidad en los libros de viajes de Bill Bryson*, as well as several articles on nineteenth- and twentieth-century travel writing.

DIEGO SANTOS SÁNCHEZ is Post-doctoral Researcher in Spanish Literature at the Autonomous University of Barcelona. He specialises in twentieth-century Spanish theatre and has published a book on the playwright Fernando Arrabal and a number of papers on theatre and censorship during the Franco regime.

ANGELINA SAULE holds an MA in Slavic Studies from Monash University in Melbourne (Australia). She has had poems and articles published in journals in Australia, Mexico and Russia, and has written about Russian literature for the Lebanese daily *Al-binaa*. She has also written about the arts for several university magazines in Australia, and has also organised several poetry events in St Petersburg (Russia).

CARMEN SERVÉN is a Senior Lecturer in Spanish Literature at the Autonomous University of Madrid, where she is also a member of the board of the "Instituto Universitario de Estudios de la Mujer". She has published a number of scholarly essays on nineteenth- and twentieth-century Spanish fiction.

GABRIELA STEINKE is a Senior Lecturer in English at the University of Wolverhampton (England). She has published articles on German women writers and German, Austrian and British children's literature.

AMILCAR TORRÃO FILHO is Lecturer in Theory and Modern History at the Pontifical Catholic University of São Paulo (Brasil). He is also the author of *A arquitetura da alteridade: a cidade luso-brasileira na literatura de viagem (1783-1845)*, and of several books and articles on travel literature, urban planning and cities.